Lecture Notes in Artificial Intelligence 4722

Edited by J. G. Carbonell and J. Siekmann

Subseries of Lecture Notes in Computer Science

Catherine Pelachaud   Jean-Claude Martin
Elisabeth André   Gérard Chollet
Kostas Karpouzis   Danielle Pelé (Eds.)

Intelligent
Virtual Agents

7th International Conference, IVA 2007
Paris, France, September 17-19, 2007
Proceedings

 Springer

Series Editors

Jaime G. Carbonell, Carnegie Mellon University, Pittsburgh, PA, USA
Jörg Siekmann, University of Saarland, Saarbrücken, Germany

Volume Editors

Catherine Pelachaud
IUT de Montreuil, Université de Paris 8, Montreuil, France
E-mail: pelachaud@iut.univ-paris8.fr

Jean-Claude Martin
LIMSI-CNRS, Orsay, France
E-mail: martin@limsi.fr

Elisabeth André
University of Augsburg, Multimedia Concepts and Applications, Augsburg, Germany
E-mail: andre@informatik.uni-augsburg.de

Gérard Chollet
LTCI - CNRS UMR 5141, GET - ENST, Paris, France
E-mail: gerard.chollet@enst.fr

Kostas Karpouzis
ICCS, National Technical University of Athens, Zografou, Greece
E-mail: kkarpou@softlab.ece.ntua.gr

Danielle Pelé
France Télécom, Orange Labs, Cesson-Sévigné, France
E-mail: danielle.pele@orange-ftgroup.com

Library of Congress Control Number: 2007934981

CR Subject Classification (1998): I.2.11, I.2, H.5, H.4, K.3

LNCS Sublibrary: SL 7 – Artificial Intelligence

ISSN   0302-9743
ISBN-10   3-540-74996-9 Springer Berlin Heidelberg New York
ISBN-13   978-3-540-74996-7 Springer Berlin Heidelberg New York

Springer is a part of Springer Science+Business Media

springer.com

© Springer-Verlag Berlin Heidelberg 2007
Printed in Germany

Typesetting: Camera-ready by author, data conversion by Scientific Publishing Services, Chennai, India
Printed on acid-free paper   SPIN: 12161539   06/3180   5 4 3 2 1 0

Preface

The Intelligent Virtual Agents conference started in 1999 in Salford in Manchester, UK. It was a biannual event: in 2001, the conference was held in Madrid, Spain; in 2003 in Irsee, Germany; in 2005 on Kos, Greece. Since IVA 2006 held in Marina del Rey, California, USA, the conference has become an annual event.

Intelligent Virtual Agents (IVAs) are autonomous, graphically embodied agents in an interactive, 2D or 3D virtual environment. They are able to interact intelligently with the environment, other IVAs, and especially with human users. The conference is an interdisciplinary forum for researchers and practitioners in computer graphics, animation, computer games, virtual environments, artificial intelligence, natural language processing, cognitive modeling, human – computer interaction and artificial life. Since the first IVA back in 1999, firm lines of research have been established, but there is much that the graphics and AI communities can learn from each other.

This volume contains the proceedings of the Seventh International Conference on Intelligent Virtual Agents, IVA 2007, held in ENST, Paris, France September 17–19. As in 2005 and 2006, IVA hosted the Gathering of Animated Lifelike Agents (GALA 2007), an annual festival to showcase the latest animated lifelike agents created by university students and academic or industrial research groups. IVA 2007 received 100 submissions from all over the world. From these submissions, 19 are published as long and 12 as short papers. In addition, 32 posters were selected for presentation at the poster sessions and are published as 2-page descriptions. Finally, five industrialists were invited to demonstrate their products of which short descriptions appear in the proceedings. Apart from the short and long papers, three invited conferences were held: Luc Steels, Sony CSL Paris, France; Sotaro Kita, University of Birmingham, UK; and Drifa Benseghir, animator, France.

This conference could only happen thanks to the help of a large number of people. In particular we would like to thank the Program Committee, whose hard and contentious work allowed us to select the best submitted papers for presentation. We are also very grateful to all the authors that submitted so many high-quality papers. Their willingness to share ideas and projects together ensured the richness of the conference. We are very thankful to all the attendees of the conference. Special thanks go to the conference committee and local organizers—Martine Charrue, Lori Malatesta, Sophie Pageau-Maurice, Catherine Vazza and all the volunteer students—that made it possible to prepare and run the conference smoothly. We are indebted to our sponsors, &ftgroup France Telecom and the European Project IST FP6 IP Callas. And last but not least we are very grateful to University Paris 8, CNRS-LIMSI, Augsburg University, and the National Technical University of Athens, and more particularly to ENST that hosted the conference.

September 2007

Catherine Pelachaud
Jean-Claude Martin
Elisabeth André
Gérard Chollet
Kostas Karpouzis
Danielle Pelé

Organization

General Conference Chairs

Catherine Pelachaud (University of Paris 8)
Jean-Claude Martin (LIMSI-CNRS)
Elisabeth André (University of Augsburg)
Gérard Chollet (ENST)
Kostas Karpouzis (ICCS, National Technical University of Athens)
Danielle Pelé (France Telecom)

General Committee

Ruth Aylett (Heriot-Watt University)
Jonathan Gratch (University of Southern California)
Patrick Olivier (University of Newcastle Upon Tyne)
Stefan Kopp (University of Bielefeld)

Scientific Committee

Jan Allbeck
Jens Allwood
Elisabeth André
Norman Badler
Jeremy Bailenson
Amy Baylor
Gaspard Breton
Joanna Bryson
Stéphanie Buisine
Felix Burkhardt
Lola Cañamero
Justine Cassell
Marc Cavazza
Zhigang Deng
Angélica de Antonio
Fiorella de Rosis
Patrick Gebhard
Marco Gillies
Art Graesser
Dirk Heylen
Adrian Hilton

Katherine Isbister
Mitsuru Ishizuka
Kostas Karpouzis
Michael Kipp
Martin Klesen
Stefan Kopp
Nicole Kraemer
Brigitte Krenn
James Lester
Brian Loyall
Steve Maddock
Andrew Marriot
Jean-Claude Martin
Stacy Marsella
Yukiko Nakano
Anton Nijholt
Toyoaki Nishida
Wenji Mao
Ana Paiva
Maja Pantic
Catherine Pelachaud

Danielle Pelé
Sylvie Pesty
Christopher Peters
Paolo Petta
Isabella Poggi
Helmut Prendinger
Stephen Read
Matthias Rehm
Thomas Rist
Zsofia Ruttkay
Marc Schröder
Jianhua Tao
Daniel Thalmann
Kris Thórisson
Henriette C. van Vugt
Hannes Vilhjálmsson
Spyros Vosinakis
Nigel Ward
Ian Wilson

Additional Reviewers

Elisabetta Bevacqua
Klaus Bruegmann
Nate Cantelmo
Betsy van Dijk
Alastair Gill
Qin Gu
Francisco Iacobelli
Florian Joffrin
Brent Lance

Jina Lee
Qing Li
Sandy Louchart
Maurizio Mancini
Radoslaw Niewiadomski
Magalie Ochs
Stavros Petridis
Mark Riedl
Kristina Striegnitz

Tanasai Sucontphunt
Ivo Swartjes
Marion Tellier
Paul Tepper
Mariet Theune
Nancy Wang
Chang Yun
Job Zwiers

Sponsoring Institutions

&ftgroup France Telecom
European Project IST FP6 IP Callas

In Association with

Springer
Association for the Advancement of Artificial Intelligence
Eurographics
FP6 IST Humaine Network of Excellence
SIGCHI the ACM Special Interest Group on Computer-Human Interaction
SIGART the ACM Special Interest Group on Artificial Intelligence

Organized By

Université Paris 8
LIMSI-CNRS
University of Augsburg
ENST
National Technical University of Athens
France Telecom

Table of Contents

Feedback Models

Dialogues

Applications

Evaluation

Gaze Models

Emotions

Poster Session

Industrial Demos

Simulation Level of Detail for Virtual Humans

Cyril Brom, Ondřej Šerý, and Tomáš Poch

Charles University in Prague, Faculty of Mathematics and Physics
Malostranské nám. 2/25, Prague, Czech Republic
brom@ksvi.mff.cuni.cz

Abstract. Graphical level of detail (LOD) is a set of techniques for coping with the issue of limited computational resources by reducing the graphical detail of the scene far from the observer. Simulation LOD reduces quality of the simulation at the places unseen. Contrary to graphical LOD, simulation LOD has been almost unstudied. As a part of our on-going effort on a large virtual-storytelling game populated by tens of complex virtual humans, we have developed and implemented a set of simulation LOD algorithms for simplifying virtual space and behaviour of virtual humans. The main feature of our technique is that it allows for several degrees of detail, i.e. for *gradual* varying of simulation quality. In this paper, we summarise the main lessons learned, introduce the prototype implementation called IVE and discuss the possibility of scaling our technique to other applications featuring virtual humans.

1 Introduction

Virtual humans are typically thought of as software components *imitating* behaviour of a human in a virtual world in a *believable* manner. Virtual humans are equipped with a *virtual body* which is graphically visualised. As the research and development in this field is maturing, increasingly large virtual environments are starting to be populated by virtual humans (v-humans), e.g. [2, 15, 17]. A lot of effort has been invested to examining graphical level of detail (LOD) to capitalise from the scene-believability/computational-complexity trade-off. However, almost nothing has been done *outside frustum* to cope with the problem of limited memory and processor resources, despite the growing need for such solutions, at least in the fields of computer and serious games.

One possible approach to the problem with limited resources is to optimise the algorithms needed, both graphical and others, as demonstrated to a large extent e.g. in [17]. However, obviously, we can not optimise beyond some limit. After we reach it, we are forced to commit ourselves to the *simplification* approach. This line of thinking compels us to gain computational resources on the expense of quality of the simulation at the places that are unimportant (and unseen) at a given instant, leading us to *simulation LOD*. As simulation quality can be degraded to nothingness, this method can be used for environments of almost any size.

Degradation of simulation quality makes this approach inapplicable when the simulation is aimed to *compute* a result, for example for large social or economic simulations, e.g. [12]. In such a case, the simulation typically must run distributively on more PCs instead. Fortunately, in the domain of v-humans, quality of the

C. Pelachaud et al. (Eds.): IVA 2007, LNAI 4722, pp. 1–14, 2007.
© Springer-Verlag Berlin Heidelberg 2007

simulation out of the scene is not the issue, *provided a user at the scene experiences the right thing* [11]. Hence, the question behind simulation LOD is how to save resources by degrading quality, but keeping the *illusion* of quality, i.e. *believability*.

We have addressed this question as a part of our effort at a large educational storytelling game populated by tens of complex virtual humans [7] by:

1. Proposing an abstract framework for simulation LOD. We intended this framework to be implemented in our storytelling application, and also possibly scaled for other applications. It had to allow for simplifying space (hence, *space LOD*) and behaviour of v-humans (*LOD AI*) at the unimportant places. We demanded varying the detail of the simulation at all places *gradually*, i.e. we required several levels of detail, which has two advantages discussed later.
2. Implementing a prototype.
3. Implementing the technique in our storytelling application.

As our scope is games, the technique is aimed at RPG-like *large* environments, i.e. worlds including tens of different areas, e.g. a region with villages, fields, and meadows. These worlds are inhabited by tens of *complex* v-humans, i.e. v-humans performing in real time several, at least two, complex tasks that are possibly conflicting (adopted according to [9]). Typically, these tasks last minutes, include manipulation with several objects, and apparently require human-level cognitive abilities. An example of such a task is harvesting or watering the garden (as opposed to obstacle avoidance or crowding). The framework is further required to be universal in the sense that it can handle different complex tasks provided as data.

We stress the scope, since recently, applications featuring different kinds of large environments have appeared—e.g. towns where all the actors "only" walk along the streets avoiding each other and not entering the houses (not that these are simple!). Perhaps, these applications can also benefit from a simulation LOD, but one concerning steering, crowding etc. Our LOD is focused on complex cognitive tasks instead.

Recently, we have completed Point 2, i.e. prototyped the simulation LOD in our toolkit for v-humans investigation called IVE [8], and our on-going work is concerned with Point 3. In the course of prototyping, we have focused on the gist of the issue, i.e. on the simulation LOD itself, and abstracted from "other v-humans issues" we would have faced when developing a full application. This, above all, means that we have intentionally avoided 3D implementation. The LOD model is implemented as a sort of abstract machine with a grid-world environment (but still with embodied v-humans). To use a 3D world would only have distracted us from the problems that are simulation LOD relevant to the problems that are 3D world relevant, e.g. to the obstacle avoidance problem, the visibility problem etc. These issues are not of much relevance when degrading simulation detail, at least in typical cases. Similarly, our v-humans have presently only limited emotions and no social relationship to the others. Scaling the technique to a 3D world and equipping our agents with relationships and emotions, using our emotional model developed in parallel [4], is a part of our on-going work on Point 3.

Goal of the Paper. During prototyping, we have stumbled on several inherent simulation LOD issues stemming from the gradualness requirement, some of which we have solved. They are mostly representational problems (both space and behavioural), and issues concerning retaining information when simulation is degraded to be able to reconstruct (to some extent) the full simulation when the detail elevates. We believe that the most important contribution of our work is not the set of particular methods we have developed, but *uncovering* of the very issues.

In this paper, our aim is to provide the reader with insight into the problematic, helping the reader to adopt the gradual simulation LOD technique for his or her application if needed. Hence, we present our technique as a general framework for thinking about the topic rather than a set of formal algorithms addressing particular issues. However, some of our solutions are also presented.

Section 2 introduces simulation LOD in general. Simulation LOD is contrasted with graphical LOD, various simulation LODs that have been already proposed in literature are discussed, an example scenario on *gradual* simulation LOD introduced, and issues of this technique are detailed. Section 3 is devoted to explanation of our framework. In Section 4, our prototype is introduced. Section 5 discusses strengths and weaknesses of our technique, shedding light on its scalability and viability.

2 Simulation LOD Overview

When speaking about LOD techniques, it is good to start with the distinction between graphical and simulation LOD. Basically, while graphical LOD concerns the simplification of portrayal of what happens in the world model, simulation LOD concerns AI of v-humans and virtual world dynamic, i.e. what happens *per se*. This (simplified) distinction between graphical and simulation LOD is mirrored in the explanatory (and again simplified) "two-layer" metaphor regarding applications featuring v-humans as being comprised of: (1) a simulator of a world model and AI of v-humans, and (2) a GUI depicting the outcome of the simulator.

Basically, graphical LOD helps to reduce the detail of the scene out of the scope of the observer. This technique can be to great advantage applied not only to the walls and objects, but to v-humans bodies as well. For example, inspired by the authors of ALOHA system [15], we can speak about a geometrical, animation, and gesture and conversational LOD used for the bodies (apparently, we do not need to care much about facial expression and non-verbal gestures for background characters, saving the resources for the foreground characters). Even gesture and conversation LOD, however, deals only with the situation, when the v-humans are *at* the scene. Once we are aiming at a simulation of a large world with tens of complex v-humans, we will surely have v-humans that are also *out of* the frustum at some particular moments. At this point, simulation LOD comes into play (Fig. 1). The purpose of this branch of techniques is to further capitalise from simplifying the simulation out of frustum.[1]

In the rest of this section, we aim at providing the reader with a general intuition behind simulation LOD. We detail several relatively simple simulation LOD approaches, presenting a ground for thinking about limitations and possible improve-ments, and then, we explain requirements on our *gradual* method using an example scenario.

---

[1] It may be argued that simulation LOD may also concern what happens at the scene. E.g., the mentioned gesture and conversation LOD may be regarded as an "at the border" technique. See [14] for another example. Here, we will disregard this terminological issue for brevity.

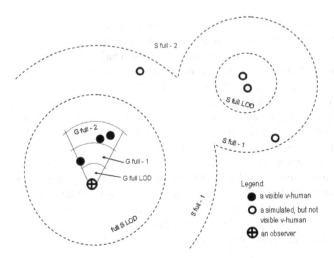

Fig. 1. The relation between graphical levels of detail (G LOD) and simulation levels of detail (S LOD) is depicted from the bird-eye view. "Full" denotes the full level of detail, "full-1" denotes the detail full minus 1 etc. As it can be seen, a place out of the frustum simulated in the full simulation detail can exist. This place may be important e.g. from the plot point of view.

Related Work. Computer games with large environments typically use a simulation LOD in addition to a graphical LOD, however, only to a limited extent. Either an *ad hoc* LOD is used, or, more often, the places in the frustum and next to it are simulated in the full detailed, while the places out of the sight not at all, e.g. [1, 13] (Fig. 2_1). Though this "all—nothing" method may fit for some games, it causes scenic inconsistencies in games emphasising a story, e.g. when a user expect a v-human to return to the scene. Moreover, this approach allows for only one place simulated in "full" detail: the place observed by the user. However, once we have a story, a drama manager may need to determine another place of importance due to course of the story reasons. Finally, "all—nothing" approach typically brings a high overhead of changing the focus of attention, since the simulation at the new centre must start from scratch, as opposed to gradual approach, where something is already simulated.

We may imagine an approach allowing for more important places (Fig. 2_4), or gradual simulation around the scene (2_5), but what we are looking for is actually a combination of both (Fig. 1, 2_3). This will help us to diminish the story inconsistencies and to keep the overhead in control. Such an approach has been presented in [5], however, it covers only combat and interaction behaviour of creatures from a real-time strategy game. Similarly, a gradual simplification has been already introduced for traffic simulation [11]. As opposed to these, we are interested in a general technique focused on complex v-humans.

In this domain, the ALOHA system has presented a robust simulation LOD using a role-passing technique [15]. When a v-human is far from the observer, it performs only a basic behaviour (staying, walking etc.). When the user approaches, each influenced v-human overtakes a role describing a domain specific behaviour, e.g. a bar-patron role. Additionally, path-finding for v-humans out of the frustum is simplified. Though this approach clearly brings new possibilities, the issue of partial behaviour is challenged only to limited extent. It likely would not be a problem to overcome the "see—not see" aspect of this method, but it is not clear how to scale the method to cope with performing a role only *partially*. Basically, ALOHA allows just for three simulation details: "full" (a v-human has taken a role), "medium" (it performs only basic behaviour), and "nothing". Additionally, ALOHA is concerned with LOD AI, but we are interested also in simplifying virtual space.

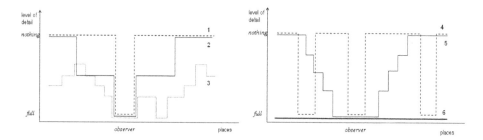

Fig. 2. Illustration of different simulation LOD approaches. 1) "see—not see" + "all—nothing", 2) ALOHA LOD, 3) gradual LOD with more partially important places, 4) "all—nothing" with more fully important places, 5) "see—not see" gradual, 6) full simulation.

Gradual Simulation LOD Example. To allow for comparison with ALOHA [15], we now demonstrate on a pub-scenario how we intended our gradual LOD to work. (We have implemented this scenario in our prototype with some minor distinctions).

Imagine a pub with a waiter and miners enjoying by drinking, chatting, watching TV, dancing etc. We will concentrate on "drinking at a table" behaviour (Fig. 3). If the pub is simulated in the detail "full", each miner should sit at a table, chat with his colleagues, sip of his beer from time to time, ask the waiter for a new beer when the old one is emptied, go to the toilet when nature calls, etc.

Assume that when the user leaves the pub and starts roaming around it, the detail in the pub is decreased to "full-1". What should happen? The miners should stop chatting and sipping of beer, instead, each should empty his glass at once every half an hour or so. After that, he should order a new beer, and the waiter should give it to him instantly, which means that he should not walk to the table, but move from the pipe to the miner in a one "giant step", and swap the glasses at once. Similarly, when nature calls, the miner in question should move to the toilet instantly.

Assume that when the user is in the farther part of the village, the detail in the pub is decreased to "full-2". At this detail, every room in the pub should be abstracted to a single point, and the glasses should cease to exist (i.e. simplifying space). However, the miners should still stay at their tables, and the waiter should decrease a bit beer level in the barrel every hour or so (instead of serving beer). Additionally, each miner still should be allowed to decide to change his activity—e.g. to start to play billiard, or to go to the toilet. At "full-3" detail, the whole pub should become a single point, and the tables and the chairs should cease to exist. Still, the miners and the waiter should stay in the pub and, of course, they should be allowed to go home, or a new person should be allowed to enter the pub, each using "giant steps" when moving.

Notice three important things. First, as the miners' behaviour is simplified, the processor load should decrease (which is the case, see Sec. 4). Second, the result of the simulation in "full" detail may differ from the simulation in a partial detail. However, third, believability is retained to large extent: when the user returns to the pub, he or she will find the miners in a consistent situation (more or less). Consider two scenarios. 1) If the user roams at the second part of the village, the detail is only "full-2", which means that when the user returns, the miners will still sit behind the

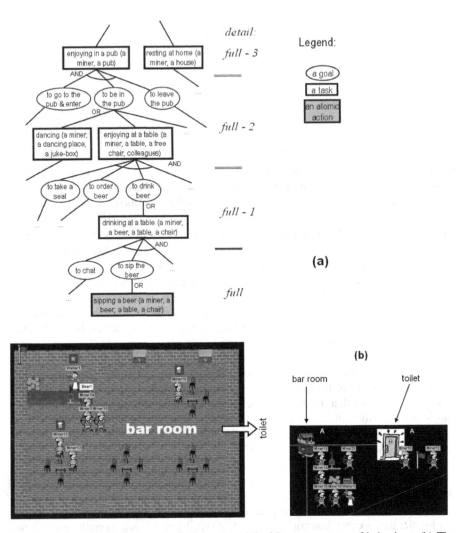

Fig. 3. (a) A part of pub behaviour. Notice the AND-OR tree structure of behaviour. (b) The pub scenario in IVE. In this particular scenario, there is no user avatar, but the user can set the LOD using a "red flag". Left: the bar room, "full" detail. Right: the same situation depicted, but the detail is lowered: both the bar room and the toilet are abstracted to a single point (note the **A** mark).

same tables as before (or they will perform another activity, but the same as they would perform in the case of the full simulation during the user's absence). 2) If the user leaves the village at all ("full-3"), the sitting positions are not remembered and must be generated randomly: but sooner than s/he enters the pub again; actually, when s/he enters the village. Because of this, it is guaranteed that the simulation will have been running for a while with the new positions before s/he enters the pub. Moreover, the user will still find in the pub some of the old guys, who have not gone home.

Gradual Simulation LOD Problem Detailed. The sketched gradual LOD raises several questions, among which the most striking are:

1. How many levels of detail shall we have and how to simplify the space?
2. If we simplify a location, what shall we do with the objects in there?
3. How to vary behavioural complexity of v-humans?
4. How to assign importance to the places and what to do when the importance is being changed?
5. How to retain information to be able to reconstruct the full simulation?

These issues must be addressed when one aims at a gradual simulation LOD.

3 Proposed Simulation LOD Framework

This section introduces our framework, being structured according to Question (1) – (5). We remark that following our "GUI—simulator" explanatory metaphor for applications featuring v-humans, what we introduce here can be seen as a proposal of an abstract world simulator that presents a lower layer for a 3D GUI.

Questions (1): Space Representation. In our framework, space is represented hierarchically, each layer presenting an additional level of a logically coherent space abstraction. The layers typically mirror the following line: places/parts of rooms/ rooms/houses/suburbs/villages etc. Each layer also presents one possible simulation detail. A bar room from the example above is an area from the layer "full-2", while the pub is from "full-3". The number of details depends on the complexity and size of the world. Our example scenario has five levels, with four villages at the top.

We call the leaves of the hierarchy, i.e. the discrete ground constituting a world, *way-places* (or *tiles*). A non-leaf node is called an *area*, and the root represents the whole world. In addition to the tree structure, each layer is organised in a graph, whose edges afford passage to a neighbouring way-place/area (Fig. 4a). Upon this structure, hierarchical A* can be used, and a pseudo-continuous 3D world developed.

To describe how to simplify space we use a *membrane metaphor*—imagine an elastic membrane cutting through the hierarchy of way-places and areas (Fig. 4b) that can be reshaped in every time step. Each area or place that is at the membrane at a particular instant is simulated as an abstract point, and nothing "below" it exists. This means that the whole world is simulated in "full" detail when the membrane crosses just way-places. If it crosses an area, the detail is decreased there.

For the purposes of coherence, there is need to settle the following *shaping rules*:

- If an area or a way-place x is at the membrane, every neighbouring area or way-place with the same parent as x is at the membrane too.
- If an area y is above the membrane, every neighbouring area with the same parent as y is above or at least at the membrane too.

For example, if a way-place from the bar room is at the membrane, all its way-places will be at the membrane too. This ensures that when the simulation runs in "full" detail somewhere in the bar room, it will run in "full" detail everywhere here. As the bar room itself is above the membrane in this case, all rooms from the pub must be simulated at least as abstract points (because the pub is their common parent). Similarly, if there is a suburb that includes this pub and near houses, all the houses must be simulated at least as abstract points. This ensures that at least something happens in the areas near to the centre of attention, which helps with the issues of story consistency and overhead during reshaping, as discussed later.

Question (2): Objects. *Objects* are represented as abstract entities (which cannot be decomposed to sub-objects presently). Bodies of v-humans are represented as objects. Each v-human is driven by its autonomous action selection mechanism (ASM). The problem with the objects is: what shall we do with them when the detail is low?

In our framework, if an area is fully simulated, the object is located at a way-place or at/on another object, e.g. at the table. If the detail is decreased, the object can either cease to exist, or it can be positioned at the area (or at/on another object that exists) (Fig. 4b). In the example from Sec. 2, with the detail "full-2", the chairs are placed at the tables; the tables, the barrel, and the actors are in the pub; and the glasses do not exist. To settle which of these possibilities apply for a particular object, we assign an *existence level* and a *view level* to every object. If the detail decreases below existence level, the object ceases to exist, otherwise, it is simulated. *View level* then determines detail required by the object after it starts to be simulated (hence, it is always equal to or higher than existence level). For example, if a waiter has "full-1" view level and "full-3" existence level, it will not exist if the detail is lower then "full-3", but if the detail elevates to "full-3", it must be further increased to "full-1" (which includes increasing the detail in the neighbouring areas according to the shaping rules). The algorithm for determining exact detail after an increase is detailed in [18].

Though this seems simple, three problems rise: A) how to remember detailed positions of objects being removed? B) how to place the objects during elevating the detail? C) what to do when an object is moving between areas with different details?

We have adopted following solutions (the description is simplified for brevity). A) Every object existing at a low detail remembers its own positions at all possible higher details. Concerning the non-simulated objects, we distinguish between *area-native* and *area-foreign* objects (a glass or a table is area-native in a pub, as opposed to a watering can). Area-native objects are destroyed in the sense of object oriented programming and only their total number is remembered by the area. The position and state information of area-foreign objects are stored by the area.

B) In this situation, we have an area being expanded. Hence, we must find exact positions for (a) already simulated objects that remembers their detailed position, (b) already simulated objects that does not remember their detailed position (for they came into the area when the detail was low), (c) presently not-simulated area-foreign objects that have to become simulated, (d) like (c) but area-native. The objects from categories (a, c) are placed according to their remembered positions, while (b, d) using a "room-specific" placing algorithm implemented for each area. Generally, this algorithm uses the strategy of generating objects randomly around fixed places (e.g. glasses somewhere at the bar). At the extreme, objects might be placed to exact preset positions (e.g. a table that never move to the way-place <12, 14>). Note, that for some objects of the category (d), it may be beneficial to remember their positions as well (e.g. for tables that can be moved, which are however moved only rarely). This last point is however unimplemented presently.

C) When an object is moving between areas with different details, following three cases may occur. (a) If the target area has sufficient detail – higher than object's *view level* – the object is just placed at the area. (b) If the area detail is too low – lower than object's *existence level* – the object ceases to exist. Finally (c), if the area detail is between object's *existence level* and *view level*, the detail in the target area is increased. The area is thus expanded to subareas and the object is placed into one of them. The exact algorithm is detailed in [6].

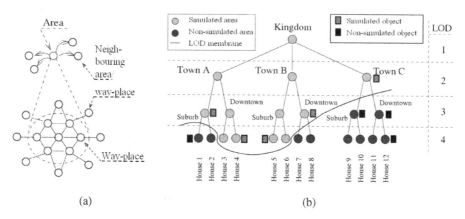

(a)   (b)

Fig. 4a (left). A part of a space hierarchy. The area comprises a set of way-places. Both the area and the way-places point to neighbouring areas or way-places respectively. **4b (right).** Space representation with the LOD membrane, and several simulated and non-simulated objects.

Question (3): Representation of Behaviour and ASM. Perhaps the most important issue is varying the complexity of behaviour. We need a hierarchical representation, with additional layers representing additional levels of behavioural complexity. We have adopted AND-OR trees as the representational concept, and reactive planning as the action selection mechanism (which is a relatively typical present day solution).

Basically, the AND-OR tree metaphor works with abstract goals representing *what* shall be achieved, and tasks representing *how* to achieve it. Typically, every goal can be accomplished by several tasks, while every task can be achieved by adopting some sub-goals. A v-human needs to perform only one task to achieve a goal (provided there is no failure), but to fulfil all sub-goals to solve a task. Hence, goals are represented as OR nodes, while tasks as AND nodes (Fig. 3a). The tasks that cannot be further decomposed are *atomic actions*, i.e. primitives changing the world-state.

In a typical simulation employing AND-OR trees, the ASM adopts a top-level goal, and recursively finds an atomic action for it. This is performed reactively in every time step, assuring that important external and internal events are taken into consideration. In our model, this is performed as well, but only when the simulation runs in "full" detail. If the detail is lowered, the ASM does not find sub-goals below a particular layer of the AND-OR tree (dependent on the detail), and instead, it executes the task at the lowest visited layer as it is atomic (Fig. 5a). E.g., when "drinking at a table" is executed atomically, the miner will empty the glass after half an hour instantly, and its bladder need will increase.

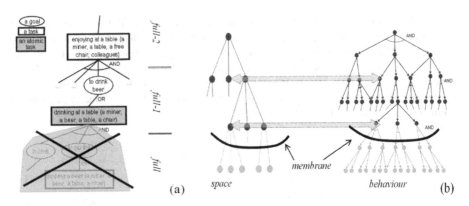

Fig. 5a. Performing a task atomically. **5b.** Layers of space hierarchy correspond with layers of behavioural representation (in reality, the correspondence can be a little more complicated).

How to specify which task shall be atomic at which detail? This can be settled simply by coupling the layers from the AND-OR tree with the layers of the hierarchy of areas and way-places (Fig. 5b). This projection can be read as "ability of the areas to afford what can be done in there" (a pub affords "enjoying in the pub", a bar room affords "enjoying at a table" etc.). If an area is not simulated, the respective tasks are not afforded. In our example, if the pub is shrunk to a point, which is a detail "full-3", "enjoying at a table" will not be possible to execute, instead, atomic execution of "enjoying in a pub" will be allowed. All what is needed is to carefully design existence level of every object so that the object is simulated when a task it is involved in can be performed. Note, however, that this is not a simple task.

Questions (4): Reshaping. We now turn our attention to changing detail. Basically, the importance of places originates in movement of important objects, which reshape the membrane. The mechanism for annotating important objects is view level. An example of an object always having "full" view level is the user avatar. Additionally, the drama manager is supposed to vary the detail (this is currently imitated manually). When detail in a particular area is elevated, objects must be placed and already executed atomic tasks must be "broken down" as described below. When detail decreases, we could adopt either of two mechanisms. First, we might immediately shrink the area, relocate objects in there or stop simulating them (depending on their existence level), interrupt currently running atomic tasks/actions and start the tasks from the higher layer of the AND-OR tree atomically. Second, we might adopt a "garbage collector" approach, which means to perform exactly the same, but not until processor resources are need. We have employed the latter mechanism for it helps us to keep down overhead in the case of a user roaming at the border of two areas.

From the implementation point of view, a discrete simulation paradigm was used. When an atomic action or an atomic task is to be started, its *end time* is estimated and hooked to a calendar as an event (e.g. end of "drinking at a table" is hooked at about 30 minutes from start of the task, Fig. 6). When the event is invoked, the result of the action/task is committed. If a conflict between two actions/tasks occurs, it must be handled in the time of occurrence, which may lead to unhooking the previously hooked ends of these two actions/tasks, and to hooking the end of a new action/task.

Consider now a task T that is executed atomically, but the simulation detail is increased before its end time (the end time is denoted as (2) and the time of expansion as (1) in Fig. 6). Two things now happen. First, T is *partially evaluated*. Second, simulation is started at the higher level of complexity, which means a sub-goal G for T is chosen, and a sub-task/action for G found and its end hooked ((3) in Fig. 6). Since T is likely half-finished after the partial evaluation, this sub-goal must be found carefully, otherwise believability may sustain a loss (e.g. chatting of the miners at a table should start in the middle). The case of decreasing the detail is handled similarly.

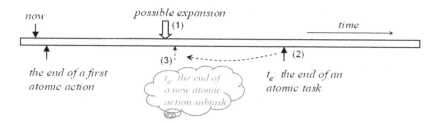

Fig. 6. Every end of an action or a task being performed is hooked in the calendar. Let an end of the task T be hooked at t_e. If detail elevates at moment (1), this event (i.e. end of "T") must be unhooked (2), T must be partially committed, its subgoals must be found, one of them chosen, and an atomic action or a task for the chosen subgoal must be found. The end of this newly found action/task is them hooked at time t_a (3).

Question (5): Information Retention. Perhaps the most important problem of simulation LOD is how to keep information about the situation in an area for the period of the simulation being stopped, or how to keep illusion that the situation is evolving. Our framework diminishes this issue, since it allows for partial simulation. Though in a coarse-grained way, the original situation can still be evolved, and some of the objects are still placed or their positions are remembered. When we decrease the detail in the pub from "full" to "full-1", miners will continue what they were doing before the decrease, skipping only the atomic actions. Some detail may be lost, but this may not matter as the user is far away. We remark that this "retain of information" is very problematic to achieve using "all—nothing" approach.

4 Prototype Implementation

We have implemented a simulation LOD prototype scenario using our Java toolkit for v-humans ASMs investigation called IVE [8] (Fig. 3b), which is also being used for the storytelling experiments presently [7]. IVE can be downloaded freely.

The scenario comprises of about 100 v-humans (miners and waiters) acting in four villages; each with a pub, five mines, and nine houses. Five levels of detail/layers of the space hierarchy have been used (a place, a room, a house or a mine, a village, the world). Way-places are square tiles. For experimental purposes, the detail is currently elevated only on the supervisor's demands and in accord with view levels of objects.

Several experiments measuring the speed and memory requirements have been carried out [6]. The results have not only revealed that the simulation runs faster at lower details, but also that when the world is simulated in "full" detail, where the v-humans are driven by about 5 000 reactive rules altogether, the simulation takes only about 5-10% of the maximum processor load at a 3GHz PC (the whole world at "full-1" detail takes about 0.1-0.5% with about 2 500 rules, and less then a third of all objects). The results of reshaping overhead measuring clearly showed that our approach keeps overhead more in control comparing to "all—nothing" approach, owing to the fact that it allows for allocating the overhead to several time steps (the detail from "nothing" to "full" can be increased through the intermediate details).

The increase of scripting-time of behaviour due to simulation LOD is about 50% (a rough estimate), which is acceptable. After we develop a 3D world, we plan to conduct an elaborate study of believability.

5   Discussion and Future Work

In this paper, we presented our simulation LOD technique as a general framework for thinking about how to save computational resources in a large application featuring complex virtual humans on the expense of decreasing quality of the simulation out of the frustum. The most remarkable feature of the technique is that it allows for *gradual* simplification of the simulation, which helps to keep reshaping overhead in control, and to avoid story inconsistencies. These issues are almost unsolvable when one commits herself to "all—nothing" approach.

The results we gained from our grid-world prototype allow us to conclude that our technique performs well to be scaled for our on-going storytelling game [7]. However, the question of scaling the technique to *other* applications remains to be answered, together with highlighting limits of the technique.

1. The technique relies on a tree-based space representation. This fits well for closed areas, i.e. rooms or corridors, but may bring troubles for open areas. We have an idea how to address this issue using fuzzy borders between areas, however, this is out of scope of this paper.
2. Representation of behaviour is based on AND-OR trees. We think that other strictly hierarchical representations, e.g. hierarchical state machines (HFSMs), can be used, provided the hierarchy has enough layers. Actually, a LOD AI for a first-person shooter agent that uses HFSMs has been already sketched in [10] (but to our knowledge, not further explored). However, combining our technique with heterarchies, neural networks or free-flow hierarchies, e.g. [16], may be problematic.
3. The technique is focused on general behaviour. For some specific behaviours, e.g. for conversation behaviour, a "domain-specific" simulation LOD may be vital. We have also not employed emotions and social relationships; exploring how these affect simulation LOD is a part of our on-going work. We plan to use our emotional model develop previously [4].
4. Our prototype uses a grid world, but not a 3D world. This was certainly beneficial for prototyping purposes, but surely, we cannot live with a grid world for ever. This scaling may bring new problems, e.g. visibility ones, which remains to be tackled.

Some advanced "optimisation" issues inherent to our technique also exist. For example, a procedure for atomic execution of each task must be written manually. It is intriguing to think about whether it would be possible to generate these scripts automatically based on the results of many simulations performed in the full detail. Apparently, this presents a tough problem, currently not addressed. However, some advanced issues related to better membrane shaping are under investigation [6].

To conclude, we think that the technique is mature enough to be scaled to any application featuring a world complex in size and behavioural possibilities, provided the areas are (more or less) close, and behaviour can be represented in a strictly hierarchical fashion. Some particular issues may arise during scaling to 3D, and during equipping virtual humans with emotions and relationships, but we think these can be overcome relatively easily.

Acknowledgments. This work was partially supported by the Ministry of Education of the Czech Republic (grant MSM0021620838), and by the Program "Information Society" under project 1ET100300517, and GA UK 351/2006/A-INF/MFF. Authors would like to thank to Brian Mac Namee for his comments.

References

1. Adzima, J.: AI Madness: Using AI to Bring Open-City Racing to Life. In: Gamasutra Online (January 24, 2001) [6.3.2007] (2001)
2. Alelo Inc.: Tactical Iraqi: a learning program for Iraqi Arabic [18.11.2006] (2005), http://www.tacticallanguage.com
3. Aylett, R.S., Louchart, S., Dias, J., Paiva, A., Vala, M.: FearNot! – An Experiment in Emergent Narrative. In: Panayiotopoulos, T., Gratch, J., Aylett, R., Ballin, D., Olivier, P., Rist, T. (eds.) IVA 2005. LNCS (LNAI), vol. 3661, pp. 305–316. Springer, Heidelberg (2005)
4. Bída, M.: Emotion bots in Unreal Tournament (in Czech) Bachelor thesis. Faculty of Mathematics-Physics. Charles University in Prague (2006)
5. Brockington, M.: Level-Of-Detail AI for a Large Role-Playing Game. In: AI Game Programming Wisdom I, pp. 419–425. Charles River Media, Inc, Hingham, Mas (2002)
6. Brom, C.: Action Selection for Virtual Humans in Large Environments (in Czech) PhD thesis. Faculty of Mathematics-Physics. Charles University in Prague (2007)
7. Brom, C., Abonyi, A.: Petri-Nets for Game Plot. In: Proceedings of AISB Artificial Intelligence and Simulation Behaviour Convention, Bristol, vol. 3, pp. 6–13 (2006)
8. Brom, C., Lukavský, J., Šerý, O., Poch, T., Šafrata, P.: Affordances and level-of-detail AI for virtual humans. In: Proceedings of Game Set and Match 2, The Netherlands, Delft (2006), http://urtax.ms.mff.cuni.cz/ive/public/about.php [6-3-2007]
9. Bryson, J.J.: Intelligence by Design: Principles of Modularity and Coordination for Engineering Complex Adaptive Agents. PhD thesis, Mas. Institute of Technology (2001)
10. Champandard, A.J.: AI Game Development: Synthetic Creatures with learning and Reactive Behaviors. New Riders, USA (2003)
11. Chenney, S.: Simulation Level-Of-Detail. In: GDC (2001), http://www.cs.wisc.edu/~schenney/research/culling/chenney-gdc2001.pdf [6-3-2007]
12. Gilbert, N., den Besten, M., et al.: Emerging Artificial Societies Through Learning. The Journal of Artificial Societies and Social Simulation, JASSS, 9(2) (2006)

13. Grinke, S.: Minimizing Agent Processing in "Conflict: Desert Strom". In: AI Game Programming Wisdom II, pp. 373–378. Charles River Media, Inc, Hingham, Mas (2004)
14. Jan, D., Traum, D.R.: Dialog Simulation for Background Characters. In: Panayiotopoulos, T., Gratch, J., Aylett, R., Ballin, D., Olivier, P., Rist, T. (eds.) IVA 2005. LNCS (LNAI), vol. 3661, Springer, Heidelberg (2005)
15. McNamee, B., Dobbyn, S., Cunningham, P., O´Sullivan, C.: Men Behaving Appropriately: Integrating the Role Passing Technique into the ALOHA system. In: Proceedings of the Animating Expressive Characters for Social Interactions (2002)
16. de Sevin, E., Thalmann, D.: A motivational Model of Action Selection for Virtual Humans. In: Computer Graphics International, IEEE Computer Society Press, New York (2005)
17. Shao, W., Terzopoulos, D.: Environmental modeling for autonomous virtual pedestrians. In: Proceedings of 2005 SAE Symposium on Digital Human Modeling for Design and Engineering, Iowa City, Iowa (June 2005)
18. Šerý, O., Poch, T., Šafrata, P., Brom, C.: Level-Of-Detail in Behaviour of Virtual Humans. In: Wiedermann, J., Tel, G., Pokorný, J., Bieliková, M., Štuller, J. (eds.) SOFSEM 2006. LNCS, vol. 3831, pp. 565–574. Springer, Heidelberg (2006)

Towards Natural Gesture Synthesis: Evaluating Gesture Units in a Data-Driven Approach to Gesture Synthesis

Michael Kipp[1], Michael Neff[2], Kerstin H. Kipp[3], and Irene Albrecht[4]

[1] DFKI, Germany
michael.kipp@dfki.de
[2] UC Davis, USA
neff@cs.ucdavis.edu
[3] Saarland University, Experimental Neuropsychology Unit, Germany
k.kipp@mx.uni-saarland.de
[4] TomTec Imaging Systems GmbH, Germany
ialbrecht@tomtec.de

Abstract. Virtual humans still lack naturalness in their nonverbal behaviour. We present a data-driven solution that moves towards a more natural synthesis of hand and arm gestures by recreating gestural behaviour in the style of a human performer. Our algorithm exploits the concept of gesture units to make the produced gestures a continuous flow of movement. We empirically validated the use of gesture units in the generation and show that it causes the virtual human to be perceived as more natural.

Keywords: Embodied Conversational Agents, Nonverbal Behavior Generation, Gesture Synthesis.

1 Introduction

Researchers and users agree that interactive Virtual Characters (VCs) still lack naturalness in their movements, be it facial expression, gesture or posture changes. A recent state-of-the-art report [1] describes VCs as "wooden" and lacking variety in response, whereas human beings are all unique and have limitless variety. Although photorealism of computer graphics is steadily advancing "behavior may be more important than the visual realism of the character". Psychologists [2] and animators [3] alike confirm the important role of a visible and consistent personality for an animated character to make it more human-like and appealing. While research in the area of gesture synthesis has been active and successful for over two decades [4,5] we believe that current research systems can be pushed in a variety of ways. First, most systems use a limited range of gestures and only a few systems can produce variants consistent with an individual style. Second, the produced gestures are rarely connected to form a fluid stream of gestures [6]. Finally, it is still hard to evaluate how natural the generated gestures are and to what aspects this naturalness is owed [7,2].

C. Pelachaud et al. (Eds.): IVA 2007, LNAI 4722, pp. 15–28, 2007.

In this paper we present a data-driven approach to synthesize gestures for a VC using procedural animation[1] [8,9,10]. Our approach features the recreation of the gesture style of a human performer, the production of a broad range of gestures, automatic synchronization with speech and the use of dynamic animation. While all technical details of the system are covered by Neff et al. [8], this paper can be regarded as a complement, giving a high-level overview, to then zoom in on gesture unit production. This sets the background for a new user study that validates the hypothesis that using gesture units makes the speaker appear more natural.

A *gesture unit* (g-unit) is a sequence of contiguous gestures where the hands only return to a rest pose at the end of the last gesture [11]. The concept stems from a proposed hierarchy of levels: on the lowest level, movement is seen as consisting of so-called *g-phases* (preparation, stroke, hold etc.), on the middle level these g-phases form whole gestures, called *g-phrases*, and on the top level gestures are grouped to *g-units* [12,6]. In his extensive gesture research, McNeill [12] found that most of his subjects performed only a single gesture per g-unit most of the time; we call such gestures *singletons*. When we analyzed our speakers Jay Leno (JL) and Marcel Reich-Ranicki (MR), both well-known TV talk show hosts with active and appealing gesture behaviour, we found a different distribution (column N displays the percentage of g-units containing N gestures, first row taken from [12]):

	1	2	3	4	5	6	>6
McNeill's subjects	56	14	8	8	4	2	8
Speaker JL	35.7	15.7	17.1	5.7	11.4	5.7	8.6
Speaker MR	33.3	16.7	11.1	14.8	9.3	3.7	11.1

JL and MR preferred "longer" g-units, and we wondered whether this was one of the reasons why their gestures were much more interesting to watch than those of the average layperson. Therefore, we not only integrated the production of g-units in our gesture generation algorithm but also conducted a user study to examine the effect of g-units on the perception of the VC.

2   Related Work

Data-driven approaches based on motion capture can produce high quality movement, but motion variation is limited. Stone et al. [13] achieve some variability and gesture-speech synchrony by splicing and warping motion captured pieces, but as the authors indicate, the system does not have the generality of procedural animation. Our approach is also data-driven, but we annotate a higher level gesture representation that allows us to make use of the flexibility of procedural animation, rather than relying on replaying low-level motion data.

Kopp et al. [14] based their system on the *Sketch Model* [15] and can create gestures from arbitrary form specifications and handle co-articulation. While

---

[1] Video samples of animations can be found on http://www.dfki.de/˜kipp/iva07

they focus on iconic gestures in spatial domains where the form-meaning relationship between speech and gesture is quite clear, we focus on metaphoric gestures where this relationship is less clear and therefore, lends itself to statistical modeling. We share with the *Sketch Model* the processing of underspecified gesture frames that are gradually enriched in the planning process.

While many systems require a complex input specification, the BEAT system [16] works on plain input text and reconstructs linguistic features (e.g., theme/rheme) to generate synchronized gestures. Our system shares this general concept but instead of using hand-made, hard-coded rules for gesture generation we automatically extract them from video data of human speakers. Lee and Marsella [17] also systematically examine a video corpus but their generation rules are still hand-made. While they do not explicitly model personal style they take the *affective state* into account. However, compared with these two approaches, our animation engine allows a more fine-grained specification of gesture phase structure, similar to [18,14]. Like our system, Hartman et al. [18] can generate *multiple strokes* as part of their expressivity parameters, but our system includes more detail concerning phase structure and timing. Several previous systems have been designed to animate expressive arm gestures (e.g. [19,20,21]). Our controller-based approach to physically simulated animation builds on similar work with hand-tuned controllers [22,23] and using controllers to track motion capture data [24], but is the first animation system to use controllers to synchronize body movement with speech.

There is limited other work on modeling the gesturing style of a specific performer, although more abstract models are starting to appear [25]. We propose modeling specific human performers as a way to achieve more natural and varied behaviour. While sharing aspects with other gesture systems, we are the first to explicitly produce g-units and to evaluate the impact of g-units in a separate user study.

3   Gesture Generation and Animation

Our approach is mainly data-driven, using a video corpus of the human performer, but also incorporates general, character-independent mechanisms. A labour-intensive *offline* or preprocessing phase has to be completed once for each new human speaker (Figure 1). It results in a *gesture profile* of this particular speaker and an updated *animation lexicon*. The actual runtime or *online* system can then produce gestures in the style of one of the modeled performers for any input text (Figure 2).

3.1   Offline: Annotation of Speech and Gesture

Our corpus consists of about 18 minutes of digitized video, 9 mins per speaker, from regular TV material where the speaker's face, torso and hands are visible. To prepare the video corpus for automatic analysis, a human coder transcribes speech and gestures according to our annotation scheme [9]. The transcription of

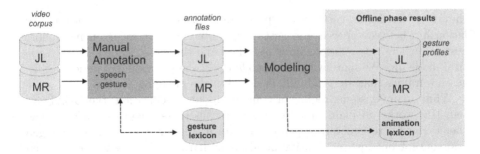

Fig. 1. Offline phase workflow: For every human speaker this work pipeline has to be completed once. The resulting data is used in the online system to generate gestures in the style of the modeled speaker for arbitrary input texts.

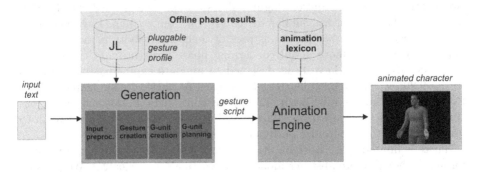

Fig. 2. Online processing: The runtime system can take arbitrary input texts (containing additional mark-up, see Section 3.3) and produce synchronized conversational gestures in the style of a modeled human performer. Gesture profiles can easily be exchanged and even mixed.

this corpus results in 229 gestures (70 g-units) for speaker JL, and 192 gestures (54 g-units) for MR.

Coding starts with transcribing speech in the PRAAT[2] tool [27]. The transcript is imported to the ANVIL[3] tool [28] where gesture annotation is performed on three separate tracks, as shown in Fig. 4. On the first track, *g-phases* (preparation, stroke, hold etc.) are transcribed [6,29]. In the track below the coder several of these phases into a *g-phrase* which basically corresponds to the notion of a "gesture" in everyday language.

On this track, the bulk of the annotation work takes place: selecting the lexeme, specifying form parameters and the link to speech. The *lexeme* refers to an entry in a *gesture lexicon* [10,26] that we assembled beforehand, where 39 gestural prototypes, i.e. recurring gesture patterns, are described by form constraints and illustrations (Figure 3). These lexemes were partly taken from the gesture literature and partly extracted from our corpus. Of the 39 entries in our

---

[2] http://www.praat.org
[3] http://www.dfki.de/~kipp/anvil

Fig. 3. Screenshots showing four lexemes from our gesture lexicon. The upper row shows samples performed by MR, the lower row shows schematic drawings (for readability) of speaker JL performing the same lexemes. The gesture lexicon contains additional textual descriptions on handshape, palm orientation, trajectory etc.

lexicon, 27 are used by both speakers, which is a large overlap that demonstrates a certain generality of the approach.

To describe gesture form the coder specifies handedness (RH, LH, 2H), trajectory (straight or curved), and the hand/arm configuration at the beginning and end of the stroke (only at the beginning of the hold for stroke-less gestures). The latter is specified with 4 attributes: three for the position of the hand and one for arm swivel. Finally, to mark the gesture's relation to speech we encode the *lexical affiliate* which is the word(s) whose meaning is most closely related to the gesture [30,29] as a symbolic link to the respective word(s) on the speech track. For temporal reasoning we also encode the word(s) that co-occur with the gesture stroke. In the third track the gesture phrases are again combined to make up *g-units* [11,6,12]. See [9] for a full description of the coding scheme.

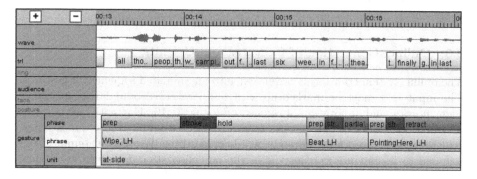

Fig. 4. Manual annotation was done in the ANVIL video annotation tool [28] on separate tracks for speech transcription and gesture annotation. Gestures were annotated on three hierarchically organized tracks for *phase, phrase* and *unit*.

3.2   Offline: Modeling Gesture Behaviour

In the modeling phase we build a *gesture profile* from the annotations. First, the speech transcription is preprocessed to abstract away from surface text. The words are reduced to their word stem and then mapped to so-called *semantic tags* like AGREEMENT ("yes"), PROCESS ("create", "manage"), QUEST_PART ("why"), and PERS_NAME ("Michael Jackson"). The tags form a thin semantic layer between surface text and gestures, containing aspects of communicative function (e.g. AGREEMENT, QUEST_PART) and semantics (e.g. PROCESS).

After preprocessing we use the annotated *lexical affiliate* links between gesture and speech to compute the conditional probability that gesture g occurs given semantic tag s. We also build a bigram model of gesture sequence, i.e. conditional probabilities that gesture g_i follows g_{i-1}. We do the same for *handedness*, i.e. we model the probability that gesture g is performed with the right, left or both hand(s), and store a bigram model of handedness sequences. Finally, we store the average number of multiple strokes and the average distance between stroke and co-occurring word per lexeme, and the general gesture rate (details in [8]). In the *GestureDB* we store every gesture occurrence, together with the spatial data from the manual annotation. It is *not* a collection of animation clips but rather contains essential form data about the gesture's expressive phase. This data includes spatial "pass through" points, indicating hand positions at the beginning and end of the stroke, and the shape of the movement trajectory (straight or curved).

In conjunction with the gesture lexicon we created an *animation lexicon* where animation-relevant data is stored for each lexeme, including palm orientation and posture changes, as well as warps to the motion envelope. For each new speaker, the lexicon can be (manually) enriched with character specifc information, including a default posture and succession pattern. The animation lexicon also defines the form of the *after-strokes* in a multiple stroke. A *multiple stroke* in a gesture contains many strokes: We call the first of these strokes *main stroke* and the subsequent ones *after-strokes*. After-stroke information generally involves small hand and forearm movements and specifying whether a hold phase is present.

3.3   Online: Generation of Gestures and G-Units

The online system transforms novel text into an animated sequence of gestures. The input text must be marked-up with temporal word boundaries, utterance segmentation and annotation of rheme and focus [31,16]. Currently, we add this information manually. The text is transformed to a graph where nodes represent time points and arcs represent words or gestures. Words are stemmed and mapped to a semantic tag, just as in the modeling step. The generation then proceeds in two steps: gesture creation/selection, and g-unit formation.

Gesture Creation and Selection. Using the speaker's gesture profile, we first create a large number of underspecified gesture frames which are then thinned out by a selection criterion. Gesture candidates are all gestures whose conditional probability to co-occur with a semantic tag exceeds a threshold of 0.1. One copy of the gesture is placed over the semantic tag in the graph. If the semantic tag is within a rheme, another copy is placed on the *focus* of the rheme [31]. For selection, we utilize the *n-gram* models to construct a sequence with maximum likelihood that observes the speaker's gesture rate. We use a similar approach to determine the handedness. Handshape is added according to our animation lexicon. After this step, we have a sequence of underspecified gesture frames that contain lexeme, handedness and handshape. The position in the graph determines the word(s) the gesture has to be synchronized with.

G-Unit Formation. The gesture hierarchy of phases, phrases and units is hypothesized to correspond to levels of speech phrase organisation. For instance, Kendon [11,32] suggested a correlation between *intonation units* and g-units. Such concepts go back to the hypothesis that speech and gesture originate from a single source, called *growth point* [12] or *idea unit* [32]. In our algorithm we try to approximate these concepts.

We "grow" g-units by merging neighbouring gestures (distance < 1.5 sec) within a single utterance segment, taking utterance segmentation as a crude approximation of intonation units. Note that the distance criterion is not speaker-dependent but could be made so to model the fact that speakers prefer longer or shorter g-units. Now, gesture phases, spatial parameters, and gesture-speech timing remains to be specified. Phase structure is determined as follows: If, for two consecutive gestures g_{i-1} and g_i, there is time for a preparation (.5 sec), then insert one. If not, insert a spatial constraint marker that g_i's start position must match g_{i-1}'s end position. Now find a suitable gesture, using lexeme and spatial constraints, from GestureDB (randomize over possible options) and generate multiple strokes randomly using the speakers mean value and standard deviation for this lexeme. Resulting temporal conflicts with the succeeding gesture g_i are resolved by either moving g_i back in time (up to a certain limit) or eliminating it altogether.

We synchronize gesture and speech by positioning the end of the stroke at the end of the corresponding word, using a random offset based on the speaker's mean value. For multiple strokes we synchronize all after-strokes with word end times of subsequent words, enforcing a minimum time span. For stroke-less gestures we synchronize the *start* of the independent hold [6] with the start of the word. In a final wrap-up phase we subtract 0.3 sec from all main stroke times (0.12 sec for after-strokes in a multiple stroke) as we empirically found this offset necessary to make the gesture timing look natural, and fill in all gaps within a g-unit with holds.

As Kendon [11] pointed out, the retraction phase is a property of the g-unit and *not* of a single gesture because within-unit gestures cannot have a full retraction by definition. We therefore generate a retraction phase for each g-unit using a simple heuristic to determine the rest position: if the distance to the following g-unit is small, retract to 'clasped', if medium retract to 'at side', if large retract to 'in pockets'. The results of the gesture generation are written to a *gesture script* containing the lexeme, timing and spatial information computed above.

3.4   Procedural Animation

The role of the animation engine is to take the gesture script as input and output a final animation. It does this in three main steps. First, it computes additional timing data and adds information from the animation lexicon (Section 3.2). Second, it maps all data to a representation suitable for generating animation. This representation is essentially a keyframe system and has tracks for every Degree of Freedom (DOF) of the character's body. The tracks are populated with desired angles at specific points in time and transition curves that specify how the DOF values should change over time. The basic keyframe representation is augmented with offset tracks (see below) that are summed with the main tracks to determine the final desired values for the joints. Additional tracks are used to control real time behaviour, such as gaze tracking. Once this representation has been populated, the third and final step is to generate the actual animation. The system can generate either dynamic, physically simulated skeleton motion, or kinematic motion. The system also produces eye brow raises on stressed phonemes and lip synching . Some of the key components of the system will be described below. Further details can be found in [8].

The gesture script does not contain all the data necessary for defining an animation and is hence augmented by the animation engine. The first step in this process is to complete the timing information. The animation engine also resolves possible spatial conflicts. These occur due to the coarse-grained spatial annotation, which can fail to record small hand separations and movements. Offsets are automatically added to deal with these cases. The rest of the augmentation involves adding the gesture-specific data from the animation lexicon, all of which is taken into account when the gesture poses are solved for and written into the low-level representation.

A pose is calculated at each phase boundary (e.g. the start and end of a stroke) using a series of local IK routines for the arms, wrists and lower-body chain. This is augmented with a feedback based balance controller and automatic collarbone adjustment based on the height of the hands. The wrist targets are defined in a body relative way, which is important for allowing the gestures to move appropriately with the body. Realtime processes provide gaze tracking and balance adjustment.

The offset tracks are used to layer different specifications together, such as when combining body rotation with gestures. They are also used to curve the spatial trajectory of motions by adding offsets in joint space. This allows a stroke to be specified with a straight or curved trajectory. It also allows the creation of more complicated gestures such as progressives, which feature the forearm and hand making circular motions.

When computing physically simulated animation, we use a controller based approach whereby an actuator is placed at each DOF which calculates the torque required to move the character towards the desired configuration. We use an antagonistic formulation of proportional-derivative control, following [33]. In order to synchronize the gesture timing with the specified timing and to preserve the spatial extent of the motions, we both shift the start time earlier and shorten the duration of each movement when doing dynamic simulation. The dynamic animations contain additional effects due to momentum, such as pendular motion when a character brings his hand to his side or wrist overshoot when the forearm is moved rapidly. A variable time step Rosenbrock integrator [34] is used to compute the motion using simulation code from SD/Fast [35]. Whereas kinematic animation runs in real time, physical simulation is only about one tenth real time so must be pre-computed and played back when needed.

3.5   Validation: Recognizability of Gesture Style

We validated the system with an emprical study where 26 subjects were exposed to video clips of generated gestures [8]. After a short training phase where the subjects watched original clips of the performers JL and MR, they went through two tests. In Test 1 the subjects watched a single animation, produced on a novel, synthesized text (prologue from "Star Wars"), and were asked which performer (JL or MR) it was based on. In Test 2 they saw a side-by-side screening of animations based on each model and were asked to identify which was which. In Test 1, subject selected the correct performer 69% of the time ($t(25)=2.083$; $p < .05$). In Test 2, subjects achieved, as expected, a higher success rate of 88% ($t(25)=6.019$; $p < .001$). These results show that the subjects were able to recognize the human original, based on only the gesture behaviour.

4   Evaluating Gesture Units

Despite the encouraging validation of our approach, evaluating nonverbal behaviour of VCs remains a difficult task [7,2]. One strategy is to single out one parameter in the generation process. In our approach, a major decision was to generate g-units instead of singletons. So our underlying hypothesis was: Using g-units makes our VC look more natural.

To test the impact of g-units beyond naturalness we selected a number of dimensions for personlity perception. We picked three dimensions from the "Big Five" [36] (friendliness, nervousness, extrovertedness) and added dimensions of potential relevance for VC applications, and arrived at 6 dimensions: naturalness, friendliness, nervousness, extrovertedness, competence, and trustworthiness.

4.1   Method

25 subjects (12 female) participated in this experiment. 14 subjects were recruited in Germany, 11 in the US.

Material. We prepared video material with a virtual character gesturing in two different ways for the same verbal material[4] (some English, some German). In the

---

[4] Samples of this material can be found on http://www.dfki.de/~kipp/iva07

U(nit) version we used the g-units generated by our system. In the S(ingleton) version we modified the animations so that only singleton gestures occur. For this, we replaced every hold that separated two gestures with a retraction. We left multiple strokes intact where possible and only removed enough after-strokes to make room for a retraction. In both versions, we replaced all rest poses with the "hands at side" rest pose, to make the effect of returning to rest pose clearer. We cut the material to 11 pieces of length 11-28 sec for each version (total of 2:58 min). In each piece we tried to include 2-3 g-units since in pilot studies too short clips did not show the effect of g-units clearly enough, as frequently returning to rest pose does not seem odd in a short clip. However, much longer clips would have made it hard to remember the impression of the first clip after viewing the second. We considered a side-by-side presentation which makes the difference between the two versions very clear but weakens the generality of the result. Pilot studies also caused us to block out the face of the VC (see Figure 5) since subjects reported being quite absorbed by facial expressions and head movement (gaze). The 11 clip pairs were presented in random order. Within-pair order (S-U or U-S) was balanced across subjects.

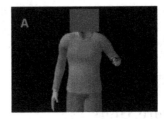

Fig. 5. In the g-unit experiment the face was blocked out to reduce distraction

Procedure. In the instruction the subject was informed that s/he was to compare two versions of the same virtual character and decide in which of the versions the character's behaviour was more natural, more friendly, more nervous, more extroverted, more competent, and more trustworthy. Subjects were explicitly requested to judge "intuitively" and to focus on the bodily behavior.

Each subject went through 11 rounds. In each round, both animation versions, labeled "A" and "B", were shown consecutively. Afterwards, a questionaire appeared with the options "A", "B" or "undecided" for each dimension. How much of the speech was understood was asked on a 3-point scale. In each round, the two versions could be played repeatedly. After the experiment the subjects were interviewed about perceived differences and answering strategies.

4.2   Results

Since our subjects came from two countries (US/Germany) we checked for differences between the two populations with a Mann-Whitney U-test which did not reveal differences on any of the dimensions. Separating the data according to "speech understanding" did not reveal any differences (2-factorial ANOVA).

Looking at all clips and all subjects[5], the **U** version was selected significantly more often (60% vs. 40%) to be *more natural* than the **S** version (1-tailed t-test[6]: t(24)=3.1062; $p < .01$). For the other five dimensions we found the following results: Subjects picked the **U** version significantly more often as *more friendly* (2-tailed t-test: t(24)=4.2774; $p < .001$), *more trustworthy* (t(24)=4.3085; $p < .001$), and tendentially more often as *more competent* (t(24)=1.7220; $p = .10$). The **S** version was perceived significantly more often as *more nervous* (t(23)= 3.7999; $p < .001$)[7]. There was no significance either way for *extroversion*.

We then tested whether any of the dimensions were correlated in the sense that subjects consistently made the same decision on two dimensions (e.g., natural and friendly). We conducted a unidimensional χ^2 test[8] on all possible dimension pairs. The results (Table 1) show that naturalness, friendliness, competentence and trustworthiness are positivly correlated with each other, whereas nervousness is negatively correlated with all of these. Extrovertedness is only directly correlated with nervousness.

Table 1. Relative frequencies of equal decisions when comparing dimensions. (+) means that subjects made the same decision, (−) means they made the opposite decision *significantly* often (all highly significant, $p < .001$; χ^2 values omitted for readability).

	friendly	nervous	extrovert	competent	trustworthy
natural	(+) .89	(−) .20	.49	(+) .83	(+) .92
friendly		(−) .17	.44	(+) .75	(+) .85
nervous			(+) .62	(−) .23	(−) .19
extrovert				.54	.48
competent					(+) .83

4.3   Discussion

Using gesture units makes a virtual character look more natural. Our results clearly confirmed this hypothesis. However, our interviews revealed that the effect is very subtle. Only one of the subjects was able to explicitly tell the difference between versions. Most subjects said that the difference was very hard to see, some plainly said they saw no difference. Those who saw differences assumed that they were in the timing, extent or smoothness of movements, synchronization with speech or torso deformations – these aspects were exactly equal in both versions.

---

[5] The "undecided" category was not considered in the analysis. For dimension naturalness, we had 14% "undecided" cases. For all other dimensions 20–28%.

[6] Since the data was normally distributed (verified with Kolmogorov-Smirnov one-sample test/Lilliefors probabilities), parametric methods were applicable.

[7] One subject chose "undecided" on this dimension for all clips.

[8] Because of the small sample we could not assume normal distribution of the basic population.

Our collected evidence suggests that for creating a friendly, trustworthy and natural VC, the use of g-units plays a subtle yet important role. G-units may also have a positive impact in terms of competence. If a more nervous or even unnatural character is desired, singleton gestures should be preferred. However, our experiment only discriminates between singleton gestures and g-units of length > 1. More precise effects of g-unit length remain to be examined. It is interesting to note that in the context of "gestural behaviour of virtual characters" the dimensions naturalness, friendliness, trustworthiness and competence seem to form one cluster where one implies the other. Nervousness stands in an inverted relationship with each of these, and finally, extroversion is a dimension that was left totally unaffected by the g-unit condition.

Although our goal was to make *virtual* humans look more natural, our results may have implications for *real* humans. For instance, based on our results, a rhetorics teacher could recommmend her students to "connect" gestures in order to appear less nervous. While this needs to be complemented by studies on how far the results with virtual characters transfer to human-human interaction [2], a VC may prove an ideal research tool for the social sciences [37,38,39].

5   Conclusion

We presented a data-driven approach to gesture synthesis that allows the synthesis of gestures on novel input text in the style of a modeled human performer, including a validation study on the "recognizability" of the produced gesture style. The approach not only creates a broad range of gestures but also connects the generated gestures into *gesture units* to produce a smooth and fluid stream of gestures.

We validated the positive effect of producing g-units as opposed to producing mere singleton gestures in a user study and found that the g-unit version was perceived as more natural, more friendly, more trustworthy and less nervous. While the study confirmed our hypothesis that generating g-units is a definite advantage, there is much room for further empirical exploration. The effect of different g-unit lengths and also decisions on handshape selection or the use of multiple strokes and various animation parameters could be studied to arrive at a more complete set of validated principles for gesture synthesis.

Acknowledgments. We would like to thank all the subjects who participated in our user studies, and Nuance Communications Inc. for providing us with a text-to-speech synthesis software.

References

1. Vinayagamoorthy, V., Gillies, M., Steed, A., Tanguy, E., Pan, X., Loscos, C., Slater, M.: Building Expression into Virtual Characters. In: Eurographics Conference State of the Art Report, Vienna (2006)

2. Nass, C., Isbister, K., Lee, E.J.: Truth is beauty: Researching embodied conversational agents. In: Cassell, J., Sullivan, J., Prevost, S., Churchill, E. (eds.) Embodied Conversational Agents, pp. 374–402. MIT Press, Cambridge, MA (2000)
3. Thomas, F., Johnston, O.: The Illusion of Life: Disney Animation. Hyperion Press, New York (1981)
4. Cassell, J., Pelachaud, C., Badler, N., Steedman, M., Achorn, B., Becket, T., Douville, B., Prevost, S., Stone, M.: Animated Conversation: Rule-Based Generation of Facial Expression, Gesture & Spoken Intonation for Multiple Conversational Agents. In: Proceedings of SIGGRAPH '94, pp. 413–420 (1994)
5. Gratch, J., Rickel, J., André, E., Badler, N., Cassell, J., Petajan, E.: Creating interactive virtual humans: Some assembly required. IEEE Intelligent Systems, 54–63 (July/ August, 2002)
6. Kita, S., van Gijn, I., van der Hulst, H.: Movement phases in signs and co-speech gestures, and their transcription by human coders. In: Wachsmuth, I., Fröhlich, M. (eds.) Gesture and Sign Language in Human-Computer Interaction, pp. 23–35. Springer, Berlin (1998)
7. Ruttkay, Z., Pelachaud, C. (eds.): From Brows to Trust: Evaluating Embodied Conversational Agents. Kluwer Academic Publishers, Dordrecht (2004)
8. Neff, M., Kipp, M., Albrecht, I., Seidel, H.-P.: Gesture Modeling and Animation Based on a Probabilistic Recreation of Speaker Style. Transactions on Graphics (2007, accepted)
9. Kipp, M., Neff, M., Albrecht, I.: An Annotation Scheme for Conversational Gestures: How to economically capture timing and form. Journal on Language Resources and Evaluation - Special Issue on Multimodal Corpora (2007)
10. Kipp, M.: Gesture Generation by Imitation: From Human Behavior to Computer Character Animation. Dissertation.com, Boca Raton, Florida (2004)
11. Kendon, A.: Gesture – Visible Action as Utterance. Cambridge University Press, Cambridge (2004)
12. McNeill, D.: Hand and Mind: What Gestures Reveal about Thought. University of Chicago Press, Chicago (1992)
13. Stone, M., DeCarlo, D., Oh, I., Rodriguez, C., Stere, A., Lees, A., Bregler, C.: Speaking with hands: Creating animated conversational characters from recordings of human performance. In: Proc. SIGGRAPH 2004, pp. 506–513 (2004)
14. Kopp, S., Wachsmuth, I.: Synthesizing multimodal utterances for conversational agents. Computer Animation and Virtual Worlds 15(1), 39–52 (2004)
15. de Ruiter, J.P.: The production of gesture and speech. In: McNeill, D. (ed.) Language and Gesture: Window into Thought and Action, pp. 284–311. Cambridge University Press, Cambridge (2000)
16. Cassell, J., Vilhjálmsson, H., Bickmore, T.: BEAT: the Behavior Expression Animation Toolkit. In: Proceedings of SIGGRAPH 2001, pp. 477–486 (2001)
17. Lee, J., Marsella, S.: Nonverbal behavior generator for embodied conversational agents. In: Proc. of the 6th International Conference on Intelligent Virtual Agents, pp. 243–255. Springer, Heidelberg (2006)
18. Hartmann, B., Mancini, M., Buisine, S., Pelachaud, C.: Design and evaluation of expressive gesture synthesis for ecas. In: Proc. AAMAS (2005)
19. Chi, D.M., Costa, M., Zhao, L., Badler, N.I.: The EMOTE model for effort and shape. In: Proc. SIGGRAPH 2000, pp. 173–182 (2000)
20. Hartmann, B., Mancini, M., Pelachaud, C.: Implementing Expressive Gesture Synthesis for Embodied Conversational Agents. In: Gibet, S., Courty, N., Kamp, J.-F. (eds.) GW 2005. LNCS (LNAI), vol. 3881, pp. 188–199. Springer, Heidelberg (2006)

21. Neff, M., Fiume, E.: AER: Aesthetic Exploration and Refinement for expressive character animation. In: Proc. ACM SIGGRAPH / Eurographics Symposium on Computer Animation 2005, pp. 161–170. ACM Press, New York (2005)

22. Hodgins, J.K., Wooten, W.L., Brogan, D.C., O'Brien, J.F.: Animating human athletics. In: Proc. SIGGRAPH 1995, pp. 71–78 (1995)

23. Faloutsos, P., van de Panne, M., Terzopoulos, D.: The virtual stuntman: Dynamic characters with a repertoire of autonomous motor skills. Computers & Graphics 25(6), 933–953 (2001)

24. Zordan, V.B., Hodgins, J.K.: Motion capture-driven simulations that hit and react. In: Proc. ACM SIGGRAPH Symposium on Computer Animation, pp. 89–96. ACM Press, New York (2002)

25. Noot, H., Ruttkay, Z.: Gesture in style. In: Camurri, A., Volpe, G. (eds.) GW 2003. LNCS (LNAI), vol. 2915, pp. 324–337. Springer, Heidelberg (2004)

26. Webb, R.: Linguistic Properties of Metaphoric Gestures. UMI, New York (1997)

27. Boersma, P., Weenink, D.: Praat: doing phonetics by computer (version 4.3.14) [computer program] (2005), Retrieved from, http://www.praat.org/

28. Kipp, M.: Anvil – a Generic Annotation Tool for Multimodal Dialogue. In: Proceedings of Eurospeech, pp. 1367–1370 (2001)

29. McNeill, D.: Gesture and Thought. University of Chicago Press, Chicago (2005)

30. Schegloff, E.A.: On some gestures' relation to talk. In: Atkinson, J.M., Heritage, J. (eds.) Structures of Social Action, pp. 266–296. Cambridge University Press, Cambridge (1984)

31. Steedman, M.: Information structure and the syntax-phonology interface. Linguistic Inquiry 34, 649–689 (2000)

32. Kendon, A.: Gesticulation and speech: Two aspects of the process of utterance. In: Key, M.R. (ed.) Nonverbal Communication and Language, pp. 207–227. Mouton, The Hague (1980)

33. Neff, M., Fiume, E.: Modeling tension and relaxation for computer animation. In: Proc. ACM SIGGRAPH Symposium on Computer Animation 2002, pp. 81–88. ACM Press, New York (2002)

34. Press, W.H., Tukolsky, S.A., Vetterling, W.T., Flannery, B.P.: Numerical Recipes in C: The Art of Scientific Computing, 2nd edn. Cambridge University Press, Cambridge (1992)

35. Hollars, M.G., Rosenthal, D.E., Sherman, M.A.: SD/FAST User's Manual. Symbolic Dynamics Inc. (1994)

36. McCrae, R.R., John, O.P.: An Introduction to the Five-Factor Model and Its Applications. Journal of Personality 60, 175–215 (1992)

37. Martin, J.C., Niewiadomski, R., Devillers, L., Buisine, S., Pelachaud, C.: Multimodal Complex Emotions: Gesture Expressivity And Blended Facial Expressions. Special issue of the Journal of Humanoid Robotics 3, 269–291 (2006)

38. Krämer, N.C., Tietz, B., Bente, G.: Effects of embodied interface agents and their gestural activity. In: Rist, T., Aylett, R., Ballin, D., Rickel, J. (eds.) IVA 2003. LNCS (LNAI), vol. 2792, pp. 292–300. Springer, Heidelberg (2003)

39. Frey, S.: Die Macht des Bildes: der Einfluß der nonverbalen Kommunikation auf Kultur und Politik. Verlag Hans Huber, Bern (1999)

3D Audiovisual Rendering and Real-Time Interactive Control of Expressivity in a Talking Head

Jean-Claude Martin, Christophe d'Alessandro, Christian Jacquemin, Brian Katz, Aurélien Max, Laurent Pointal, and Albert Rilliard

LIMSI-CNRS, BP 133, 91403 Orsay Cedex, France
{martin,cda,jacquemin,katz,aurelien.max,laurent.pointal, rilliard}@limsi.fr

Abstract. The integration of virtual agents in real-time interactive virtual applications raises several challenges. The rendering of the movements of the virtual character in the virtual scene (locomotion of the character or rotation of its head) and the binaural rendering in 3D of the synthetic speech during these movements need to be spatially coordinated. Furthermore, the system must enable real-time adaptation of the agent's expressive audiovisual signals to user's on-going actions. In this paper, we describe a platform that we have designed to address these challenges as follows: (1) the modules enabling real time synthesis and spatial rendering of the synthetic speech, (2) the modules enabling 3D real time rendering of facial expressions using a GPU-based 3D graphic engine, and (3) the integration of these modules within an experimental platform using gesture as an input modality. A new model of phoneme-dependent human speech directivity patterns is included in the speech synthesis system, so that the agent can move in the virtual scene with realistic 3D visual and audio rendering. Future applications of this platform include perceptual studies about multimodal perception and interaction, expressive real time question and answer system and interactive arts.

Keywords: 3D animation, voice directivity, real-time and interactivity, expressiveness, experimental studies.

1 Introduction

Current applications of talking heads are mostly designed for desktop configurations. Mixed and virtual reality applications call for coordinated and interactive spatial 3D rendering in the audio and visual modalities. For example, the rendering of the movements of a virtual character in a virtual scene (locomotion of the character or rotation of its head) and the binaural rendering in 3D of the synthetic speech during these movements need to be coordinated. Furthermore, the expressiveness of the agent in the two modalities needs to be displayed appropriately for effective affective interactions, and combined with audiovisual speech. This requires experimental investigations on how to control this expressiveness and how it is perceived by users.

Since the 70's, research in audiovisual speech uses model-based approaches, and image / video-based approaches [1]. Control models have been defined using visemes,

C. Pelachaud et al. (Eds.): IVA 2007, LNAI 4722, pp. 29–36, 2007.

co-articulation models [2], n-phones models grounded on corpora [3], or a combination of rule-based and data-driven articulatory control models [4]. For example, a set of four facial speech parameters have been proposed in [5]: jaw opening, lip rounding, lip closure and lip raising. Expressive qualifiers are proposed by [6] to modulate the expressivity of lip movements during emotional speech. Audiovisual discourse synthesis requires the coordination of several parts of the face including lips, but also brows, gaze and head movement [7]. With respect to facial animation [8], one reference formalism is MPEG-4 that defines a set of Face Animation Parameters (FAPs) deforming a face model in its neutral state [9]. FAPs are defined by motion of feature points, vertices that control the displacement of neighboring vertices through a weighting scheme. An overview of expressive speech synthesis can be found in [10].

Few of these studies and systems enable the coordinated display of 3D speech and facial expressions (directivity measurement of a singer was computed by Kob and Jers [11]), nor propose real-time interactive means for controlling expressive signals. Moreover, several systems are limited to a single face model where experimental studies and various interactive applications require the use of several models at different resolutions.

Our goal is to enable this coordinated spatial rendering in 3D of the speech and face of a talking head, and to provide means for real-time interactive control of its expressive signals. With respect to visual rendering, we aim at real time 3D rendering of different models at different resolutions that can be easily embedded in different mixed reality applications. In this paper we describe the components that we have developed in order to meet our research goals and the current state of their integration within an experimental platform for conducting perception studies about audiovisual expressive communication.

Section 2 describes the modules enabling real time synthesis and head orientation dependant audio rendering of expressive speech. The modules for 3D visual real time rendering of facial expressions are detailed in section 3. An overview of the platform integrating both audio and visual components enabling interactive control for experimental studies is provided in section 4. Although our short term goal is to use this platform for experimental studies, we explain in section 5 how we plan to use it for interactive applications.

2   Real Time Synthesis and 3D Rendering of Expressive Speech

The core component for synthetic speech generation is LIMSI's selection / concatenation text-to-speech synthesis system (SELIMSI). This core system has been augmented with three specific components: a radiation component accounting for relative head orientation and spatial motion of the virtual agent; a gesture control device allowing for direct control and animation of the virtual agent and a phoneme-to-viseme conversion module allowing for speech sounds and lips movements' synchronization.

The text-to-speech synthesis system [12] is based on optimal selection and concatenation of non-uniform units in a large speech corpus. The system contains two main components: text-to-phoneme conversion using approximately 2000 linguistic rules and non-uniform unit selection and concatenation. The annotated speech corpus

(1 hour) contains read text and additional material such as numbers, dates, time. The selection algorithm searches for segments in the corpus according to several criteria and cost functions for ensuring optimal prosodic rendering and segmental continuity. The system receives text as input and outputs the audio speech signal together with a text file describing the phonemic content and the prosody of the utterance.

Special attention is paid to the directional characteristics of the synthetic speech. Realistic rendering of a moving speaking agent in 3D space requires the acoustic signal to be adapted according to the relative position and orientation of the speaker and listener. A broad study of time-varying speech radiation patterns has been conducted [13]. For speech synthesis, these results provide phoneme-dependant 3D radiation patterns that are integrated as post-processing of the synthetic speech signals. This enables visual movements of the agent to be accompanied by correlated audio movements.

Real-time interactive control of expressive speech signals is managed in the system by a direct gesture interface [14]. The agent is considered as an "instrument" driven by an operator through a manual interface: as a joystick controls the head position, the expressivity of speech may be controlled using hand gestures via a graphic tablet. The gesture input enables interactive control of expressive parameters of the speech signal like fundamental frequency and voice source parameters (amplitude, spectral tilt, open quotient, noise in the source). Expression is controlled through subtle real-time variations according to the context and situation. In our application, as in real life communication, the vocal expression of strong emotions like anger, fear, or despair are more the exception than the rule [15, 16]. As such, the synthesis system should be able to deal with subtle and continuous expressive variations rather than clear cut emotions. Expressive speech synthesis may be viewed from two sides: on the one hand is the question of expression specification (what is the suited expression in a particular situation?) and on the other hand is the question of expression realization (how is the specified expression actually implemented). Our gesture interface is a research tool for addressing the second problem. Finally, phoneme to viseme conversion is handled by a set of rules, and audio and visual speech streams are synchronized using the prosodic description provided by the text-to-speech module. Experiments on hand gestures intonation reiteration showed that the performance levels reached by hand-made and vocal reiterated intonation are very comparable [17]. This could suggest that intonation, both on the perceptual and motor production aspects, is processed at a relatively abstract cognitive level, as it seems somehow independent of the modality actually used. Hand-controlled speech is a new tool for studying expressive speech synthesis [18], modeling expressive intonation, designing new interfaces for musical expression [19].

3   A Module for 3D Real Time Rendering of Facial Expressions

The graphic engine used for rendering our animated face is a multi-purpose, robust, and flexible environment for the synthesis and control of audiovisual speech. These requirements have led us towards MPEG-4, the standardized formalism for face animation [20]. It relies on a predefined set of standard control points, a set of weights that defines the influence of the control points on face vertices, and interpolation mechanisms that are used to combine multiple control point displacements for audiovisual speech [6] and emotion synthesis [21]. We can use a face mesh at any level of detail (LOD) and define feature points through Xface [22]. Weight computation is automatic: weights are proportional to the inverse of a distance from feature points as defined in [23].

We intend to develop faces with lower LODs for applications with critical computing resources such as animations for portable devices. Conversely, for applications with high requirements for realism such as interactive expressive avatars for artistic applications or high resolution rendering, we can design faces with higher LODs. Variation of LOD will not have any impact on the scripting of the animation. In case of lower LOD, unused controlled points will be ignored. Automatic animations of additional control points through interpolations of existing ones will be added in case of higher LODs. Ongoing work on the enhancement of the skin and wrinkle rendering is also used to increase the realism of high definition faces.

With the same purpose of standardization in mind, graphical rendering relies on Virtual Choreographer (http://virchor.sourceforge.net/) (VirChor) a 3D engine based on an extension of X3D (http://www.web3d.org/). VirChor is a generic 3D engine, but has specific data structure and behaviors for face animation. The data structures define the control points and the associated weights on the vertices of a 2D or 3D mesh. The behavior is defined through an event based scripting language.

The steps for the design of a talking head are the following. First, XFaceEd (http://xface.itc.it/) is used to define the MPEG-4 control points and their weights on the vertices of the face mesh. XFaceEd has been enhanced to compute weights automatically through Voronoi distances. It has also been enriched to generate automatically the XML encoding of the face, its control points, and its weighting scheme in VirChor formalism. The automatic weight computation and the automatic code generation associated with the intuitive interface of XfaceEd allow for a fast and efficient transformation of any face mesh into an MPEG-4 ready mesh.

Second, a set of visemes and/or expressions can be defined as displacement vectors of the MPEG-4 control points. For this purpose, we have designed a Python-Tcl/Tk interface for the modification of the control point displacement to generate face animation targets. Through sliders, the control points are translated by sending commands to VirChor via UDP (**Fig. 1**). In the final step, animations are defined as sequences of scheduled targets.

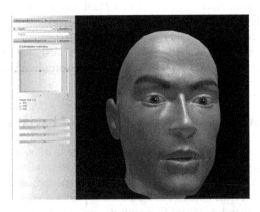

Fig. 1. Displaying facial expressions using VirChor real time engine

Since real time interactivity was also one of our requirements, facial animation in VirChor is implemented in the Graphic Processing Unit (GPU) [24]. The frame rate is approximately 10 times faster than when animation is performed in the CPU: 165 fps instead of 15 for an 8k face and 4k vertex mesh. Through GPU-rendering, both vertex position and normal are computed without the need to transfer the geometry through the graphic bus. At each time step, the interpolation coefficient is computed and sent to the GPU. If a keyframe is reached, the current state of the interpolation is saved as the future source frame in order to ensure a smooth transition between the current interpolation and the subsequent one. The source frame and the target frame are both sent as parameter tables to the vertex shader.

4 Platform Overview

The components described in the previous sections are integrated within a software platform made of five modules described in Fig. 2. They communicate through simple text/xml data exchanged with UDP packets between modules and via files for voice synthesis sound. The application model is expected to produce tagged strings [message 1] for the multimodal module. Text is then sent [message 2] to our TTS which produces [message 3] a sound file and returns a set of lexeme descriptions. From these lexemes the multimodal module requests [message 4] the MPEG4Decoder application to build the corresponding visemes set with timings and send them [message 5] to the VirChor engine. Sound file references produced by the TTS are also sent to the 3D

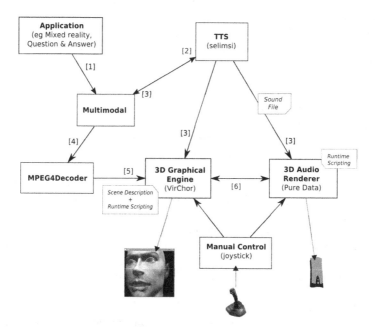

Fig. 2. A platform for 3D audiovisual rendering and real-time interactive control of expressive signals in a talking head

audio PureData module, together with 3D coordinates of the virtual character for 3D audio rendering. Once VirChor and PureData have both visual and sound rendering information, they [message 6] start to play, considering possible real-time interaction coming from external events at runtime such as a joystick.

5   Conclusions and Future Directions

We have described a platform that addresses several challenges of mixed reality interactive applications: 1) coordination of the visual display of a 3D talking head and the corresponding binaural rendering in 3D of the synthesized speech, 2) real-time interactive control of expressive signals, and 3) management of different head models at different resolution.

For the definition of synthetic visemes or expressions we rely on video-captured expressions [25]. We have recorded a first video corpus of visemes that suit our goals and our platform. This corpus was used for the definition of a first set of visemes that is used by the talking head. We intend to collect further data to improve the temporal description of the visemes and their co-articulation. We also intend to define expressions of emotion to be displayed with the 3D graphical engine. In order to study expressive speech, we plan to have two separate channels of animations sent to VirChor (one for lip movements, one for the expression of emotion) and explore different directions for their combinations thanks to our experimental platform.

The quality of the visual speech has not yet been evaluated *per se* but the animated face has already been used in an application for interactive affective communication [26]. The qualitative evaluation accompanying this work through a questionnaire on users' satisfaction shows that the users have appreciated the interface for its reactivity, its progressiveness, and its malleability. The smoothness of the animation and its high frame rate make it appropriate for an application on dialogic information querying such as ours. The 3D face can convey subtle and complex expressions, it can be accurately synchronized with speech signal, and its animation can be interrupted and redirected towards new targets.

We intend to use the platform not only for experimental studies but also for the design of interactive applications such as artistic applications or cooperative information retrieval applications. The information retrieval paradigm, exemplified by Internet search engines, which return a list of candidate documents matching a query made up of keywords, is evolving towards so-called Question Answering (QA) systems. It is important that the system indicates its level of confidence into its answers or justify them with evidence in order to retain the user's trust. Future advances in QA are likely to take the form of *cooperative QA* [27], whereby answers can be augmented with information likely to be of interest to the user (e.g. suggestions, corrections to a previous result) [28]. In an attempt to make such systems more natural to use, speech can be used as the input and output modality [29, 30]. A recent study [31] shows that facial expressions can be better interpreted than linguistic cues for transmitting the certainty of a QA system. It is therefore interesting to consider adding a talking head as a modality to an interactive QA system, and to study the impact on the perceived cooperativity of the system. As an initial application, we intend to use the Ritel system developed at LIMSI [30]. Ritel is an open-domain dialogic QA system for French which uses speech as its input and output modalities, and which thus runs under strict time constraints.

Ongoing work on interactive control of expressive facial animation not only includes a joystick, but also an anthropomorphic tangible interface that dynamically controls the animation of the 3D face. The evaluation of this experiment showed that the tactile control of a face can be experienced as a unique affective communication medium. Since VirChor is a generic 3D engine for Mixed Reality, animated faces at different resolution can be made available for a large scale of applications without efforts. They are 3D component that can be embedded into 2D/3D scenes and interact with other scene parts.

References

1. Bailly, G., Bérar, M., Elisei, F., Odisi, M.: Audiovisual Speech Synthesis. International Journal of Speech Technology. Special Issue on Speech Synthesis: Part II. 6(4) (2003)
2. Cohen, M.M., Massaro, D.W.: Modeling coarticulation in synthetic visual speech. Models and Techniques in Computer Animation. AAAI/MIT Press, Cambridge (1993)
3. Ma, J., Cole, R., Pellom, B., Ward, W., Wise, B.: Accurate automatic visible speech synthesis of arbitrary 3D models based on concatenation of diviseme motion capture data. Computer Animation and Virtual Worlds, 15(5) (2004)
4. Beskow, J.: Talking Heads - Models and Applications for Multimodal Speech Synthesis. PhD Thesis. Stockholm (2003), http://www.speech.kth.se/~beskow/thesis/index.html
5. Reveret, L., Essa, I.: Visual Coding and Tracking of Speech Related Facial Motion, Hawai, USA
6. Bevacqua, E., Pelachaud, C.: Expressive audio-visual speech. Comp. Anim. Virtual Worlds, 15 (2004)
7. DeCarlo, D., Stone, M., Revilla, C., Venditti, J.: Specifying and Animating Facial Signals for Discourse in Embodied Conversational Agents. Computer Animation and Virtual Worlds 15(1) (2004)
8. Cohen, M., Beskow, J., Massaro, D.: Recent developments in facial animation: an inside view. In: AVSP'98 (1998)
9. Ostermann, J.: Animation of synthetic faces in MPEG-4. In: Computer Animation'98, Philadelphia, USA, pp. 49–51 (1998)
10. Schröder, M.: Speech and Emotion Research: An overview of research frameworks and a dimensional approach to emotional speech synthesis. PhD Thesis (2004)
11. Kob, M., Jers, H.: Directivity measurement of a singer. Journal of the Acoustical Society of America 105(2) (1999)
12. Prudon, R., d'Alessandro, C.: selection/concatenation text-to-speech synthesis system: databases development, system design, comparative evaluation. In: 4th ISCA/IEEE International Workshop on Speech Synthesis, IEEE Computer Society Press, Los Alamitos (2001)
13. Katz, B., Prezat, F., d'Alessandro, C.: Human voice phoneme directivity pattern measurements. In: 4th Joint Meeting of the Acoustical Society of America and the Acoustical Society of Japan, Honolulu, Hawaï 3359 (2006)
14. D'Alessandro, C., D'Alessandro, N., Le Beux, S., Simko, J., Cetin, F., Pirker, H.: The speech conductor: gestural control of speech synthesis. In: eNTERFACE 2005. The SIMILAR NoE Summer Workshop on Multimodal Interfaces, Mons, Belgium, pp. 52–61 (2005)

15. Campbell, N.: Speech & Expression; the value of a longitudinal corpus. In: LREC 2004, pp. 183–186 (2004)

16. Martin, J.-C., Abrilian, S., Devillers, L.: Annotating Multimodal Behaviors Occurring during Non Basic Emotions. In: Tao, J., Tan, T., Picard, R.W. (eds.) ACII 2005. LNCS, vol. 3784, pp. 550–557. Springer, Heidelberg (2005)

17. d'Alessandro, C., Rilliard, A., Le Beux, S.: Computerized chironomy: evaluation of hand-controlled Intonation reiteration. In: Interspeech 2007, Antwerp, Belgium (2007)

18. Le Beux, S., Rilliard, A.: A real-time intonation controller for expressive speech synthesis. In: 6th ISCA Workshop on Speech Synthesis (SSW-6), Bonn, Germany (2007)

19. d'Alessandro, N., Doval, B., d'Alessandro, C., Beux, L., Woodruff, P., Fabre, Y., Dutoit, T.: RAMCESS: Realtime and Accurate Musical Control of Expression in Singing Synthesis. Journal on Multimodal User Interfaces 1(1) (2007)

20. Pandzic, I.S., Forchheimer, R.: MPEG-4 Facial Animation. The Standard, Implementation and Applications. John Wiley & Sons, LTD, Chichester (2002)

21. Tsapatsoulis, N., Raouzaiou, A., Kollias, S., Cowie, R., Douglas-Cowie, E.: Emotion Recognition and Synthesis based on MPEG-4 FAPs. MPEG-4 Facial Animation. John Wiley & Sons, Chichester (2002)

22. Balci, K.: MPEG-4 based open source toolkit for 3D Facial Animation. In: Working conference on Advanced visual interfaces, New York, NY, USA, pp. 399–402 (2004)

23. Kshirsagar, S., Garchery, S., Magnenat-Thalmann, N.: Feature Point Based Mesh Deformation Applied to MPEG-4 Facial Animation. In: IFIP Tc5/Wg5.10 Deform'2000 Workshop and Avatars'2000 Workshop on Deformable Avatars, pp. 24–34 (2000)

24. Beeson, C.: Animation in the "Dawn" demo. GPU Gems, Programming Techniques, Tips, and Tricks for Real-Time Graphics. Wiley, Chichester, UK (2004)

25. Fagel, S.: Video-realistic Synthetic Speech with a Parametric Visual Speech Synthesizer. In: International Conference on Spoken Language Processing (INTERSPEECH/ICSLP 2004) (2004)

26. Jacquemin, C.: A tangible cephalomorphic interface for expressive facial animation. In: Paiva, A., Prada, R., Picard, R.W. (eds.) ACII 2007. LNCS, vol. 4738, pp. 558–569. Springer, Heidelberg (2007)

27. Benamara, F.: WebCoop: un système de Questions-Réponses coopératif sur le Web. PhD Thesis (2004)

28. Bosma, W.: Extending answers using discourse structure. In: Proceedings of RANLP workshop on Crossing Barriers in Text Summarization Research, Borovets, Bulgaria (2005)

29. Boves, L., den Os, E.: Interactivity and multimodality in the IMIX demonstrator. In: IEEE conference on Multimedia and Expo (ICME 2005) (2005)

30. Rosset, S., Galibert, O., Illouz, G., Max, A.: Integrating spoken dialog and question answering: the Ritel project. In: Interspeech'06, Pittsburgh, USA (2006)

31. Marsi, E., van Rooden, F.: Expressing uncertainty with a Talking Head in a Multimodal Question-Answering System, Aberdeen, UK

Semantic Segmentation of Motion Capture Using Laban Movement Analysis

Durell Bouchard and Norman Badler

Center for Human Modeling and Simulation, University of Pennsylvania
200 S. 33rd St. Philadelphia, PA 19104, USA
durell@cis.upenn.edu, badler@seas.upenn.edu
http://cg.cis.upenn.edu/hms/

Abstract. Many applications that utilize motion capture data require small, discrete, semantic segments of data, but most motion capture collection processes produce long sequences of data. The smaller segments are often created from the longer sequences manually. This segmentation process is very laborious and time consuming. This paper presents an automatic motion capture segmentation method based on movement qualities derived from Laban Movement Analysis (LMA). LMA provides a good compromise between high-level semantic features, which are difficult to extract for general motions, and low-level kinematic features which, often yield unsophisticated segmentations. The LMA features are computed using a collection of neural networks trained with temporal variance in order to create a classifier that is more robust with regard to input boundaries. The actual segmentation points are derived through simple time series analysis of the LMA features.

Keywords: Human motion, motion capture, motion segmentation, Laban Movement Analysis, LMA.

1   Introduction

The increasing use of 3D computer generated animation for virtual agents coupled with the decreasing cost of motion capture production are driving a need for more sophisticated tools to process and analyze motion capture data. Many of these motion capture tools, such as gesture recognition and motion retargeting, require small, discrete, semantically sophisticated segments of input motion capture in order to function properly. However, in order to create quality motion capture data efficiently, capture sessions typically produce long streams of motion capture data. The solution is to preprocess the long motion capture data stream by breaking it up into short segments that are appropriate for an analysis tool. This process is often done manually, but it is a very laborious and time consuming process. A better solution is to create tools that automate the segmentation process.

Automated segmentation is also more deterministic than manual segmentation due to low interannotator and intra-annotator agreement in manual segmentation. An automatic segmentation program will produce the same segmentation

C. Pelachaud et al. (Eds.): IVA 2007, LNAI 4722, pp. 37–44, 2007.

given the same input motion capture. Different people given the same motion capture data, on the other hand, will produce different segmentations. In addition a person will often produce different segmentations of identical motion capture data. Figure 1 shows the result of having one person segment 3 different groups of motion capture data 6 times each. The median of each segment boundary was computed and then the distance of each boundary from the median was computed and graphed as a histogram. The result is a standard deviation of 15.4 frames or about a half second. The annotator agreements can be increased if the motion capture sample rate is decreased; however, it will also introduce shift error into the segment points. The performance of some classifiers is dependent on the selection of segment points. Figure 2 shows the effect of changing the segment boundaries on the performance of a neural net. A shift of 5 frames of the segment boundaries can change the error rate from 15% to 55%. Deterministic segmentation, and therefore automated segmentation, can improve the performance of classifiers.

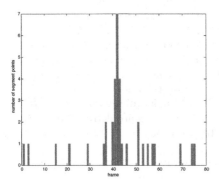 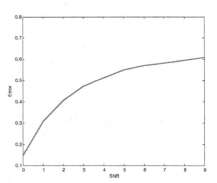

Fig. 1. Manual Segmentation Boundary Deviance Histogram

Fig. 2. Classifier Performance

To segment motion capture data is to produce a collection of smaller motion capture data segments that consist of contiguous portions of the original motion capture data. A semantic segmentation is a high-level segmentation, where segments correlate to a semantic labeling of the motion, such as throwing a ball with great force. A kinematic segmentation is a low-level segmentation, where segments correlate to a kinematic description of a motion, such as a high velocity sagittal motion. The generality of motion capture data refers to the diversity of motions. General motion capture consists of any motion that can be performed by a person. Motion capture that is not general is limited to classes of motions such as locomotion or dancing. Current methods of automatic motion capture segmentation tend to either be effective for general motions, but do not produce semantic segmentations, or produce semantic segmentations, but are not useful for general motions. The goal of automatic motion capture segmentation is to produce semantic segmentation of general motion capture data.

A naïve solution to the segmentation problem is to create a classifier and apply it to all possible segments. Any segments that are properly classified are considered segments. There are multiple problems with this approach. It would be extremely slow, and it requires an extremely sophisticated classifier. The classifier must be robust enough to take poorly segmented data as an input. This is difficult because the performance of a classifier is dependent on the quality of the segmentation of its input. Thus the problem is a paradox, where recognition requires segmentation and segmentation requires recognition. The following section summarizes existing methods that attempt to bypass or overcome this paradox.

2   Related Work

Many motion capture segmentation methods are based on changes in low-level kinematic features. Fod et al. [3] implement two different segmentation methods that utilize angular velocity in four different degrees of freedom in the arm. The first method chooses segments such that at least two degrees of freedom have zero velocity within three ms. of both the beginning and end of every segment. The second method tracks the sum of the four degrees of freedom's angular velocity and determines segment boundaries when the value drops below an experiment-based threshold. Osaki et al. [8] and Shiratori et al. [10] also use velocity in segmentation calculation. They calculate the linear velocity of a hand relative to the waist. Segment boundaries are velocity local minima with the added constraints that initial and ending velocity must be under some threshold, and the maximal velocity must exceed some threshold. Zhao and Badler [14] calculate segment boundaries when there is a hand linear acceleration zero crossing and curvature is above some threshold. Wang et al. [12] determine segment boundaries to be when the velocity of a hand is below a threshold at the same time as the curvature of the hand is above a threshold. Jenkins and Matarić [4,5] use a method called kinematic centroid segmentation. The segments are calculated in-line by finding a local maximum of the distance between the centroid of an arm's markers for the first frame and the centroid of each following frame. These kinematic methods are extremely efficient; however, they produce simple low-level segmentations.

There are motion capture segmentation methods that produce more high-level segmentations than the kinematic methods above by using techniques from time series database analysis. Barbič et al. [1] implement two different segmentation methods that are based on data compression. The first method segments where the projection error resulting from Principal Component Analysis (PCA) increases on incrementally larger segments of motion capture data. The second method segments by tracking changes in the distance of fitting a small segment of motion capture data to a Gaussian distribution model of the frames that precede the segment. Li et al. [13] use a similar method where segments are chosen such that they can be represented with the fewest number of linear dynamic systems. Another data analysis method, clustering, is also useful for segmenting motion capture data. When clustering is applied to motion capture segmentation the assumption is that frames of neighboring segments belong to separate clusters. Barbič et al. [1] employ expectation minimization to estimate the Gaussian Mixture Model (GMM) that corresponds to a cluster, while Lee and Elgammal [7] use k-means to estimate the GMM. These time series analysis-based methods produce more high-level segmentations than the kinematic methods produce, but they do not utilize semantic content of the motion on which they operate.

It is possible to capture some of the complexity and flexibility of decision making present in manual motion capture segmentation by using supervised learning. Kahol et al. [6] use a naïve Bayesian classifier in order to derive choreographer segmentation profiles of dance motion capture sequences. Starner and Pentland [11] and Bregler [2] implement implicit segmentation through the use of Hidden Markov Models (HMM) trained with manually segmented data. These learning-based segmentation methods are difficult to implement for general motion. In the above three examples, Kahol et al. perform tests on motion capture of dance, Starner and Pentland to sign language gestures, and Bregler to gait. Creating a general classifier for all motions is difficult because as the class of motions that can potentially be classified grows so does the number of training examples needed. In the case of a truly general classifier, the number of training motions would be enormous.

3   Hypothesis and Model

The learning based segmentation methods have the ability to create semantic segmentations, but the implementation is not feasible for general motion capture data. The above methods avoid this problem by eliminating the requirement of general motion capture and using a class of motions, such as dance, sign language, and gait. A different solution would be to use a classifier that operates on a smaller set of classes but is effective on general motions. In order for a segmentation based on this type of classifier to be useful, the subset of classes must be present in all motions, significant in meaning, and practical to classify.

A classification that fits these critera is Laban Movement Analysis (LMA) Effort classification. LMA is a rigorous system of movement study, which describes motion as a combination of four components: Body, Shape, Space, and Effort. Body, Shape, and Space define what motion is performed while Effort describes how a motion is performed. The Effort component is related to a person's intention and is itself composed of four different motion parameters: Space, Weight, Time, and Flow. Each parameter is a continuum between diametric extremes. The Effort of any motion can be described as four values on the four different Effort dimensions.

4   Method

The advantage of LMA Effort as a basis for motion capture segmentation is that it is more meaningful than kinematic features, and it is easier to compute for general motions than semantic features. Therefore, it has the potential to create semantic segmentations for general motion. In order to test this hypothesis, an LMA Effort classifier must be constructed and used to segment a collection of general motions.

4.1   LMA Effort Classifier

The classifier implemented is based on the LMA classification work of Zhao and Badler [14], and is a set of four neural networks, one for each LMA Effort parameter, which outputs three values between 0 and 1 for indulging, neutral, and condensing. The first step in creating the neural networks was to collect the training motion capture data. In order to accomplish this two LMA experts assisted in creating a repertoire of 12 motions that span a set of primitive motions defined in LMA. Each of the motions was performed 12 times in order to isolate and emphasize the 4 different LMA Effort parameters (Space, Time, Weight, and Flow) and at 3 intensities (condensing, neutral, and indulging). In total, 288 different motions were captured using Ascension Technology's active optical motion capture system, the ReActor. The system tracks 30 markers at 30 Hz. with an accuracy of 3 mm.

The neural network training motions were normalized and manually segmented. In order to abstract the motions from positional information, displacement, velocity, acceleration, distance, curvature, and torsion time series were computed for the joints of the right arm and the sternum. Experiments showed that some subsections of these kinematic time series were more important than others. For example, the Flow parameter is very dependent on the end of a motion, while the Time parameter is sensitive to the beginning of the motion. Therefore, front, back, and center weighted masks, were applied to each kinematic time series. Lastly, scalar kinematic features were generated by computing the average, minimum, maximum, and sum of each of the weighted time series.

In total, 4788 different features were calculated, too many for a an effective neural network. In order to select the most salient features, a method from Ruck et al. [9] was implemented. The method associates feature saliency with changes in the weights of the hidden layers of the neural networks during training. In order to find the optimum number of inputs the neural networks were trained with an increasing number of the most salient features until performance reach a maximum. The Space, Time, Weight, and Flow neural networks had 84, 72, 75, and 57 inputs, respectively. In order to further optimize the performance of the neural networks PCA was performed on these inputs to create a set of inputs with 95% variance, which reduced the number of inputs to 36, 23, 33, and 25, respectively. Finally, the optimum number of hidden layer units was determined by performing PCA on the hidden layer weights.

The average performance of the neural networks is summarized under the heading 'Static Boundary' in Table 1. The neural networks performed more poorly than expected on data that they were not trained on due to error induced by manual segmentation boundary shift in the test data. When the neural networks were tested on the data they were trained on, there was no perturbation in the segment boundary points. However, as was demonstrated in the introduction, the performance of a motion capture classifier is very sensitive to test data boundary points, and manual segmentation produces irregular boundary points. Experiments showed that the majority of boundary shift error occurs within a window of 11 frames. In order to minimize the error due to segment boundary inconsistencies, 121 sets of neural nets were trained with motion capture data; all permutations of boundary points were shifted by at most 5 frames. Then, the boundaries of every test motion capture segment were shifted in the same 121 ways and the output of the 121 neural networks was summed for a final output. The result, summarized under the heading 'Variable Boundary' in Table 1, is a reduction in the difference between training data error and test data error from 26.2% to 4.3%.

Table 1. Neural Network Average Percent Correct

Static Boundary		Variable Boundary	
Training Data	Test Data	Training Data	Test Data
91.2%	65.0%	92.3%	88.0%

4.2   Segmentation Determination

Once the neural networks were trained, the final step was to incorporate them into a segmentation scheme. Using the neural networks to find segments by exhaustive search yielded many false positives. In a 25 second test motion capture sequence, which consisted of a person repeatedly throwing a ball, applying the neural networks to all segments between $\frac{2}{3}$ and $3\frac{1}{3}$ seconds resulted in 26,493 segments. The large number of segments is because segments with similar start and end frames produce similar neural network outputs, and, therefore, if one segment makes a good segment, its neighboring segments will as well. This local similarity can be taken advantage of by assuming that a frame that is a good segment boundary will appear in many other good segments. This is accomplished by producing a histogram where the value of bin i is the number of segments in the set of 26,493 segments that begin at frame i. The histogram of the test motion capture sequence is shown in Fig. 3(a). There is a strong correlation between the peaks of this histogram and the peaks of the histogram in Fig. 3(b), which is of 20 manual segmentations of the same sequence.

   Two different methods were implemented in order to convert the segment histogram into segment boundaries. The first method finds peaks in the neural network output histogram of a minimum size by using a pair of dynamic thresholds. A dynamic threshold is calculated for every frame of the sequence as the average of its neighboring 100 frames. The upper and lower thresholds are calculated by shifting the dynamic threshold up and down by half of the experimentally determined minimum peak size. Segment boundares are calculated as the maximum histogram value in between the points where the histogram transitions from below the lower threshold to above the upper threshold to below the lower threshold again.

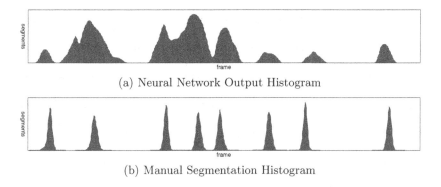

(a) Neural Network Output Histogram

(b) Manual Segmentation Histogram

Fig. 3. Neural Network Output and Segmentation Correlation

The second method for calculating the segment boundaries from the segment histogram uses local maxima and minima. The method begins by calculating all of the local maxima and minima of the segment histogram. The local maxima and minima are then pruned such that the distance in height between two consecutive points must be above some experimentally determined threshold. The segment boundary points are the same as local maximum points.

5   Analysis

Both of the above methods for calculating segment boundaries produced all of the same segment points as manual segmentation in the 25 second test sequence. The average distance between automatically calculated segment points and the manual segment points is 8.5 frames for the threshold method and 9 frames for the local maximum method. In experiments with manual segmentation, it was found that segment points varied by 9.2 frames on average. Therefore, the error of the automatically generated segment points for this example is within the error that is produced by manual segmentation.

The preliminary results demonstrate that using LMA Effort parameters as the basis for segmenting motion capture data produces results that are on par with manual segmentation in at least this one example. In order to demonstrate that this method is effective on general motions it should be extended to analyze the entire body and should be tested on longer and more general sets of motions. The performance metric should also be changed from a subjective manual comparison to an evaluation of performance when integrated into real applications.

References

1. Barbič, J., Safonova, A., Pan, J.Y., Faloutsos, C., Hodgins, J.K., Pollard, N.S.: Segmenting motion capture data into distinct behaviors. In: Proceedings of Graphics Interface (GI'04) (2004)

2. Bregler, C.: Learning and recognizing human dynamics in video sequences. In: IEEE Conference on Computer Vision and Pattern Recognition, pp. 568–574 (1997)
3. Fod, A., Matarić, M.J., Jenkins, O.C.: Automated derivation of primitives for movement classification. Autonomous Robots 12(1), 39–54 (2002)
4. Jenkins, O.C., Mataric, M.J.: Automated derivation of behavior vocabularies for autonomous humanoid motion. In: Proceedings of the second international joint conference on Autonomous agents and multiagent systems, pp. 225–232 (2003)
5. Jenkins, O.C., Matarić, M.J.: A spatio-temporal extension to isomap nonlinear dimension reduction. ACM International Conference Proceeding Series (2004)
6. Kahol, K., Tripathi, P., Panchanathan, S.: Automated gesture segmentation from dance sequences. In: Automatic Face and Gesture Recognition, 2004. Proceedings. Sixth IEEE International Conference, pp. 883–888 (2004)
7. Lee, C.S., Elgammal, A.: Human motion synthesis by motion manifold learning and motion primitive segmentation. In: Perales, F.J., Fisher, R.B. (eds.) AMDO 2006. LNCS, vol. 4069, pp. 464–473. Springer, Heidelberg (2006)
8. Osaki, R., Shimada, M., Uehara, K.: A motion recognition method by using primitive motions. In: Proceedings of the Fifth Working Conference on Visual Database Systems: Advances in Visual Information Management, pp. 117–128 (2000)
9. Ruck, D.W., Rogers, S.K., Kabrisky, M.: Feature selection using a multilayer perceptron. Journal of Neural Network Computing 2(2), 40–48 (1990)
10. Shiratori, T., Nakazawa, A., Ikeuchi, K.: Rhythmic motion analysis using motion capture and musical information. In: IEEE International Conference on Multisensor Fusion and Integration for Intelligent Systems (MFI), pp. 89–94 (2003)
11. Starner, T., Pentland, A.: Visual recognition of american sign language using hidden markov models. Master's thesis, Massachusetts Institute of Technology, Program in Media Arts and Sciences (1995)
12. Wang, T.S., Shum, H.Y., Xu, Y.Q., Zheng, N.N.: Unsupervised analysis of human gestures. In: IEEE Pacific Rim Conference on Multimedia, pp. 174–181 (2001)
13. Shum, H.-Y., Li, Y., Wang, T.: Motion texture: a two-level statistical model for character motion synthesis. In: siggraph2002, pp. 465–472 (2002)
14. Zhao, L., Badler, N.: Acquiring and validating motion qualities from live limb gestures. Journal of Graphical Models (2005)

A Computational Model of Culture-Specific Conversational Behavior

Dušan Jan[1], David Herrera[2], Bilyana Martinovski[1],
David Novick[2], and David Traum[1]

[1] Institute for Creative Technologies, Los Angeles, CA
[2] The University of Texas at El Paso, El Paso, TX

Abstract. This paper presents a model for simulating cultural differences in the conversational behavior of virtual agents. The model provides parameters for differences in proxemics, gaze and overlap in turn taking. We present a review of literature on these factors and show results of a study where native speakers of North American English, Mexican Spanish and Arabic were asked to rate the realism of the simulations generated based on different cultural parameters with respect to their culture.

Keywords: Conversational agents, proxemics, gaze, turn taking, cultural model.

1 Introduction

Virtual agents are often embedded in life-like simulations and training environments. The goal is to immerse the user in the virtual environment, to provide an experience that is similar to what they could experience in the real world. There are many factors that influence how believable the virtual experience is. It is influenced by the visual appearance of the world and its soundscape, but the virtual agents also have to behave and interact with each other in a manner that fits in the environment. If the user is on a virtual mission in a small town in the Middle East he will expect to see Arab people on the streets. The experience will be much different than a similar setting in the suburbs of a western city. There will be many differences in how people behave in each environment. For instance when people interact with each other there will be differences in how close to each other they stand and how they orient themselves. Their gaze behavior will be different and there could even be differences in turn taking and overlap.

It is important then for the virtual agents to behave in a culturally appropriate manner depending on where the virtual experience is situated. There has been increasing interest in culturally adaptive agents e.g. [1]. In most cases the agents are built to target a particular culture. When applying this kind of agent to a new virtual setting its behavior has to be modified. To minimize the amount of work required for this modification, the agent architecture can be designed in a modular fashion so that only the mappings of functional elements to their

C. Pelachaud et al. (Eds.): IVA 2007, LNAI 4722, pp. 45–56, 2007.

culture-specific surface behaviors have to be changed as is the case for REA [2]. On the other hand the agents can be made to adapt to different cultural norms. At one extreme they could be able to observe the environment and decide how to behave. A more feasible alternative however is for the agent's designer to provide this information as is proposed for GRETA [3]. The goal is for the agent architecture to provide a set of parameters that can be modified in order to generate the behavior that is culturally appropriate for the agent in a given scenario.

In our work toward augmenting our agents with culture-specific behavior we have first focused on a small subset of cultural parameters. We have created a model that can express cultural differences in agent's proxemics, gaze and overlap in turn taking. This cultural model is an extension to the personality model we used previously for the agents in face-to-face conversation simulation [4]. We assigned the values for these cultural parameters based on reviewed literature to model Anglo American, Spanish-speaking Mexican and Arab agents. To test whether the differences are salient to the user in a virtual world we performed an experiment where we showed multi-party conversations based on different cultural models to subjects from different cultural backgrounds and asked them to rate the realism of overall animation, agent's proxemics, gaze behavior and pauses in turn taking with respect to their culture.

In this paper we first provide an overview of the conversation simulation in section 2. In section 3 we continue with review of literature on cultural variations in proxemics, gaze and turn taking for our three target cultures and show how this influenced the design of cultural parameters in section 4. Section 5 presents the results of the experiment and section 6 concludes with our observations and plans for future work in this area.

2 Conversation Simulation

The simulation of face-to-face interaction we are using is an extension of prior work in group conversation simulation using autonomous agents. Carletta and Padilha [5] presented a simulation of agents engaged in a group conversation, in which the group members take turns speaking and listening to others. The discussion was only simulated on the level of turn taking, there was no actual speech content being generated in the simulation. Previous work on turn taking was used to form a probabilistic algorithm in which agents can perform basic behaviors such as speaking and listening, beginning, continuing or concluding a speaking turn, giving positive and negative feedback, head nods, gestures, posture shifts, and gaze. There was no visual representation of the simulation, the output of the algorithm was a log of different choices made by the agents.

Behaviors were generated using a stochastic algorithm that compares randomly generated numbers against parameters that can take on values between 0 and 1. These parameters determine the likelihood of wanting to talk, how likely the agents are to produce explicit positive and negative feedback, and turn-claiming signals. They determine how often the agents will interrupt others and duration of speech segments. The parameters of this algorithm are used to define the personality of the agents. There are great variations present between individuals, even within a single culture, although cultural biases are also possible and would require further investigation.

This work was extended in [6], which tied the simulation to the bodies of background characters in a virtual world [7] and also incorporated reactions to external events as part of the simulation. This kind of simulation allowed middle-level of detail conversations, in which the characters are close enough to be visible, but are not the main characters in the setting. Their main role is not to interact with the user, but rather maintain the illusion of a realistic environment where the user is situated.

Further improvements to the simulation were made by using new bodies in the Unreal Tournament game engine and adding support for dynamic creation of conversation groups [4]. This allowed dynamic creation, splitting, joining, entry and exit of sub-conversations, rather than forcing the entire group to remain in one fixed conversation. Other extensions to the simulation were made to add support for movement of the agents by adding a movement and positioning component that allows agents to monitor "forces" that make it more desirable to move to one place or another, iteratively select new destinations and move while remaining engaged in conversations [8].

3   Aspects of Culture-Specific Behavior

Our current focus of investigation is on cultural variation of non-verbal behaviors in conversation. We were interested in factors that play an important role in face to face conversation and are mainly controlled and learned on a rather subconscious level. As a first step we examined differences in proxemics, gaze and pauses between turns. While other factors such as gestures also have significant cultural variation and are salient for the outward appearance of conversation, we restricted our investigation to some of the factors where we did not have to alter the art used in the simulation.

Our goal was to create a cultural model and provide examples for Anglo American, Spanish-speaking Mexican and Arab cultures. In order to accomplish this we reviewed relevant literature and we report on our findings in the rest of this section.

3.1   Proxemics

Proxemics relates to spatial distance between persons interacting with each other, and their orientation toward each other. Hall writes that individuals generally divide their personal space into four distinct zones [9]. The intimate zone is used for embracing or whispering, the personal zone is used for conversation among good friends, the social zone is used for conversation among acquaintances and the public zone for public speaking. While the proxemics are culturally defined, there are also variations based on sex, social status, environmental constraints and type of interaction.

Baxter observed interpersonal spacing of Anglo-, Black-, and Mexican- Americans in several natural settings [10]. He classified subjects by ethnic group, age, sex and indoor/outdoor setting. Results for Anglo- and Mexican-American adults are listed in table 1.

Table 1. Mean Interpersonal Distance in Feet [10]

Ethnic Group	Sex Combination	Indoor Adults	Outdoor Adults
Anglo	M-M	2.72	2.72
Anglo	M-F	2.33	2.59
Anglo	F-F	2.45	2.46
Mexican	M-M	2.14	1.97
Mexican	M-F	1.65	1.83
Mexican	F-F	2.00	1.67

Graves and Watson [11] observed 32 male Arab and American college students in pairs (6 possible combinations) for 5 minutes after 2 minute warm-ups. They found that Arabs and Americans differed significantly in proxemics, the Arabs interacting with each other closer and more directly than Americans. They also report that differences between subjects from different Arab regions were smaller than for different American regions. While the study confirms that Arabs interact much closer to each other we cannot use their measurements as all their subjects were seated. In a similar experiment Watson studied 110 male foreign students between spring of '66 and '67 at the University of Colorado. He found that Latin Americans exhibit less closeness than Arabs, but still interact much closer than Anglo Americans [12].

Shuter's investigation of proxemic behavior in Latin America gives us some useful data about proxemics in Spanish cultures. He was particularly interested in changes between different geographical regions. In his study he compared proxemics of pairs involved in conversation in a natural setting [13]. He concluded that interactants stand farther apart and the frequency of tactile contact diminishes as one goes from Central to South America. Table 2 lists the distances recorded in his study.

Table 2. Mean Interpersonal Distance in Feet [13]

Sex Combination	Costa Rica	Panama	Colombia
M-M	1.32	1.59	1.56
M-F	1.34	1.49	1.53
F-F	1.22	1.29	1.40

McCroskey et al. performed an interesting study investigating whether real life proxemic behavior translates into expected interpersonal distances when using a projection technique [14]. Their main goal was to get more data on proxemics as it relates to differences in subjects that are hard to measure in naturalistic observations. They asked subjects to place a dot on a diagram of a room where they would prefer to talk with a person of interest. The results for projection technique were in agreement with findings of real observations. Similar finding of translation of proxemic behavior to a virtual setting is reported by Nakanishi in analysis of proxemics in virtual conferencing system [15].

3.2 Gaze

Most data on gaze is available for dyadic conversations. Kendon writes that gaze in dyadic conversation serves to provide visual feedback, to regulate the flow of conversation, to communicate emotions and relationships and to improve concentration by restriction of visual input [16].

Argyle and Cook provide a number of useful data on gaze measurements in different situations [17]. While most of it is dyadic, there is some data available for triads. They compare gaze behavior between triads and dyads as reported in studies by Exline [18] and Argyle and Ingham [19]. Table 3 shows how the amount of gaze differs between the two situations (although the tasks and physical conditions in the two studies were different so group size may not be the only variable). In dyadic conversation people look nearly twice as much when listening as while speaking.

Table 3. Amount of gaze (%) in triads and dyads [17]

	Triads		Dyads	
Sex Combination	MMM	FFF	MM	FF
Average amount of gaze by individuals	23.2	37.3	56.1	65.7
Looking while listening	29.8	42.4	73.8	77.9
Looking while talking	25.6	36.9	31.1	47.9
Mutual Gaze	3.0	7.5	23.4	37.9

A study by Weisbrod looked at gaze behavior in a 7-member discussion group [20]. He found that people looked at each other 70% of the time while speaking and 47% while listening. Among other things, he concluded that to look at someone while he is speaking serves as a signal to be included in the discussion, and to receive a look back from the speaker signals the inclusion of the other. Kendon [16] attributes this reversal of the pattern as compared to dyadic situation to the fact that in multiparty situation the speaker must make it clear to whom he is speaking.

There is some data available on cultural differences in gaze behavior. In a review by Matsumoto [21] he reports that people from Arab cultures gaze much longer and more directly than do Americans. In general contact cultures engage in more gazing and have more direct orientation when interacting with others.

3.3   Turn Taking and Overlap

According to Sacks, Schegloff and Jefferson [22], most of the time only one person speaks in a conversation, occurences of more than one speaker at a time are common, but brief, and transitions from one turn to next usually occur with no gap and no overlap, or with slight gap or overlap. The low amount of overlap is possible because participants are able to anticipate transition-relevance place, a completion point at which it would be possible to change speakers.

However, in actual conversations this is not always the case. Berry [23] makes a comparison between Spanish and American turn-taking styles and finds that amount of overlap in Spanish conversation is much higher than predicted by Sacks et al. One of the reasons for this behavior is presence of collaborative sequences. These are genuinely collaborative in nature and include completing another speaker's sentence, repeating or rewording what a previous speaker has just said, and contributing to a topic as if one has the turn even though they don't. Also when simultaneous speech does occur, continued speaking during overlap is much more common in Spanish conversation.

3.4   Overall Evaluation of Literature

The literature provides enough information to create a general framework for a simple computational model. However, in the process of specifying specific values for the cultural parameters we found that a lot of the needed information is missing.

Most of the data on proxemics only has information on mean distance between observed subjects. Information about values for different interaction zones is rare and for North American most agree with values reported by Hall. Data for Mexican and Arab culture is much more scarce. While we did find some information in Spanish literature on interaction distances for different zones, it was not clear whether they were reporting values specific to Spanish cultures or just in general.

Literature on cultural differences of gaze and overlap in turn taking is rare and generally lacks quantitative data. The only culture-specific information we found on gaze indicated that gaze is more direct and longer in contact cultures. While data on overlap in turn taking suggested that Spanish cultures allow for more overlap than English, we did not find any comparative analysis for Arab culture.

4   Computational Model

Before we could apply cultural variations to the simulation we had to make some changes in the computational model so that it was better able to express the cultural differences. The ability to provide proxemic parameters to the simulation is provided by the movement and positioning algorithm [8]. It takes 3 inputs; maximum distance for intimate zone, maximum distance for personal zone and maximum distance for social zone. Each agent maintains a belief about relationship with other agents. They will choose appropriate interactional distance based on this information. If at some point during the conversation an agent gets out of his preferred zone for interaction he will adapt by repositioning himself. He will do this while balancing requirements for proxemics with other factors that influence positioning, such as audibility of the speaker, background noise and occlusion of other participants in the conversation.

To express the differences in gaze behavior and turn taking overlap we had to make some changes to the simulation. Previously the conversation simulation employed a uniform gazing behavior. In order to differentiate gazing behavior of agents that are speaking and listening we designed a probabilistic scheme where agents transition between different gaze states. We identified 5 different states: 1) agent is speaking and the agent they are gazing at is looking at the speaker, 2) agent is speaking and the agent they are gazing at is not looking at the speaker, 3) agent is speaking and is averting gaze or looking away, 4) agent is listening and speaker is gazing at him, 5) agent is listening and speaker is not gazing at him. In each of the states the agent has a number of possible choices. For example in state 1 he can choose to keep gazing at the current agent, he can choose to gaze at another agent or gaze away. Each outcome has a weight associated with it. If the weights for these 3 outcomes are 6, 2 and 2 respectively, then the speaker will choose to keep gazing at their current target 60% of the time, in 20% he will pick a new agent to gaze at and in the remaining 20% he will look away. The decision on whether to transition between states is performed about every 0.5 seconds of the simulation. In addition to these weights we introduced another modifier based on our informal observations that makes it more likely for agents to look at agents that are currently gazing at us.

Last, the overlap between turns was redesigned to follow gaussian distribution [24], with mean and variation as parameters that can be culturally defined. Whenever the agent decides to take a turn at a pre-TRP signal (a cue by which the agents are able to predict when the next transition relevance place will occur), it picks a random value based on this distribution and uses this value to queue when he's going to start his turn speaking.

The parameters defining the cultural variation are represented in XML format with sections for proxemics, gaze and silence and overlap. The following is an example XML culture description for the Anglo American model. The distance for proxemics are expressed in meters. The gaze section starts with GazingAtMeFactor which specifies the modifier making it more likely to gaze at someone that is currently looking at the agent. Following are the distributions for the gaze behavior for each of the 5 gaze states (Speaker/Attending, Speaker/NonAttending, Speaker/Away, Addressee, Listener). The choices for which the weights can be specified are: Speaker - agent that is speaking, Addressee - agent that speaker is gazing at, Random - random conversation participant, Away - averting gaze or looking away. The last section, Silence, includes the before mentioned parameters influencing the gaussian distribution for overlap between turns.

```
<Culture>
  <Proxemics>
    <IntimateZone>0.45</IntimateZone>
    <PersonalZone>1.2</PersonalZone>
    <SocialZone>2.7</SocialZone>
  </Proxemics>
  <Gaze>
    <GazingAtMeFactor>1.5</GazingAtMeFactor>
    <Speaker>
      <Attending>
        <Addressee>6.0</Addressee>
        <Random>2.0</Random>
        <Away>2.0</Away>
      </Attending>
      <NonAttending>
        <Addressee>1.0</Addressee>
        <Random>8.0</Random>
        <Away>1.0</Away>
      </NonAttending>
      <Away>
        <Random>9.0</Random>
        <Away>1.0</Away>
      </Away>
    </Speaker>
    <Addressee>
      <Speaker>8.0</Speaker>
      <Random>1.0</Random>
      <Away>1.0</Away>
    </Addressee>
    <Listener>
      <Speaker>6.0</Speaker>
      <Addressee>2.0</Addressee>
      <Random>1.0</Random>
      <Away>1.0</Away>
    </Listener>
  </Gaze>
  <Silence>
    <StartOffset>0.0</StartOffset>
    <StartVariation>0.5</StartVariation>
  </Silence>
</Culture>
```

We tried to back most of the values for cultural parameters with data from the available literature, but in many cases we had to resort to approximations based on available qualitative descriptions. For proxemics of North American culture we used the values reported by Hall and are used as shown in the above example

XML. To overcome the lack of data for zone distances of Arab and Mexican culture we used differences in mean distances from reported studies and used them to modify distances for all zones. For Mexican Spanish we used the values of $0.45m$ for intimate, $1.0m$ for personal and $2.0m$ for social zone and $0.45m$, $0.7m$, $1.5m$ for respective zones in Arab model.

To model the more direct gaze of contact cultures we increased the weight corresponding to gaze at the speaker in the Mexican and Arab model. We have decided not to make any differences in overlap of turn taking because we did not get any data for Arab culture.

In the end the cultural models are richer in respect to proxemics due to lack of exact studies on cultural aspects of gaze and overlap in turn taking. While it is unfortunate that we do not have more data this gives us an opportunity to verify if the virtual reality simulation reflects cultural phenomena which are recognized by the subjects. If the subjects are asked to evaluate the parameters in respect to their culture even for the parameters that we do not vary between cultures, then we should expect more cultural differences with respect to proxemics than with respect to gaze and overlap in turn taking.

5   Evaluation

To test whether the proposed extension of the conversational simulation can saliently represent the cultural differences we conducted a cross-cultural study of the perceptions of non-verbal behaviors in a virtual world. Native speakers of American English, Mexican Spanish, and Arabic observed six two-minute silent animations representing multi-party conversation created by running the simulation with different parameters. We also identified age and sex of the participants and where they attended high school. In the study we had 18 native English speakers, 22 to 70 years old, who all attended high school in the US. 12 Arab subjects were in the range from 21 to 48 years old and most attended high school in the Middle East (Lebanon, Qatar, Syria, Kuwait, Palestine, Morocco, Egypt). All except one out of 10 Mexican subjects attended high school in Mexico and ranged from 19 to 38 years old.

While all of the animations had Afghani characters in a Central Asian setting, the parameters of the characters' non-verbal behaviors were set to values based on the literature for Americans, Mexicans, and Arabs. The animations differed mainly with respect to proxemics. While the Mexican and Arab model had more direct gaze at the speaker, that aspect was not always easily observable given the location of the camera. Two different animations for each culture were presented to each observer, and the order of presentations was balanced across observer groups. The observers were asked to rate the realism with respect to their culture of the overall animation, the characters' proxemics, the characters' gaze behaviors, and the characters' pauses in turn-taking. They were also asked to describe what differences they noticed between the movies and what elements they thought weren't appropriate for their culture.

Fig. 1. These are two examples taken from the animations used in the evaluation. Left picture is from the North American model and right picture from the Arab model.

The results contained both expected and unexpected elements. Arab subjects judged the Arab proxemics to be more realistic than both American and Mexican proxemics ($p < 0.01$). Arab subjects also judged the Arab animation more realistic overall than the American animation ($p < 0.01$). Arab subjects did not judge American proxemics to differ from Mexican proxemics. And judgments of Arab subjects about gaze and pause did not show significant differences across cultures, which was expected because these parameters did not significantly differ across the animations. The judgments of the Mexican and American subjects did not show differences between any of the cultures with respect to proxemics or overall realism. In the aggregate the subjects saw significant differences between some of the individual animations, even if they did not see significant differences between the sets of animations representing the different cultural parameters. For example, the aggregated subjects judged the proxemics of animation "Arab 1" to differ significantly from those of both "American 1" and "Mexican 2" ($p < 0.001$). There was suggestive evidence ($p < 0.5$) that American subjects distinguished the proxemics of "Arab 1" from "American 1", but Mexican subjects apparently did not perceive these differences ($p > 0.59$). There is suggestive evidence that Mexican subjects distinguished "Arab 1" from "Mexican 2" ($p < 0.13$), but Mexican subjects did not distinguish the pairs of Arab and Mexican animations.

The significant differences in perceptions of the individual animations suggest that the animations differed from each other along dimensions other than proxemics, gaze and inter-turn pause length. Possible factors include gesture, coincidental coordination of gesture among the characters, and limitations of the virtual world, which may have affected the representations of the different cultural models in different ways. This is also confirmed by qualitative responses from the subjects that were asked to note any factors they thought did not fit their culture. Some Arab subjects noted that there wasn't enough tactile contact between the characters. One thought that characters conversing in diads in one particular movie was not culturally appropriate. Some were also distracted by the clothes the characters were wearing.

6 Conclusion

In this paper we have presented an extension of a conversation simulation that can express cultural differences in conversation. We presented the data used to create the model and an example XML representation of the cultural parameters. The results of the evaluation have shown that subjects were able to distinguish between simulations generated with different parameters in regard to culture-appropriateness, which suggests that the simulations do reflect culturally specific behaviors which are observable by the viewers of same or other cultures.

To further the study of cross-cultural differences in conversation we could pursue research in several directions. More studies are needed on culture-specific data on duration of gaze before transition, on turn taking, pauses and overlap. We could explore other factors that change across cultures including gestures and other non-verbal behaviors or investigate in cultural difference in goal oriented conversations as opposed to the free-form conversations in the current simulation. We could also expand the analysis to include more cultures than the ones we examined. In order to achieve many of these goals it would be helpful to have an audiovisual corpus for analyzing non-verbal behaviors, particularly in multi-party interaction. Another way to achieve the same goal could also be to let the subjects of different cultures experiment with the parameters of the simulation in some way and set the parameters themselves.

Acknowledgments. The project described here has been sponsored by the U.S. Army Research, Development, and Engineering Command (RDECOM). Statements and opinions expressed do not necessarily reflect the position or the policy of the United States Government, and no official endorsement should be inferred.

References

1. O'Neill-Brown, P.: Setting the stage for the culturally adaptive agent. In: Proceedings of the 1997 AAAI Fall Symposium on Socially Intelligent Agents, pp. 93–97. AAAI Press, Menlo Park, CA (1997)
2. Cassell, J., Bickmore, T., Billinghurst, M., Campbell, L., Chang, K., Vilhjálmsson, H., Yan, H.: Embodiment in conversational interfaces: Rea. In: Proceedings of the SIGCHI conference on Human factors in computing systems: the CHI is the limit, pp. 520–527 (1999)
3. de Rosis, F., Pelachaud, C., Poggi, I.: Transcultural believability in embodied agents: a matter of consistent adaptation. In: Agent Culture: Designing Human-Agent Interaction in a Multicultural World, Laurence Erlbaum Associates, Mahwah (2003)
4. Jan, D., Traum, D.R.: Dialog simulation for background characters. In: Panayiotopoulos, T., Gratch, J., Aylett, R., Ballin, D., Olivier, P., Rist, T. (eds.) IVA 2005. LNCS (LNAI), vol. 3661, pp. 65–74. Springer, Heidelberg (2005)
5. Padilha, E., Carletta, J.: A simulation of small group discussion. In: Proceedings of EDILOG 2002: Sixth Workshop on the Semantics and Pragmatics of Dialogue, pp. 117–124 (2002)

6. Patel, J., Parker, R., Traum, D.R.: Simulation of small group discussions for middle level of detail crowds. In: Army Science Conference (2004)
7. Swartout, W., Hill, R., Gratch, J., Johnson, W., Kyriakakis, C., Labore, K., Lindheim, R., Marsella, S., Miraglia, D., Moore, B., Morie, J., Rickel, J., Thiebaux, M., Tuch, L., Whitney, R., Douglas, J.: Toward the holodeck: Integrating graphics, sound, character and story. In: Proceedings of 5th International Conference on Autonomous Agents (2001)
8. Jan, D., Traum, D.R.: Dynamic movement and positioning of embodied agents in multiparty conversations. In: AAMAS 2007: Proceedings of the Sixth International Joint Conference on Autonomous Agents and Multi-Agent Systems (2007)
9. Hall, E.T.: Proxemics. Current Anthropology 9(2/3), 83–108 (1968)
10. Baxter, J.C.: Interpersonal spacing in natural settings. Sociometry 33(4), 444–456 (1970)
11. Watson, O.M., Graves, T.D.: Quantitative research in proxemic behavior. American Anthropologist 68(4), 971–985 (1966)
12. Watson, O.: Proxemic Behavior: A Cross-cultural Study. Mouton (1970)
13. Shuter, R.: Proxemics and Tactility in Latin America. Journal of Communication 26(3), 46–52 (1976)
14. McCroskey, J.C., Young, T.J., Richmond, V.P.: A simulation methodology for proxemic research. Sign Language Studies 17, 357–368 (1977)
15. Nakanishi, H.: Freewalk: a social interaction platform for group behaviour in a virtual space. Int. J. Hum.-Comput. Stud. 60(4), 421–454 (2004)
16. Kendon, A.: Some functions of gaze-direction in social interaction. Acta Psychol (Amst) 26(1), 22–63 (1967)
17. Argyle, M., Cook, M.: Gaze and Mutual Gaze. Cambridge University Press, Cambridge (1976)
18. Exline, R.V.: Explorations in the process of person perception: Visual interaction in relation to competition, sex, and need for affiliation. Journal of Personality 31 (1960)
19. Argyle, M., Ingham, R.: Gaze, mutual gaze, and proximity. Semiotica 6(1), 32–50 (1972)
20. Weisbrod, R.M.: Looking behavior in a discussion group (1965) (unpublished paper)
21. Matsumoto, D.: Culture and Nonverbal Behavior. In: The Sage Handbook of Nonverbal Communication, Sage Publications Inc, Thousand Oaks, CA (2006)
22. Sacks, H., Schegloff, E., Jefferson, G.: A simplest systematics for the organization of turn-taking for conversation. Language 50(4), 696–735 (1974)
23. Berry, A.: Spanish and American turn-taking styles: A comparative study. Pragmatics and Language Learning, monograph series 5, 180–190 (1994)
24. ten Bosch, L., Oostdijk, N., de Ruiter, J.: Durational Aspects of Turn-Taking in Spontaneous Face-to-Face and Telephone Dialogues. In: Sojka, P., Kopeček, I., Pala, K. (eds.) TSD 2004. LNCS (LNAI), vol. 3206, pp. 563–570. Springer, Heidelberg (2004)

Ethnic Identity and Engagement in Embodied Conversational Agents

Francisco Iacobelli and Justine Cassell

Northwestern University
Frances Searle Building 2-343. 2240 Campus Drive. Evanston, 60208-2952
[f-iacobelli,justine]@northwestern.edu

Abstract. In this paper we present the design, development and initial evaluation of a virtual peer that models ethnicity through culturally authentic verbal and non-verbal behaviors. The behaviors chosen for the implementation come from an ethnographic study with African-American and Caucasian children and the evaluation of the virtual peer consists of a study in which children interacted with an African American or a Caucasian virtual peer and then assessed its ethnicity. Results suggest that it may be possible to tip the ethnicity of a embodied conversational agent by changing verbal and non-verbal behaviors instead of surface attributes, and that children engage with those virtual peers in ways that have promise for educational applications.

Keywords: Virtual Peers, Embodied Conversational Agents, Culture, Ethnicity.

1 Introduction and Background

Although a number of researchers have addressed the issue of embodied conversational agents that exhibit culturally authentic traits [for example 1, 10, 11], the majority of those studies have modeled culture only through surface traits such as skin color, hair style, clothing, etc. Additionally, the majority of these studies have targeted the issue of whether adults prefer to interact with a same or different racially-identified agent. However, research on Embodied Conversational Agents (ECAs) shows that users prefer ECAs that display verbal behaviors that are consistent with their non verbal behaviors. This suggests that in order to build a ethnically authentic ECA one needs to model verbal and non verbal behaviors that are consistent with one another and with the ethnicity that one wishes to emulate.

A number of researchers have studied user reactions to culturally diverse embodied conversational agents (ECAs). The design of these agents has primarily consisted of external features such as skin color or appearance [for example 1, 9, 11]. Baylor [1], for example, implemented ECAs that varied in skin color and hairstyle to represent Caucasian and African American agents. She found that African-American students may affiliate more strongly with an African-American agent, perceive it as more engaging and as more facilitating of learning; however, no evidence of increased learning outcomes was found. Nass and colleagues [11] evaluated a Korean and a Caucasian agent and found that participants judged the agent of their same ethnicity to be more trustworthy, attractive and competent. Nass also found that participants

C. Pelachaud et al. (Eds.): IVA 2007, LNAI 4722, pp. 57–63, 2007.
© Springer-Verlag Berlin Heidelberg 2007

conformed more to the decision of agents of the same ethnicity. In Nass' study, only physical appearance was altered to represent ethnicity. Prior research on Embodied Conversational Agents (ECAs) shows, however, that users prefer ECAs that displays verbal behaviors that are consistent with their non verbal behaviors [11]. Along these lines, Maldonado and colleagues [10] implemented three pedagogical agents that represented adolescent girls from Venezuela, Brazil and the United States. Nevertheless no empirical evaluation was carried out with these agents, and it is unclear where the authors derived the traits that they attribute to each ethnicity.

In general, the term "race" is associated with biology while "ethnicity" is associated with culture. Since recent scholarship questioned whether the human race can be divided into biological groups [8], in this paper we concern ourselves with ethnicity, which may be thought of as a set of traits that index to other members of the group, and to members of other groups, one's cultural community membership. Physical appearance is not the most reliable index of ethnicity. On the other hand, we claim that the combination of verbal and non-verbal behaviors can be a reliable index of ethnicity. For example, African Americans may speak a dialect of English known as African American Vernacular English, with its own syntax, morphology and lexicon, and they also may produce non-verbal behaviors that are different from those used by Caucasians in similar situations [6]. Identity is thus constructed on the cultural level and on the micro-interpersonal level and the two are brought together in moment-by-moment behavior in conversation [7]. To address the problem of cultural authenticity and the development of ethnic diversity in ECAs, then, we argue that the design process must be informed by careful research on actual communities of people in particular contexts, and must depend on a model that is derived from the verbal and non verbal behaviors that signal ethnic identity in those contexts.

The study reported here is a part of a larger research program into the development of virtual peers (lifesize child-like ECAs) to scaffold the development of literacy skills in children from different populations. In the study reported here we assess whether children are able to attribute ethnic identity to an ECA based on behavior and not skin color. We do this by having children interact with two virtual peers which have an identical appearance but of which one speaks African American Vernacular English, and uses nonverbal behaviors based on a study of African-American children, and the other speaks and uses non-verbal behavior from Caucasian children who speak Standard American English. We believe that children will be able to assess ethnicity on the basis of these kinds of identity features, and that they will be more engaged with ECAs of their own ethnicity.

2 Methodology

In order to test our hypotheses we implemented two virtual peers by applying two models of behaviors to an existing virtual child with a racially-ambiguous appearance [5]. The Caucasian peer was implemented on the basis of the narrative model described by Wang and Cassell [12]. Several dyads of Caucasian children who spoke Standard American English (SAE) were videotaped playing with a doll house and figurines. Wang and Cassell coded narrative roles, speech acts, eye gaze patterns and other non-verbal behaviors. In order to construct the African-American model of behavior we observed and coded the verbal and non-verbal behaviors of seven African American children who were monolingual speakers of African American Vernacular English (AAVE), during spontaneous play. We coded narrative roles, speech acts and eye gaze patterns, and identified those verbal and nonverbal behaviors that were maximally distinctive from the Caucasian children. An excerpt from this model is given in Table 1. Under the "*Non-Verbal*" column, asterisks (*) indicate those behaviors maximally distinctive from Caucasian children who speak SAE [6]. For example, the African-American children were more likely to gaze at the toys than one another, which was not the case for Caucasian children who spoke SAE.

The African-American and Caucasian models of behavior were then implemented in virtual peers. The virtual peer was displayed on a back projection screen with a wooden doll house placed against the screen. Overall, the environment looked as if the virtual child and the real child were playing, facing each other (see Figure 1). The doll house contained figurines and play furniture, and children were invited to tell stories with the virtual peer.

Table 1. Excerpt from model of African American children's collaborative storytelling

Roles	Speech Act	Spe aker	Function	Non-Verbal
Critics and Authors	Suggest	Critic	To suggest an event or idea to the story	Eye gaze towards toy (66.3% of the tim)e. Towards author (33.3%)
	Correct	Critic	To correct what has been said	*Eye gaze on toy and remains there (50%). Eye gaze towards author and then turns towards t oy (25%).
	Question	Critic	Seek clarification or missing informatio n	Eye gaze towards toy 100% of the time.
	Answer	Both	To clarify or supply missing information	*Eye gaze to doll house or toy (66%). Gaze towards camera (33%)
	Elaborate	Author	Additions to story	Eye gaze on toy or house (79%)
Co-Authors	Role-Play	Both	Play role of characters in story	Eye gaze towards own toy (78%).
	Simultaneous Turns	Both	Compete for turn	Eye gaze towardes own toy (71%).
Nonstory	Direct	Both	Suggest position of toys or behavior	Eye gaze towards other and then quickly turns to house or toys (56%)
	Comment	Both	Comment unrelated to story	Eye gaze to toy or house (80%). Gaze towards other speaker (10%).
	Idiosyncratic	Both	Uutterance unrelated to story	Eye gaze to the toy or house (68%). Gaze to other speaker (10%).

Below we report the results of a pilot study to determine if we were successful in changing the perceived ethnicity of the virtual peer by changing its verbal and non-verbal behaviors, and how African-American children engaged with the two models.

29 third graders (ages 9-10) from a public school in Chicago participated. 100% of the students of the school are African American and 95.3% are low income. All participants are mono-lingual speakers of AAVE. 20 of the participants are taught by an African American speaker of AAVE while 9 belonged to a class with a Caucasian

SAE-speaking teacher. 15 participants were girls. We used the scores of the Stanford Learning First standardized test to make sure that the distribution of children to each condition was diverse with respect to academic performance.

In this study, we examined one independent variable: ethnicity of the virtual peer: one virtual peer was modeled after Caucasian children that speak Standard American English (SAE VP) and one was modeled after African American children that speak African American Vernacular English (AAVE VP).

Instructions to the children were given as follows: First, the experimenter, who is Hispanic, and speaks with a slight Hispanic accent, introduced the virtual peer and invited children to tell stories with it; he then left the children alone. The virtual peer, who was operated by another experimenter in a Wizard of Oz mode (following the rules of either AAVE or SAE model), told one story and then elicited a story from the child. While the child was speaking, the VP gave feedback ("what happened next?", "for real?"). Once the child finished the virtual peer told a second story, and then elicited a second story from the child. The virtual peer then said goodbye and the experimenter entered the room. The participant was then asked to complete a sorting task that demonstrates ability to find similarity along more than one dimension in order to ensure that the child was capable of understanding multiple dimensions of similarity [2], and finally the child was asked which of two family strips (pictures of a family; in this case African-American and Caucasian appearance) represented the family that "came to take Alex, the virtual peer, home from school" [2]. Finally, in order to ensure that the family-matching task was picking up on ethnicity, we asked children which family strip would pick them up from school [2].

Due to the long-running nature of data collection, five experimenters ran the Wizard of Oz on different days. In order to ensure comparability, we looked at the mean number of feedback utterances by the VP, using pairwise t-tests. A significant effect pointed to one experimenter, a non-native speaker of English, in the US for 4 months. The data collected in those sessions was therefore not considered here. Additionally, in one case the child did not complete the tasks assigned and in another the experimenter did not explain a task properly. This left us with 17 participants of which 9 were assigned to the AAVE VP condition and 8 to the SAE VP condition.

3 Results

Results from the ethnic assessment task are presented in Figure 2. A power analysis reveals that significance would require 28 participants in each condition. Our sample size was significantly smaller; therefore, most of the results presented simply represent interesting trends. As seen in Figure 2, 56% of the AAVE VP children perceived the virtual peer as having African American parents versus 12% in the SAE condition. 83% of children in the SAE condition judged the VP as having Caucasian parents. This result did not reach significance (p=0.15, Fisher's Exact; hybrid version), but it should be noted that it might have had we included the children who quickly changed their minds from saying that Alex would be picked up by the Caucasian family to saying that Alex would be picked up by the African American family (no child changed his or her mind in the other direction). This suggests that our model is not complete, and that while the SAE VP was accurately judged as ethnically

Caucasian, the AAVE VP was not as convincingly African American. This is not particularly surprising since the current AAVE model contains fewer observations of nonverbal behaviors than the SAE model. Future work includes running a bigger study with a VP that incorporates a more complete model of African American interactions and a wider range of AAVE utterances and stories.

Fig. 1. Layout of experiment   **Fig. 2.** Perception of ethnicity by condition

In order to test whether children are more engaged when interacting with agents of their own ethnicity, it is valid to use the modeled ethnicity of the VP as the independent variable. However, because we were not able to emulate ethnicity in a convincing way, this independent variable does not fully capture the concept of an agent of the same ethnicity as the child. For this reason, below we present results both as a function of the condition "ethnicity of VP" *and* as a function of the ethnicity that the child attributed to the agent.

Our first analysis looks at the duration of the children's stories in number of seconds; a trend suggests that the *first* stories told with the AAVE VP were longer $t(16)=1.52$, $p<0.08$). The duration of the second story, however, was not significantly different. In addition, a re-analysis of these results in terms of *perceived* ethnicity is also not significant. However, in children's play, engagement is signaled by duration of play, complexity of stories, and also the amount of thematic overlap between the two children. That is, when children are very engaged, they pick up on one another's language [3]. In order to test for this, we coded instances in which the child mimics Alex's lexical or thematic choices [4]. Looking at the proportion of total utterances that mimic Alex, we found a trend that suggests that children in the SAE VP condition produce a higher proportion of mimicking utterances in Story1. $t(15)=-1.5, p<0.07$ (see Figure 3). This trend remains, albeit to a lesser degree, in the second story. Re-analyzing these results as a function of *perceived* ethnicity demonstrates that children do mimic the virtual peer significantly more when they perceive it as Caucasian. $t(14)=-2.51$; $p<0.02$ (see Figure 4).

In order to assess the effect of ethnicity of the virtual peer on the children's language, we also coded instances where the children produced SAE linguistic features in their talk. We used the two most common AAVE-SAE contrasts for third grade children: (a) zero copula (e.g. she drinking instead of she is drinking) and (b) subject-verb agreement (e.g. he sleep every night instead of he sleeps every night) [6]. We found that children who interacted with an SAE-speaking peer produced a mean of .04 SAE features as opposed to .02 for children who interacted with the AAVE-speaking peer. This difference was not, however, significant. Re-analysis of these results in terms of the perceived ethnicity of the virtual peer was still not significant. However, in the second story, we observed that children who perceived the VP as African American produced an average of 0.015 SAE utterances, whereas children who perceived the VP as Caucasian produced a mean of 0.042 SAE utterances.

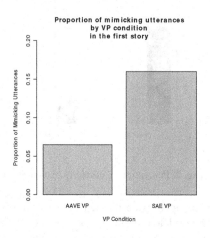

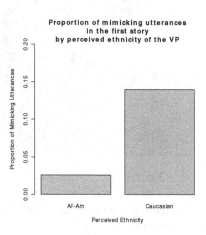

Fig. 3. Proportion of child's utterances in Story1 that mimicked Virtual Peer, by VP condition (p<0.07)

Fig. 4. Proportion of child's utterances in Story1 that mimicked Virtual Peer, by perceived ethnicity of the VP (p<0.02)

4 Conclusion

In this study we set out to assess whether we could tip the perceived ethnicity of an embodied conversational agent, specifically a virtual peer (VP), by changing the verbal and non verbal behaviors and leaving the appearance constant. The ethnicities we chose to model were an African American speaker of African American Vernacular English (AAVE) and a Caucasian American speaker of Standard American English (SAE). Our results were very partial, but do illustrate differences in kinds of engagement between versions of the VP. This exploratory study is a part of an iterative design process, and the next step is to go back to the original data of child-child African-American interaction in order to better understand the nature of linguistic and nonverbal features that signify African-American identity.

As well as investigating how children assessed their ethnicity, we also examined the effects of interaction with VPs on language use. We found that the African American children tend to spend more time telling stories with the African American VP, although since this is only true for Story1, this effect may wear off. However,

African American children mimicked the Caucasian peer more often. Our ultimate goal is to implement an African-American virtual peer capable of sustaining engagement with a child such that the VP can model and scaffold the use of code-switching between AAVE and SAE, to increase school-based literacy. The current results suggest that an AAVE-speaking VP will indeed be able to sustain engagement, and that an SAE VP will encourage children to mimic its language and trigger code-switching behaviors. Both of these results are extremely promising for future research.

Acknowledgments. We thank Andrea Tartaro, Joris Janssen, Nathan Cantelmo, Deb Zutty and the other members of the Articulab for their help. This study was made possible by grants from the National Science Foundation.

References

[1] Baylor, A., Kim, Y.: The Role of Gender and Ethnicity in Pedagogical Agent Perception. In: Proceedings of ELearn World Conference on ELearning in Corporate, Government, Healthcare, & Higher Education, Phoenix, AZ (2003)

[2] Bigler, R.S., Liben, L.S.: A Cognitive-Developmental Approach to Racial Stereotyping and Reconstructive Memory in Euro-American Children. Child development 64, 1507 (1993)

[3] Cassell, J.: Towards a Model of Technology and Literacy Development: Story Listening Systems. Journal of Applied Developmental Psychology 25, 75–105 (2004)

[4] Cassell, J., Ryokai, K.: Making Space for Voice: Technologies to Support Children's Fantasy and Storytelling. Personal Technologies 5, 203–224 (2001)

[5] Cassell, J., Tartaro, A., Oza, V., Rankin, Y., Tse, C.: Virtual Peers for Literacy Learning. Educational Technology, Special Issue on Pedagogical Agents XLVII, 39–43 (2007)

[6] Craig, H.K., Washington, J.A.: Malik goes to school: Examining the language skills of African American students from preschool-5th grade. Lawrence Erlbaum, New York (2005)

[7] Eckert, P.: Variations, conventions and social meanings. In: Proceedings of Linguistic Society of America, Oakland, CA (2005)

[8] Gould, S.J.: The mismeasure of man, 1st edn. Norton: New York (1981)

[9] Hayes-Roth, B., Maldonado, H., Moraes, M.: Designing for diversity: Multi-cultural characters for a multi-cultural world. In: Proceedings of IMAGINA 2002, Monte Carlo, Monaco (2002)

[10] Maldonado, H., Hayes-Roth, B.: Toward Cross-Cultural Believability in Character Design. In: Payr, S., Trappl, R. (eds.) Agent Culture: Human-Agent Interaction in a Multicultural World, pp. 143–176. Lawrence Erlbaum Associates, New Jersey (2004)

[11] Nass, C., Isbister, K., Lee, E.-J.: Truth is Beauty: Researching Embodied Conversational Agents. In: Cassell, J., Sullivan, J., Prevost, S., Churchill, E. (eds.) Embodied Conversational Agents, pp. 374–402. MIT Press, Cambridge, MA (2000)

[12] Wang, A., Cassell, J.: Co-authoring, Corroborating, Criticizing:Collaborative Storytelling for Literacy Learning. In: Payr, S., Trappl, R. (eds.) Vienna Workshop '03: Educational Agents - More than Virtual Tutors, Vienna, Austria (2003)

Neuroticism – A Competitive Advantage (Also) for IVAs?

Christoph Hermann[1], Helmuth Melcher[1], Stefan Rank[1], and Robert Trappl[1,2]

[1] Austrian Research Institute for Artificial Intelligence (OFAI), Freyung 6/6,
A-1010 Vienna, Austria
[2] Institute for Medical Cybernetics and AI, Center for Brain Research,
Medical University of Vienna, Austria
Firstname.Secondname@ofai.at

Abstract. Real-Time Strategy (RTS) games are a challenging genre for the design of Intelligent Virtual Agents. We were interested whether incorporating a simple emotional model to an existing bot-script improves playing strength. We implemented a bot for Microsoft's RTS game "Age of Mythology". The emotional model is based on the "Big-Five" and the Emotion-Connectionist Model. Four variants of the bot were evaluated, each using different personality parameters; one of the variants was designed to show "neurotic" behaviour. The emotion-driven bots were evaluated in a bot-versus-bot setup, playing matches against the game's default script. Evaluation results indicate a significant increase in playing strength, the "neurotic" bot being the strongest one.

Keywords: Neurotic agent, bot, emotion, artificial intelligence, real-time strategy game.

1 Introduction

The market of interactive games, being played on PCs, game consoles or mobile phones, is booming. In these games already semi-intelligent agents are employed to steer virtual actors, especially opponents of human gamers. However, their "personality structure" is quite simple, their motivation is fast winning. Since the human player is only challenged with respect to rational, strategic behaviour, the attraction of games may be increased by using emotional and/or partially "neurotically" acting agents.

However, such an agent may fare worse than a rational one. Therefore, an AI script for the real-time strategy game "Age of Mythology" was created, i.e. an emotional bot that could also act "neurotically" (see section 5). The underlying hypothesis is that "neurotic" behaviour could make it also more fun to play against this bot.

In order to build this bot, we designed and implemented a general personality and emotion model which was based on the Big-Five and the Emotion-Connectionist Model; perceptions and personality of the bot influence its emotions, and those in turn influence its actions. We presume that we can then create "neurotic" bots by extreme parameterisation of the personality model. The effects and consequences of the emotional bots are evaluated and discussed in section 7.

C. Pelachaud et al. (Eds.): IVA 2007, LNAI 4722, pp. 64–71, 2007.
© Springer-Verlag Berlin Heidelberg 2007

2 The Game

The game "Age of Mythology" was published by Microsoft Game Studios in 2002 and falls into the category of real-time strategy (RTS) games. The player is the leader of one of several peoples (Vikings, Greeks, or Egyptians) whose members he can command. He can make use of military units (infantry, cavalry, siege weapons, etc.) and civilian units (villagers) to lead battles, erect buildings, gather resources, and worship their gods. Also, he can extend his people's abilities by pushing the technological progress (in the form of so-called "Ages"): He can train new, improved units, build more effective production facilities and new building types. By worshiping the people's gods, miracles (like freezing the enemy's units or calling walking trees to help in battle) can be conjured and mythological creature units can be summoned.

3 The AI Scripting Language

3.1 Introduction

The AI players in Age of Mythology are controlled by a script system. The language syntax is close to C. The standard AI scripts of the game comprise about 3000 lines of code, where only a small part of the scripts really deals with "intelligent acting" of the player. Accordingly, the AI-driven players are quite weak in comparison with the human players. The emotional model is to be integrated into the existing AI scripts of the game.

3.2 AI Actions

The AI scripts can in principle perform all actions that a human player can execute in the GUI. This also comprises "low level" actions like moving single units. Because of efficiency considerations the asserted intention of the Age of Mythology developers is to keep the actions used in AI scripts on an abstraction level as high as possible.

3.3 Predefined Functions

The script system provides a repertoire of about 600 functions. These functions mirror, amongst other things, the most important actions that are provided to the human player via the user interface. Apart from simple actions these functions also allow access to plans, rules, and the knowledge base.

3.4 Perception of the AI

In principle, all "raw information" that a human player gets over the GUI is retrievable for the AI via a so-called knowledge base. This comprises amongst others:

- Position / status / activity of own / visible units
- Consistence of the environment
- Retrieval of basic game information (technology tree, etc.)
- Assessment of the enemy's state. The knowledge base manages a model of the seen enemy units. Thereby, it can be estimated which units the enemy probably has.

4 Calculation of the Perceptions

The basic calculation of the perceptions is done quite uniformly. A weighted average of the respective game state value over the past development of the state is calculated. In the calculation of the current perception, the weighted average is then compared with the current value.

The following perceptions are calculated: Pleasure / Pain, and Clarity / Confusion.

5 The Emotional Agent

It was based on the paper "Emotional agents: how personalities change behaviour" by G. Meyer [1]. However, neither the Emotion-Connectionist Model [2] nor the OCC Emotion Model [3] was found to be fully suitable for the game environment. The main limitations for implementing an emotion model were the computational resources available to the scripting language in the game. A model of emotion that represents the current state of a player in a low-dimensional space with straight-forward updating rules seemed most appropriate. (But see the conclusion section for plans to integrate elements of appraisal theories of emotion [4, 5]).

Therefore aspects of both these models [2] and [3] were combined and adapted to the possibilities of the game. It was furthermore assumed that the personality of emotional agents influences their behaviour patterns. The model used for personality description is the Five Factor Model (FFM). As in [2], the following emotion components were distinguished: Arousal, Pain, Pleasure, Confusion, and Clarity.

The pairs pain / pleasure and confusion / clarity had to be implemented as separate scales, as it actually is possible to feel both pain and pleasure at a time (e.g. someone loses units in battle but also rejoice when winning). As in the Emotion Connectionist Model, pain, pleasure, confusion and clarity govern the state of arousal. Arousal then weights the actual influence of the personality model on the course of the game.

In this implementation, all emotions are represented as values within the interval of [0; 1], the higher the value, the stronger the emotion.

It is assumed that, by changing the weighting factors in the personality model, any artificial opponent can be simulated ranging from rational to neurotic. The necessary weighting factors are derived from personality tests like NEO-FFI [6].

5.1 The Personality Model

The following personality factors were modelled: Extraversion (EX), Agreeableness (AG), conscientiousness (CO), Neuroticism (NE), Openness (OP).

As an Example the Neuroticism level leads to the following reactions:

High	Low
– irrational assessment of resource value; e.g. value of timber is over assessed – tend to resort to extreme playing styles: aggressive vs. defensive	– rational adjusting of assessed resource value → retrieve game statistics

5.2 The Emotion Model

The emotion model determines the intensity of all emotional states possible for the computer opponent. A change in emotion is the result of an environmental factor (a perception). The strength of emotional change is influenced by the personality.

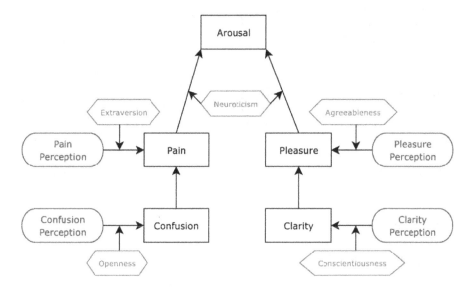

Fig. 1. Factors influencing emotions

6 Four Character Types

This chapter gives an overview of four different character configurations that we selected for running test and their expected significance in the games the bot plays using this personality.

Defensive Character
Character configuration: EX = 0.0, AG = 1.0, CO = 1.0, NE = 0.5, OP = 1.0

   Due to high values for agreeableness and openness the bot tends to give more attention to developing economics in the early game stage. It is spending more resources on researching technology early and building less military in early ages. To make up for the military sacrifices, the defensive bot builds defensive structures to protect his town.

   The basic game idea for this bot is to achieve a technologic/economic advantage over the enemy by pushing the economy early in the game. Later in the game, its economic power is converting into military strength.

Aggressive Character
Character configuration: EX = 1.0, AG = 0.0, CO = 0.5, NE = 0.5, OP = 0.0

The aggressive bot is basically the counterpart to the defensive one. It sacrifices early economic development for fast attacks. High extraversion causes it to do much scouting, and eventually build aggressive "forward bases" next to the enemy's base. The basic game-idea of this bot is to cause early economic damage to the enemy, trying to make up for the own economic sacrifices.

Normal Character
Character configuration: EX = 0.5, AG = 0.5, CO = 0.5, NE = 0.5, OP = 0.5

The normal character is the balanced combination of the defensive and aggressive approaches. The bot is expected to adapt its actual playing style during game-time depending on emotional actions.

Neurotic Character
Character configuration: EX = 0.5, AG = 0.5, CO = 0.5, NE = 1.0, OP = 0.5

The neurotic character bot is very similar to the normal character. The boost on Neuroticism enables some rules to "confuse" the emotional state from time to time. We were expecting these settings to trade off playing strength for "interesting behaviour", making irrational decisions that appear interesting but decrease playing strength.

7 Evaluation

7.1 Conditions/Constraints

The experiment was to be conducted under the following conditions:

2 players. The test scenario was limited to 2 players per game. More than 2 players in a game were not tested to keep the scenario as simple as possible.

Odin's Vikings. Every player had to use Odin's Vikings as their race because the programming effort to adjust our script to all races is quite high but has nothing to do with our topic.

Difficulty "hard". The difficulty level was set to "hard" because in the other levels the standard AI is restricted in its "intelligence".

Strategy "normal". The strategy for the standard AI and the initial state for our bot were set to be "normal" (as opposed to "aggressive", "defensive" ...). The strategy of our bot could change during the game due to its emotions.

Map "Alfheim". The game was set on a randomized "Alfheim" map. Random maps in Age of Mythology are "random" in their arrangement but they must contain a fixed number of resources, area types, etc., so they are strongly standardised.

7.2 Assessment

To qualitatively assess the success of the standard AI and of the Emo-Bot we used the game scores that are generated for different areas of the game. There is an overall score and scores for the following categories, which were computed from the given criteria:

Economy: Gathered resources (food, wood, and gold), gold from trade, donated resources, and maximum number of civilian units.

Military: Trained units, killed (enemy) units, destroyed (enemy) buildings, lost (own) units and lost (own) buildings.

Technological progress: Time until the different ages were reached and number of the technological improvements (e.g. plough).

Mythology: Conquered settlements and recovered relics.

These statistics, however, present difficulties for assessing relative player strength. Online communities of RTS-game players use a system based on Elo ratings [7, 8]. These ratings were originally developed to rate chess players but have been used for many other two-player games and, further, have been extended to be usable for multi-player games.

The Elo system takes into account the previous rating of the competing players and adjusts their scores after a game or tournament depending on the number of wins, losses, or draws. We therefore approximated relative playing strength by the ratio of wins and losses during our test games.

7.3 Test Results

4 defined character settings were tested against the default Age of Mythology AI script. Each character setting completed 7 test games. All of the character settings performed very well against the default AI, with each bot version scoring a minimum of 6 wins out of 7 matches, altogether 26 wins out of 28 games ($p < 0.0001$).

We observed two losses in the evaluation series, both caused by attack plans stuck during execution, resulting in the loss of all attacking troops without causing any damage to the opponent. The actual execution of attacks is handled by game-integrated plans, and is independent of the settings in the emotional model. Therefore, the chance of observing bugged attacks should be equal for all character settings.

- Aggressive: This setting performed worst, compared to the other ones. Although winning all the evaluation games, two of the games were rather close. It is notable that these 2 games did not include the attack-plan bug described above. We think that the nature of AI scripts in AoM, with the low amount of micromanagement being performed, handicaps early attacks by AI players. This is because early attacks rely on lower numbers of units, making the management of single units more important. As the AI scripts are not able to do any reasonable combat-handling of the units, the Aggressive bot loses too many of its early units to enemy buildings, preventing it from doing the desired economic damage to the opponent.
- Defensive: This setting was performing quite well, probably caused by the handicapped early attacking capabilities described above. This favours a defensive playing style. The bot was able to build up a strong economy in second age, advance to third age and then use the technologic advantage to decide the games in its favour.
- Normal: The games played by the Normal bot were quite similar to the Defensive games. The Normal bot usually achieved a decent military advantage over the enemy early, but it took more time to advance to third age, therefore causing longer games.

- Neurotic: The results of the neurotic bot were quite surprising. We were expecting it to play significantly worse than the other character-settings. In fact, it won all of its test games very clearly and in the shortest total amount of time.

Table 1. Gametime statistics for the test games

Setting	Wins : Losses	Average winning time
Aggressive	7 : 0	44:35 min
Defensive	6 : 1	35:17 min
Normal	6 : 1	40:34 min
Neurotic	7 : 0	31:45 min

The above test series indicates that our AI script has a significantly improved playing strength. Since we observed only 2 losses in 28 test games played with the final version of the emotional bot, the difference in playing strength could be expressed as at least 232 Elo points (the lower bound of a 95% confidence interval for winning 26 out of 28 games).

8 Conclusion and Further Work

We have been able to significantly improve the playing strength of the Age of Mythology default AI script, by adding an emotional model and a simple set of actions. These actions allow the bot to adapt the playing style during game-time depending on the state of the emotional model. While the increase in playing strength is certainly significant in comparison to existing game-AIs, the bot is still far away from the level of trained human players.

What could be done to further improve the playing strength?

- Manage the build-up process more tightly. The AI script is using a very loosely defined build-up sequence to advance to the second age, while most expert human players prefer tightly defined, optimized build-up sequences to advance to the second age. Several of those optimized build-up sequences could be implemented to improve the early playing strength of the AI.
- Raiding. Despite numerous attempts to select the targets of raiding attacks in a more intelligent way, the attack-goals refuse accept enemy villagers as attack target. By fixing this, the playing strength in age 2 and 3 could be significantly increased.

A further aspect we are investigating is the operationalisation of an appraisal model of emotion adapted for the specific environment of RTS games. This would not only allow more fine-grained evaluations of the game situation, it would also allow a more direct influence of personality parameters on action execution of the bot. It could furthermore also increase the attractiveness of the game [9]. The results of this project will be presented in a future paper.

Acknowledgement. The financial support of this project by the Austrian Federal Ministry of Transport, Innovation, and Technology is greatly appreciated.

References

1. Meyer, G.: Emotional agents: how personalities change behaviour. In: 1st Twente Student Conference on IT, Enschede, 14 June 2004. University of Twente, Faculty of Electrical Engineering, Mathematics and Computer Science (2004)
2. Chown, E., Jones, R.M., Henninger, A.E.: An architecture for emotional decision-making agents. In: Proceedings of Autonomous Agents and Multi-Agent Systems (2002)
3. Ortony, A.: On making believable emotional agents believable. In: Trappl, R., Petta, P., Payr, S. (eds.) Emotions in Humans and Artifacts, pp. 189–211. MIT Press, Cambridge (2003)
4. Scherer, K.R.: What are emotions? And how can they be measured? Social Science Information 44(4), 695–729 (2005)
5. Frijda, N.H.: The Laws of Emotion. Lawrence Erlbaum Associates, Mahwah NJ USA/London UK (2007)
6. Costa Jr, P.T., McCrae, R.R.: Revised neo personality inventory (neo-pi-r) and the neo five-factor inventory (neo-ffi): Professional manual. Psychol. Assessment Resources, Inc (1992)
7. Elo, A.E.: The Rating of Chess Players, Past and Present. Arco Publishing, New York (1978)
8. Glickman, M.E.: A Comprehensive Guide to Chess Ratings, American Chess. Journal 3, 59–102 (1995)
9. Isbister, K.: Better Game Characters by Design. Elsevier, San Francisco (2006)

Emotionally Expressive Head and Body Movement During Gaze Shifts

Brent Lance and Stacy C. Marsella

University of Southern California
Information Sciences Institute
4676 Admiralty Way Suite 1001
Marina Del Rey, CA 90292
{brent,marsella}@isi.edu

Abstract. The current state of the art virtual characters fall far short of characters produced by skilled animators. One reason for this is that the physical behaviors of virtual characters do not express the emotions and attitudes of the character adequately. A key deficiency possessed by virtual characters is that their gaze behavior is not emotionally expressive. This paper describes work on expressing emotion through head movement and body posture during gaze shifts, with intent to integrate a model of emotionally expressive eye movement into this work in the future. The paper further describes an evaluation showing that users can recognize the emotional states generated by the model.

1 Introduction

The manner of a persons gaze, how it is performed, reveals much about their inner state and intent. In fact, a key role of gaze in human interaction is to express the feelings and attitudes of the individual gazing. This role is revealed in the rich vocabulary used to describe a person's gaze. Phrases such as glare, gawking, furtive glance, etc. all indicate different ways of looking based on the emotional and cognitive state of the individual gazing. In this research, we are interested in how to create a virtual human capable of revealing its emotional states through the manner of its gaze behavior. We define the manner of gaze behavior as changes in physical parameters of individual movements, such as the velocity of the head in a single gaze shift, as opposed to changes in specific properties such as the target or time of occurrence of a gaze shift.

While there are many potential influences on gaze behavior [2], [10], we will only be looking at a subset of these. Specifically, we will be looking at how emotion affects the manner of gaze behavior. We have chosen to examine emotional factors for a number of reasons. In our previous work on gaze behavior manner [13], we found a greater association between physical parameters and emotion than between physical parameters and the other gaze-affecting factors that we examined, such as speech-related gaze shifts. More importantly, we found that the manner of gaze is a highly expressive signal. Despite findings from psychological research that show the importance of gaze manner in displaying emotion [2], [12], its recognized importance

C. Pelachaud et al. (Eds.): IVA 2007, LNAI 4722, pp. 72–85, 2007.
© Springer-Verlag Berlin Heidelberg 2007

in animation [23], and our own findings [13], little work in the virtual humans community has been done on using gaze manner to express emotion.

A key challenge that arises in developing such a model of gaze manner is that gaze is not simply eye movement. Gaze is a complex of behaviors that can include eye, head, posture, and even stepping or standing, and all of these components must be taken into account. In addition, these behaviors are not independent from each other [16]. The importance of both appropriate manner for gazing behaviors and of appropriate physical interrelations between distinct body components can be seen in a number of virtual human designs, as well as in some computer graphic animated films. The result is that independent behaviors seem robotic and unnatural, and their relationship appears random and disjointed. This effect is immediately disconcerting to the viewer. As an example, consider the film "The Polar Express," in which the characters were animated through motion capture, except for the eyes, which were separately hand-animated. One reviewer noted "Although the human characters look about 90% lifelike, it is that darn 10% (mostly the lifeless eyes) that winds up making them seem really creepy," [22]. Other reviewers agreed, describing unnatural eyes, and referring to the animated characters as "zombies" or "creepy."

This paper addresses the problem of emotionally expressive gaze manner by describing a preliminary approach for expressing emotion during gaze behaviors. This approach is described as follows: first, recordings of head, eye, and body movement are made of actors performing emotionally expressive and emotionally neutral gaze shifts. Then, parameters describing how the emotionally expressive gaze shifts differ from neutral gaze shifts are extracted. This parameterization is then applied to emotionally neutral gaze shifts at different targets from the emotional gaze shifts, transferring the physical properties of the emotional gaze to the neutral gaze. Finally, the emotional content of these generated shifts are evaluated. While this approach only describes a subset of a dimensional model of emotion and does not address the problem of emotionally expressive eye movement, the preliminary results described here show promise for future research.

While it may seem counterintuitive to discuss generating gaze while not discussing the generation of eye movement, we believe that modeling eye movement and modeling movement of the head and body require different approaches, due to the physical differences between the two types of movement. We are currently developing a model of emotionally expressive eye movement, derived in part from the eye data collected while performing this work, which will be integrated with this work once it is completed.

2 Related Work

Gaze has many uses in human interaction. Much research has been done on how gaze regulates interaction between individuals, as well as the use of gaze to signal communicative acts [10]. However, in this work, we are more interested in how gaze is used to display relational attitudes and affective states, specifically dominance/ submissiveness, arousal/relaxation, and pleasure/displeasure. Dominance is a signal sent through gaze [7], head movement [18], and posture [5]. For example, displaying increased gaze while speaking, a raised head, and upright posture all signal dominance, while the opposite behaviors signal submission.

Arousal is also closely related to gaze [2]. While there has been little work on how arousal and relaxation are specifically related to head movement, velocity has been shown to be an indicator of arousal [19]. Evidence for the relationship of gaze to the display of pleasure/displeasure is more limited. In fact, as reported in [12], some have argued that gaze is incapable of displaying emotional valence. However, the head [18], and the body [6], have both been shown to reveal pleasure/displeasure, although there is overlap with the behaviors which reveal dominance/submissiveness.

There have also been many implementations of gaze behaviors in real-time applications, such as Embodied Conversational Agents. Many of these implementations are based on communicative signals, such as [3], [20]. Other models of gaze have been developed for agents that perform tasks, interacting with an environment instead of with other characters or users [21]. Further models have simulated resting gaze, when the eye is performing no other tasks [14], or models of gaze based on realistic models of saliency [11].

In addition to models of gazing behavior, there has also been work focused on the manipulation of parameters describing the way in which movement is performed. This concept is referred to as "manner" or "style." One of the primary works on style uses what are called "style machines," combinations of statistical Hidden Markov Models, to allow for easily modifying a style, or learning a style, such as "angry," from one movement and applying it to another movement [4]. Other style research includes applying different styles to walking behaviors [15], or using style to express emotion, although through gesture instead of gaze, as described in [25], and [1]. The research in [1] employs a similar technique to ours, but focuses on a simple door-knocking movement, as opposed to our work, which focuses on the greater emotional expressivity possible through gaze.

Despite the numerous models of gaze in virtual agents, and the work done on transferring manner from one movement to another, there currently has been no exploration of how changes in emotional state affect changes in the manner of gazing behavior. This work is intended to begin this exploration.

3 Approach

Our approach to realizing a model of emotionally expressive head and body movement during gaze shifts is based on deriving a Gaze Warping Transformation (GWT), a combination of temporal scaling and spatial transformation parameters that describe the manner of an emotionally expressive gaze shift. This transformation, when applied to an emotionally neutral gaze shift (created procedurally or through motion capture); will modify that neutral gaze shift into one which displays the same emotion as the original shift. A small number of transformations would then be used to produce gazes displaying different emotional content that vary in the directionality of the gaze. It is currently unclear to what extent emotional expression can be transferred between different categories of gaze. For example, if an individual is interacting with another individual on a catwalk high above her, how is her gaze behavior different from that of two people speaking face to face? Due to this, the scope of this paper is the display of a few emotional dimensions through head and body movement during gaze attractions and gaze aversions in face-to-face interaction.

In order to find a GWT we first use psychological research into expressive gaze manner to generate a series of guidelines describing how emotional state affects gaze behavior. These guidelines are provided to actors, whose performances of the behaviors result in three sets of collected motion capture data. The first set consists of emotionally expressive gaze shifts and emotionally neutral gaze shifts directed at a single target. From this data, we derive the GWT. This transformation is then applied to the second set of motion capture data, which consists of emotionally neutral gaze shifts averting from that target, transferring expressive manner to the neutral gazes. Finally, animations are generated from these modified gaze shifts, and compared to a set of emotionally expressive gaze shifts collected for evaluation.

3.1 Emotion Model

The first step in this procedure is to construct a set of guidelines for how emotional state affects expressive gaze manner. In order to do this, a model of emotion is used as a framework for the gaze behavior. We are using the model of emotion described in [17], which is a dimensional model of emotion, one that views the set of emotions as a space described with a small number of dimensions.

This model of emotion is called the Pleasure-Arousal-Dominance, or PAD model, which are the three emotional dimensions comprising the model. The intuitive categories of emotion, such as anger, fear, or happiness, are represented in this model by subregions in the space defined by the emotional dimensions.

For example, anger is defined as negative pleasure, positive arousal, and positive dominance (see [9] for a categorization of the PAD model for use in a computational model of emotion).

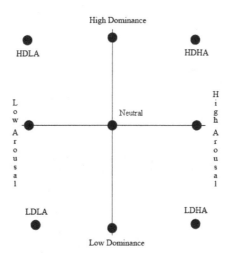

Fig. 1. Dimensional Model of Emotion

There are many alternative emotional models, such as models where emotions are viewed as discrete categories, or appraisal models, which use appraisal variables to define emotional states. We chose the PAD model because it is composed of a small number of dimensions, each of which have a background of research describing how gaze behaviors vary along the dimension [2], [7], [12]. This will allow us to develop a model of how expressive gaze behavior of a character varies based on the location of that character's emotional state in the PAD space.

We have so far used only the Arousal and Dominance dimensions of the model, dividing each dimension into discrete high and low values. This gives us nine distinct regions of the emotional space: Neutral Dominance and High Arousal (NDHA), Neutral Dominance and Low Arousal (NDLA), Neutral Arousal and High Dominance (NAHD), Neutral Arousal and Low Dominance (NALD), High Arousal and High Dominance (HAHD), High Arousal and Low Dominance (HALD), Low Arousal and High Dominance (LAHD), Low Arousal and Low Dominance (LALD), and the emotionally neutral origin, as shown in Fig. 1.

3.2 Data Description

The data for this work was collected by motion capture from gaze shifts performed by an actor who was provided with the set of performance guidelines shown in Table 1. For the basis of these guidelines, we use the findings that coders will rate an individual with upright head and posture as more dominant than one slouching forwards [5], [18], as well as results showing that velocity is clearly identified with arousal (for example in gesture [19]). Our interest is in arousal and dominance as signals, and thus the focus here is on those physical properties that are reliably decoded by observers, as opposed to how dominance and arousal are actually encoded in behavior, which is a more complex relationship [7].

Table 1. Predicted Physical Behaviors

Emotional Dimension	Behavior Guidelines
High Dominance (NAHD)	Upright Posture Head Turns Upwards Face Is Towards Other Individual
Low Dominance (NALD)	Hunched Forward Posture Head Turns Downwards Face Is Turned Away from Other Individual
High Arousal (NDHA)	Faster Movement Increased Blink Rate Body Moves Forward Slightly
Low Arousal (NDLA)	Slower Movement Decreased Blink Rate Body Moves Backward Slightly

Using these guidelines, the three sets of motion capture data are collected. For the first set, an actor is provided with the guidelines and demonstrates these behaviors while performing four to six gaze shifts from a target 90 degrees to the side of the actor to another target in front of the actor. The actor also performs this same gaze shift while displaying no emotion. The GWT is drawn primarily from this set.

The second set of motion capture data consists of emotionally neutral gaze shifts at different targets. For this, the actor also performs gaze shifts at three targets - one directly in front of the actor, one twenty degrees to the side of the actor, and one 45 degrees to the side - while demonstrating no predicted behaviors, and attempting to display no emotion. These are intended to simulate different levels of gaze aversion, where the character looks away from the user. These are the gaze shifts that will be converted into emotional gaze shifts using the GWT. This means that we will be emotionally transforming these aversion gaze shifts based on GWT's drawn from attraction gaze shifts, where the character looks at a user, in order to test the capability of the GWT's. Finally, the third set of data consists of the actor performing the combined behaviors for HAHD, HALD, LAHD, and LALD while shifting gaze from a target 90 degrees to the actor's side to a target to their front. This set provides additional data for determining the GWT, and will be compared to the converted emotional gaze shifts for evaluation purposes.

Recordings of the position of the head, body, and eyes are made throughout the gaze shifts. The data is collected as a set of time-series data points from three motion sensors: one on the head, one at the base of the neck, and one at the base of the spine. Each of the sensors records a time stamp, along with the position of the sensor in (x,y,z) coordinates, where the x axis runs laterally, with regard to the actor, the y axis runs from the actor's back to their front, and the z axis records vertical movement. This is followed by the orientation of the sensor as an Euler angle, resulting in eighteen total recorded degrees of freedom (DOF). Although the work reported here focuses on the head and body movements, the eyes were also recorded as an (x, y) coordinate representing the eye's angular position. Each DOF is represented as a separate two-dimensional curve (x_i, t_i), with the value of the sensor (x_i) plotted against the time of the reading (t_i). The head and body movement are captured with Ascension Flock of Birds electromagnetic sensors, while the eye movement is captured with an Applied Science Laboratories H-6 head-mounted eye tracker.

After capturing the data, it needs to be evaluated in order to avoid developing a model of gaze manner based on incorrect expectations. It is possible that our guidelines as to how emotional dimensions can be decoded from gaze behaviors are incorrect, or that the actor's performance is lacking, leading to an unclear emotional display, or a different emotion being displayed. For the evaluation, animations generated directly from first set of motion captures were displayed in pairs to eleven coders, who rated each animation individually on 5-point Likert scales of dominance and arousal. Each coder saw each animation three times.

We then performed two analyses of variance (ANOVAs), comparing the ratings of animations along the emotion scales. Ratings of NALD animations on the dominance scale ($M = 2.515$) were significantly different from ratings of NAHD animations ($M = 3.727$), and from ratings of animations neutral on the dominance scale ($M = 3.348$), $F(2, 131) = 12.1474$, $p < .01$, although NAHD animations were not significantly different dominance-neutral animations.

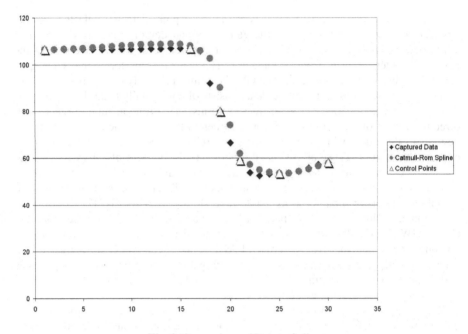

Fig. 2. Comparison of Data to Spline

Similarly, ratings of NDHA animations on the arousal scale (M = 3.909) were significantly different from ratings of NDLA animations (M = 2.727) and from animations neutral on the arousal scale (M = 2.803), $F(2, 131)$ = 12.2311, $p < .01$, though NDLA and arousal-neutral animations did not significantly differ.

Because coders differentiated between low and high values for both dominance and arousal, and the neutral animations for each scale fell between low and high, we drew our GWTs from these animations. Had the coders been unable to distinguish either scale, we would have revised our behavior guidelines, and collected new data.

3.3 Gaze Warping Transformation

After evaluating the motion capture data, the GWT was derived from the first and third motion capture sets, which consisted of four to six motion captures of the actor looking from a target 90 degrees to their left to a target directly in front of them, for each point in the emotional space (Fig. 1), including an emotionally neutral gaze. The GWT is found through the following process:

1. The representation of animation curves in each gaze shift is changed to a spline, effectively down-sampling the curve to a set of control points
2. The point-to-point transformations between down-sampled emotionally expressive and emotionally neutral gaze shifts are found.
3. The transformations that significantly differ along emotional dimensions are found.
4. The GWT for an emotional category is assembled from the point-to-point transformations for an entire DOF where a plurality of the transformations for that DOF significantly differ along the emotional dimensions comprising that category.

First, we represent our data with cubic interpolating splines: parametric cubic functions defined using a set of control points. We do this because the spline functions as smoothing, cleaning up noise and outliers. It also effectively down-samples the data, giving us a sparser representation for determining the GWT, while keeping some of the time variability of the data. Finally, it allows the GWTs to be easily applied to new gaze shifts.

While splines are commonly used in animation, these splines are often multilevel B-splines. We use Catmull-Rom splines [8], which are mathematically simpler, but serve our purpose as they are interpolating splines that pass through all of their control points. If there are not enough control points, the spline will not closely fit the collected data, but if there are many, then the data is not adequately down-sampled. Fig. 3 shows a comparison of a data curve to a Catmull-Rom curve with six control points. While six points has shown adequate performance so far, modeling more complex gaze behavior may require either increasing the number of control points, or segmenting the complex behavior into simpler gaze shifts.

In order to determine the proper location for the control points, we first find the locations of the control points on the animation curve representing the direction in which head rotation is the largest, as the head performs the easiest to distinguish and largest amplitude movements during many gaze shifts. Since these are single gaze shifts, the curve representing the angle the heard turns through resembles an S-curve.

The control points are placed to minimize least squared error while meeting a number of constraints, so that of the six control points, one point represents the start, one the end, two points bracket the first curve, and two points bracket the second. Then, we place control points in all of the other animation curves in the gaze shift at the same temporal location as these six.

Fig. 3. Animated Model showing High (left) and Low (right) Dominance

As the GWT is a set of point-to-point transformations, the control points on each individual gaze shift need to align, and increasing the accuracy of alignment will result in increased accuracy in the transformation. Currently, the constrained least squares minimization method only produces an approximate alignment.

The next step is to find, for each emotionally expressive gaze shift, the motion warping [24] functions that transform the control points for that shift into the control points for an emotionally neutral gaze shift following the same path. A motion warping function provides a pointwise transformation from one animation curve $x(t)$ that consists of a set of (x_i, t_i) pairs to a new motion $x'(t')$. The first function is $t = g(t')$, where given an actual frame time t', g describes where in the unwarped motion curve to obtain x. We use $g(t')=ct$, where c is a time scaling parameter. The other function is $x'(t) = a(t)x(t) + b(t)$, where $a(t)$ is a scaling function, and $b(t)$ is an offset function. However, $a(t)$ and $b(t)$ are not uniquely determined for a single x'. In [24], the user selected one of the two values to use, and one to hold constant. We currently use the offset function $b(t)$, and hold $a(t)$ constant, but either would work.

So, to convert the six control points for a DOF in an emotionally expressive gaze shift into the six points for that DOF in an emotionally neutral shift, we find, for each pair of points, the spatial offset parameter $b(t)$, and the time scaling parameter c that would transform between them. By doing this for each DOF in the gaze shift, we end up with nineteen sets - one set for each DOF, and one set for the time scaling parameter - of six motion warping parameters - one for each control point - for each gaze shift.

The next step is to find which of the motion warping parameters are significant for which emotional dimensions. While all of the motion warping parameters could be included, we would prefer sparse GWTs, as this makes them easier to combine. To do this we perform a series of ANOVAs across multiple animations that compare the motion warping parameters for the different emotional states to each other. This tells us which of the motion warping parameters are significantly different across different states along an emotional axis. We compared twelve low arousal motion warping parameter sets to twelve high arousal parameter sets ($n = 24$), and twelve low dominance sets to fourteen high dominance sets ($n = 26$), running one ANOVA for each DOF and control point combination. A subset of the results of these ANOVAs can be seen in Table 2, which shows some significant relationships between motion DOF's, and emotional dimensions.

Each row in the table shows the emotional dimensions that had a difference significant to $p < 0.05$ between its low and high values for that degree of freedom. Additionally, the behavior guidelines described in Table 1 can be seen in the subset of parameters in Table 2. For example, the guidelines called for changes in speed and forwards/backwards position of the body to show arousal, which is what we found. In addition, dominance was significantly related to head pitch and body vertical position. The warping parameters thus provide specific values for the abstract, general guidelines expressed in Table 1.

The GWT was assembled from the motion warping parameters for each DOF that had a plurality of control points significant to that dimension. Entire DOF's were used to increase the smoothness of movement.

Table 2. Some Significant Emotional and Movement Relationships

Movement Dimension	Emotional Dimension	Observed Change
Speed	Arousal	Low Arousal Animations are 80% slower than High Arousal Animations
Head Rotation - Pitch	Dominance	Low Dominance Head Pitch is 25 degrees lower than High Dominance
Body Movement - Front/Back	Arousal	The body moves forwards 1.5 inches more in High Arousal than Low Arousal Animations
Body Movement - Vertical	Dominance	The body moves down 1 inch more in Low Dominance than High Dominance Animations

The final GWTs were then used to warp neutral gaze shifts into emotionally expressive gaze shifts. We note that using individual motion warping transformations in this way assumes independence between the transformations, which is currently an untested assumption

3.4 Producing Emotionally Expressive Animations

After obtaining the GWT for emotionally expressive head and body manner during gaze shifts, new movements can be generated. Because the GWT is a set of motion warping parameters, an emotionally neutral gaze shift is down-sampled to six control points, and then the parameters are used to warp the neutral gaze shift control points. Finally, interpolation generates an emotionally expressive gaze shift. In addition, GWTs describing different emotional dimensions can be combined. Currently, there is no overlap in the arousal and dominance parameters, simplifying combination. In the future, better methods for combining parameters will be needed.

For evaluation we generated animations of HDHA, HDLA, LDHA, and LDLA by warping three gazes: one straight ahead of the actor, one 20° to the actor's left, and one 45° to the actor's left. This results in manner parameters taken from attraction gazes, looking at a target directly ahead of the actor, placed onto aversion gazes looking away from this target. We also used combinations of gaze warping transformations, instead of individual transformations; for example, combining the GWTs from NAHD and NDHA instead of using the collected HDHA gazes. The purpose of this was to provide a broader evaluation of the performance of GWTs. The result of applying the gaze warping parameter to the Head Rotation – Pitch DOF can be seen in Figure 4, and the resulting change in generated gaze can be seen in Figure 3.

After applying the transformations, constraints are applied to ensure that the motion warping does not cause physically impossible motions. This is needed because motion warping is a geometric, not a physically-based, technique. We are currently using ad-hoc constraints drawn from motion capture where an actor performed motions to explore the limits of their movement. Finally, the new emotionally expressive gaze shifts are animated on a very simple model in Maya (Figure 3). The model is intended to ablate nonverbal signals that are not being examined in the course of this research, such as facial expression or hand gesture.

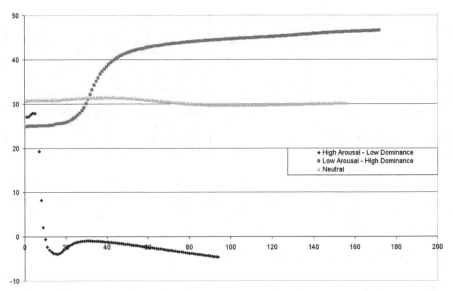

Fig. 4. Head Rotation –Pitch Showing Transformation from Neutral to HALD and LAHD

4 Evaluation

We then evaluated the animations to determine if the emotional signals in the generated animations for HDHA, HDLA, LDHA, and LDLA were coming through as strongly as the emotional signals in motion-captured animations of the same emotional states. To do this, we provided the videos and a questionnaire to 21 coders. Ten coders saw the set of twelve generated animations, while eleven coders saw the set of four motion-captured animations. Animations were displayed to coders in pairs, differing along a single emotional dimension, e.g. HDHA vs. HDLA. The set of animations is arranged according to a Latin Square. The coders chose the animation that showed higher arousal, and the animation that showed a more dominant character. Then, they rated the arousal and dominance of each animation individually on five-point Likert scales. Each coder saw each animation twice, but rated it only once on dominance, and once on arousal.

The result of this evaluation showed that coders significantly distinguished between low and high arousal; and between low and high dominance for both the generated and motion captured animations, as shown by a Chi squared test. The ability to distinguish arousal was similar for both the generated and captured animations (see Table 3). When asked to select the more highly aroused animation, the coders selected the generated animation intended to display high arousal 85% of the time, while the percentage was 86% for the captured animations.

Table 3. Evaluation Results - Arousal

Arousal		
Statistic	Generated Animations	Captured Animations
Number of Comparisons	60	22
Comparison Recognition	85%	86%
Comparison p	<.01	<.01
Number of Ratings	120	44
Low Arousal Mean Rating	3.000	2.80
High Arousal Mean Rating	3.817	3.70
F	9.045	15.2821
ANOVA p	<.05	<.01

The results for dominance can be seen in Table 4. Unlike arousal, the recognition for dominance, while still significant, was lower for the generated animations (66%) than for the captured animations (90%).

A within-subject Multivariate ANOVA showed that ratings on the Likert scales were also significantly ($p < .05$) different for low and high arousal animations. However, the Likert scale ratings were not significantly different, for low and high dominance in the animations generated with the GWT, although they were for the motion-captured animations. The interaction effects were also not significant.

The evaluation results show that we have transferred the manner of emotionally expressive gaze shifts to different emotionally neutral gaze shifts in such a way that the signal can still be recognized. It also reveals that there is room for improvement, specifically with regards to the signaling of dominance. The dominance animations that obtained the lowest recognition were those where the movement was quick and the animation did not end facing straight ahead. During debrief, coders explained that the character appeared to be looking at objects instead of expressing emotion.

One cause of this is the lack of a model of eye movement. We are currently working on a model of expressive eye movement, drawing from the same motion capture data, to merge with this model of head and body movement during gaze shifts. Another likely cause is the transfer of manner from the captured attraction gaze to the generated aversive gaze which was performed to test the ability of GWTs to generalize between different types of gaze. This transformation of a gaze, based on the emotional content of a very different type of gaze, could cause the decrease in recognition.

Table 4. Evaluation Results - Dominance

Dominance		
Statistic	Generated Animations	Captured Animations
Number of Comparisons	60	22
Comparison Recognition	66%	90%
Comparison p	<.01	<.01
Number of Ratings	120	44
Low Dominance Mean Rating	3.000	2.55
High Dominance Mean Rating	3.333	3.70
F	2.250	30.9729
ANOVA p	.168	<.01

5 Conclusion

There has been little prior work on using the expressive gaze manner of characters to display their emotional state. In this work we have described the Gaze Warping Transformation, a method for combining and transferring expressive gaze manner from emotional gazes to neutral gazes, and performed an evaluation showing that the encoded emotional dimensions can be recognized. There are improvements that need to be made, the most pressing of which is the integration of a model of expressive eye movement. In addition, the pleasure dimension of the PAD model needs to be integrated, and the relationship between expressive behavior and PAD space needs to be explored. Finally, implementation details such as improving point-to-point alignment and determining to what extent to down-sample animation curves must be addressed. Yet, the performed evaluation demonstrates the utility of our model, and we will continue to build upon it.

Acknowledgements

We would like to thank Mei Si and Sinhwa Kang for sharing their knowledge of statistical analysis, Tiffany Cole for her acting knowledge, and Dr. Bosco Tjan and Dr. Skip Rizzo for the use of their data recording hardware.

This work was sponsored by the U.S. Army Research, Development, and Engineering Command (RDECOM), and the content does not necessarily reflect the position or the policy of the Government, and no official endorsement should be inferred.

References

[1] Amaya, K., Bruderlin, A., Calvert, T.: Emotion From Motion. In: Proceedings of the 1996 Conference on Graphical Interface, pp. 222–229 (1996)

[2] Argyle, M., Cook, M.: Gaze and Mutual Gaze. Cambridge University Press, Cambridge (1976)

[3] Bickmore, T., Cassell, J.: Social Dialogue with Embodied Conversational Agents. In: Bernsen, N. (ed.) Natural, Intelligent and Effective Interaction with Multimodal Dialogue Systems, pp. 23–54. Kluwer Academic Publishers, Dordrecht (2004)

[4] Brand, M., Hertzmann, A.: Style Machines. In: Proceedings of SIGGRAPH, ACM Press, New York (2000)

[5] Carney, D.: Beliefs About the Nonverbal Expression of Social Power. Journal of Nonverbal Behavior. 29(2), 105–123 (2005)

[6] Coulson, M.: Attributing Emotion to Static Body Postures: Recognition Accuracy, Confusions, and Viewpoint Dependence. Journal of Nonverbal Behavior 28(2) (2004)

[7] Exline, R.: Visual Interaction: The Glances of Power and Preference. In: Weitz, S. (ed.) Nonverbal Communication: Readings with Commentary, Oxford University Press, Oxford (1974)

[8] Foley, J., van Dam, A., Feiner, S., Hughes, J.: Computer Graphics: Principles and Practice, 2nd edn. Addison-Wesley Publishing Company, Redwood City, CA, USA (1997)

[9] Gebhard, P.: ALMA: A Layered Model of Affect. In: Proceedings of AAMAS, ACM Press, New York (2005)

[10] Kendon, A.: Some Functions of Gaze Direction in Two-Person Conversation. In: Kendon, A. (ed.) Conducting Interaction: Patterns of Behavior in Focused Encounters (1990)

[11] Kim, Y., Hill. Jr., R., Traun, D.: A Computational Model of Dynamic Perceptual Attention for Virtual Humans. Proceedings of the 14th Conference on Behavior Representation in Modeling and Simulation. May (2005)

[12] Kleinke, C.: Gaze and Eye Contact: A Research Review. Psychological Bulletin. v. 100(1), 78–100 (1986)

[13] Lance, B., Marsella, S., Koizumi, D.: Towards Expressive Gaze Manner in Embodied Virtual Agents (2004)

[14] Lee, S., Badler, J., Badler, N.: Eyes Alive. ACM Transactions on Graphics 21(3), 637–644 (2002)

[15] Liu, C.K., Hertzmann, A., Popović, Z.: Learning Physics-Based Motion Style with Nonlinear Inverse Optimization. In: Proceedings of SIGGRAPH, ACM Press, New York (2005)

[16] Marsella, S., Gratch, J., Rickel, J.: Expressive Behaviors for Virtual Worlds. In: Prendinger, H., Ishizuka, M. (eds.) Life-Like Characters. Tools, Affective Functions, and Applications, Springer, Heidelberg (2003)

[17] Mehrabian, A.: Silent Messages: Implicit Communication of Emotions and Attitudes, 2nd edn. Wadsworth Publishing Company (1981)

[18] Mignault, A., Chaudhuri, A.: The Many Faces of a Neutral Face: Head Tilt and Perception of Dominance and Emotion. Journal of Nonverbal Behavior 27(2) (Summer 2003)

[19] Paterson, H., Pollick, F., Sanford, A.: The Role of Velocity in Affect Discrimination. In: Proceedings of the 23rd Annual Conference of the Cognitive Science Society (2001)

[20] Pelachaud, C., Bilvi, M.: Modelling Gaze Behavior for Conversational Agents. In: Rist, T., Aylett, R., Ballin, D., Rickel, J. (eds.) IVA 2003. LNCS (LNAI), vol. 2792, pp. 93–100. Springer, Heidelberg (2003)

[21] Rickel, J., Johnson, W.L: Animated Agents for Procedural Training in Virtual Reality: Perception, Cognition, and Motor Control. Applied Artificial Intelligence 13(4-5), 343–382 (1999)

[22] Sobczynski, P.: Polar Express, The (November 2004), http://www.efilmcritic.com/review.php?movie=10918&reviewer=389

[23] Thomas, F., Johnston, O.: The Illusion of Life: Disney Animation. Walt Disney Productions (1981)

[24] Witkin, A., Popovic, Z.: Motion Warping. In: Proceedings of SIGGRAPH, ACM Press, New York (1995)

[25] Zhao, L., Badler, N.: Acquiring and Validating Motion Qualities from Live Limb Gestures. Graphical Models 67(1), 1–16 (2005)

Fuzzy Similarity of Facial Expressions of Embodied Agents

Radosław Niewiadomski and Catherine Pelachaud

IUT de Monreuil, Université Paris 8, France
{niewiadomski,pelachaud}@iut.univ-paris8.fr

Abstract. In this paper we propose an algorithm based on fuzzy similarity which models the concept of resemblance between facial expressions of an Embodied Conversational Agent (ECA). The algorithm measures the degree of visual resemblance between any two facial expressions. We also present an evaluation study in which we compared the users' perception of similarity of facial expressions. Finally we describe an application of this algorithm to generate complex facial expressions of an ECA.

Keywords: Embodied Conversational Agents, facial expressions, fuzzy similarity.

1 Introduction

The mystery of the human face inspired artists and psychologists for centuries. Recently it has become also an object of interest of computer scientists. Embodied conversational agents (ECAs) – programs that focus on multimodal communication between humans and machines – display facial expressions to communicate. In this paper we focus on modelling the concept of similarity between any two facial expressions of emotion of an ECA. Despite facial expressions are complex objects it is quite natural and easy for human beings to decide if any two facial expressions are similar or not. Our aim is to build an algorithm that simulates this human's skill.

Establishing the degree of similarity between facial expressions can be very useful for an ECA designer. Often the knowledge about facial expressions is restricted only to some particular cases. Despite the evidence that many facial expressions exist [13,15,19] most of researchers (e.g. [3,10,11]) limit their research only to six of them, namely: anger, disgust, fear, joy, sadness, and surprise. Other facial expressions were rarely studied, and as consequence they are difficult to model. We used the algorithm presented in this paper to model different types of facial expressions like fake or inhibited expressions for the expressions like embarrassment, disappointment or contempt (see section 5).

Generally, similarity is very difficult to measure. It is a quantity that reflects the strength of relationship between two objects. The similarity between two objects is measured by comparing their attributes. Two cars are similar if both have the same number of doors, are about 4 meters long, and both are red.

C. Pelachaud et al. (Eds.): IVA 2007, LNAI 4722, pp. 86–98, 2007.

Traditionally the similarity between, two objects is expressed through a *distance function*. In this geometrical tradition two objects are similar if the distance between them is small [25]. On the other hand, *fuzzy similarity* [5] is used to work with objects characterised by loose description. Each object or feature that does not have a precise definition can be described by a fuzzy set. Fuzzy similarity allows for the comparison of any two fuzzy sets. It takes into consideration the various features of objects that characterise them at least partly. Various measures have been proposed to compare any two fuzzy sets [5].

For the purpose of comparing computer generated facial expressions we decided to use fuzzy similarity. It allows us to define attributes of an object by fuzzy sets instead of using precise values. On the other hand, according to many researchers (e.g. [10,16]) each "distinct and labelled expression of emotion" like "expression of anger" or "expression of contempt" is rather a "class" or a "set" of different but similar configurations of facial muscles actions (or a set of different *facial displays*). Indeed, there is not one precise smile or a frown. Each smile is a little bit different but "all smiles" have some characteristics in common. The boundary between smiling and not smiling is also imprecise. Different facial displays of different intensities are classified as smiles. Indeed, in many experiments (e.g. [2,11]) different facial displays involving the same group of muscle contractions were described by subjects with the same label, so an expression of an emotion e.g. "expression of anger" is not a precise concept. It has an imprecise "fuzzy" definition (see also [26]). On the other hand, all facial displays that belong to one category like "happiness", "anger", or "embarrassment" have some common features. Therefore, any category can be defined by a set of fuzzy sets that corresponds to these features.

Our approach follows the results from the psychological theory and experiments. It is based on the *discrete-emotion approach* represented among others by Paul Ekman [7,10]. According to this theory there is only a discrete number of expressions that can be universally recognized by humans. Ekman focuses his research on the six facial expressions mentioned above. We decided not to restrict ourselves to this small set. Thus our algorithm of similarity should work properly with any facial expression as, for example, those described in [13,18,19].

Thus we aim at building an algorithm that:

- is coherent with the discrete-emotion approach and with the results of the experiments about the perception of facial expressions,
- works for any facial expression,
- preserves the fuzziness of the concept of facial expression,
- preserves the different degrees of similarity between facial expressions.

The remaining part of this paper is structured as follows. In next section we present some theoretical aspects of comparing facial expressions. In section 3 we present our algorithm and in section 4 the evaluation study. The section 5 is entirely dedicated to the applications of our algorithm. Finally conclusion and future work are presented is section 6.

2   Fuzzy Similarity

Fuzzy similarity offers a set of methods to compare two objects. As opposed to distance-based similarity, each feature of an object is represented by a fuzzy set. Two fuzzy sets can be compared using *M-measure of comparison* [5]. It expresses the strength of the relationship between the features of two objects. There are different types of the M-measures of comparison. For our application we chose the M-measure of resemblance [5]. It is used for comparing objects of the same level of generality. Using this M-measure it is possible to check whether two objects "have many characteristics in common" [5]. It is often used in case-based reasoning systems. Each M-measure of resemblance S has also two other properties:

- reflexivity: $S(A, A) = 1$,
- symmetry: $S(A, B) = S(B, A)$.

These properties characterise also the process of comparing facial expressions. First of all, comparing facial expressions means to compare objects of the same level of generality. Following Ekman's theory [10] all expressions are equi-important and distinct. Moreover, in [20] it was found that the perception of similarity between unlabelled facial expressions is symmetrical, i.e. expression A is similar to expression B to the same degree as B is similar to A [20].

In [5] different M-measures of resemblance are proposed. For our application we chose the measure of resemblance S defined by:

$$S(A, B) = \frac{(M(A \cap B))}{(M(A \cup B))} \tag{1}$$

where A and B are two fuzzy sets (μ_A is membership function of A) and M is the fuzzy measure on Ω:

$$M(A) = \int_\Omega \mu_A(x)dx \tag{2}$$

This choice was made mainly because of practical consequences. This concrete measure is easy to implement and the process of computation is relatively simple. As a result we obtain the value of comparison $x_i \in [0,1]$ for each pair of attributes. Following the approach proposed in [23] we use *Ordered Weighted Averaging* (OWA) operator to aggregate all values $x_1,...,x_n$. The OWA, $h_W : [0,1]^n \to [0,1]$, is defined as:

$$h_W = \sum_{i=1}^{n} w_i b_i \tag{3}$$

where b_i be i-th biggest value between $x_1,...,x_n$ and $W = \{w_1,....,w_n\}$ is a set of weights with $w_i \in [0,1]$ and such that $\sum_{i=1}^{n} w_i = 1$ [23]. Finally, we use trapezoid fuzzy sets in order to describe the features of facial expressions as shown in Figure 1. This shape renders the experimental results about perception of facial expressions [2,27]. On the other hand, it is characterised by computational facility.

3   Similarity of Facial Expressions in an Embodied Conversational Agent

In order to implement and test our algorithm we used an existing ECA architecture called Greta [4]. Facial expressions of Greta are described in terms of facial animation parameters (FAPs) [21]. Originally Greta did not offer fuzzy definitions of facial expressions. The static expressions used by Greta needed to be fuzzified. For each FAP of each expression we have defined the fuzzy set of plausible values. First, we have established for each facial feature (i.e. single FAP) the amplitude of values that preserves the reliability and plausibility of a particular movement. It means that for any feature we have established the minimum x_1 and the maximum x_2 plausible values for any expression. Beyond this range the movement is perceived as unnatural. Each fuzzy set FAP_k of a particular facial expression depends on this amplitude of plausible values. We have established that membership is a symmetrical trapezoid with the centre in the point v, where v is a value of the original expression (see Figure 1). The dimensions of the trapezoid depend on the absolute value of the difference: $|x_2 - x_1|$. Using fuzzy definitions of facial expressions we count the value of sim-

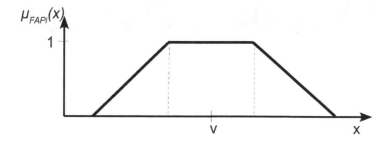

Fig. 1. A fuzzy set of FAP_i

ilarity between them. For that purpose we use the procedure described in the previous section. Let $FS(Exp(E_i),Exp(E_j))$ be the value of similarity between two expressions $Exp(E_i)$ and $Exp(E_j)$. For each FAP_k of $Exp(E_i)$ and $Exp(E_j)$ we have:

$$fs_k = \frac{M(FAP_k(E_i) \cap FAP_k(E_j))}{M(FAP_k(E_i) \cup FAP_k(E_j))} \qquad (4)$$

where $k = 1,...,n$. Then:

$$FS(Exp(E_i), Exp(E_j)) = h_w(fs_1, ..., fs_n) \qquad (5)$$

where h_w is OWA operator with the weights $w_k = \frac{1}{n}$ (see section 2).

Recapitulating, our algorithm works as follow: let E_u and E_w be two emotions whose expressions we want to compare. Thus we want to establish fuzzy similarity between two static expressions: $Exp(E_w)$ and $Exp(E_u)$. Each $Exp(E_i)$ is associated with a number of fuzzy sets such that all plausible *facial displays*

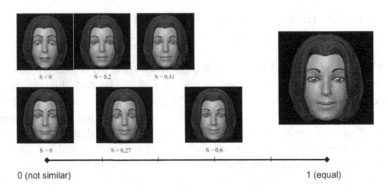

Fig. 2. Fuzzy similarity of facial expressions of Greta agent

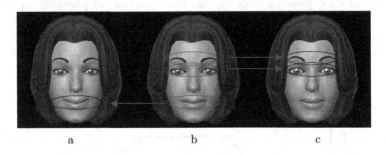

Fig. 3. The example of comparing facial expressions

(in the sense of muscle contractions) for the emotion E_i are defined. That is, for each parameter k of an expression of E_i there is a fuzzy set FAP_k that specifies its range of plausible values. Then the value of fuzzy similarity for each parameter of $Exp(E_w)$ and $Exp(E_u)$ is established. The M-measure of resemblance S is used to find these similarity values. Finally, in the third step, all values are combined by means of the aggregation operator h_w (3).

Let us compare the three facial expressions shown in Figure 3. The values of similarity between them are: S(A,B) = 0.6 and S(B,C) = 0.4. That is, the expression A is more similar to B than C is to B. In Figure 3a, the lips are extended with greater intensity than in Figure 3b. When comparing Figure 3b and Figure 3c, the eye aperture in Figure 3b is more closed than in Figure 3c. Moreover, in these two images, the eyebrows have different shapes. This explains why the similarity between B and C is less than between A and B. The areas of the facial expressions that vary among the three images are marked by a circle.

4   Evaluation

We have conducted an evaluation study to check if our algorithm models adequately the concept of the resemblance of static computer generated facial expressions. We are unaware of any similar experiment made on computer generated expressions of emotions. Previous evaluation studies of embodied agents ([2,6,17]) mainly analysed the perception of emotions from the computer generated facial expressions. Instead we focus on the process of comparison of any two facial expressions (i.e. the perception of the common features and the differences between them). We avoid considering the problem of interpretation of these facial expressions.

Our main aim is to verify if the values of the similarity established by our algorithm are consistent with human perception of the resemblance between facial expressions. Our hypothesis was that values of fuzzy similarity are proportional to those found by human's perception. In particular, we expected to find that our algorithm and human perception are concordant not only in evaluating if any two expressions are similar to each other or not, but also that different degrees of resemblance perceived are adequately modelled in our algorithm.

4.1 Objects of Comparison

Our objects of comparison are images the emotional facial expressions of the Greta agent. Each image depicting facial expressions follows the same setting:

- each image presents one facial expression of Greta,
- only the face is visible in the image,
- the face is directed at the observer,
- a black background was used.

Each image was saved in jpeg format. An example of the image is presented in Figure 4. In the experiment we used 22 different facial expressions. Each expression is defined by a different combination of FAP parameters and by their values. The expressions are created according to the descriptions presented in the literature. Among others, we used all six facial expressions proposed by Ekman as *universally recognized expressions* of emotions [7,10]. We used other distinct facial expressions (e.g. [18]), as well as some variations of one expression like "low-intensity-joy" and "high-intensity-joy". The neutral expression is also included (see [11]).

Fig. 4. An example of facial expression used in the evaluation study

4.2   Procedure

In our evaluation study we asked participants to rate the degree of similarity between different facial expressions. For this purpose we ascribed the images, prepared according the procedure presented in the previous section, to ten sets. Each set s_l, $l = 1,...,10$, is composed of one *reference expression* and six facial expressions that have to be *compared* with the reference one. It means that each experiment session consists of 60 operations of comparison (i.e. ten sets of six comparison pairs each). To have access to a greater number of participants, we set up our experiment on the web.

One experiment session consists in passing through 10 different web pages. Each of them presents one set of images s_l (i.e. seven facial expressions). The reference image is signalled by a yellow border and it is placed in the first row. The next two rows contain expressions to be compared with the reference one. After deciding the similarity degrees for all six pairs, subjects can pass to another set. They cannot come back to the preceding sets (i.e. s_1 - s_{l-1}) and they cannot jump to the next set s_{l+1} without providing answers to the current one.

The single images as well as sets of images s_l were displayed in a random order. Images were not labelled. The participation in the experiment was anonymous. For each pair of images (i.e. reference object, compared object) subjects had to choose the degree of similarity by using a set of predefined expressions defined in natural language (five-point Likert scale, ranging from "not similar" to "equal"). In the experiment we decided to avoid the use of numerical description of the level of similarity as it is not used by people to refer to similarity.

Sixty persons participated in the experiment, but only 46 of them went through all ten sets of images. We focused only on complete responses. Twenty three participants from the 46 classified were women, the other 18 - men. The remaining 5 persons did not specify their gender.

4.3   Results

The total number of answers was 2760. First of all, we found that different labels were used by subjects with different frequency. The first label: "1 - Not at all" that corresponds to the lowest degree of similarity occurred in nearly half of all answers (46%). Other labels occurred from 10% to 16% of all responses.

In order to interpret the subjects' answers we compared them with the values returned by our algorithm. For this purpose we changed the responses given by the subjects into numeric values. Then, we compared them with the values of fuzzy similarity. We translated a discrete set of answers given by participants to one value in the interval [0,1]. We assumed that labels are evenly placed along this interval and for each degree of similarity we associated a weight. More formally, for the purpose of measuring the answers of participants we introduced the *average similarity index*. Let *(A, B)* be a pair of expressions in which A is the reference and B is the compared object. Then u_i is the number of answers using a given label, i.e. u_1 corresponds to the label "1 – Not at all" and u_5 to the "5 – Equal". The average similarity index, y_{AB}, is:

$$y_{AB} = \frac{\sum\limits_{i}^{5}(w_i u_i) - w_1 \sum\limits_{i}^{5} u_i}{(w_5 - w_1) \sum\limits_{i} u_i} \qquad (6)$$

where $w_i = i$ is the weight that corresponds to u_i. Let us notice that the values of y_{AB} and the values of fuzzy similarity FS (see section 3) are in the interval [0,1]. Let the vector $[a_i]$ contains the values of our fuzzy similarity FS such that: $a_i = FS(A_i, B_i)$ and let the vector $[b_i]$ be such that: $b_i = y_{A_i B_i}$. First of all, we measured the correlation between $[a_i]$ and $[b_i]$. The overall value of correlation (r) is 0.89. The *average similarity index*, y_{AB} (i.e. subjects' answers) is more or less proportional to the fuzzy similarity values (see Figure 5). The higher the index value is, the higher the fuzzy similarity value is as well. On the other hand, certain pairs were evaluated significantly higher by the participants than by the fuzzy similarity. For this reason we measured also the discrepancy between values b_i and a_i. The mean difference between b_i and a_i:

$$\frac{\sum\limits_{i}^{n}(b_i - a_i)}{n} \qquad (7)$$

is 0.09. At the same time the standard deviation of the difference $[a_i]$ and $[b_i]$ is 0.15. Finally, the average value of y_{AB} is 0.35.

4.4 Discussion

The aim of our experiment was to verify if the degrees of the similarity of computer generated facial expressions established by our algorithm are consistent with human perception of this phenomenon. Firstly, we compared the weighted average of the subjects' answers with the values of our algorithm. We found that the human's answers and our algorithm results are positively correlated and that the correlation coefficient is high (0.89). Also other results show that the human perception of the resemblance of facial expressions is modelled correctly by our algorithm. The average similarity index for 80% of the considered pairs is different from the perfect value (represented by the main diagonal) by 0.2 at most. Moreover, the mean difference between subjects' responses and our algorithm results is relatively small (i.e. 0.09). It is less than half of the distance between any two neighbouring degrees of similarity on the scale used by subjects in this experiment. Thus, we can say that the values of fuzzy similarity tend to be proportional to the subjects' answers. The coarse-grained scale of similarity used in this experiment probably influenced this result negatively. Subjects had to choose from a discrete set of labels, as a consequence their answers can only approximate the values of FS. The result is also influenced by the choice of the method of ranking the subjects' answers (i.e. y_{AB}). In particular, we assumed arbitrally that the distance between any two degrees of similarity was constant.

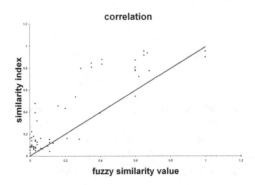

Fig. 5. Correlation between the fuzzy similarity and the average similarity index

On the other hand, the mean difference between subjects' responses and our algorithm results is positive. It means that the algorithm has a tendency to evaluate certain pairs of expressions as less similar in comparison with the subjects' choices. Indeed, we noticed certain pairs that have the fuzzy similarity value in the interval [0.3,0.5] were evaluated as relatively more similar than our algorithm indicates. Indeed, as shown in Figure 5 more points in this interval are situated above the diagonal than under it.

5   Application

In the previous section we have presented an innovative algorithm, which allowed us to compare any two facial expressions of an embodied agent. In this section we present an example of its application. We use it to generate different types of facial expressions (e.g. expressions of masking or fake expressions). Previous models [1,26] of facial expressions deal with the display of emotional states. They are based on the assumption that emotions which are similar (for instance in terms of valence or arousal values) have also similar expressions. On the contrary, we propose that the visual resemblance between two facial expressions is the measure that can be used in order to generate a new expression. We used our fuzzy similarity based algorithm in order to generate different types of facial expressions.

There is a large amount of evidence in psychological research that human's repertoire of facial expressions is very large [9,15,22]. Facial expressions do not always correspond to felt emotions but they can be fake (showing an expression of an unfelt emotion), masked (masking a felt emotion by an unfelt emotion), superposed (showing a mixed of felt emotions), inhibited (masking the expression of emotion with the neutral expression), suppressed (de-intensifying the expression of an emotion), or exaggerated (intensifying the expression of an emotion) (see [20] for detailed discussion). We called *complex facial expressions* expressions that are combinations of several facial displays. It was shown that humans can distinguish the expression of felt emotion from the expression of fake emotion or from a masked one [9,12,14,22]. In fake expressions some elements of the original expression are missing [10], while certain elements of expression of the felt emotion can be still visible even if that expression is masked or inhibited [8]. We proposed [4] a model to generate complex facial expressions (e.g. fake expression of anger or expression of sadness masked by joy) on the basis of simple expressions (e.g. sadness, joy). This model of complex facial expressions is based on Ekman's results [7,10].

We model complex facial expressions using a face partitioning approach. The face is divided in eight facial areas F_i, i= 1,..,8 (i.e., F_1 - brows, F_2 - upper eyelids, F_3 - eyes, F_4 - lower eyelids, F_5 - cheeks, F_6 - nose, F_7 - lips movement, F_8 - lips tension, see Figure 6). Each facial expression is a composition of these facial areas, each of which can display signs of emotion. For complex facial expressions, different emotions (as in an expression masked another one) can be expressed on different areas of the face (in the example of sadness masked by anger, anger is shown on the eyebrows area while sadness is displayed on the mouth area). In our model complex facial expressions, involving one or more emotions, are composed of the facial areas of the input expressions using a set of rules. Our model can be used to generate different displays for the facial expressions of masking, as well as fake and inhibited expressions. These complex facial expressions involving the six emotions (anger, disgust, fear, joy, sadness, and surprise) are described in the literature [7,10]. For each type of expression we have defined a set of fuzzy rules that describes its characteristic features in terms of facial areas. To each emotion corresponds a rule. Thus we have defined six rules for each type of complex facial expression. In case an input expression for which the deceptive facial expression is not defined explicitly by our rules (e.g. expressions of contempt or disappointment) our fuzzy similarity based algorithm presented in the previous sections is used in order to establish the degree of similarity between the input expression and the expressions whose complex facial expressions are described by our rules. Once the most similar expression (chosen among the 6 ones) is known, we can apply the corresponding rules to our input expression. For example, when we want to compute the complex facial expression of contempt or of disappointment, we look to which expression of the six-elements set mentioned above it is the most similar to and we use the associated rule. Thus masked,

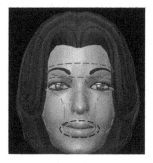

Fig. 6. The partition of the face

inhibited or fake facial expressions of two *similar* facial expressions are created using the same rules.

Figure 7b presents the agent displaying the expression of disappointment masked by a fake happiness. Our rules describe the expression of masked sadness but they do not define masked disappointment. We applied algorithm fuzzy similarity and found that disappointment has a facial expression very similar to sadness. According to Ekman [10,7] the features of felt sadness that leak over the masking expression are: forehead, brows, and upper eyelids. In our model these elements of expression are represented by the facial areas F_1(forehead and brows) and F_2 (upper eyelids). As a consequence, they can be observed in masked sadness. On the other hand, the expression of disappointment (Figure 7a) is very similar (according to the algorithm described in section 3) to the expression of sadness and so the rules of sadness will be applied also in the case of disappointment expression. Indeed in the expression of disappointment masked by fake joy (Figure 7b) we can notice the movement of brows, which is characteristic of disappointment. On the other hand the mouth area displays a smile (sign of happiness).

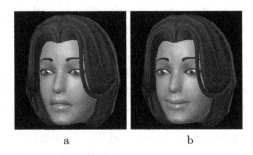

a   b

Fig. 7. Examples of expressions: a) disappointment and b) disappointment masked by a happiness

6   Conclusion

In this paper we have presented how fuzzy similarity can be used to compare facial expressions of an embodied agent. In our approach any facial expression is described by a set of fuzzy sets. Using our algorithm we are able to compare expressions i.e. the vague and imprecise objects described by certain labels. The main advantage of this approach is that slightly different facial displays can be described by one significant label. Then using fuzzy similarity we compare these imprecise definitions and establish the degrees of similarity between them. We are unaware of any other applications of the fuzzy similarity for the purpose of comparing facial expressions.

We have also conducted a test to measure the perception of similarity between facial expressions. We checked if the perception of similarity between computer generated facial expressions is consistent with the values that are obtained with our algorithm. The results of the test showed that the algorithm based on the fuzzy similarity meets our expectations. Finally we have also presented an application of our algorithm for generating facial expressions.

It is important to stress that in a more realistic model of similarity one should take into consideration also the probability of occurrence of certain values for a FAP. It means that even if a fuzzy set defines plausible values for a certain expression it does not mean that all these values occur with the same frequency. The similarity between two objects has to take into account the probability of occurrence of the values from the given interval (see [24]) to avoid for instance that two attributes "become similar" because of similar values but that occur very seldom. Unfortunately, we do not have the data of this type for facial expressions. In this situation we assumed that all values are equi-probable.

In the future, we aim to create fuzzy definitions of facial expressions based on empirical data. Consequently, the shapes of the fuzzy sets that describe the features of facial expression will be uniquely defined for each expression (see [26]). All parts of the face are considered as equi-important in our similarity algorithm at current stage of development. However, it is known that each face areas of the face can have a different role in the perception of emotion ([3,6]). We want to test if it is also the case for the perception of similarity.

Acknowledgement. We are very grateful to Giulianella Coletti and to Andrea Capotorti for their help on fuzzy methods. We also thank Elisabetta Bevacqua and Maurizio Mancini for implementing the Greta system. Part of this research is supported by the EU FP6 Network of Excellence HUMAINE (IST-2002-2.3.1.6) and by the EU FP6 Integrated Project Callas (FP6-2005-IST-5).

References

1. Albrecht, I., Schröder, M., Haber, J., Seidel, H.: Mixed feelings: expression of non-basic emotions in a muscle-based talking head. Virtual Reality 8(4), 201–212 (2005)
2. Bartneck, C., Reichenbach, J.: Subtle emotional expressions of synthetic characters, International. Journal Human-Computer Studies 62(2), 179–192 (2005)
3. Bassili, J.N.: Emotion recognition: the role of facial movement and the relative importance of upper and lower areas of the face. Journal of Personality and Social Psychology 37(11), 2049–2058 (1979)
4. Bevacqua, E., Mancini, M., Niewiadomski, R., Pelachaud, C.: An expressive ECA showing complex emotions. In: Proceedings of the AISB Annual Convention, Newcastle, UK, pp. 208–216 (2007)
5. Bouchon-Meunier, B., Rifqi, M., Bothorel, S.: Towards general measures of comparison of objects. Fuzzy sets and systems 84(2), 143–153 (1996)
6. Constantini, E., Pianesi, F., Prete, M.: Recognizing Emotions in Human and Synthetic Faces: The Role of the Upper and Lower Parts of the Face. In: Proceedings of the 10th International Conference on Intelligent User Interfaces, San Diego, California, USA, January 10-13, pp. 20–27 (2005)
7. Ekman, P.: The Face Revealed. Weidenfeld & Nicolson, London (2003)
8. Ekman, P.: Darwin, deception, and facial expression, Ann. N.Y. Acad. Sci. 1000, 205–221 (2003)

9. Ekman, P., Friesen, W.V.: The Repertoire of Nonverbal Behavior's. Categories, Origins, Usage and Coding, Semiotica 1, 49–98 (1969)
10. Ekman, P., Friesen, W.V.: Unmasking the Face. A guide to recognizing emotions from facial clues. Prentice-Hall, Inc, Englewood Cliffs, New Jersey (1975)
11. Etcoff, N., Magee, J.: Categorical perception of facial expressions. Cognition 44(3), 227–240 (1992)
12. Frank, M.G., Ekman, P., Friesen, W.V.: Behavioral Markers and Recognizability of the Smile of Enjoyment. In: Ekman, P., Rosenberg, E.L. (eds.) What the Face Reveals: Basic and Applied Studies of Spontaneous Expression Using the Facial Action Coding System (FACS), Oxford University Press, Oxford (1995)
13. Gonzaga, G.C., Keltner, D., Londahl, E.A., Smith, M.D.: Love and commitment problem in romantic relation and friendship. Journal of Personality and Social Psychology 81(2), 247–262 (2001)
14. Gosselin, P., Kirouac, G., Doré, F.Y.: Components and Recognition of Facial Expression in the Communication of Emotion by Actors. In: Ekman, P., Rosenberg, E.L. (eds.) What the Face Reveals: Basic and Applied Studies of Spontaneous Expression Using the Facial Action Coding System (FACS), pp. 243–267. Oxford University Press, Oxford (1995)
15. Haidt, J., Keltner, D.: Culture and facial expression: Open-ended methods find more expressions and a gradient of recognition. Cognition and Emotion 13(3), 225–266 (1999)
16. Izard, C.E.: Human emotion, Plenum Press, New York (1977)
17. Kätsyri, J., Klucharev, V., Frydrych, M., Sams, M.: Identification of synthetic and natural emotional facial expressions. In: ISCA Tutorial and Research Workshop on Audio Visual Speech Processing (AVSP'03), St. Jorioz, France, pp. 239–244 (2003)
18. Keltner, D.: Signs of appeasement: Evidence for the distinct displays of embarrassment, amusement, and shame. Journal of Personality and Social Psychology 68, 441–454 (1992)
19. Matsumoto, D.: More evidence for the universality of a contempt expression. Motivation and Emotion, 16(4), 363–368 (1992)
20. Niewiadomski, R.: A model of complex facial expressions in interpersonal relations for animated agents, Ph.D. thesis, University of Perugia (2007)
21. Ostermann, J.: Face Animation in MPEG-4. In: Pandzic, I.S., Forchheimer, R. (eds.) MPEG-4 Facial Animation - The Standard Implementation and Applications, pp. 17–55. Wiley, England (2002)
22. Poggi, I.: Interacting bodies and interacting minds. In: 2nd lInternational Society for Gesture Studies (ISGS) Conference Interacting Bodies, Lyon, pp. 15–18 (2005)
23. Rifqi, M.: Mesures de comparaison, typicalité et classification d'objets flous: théorie et pratique, Ph.D Thesis (1996)
24. Scozzafava, R., Vantaggi, B. (eds.): Fuzzy Relations in a Coherent Conditional Probability Setting, 7th International Conference on Information and Management Sciences (IMS), Chengdu, China, pp. 496–500 (2006)
25. Teknomo, K.: Similarity Measurement, http://people.revoledu.com/kardi/tutorial/Similarity/index.html
26. Tsapatsoulis, N., Raouzaiou, A., Kollias, S., Crowie, R., Douglas-Cowie, E.: Emotion Recognition and Synthesis Based on MPEG-4 FAPs. In: Pandzic, I., Forchheimer, R. (eds.) MPEG-4 Facial Animation - The standard, implementations, applications, John Wiley & Sons, UK (2002)
27. Young, A.W., Rowland, D., Calder, A.J., Etcoff, N.L., Seth, A., Perrett, D.I.: Facial expression megamix: tests of dimensional and category accounts of emotion recognition. Cognition 63(3), 271–313 (1997)

The Behavior Markup Language:
Recent Developments and Challenges

Hannes Vilhjálmsson[1], Nathan Cantelmo[2], Justine Cassell[2], Nicolas E. Chafai[3],
Michael Kipp[4], Stefan Kopp[5], Maurizio Mancini[3], Stacy Marsella[7],
Andrew N. Marshall[7], Catherine Pelachaud[3], Zsofi Ruttkay[6], Kristinn R. Thórisson[1],
Herwin van Welbergen[6], and Rick J. van der Werf[6]

[1] CADIA, Reykjavik University, Iceland
{hannes,thorisson}@ru.is
[2] ArticuLab, Northwestern University, USA
{n-cantelmo,justine}@northwestern.edu
[3] IUT de Montreuil, University de Paris 8, France
{n.chafai,m.mancini,pelachaud}@iut.univ-paris8.fr
[4] DFKI, Germany
Michael.kipp@dfki.de
[5] Artificial Intelligence Group, University of Bielefeld, Germany
skopp@techfak.uni-bielefeld.de
[6] Human Media Interaction, University of Twente, The Netherlands
{z.m.ruttkay,h.vanwelbergen,werf}@ewi.utwente.nl
[7] Information Sciences Institute, University of Southern California, USA
{marsella,amarshal}@isi.edu

Abstract. Since the beginning of the SAIBA effort to unify key interfaces in
the multi-modal behavior generation process, the Behavior Markup Language
(BML) has both gained ground as an important component in many projects
worldwide, and continues to undergo further refinement. This paper reports on
the progress made in the last year in further developing BML. It discusses
some of the key challenges identified that the effort is facing, and reviews a
number of projects that already are making use of BML or support its use.

1 Introduction

The goal of the SAIBA effort is to create a representational framework for real-time
multimodal behavior generation in embodied conversational agents. Its members
have proposed knowledge structures that describe the form and generation of
multimodal communicative behavior at different levels of abstraction. The levels
represent the interfaces between the stages for (1) planning communicative intent, (2)
planning multimodal realization of this intent, and (3) the realization of the planned
behaviors (see Fig. 1). Mediating between the first two stages is the Functional
Markup Language (FML) that describes intent without reference to surface form; the
FML still remains largely undefined. Between the last two stages sits the Behavior
Markup Language (BML) that describes human nonverbal and verbal behavior in a
manner independent of the particular realization (animation) method used.

C. Pelachaud et al. (Eds.): IVA 2007, LNAI 4722, pp. 99–111, 2007.

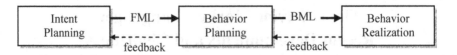

Fig. 1. The three stages of behavior generation in the SAIBA framework and the two mediating languages FML and BML

This is an ongoing effort that was officially kicked off when a group of international researchers in the area of multimodal communication and computer animation came together at Reykjavik University in April 2005. A paper published at IVA in 2006 introduces the framework and describes the first iteration of the Behavior Markup Language [5] and a wiki site hosted by the Mindmakers community portal tracks its development[1]. An active discussion forum and a mailing list are linked off the wiki site and we invite all interested to join and participate in the discussions. The material in this paper is mainly drawn from the most recent workshop which was hosted by OFAI in Vienna, Austria, in November 2006. The next workshop on BML will take place in Paris, France, in June 2007.

The paper is organized as follows: First we give a quick overview of BML in section 2 and then focus on some of the recent developments in section 3. Noteworthy challenges that we have identified are described in section 4. A review of a range of research projects that are pioneering the use of BML is provided in section 5 and finally some conclusions wrap up the paper in section 6.

2 Quick Overview of BML

BML is an XML based language that can be embedded in a larger XML message or document simply by starting a <bml> block and filling it with behaviors that should be realized by an animated agent.

For example:

```
<bml>
   <speech id="s1" type="application/ssml+xml">
     <text>This is an <mark name="wb3"> example</text>
   </speech>
   <head id="h1" type="NOD" stroke="s1:start"/>
   <gesture id="g1" stroke="s1:wb3" relax="s1:end" type="BEAT">
     <description level="1" type="MURML">...
     </description>
   </gesture>
   <gaze id="z1" target="PERSON1" stroke="g1:stroke-0.1"/>
   <body id="p1" posture="RELAXED" start="after(s1:end)"/>
   <cadia:operate target="SWITCH1" stroke="p1:ready"/>
</bml>
```

---

[1] http://wiki.mindmakers.org/projects:BML:main

This block coordinates speech, gesture, gaze, head and body movement by including a set of corresponding behavior elements inside a single <bml> element. Other possible behavior elements include torso, face, legs, lips and a wait behavior. Every behavior is divided into six animation phases. Each phase is bounded by a *sync-point* that carries the name of the motion transition it represents. The seven sync-points are: *start, ready, stroke-start, stroke, stroke-end, relax* and *end*. Synchrony between behaviors is achieved by assigning the sync-point of one behavior to a sync-point of another, causing the two to align at that point in time. In the example above, the stroke (most effortful part) of the head nod occurs exactly when the speech starts. An SSML annotation of the text to be spoken generates a new sync-point called *wb3*, which the gesture aligns its stroke with. The gaze uses a negative offset of 100 ms to make sure it rests on its target named PERSON1 just before the stroke of the gesture.

The body behavior uses a new feature to indicate that it can occur any time after the speech ends. This feature and other recent synchronization developments are discussed further in section 3.3. An important recent addition to BML is levels of description, which provide a way to describe a behavior in more detail than is possible with the core set of BML tags and attributes (see Fig. 2). Here a MURML type description of the gesture is included (not shown in full) with the core BML gesture element. Section 3.1 will explain the new levels of description in more detail. In order to introduce candidates for core BML extensions, namespaces can be used, as demonstrated by the hypothetical *operate* behavior above which is qualified with a CADIA specific namespace. This feature is covered in section 3.2.

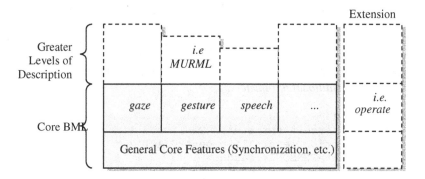

Fig. 2. The core BML specification of a behavior can be further refined through greater levels of description, while namespaces can provide general extensions

3 Recent Developments

3.1 Levels of Description

When describing behavior in great detail for animation, it makes good practical sense to use whatever advanced capabilities the character animation engine might support, such as a particularly high level of articulation or a simulation of physical dynamics. Furthermore, a behavior planner may want to generate behavior at multiple levels of detail so that a behavior realizer can adjust the required realization effort based on some chosen level of detail in the environment. Just as it would make little sense to cover all interaction over the Internet in a mail protocol, it would be an impossible task to cram the entire range of parameters required to address a variety of advanced animation methods and levels of detail into the core BML specification. One reason is that without a very specific goal, it is difficult to select between the many options for describing a particular behavior at a particular level of detail. One way is to put a large number of alternatives into the same language, but then we would quickly end up with a bloated specification language, trying to be everything to everyone and ending up being abandoned by all.

Instead of this route, it was decided to introduce levels of description to BML and define a core BML specification that would be kept completely independent of animation engines and developed to strike a good balance between being expressive and being lean. Additional levels can include a more detailed or a more engine specific description of the behavior already described in core BML. It is still an objective to allow re-use at the other description levels and the aim is to see the emergence of a set of description methods corresponding to some of the major animation techniques. Whether we can achieve a unified ontology of detail across multiple levels remains to be seen, but to begin with we can see the various descriptions as kinds of "plug-ins" for the various techniques.

The core BML description corresponds to the basic behavior elements and attributes introduced in [5] and the online reference[1]. Additional levels are embedded within a behavior element as an XML *description* element that can contain arbitrary XML. The type attribute of the description element should identify the type of content, indicating how it should be interpreted and executed by the behavior realizer.

This example shows BML describing gaze towards another character called PERSON1. *The attributes inside the <gaze> element are part of core BML while the embedded description levels of type* RU.ACT *and* ISI.SBM *(names identifying projects) provide additional parameters.*

```
<bml id="bml1">
  <gaze id="gaze1" target="PERSON1">
    <description level="1" type="RU.ACT">
      <target>PERSON1</target>
      <intensity>0.6</intensity>
      <lean>0.4</lean>
    </description>
    <description level="2" type="ISI.SBM">
      ...
    </description>
  </gaze>
</bml>
```

If additional levels of description cannot be interpreted by a realizer, it needs to be able to fall back on the core BML which should still provide a reasonable, if a somewhat simpler, description. Therefore, core BML needs to be present, even if higher levels of description make it redundant. This is crucial for the portability of a behavior planner, since you can't know for sure what levels beyond the core other realizers support.

All BML-compliant behavior realizers have to guarantee that they can interpret core BML behavior descriptions and display them correctly. In those cases where a realizer is only providing a special subset of BML, for example a talking head, it should be made very clear and behaviors that are not realized should produce appropriate feedback messages (see 3.4). Those realizers that can interpret any of the higher levels of description should make use of those. If a realizer is expecting a description of a certain level but does not receive it, it should default to the core description.

Numbered description levels imply a particular order, and generally higher numbers can be associated with richer descriptions. In that sense, the numbers can be seen either as a priority, where richer descriptions would be picked before poorer ones, or as roughly corresponding to a level of detail. However, even if behavior planners request a performance at a certain description level, a realizer may end up picking a description based on its own capabilities (sending a warning message back to the behavior planner). The overall effort will now focus on solidifying the first version of the core BML specification and allow working groups to discuss other levels of description pertinent to their specific research interests.

3.2 Namespace Extensions

The core BML behavior elements will continue to grow with new versions of the specification because the ongoing work behind BML involves identifying and defining a broad and flexible library of behaviors. Implementers are encouraged to explore new behavior elements and specialized attributes when making use of BML. Any such experimental components that cannot be embedded within a special level of description, should be identified as non-standard BML by utilizing XML namespaces to prefix the elements and attributes.

This example utilizes customized behaviors from the Smartbody project. Here, we use the namespace sbm *(short for SmartBody Module).*

```
<bml>
  <sbm:animation name="CrossedArms_RArm_beat"/>
  <gaze target="PERSON1"
      sbm:joint-speeds="100 100 100 300 600"/>
</bml>
```

3.3 Special Synchronization Features

BML provides special sync-points with every behavior block, *bml:start* and *bml:end*, that refer to the start of the earliest behavior in the request and the end of the latest behavior. Aligning to *bml:start* and *bml:end* requires special precautions. If there is no offset specified, only *start* sync-points can be aligned to *bml:start*, and only *end* sync-points can be aligned to *bml:end*. If there is an offset specified, it must be positive when referring to *bml:start* and negative when referring to *bml:end*. This constraint ensures that *bml:start* and *bml:end* properly point at the very start and end of the behavior request.

Aligning sync-points provides exact timing information, but there are times when a behavior planner only cares about the order in which behaviors occur and not so much about the exact moments in time they occur. To allow for this flexibility BML now allows under specified timing constraints in the form of the predicates *before()* and *after()*. The time *before(sync-point)* occurs at any point before the indicated sync-point and the time *after(sync-point)* occurs at any point after the indicated sync-point.

3.4 Feedback

It is important that the behavior planner get information back from the behavior realizer about the success or failure of various behavior requests in order to successfully plan subsequent action. This is particularly true for real-time systems that incrementally generate behavior.

Three main kinds of feedback have been identified and have received a special element in the core specification, while the particular system-level messaging protocol is not being defined by BML. The first kind is the regular `<event>` message, which can be scheduled to be emitted upon successfully reaching any sync-point in a behavior block and is automatically sent when an entire block successfully finishes. A special `<warning>` message is sent whenever the behavior realizer is unable to 100% comply with a behavior request, but was able to work within permissible soft boundaries. For example, a warning is issued if a soft timing constraint could not be honored or a behavior could not be performed at a recommended level of description. Finally, an `<exception>` message is returned when a behavior or a block of behaviors had to be cancelled because hard constraints could not be honored or because of an interrupt or other kinds of realization problems.

4 Open Challenges

4.1 Maintenance of Behavior

If one thinks about behavior as something that has a fixed duration and does not have a lasting impact of any kind, it is straight-forward to keep track of what the body is doing. At any given time, one can simply sum up all the behaviors currently executing to see exactly what is going on. However, reality is not that simple. When a behavior command is completed, the body is typically left in a new state, possibly even maintaining the behavior until another behavior replaces it.

One example is the gaze behavior. If a character is asked to gaze at a certain target with the command `<gaze target='person1' stroke='g1:stroke'/>`, it is clear that the gaze will fully rest on the target at exactly the same time another behavior (g1) reaches its own moment of greatest effort. However, it is completely left undetermined what happens next. Does the character continue to look at *person1*? If *person1* starts moving, should the character adjust its gaze accordingly? If the character is being requested to track *person1* with its gaze, how should that be indicated and how long should it last? What would then happen if *person1* left the scene? What if during tracking there was request for a short glance at the watch – would the gaze return to tracking *person1* after the glance? If not, where should the gaze go after looking at the watch?

Clearly there is a lot left undetermined here and the behavior realizer has a great deal of flexibility to fill in the missing pieces. However, it is reasonable for a behavior planner to want to know what happens between behavior requests or even to be able to describe what should happen. One way to approach this is for the behavior planner to describe to the realizer (a) rules for maintaining behaviors, such as "keep doing this until I tell you otherwise" and (b) default behavior states that the body should return to when other behaviors run their course. No structure to do this is part of BML yet, except for a few special behaviors that assume continuous maintenance like `<body pose='sit'/>`. Another way is to have a much tighter command-feedback cycle where the planner takes charge of all decisions and continuously reacts to events from the world and from the realizer. That approach is already possible with BML and needs to be maintained as an equally valid approach.

4.2 Constraints and Synchronization

The synchrony achieved through aligning behavior sync-points demonstrates one type of timing constraint, but it is important to consider other types as well. These include:

- *Physical characteristics constraints:* Limitations on body movement speed.
- *Rhythmic constraints:* Requirement that different modalities stay in perfect synchrony.
- *Global rule constraint:* A general synchrony rule that is meant to hold true for all behaviors in a set of behaviors (such as stating that all gesture strokes should coincide or precede emphasized syllables).
- *Fixed signal constraint:* Synchronization to an external source with a fixed timing pattern (such as clapping to music).
- *Perceptual signal constraint:* Synchronization to an external signal with unknown timing (such as the actions of another person).

While it is evident that all these kinds of timing constraints 'make sense' for Virtual Humans, they raise some challenges for the SAIBA framework:

- *Where, and how should the different constraints be declared?* Should their description be deferred to FML or should specification of character state for example become part of BML?
- *What type of constraints are necessary, as of the numerically and of strength?* As of the nature of the constraints, the linear interval constraints (on sync-points of gestures), similar to ones used for facial expressions seem to be expressive enough. Two categories are needed though: hard and soft constraints. The latter might need ranks, indicating how important a certain constraint is. Another option would be to consider the precision of constraints: even if a gesture cannot be scheduled to the required time, effort could be made to schedule it 'as close as possible'.
- *Where and how can they all be examined together for making final timing decisions ?* A behavior planner or a behavior realizer may need to collect all timing constraints from various sources for combining redundant ones, resolving possible conflicts and for finally providing a flattened uniform representation for correct and efficient temporal scheduling.
- *What solution principles should be used to cope with under-constrained and over-constrained cases?*

The declaration and manipulation of constraints is related to levels of description. If only core BML gestures are available from a particular gesture repository, it is possible to omit the prescription of constraints that assure subtle variants of those gestures. A conceptually clear and computationally efficient way to handle all these possible constraints is needed and is currently being explored.

5 Current Projects and Tools

This section reviews a few projects that incorporate BML. These projects are tentatively classified into: Full ECA systems, behavior planners, behavior realizers, repositories and tools. This is informal, and only meant to demonstrate the range of projects and how they potentially fit together in the SAIBA framework (see Fig. 1).

5.1 Full ECA Systems

RVT: The Reactive Virtual Trainer[2]. The *Reactive Virtual Trainer* (RVT) [10] is an ECA capable of presenting physical exercises that are to be performed by a human, while monitoring the user and providing feedback. The reactivity of the RVT is manifested in natural language comments, readjusting the tempo, pointing out mistakes or rescheduling the exercises. These exercises can be performed to the beat of a user's favorite music. Exercises describe a mix of behaviors in different modalities, including exercise movement, sound (such as clapping, feet tapping), speech and music. The main extension to core BML is the *observer* behavior. The observer is used to provide coordination with outside world events that are predictable and possibly repeat themselves, such as the beat in music. Such synchronization can not be achieved by the event/wait system described in core BML since BML events are, by design, non-repeatable and unpredictable.

This example shows counting at the beat of beatObserver1.

```
<bml>
  <bmlt:observer id="beatObserver1"/>
  <speech id="s1" start="beatObserver1:1">One</speech>
  <speech id="s2" start="beatObserver1:2">Two</speech>
  <speech id="s3" start="beatObserver1:3">Three</speech>
</bml>
```

Ambulation Agents[3]. *EVE-Online* is a massively multiplayer online role playing game (MMORPG) where over 30.000 simultaneous players travel through a vast galaxy in custom configured ships, seeking fame and fortune through exploration, trade, conflict and political power. So far, players have been bound to their ships, but the developer of this game, CCP Games, has decided to develop an addition to this game called *Ambulation* that allows players to exit their ships at space stations and mingle with other players and fully autonomous agents, represented by animated graphical avatars. To achieve believable interactions between characters, this project will rely on automating the coordination of nonverbal social behavior. A special

---

[2] Developed at Human Media Interaction, University of Twente.
[3] Developed jointly by CADIA, Reykjavík University and CCP Games.

version of the game client is being equipped with a BML interface, so that behavior planning can be fully implemented within the SAIBA framework, both ensuring CCP access to existing domain expertise and ensuring that new results from this project will immediately be available to the research community. It is expected that this work will particularly contribute to BML by exploring support for tight perception-action loops in a highly dynamic social environment.

SuperRadioHost[4]. *SuperRadioHost* is an autonomous radio show host designed to create a radio program from scratch and execute it in real-time – on the air – including creating song introductions and conducting interviews with real people. The system perceives its own on-air transmissions including its own speech content and prosody. For interviews it employs a new model of turntaking that goes well beyond what has been built in the past [11]. The system's planning mechanisms embody a version of the SAIBA framework and propose a mixture of opportunism and predefined plans. Naturally the system only uses speech-related markup for describing its behaviors. Among the key research topics addressed is opportunistic planning in real-time dialogue and holistic models of cognitive agents.

5.2 Behavior Planners

NVB: Non-verbal Behavior Generator[7]. The *Non-Verbal Behavior Generator* (NVB) [7] is a rule-based behavior planner, inspired by BEAT [1], that analyses a virtual human's communicative intent, emotional state, and text (dialog) and generates appropriate nonverbal behaviors. The inputs are described using a preliminary version of the FML format and the final behavior commands are specified in BML, which are passed to *SmartBody*. The NVB generator is designed for portability and for being imported into different virtual human systems with different animation schemes by simply changing the names of the behaviors in the behavior description repository without modifying the nonverbal behavior rules. NVB is used in the SASO-ST, ELECT and Virtual Patient systems, among others.

NOVA: Nonverbal Action Generator[5]. NOVA is a system able to recreate the gesture behaviour of a specific human performer using statistical models, a fixed repertoire of gestures and procedural animation [8]. It is intended as an alternative/complement to rule-based approaches to generate a varied and natural looking "baseline" behaviour. With respect to SAIBA, we plan to (1) translate the descriptions of our gesture repertoire to emerging BML descriptors and (2) make our planner communicate to the realizer using BML. A central research challenge for NOVA will be the merging of two BML streams to combine our probabilistic approach with rule-based ones.

5.3 Behavior Realizers

ACE: The Articulated Communicator Engine[6]. The *Articulated Communicator Engine* (ACE) is a behavior realization engine that allows the modeling of virtual

---

[4] Developed at CADIA, Reykjavík University.
[5] Developed jointly at DFKI and UC Davis.
[6] Developed in the Artificial Intelligence Group, University of Bielefeld.

animated agents, independent of a graphics platform, and to synthesize multimodal utterances with prosodic speech, body and hand gesture, or facial expressions [6]. ACE has been used in several conversational agents, e.g., the museum guide MAX and the direction giving information kiosk NUMACK. One hallmark of ACE is its tight coupling of behavior realization, including speech synthesis and animation planning, and behavior execution, which enables smart scheduling and blending/co-articulation of gesture and speech. Assuming that uttering runs incrementally in chunks, animations are formed such that the gesture spans the co-expressive word or sub-phrase within each chunk; between successive chunks, transition movements and silent pauses in speech are adjusted to prepare the synchrony of upcoming behaviors. Originally, the input for ACE was specified in MURML, a representation language addressing the same level of abstraction as BML. ACE is now being made BML-compliant. For BML, this work will result in proposals for new levels of fine-grained, yet player-independent, feature-based gesture description, and for an extension towards complex utterances that consist of multiple "chunks" of coordinated multimodal behavior.

SmartBody[7]. *SmartBody* [4] is an open source modular framework for animating embodied characters, based on motion controllers that can be hierarchically interconnected in real-time in order to achieve continuous motion. Controllers can employ arbitrary animation algorithms, such as key frame interpolation, motion capture or procedural animation, as well as schedule or blend other controllers. *SmartBody* was designed around the BML standard and currently supports eight types of BML behaviors: body postures, full or partial body animations, gaze, head motions like nodding and shaking, facial expressions based on action units, speech, event or progress notifications, and the interruptions of prior behaviors. Most behaviors map directly to single motion controllers. SmartBody has been used in a growing number of research projects and training applications, including the SASO-ST virtual human research platform, the ELECT negotiation trainer, the Virtual Rapport studies and the Virtual Patient demonstration.

5.4 Repositories and Tools

The Expressive Gesture Repository[8]. In this work, the aim is to help ECAs produce varied gestures from a single representation, based on the agent's expressivity and the relevant semantic dimensions of those gestures. The SAIBA framework supports the inclusion of a BML based gesture repository, either at the behavior planning stage or at behavior realization. An ECA can reproduce gestures from this repository but their application may be limited. Expressivity of behavior is an integral part of the communication process as it can provide information on the current emotional state, mood, and personality of the agents. A set of parameters that affect the qualities of the agent's behavior such as its speed, spatial volume, energy, fluidity have been defined and implemented [3]. During communication, the agent retrieves the gestures definition from the repository and then applies these dynamic variations to the gestures execution.

---

[7] Developed at the Information Sciences Institute and the Institute for Creative Technologies, University of Southern California.

[8] Developed at IUT de Montreuil, Université de Paris 8.

Moreover, a communicative gesture can have a number of possible meanings, so we have to make sure that a gesture description includes its semantic dimensions. As a first step, we have defined a set of gesture primitives for action gestures that relate to parts of the human body [2], and as a second step, we are currently working on the definition of the relevant dimensions for a family of gestures produced in the space in front of the speaker (gestures with meaning related to: temporal relations, refusal or negation). These descriptions extend possible applications of gestures in the repository, especially when one wants to introduce levels of detail or create variations from a single entry while concerving the meaning of a gesture.

ECAT: The ECA Toolkit[9]. The *ECA Toolkit* (ECAT) aims to allow ECA developers to easily connect any BML behavior-generating system to any behavior realization system. This toolkit assumes that in addition to the three-stage model proposed in the SAIBA framework, the behavior realization stage may be further divided into three distinct processing stages. The first of the three stages is called interpretation, which makes it possible to convert behavior description languages that are not already in BML into well formed BML. The second stage, called compilation, turns BML into low level joint rotations, facial deformations and audio playback directives. Translation, the final stage, involves the rendering of these low level behaviors. Interpreters for different behavior languages and translators for different behavior realizers are being developed.

BCBM Behavior Rule Builder[10]. The Rule Builder is a graphical user interface that allows someone who is not a programmer or an animator to link communicative intent of an animated character to its nonverbal expression of that intent, given a certain context. This linkage is established by way of "rules" authored by the user in a point-and-click manner. The communicative intent is expressed using a preliminary version of FML and the resulting nonverbal behavior is expressed BML. The context can be constructed as an arbitrary XML structure. Both FML and BML are dynamically read into the application from schemas, and therefore the Rule Builder will continue to grow with the development of these standards. The Rule Builder can connect directly to a game engine to provide a real-time preview of resulting behavior. By default behaviors are sent in BML format, but users can specify an XSLT file for translating BML into proprietary animation languages. The Rule Builder has been used with *SmartBody* (using BML) and the Alelo Virtual Culture engine (using Gamebots). The Rule Builder is a part of a behavior generation and authoring toolkit for social training environments that includes a Dialog Builder as described in [12].

6 Conclusion

The SAIBA effort, and BML in particular, is gathering momentum as seen by the ongoing developments and the number of projects that already commit to the

---

[9] Developed at ArticuLab, Northwestern University.
[10] Developed jointly at University of Southern California and Micro Analysis and Design, currently maintained by CADIA.

framework. Being able to mix and match behavior planners and realizers from a list like the one in the section above and have them work together may be around the corner. However, it is unlikely that the first interoperability attempts will immediately succeed, as integration may reveal unforeseen factors that then need addressing in the framework. It is therefore important to ensure that BML can continue to grow while remaining focused on the interoperability goals. Lessons from integration tests await future publication, but today the prospects for achieving general ECA module interoperability are better than ever, driven by a strong desire to literally build on each other's work.

Acknowledgements. The authors would like to thank those that attended the Vienna workshop as well as those that participated in previous gatherings and online discussions. Particular thanks go to the coordinators of the Vienna and Paris workshops and the EU Network of Excellence HUMAINE (IST-507422) for meeting support. All the individual projects mentioned in this paper are grateful to their respective members for their work and sponsors for their support.

References

1. Cassell, J., Vilhjalmsson, H., Bickmore, T.: BEAT: the Behavior Expression Animation Toolkit. In: Proceedings of ACM SIGGRAPH, Los Angeles, August 12-17, pp. 477–486 (2001)
2. Chafai, N.E., Pelachaud, C., Pelé, D.: A semantic description of gesture in BML. In: Proceedings of AISB'07 Annual Convention Workshop on Language, Speech and Gesture for Expressive Characters, Newcastle, UK (2007)
3. Hartmann, B., Mancini, M., Pelachaud, C.: Design and evaluation of expressive gesture synthesis for embodied conversational agents. In: Proceedings of the 3rd International Joint Conference on Autonomous Agents and Multi-Agent Systems, Utrecht, The Netherlands (2005)
4. Kallmann, M., Marsella, S.: Hierarchical Motion Controllers for Real-Time Autonomous Virtual Humans. In: Panayiotopoulos, T., Gratch, J., Aylett, R., Ballin, D., Olivier, P., Rist, T. (eds.) IVA 2005. LNCS (LNAI), vol. 3661, pp. 253–265. Springer, Heidelberg (2005)
5. Kopp, S., Krenn, B., Marsella, S., Marshall, A., Pelachaud, C., Pirker, H., Thórisson, K., Vilhjalmsson, H.: Towards a Common Framework for Multimodal Generation in ECAs: The Behavior Markup Language. In: Gratch, J., Young, M., Aylett, R., Ballin, D., Olivier, P. (eds.) IVA 2006. LNCS (LNAI), vol. 4133, pp. 205–217. Springer, Heidelberg (2006)
6. Kopp, S., Wachsmuth, I.: Synthesizing Multimodal Utterances for Conversational Agents. In The Journal of Computer Animation and Virtual Worlds 15(1), 39–52 (2004)
7. Lee, J., Marsella, S.: Nonverbal Behavior Generator for Embodied Conversational Agents. In: Gratch, J., Young, M., Aylett, R., Ballin, D., Olivier, P. (eds.) IVA 2006. LNCS (LNAI), vol. 4133, pp. 243–255. Springer, Heidelberg (2006)
8. Neff, M., Kipp, M., Albrecht, I., seidel, H.-P.: Gesture Modeling and Animation Based on a Probabilistic Recreation of Speaker Style. In: Transactions on Graphics, ACM Press, New York
9. Ruttkay, Zs.: Constraint-based facial animation. Int. Journal of Constraints, 6, 85–113 (2001)

10. Ruttkay, Z.s., Zwiers, J., van Welbergen, H., Reidsma, D.: Towards a Reactive Virtual Trainer. In: Gratch, J., Young, M., Aylett, R., Ballin, D., Olivier, P. (eds.) IVA 2006. LNCS (LNAI), vol. 4133, pp. 292–303. Springer, Heidelberg (2006)
11. Thórisson, K.R.: Natural Turn-Taking Needs No Manual: Computational Theory and Model, from Perception to Action. In: Granström, B., House, D., Karlsson, I. (eds.) Multimodality in Language and Speech Systems, pp. 173–207. Kluwer Academic Publishers, The Netherlands (2002)
12. Warwick, W., Vilhjalmsson, H.: Engendering Believable Communicative Behaviors in Synthetic Entities for Tactical Language Training: An Interim Report. In: Proceedings of Behavior Representation in Modeling and Simulation, Universal City, CA (2005)

Dynamic Behavior Qualifiers
for Conversational Agents

Maurizio Mancini and Catherine Pelachaud

University of Paris 8, France

Abstract. We aim at defining conversational agents that exhibit qualitatively distinctive behaviors. To this aim we provide a small set of parameters to allow one to define behavior profiles and then leave to the system the task of animating the agent. Our approach is to manipulate the behavior tendency of the agent depending on its communicative intention and emotional state.

In this paper we will define the concepts of *Baseline* and *Dynamicline*. The Baseline of an agent is defined as a set of fixed parameters that represent the personalized agent behavior, while the Dynamicline, is a set of parameters values that derive both from the Baseline and the current communicative goals and emotional state.

1 Introduction

We present a model for the definition of conversational agents that exhibit *distinctive* behaviors. It means that even if the communicative intentions and/or emotional states of two agents are exactly the same they will behave in a different way according to their general and current behavior tendencies. Differences will be noticeable both in the signals chosen by the agents to communicate and in the quality of behavior.

Human communication involves verbal and non-verbal behaviors. People communicate through several modalities like face, gestures, posture. The same beliefs and goals can be communicated in different personalized ways, and the interaction with other people will be always influenced by personal behavior tendencies. For example we are able to give a quick but usually very precise definition of the general behavior tendency of a person: we say "this person *never* moves, she is expressiveless" or "he is very expansive and gestures a lot while talking" and so on. Some people may tend to use one modality more than the others, other people may often use more than one modality at the same time and so on. For example let us consider a person that gestures a lot while speaking. This is a basic trait of that person, we can expect that in general circumstances she prefers to convey non-verbal signals more on the gesture modality than another modalities. That is the idea we want to capture with the concept of *Baseline* for virtual agents. On the other hand there can be some events or situations in which one's basic tendencies change, and one gesture in a greatly different way. For example a person that never does hand/body gestures while she talks may

C. Pelachaud et al. (Eds.): IVA 2007, LNAI 4722, pp. 112–124, 2007.

change her behavior if she is very angry at someone. We embody the current tendency of behavior with the concept of *Dynamicline* of a virtual agent.

In the next Section we will give a brief description of other systems that implemented agents that exhibit distinctive behaviors. Section 3 will give some details about the definition of the modalities preferences and the expressivity parameters. In Section 4 and 5 we will explain how Baseline and Dynamicline are used to generate the final agent's behavior. Then we will give an example of our system and we will conclude the paper.

2 State of the Art

Several researchers have addressed the problem of defining conversational agents that exhibit distinctive behaviors. Some of them have applied psychological theories to the creation of models that simulate personality, mood and emotion [3]. Others have defined parameters that aim at modifying the quality of movement dynamically to increase the expressivity of the agent [4,13] [11]. In other systems, the agent's behavior, previously stored in script files manually or statistically computed, is selected during the interaction with the user [9,2].

Ruttkay et al. [15,14] propose the idea of behavior style, defined in terms of when and how the ECA (Embodied Conversational Agent) uses certain gestures. Styles are implemented by selecting gestures from a *style dictionary* that defines both which gestures an agent has in his repertoire and its habits in using them. The style dictionaries are written in GESTYLE. This language specifies which modalities should be used to display non-verbal behaviors and is also used to annotate the text that the agent has to utter. Ball and Breese [3] propose a model for individualization for virtual agents in which the final behavior is computed depending on the agent's actual emotional state and personality by choosing the most appropriate style. The PAR model of Allbeck et al. [1] offers a parameterization of actions. The actions that the agent is able to carry out are defined together with the conditions that need to be true in order to perform the actions. Conditions can refer to the state of other agents or objects in the agent's environment. EMOTE [4] is a system for creating differentiated gestures. Starting from Laban's annotation scheme, gestures are defined in terms of *Effort* and *Shape*. Effort gives information about the sense of impact (delicate vs strong), speed (indulging vs urgent/sudden) and control (uncontrolled/abandoned vs controlled/tense) of movement. space, weight, time and flow. Shape defines the movement path in the 3D space. Neff et al. [13] found out some key movement properties by reviewing arts and literature, for example from theater and dance. They found that body and movement characteristics such as balance, body silhouette (contour of the body), position of torso and shoulder, etc. influence the way in which people perceive the others. They have implemented three motion properties into animated characters: the pose of the character, the timing of movements and the transition from one pose to another. In this model physical constraints are also considered, for example gravity and body balance, to obtain a very realistic animation. In André et al. [2] the agent's behavior depends both on a script that describes what the agent has to communicate to the user (for example how to do a reservation for a room in a hotel's website) and its personalized behavior. The last one includes idle movements like for example tapping with its foot while the user does nothing or jumping when the mouse passes over the agent's figure. Maya et al. [11] define a taxonomy to classify the influences on people's behavior. Intrinsic influences are personal habits that derive from personality, culture, gender, etc. Contextual influences come from the physical environment in which the person is acting. Finally dynamic influences represent the person's emotional states, beliefs and goals during the conversation. In our model we also use the notion of dynamic influence but we look at how these influences can be computed in term of movement quality and modalities preference without looking at the factors that could have caused them. In Michael Kipp's work [8] the author presents a gesture animation system based on statistical models of human speakers gestures. Videos of interviewed people have been manually annotated in terms of gestures types (iconic, deictic, etc. [12]), together with their frequency of occurrence and timing (that is the synchronization between the gesture stroke and the most emphasized syllable of the sentence). The statistics on the speaker's gestures are then used to model the agent's set of preferred gestures (the probabilities of their occurrence is computed from the annotated gesture frequency) and synchronization tendency (for example an agent can perform gesture strokes always synchronized with speech emphasis). In a more recent work [9], the agent's gestures selection can be human authored or automatically learned using machine learning algorithms on the basis of previously annotated scripts. In our work we look at behavior qualitative differences rather than gesture types differences. Kipp's approach and ours are thus complementary. Similarly to our work, M. Kipp does not model the possible causes of visible variations in behaviors.

3   Modalities Preferences and Behavior Expressivity

Conversational agents are graphical representations of humans that are increasingly used in a large variety of applications to help, assist or direct the user in performing a wide number of tasks. They can communicate to the user multimodally, that is by using many modalities at the same time. In our work, agents produce signals on the following modalities:

- face (eyebrows/eyelids/mouth/cheek movements)
- head movement (head direction and rotation, such as nods and shakes)
- gestures (arms and hands movements)
- body posture (upper part of the body movements)

People differ in the way they use their modalities: one can be very expressive on the face, another can gesture a lot. The concept of *Modalities preferences* encompasses this variability in the modalities use. People can also differ in the quality of their behavior. For example, one can have the tendency to do large hand gestures at a fast paste. Thus behavior expressivity is also a characteristic of an agent.

3.1   Modalities Preferences

People can communicate by being more or less expressive in the different modalities. The modalities preferences represent the agent's degree of preference of each available modality. If for example we want to specify that the agent has the tendency to mainly use hand gestures during communication we assign a high degree of preference to the *gesture* modality, if it uses mainly the face, the face modality is set to a higher value, and so on. For every available modality (face, head movement, gesture, posture), we define a value between 0 and 1 which represents its preferability. Agents can also use two or more modalities with the same degree of preference. This means that the agent will communicate with these modalities equally.

3.2   Behavior Expressivity

Expressivity of behaviour is an integral part of the communication process as it can provide information on the current emotional state, mood, and personality of the agents [17]. We view it as the "How" the physical behaviour is executed. Starting from the results reported in [17], we have defined and implemented [7,6] a set of parameters that affect the qualities of the agent's behavior such as its speed, spatial volume, energy, fluidity. Thus, the same gestures or facial expressions are performed by the agent in a qualitatively different way depending on the following parameters:

- *Overall activation (OAC)*: amount of activity (quantity of movement) across several modalities during a conversational turn (e.g., simultaneous use of facial expression, gaze, gesture to visualize communicative acts passive/static or animated/engaged).
- *Spatial extent (SPC)*: amplitude of movements (e.g., amount of space taken up by body; amplitude of eyebrow raise)
- *Temporal (TMP)*: duration of movements (e.g., quick versus sustained actions)
- *Fluidity (FLD)*: smoothness and continuity of overall movement (e.g., smooth, graceful versus sudden, jerky)
- *Power (PWR)*: dynamic properties of the movement (e.g., weak/relaxed versus strong/tense)
- *Repetitivity (REP)*: tendency to rhythmic repeats of specific movements along specific modalities.

4   Baseline and Dynamicline

In our model for conversational agents exhibiting distinctive behavior we want to capture the idea that people have tendencies that characterise globally their behavior, but these tendencies can change in situations rising after some particular events. To encapsulate this global and local qualities we have introduced the concepts of Baseline and Dynamicline, which both contain information on

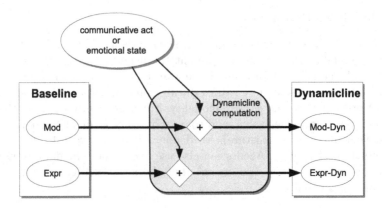

Fig. 1. The agent's Baseline, communicative act and/or emotional state determine the computation of the agent's Dynamicline

the agent's modalities preferences and expressivity but with different time span: while the Baseline is the overall definition of how the agent behaves in general situation, the Dynamicline is the *local* specification of the agent's behavior (for example during a given agent's emotional state).

In our model, Baseline and Dynamicline do not only differ by their meaning (global vs local behavior tendency) but also by the fact that the Baseline is an input parameter, that is, it is used to define some characteristics of an agent, while the Dynamicline is automatically computed by the system at runtime, depending on the current agent's communicative intention and/or emotional state. To use our system, the Baseline for each agent has to be defined manually before running the system. The system is left with the task of computing automatically the agent's behavior.

We define the Baseline by the pair *(Mod,Expr)* where:

- *Mod*: this parameter represent the modalities preferences. As described in Section 3.1 this is the agent's tendency to use its modalities during communication. The modalities preferences are defined by assigning a real value between 0 and 1 to each modality.
- *Expr*: is the behavior expressivity. This is the set of expressivity values (see Section 3.2) that represents the base behavior tendency of the agent. An agent could for example tend to do slow and smooth gestures while another agent could tend to move in a fast and jerky manner. Note that we implemented expressivity separately for each modality, that is there is a set of expressivity parameters for each modality.

Figure 1 outlines how the Dynamicline is computed at runtime. The data in input is: the agent's Baseline and the agent's communicative act or emotional state. So, each time a new communicative intention and/or emotional state arrives in input, our system will compute a new Dynamicline for the agent.

Dynamicline is modeled by the pair *(Mod-Dyn,Expr-Dyn)* where:

- *Mod-Dyn*: the current agent's modalities preferences. It represents the agent's tendency to use its modalities given a certain communicative intention and/or emotional state. It is obtained by modulating the modalities preferences *Mod* of the Baseline depending on the actual communicative act and/or emotional state.
- *Expr-Dyn*: the current agent's expressivity parameters. It represents the agent's expressivity of movements given a certain communicative intention and/or emotional state. It is obtained by modulating the expressivity parameters *Expr* of the Baseline depending on the actual communicative act and/or emotional state.

In the next Section we will see in detail how the Dynamicline is computed by our system.

5   Dynamicline Computation

The *Dynamicline computation* module of Figure 1 performs the computation of the content of the Dynamicline (see previous Section for a description of the Dynamicline). During the process, the modalities preferences and the expressivity parameters contained in the Baseline are modulated depending to the agent's actual communicative intention and/or emotional state and the resulting values are stored in the Dynamicline. It means that communicative intention and/or emotional state will have different impact on the Dynamiclines of two agents having different Baselines. For example, if an agent has a general tendency (Baseline) to perform movements with average speed/amplitude and to use hand gestures moderately then in a sad state it will do very few hand gestures with very low amplitude and speed. On the other hand, an agent with a general tendency of gesturing a lot with fast and large movements even when being sad, it will continue doing gestures in a less number and with a less expressivity (average speed and amplitude). In the following sections we will introduce a computational model for the definition of the agent's Baseline and for the determination of the Dynamicline that corresponds to a particular communicative intention or emotional state. All the structures presented in the next sections have been defined using XML Schema Definitions (XSDs). This allows us to have a safer system, because we can perform a very efficient data type and syntax check before starting the computation. Moreover, the system is easily extensible for adding new entities and parameters in the future.

5.1   Baseline and Dynamicline Specification

In Section 4 we have given the definition of Baseline and Dynamicline for a conversational agent. Here we will present an XML-based specification of these two entities. First of all, we may notice that the meaning of the concepts of Baseline and Dynamicline is slightly different, because the first one is a static global parameter while the second one is dynamically changing element. Anyway, from a

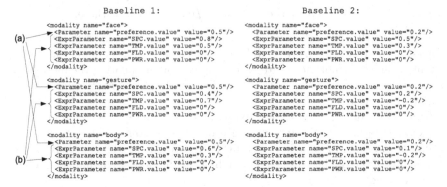

Fig. 2. XML-based definition of the Baseline: a more active agent on the left, and less active, static agent on the right. The arrows starting from (a) indicate the modalities preferences while the arrows starting from (b) highlight the sets of expressivity parameters for each modality.

structural point of view, they can be modeled exactly in the same way, in fact, as explained in Section 4, they both represent (a) the agent's degree of preference for each modality and (b) the expressivity parameters for each modality. Figure 2 illustrates an example of two Baselines: the one on the left represents an agent that has a tendency to be very activated on each modality; the one on the right, instead, refers to an agent which is less active. Arrows marked by (*a*) and (*b*) highlight respectively the rows defining the modalities preferences and the sets of expressivity parameters for each modality. The language in the example has been developed following the definition of Baseline and Dynamicline given in Section 4:

- a Baseline/Dynamicline is a list of modalities;
- a modality is composed by a preference factor and a list of expressivity parameters;
- an expressivity parameter is one of the parameters listed in Section 3.2.

5.2   Behavior Qualifiers

Communicative intentions and emotional states may influence the way one tends to communicate non-verbally. We call *behavior qualifier* the set of *modulations* that, given an emotional state or a communicative intention, acts on the behavior tendency of a conversational agent. A *modulation* is defined as a variation over one of the parameters contained in the Baseline of an agent. It is represented by the following components:

- *destination*: it is the parameter in which the result of the modulation will be stored. For example it can be one of the modalities preference, or an expressivity parameter.
- *operator*: it specifies which operation should be performed between the terms listed in the modulation definition. The actual operators implemented in

our system are simple mathematical operations like addition, subtraction, multiplication, division, scaling. We have also defined an assignment operator to copy values between parameters. Moreover, new operators can easily be added by defining their C++ implementation in the source code of the system.

– *list of terms*: it is the list of the modulation terms. Each term can be one of the modality preference, an expressivity parameter, or a numeric value. The number of terms depends on the operator, for example a simple assignation (e.g., $SPC = 1.0$) will need just one term, while a sum (e.g., $SPC = SPC + 0.5$) will need two terms.

As an example, let us see how we define a behavior qualifier that represents the following description:

"a hot anger state (i) increases the degree of bodily activation and at the same time (ii) the speed, amplitude and power of movements will be very high".

Let us notice that the modulations described in this behavior qualifier are of two kinds: *relative* and *absolute*. In the example, part (i) of the qualifier says that the degree of bodily activation increases. This is a relative variation since it gives an indication of the local behavior tendency (Dynamicline) in terms of the global tendency (Baseline). Instead, part (ii) of the qualifier indicates that speed, amplitude and power of movement should be very high: in this case it refers to absolute values, that is the local behavior tendency (Dynamicline) is explicitly defined, and it does not refer to the global tendency (Baseline). Figure 3 shows the code representing this behavior qualifier. The code is written in an XML-based *ad-hoc* language.

In Figure 3, lines 3-28 describe the modulations that act on the *Overall activation* expressivity parameter of the agent's *body*, *face* and *gesture* modalities by multiplying it by 1.5. These *relative* variations are described in part (i) of

```
01 <qualifier name="hot anger">
02
03     <modulation>
04         <destination>body</destination>
05         <parameter>OAC.value</parameter>
06         <operator>MULT</operator>
07         <term1name>body</term1name>
08         <term1attribute>OAC.value</term1attribute>
09         <term2value>1.5</term2value>
10     </modulation>
11
12     <modulation>
13         <destination>face</destination>
14         <parameter>OAC.value</parameter>
15         <operator>MULT</operator>
16         <term1name>face</term1name>
17         <term1attribute>OAC.value</term1attribute>
18         <term2value>1.5</term2value>
19     </modulation>
20
21     <modulation>
22         <destination>gesture</destination>
23         <parameter>OAC.value</parameter>
24         <operator>MULT</operator>
25         <term1name>gesture</term1name>
26         <term1attribute>OAC.value</term1attribute>
27         <term2value>1.5</term2value>
28     </modulation>

29     <modulation>
30         <destination>gesture</destination>
31         <parameter>TMP.value</parameter>
32         <operator>VAL</operator>
33         <term1value>0.9</term1value>
34     </modulation>
35
36     <modulation>
37         <destination>gesture</destination>
38         <parameter>SPC.value</parameter>
39         <operator>VAL</operator>
40         <term1value>0.9</term1value>
41     </modulation>
42
43     <modulation>
44         <destination>gesture</destination>
45         <parameter>PWR.value</parameter>
46         <operator>VAL</operator>
47         <term1value>0.9</term1value>
48     </modulation>
49
50 </qualifier>
```

(i)   (ii)

Fig. 3. Example of behavior qualifier definition

the behavior qualifier of 'hot anger'. On the other hand, lines 29-48 describe the modulations that assign the value 0.9 in the *Temporal, Spatial* and *Power* expressivity parameters of the agent's gesture modality. These *absolute* variations are described in part (ii) of the example.

Starting from the studies reported in Wallbott [16] and Gallaher [5], and from our previous works [6,10] we have written a library of behavior qualifiers that correspond to the set of some emotional states and some communicative functions using the language in Figure 3. From the point of view of the Dynamicline computation module, behavior qualifiers are predefined input parameters that determine how the Dynamicline is computed from the Baseline. In our current implementation the definition of these behavior qualifiers is fixed. It will always be used in the Dynamicline computation. In the future it would be possible to dynamically compute the definition of behavior qualifiers to take care of individual differences and thus allow for more behavior variability.

5.3   Dynamicline Computation Example

In the previous sections we have introduced the specification of the Baseline and Dynamicline for a conversational agent, then we have explained how behavior qualifiers can be described through an XML-based language. In the present Section we will describe an example of Dynamicline computation.

Let us consider the Baseline on the left side of Figure 2, and the qualifier defined in Figure 3. We also suppose that the current emotional state of the agent corresponds to the one defined in the qualifier, that is the agent is in an *hot anger* emotional state. So, the *Dynamicline computation* module of Figure 1 decides to apply the behavior qualifier to the Baseline of Figure 2, by performing the operations specified in the qualifier. The result of this computation is the Dynamicline shown on the left column of Figure 4.

```
        Dynamicline 1:                      Dynamicline 2:

01 modality: body                 01 modality: body
02         FLD.value=0.00         02         FLD.value=0.00
03         OAC.value=1.00         03         OAC.value=0.30
04         PWR.value=0.00         04         PWR.value=0.00
05         SPC.value=0.60         05         SPC.value=0.10
06         TMP.value=0.30         06         TMP.value=-0.20
07         preference.value=0.50  07         preference.value=0.20
08                                08
09 modality: face                 09 modality: face
10         FLD.value=0.00         10         FLD.value=0.00
11         OAC.value=1.00         11         OAC.value=0.75
12         PWR.value=0.00         12         PWR.value=0.00
13         SPC.value=0.80         13         SPC.value=0.50
14         TMP.value=0.50         14         TMP.value=0.30
15         preference.value=0.50  15         preference.value=0.20
16                                16
17 modality: gesture              17 modality: gesture
18         FLD.value=0.00         18         FLD.value=0.00
19         OAC.value=1.00         19         OAC.value=0.45
20         PWR.value=0.90         20         PWR.value=0.90
21         SPC.value=0.90         21         SPC.value=0.90
22         TMP.value=0.90         22         TMP.value=0.90
23         preference.value=0.50  23         preference.value=0.20
```

Fig. 4. Example of Dynamiclines for an *hot anger* state

The parameters affected by the qualifier are highlighted in bold. For example lines 03, 11 and 19 represent the *Overall activation* expressivity parameter for the three modalities, and they have been obtained from the values in the Baseline by multiplying them by a factor of 1.5, as defined in the qualifier (Figure 3). Instead, the gesture expressivity parameters in lines 20 - 22 are not related to the Baseline, as they are explicitly determined by the qualifier.

Let us consider a different Baseline, the one on the right side of Figure 2. After applying the same qualifier, the resulting Dynamicline is the one reported in the right column of Figure 4. We may notice that the *Overall activation* parameters are different from the previous Dynamicline, because they have been generated from a different Baseline. Anyway, the three expressivity parameters in lines 20 - 22 have the same values, so these values have "overridden" the behavior tendency of the agent, no matter how it was.

Let us now consider the APML input file in Figure 5. As highlighted in bold, the APML file specifies that the agent has to show an *hot anger* emotional state and then *inform* the user about something. Let us imagine to define two agents with the Baselines of Figure 2, and to give them as an input to our system together with the APML file of the example. Figure 6 shows both the Baselines and the evolution of the Dynamiclines of the two agents. To simplify things in the diagrams we focus only on two expressivity parameters: Overall activation (OAC) for the body modality (diagram on the left) and Spatial (SPC) for the gesture modality (diagram on the right). From the diagrams we may notice that for example the *hot anger* state sets the SPC parameter of both Dynamiclines (diagram on the right) to the same value, following the corresponding qualifier definition. On the other hand, for the same *hot anger* state, the OAC parameter of both Dynamiclines (diagram on the left) is a modulation of the Baseline value.

APML input:

```
<?xml version="1.0"?>
<!DOCTYPE apml SYSTEM "apml.dtd" []>

<apml xml:lang="en">

<performative>
    <rheme affect="hot anger">
        what are you<emphasis x-pitchaccent="Hstar">doing</emphasis>
        here
        <boundary type="HH"/>
    </rheme>
</performative>

<performative type="inform">
    You should
    <rheme> leave this place
    <emphasis x-pitchaccent="Hstar">immediately</emphasis>
    <boundary type="H"/>
    </rheme>
</performative>

</apml>
```

Fig. 5. Example of an APML input file

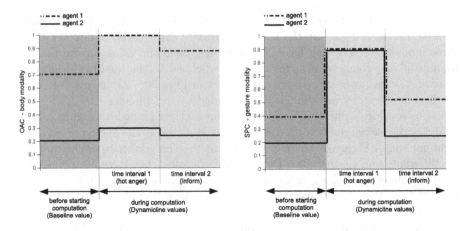

Fig. 6. Evolution of two expressivity parameters (OAC for the body modality on the left diagram and SPC for the gesture modality on the right diagram) for two agents with different Baselines. The diagrams show both the Baselines and the evolution of the Dynamiclines of the two agents.

Fig. 7. Frames taken from two example videos: (1) a very aroused agent; (2) a less expressive agent

5.4 Demo Videos

Two demonstration videos are available for showing the different behaviors obtained from the two Baselines. To generate these videos we have given to our agent a sentence to be spoken, together with the associated communicative intentions and emotional states. We then generated one video for each of the Baselines considered in the example above. Some frames of the two videos are shown in Figure 7. The animations can be seen by downloading the following files from the Internet:

http://www.iut.univ-paris8.fr/greta/clips/gw2007/exuberant.mpg
http://www.iut.univ-paris8.fr/greta/clips/gw2007/indolent.mpg

6   Conclusion

In order to improve the effectiveness of communication of conversational agents we have presented a system in which agents show *distinctive* behaviors. We have defined the concept of Baseline as the general agent's expressivity and tendency in using communicative modalities. Depending on the agent's Baseline, communicative intention and emotional state, our system computes the Dynamicline, which is then used in the processes of behavior selection and generation. The consequence is that we may be able to distinguish the behavior of two agents that have been defined with different Baselines, even if their communicative intentions and/or emotional states are the same.

Acknowledgements

Part of this research is supported by the EU FP6 Network of Excellence HUMAINE (IST-2002-2.3.1.6) and by the EU FP6 Integrated Project Callas (FP6-2005-IST-5).

References

1. Allbeck, J., Badler, N.: Toward representing agent behaviors modified by personality and emotion. In: Workshop on Embodied Conversational Agents - Let's specify and evaluate them!, ACM Press, New York (2002)
2. André, E., Rist, T., Müller, J.: Integrating reactive and scripted behaviors in a life-like presentation agent. In: Second International Conference on Autonomous Agents, pp. 261–268 (1998)
3. Ball, G., Breese, J.: Emotion and personality in a conversational agent. In: Cassell, J., Sullivan, J., Churchill, E. (eds.) Embodied Conversational Characters, MIT Press, Cambridge (2000)
4. Chi, D., Costa, M., Zhao, L., Badler, N.: The EMOTE model for effort and shape. In: Proceedings of the 27th annual conference on Computer graphics and interactive techniques, pp. 173–182. ACM Press/Addison-Wesley, New York (2000)
5. Gallaher, P.E.: Individual differences in nonverbal behavior: Dimensions of style. Journal of Personality and Social Psychology 63(1), 133–145 (1992)
6. Hartmann, B., Mancini, M., Buisine, S., Pelachaud, C.: Design and evaluation of expressive gesture synthesis for embodied conversational agents. In: Third International Joint Conference on Autonomous Agents & Multi-Agent Systems, Utretch, July 2005 (2005)
7. Hartmann, B., Mancini, M., Pelachaud, C.: Towards affective agent action: Modelling expressive ECA gestures. In: International conference on Intelligent User Interfaces - Workshop on Affective Interaction, San Diego, CA (2005)
8. Kipp, M.: Gesture Generation by Imitation. Dissertation.com (2005)
9. Kipp, M.: Creativity meets automation: Combining nonverbal action authoring with rules and machine learning. In: Gratch, J., Young, M., Aylett, R., Ballin, D., Olivier, P. (eds.) IVA 2006. LNCS (LNAI), vol. 4133, pp. 230–242. Springer, Heidelberg (2006)

10. Mancini, M., Bresin, R., Pelachaud, C.: From acoustic cues to an expressive agent. In: Gibet, S., Courty, N., Kamp, J.-F. (eds.) GW 2005. LNCS (LNAI), vol. 3881, pp. 280–291. Springer, Heidelberg (2006)
11. Maya, V., Lamolle, M., Pelachaud, C.: Influences on embodied conversational agent's expressivity: Towards an individualization of the ecas. In: Proceedings of the Artificial Intelligence and the Simulation of Behaviour, Leeds, UK (2004)
12. McNeill, D.: Hand and Mind: What Gestures Reveal about Thought, p. 423. University Of Chicago Press, Chicago (1992)
13. Neff, M., Fiume, E.: AER: Aesthetic Exploration and Refinement for Expressive Character Animation. In: Proceedings of the 2005 ACM SIGGRAPH/Eurographics symposium on Computer animation, pp. 161–170. ACM Press, New York, USA (2005)
14. Noot, H., Ruttkay, Z.: Gesture in style. In: Camurri, A., Volpe, G. (eds.) Gesture-Based Communication in Human-Computer Interaction - Gesture Workshop 2003. LNCS (LNAI), vol. 2915, pp. 324–337. Springer, Heidelberg (2004)
15. Ruttkay, Z., Pelachaud, C., Poggi, I., Noot, H.: Exercises of style for virtual humans. In: Canamero, L., Aylett, R. (eds.) Animating Expressive Characters for Social Interactions, J. Benjamins Publishing
16. Wallbott, H.G.: Bodily expression of emotion. European Journal of Social Psychology 28, 879–896 (1998)
17. Wallbott, H.G., Scherer, K.R.: Cues and channels in emotion recognition. Journal of Personality and Social Psychology 51(4), 690–699 (1986)

Creating Rapport with Virtual Agents

Jonathan Gratch, Ning Wang, Jillian Gerten, Edward Fast, and Robin Duffy

University of Southern California
Institute for Creative Technologies
13274 Fiji Way, Marina del Rey, CA, 90405, USA
{gratch,nwang,gerten,fast}@ict.usc.edu

Abstract. Recent research has established the potential for virtual characters to establish rapport with humans through simple contingent nonverbal behaviors. We hypothesized that the contingency, not just the frequency of positive feedback is crucial when it comes to creating rapport. The primary goal in this study was evaluative: can an agent generate behavior that engenders feelings of rapport in human speakers and how does this compare to human generated feedback? A secondary goal was to answer the question: Is contingency (as opposed to frequency) of agent feedback crucial when it comes to creating feelings of rapport? Results suggest that contingency matters when it comes to creating rapport and that agent generated behavior was as good as human listeners in creating rapport. A "virtual human listener" condition performed worse than other conditions.

Keywords: Rapport, virtual agents, evaluation.

1 Introduction

You know that harmony, fluidity, synchrony, flow one feels when engaged in a good conversation with someone? Known formally as *rapport*, these features are prototypical characteristics of many successful interactions. Speakers seem tightly enmeshed in something like a dance. They rapidly detect and respond to each other's movements. Tickle-Degnen and Rosenthal [1] equate rapport with behaviors indicating positive emotions (e.g. head nods or smiles), mutual attentiveness (e.g. mutual gaze), and coordination (e.g. postural mimicry or synchronized movements). Numerous studies have demonstrated that, when established, rapport facilitates a wide range of social interactions including negotiations [2], management [3], psychotherapy [4], teaching [5] and caregiving [6].

Several research groups are currently exploring the potential of embodied agents to establish rapport with humans through simple contingent nonverbal behavior. Such systems, for example, can generate positive feedback (e.g., nods) by recognizing and responding to vocal or behavioral cues of a human speaker [7-13]. Further, there is growing empirical evidence that such simple contingent behaviors can make agents more engaging [9, 14, 15] and persuasive [13], promote fluent speech [9, 14] and reduce user frustration [12]. These effects can be subtle; many studies indicate the benefits of such feedback fall outside of conscious awareness in that people often show measurable impacts on their observable behavior without reporting significant differences when introspecting upon their experience.

C. Pelachaud et al. (Eds.): IVA 2007, LNAI 4722, pp. 125–138, 2007.
© Springer-Verlag Berlin Heidelberg 2007

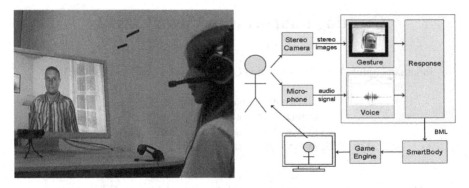

Fig. 1. A speaker interacting with the Rapport Agent (left) and the system architecture (right)

Our research on the Rapport Agent [9] investigates how virtual characters can elicit the harmony, fluidity, synchrony, flow one feels when achieving rapport. Among human dyads, rapport can be conceptualized as a phenomenon occurring on three levels: the emotional, the behavioral, and the cognitive. Emotionally, rapport is an inherently rewarding experience; we feel a harmony, a flow. Cognitively, we share an understanding with our conversation partner; there is a convergence of beliefs or views, a bridging of ideas or perspectives. Behaviorally (or interactionally), there is a convergence of movements with our conversational partner; observers report increased synchrony, fluidity and coordination in partners' movements. Are virtual characters capable of establishing rapport with us, on each of these levels, when we are their conversation partners?

Although our primary goal in this study was evaluative (i.e., can agent-generated behavior engender feelings of rapport in human speakers comparable to that of real human listeners?), a secondary goal of ours was to attempt to answer the question: Is contingency, not just the frequency of positive feedback in agents, crucial when it comes to creating feelings of rapport? We define *contingent feedback* as nonverbal movements by a listener (e.g, nods or posture shifts) that are tightly coupled to what the speaker is doing in the moment and *non-contingent feedback* as listener movements that share the same frequency and characteristics of contingent feedback divorced from what the speaker is doing in the moment. In other words, does feedback have to be tightly coupled to what the speaker is doing *in the moment* (imposing fairly challenging computational requirements) or would random positive feedback suffice (greatly simplifying the task of embodied agent design)? This article describes our current progress on addressing these questions.

Rapport Agent and Prior findings

The Rapport Agent is designed to elicit rapport from human participants within the confines of a dyadic narrative task. In this setting, a speaker (the narrator) retells some previously observed series of events (i.e., the events in a sexual harassment awareness and prevention video) to a graphical character. The speaker is led to believe that the character accurately reflects the nonverbal feedback of a human listener. In fact, these movements are generated by the Rapport Agent (see Figure 1).

The central challenge for the rapport agent is to provide the nonverbal listening feedback associated with rapportful interactions. Such feedback includes the use of backchannel continuers [16] (nods, elicited by speaker prosodic cues, that signify the communication is working), postural mirroring, and mimicry of certain head gestures (e.g., gaze shifts and head nods). The Rapport Agent generates such feedback by real-time analysis of acoustic properties of speech (detecting backchannel opportunity points, disfluencies, questions, and loudness) and speaker gestures (detecting head nods, shakes, gaze shifts and posture shifts).

Prior evaluations have demonstrated the Rapport Agent's social impact at the emotional and behavioral levels when contrasted with either an "unresponsive agent" that produced random, neutral (as opposed to positive) behaviors or with visible human listeners [9, 14]. The Rapport Agent produced benefits at the emotional level through increased speaker engagement (as indexed by duration of the interaction and the number of meaningful words produced). It produced improvements at the behavioral or interactional level when compared with the unresponsive agent (as indexed by the number and rate of disfluencies). We have not addressed the question of influences at the cognitive level.

Although these prior studies have demonstrated a social impact, it is less clear what aspects of agent behavior are critical and where improvements can be made. One relevant fact is the *form* of the feedback. People utilize a variety of behavioral movements, posture shifts, and facial expressions, and some research has shown that subtle features of how these behaviors are expressed can influence interpretation. For example, Krumhuber et al. showed that variation in the onset and offset rates of facial expressions would influence interpretations of trust and sincerity [17]. One way to gain insight into such factors is to capture the actual nonverbal feedback displayed by human listeners and use this to drive the behavior of virtual characters.

Another relevant factor in the establishment of rapport is the *contingency* of feedback: does listener feedback have to be contingent on speaker behavior? Few empirical studies of embodied agents have specifically controlled for the contingency of behavior. For example, studies of the Rapport agent [9, 14] did not control separately for the contingency and the distribution of feedback, leaving open the possibility that *frequency of feedback* is the crucial variable when it comes to creating rapport and that non-contingent (i.e., randomly timed) head nods and posture shifts could be just as effective as well-timed feedback when it comes to creating feelings of rapport, obviating the need for complex techniques for sensing user behavior.

When contingency has been carefully controlled, empirical findings are mixed. For example, Bailenson and Yee found a significant increase in the persuasiveness of virtual characters if they mirrored a human listener's head motion with a four second delay [13]. On the other hand, Burleson found no significant difference on a number of dependent variables from a similar mirroring intervention [18], though a recent post-hoc analysis suggests an interaction dependent on gender [12]. Research on delays in human-to-human interaction also has shown a mixed relationship with rapport. [19]. Collectively, such findings point to a need to further investigate the role of contingency in the context of listener feedback.

The present study seeks to deepen and generalize our prior findings on the cognitive, emotional and behavioral impact of rapport and to specifically investigate the role of contingency.

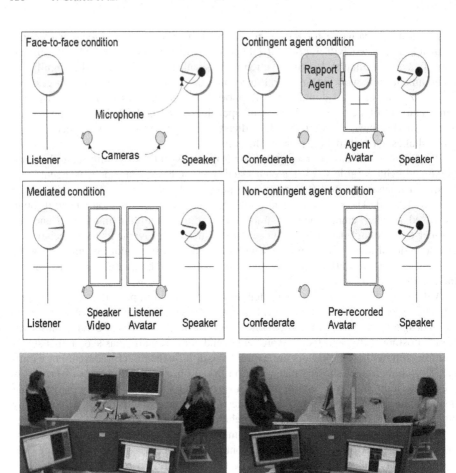

Fig. 2. Graphical depiction of the four conditions. The actual face-to-face condition is illustrated on the lower left and the setup for the other three conditions on the lower right.

2 Method

One-hundred thirty-one people (61% women, 39% men) from the general Los Angeles area participated in this study. They were recruited by responding to recruitment posters posted on Craigslist.com and were compensated $20 for one hour of their participation. On average, the participants were 37.5 years old ($min = 18$, $max = 60$, $std = 11.3$) with 15.6 years of education ($min = 5$, $max = 24$, $std = 3.0$). For female subjects, the average age is 38.7 ($min = 20$, $max = 60$, $std = 11.4$), and the average years of education is 15.7 ($min = 5$, $max = 24$, $std = 3.3$). For male subjects, the average age is 35.7 ($min = 18$, $max = 59$, $std = 11.1$), and the average years of education is 13.7 ($min = 10$, $max = 20$, $std = 2.5$).

Design

To investigate the importance of feedback form and contingency, we studied two kinds of virtual characters: one, a "good virtual listener" (the "Responsive" condition) using the Rapport Agent to synthesizes head gestures and posture shifts in response to features of a real human speaker's speech and movements, and the other, a "virtual representation of a real listener" (the "Mediated" condition), which reproduces the actual head movements and posture shifts of a real human listener. To investigate whether these two characters could engender feelings of rapport in human speakers comparable to that of real human listeners, we added a "face-to-face" condition, in which speakers spoke directly to real human listeners, for comparison. In a fourth condition, we created "a non-contingent response virtual listener" that provided positive feedback that was un-synchronized with the speaker's movements and speech. Equivalence in feedback frequency across conditions was created by experimental design.

The study design was a between-subjects experiment with four conditions: Face-to-face (n = 40: 20 speakers, 20 listeners), Mediated (n = 40: 20 speakers, 20 listeners), Responsive (n = 24), and Non-contingent (n = 24), to which participants were randomly assigned using a coin flip. A confederate listener was used in the Responsive and Non-Contingent conditions.

Face to Face. In the Face-to-face condition, the participant talked to a human listener face-to-face.

Mediated. In the Mediated condition, the participant interacted with a virtual character whose head movements and posture were copied from the movements of a real human listener. Through the use of stereo camera and image-based tracking software, the head position and orientation of the listener were captured and displayed by a virtual human character to the speaker. Facial expression feedback was not recognized or displayed.

Responsive. In the Responsive condition, the participant interacted with a virtual character displaying proper listening behaviors. These behaviors were contingent on the recognition of features of the participant's speech (acquired by microphone) and head movements (acquired by a stereo camera) and driven according to predefined behavior-mapping rules (see [9]). For example, certain prosodic contours in the speaker's voice would cause the character to nod and mirror posture shifts. Facial expressions were not generated.

Non-contingent. Finally, in the Non-contingent condition, the participant interacted with a virtual character whose behaviors are identical to the responsive condition in terms of their frequency and dynamics, but not contingent on the behaviors of the speaker. Each subject is presented with a pre-recorded behavior sequence taken from the responsive condition. Equivalence in feedback frequency across conditions was created by experimental design: Following the "yoking" design of Bailenson and Yee [13], the behavior corresponded to what was seen by the previous speaker in the Responsive condition (i.e., each Non-contingent speaker was paired with a Responsive speaker, and saw their feedback).[1]

---

[1] In the case where duration of the Non-contingent session is longer than the last Responsive session, the system would loop to the beginning of the recording.

Procedure

Participants in groups of two entered the laboratory and were told they were participating in a study to evaluate a communicative technology. The experimenter informed
participants:

*The study we are doing here today is to evaluate a communicative technology that's
developed here. An example of the communicative technology is a web-camera used
to chat with your friends and family.*

After subjects signed the consent form and completed the pre-questionnaire, the
experimenter asked the question "what's your favorite animal?" The subject whose
answer came first alphabetically was assigned the speaker role and the other subject
was assigned the listener role. In the Responsive and Non-contingent conditions, the
confederate always gave the answer "zebra" to ensure their being assigned to the
listener role.

Next, subjects were led to two separate side rooms to fill out the pre-questionnaire.

After both subjects completed the pre-questionnaire, subjects were led into the
computer room. The experimenter then explained the procedure and introduced participants to the equipment used in the experiment.

Next, the speaker remained in the computer room while the listener was led to a
separate side room to wait. The speaker then viewed a short segment of a video clip
taken from the Edge Training Systems, Inc. Sexual Harassment Awareness video. The
video clip was merged from two clips: The first, "CyberStalker," is about a woman at
work who receives unwanted instant messages from a colleague at work (CLIP 1),
and the second, "That's an Order!", is about a man at work who is confronted by a
female business associate, who asks him for a foot massage in return for her business
(CLIP 2).

After the speaker finished viewing the video, the listener was led back into the
computer room, where the speaker was instructed to retell the stories portrayed in the
clips to the listener.

Speakers in all conditions (except the face-to-face condition) sat in front of a 30-
inch computer monitor and sat approximately 8 feet apart from the listener, who sat in
front of a 19-inch computer monitor. They could not see each other, being separated
by a screen. The speaker saw an animated character displayed on the 30-inch computer monitor. Speakers in all conditions (but the face-to-face condition) were told
that the avatar on the screen represents the human listener. While the speaker spoke,
the listener could see a real time video image of the speaker retelling the story displayed on the 19-inch computer monitor. The monitor was fitted with a stereo camera
system and a camcorder. For capturing high-quality audio, the subject wore a light-
weight close-talking microphone and spoke into a microphone headset.

Next, the experimenter led the speaker to a separate side room. The speaker completed the post-questionnaire while the listener remained in the computer room and
spoke to the camera what he/she had been told by the speaker.

Finally, participants were debriefed individually and probed for suspicion using the
protocol from Aronson, Ellsworth, Carlsmith, and Gonzales [20]. No participants
indicated that they believed the listener was a confederate in the study.

Equipment

To produce listening behaviors, the Rapport agent first collects and analyzes the features from the speaker's voice and upper-body movements. Two Videre Design Small Vision System stereo cameras were placed in front of the speaker and listener to capture their movements. Watson, an image-based tracking library developed by Louis-Phillipe Morency, uses images captured by the stereo cameras to track the subjects' head position and orientation [21]. Watson also incorporates learned motion classifiers that detect head nods and shakes from a vector of head velocities. Both the speaker and listener wore a headset with microphone. Acoustic features are derived from properties of the pitch and intensity of the speech signal using a signal processing package, LAUN, developed by Mathieu Morales [9].

Three Panasonic PV-GS180 camcorders were used to videotape the experiment: one was placed in front the speaker, one in front of the listener, and one was attached to the ceiling to record both speaker and listener. The camcorder that was in front of the speaker was connected to the computer monitor in front of the listener, in order to display video images of the speaker to the listener.

Four desktop computers were used in the experiment: two DELL Precision 670 computers, one with Intel Xeon 3.2 GHz CPU and 2 GB of RAM (for speaker) and another one with Intel Xeon 3.80 GHz CPU and 2 GB of RAM (for listener), run Watson and record stereo camera images, one DELL Precision 690 (Intel Xeon 3.73 GHz CPU with 3 GB of RAM) runs the experiment system and one DELL Precision 530 (Intel Xeon 1.7 GHz with 1 GB of RAM) stores logs.

The animated agent was displayed on a 30-inch Apple display to approximate the size of a real life listener sitting 8 feet away. The video of the speaker was displayed on a 19-inch Dell monitor to the listener.

Measures

Rapport scale. We constructed a 10-item rapport scale (coefficient alpha = .89), presented to speakers in the post-questionnaire. This scale was measured with a 9 point metric (0 = Disagree Strongly; 8 = Agree Strongly). Sample items include: "I think the listener and I established a rapport" and "I felt I was able to engage the listener with my story."

Emotional rapport. We indexed the emotional component of rapport using the item "I felt I had a connection with the listener." This is taken from the Rapport scale listed above.

Cognitive rapport. We indexed the cognitive component of rapport using the item "I think that the listener and I understood each other." This is taken from the Rapport scale listed above.

Behavioral or interactional rapport. Behavioral or interactional measures of rapport included duration or speech, word count, number of pausefillers, number of prolonged words, number of incomplete words, number of disfluencies (pausefillers + incomplete words), number of meaningful words (wordcount-pausefillers-incomplete words), and variations thereof (i.e., calculations per word and per minute).

Helpfulness, distraction, agent naturalness. For helpfulness and distraction scla, we constructed 2 items for each scale, with Cronbach's alpha coefficient of .64 and .49, respectively. These scales were measured with a 9 point metric (0 = Disagree Strongly; 8 = Agree Strongly). We also constructed a 6-item agent naturalness scale, with Cronbach's alpha coefficient of .77. This scale was measured with a 9 point metric (0 = Disagree Strongly; 8 = Agree Strongly). These three scales were issued to speakers in the post-questionnaire. These scales indexed how helpful the listener's feedback was, how distracting the listener's feedback was, and how natural the agent appeared to be, respectively.

Performance. Speakers' self-assessed performance in the speaking task was measured using this scale we constructed (coefficient alpha = .85). Sample items include: "I think I did a good job telling the story" and "I had difficulty explaining the story" (reverse coded). This scale was issued in the post-questionnaire.

Trustworthiness and Likableness. Speakers from all conditions were asked to evaluate the listener on these traits, using the items 'likeable' and 'trustworthy' taken from the dependent measure used in the Krumhuber, Manstead, Cosker, Marshall, and Rosin study [17]. This scale was measured with an 8 point metric (0 = Not At All; 7 = Very). These items were issued in the post-questionnaire packet.

Pre-questionnaire packet. In addition to the scales listed above, the pre-questionnaire packet also contained questions about one's demographic background, personality [22], self-monitoring [23], self-consciousness [24] and shyness [25]. Scales ranged from 1 (disagree strongly) to 5 (agree strongly). Speakers and listeners from all conditions filled out the pre-questionnaire.

Post-questionnaire packet. In addition to the scales listed above, the post-questionnaire packet also contained questions to examine speaker self-focus, other-focus, embarrassment, and speaker's goals while explaining the video. Scales from [17] range from 0 (not at all) to 7 (very). Other scales ranged from 0 (disagree strongly to 8 (agree strongly). It was completed by speakers across all conditions.

3   Results

Although our primary goal in this study was evaluative (i.e., do the agents we created engender feelings of rapport in human speakers comparable to that of real human listeners?), a secondary goal of ours was to attempt to answer the question: Is contingency, not just the frequency of feedback in agents, crucial when it comes to creating feelings of rapport?

To investigate whether embodied agents could engender feelings of rapport in human speakers comparable to that of real human listeners, we performed a pairwise means analysis on rapport means across these 4 conditions using the Tukey test (see Table 1). Results indicate that the responsive agent was as good as human listeners in creating rapport, but that the mediated avatar was not, with the mediated avatar eliciting less rapport, as captured by our self report scale, and more pause fillers (each in terms of raw counts, rate, and per word) than a real human listener. The mediated avatar also elicited more prolonged words (each in terms of raw counts, rate, and per word) than in the responsive condition. As compared with real human listeners in the face-to-face condition, the non-contingent agent elicited more speaker pause fillers. Although the mediated avatar was as likeable and trustworthy, it was found to be less helpful and more distracting than either a real human listener or the responsive agent, and to be less natural than the responsive agent. The non-contingent agent was also found to be more distracting than a real human listener. The responsive agent, however, was found to be less trustworthy than human listeners. Speakers rated themselves as performing equally well across all conditions.

Table 1. Tukey Table of Means for Speakers

Measures	Non-Contingent	Responsive	Mediated	F-to-F
Helpful	5.44	5.73b	4.43b,c	5.85c
Distracting	3.64a	2.62b	4.15b,c	2.45a,c
Trustworthy	4.56	3.65d	4.40	4.89 d
Likeable	4.67	4.15	4.55	4.63
Natural Agent	3.12	3.79b	2.63b	NA
Performance	5.20	5.22	5.50	5.52
Rapport Scale	4.79	5.04	4.46c	5.53c
Emo Rapport	4.56	4.65	4.20	5.60
Cog Rapport	4.88	5.35	4.80	5.55
Beh Rapport:				
Duration	144	131	139	115
Word Count	403	345	353	319
Pausefiller Count	14.00a	13.08	15.40c	6.75a,c
Prolonged Count	3.96	3.00b	7.00b	4.60
Incomplete Word Count	5.56	3.92	3.70	4.55
Disfluency Count	19.56	17.00	19.10	11.30
Meaningful Word Count	384	328	334	308
Word Rate	166	158	152	169
Pausefiller Rate	6.08	5.66	6.89c	3.60 c
Prolonged Rate	1.56	1.40b	2.82b	2.12
Incomplete Word Rate	2.26	1.75	1.53	2.26
Disfluency Rate	8.33	7.41	8.42	5.86
Meaningful Rate	157	151	144	163
Pausefiller per Word	.04	.04	.05c	.02c
Prolonged per Word	.01	.01b	.02b	.01
Incomplete Wd per Word	.01	.01	.01	.01
Disfluency per Word	.05	.05	.06	.03
Meaningful per Word	.95	.95	.94	.97

Note, columns share the same subscripts connote a significant difference at an alpha level of .05 between them.

To answer the question as to whether contingency of feedback is crucial when it comes to creating feelings of rapport, participants across the Non-contingent agent and Responsive agent conditions were paired by feedback frequency, and a dependent samples t-test was conducted, comparing the rapport means across conditions. This analysis was chosen because equivalency in feedback frequency across conditions was created by experimental design: A feedback recording taken from the Agents in the Responsive condition was replayed to speakers in the Non-contingent condition.[2] However, because the same feedback tape from the Responsive condition was sometimes played to more than one participant in the Non-Contingent condition, to obtain one-to-one correspondence for this analysis, a randomly selected subsample of participants was drawn from those participants who shared the same feedback tape. Using this procedure, in effect, controlling for feedback frequency, all rapport variables were examined. Figure 3 shows that the total number of words spoken was significantly greater for speakers interacting with non-contingent agent ($M = 458.83$) than with the responsive agent ($M = 299.17$, $t (11) = 2.17$, $p = .05$), the raw number of pause fillers was significantly greater for speakers interacting with the non-contingent agent ($M = 15.75$) than with the responsive agent ($M = 8.00$, $t (11) = 3.06$, $p = .01$), the pause filler rate was significantly greater for speakers interacting with the non-contingent agent ($M = 6.11$) than with the responsive agent ($M = 3.80$, $t (11) = 2.44$, $p = .03$), and the raw number of disfluencies was significantly greater for speakers interacting with the non-contingent agent ($M = 22.17$) than with the responsive agent ($M = 11.75$, $t (11) = 2.30$, $p = .04$), suggesting that contingency matters.

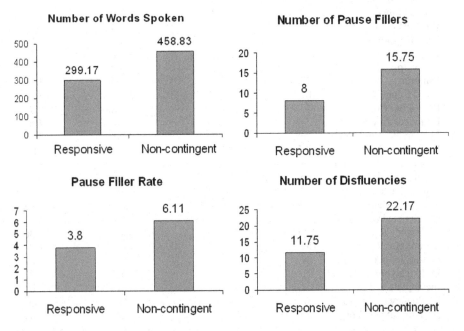

Fig. 3. Significant differences were found in number of words spoken, number of pause fillers, pause filler rate and number of disfluencies between speakers interacting with Responsive agent and with the Non-contingent agent

---

[2] As individual speakers vary in the length of their narrative, the frequency of feedback is not strictly identical as the non-contingent behavior may be either a shortened or looped display of the Responsive behavior.

4   Discussion and Future Work

The primary goal in this study was evaluative: Do the two agents we created engender feelings of rapport in human speakers comparable to that of real human listeners? A secondary goal was to answer the question: Is contingency (as opposed to frequency) of agent feedback crucial when it comes to creating feelings of rapport?

Results indicate that the responsive agent was as effective as human listeners in creating rapport, but that the mediated avatar was not as effective, with the mediated avatar eliciting less rapport, as captured by our self report scale, and by some of our behavioral/interactional indices. Although the mediated avatar was as likeable and trustworthy, it was found to be less helpful and more distracting than either a real human listener or the responsive agent we created. Several factors could have contributed to relatively poor performance of the mediated condition. It is possible that listeners in the mediated condition gave less visible feedback. For example, the Rapport Agent always generates bodily feedback (nods, posture shifts) in response to speaker cues; however human listeners often responded with facial feedback that would be seen in the face-to-face condition but was not recognized or displayed in the mediated condition. Listeners may have also felt less engaged from watching a video than listeners in the face-to-face condition and therefore exhibited less feedback. Finally, there may have been subtle errors introduced by the video processing equipment that disrupted rapport. A direction for future studies is to understand the factors that contributed to the lower measures for the mediated condition.

Controlling for the frequency of feedback, some behavioral indices of rapport were significantly greater for speakers interacting with the non-contingent agent than with the responsive agent, suggesting that contingency of agent feedback matters when it comes to creating virtual rapport. This is the first experimental evidence supporting this (often unspoken) assumption of much embodied agent research.

Several open questions remain for future work. The current study reveals interesting differences in the impact of virtual character behavior on rapport-related variables when compared with our prior experimental findings. For example, a previous study [14] found that subjects spoke significantly longer in the responsive condition when compared to face-to-face, whereas the current study found no significant difference on this dimension. One key difference in the current study is the use of more provocative narrative content – a sexual harassment video as opposed to a funny cartoon. One may expect subjects to be less comfortable and more concerned with impression management (e.g., using "politically correct" terminology in their narratives). These factors would be expected to negatively impact rapport, though their differential impact across conditions is unclear.

Another important question is how to provide more semantically meaningful feedback to the speaker. The Rapport Agent responds without attending to the content of the speaker's narrative. Such feedback has been called *envelope feedback* [26] or *generic feedback* [27] and, despite being non-specific to the meaning of speech, plays an important interaction function. It seems to signal "everything is ok, please continue," or "I'm paying attention", and can contribute to a sense of mutual understanding and liking; factors associated with rapport. Several studies have demonstrated that envelope feedback can be woefully inadequate in certain contexts if not bolstered by *specific,* or *content feedback,* that makes reference to the content of the speech. For example, Bavelas et al. [27] found when speakers were telling personally emotional stories, storytellers expected emotional feedback to key events in the story and found it hard to construct effective narratives without it. A major challenge is how to recognize and respond meaningfully to a speaker with the rapidity seen in human dyads. See [28, 29] for some initial explorations in this direction.

Finally, within the virtual human's community, rapport has been conceptualized as short-term construct that arises in a single interaction, as discussed here, or as a deepening sense of interdependence that arises over time [30, 31]. Both approaches, however, demand greater attention to multi-modal recognition, a greater understanding of the functional role nonverbal behavior plays in co-construction of meaning and deeper models of the social cognitions that underlie the generation and interpretation such reciprocal behaviors. As such, rapport can serve as a productive theoretical construct to propel the advancement of virtual human research.

Overall, the current study and related findings add further evidence that the nonverbal behavior of virtual characters influence the behavior of the humans that interact with them. This gives confidence that embodied agents can facilitate social interaction between humans and computers, with a host of implications for application and social psychological research.

Acknowledgments. We are grateful for the substantive contributions of a number of individuals. Wendy Treynor played an indispensable role in the experimental design and data analysis, and contributed to the draft. Jeremy Bailenson, Anya Okhmatovskaia and Alison Wiener also gave valuable input to the experimental design. Sue Duncan, Nicole Kraemer and Nigel Ward informed the theoretical underpinnings of the work. We also thank Edge Training Systems, Inc., 9710 Farrar Court, Suite P, Richmond, VA 23236, for granting us the right to use their vignettes in our research. This work was sponsored by the U.S. Army Research, Development, and Engineering Command (RDECOM), and the content does not necessarily reflect the position or the policy of the Government, and no official endorsement should be inferred.

References

1. Tickle-Degnen, L., Rosenthal, R.: The Nature of Rapport and its Nonverbal Correlates. Psychological Inquiry 1(4), 285–293 (1990)
2. Drolet, A.L., Morris, M.W.: Rapport in conflict resolution: accounting for how face-to-face contact fosters mutual cooperation in mixed-motive conflicts. Experimental Social Psychology 36, 26–50 (2000)
3. Cogger, J.W.: Are you a skilled interviewer? Personnel Journal 61, 840–843 (1982)
4. Tsui, P., Schultz, G.L.: Failure of Rapport: Why psychotheraputic engagement fails in the treatment of Asian clients. American Journal of Orthopsychiatry 55, 561–569 (1985)
5. Fuchs, D.: Examiner familiarity effects on test performance: implications for training and practice. Topics in Early Childhood Special Education 7, 90–104 (1987)
6. Burns, M.: Rapport and relationships: The basis of child care. Journal of Child Care 2, 47–57 (1984)
7. Tosa, N.: Neurobaby. In: ACM SIGGRAPH, pp. 212–213 (1993)

8. Breazeal, C., Aryananda, L.: Recognition of Affective Communicative Intent in Robot-Directed Speech. Autonomous Robots 12, 83–104 (2002)
9. Gratch, J., et al.: Virtual Rapport. In: Gratch, J., Young, M., Aylett, R., Ballin, D., Olivier, P. (eds.) IVA 2006. LNCS (LNAI), vol. 4133, Springer, Heidelberg (2006)
10. Cassell, J., Thórisson, K.R.: The Power of a Nod and a Glance: Envelope vs. Emotional Feedback in Animated Conversational Agents. International Journal of Applied Artificial Intelligence 13(4-5), 519–538 (1999)
11. Brand, M.: Voice puppetry. In: ACM SIGGRAPH, ACM Press/Addison-Wesley Publishing Co, New York (1999)
12. Burleson, W., Picard, R.W.: Evidence for Gender Specific Approaches to the Development of Emotionally Intelligent Learning Companions. In: IEEE Intelligent Systems, Special issue on Intelligent Educational Systems (July/August 2007)
13. Bailenson, J.N., Yee, N.: Digital Chameleons: Automatic assimilation of nonverbal gestures in immersive virtual environments. Psychological Science 16, 814–819 (2005)
14. Gratch, J., et al.: Can virtual humans be more engaging than real ones? In: 12th International Conference on Human-Computer Interaction, Beijing, China (2007)
15. Smith, J.: GrandChair: Conversational Collection of Family Stories, Media Lab. MIT, Cambridge (2000)
16. Ward, N., Tsukahara, W.: Prosodic features which cue back-channel responses in English and Japanese. Journal of Pragmatics 23, 1177–1207 (2000)
17. Krumhuber, E., et al.: Temporal aspects of smiles influence employment decisions: A comparison of human and synthetic faces. In: 11th European Conference Facial Expressions: Measurement and Meaning, Durham, United Kingdom (2005)
18. Burleson, W.: Affective Learning Companions: Strategies for Empathetic Agents with Real-Time Multimodal Affective Sensing to Foster Meta-Cognitive and Meta-Affective Approaches to Learning, Motivation, and Perseverance. MIT Media Lab, Boston (Unpublished PhD Thesis, 2006)
19. Manning, T.R., Goetz, E.T., Street, R.L.: Signal delay effects on rapport in telepsychiatry. CyberPsychology and Behavior 3(2), 119–127 (2000)
20. Aronson, E., et al.: Methods of Research in Social Psychology, 2nd edn. McGraw-Hill, New York (1990)
21. Morency, L.-P., et al.: Contextual Recognition of Head Gestures. In: 7th International Conference on Multimodal Interactions, Toronto, Italy (2005)
22. John, O.P., Srivastava, S.: The Big-Five trait taxonomy: History, measurement, and theoretical perspectives. Handbook of personality: Theory and research 2, 102–138 (1999)
23. Lennox, R.D., Wolfe, R.N.: Revision of the Self-Monitoring Scale. Journal of Personality and Social psychology 46, 1349–1364 (1984)
24. Scheier, M.F., Carver, C.S.: The Self-Consciousness Scale: A revised version for use with general populations. Journal of Applied Social Psychology 15, 687–699 (1985)
25. Cheek, J.M.: The Revised Cheek and Buss Shyness Scale (RCBS). Wellesley College, Wellesley MA (1983)
26. Thórisson, K.R.: Communicative Humanoids: A Computational Model of Psycho-Social Dialogue Skills. In: The Media Lab, Massachusetts Institute of Technology (1996)
27. Bavelas, J.B., Coates, L., Johnson, T.: Listeners as Co-narrators. Journal of Personality and Social Psychology 79(6), 941–952 (2000)
28. Jondottir, G.R., et al.: Fluid Semantic Back-Channel Feedback in Dialogue: Challenges and Progress. In: Pelachaud, C., et al. (eds.) IVA 2007. LNCS (LNAI), vol. 4722, pp. 154–160. Springer, Heidelberg (2007)

29. Heylen, D.: Challenges Ahead. Head Movements and other social acts in conversation. In: AISB, Hertfordshire, UK (2005)
30. Cassell, J., Bickmore, T.: Negotiated Collusion: Modeling social language and its relationship effects in intelligent agents. User Modeling and Adaptive Interfaces 12, 1–44 (2002)
31. Cassell, J., Gill, A., Tepper, P.: Conversational Coordination and Rapport. In: Proceedings of Workshop on Embodied Language Processing at ACL 2007, Prague, CZ (2007)

Incremental Multimodal Feedback for Conversational Agents

Stefan Kopp, Thorsten Stocksmeier, and Dafydd Gibbon

Artificial Intelligence Group, Faculty of Technology, University of Bielefeld
Faculty of Linguistics and Literature, University of Bielefeld
D-33594 Bielefeld, Germany
{skopp,tstocksm}@techfak.uni-bielefeld.de
gibbon@uni-bielefeld.de

Abstract. Just like humans, conversational computer systems should not listen silently to their input and then respond. Instead, they should enforce the speaker-listener link by attending actively and giving feedback on an utterance while perceiving it. Most existing systems produce direct feedback responses to decisive (e.g. prosodic) cues. We present a framework that conceives of feedback as a more complex system, resulting from the interplay of conventionalized responses to eliciting speaker events and the multimodal behavior that signals how internal states of the listener evolve. A model for producing such incremental feedback, based on multi-layered processes for perceiving, understanding, and evaluating input, is described.

1   Introduction

When humans talk to each other they regularly give feedback to the dialog partner using body movements and short utterances. This phenomenon has long been overlooked by research as it was considered a negligible by-product of the actual utterances produced by the speakers. This was changed radically by the work of Yngve [17], who put the topic of feedback (which he called back-channel) into the research limelight. Since then, a growing body of knowledge has accumulated across several disciplines.

Feedback is an important foundation for the construal of common ground between interlocutors. From this point of view communication is seen as a collaboration between interlocutors, who cooperate to establish common mutual beliefs. This involves explicit contributions that bear an acceptance phase, signaling that the hearer believes she understood the content of some other contribution [5]. More generally, feedback consists of those methods that allow for providing, in unobtrusive ways and without interrupting or breaking dialog rules, information about the most basic communicative functions in face-to-face dialogue. It consists of unobtrusive (usually short) expressions whereby a recipient of information informs the contributor about her/his ability and willingness to communicative (have contact), to perceive the information, and to understand

C. Pelachaud et al. (Eds.): IVA 2007, LNAI 4722, pp. 139–146, 2007.
© Springer-Verlag Berlin Heidelberg 2007

the information (Allwood et al., 1992). That is, feedback serves as an early warning system to signal how speech perception or understanding is succeeding. A feedback utterance can communicate to the speaker that she should, e.g., repeat the previous utterance and speak more clearly, or use words that are easier to understand. Additionally, feedback communicates whether the recipient is accepting the main evocative intention about the contribution, i.e. can a statement be believed, a question be answered, or a request be complied with. Furthermore, feedback can indicate the emotions and attitudes triggered by the information in the recipient.

The essential role of feedback in natural communication makes it a crucial issue in the development of artificial conversational agents. Yet, many conversational systems still fall silent and remain immobile while listening. Only in the last ten years or so, starting with [15], has feedback been increasingly adopted in conversational systems and this work is still in its infancy. We follow an approach that conceives feedback as resulting from an interplay of multimodal, multi-layered and incremental mechanisms involved in perceiving, understanding, and evaluating input. In this paper we present work on modeling multimodal feedback that way with our virtual human Max [10]. After discussing related work in Sect. 2, we will present in Sect. 3 an integrated model that accounts for two important origins of backchannel feedback, the latter of which has not gained sufficient attention in existing work so far: the more or less automatic ways feedback is produced to respond to eliciting cues from a speaker, and its function to signal to the speaker significant changes in the listener's mental or emotional states towards the incoming utterance. Sect. 4 will describe a first implementation of this model in the virtual human Max.

2   Related Work

A lot of work on conversational systems have, implicitly or explicitly, tackled the problem of how to generate feedback. With respect to explicit modeling attempts, most researches have concentrated on one modality at a time, often resulting from contributions of linguistics that center on verbal feedback (but see more recent work including head movements or shakes [1]). Moreover, most existing systems do not deal with feedback holistically so as to search for models that account for the basis and variety of the behavior, but concentrate on questions regarding *when* humans produce feedback or *which* feedback they perform. Ward and Tsukahara [16] describe a pause-duration model that can be stated in a rule-based fashion: After a relatively low pitch for at least 110ms, following at least 700ms of speech, and given that you have not output back-channel feedback within the preceding 800ms, wait another 700ms and then produce back-channel feedback. Takeuchi et al. [14] augment this approach with incrementally obtained information about word classes. Fujie et al. [6] employ a network of finite state transducers for mapping recognized words onto possible feedback of the robot ROBISUKE that can generate verbal backchannels along with short head nods for feedback. Evaluation studies showed that such models are able to predict feedback only to a limited extent. Cathcart et al. [4] evaluated three different approaches: (1) the baseline model simply inserts a feedback utterance every n words and achieves an accuracy of only 6% ($n{=}7$); (2) the pause duration model gives feedback after silent pauses of a certain length, often combined with part-of-speech information, and achieves 32% accuracy; (3) integrating both methods increased accuracy to 35%.

Among explicit modeling attempts, the Gandalf system [15] employs pause duration models to generate agent feedback and simulated turn-taking behavior by looking away from the listener while speaking, returning his gaze when finishing the turn. The REA system [3] built on this pause duration model and included further modalities (head nods, short feedback utterances). The AutoTutor system [7] deliberatively utilizes positive (Great!), neutral (Umm), or negative feedback (Wrong) to enhance learning by the student. Such feedback is modeled as didactic dialogue moves triggered by fuzzy production rules.

Gratch et al. [8] describe an experiment on multimodal, nonverbal agent feedback and its effects on the establishment of rapport. Their Rapport Agent gives feedback to a human speaker whose head moves and body posture is analyzed through a camera. Implementing the pitch cue algorithm of Ward and Tsukahara [16], the system determines the right moment for performing head nods, head shakes, head rolls or gaze. Humans tellers were found to use significantly more words and to tell longer recaps with the Rapport Agent. Further, subjects self-report evaluation showed higher ratings of the agents understanding of the story and a stronger feeling of having made use of the agents feedback. Remarkably, about one quarter of subjects in the baseline condition, which was simple random feedback, felt they were given useful feedback.

3   A Model for Generating Incremental Embodied Feedback

With the exception of the systems originating from Gandalf [15,3], previous approaches have relied on rules that state on a mere behavioral level how to map agent-internal or external events onto feedback reactions or responses. Evaluation studies revealed several shortcomings of this approach (see Sect. 2). We propose that multimodal feedback must also be conceptualized and structured in terms of more abstract functional notions as described in Sect. 1, which can be meaningfully tied to events occurring in a listeners attempts to perceive, understand, and respond to a speakers contribution.

3.1   Feedback Model for Max

The generation of feedback requires a *predictive* model that formulates significances upon which feedback behaviors are triggered and how they are selected. It must cover both the responsive functions of feedback, when listeners on different levels of awareness react to cues produced by the speaker, as well as the more declarative functions of feedback, when listener by themselves inform about the success of their evaluation of what a speaker is contributing. In previous work [9] we have developed a theoretical account of feedback behavior based on the theory by Allwood et al. [2] described above. Here, we follow this approach but refine it to a model for one particular version of the virtual human Max. In this system, Max is employed in a public computer museum in Paderborn (Germany) [10], where he engages visitors in face-to-face conversations and provides them with background information about the museum. Visitors enter natural language input with a keyboard, whereas Max is to respond with synthetic German speech and nonverbal behaviors like gestures, facial expressions, gaze, or locomotion. For this system, we define potential sources (or causes) of feedback:

- Contact (C): always positive, unless the visitor or Max leave the scene
- Perception (P): positive as long as the words typed in by the user are known. This evaluation runs in a word-by-word fashion, while the user is typing in.
- Understanding (U): positive if the user input can be successfully interpreted. This is mapped onto the successful derivation of a conversational function by a firing interpretation rule, which in the systems current state cannot be evaluated until the contribution is completed.
- Acceptance (A): the main evocative intention of the input must be evaluated as to whether it complies with the agents beliefs, desires, or intentions.
- Emotion and attitude (E): the emotional reaction of the agent is caused by positive/negative impulses that are sent to the emotion system upon detection of specific events as described above, e.g. when appraising the politeness or offensiveness of user input. In addition, all positive or negative C, P, U evaluations can be fused into an assessment of a general (un-)certainty the agent is experiencing in the current interlocution.

3.2   Architecture

We argue that feedback generation must account for at least two mechanisms, notably, the automatic, largely conventionalized responses to eliciting cues from the speakers, as well as the functions to signal significant changes in the listener's mental or emotional states towards the incoming utterance. For both mechanisms it is vital to cut latencies to the minimum and to avoid giving feedback at the wrong moments in conversation. To integrate these mechanisms, and to meet the requirements for incrementality and reactivity, we propose a model of feedback generation that simulates different mechanisms of appraisal and evaluation, operating on different time scales and different levels of awareness or automaticity. Importantly, all of these processes may feed into response dispositions and trigger some of the aforementioned agent feedback behaviors.

Figure 1 shows the devised architecture of the model for feedback generation, which we have largely implemented and integrated into Maxs general architectural set-up (to the extent needed for the particular system). Overall, the model comprises two layers, a planning layer at the top and a reactive layer at the bottom of Fig. 1. The planning layer consists of the processes that are concerned with (1) analyzing user input; (2) keeping track of the contact, perception, and

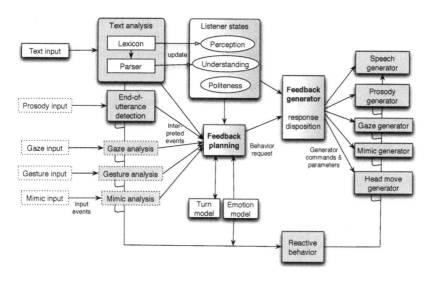

Fig. 1. Architecture of the incremental feedback generation model (dashed modules were not implemented in the current system)

understanding listener states of the agent; (3) deciding which feedback behavior to generate and when; (4) generating suitable multimodal behaviors. The central feedback planner decides upon the occurrence of intentional and aware feedback acts. It is only active when the agent is in a listening state or turn-transition phases (as indicated by the turn state model). The planner maps decisive external or internal events onto feedback acts that fulfill a required responsive or eliciting function. For example, results from input analysis can, via the state variables, give rise to feedback to signal problems with following. A generator is in charge of selecting the actual backchannel behaviors and is responsible for producing, possibly in overlap, less aware cues about the current listener state. For example, an event from the EOU module may trigger affirmative feedback, which is then enriched with prosodic cues for unsure understanding.

The reactive layer is constituted by direct connections from the input processing units to the production units. This pathway allows for incorporating feedback produced independent of the awareness and intentional control of the sender, e.g. blushing, as well as behaviors that are only potentially amenable to awareness and control, like smiles or emotional prosody. The planning layer also delegates control of behaviors with a longer duration (e.g. raising the eyebrows as long as input is not understood) to this layer. Behaviors using this path support the rest of the generated feedback instead of replacing it.

4   Module Realization in Max

Input Processing. Input processing continuously updates the listener states and sends important events directly to the feedback planner. At the moment,

Max gives feedback solely based on typed verbal input. Incoming text needs to be evaluated in a rapid and incremental fashion. Single words are the minimal unit of verbal input processing, which is accomplished by two modules, the lexicon and the parser. The lexicon determines the word class by part-of-speech tagging [12] and looks up the resulting lemma. Lookup failures lead to lowering of the perception state, if a word is found, perception is increased by the same constant. The understanding parameter is mainly coupled to syntactic-semantic analysis through parsing, which employs a shallow but robust rule-based approach. Depending on whether the word(s) in the current phrase context can be interpreted or not, i.e. interpretation rules are applicable, the understanding parameter is increased or lowered by a constant.

End-of-utterance (EOU) detection is one of the most important aspects when it comes to determining the right moment for giving feedback. Purely textual input as Max uses it at the moment can be considered an impoverished input for EOU detection, which usually draws on prosodic information. The system tries to gain as much information as possible from the words flowing into the system. End of utterance is simply signaled by enter-pressed events. In addition, appropriate places for feedback are found using the part-of-speech tags supplied by the lexicon. Feedback after e.g. articles is very improbable, while feedback after relevant content words like nouns, verbs, or adjectives is more appropriate.

Listener States. The listener states of the agent are quantified by explicit numerical parameters for contact, perception, and understanding evaluations. Perception has values between one (1.0) for excellent, flawless perception of the verbal stimulus and zero (0.0) for completely incomprehensible input. Understanding has values between one (1.0) for complete understanding of the incoming utterances in the phrasal context and zero (0.0) for unintelligible input. Future extensions may specify in similar ways parameters that carry further attitudinal or epistemic states like acceptance or uncertainty.

Feedback Planning. The feedback planner combines two approaches, a rule-based approach that connects context conditions with conventionalized multimodal feedback behaviors, and a probabilistic approach that captures not so clear-cut, less aware causal-effect structures. The current rule-based part of the planner is based on a linguistic analysis of German backchannels [9]. It states, e.g., that after a user contribution with matches in the lexicon and interpretation rule(s) verbal feedback by saying "yes", "I understand" or "'mhm" in connection with a head nod and repetition of the user's last content word should be given. The probabilistic part of the planner employs a Bayesian network to represent behavior probabilities conditioned on speaker elicitation events as well as the current listener states.

To combine feedback requests, a simple weighted-combination method is applied, in which behaviors are picked from the repertoire by order of priority, with higher levels of evaluation (understanding) yielding higher weights than lower appraisals (perception). Notwithstanding, since reception is modeled in a cascaded fashion, lower processes are faster and trigger behavior earlier than higher processes. In result, Max would at first look certain and nod due to a positive perception evaluation, but would then start to look confused once a negative understanding evaluation barged in, eventually leading to a corresponding verbal request for repetition or elaboration like 'Pardon me?'.

Feedback Generation. The feedback generator receives from the planner specific requests for verbal feedback expressions or abstract specifications of weighted to-be-achieved feedback functions (e.g. "signal-positive-understanding"). The latter are mapped onto multimodal feedback by drawing on modality-specific behavior repertoires. In addition, the listener state variables as well as the emotional state of the agent are constantly available to the generator, which sets appropriate facial expressions and overlays appropriate prosodic cues to verbal feedback requests from the planner.

The feedback generator operates a number of modality-specific generators, realized in the Articulated Communicator Engine (ACE) [11]. To be able to realize verbal backchannels with appropriate prosodic cues, ACE was extended with a novel feedback prosody generator [13] that allows fine prosody control on five parameters. The pitch *contour*, selected out of a set of six shape templates, is added to the *base frequency* of the voice and multiplied by a value to control the *slope* of the contour. Timing is adjustable by two further parameters, *duration* and *hesitation*, the latter of which controls the ratio between the first phone and the remaining phone(s), if any, in order to enable hesitative feedback. A listening study was conducted to determine the semantic potential of these parameters [13]. A long duration was found to communicate boredom, a flat pitch contour with increasing duration was evaluated as anger, and a sombrero-shape pitch contour was found to communicate agreement and a happy mood. The mean evaluations from the listening test are used as a fingerprint to pick from prosodies when producing positive verbal feedback.

5   Conclusion

We have presented work aiming at conversational agents to become more active and responsive listeners in natural human-agent interaction. Here we focused on a very important but so far too underrated aspect, the development of a model that combines rule-based, behavioral feedback responses to speaker elicitation events with the notion of a "concerned", collaborative listener that strives to keep track of what a speaker is saying. We have described a first implementation with Max in a restricted scenario (typed-in speech) and our first results with the prototype are promising to demonstrate that (and how) the actual processing of other's dialogue acts can be dynamically reflected in an agent's multimodal feedback. It remains to be shown in future work whether this makes Max a "better" listener. Future work should also concern the incorporation of further input modalities and in particular spoken language, which will then enable the use of end-of-utterance detectors as well as the generation of appropriate reactions to different types of recognition errors.

References

1. Allwood, J., Cerrato, L.: A study of gestural feedback expressions. In: Paggio, P., K. J. K., Jönsson, A.(eds.) First Nordic Symposium on Multimodal Communication, Copenhagen, 23-24 September, pp. 7–22 (2003)
2. Allwood, J., Nivre, J., Ahlsen, E.: On the semantics and pragmatics of linguistic feedback. Journal of semantics 9(1), 1–26 (1992)
3. Cassell, J., Bickmore, T.W., Billinghurst, M., Campbell, L., Chang, K., Vilhjálmsson, H.H., Yan, H.: Embodiment in Conversational Interfaces: Rea. In: Proceedings of the CHI'99 Conference, Pittsburgh, PA, pp. 520–527 (1999)
4. Cathcart, N., Carletta, J., Klein, E.: A shallow model of backchannel continuers in spoken dialogue. In: Proceedings of the 10th Conference of the European Chapter of the Association for Computational Linguistics (EACL10), Budapest, April 2003, pp. 51–58 (2003)
5. Clark, H.H., Schaefer, E.F.: Contributing to discourse. Cognitive Science 13, 259–294 (1989)
6. Fujie, S., Fukushima, K., Kobayashi, T.: A conversation robot with back-channel feedback function based on linguistic and nonlinguistic information. In: Proc. Int. Conference on Autonomous Robots and Agents (2004)
7. Graesser, A.C., Lu, S., Jackson, G.T., Mitchell, H., Ventura, M., Olney, A., Louwerse, M.M.: A tutor with dialogue in natural language. Behavioral Research Methods, Instruments, and Computers 36, 180–193 (2004)
8. Gratch, J., Okhmatovskaia, A., Lamothe, F., Marsella, S., Morales, M., van der Werf, R., Morency, L.-P.: Virtual Rapport. In: Gratch, J., Young, M., Aylett, R., Ballin, D., Olivier, P. (eds.) IVA 2006. LNCS (LNAI), vol. 4133, pp. 14–27. Springer, Heidelberg (2006)
9. Kopp, S., Allwood, J., Grammer, K., Ahlsen, E., Stocksmeier, T.: Modeling embodied feedback in virtual humans. In: Wachsmuth, I., Knoblich, G. (eds.) Modeling Communication With Robots and Virtual Humans, Springer, Heidelberg
10. Kopp, S., Gesellensetter, L., Krämer, N.C., Wachsmuth, I.: A Conversational Agent as Museum Guide – Design and Evaluation of a Real-World Application. In: Panayiotopoulos, T., Gratch, J., Aylett, R., Ballin, D., Olivier, P., Rist, T. (eds.) IVA 2005. LNCS (LNAI), vol. 3661, pp. 329–343. Springer, Heidelberg (2005)
11. Kopp, S., Wachsmuth, I.: Synthesizing multimodal utterances for conversational agents. Computer Animation & Virtual Worlds 15(1), 39–52 (2004)
12. Schmid, H.: Improvements in Part-of-Speech Tagging With an Application To German. (1995), http://www.ims.uni-stuttgart.de/ftp/pub/corpora/tree-tagger1.pdf
13. Stocksmeier, T., Kopp, S., Gibbon, D.: Synthesis of prosodic attitudinal variants in german backchannel 'ja'. In: Proc. of Interspeech 2007 (2007)
14. Takeuchi, M., Kitaoka, N., Nakagawa, S.: Timing detection for realtime dialog systems using prosodic and linguistic information. In: Proc. of the International Conference Speech Prosody (SP2004), pp. 529–532 (2004)
15. Thórisson, K.R.: Communicative Humanoids - A Computational Model of Psychosocial Dialogue Skills. PhD thesis, School of Architecture & Planning, Massachusetts Institute of Technology (September 1996)
16. Ward, N., Tsukahara, W.: Prosodic features which cue back-channel responses in English and Japanese (2000)
17. Yngve, V.H.: On getting a word in edgewise. In: Papers from the Sixth Regional Meeting of the Chicago Linguistics Society, April 16-18, pp. 567–578. University of Chicago, Department of Linguistics (1970)

Searching for Prototypical Facial Feedback Signals

Dirk Heylen[1], Elisabetta Bevacqua[2],
Marion Tellier[2], and Catherine Pelachaud[2]

[1] Human Media Interaction Group - Departement of Computer Science
University of Twente, The Netherlands
[2] LINC - IUT de Montreuil, University of Paris 8, France

Abstract. Embodied conversational agents should be able to provide feedback on what a human interlocutor is saying. We are compiling a list of facial feedback expressions that signal attention and interest, grounding and attitude. As expressions need to serve many functions at the same time and most of the component signals are ambiguous, it is important to get a better idea of the many to many mappings between displays and functions. We asked people to label several dynamic expressions as a probe into this semantic space. We compare simple signals and combined signals in order to find out whether a combination of signals can have a meaning on its own or not, i. e. the meaning of single signals is different from the meaning attached to the combination of these signals. Results show that in some cases a combination of signals alters the perceived meaning of the backchannel.

Keywords: Feedback, Facial expressions, Interpretation.

1 Introduction

In the context of working on the Sensitive Artificial Listener Agent, a Humaine examplar[1], we are compiling a list of verbal and nonverbal backchannel expressions ([BHPT07], [Hey07]). The goal of the Sensitive Artificial Listener project is to create several talking heads with different personalities that operate as chatbots inviting the human interlocutor to chat and to bring him or her in a particular mood. A particular concern of the project is to have the agent produce appropriate feedback behaviours.

The behaviours displayed by listeners during face-to-face dialogues have several conversational functions. By gazing away or to the speaker a listener signals that he is paying attention and that the communication channels are open. By nodding the listener may acknowledge that he has understood what the speaker wanted to communicate. A raising of the eye-brows may show that the listener thinks something remarkable is being said and by moving the head into a different position the listener may signal that he wants to change roles and say something

---

[1] http://www.emotion-research.net

C. Pelachaud et al. (Eds.): IVA 2007, LNAI 4722, pp. 147–153, 2007.

himself. The behaviours that listeners display are relevant to several communication management functions such as contact management, grounding, up-take
and turn-taking ([ANA93],[Yng70],[Pog05]). They are not only relevant to the
mechanics of the conversation but also to the expressive values: the attitudes
and affective parameters that play a role. Attitudes related to a whole range
of aspects, including epistemic and propositional attitudes such as believe and
disbelieve but also affective evaluations such as liking and disliking ([Cho91]).

Some important characteristics of expressive communicative behaviours are
that (a) a behaviour can signal more than one function at the same time, (b)
behaviours may serve different functions depending on the context, (c) and behaviours are often complexes composed of a number of behaviours. Moreover,
(d) the absence of some behaviour can also be very meaningful.

In this paper we describe a way to gain some further insight in the way certain
communicative feedback signals are interpreted. We have used a generate and
evaluate procedure where we have asked people to label short movies of the
Greta agent displaying a combination of facial expressions. We report here on
the second in a series of experiments ([BHPT07]). The aims of these experiments
are to get a better understanding of:

- the expressive force of the various behaviours,
- the range and kinds of functions assigned,
- the range of variation in judgements between individuals,
- the nature of the compositional structure (if any) of the expressions.

In this paper, we present the results of the second experiment where we attempted to find some prototypical expressions for several feedback functions and
tried to gain insight into the way the various components in the facial expression
contribute to its functional interpretation.

A lot has been written about the interpretation of facial expressions. This
body of knowledge can be used to generate the appropriate facial expressions for
a conversational agent. However, there are many situations for which the literature does not provide an answer. This often happens when we need to generate
a facial expression that communicates several meanings from different types of
functions: show disagreement and understanding at the same time, for instance.
We may find pointers in the literature to expressions for each of the functions
separately, but the way they should be combined may not be so easy. In another
way, we know that eye brow movements occur a lot in conversations with many
different functions. Is there a way in which a distinction should be made between
them in terms of the way and the timing of execution or the co-occurrence with
other behaviours? In general, listeners make all kinds of comments through their
facial expressions, as we will point out in the next section, but the expressions
can be subtle.

2   Recognition Test

In the previous experiment ([BHPT07]) we found that users could easily determine when a context-free signal conveys a positive or a negative meaning.

However, in order to generalise our findings the experiment needs to be performed with more subjects. Moreover as we have tested combinations of signals it occurred to us that we needed to assess the meaning of each single action. Thus, we prepared a second version of the experiment. A first question we wanted to explore with this new test is: is it possible to identify a signal (or a combination of signals) for each meaning? For example, is there a signal more relevant than others for a specific meaning or can a single meaning be expressed through different signals or a combination of signals? We hypothesised that for each meaning, we could find a prototypical signal which could be used later on in the implementation of conversational agents. A second question is: does a combination of signals alter the meaning of backchannel single signals? We hypothesised that in some cases, adding a signal to another could significantly change the perceived meaning. In that case, the independent variable is the combination of signals and the dependent variable is the meaning attributed to each signal by the subjects.

Sixty French subjects were involved in this experiment, the age mean was 20.1 years (range 18-32). They were divided randomly into two groups of thirty: group 1 and group 2.

The test used our 3D agent, Greta [PB03]. Besides the 14 movies used in the previous experiment, Greta displays 7 more movies. Table 1 shows the 21 signals, chosen among those proposed by [AC03, Pog05], that were used to generate the movies. For a more controlled procedure, we decided that participants could not rewind the movie. A list of possible meanings is proposed to the participant who, after each movie and before moving on, can select one meaning according to his/her opinion about which meaning fits that particular backchannel signal best. It is possible to select several meanings for one signal and when none of the meanings seems to fit, participants can just select either "I don't know" or "none" (if they think that there is a meaning but different from the ones proposed). As far the meanings the subjects had to choose from, we selected: *agree, disagree, accept, refuse, interested, not interested, believe, disbelieve, understand, don't understand, like, dislike.*

Table 1. Backchannel signals

1. nod	8. raise eyebrows	15. nod and raise eyebrows
2. smile	9. shake and frown	16. shake, frown and tension[2]
3. shake	10. tilt and frown	17. tilt and raise eyebrows
4. frown	11. sad eyebrows	18. tilt and gaze right down
5. tension[2]	12. frown and tension[2]	19. eyes wide open
6. tilt	13. gaze right down	20. raise left eyebrows
7. nod and smile	14. eyes roll up	21. tilt and sad eyebrows

Participants were given instructions for the test through a written text in French. They were told that Greta would display back-channel signals as if she was talking to an imaginary speaker. They were asked to evaluate these signals

---

[2] The action *tension* means tension of the lips.

by choosing one or several answers among the available list of meanings. This way we made sure that participants were aware that they were evaluating backchannel signals. The signals were shown once, randomly: a different order for each subject. As the list of possible meanings was too long (12 meanings + *none* + *I don't know*), we split it in two, for fear the list might be too long for the subjects to memorise. Each group had to choose between six possible meanings, plus *none* and *I don't know*.

2.1 Results

For each meaning, we looked both at the most chosen signals and at the distribution of answers and performed statistical paired t-tests to compare the means of given answers. We especially took a close look at the difference between signals and combinations of signals in order to find out whether adding a signal to another could alter the meaning or not. We just present here the most relevant results. Figure 1 shows the results for the positive meanings.

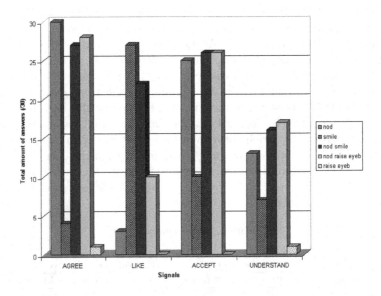

Fig. 1. Signals for positive meanings

AGREE. When displayed on its own, *nod* proved to be very significant since every subject answered "agree". *Nod and smile* (27 subjects) and *nod and raise eyebrows* (28 subjects) are also highly considered as backchannel signals of agreement. Difference between the three of them is not significant. When on its own, *smile* (4 subjects) does not mean "agree". For the meaning "agree", difference between the mean of answers for *smile* and the mean of answers for *nod and smile* is highly significant (t=9.761, p<0.0001). We obtained similar results for the meaning "accept".

LIKE. Two signals convey the meaning "like": *nod and smile* (22 answers) and *smile* (27 answers). The difference between *nod and smile* and *smile* is not significant (t=-1.980, p=0.0573). However, the difference between *nod* (3 subjects) and *nod and smile* is significant (t=-7.077, p<0.0001). This means that the signal *smile* conveys the meaning "like" on its own.

UNDERSTAND. Thirteen subjects associated nod with "understand", 16 paired *nod and smile* with this meaning and 17 found that *nod and raise eyebrows* could mean "understand". There is no statistical difference between *nod* and *nod and smile* (t=-1.795, p=0.0831). There is however a significant difference between *nod* and *nod and raise eyebrows* (t=-2.112, p=0.0434). *Raise eyebrows* on its own does not mean "understand" since only one subject gave that answer.

DISAGREE. The signal *shake* is labeled by every 30 subjects of group 1 as meaning "disagree". The combination of *shake, frown and tension* is also highly recognised as "disagree" (27 subjects). Paired T test shows that there is no significant difference between the two (t=1.795, p=0.0831). The combination of *shake and frown* is also regarded as meaning "disagree" (25 subjects) but it appears that the presence of frown alters the meaning for the difference between the mean of answers for *shake* versus *shake and frown* is significant (t=2.408, p=0.0226). The difference between *shake and frown* and *shake, frown and tension* is not significant (t=-1.439, p=0.1608). In conclusion, *shake* appears as the most relevant signal to mean "disagree", the high and significant difference between *shake, frown and tension* and *frown and tension* (t=10.770, p<0.0001) leaves no doubt about it. We obtained similar results for the meaning "refuse".

DISLIKE. *Frown and tension* appears as the most relevant combination of signals to represent "dislike" (26 answers). But when *shake* is added to *frown and tension*, it alters the meaning (16 answers). The difference between *frown and tension* and *shake, frown and tension* is significant (t=-3.808, p=0.0007). *Frown* alone is sometimes regarded as meaning "dislike" (by 17 subjects), but it is significantly less relevant than *frown and tension* (t=-3.525, p=0.0014). When displayed on its own, *tension* is also less relevant than the combination *frown and tension*, the difference is significant (t=-4.709, p<0.0001).

DISBELIEVE. Subjects considered that the combination *tilt and frown* means "disbelieve" (21 answers out of 30). It seems that it is the combination of both signals that carries the meaning since *tilt* on its own is regarded as disbelieve by only 8 subjects. Therefore, the difference between *tilt and frown* and *tilt* is significant (t=4.709, p<0.0001). Similarly, *frown* on its own means "disbelieve" for only 6 subjects and thus the difference between *frown* and *tilt and frown* is significant (t=5.385, p<0.0001). Finally, *raise left eyebrow* is also regarded by 21 subjects as "disbelieve".

DON'T UNDERSTAND. *Frown* and *tilt and frown* are both associated to the meaning "don't understand" by 20 subjects. *Tilt* is only given by 4 subjects so that we can infer that *frown* is the most relevant signal of the combination. However, when associated to other signals such as *tension* and/or *shake*, *frown* is less regarded as meaning "don't understand". Difference between *frown* and *frown and tension* is significant (t=2.693, p=0.0117). Similarly, the difference between *frown and tension* and *tension* is significant (t=2.408, p=0.0226), which proves the strong meaning conveyed by the signal *frown*. Apart from the *frown* signal, *raise left eyebrow* appears as relevant to mean "don't understand". It is given by 19 subjects.

NOT INTERESTED. For this meaning, two signals seem to be relevant: *eyes roll up* (20 subjects) and *tilt and gaze* (20 subjects). As far as *tilt and gaze* is concerned, it seems it is the combination of both signals that is meaningful since the difference between *tilt and gaze* and *tilt* (13 answers) is significant (t=-2.971, p=0.0059). Similarly, the difference between *tilt and gaze* and *gaze right down* (13 answers) is also significant (t=-2.971, p=0.0059).

2.2   Discussion

This test provides us with prototypical signals for most of our meanings. For the positive meanings, we have found that "agree" is meant by a *nod*, as well as "accept". To mean "like" a smile appears as the most appropriate signal. A nod associated to a raise of the eyebrows seem to convey "understand" but we have to point out that only 17 subjects out of 30 thought so. As for "interested" and "believe" we will have to test other signals. A combination of *smile and raise eyebrows* could be a possibility for "interested". For the negative meanings, "disagree" and "refuse" are meant by a head shake. Whereas "dislike" is represented by a *frown and tension* of the lips. A *tilt and frown* as well as a *raise of the left eyebrow* mean "disbelieve" for most of our subjects. The best signal to mean "don't understand" seem to be a *frown*. And *tilt and gaze right down* as well as *eyes roll up* are more relevant for the meaning "not interested". It also appeared that a combination of signals could significantly alter the perceived meaning. For instance, *tension* alone and *frown* alone do not mean "dislike", but the combination *frown and tension* does. The combination *tilt and frown* means "disbelieve" whereas *tilt* alone and *frown* alone do not convey this meaning. *Tilt* alone and *gaze right down* alone do not mean "not interested" as significantly as the combination *tilt and gaze*. Conversely the signal *frown* means "don't understand" but when the signal *shake* is added, *frown and shake* significantly looses this meaning. These results contribute to the building up of a library of prototypical backchannel signals.

3   Conclusion

We have presented a perceptual experiment directed to analyse how users interpret context-free backchannel signals displayed by a virtual agent. From our results we are now able to assign specific signals to most of the meanings proposed in the test and thus begin to define a library of prototypes. Recently, such an experiment has been submitted to subjects of different cultures, in Holland and in Italy. In the future we want to compare the results in order to see if backchannel signals are interpreted in the same way or if they are culture-specific. We also aim at using the set of recognizable signals, defined thanks to this test, in the implementation of a listener model for our conversational agent Greta. Not only the agent will be able to perform such backchannels but, knowing their generic meaning, it will also be able to interpret similar signals emitted by the user. Moreover, this set of recognizable backchannel signals, associated to a set of meanings, opens up further opportunities: we can, for instance, implement virtual agents who display a style of behaviour. For example we can create listeners who appear disbelieving, assertive, not interested and so on and test their effect on users interacting with them.

Acknowledgement

Part of this research is supported by the EU FP6 Network of Excellence HUMAINE (IST-2002-2.3.1.6) and by the EU FP6 Integrated Project Callas (FP6-2005-IST-5).

References

[AC03]   Allwood, J., Cerrato, L.: A study of gestural feedback expressions. In: Paggio, P., Jokinen, K., Jonsson, A. (eds.) First Nordic Symposium on Multimodal Communication, Copenaghen (September 23–24, 2003), pp. 7–22 (2003)

[ANA93]   Allwood, J., Nivre, J., Ahlsén, E.: On the semantics and pragmatics of linguistic feedback. semantics 9(1) (1993)

[BHPT07]   Bevacqua, E., Heylen, D., Pelachaud, C., Tellier, M.: Facial feedback signals for ecas. In: Proceedings of AISB'07: Artificial and Ambient Intelligence, Newcastle University, Newcastle upon Tyne, UK (April 2007)

[Cho91]   Chovil, N.: Social determinants of facial displays. Journal of Nonverbal Behavior 15, 141–154 (1991)

[Hey07]   Heylen, D.: Multimodal backchannel generation for conversational agents. In: van der Sluis, I., Theune, M., Reiter, E., Krahmer, E. (eds.) Workshop on Multimodal Output Generation, Aberdeen, Scotland (2007)

[PB03]   Pelachaud, C., Bilvi, M.: Computational model of believable conversational agents. In: Huget, M.-P. (ed.) Communication in Multiagent Systems. LNCS (LNAI), vol. 2650, pp. 300–317. Springer, Heidelberg (2003)

[Pog05]   Poggi, I.: Backchannel: from humans to embodied agents. In: Conversational Informatics for Supporting Social Intelligence and Interaction - Situational and Environmental Information Enforcing Involvement in Conversation workshop in AISB'05. University of Hertfordshire, Hatfield, England (2005)

[Yng70]   Yngve, V.: On getting a word in edgewise. In: Papers from the Sixth Regional Meeting of the Chicago Linguistic Society, pp. 567–577 (1970)

Fluid Semantic Back-Channel Feedback in Dialogue: Challenges and Progress

Gudny Ragna Jonsdottir[1], Jonathan Gratch[2], Edward Fast[2], and Kristinn R. Thórisson[1]

[1] CADIA / Department of Computer Science, Reykjavik University
Ofanleiti 2, IS-103 Reykjavik, Iceland
[2] University of Southern California, Institute for Creative Technologies,
12374 Fiji Way, Marina del Rey, CA 90292
{gudny04,thorisson}@ru.is, {gratch,fast}@ict.usc.edu

Abstract. Participation in natural, real-time dialogue calls for behaviors supported by perception-action cycles from around 100 msec and up. Generating certain kinds of such behaviors, namely envelope feedback, has been possible since the early 90s. Real-time backchannel feedback related to the content of a dialogue has been more difficult to achieve. In this paper we describe our progress in allowing virtual humans to give rapid within-utterance content-specific feedback in real-time dialogue. We present results from human-subject studies of content feedback, where results show that content feedback to a particular phrase or word in human-human dialogue comes 560-2500 msec from the phrase's onset, 1 second on average. We also describe a system that produces such feedback with an autonomous agent in limited topic domains, present performance data of this agent in human-agent interactions experiments and discuss technical challenges in light of the observed human-subject data.

Keywords: Face-to-face dialogue, real-time, envelope feedback, content feedback, interactive virtual agent.

1 Introduction

The fluidity and expressiveness of human dialogue presents significant challenges to developers of embodied conversational agents. Partners in a conversation effortlessly exchange verbal and nonverbal signals that help regulate the interaction and provide key semantic and emotional feedback. The variety of communication channels involved (speech content and prosody, facial expressions, gestures, postures, respiration, etc.) and the rapidity with which people can produce and process such information, tax the technical capabilities of autonomous agents intended to capture natural human speech. Therefore, contemporary conversational systems typically focus on a small number of channels and enforce explicit, structured turn taking. The resulting interaction is more akin to conversations with astronauts on the moon than normal face-to-face interaction, in both structure and pacing.

C. Pelachaud et al. (Eds.): IVA 2007, LNAI 4722, pp. 154–160, 2007.
© Springer-Verlag Berlin Heidelberg 2007

The present work aims to understand better key perceptual and behavior mechanisms in people's communicative behavior and to move closer to autonomous agents capable of fluid, dynamic speech interaction.

Several systems have attempted to improve the fluidity of virtual human feedback by providing back-channel feedback to non-lexical features of human speakers [1],[2],[3],[4]. Due to technological limitations the content of the speech has been largely ignored, at least as a source of realtime feedback. Thórisson's autonomous agents J. Jr. [2] and Gandalf [3] produced believable gaze, back-channel feedback and turntaking in real-time, based on automatic analysis of prosody and gesture input, without attending to speech content. People, too, can give such feedback without attending to speech content, termed *envelope feedback* by Thórisson [3],[5] or *generic feedback* by Bevales et al. [6]. Bavelas and colleagues demonstrated that people can produce well-timed nods even while engaged in a demanding distraction task that prevented them from attending to the speaker's content, in support of the Thórisson's hypothesis that separate cognitive mechanisms are responsible for envelope and semantic feedback [5]. Envelope feedback plays an important interaction function, signaling "everything is OK, please continue/I'm paying attention", and can contribute to a sense of mutual understanding and liking, factors associated with rapport [7]. Agents that provide such feedback can improve speaker engagement and speech fluency [1],[8].

Content feedback is back-channel feedback that makes reference to the content of the speech.[1] For example, Bavelas et al. [6] found that storytellers expected emotional feedback from their listeners to key events in the story and found it hard to construct effective narratives without it. In their study some listeners were required to perform a demanding distraction task while listening. The listeners were able to provide some envelope feedback (nods and vocalizations such as "mm-hmm") while listening but they were unable to produce responses related to content (such as wincing, looking surprised, etc.). Narrators found this lack of feedback disruptive, and generated less structured and less satisfying stories.

In this paper we describe our progress in allowing virtual humans to give within-utterance *content feedback* to user speech. As we will illustrate, this is a challenging problem in terms of the rapidity with which people expect such feedback. The next section describes the requirements such a system must satisfy. We describe a study that elicits content feedback and discuss the form and temporal dynamics of such behavior. Section 3 describes our results in achieving this performance through real-time speech recognition in an integrated system.

2   The Character of Content Feedback

To better support the study of the general constraints that govern the response characteristics, timing and individual variability of listeners' behavior we constructed a database of naturalistic listener feedback. The database serves as a reference point for judging the effectiveness of automated techniques.

---

[1] Bavelas et al [6] use the term "specific feedback" to refer to feedback produced in response to the content/meaning of speech. We prefer the more descriptive term "content feedback".

2.1 Human Subject Study: Listener Feedback Elicitation

The main goal of this study was to identify features of a storyteller's behavior that are correlated with content-related back-channel feedback, and that a computational system might reasonably be able to identify and react to in real-time. Eighty people (60% women, 40% men) from the general Los Angeles area participated in this study. They were recruited using Craig's List and were compensated $20 for one hour of their participation. We used a video clip taken from the *Edge Training Systems Sexual Harassment Awareness* video. The video clip was merged from two segments: The first is about a woman at work who receives unwanted attention through the Internet from a colleague at work, and the second is about a man who is confronted by a female business associate, who asks him for a foot massage in return for her business.

There were two experimental conditions: the *Face-to-face* condition (n=40) and the *Mediated* condition (n=40), to which participants were randomly assigned. In each condition, two participants were randomly assigned the role of storyteller (*Speaker*) or story listener (*Listener*).[2] In both Face-to-face and Mediated conditions the Speaker viewed the video while the Listener waited in another room. Face-to-face condition: When the Speaker had finished viewing the video, the Listener entered and the Speaker told him/her about the video. Mediated condition: When the Speaker had finished viewing the video, the Listener entered and sat across from the Speaker but separated by a physical barrier; the Listener saw a live video image of a human Speaker displayed on a large monitor; the Speaker saw a computer generated avatar that matched the Listener's head movements via a vision-based tracking system and told him/her about the video. In all conditions the Speaker and Listener were on opposite sides of a table separated by 2 meters.

2.2 Analysis and Results

No significant differences were found between the Mediated and Face-to-face conditions on the dependent variables reported below. We collapsed data across conditions for the purpose of analysis. One listener was excluded from the analysis due to a failure of the re-cording equipment yielding a final sample of thirty-nine Listeners.

Lexical Feedback Markers. There was considerable similarity in the words Speakers used to describe events. Facial expressions of Listeners would often immediately follow certain Speaker phrases; 36

Fig. 1. Subjects showed a range of facial upon hearing the term "foot massage." These included expressions of disgust, lowered brows, raised brows, gaze shifts, and various expressions of amusement. Subjects responded rapidly, within 350 milliseconds on average after "foot massage" was spoken. A quarter of the subjects showed no obvious response.

---

[2] The two conditions were created to address a secondary goal: to tease apart what aspects of listener feedback are crucial for speakers. For example, does the speaker need to see the listener or could a graphical representation of the listener be just as effective? This paper only focuses on the first goal. For the purpose of this article, the two conditions simply represent different methods to elicit feedback.

of 39 Speakers mentioned the exact phrase "foot massage" and in 26 of these Listeners rapidly thereafter displayed a visible facial expression. We refer to these key phrases as *lexical feedback markers (LFMs)*.[3]

Listener Facial Feedback: Subjects produced a variety of facial feedback during the narratives. We explored peoples' responses associated with the LFM "foot massage" and examined Listeners' facial responses to the first mention of the phrase; most conveyed some notion of surprise but the specific facial response varied widely in its form and intensity (Figure 1). Responses included raised brows (8 subjects), smiles (6 subjects), grimaces (6 subjects), gaze shifts (4 subjects), and laughter (3 subjects). In some cases there was a complex unfolding of expressions (e.g., a brow raise shortly followed by a smile) as predicted by theories of facial expressions [9].

Listener Feedback Delays: Table 1 summarizes the listener feedback delays (average for 22 subjects[4]) for the "foot massage" LFM. (Since people might understand the phrase before it is fully completed, we report reaction times from both the beginning and completion of the phrase.) Subjects showed significant variability in the timing of their responses. In general, feedback was quite rapid, within 400 msec of the completion of the LFM.[5] In two cases feedback occurred in midst of the LFM.

Table 1. Subject reaction times

	Time to Produce Lexical Feedback Marker	Delay between Lexical Feedback Marker and Listener Expression	
		From its start	From its completion
Avg time	775 msec (σ=153)	1038 msec (σ=418)	344 msec (σ=444)
Min time	550 msec	560 msec	-220 msec
Max time	1080 msec	2510 msec	1630 msec

3 System Design and Setup

We constructed a multi-module system to produce content feedback by incorporating continuous speech recognition into the Rapport Agent of Gratch et. al [1], an architecture for exploring the social impact of nonverbal behavior (see Figure 2). The agent was set up to recognize and react to the LFMs identified in the elicitation study. The agent can produce natural envelope feedback in responses to body movements and speech prosody, as well as content-related facial feedback, as seen in the human subject study. In its standard configuration, the Rapport Agent generates envelope feedback by real-time analysis solely from a narrator's speech and body movements using a prosody detector, named LAUN, including backchannel opportunity points [2],[10], disfluencies, questions, and loudness. Using the Watson vision-based gesture detector [11], it detects speaker gestures including head nods, shakes, gaze shifts and posture

---

[3] We do not claim that these terms necessarily elicited the listener feedback, but they closely preceded it and would serve as reasonable makers for a computer system to attempt to recognize and respond to as a proxy for true understanding. (See list of terms in Table 2).

[4] Accurate timing statistics for the remaining 24 subjects was not yet complete at the time of submission but results appear comparable.

[5] The machine running Dragon, on which all measurements were made, is a 2x dual core 2.61GHz Intel Pentium-class processor running Windows XP with 3.37GB RAM.

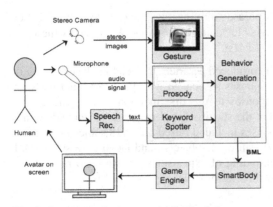

Fig. 2. Our approach to semantic feedback incorporates continuous speech recognition to the existing Rapport Agent approach to providing envelope feedback via gesture and prosody detection

shifts. Neither Watson nor LAUN can extract content or meaning from communicative behavior.

Speech Recognition. We use a continuous, large vocabulary, general-purpose dictation speech recognizer. Dragon has proven to have relatively good accuracy, and user-independence, as shown in our own test (even without the individual training recommended by the manufacturer). Normal operation of Dragon is to wait for silences before starting to process; however, between pauses (larger than 100 msecs) it produces hypotheses about what has said so far. These are less accurate than the final response, it may mean the difference of several seconds to wait for the final output. We need time-stamps and confidence of words, as well as n-best hypothesis of the uttered phrase, which Dragon provides through their API. However, the time to produce hypotheses varies considerably (see Figure 3). When the final hypothesis is released, a final timestamp estimation for each word is produced, representing the actual time (in the past) that the words were spoken by the user.

Pattern Matching. We use a continuous speech recognizer to extract text from the Speakers' speech; specialized pattern matchers extract meaning from the recognized text. Since the time to search the text is a linear function of the number of words/phrases we are looking for, we run multiple matchers in parallel, each matching a limited set of phrases with relatively simple techniques. Data collected in the human subject experiment was used to construct the patterns for detecting the LFMs.

Table 2. Accuracy of recognition per LFM category

Category	Lexical Feedback Markers	Accuracy
Foot massage	Foot massage, Foot rub, Rub her feet	63%
Harassment	Harass	94%
Sexual	Sexual	93%
Legal	Legal, Law department	92%
Quit	Quit her job, Quitting, To quit	48%
Start with	Start with that, Take it from there, Where we'll start, Going to start	47%
Stalking	Stalking	33%
Sweet	How sweet	25%

Listener feedback. All perception modules (prosody, behavior and lexical) communicate with a reactive Behavior Generation system which probabilistically selects a

Table 3. Accuracy of system modules

	Occurrences	Percentage
Recognized topics	100	66%
Missed by Speech recognizer	37	25%
Missed by pattern matchers	14	9%
False positive rate	0	0%
Total occurrences	151	100%

single appropriate feedback response given the recognized input and internal state information (details described in Gratch et al., [1]). Behaviors represented in the Behavior Markup Language (BML) [12] are passed to an animation system that seamlessly blends animations and procedural behaviors. Finally, these animations are rendered in the Unreal Tournament™ game engine and displayed to the Speaker.

3.1 System Accuracy Evaluation

To test the system's performance we ran 36 recordings of speakers telling the foot massage story through the system. Average accuracy was 66% for recognizing LFM categories (see table 3). The substantial differences in accuracy between LFM categories (e.g. foot massage vs. harassment) have two causes. First, the general vocabulary is biased – some words are more difficult to recognize than others (e.g. "stalking" misrecognized as "stocking").

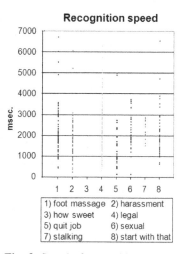

Fig. 3. Speed of recognition over 3 runs per audio file from the human-human interaction study

A high number of variations contribute to low scores in categories such as "quit" (e.g. choice of 1st person and 3rd person) were not in our set of selected LFMs and thus missed by the pattern matchers. Speed varies quite a bit between runs (Dragon's response time is fairly non-deterministic), so to test time performance we did 3 runs on the same dataset of 36 interviews: Average response time was just over 2 sec; 15% occured under 1 sec. The system is thus still far from reliably achieving natural response times of 1 sec on average.

4   Discussion and Future Work

We have described a framework intended to help with human subject dialogue experiments and in building autonomous agents and automatic dialog systems. We also described initial us of it in producing appropriate and timely content feedback. The results demonstrate progress in integrating behavioral, prosodic and lexical information to produce realtime listening feedback within a constrained setting. Although our findings indicate that significant advancements need to be made to reach human-level performance, they also highlight that embodied agents are inching towards the richness of natural conversational behavior by combining envelope and content feedback, and in the process opening up a host of new research questions, e.g. how to integrate such feedback with models of emotion [13].

An obvious next step is to improve the technology to match the speed and accuracy observed in the human-human condition. A more powerful pattern matching function would capture more surface variability in how people describe key narrative events. In the current system setup there were no false positives, but allowing for more general variations in the pattern matching will very likely raise their number; how much, however, is a function of the number of false positives in the speech recognition and the generality of the expressions allowed.

At present there is little data about how well people can adjust to delays or peculiarities of feedback produced by (virtual) humans. The role of non-lexical features in the elicitation of feedback is also unclear (e.g. speaker prosody or facial expressions)

and further work is needed to tease apart these factors. Embodied agents that react instantly and emotionally to human speech, albeit in simplified settings, have the potential to begin to address these questions, for the benefit of both autonomous agents and our understanding of human communication.

Acknowledgments. We are grateful for the substantive contributions of a number of individuals. Anya Okhmatovskaia and Alison Wiener contributed to our experimental design. Jillian Gerten, Ning Wang, and Robin Duffy assisted with the data elicitation and analysis. Jeremy Bailenson and Nicole Kraemer informed of relevant findings. This work was sponsored in part by the U.S. Army Research, Development, and Engineering Command (RDECOM), and the content does not necessarily reflect the position or the policy of the Government, and no official endorsement should be inferred. This work was in part supported by a Marie Curie European Reintegration Grants within the 6th European Community Framework Programme, and by a research project grant from RANNÍS.

References

1. Gratch, J., Okhmatovskaia, A., Lamothe, F., Marsella, S., Morales, M., van der Werf, R., et al.: Virtual Rapport. In: Gratch, J., Young, M., Aylett, R., Ballin, D., Olivier, P. (eds.) IVA 2006. LNCS (LNAI), vol. 4133, Springer, Heidelberg (2006)
2. Thórisson, K.R.: Dialogue Control in Social Interface Agents. In: Paper presented at the InterCHI Adjunct Proceedings, Conference on Human Factors in Computing Systems, Amsterdam (1993)
3. Thórisson, K.R.: Communicative Humanoids: A Computational Model of Psycho-Social Dialogue Skills. Unpublished Ph.D. thesis, Massachusetts Institute of Technology (1996)
4. Tosa, N.: Neurobaby. In: ACM SIGGRAPH, pp. 212–213 (1993)
5. Thórisson, K.R.: Natural Turntaking Needs No Manual: Computational Theory and Model, From Perception to Action. In: Granström, B., House, D., Karlsson, I. (eds.) Multimodality in Language and Speech Systems, pp. 173–207. Kluwer Academic Publishers, Dordrecht, The Netherlands (2002)
6. Bavelas, J.B., Coates, L., Johnson, T.: Listeners as Co-narrators. Journal of Personality and Social Psychology 79(6), 941–952 (2000)
7. Tickle-Degnen, L., Rosenthal, R.: The Nature of Rapport and its Nonverbal Correlates. Psychological Inquiry 1(4), 285–293 (1990)
8. Gratch, J., Wang, N., Okhmatovskaia, A., Lamothe, F., Morales, M., van der Werf, R., et al.: Can virtual humans be more engaging than real ones? In: Jacko, J. (ed.) Human-Computer Interaction, Part III, HCII 2007. LNCS, vol. 4552, pp. 286–297. Springer, Heidelberg (2007)
9. Scherer, K.R., Ellgring, H.: Are facial expressions of emotion produced by categorical affect programs or dynamically driven by appraisal? Emotion (2007)
10. Ward, N., Tsukahara, W.: Prosodic features which cue back-channel responses in English and Japanese. Journal of Pragmatics 23, 1177–1207 (2000)
11. Morency, L.-P., Sidner, C., Lee, C., Darrell, T.: Contextual Recognition of Head Gestures. In: Paper presented at the 7th International Conference on Multimodal Interactions, Torento, Italy (2005)
12. Kopp, S., Krenn, B., Marsella, S., Marshall, A., Pelachaud, C., Pirker, H., et al.: Towards a common framework for multimodal generation in ECAs: The behavior markup language. In: Gratch, J., Young, M., Aylett, R., Ballin, D., Olivier, P. (eds.) IVA 2006. LNCS (LNAI), vol. 4133, Springer, Heidelberg (2006)
13. Gratch, J., Marsella, S.: A domain independent framework for modeling emotion. Journal of Cognitive Systems Research 5(4), 269–306 (2004)

T2D: Generating Dialogues Between Virtual Agents Automatically from Text

Paul Piwek[1], Hugo Hernault[2], Helmut Prendinger[2], and Mitsuru Ishizuka[3]

[1] NLG Group, Centre for Research in Computing
The Open University, Walton Hall, Milton Keynes MK7 6AA, UK
`p.piwek@open.ac.uk`
[2] National Institute of Informatics
2-1-2 Hitotsubashi, Chiyoda-ku, Tokyo 101-8430, Japan
`{hugo,helmut}@nii.ac.jp`
[3] Graduate School of Information Science and Technology, University of Tokyo
7-3-1 Hongo, Bunkyo-ku, Tokyo 113-8656, Japan
`ishizuka@i.u-tokyo.ac.jp`

Abstract. The Text2Dialogue (T2D) system that we are developing allows digital content creators to generate attractive multi-modal dialogues presented by two virtual agents—by simply providing textual information as input. We use Rhetorical Structure Theory (RST) to decompose text into segments and to identify rhetorical discourse relations between them. These are then "acted out" by two 3D agents using synthetic speech and appropriate conversational gestures. In this paper, we present version 1.0 of the T2D system and focus on the novel technique that it uses for mapping rhetorical relations to question–answer pairs, thus transforming (monological) text into a form that supports dialogues between virtual agents.

1 Introduction

Information presentation in dialogue format is a popular means to convey information effectively, as evidenced in games, news, commercials, and educational entertainment. Moreover, empirical studies have shown that for learners, dialogues often communicate information more effectively than monologue (see e.g. [5,6]). The most well-known use of dialogue for information presentation is probably by Plato: in the Platonic dialogues, Socrates and his contemporaries engage in fictitious conversations that convey Plato's philosophy. A more recent example is Douglas Hofstadter, whose Pulitzer prize winning book *Gödel, Escher, Bach* [8] consists of chapters which are each preceded by a dialogue that explains and illuminates concepts from mathematical logic, philosophy or computer science. Most information, however, is not available in the form of dialogue. Presumably the most common way of representing information is (monological) text, for instance on the web, where textual information is abundant in quantity and diversity. Moreover, huge amounts of information are captured in databases and, with the advent of the semantic web, ontologies.

C. Pelachaud et al. (Eds.): IVA 2007, LNAI 4722, pp. 161–174, 2007.

The preparation of attractive and engaging multi-modal presentations using a team of virtual agents is a time-consuming activity that requires several skills regarding: (1) How to generate a coherent, meaningful dialogue; (2) how to assign appropriate gestures to the conversing agents; and (3) how to integrate media objects illustrating the dialogue into the presentation. Currently, most of these tasks can only be performed by a trained dialogue script writer. The wide dissemination of digital media content using life-like characters, however, would greatly benefit from an authoring tool that supports non-experts (for dialogue script writing) in generating multi-modal content.

In this paper, we focus on the issue (1) of generating coherent dialogue, and assume (monological) text as the input to dialogue generation. The next section provides an overview of and comparison with related work in this area. We then proceed to a description of version 1.0 of our implemented T2D system (Section 3). We relate the design of the system to a set of requirements that include robustness and extensibility. In Section 4 a walk-through example is described that illustrates how the system operates. Finally, Section 5 presents our conclusions and issues for further research.

2   Related Work

There are a number of studies that deal with the problem of automatically generating multi-modal dialogues between life-like animated agents. These differ, however, in the type of input they require and the techniques that are employed to map the input to multi-modal dialogue.

In Intelligent Multimedia Presentation (IMMP) systems the authoring process is automated by employing methods from artificial intelligence, knowledge representation, and planning (see [1] for an overview). An IMMP system assumes a so-called "presentation goal" and uses planning methods to generate a sequence of presentation acts. The generation of a presentation is based on dedicated information sources that encode information about presentation content and objects [2]. The difference with our proposal is that we do not require the formulation of planning operators, which assumes a background in artificial intelligence. Our proposal is solely based on existing material (currently text and, in future, possibly also associated graphics), and thus easy-to-use by non-experts and not suffering from the knowledge representation bottleneck.

Recently developed related systems include Web2TV and Web2Talkshow [12], and e-Hon [18].[1] Web2TV uses two animated characters to readout a given text in a TV-style environment. Web2Talkshow transforms a (summary) of text from

---

[1] Here, we do not review work on tutorial dialogue systems. Some of the work in that area focuses on authoring tools for generating questions, hints, and prompts. Typically, these are, however, single moves by a single interlocutor, rather than an entire conversation between two or more interlocutors. Some researchers have concentrated on generating questions together with possible answers (i.e., multiple-choice test items), but this work is restricted to a very specific type of question–answer pairs (see, e.g., [11]).

the web into a humorous dialogue between character agents. e-Hon transforms text into an easy-to-understand dialogue based on rephrasing content, and enriching it with animations. Web2Talkshow and e-Hon on the one hand, and our T2D system on the other, are similar in that they both aim to generate dialogues automatically from text. The differences lie in how text is mapped to dialogue: Firstly, Web2Talkshow and e-Hon analyze single sentences as the basis of the generated dialogue. E.g., Web2Talkshow takes declarative sentences of the form *X of the Y did Z* and transforms them into dialogue fragments of the form *A: Who is X. B: I know. X is one of the Y. A: That's right! He did Z.* The system looks for keywords called subject and content terms [12] that can fulfill the role of *X*, *Y*, and *Z*. Keywords are identified based on frequency counts and co-occurrence statistics, and presumably intended to reflect what the document is about. As a result, the approach seems to be based on, what (in linguistics) is called the *information structure* of a sentence. Information structure is orthogonal to *discourse structure*. The latter focuses on *relations* between spans of text (such as evidence, condition, justification, etc.), rather than aboutness, and applies both within and across sentence boundaries. T2D uses discourse rather than information structure to create dialogues. Secondly, whereas our aim is to faithfully render the content of the input text as a dialogue, a feature of Web2Talkshow is that it generates humorous dialogues, exploiting distortions and exaggerations of what is actually said in the input text. Furthermore, our approach is underpinned by systematic tests on a corpus of Patient Information Leaflets to verify that the mappings performed by T2D are indeed meaning-preserving and result in linguistically well-formed dialogues.

The investigations on automated generation of scripted dialogues described in [16,14] provided some of the foundations for the current work. That research also investigates the combination of information from sources other than text. In one scenario [15], the principal information is an electronic health record, and supplementary information is drawn from thesauri, wikis, and ontologies.

3   System Description

The main starting point for our system is that it should be usable by non-experts to create multi-modal dialogue from text. We identify three requirements for such a system: robustness, extensibility, and variation/control.

Firstly, the system should be able to produce a dialogue regardless of the input text. In other words, the system should be ROBUST. Secondly, the system should be EXTENSIBLE. A given input text will normally be realizable as more than just one single dialogue. Since the general task of mapping text to dialogue is a very difficult one, any current system is unlikely to cover all possible mappings from text to dialogue. The system should, however, be easily extensible in order to cover new mappings. It should be straightforward to add new mappings and replace parts of the system, as and when new technologies and techniques for particular subtasks become available (e.g., text segmentation and discourse parsing). Finally, we require that our system allows for VARIATION and

CONTROL of its outputs: An output dialogue should not contain repetitive structures that make it less appealing (e.g., 'conversational ping-pong' [7]). Ideally, choices for specific forms of expression should depend on the context and the purpose for which the dialogue is used. Here we will only discuss some very preliminary attempts to introduce variation, and leave issues of control for future work.

3.1 System Design

The system consists of three principal components:

1. ANALYZER: A component that analyses text in terms of Rhetorical Structure Theory (RST, [10]). Currently, it consists of the DAS Discourse Analyzing System [9] which builds RST structures (but without identifying nuclei and satellites), and a nucleus/satellite Identification Module;
2. MAPPER: Module that maps RST structures to DialogueNet structures (these are a specific subclass of RST structures that represent dialogue);
3. PRESENTER: A Module for translating DialogueNet structures to the Multimodal Presentation Markup Language (MPML3D) format [13]. MPML3D script specifies multi-modal dialogue performed by two 3D agents.

Both components (1) and (3) are partly of-the-shelf systems that can in principle be replaced with alternative solutions for discourse analysis and multi-modal presentation. Representations between components are exchanged in XML format. All this contributes to the EXTENSIBILITY of the system.

At the heart of the system sits the mapper from RST structures to DialogueNet structures. In the remainder of this section we introduce both RST and DialogueNet structures and then focus on the theoretical foundations underlying the T2D approach to mapping between such structures.

Rhetorical Structure Theory. RST is the most widely used descriptive theory of discourse structure. A text is presumed to be segmented into units, e.g., independent clauses, and these occupy the terminal nodes in an RST structure. For example, the text 'If you are unsure of your dosage or when to take it, you should ask your doctor' receives the following analysis in RST:[2]

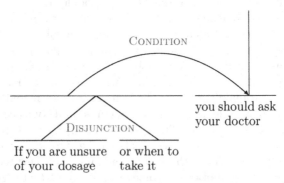

---

[2] Reitter's rst LaTeX package [17] is used for displaying RST trees.

This structure is built up of two relations that are instances of the following two generic schemas for building RST structures [10]:

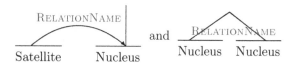

In the schema on the left-hand there is a difference in status between the items that are related: one is more essential or prominent than the other. The more important span – the *nucleus* – is distinguished graphically from the *satellite*, by being the endpoint of the arrow. A relation with a distinguished nucleus is known as mononuclear. The notion of nuclearity plays a central role in the operational definitions of discourse relations. For example, CONDITION is defined in [4, p. 51] as: 'In a CONDITION relation, the truth of the proposition associated with the nucleus is a consequence of the fulfillment of the condition in the satellite. The satellite presents a situation that is not realized.' The schema on the right-hand applies to relations that do not have a single most prominent item. For example, DISJUNCTION is '[...] is a multinuclear relation whose elements can be listed as alternatives, either positive or negative.' [4, p. 53].

DialogueNet. DialogueNet (henceforth DN) structures are the subclass of RST structures that satisfy the following definition:

DEFINITION *DN Structure*: An RST structure R is a DN structure for a text T, if and only there exists a partitioning of T into a set of non-overlapping spans $\{T_1, \ldots, T_n\}$, such that this set consists of pairs of spans $\langle T_x, T_y \rangle$ which are related in R by the RST ATTRIBUTION relation, with T_x the satellite of the ATTRIBUTION relation, in particular, a clause of the form *Speaker said*, and T_y being the nucleus.

Thus a DN Structure corresponds to a text of the form *Speaker$_1$ said P_1, Speaker$_2$ said P_2*, ..., where *Speaker$_1$, Speaker$_2$*, ... can be the same or different speakers. In the extreme, a DN structure can represent an internal monologue by a single speaker, or a conversation which has a different speaker for each span. Here, however, we deal mainly with DN Structures that have two alternating speakers.

Mapping from RST to DialogueNet Structures. Mapping RST to DialogueNet structures can be decomposed into two tasks. Firstly, we need to introduce the aforementioned ATTRIBUTION relations into the input RST structure. On its own, this would, however, not lead to very natural dialogues; rather, we would end up with a presentation of the input text by two or more speakers. To create a proper dialogue, we also need to introduce instances of the RST QUESTION-ANSWER relation into the input RST structure. Questions are characteristic of dialogue. They move the dialogue forward by at the same time introducing new topics and making requests for information. This raises the issue of how to introduce QUESTION-ANSWER relations into RST structures. Take the following flat representation of an RST structure: (1) CONDITION(P, **Q**), where bold face indicates the nucleus. A question-answer pair corresponding with this structure is: (2) QUESTION-ANSWER(What if P, **Q**). We use this example to illustrate two problems. Firstly, how do we arrive at the question-answer pair, and, secondly, given our commitment to information preserving mappings, what is the formal correlate of information preservation from (1) to (2)? (1) and (2) are supposedly carrying the same information, but they do not even have an RST relation in common.

To address this problem, we use a tool from mathematical logic, called λ-abstraction. One problem with (2) is that it obscures the fact that there there is an underlying CONDITION relation. Instead, let us write

$$(3) \text{ QUESTION-ANSWER}(\lambda x. \text{ CONDITION}(P,x),\mathbf{Q}).$$

Thus, in (2) we replaced 'What if P' with $\lambda x.$CONDITION(P,x). The latter is a formal representation of the former. The question is now analyzed as an abstraction over one of the arguments of the CONDITION-relation. Abstraction is the sister of application. If we apply a lambda expression $(\lambda x.M)$ to another expression N, the result is defined as follows: $(\lambda x.M)N \mapsto M[x := N]$. This now allows us to explicate in what sense (1) and (3) are equivalent. For that purpose, our formal interpretation of the QUESTION-ANSWER relation is application, and consequently: $\lambda x.$CONDITION(P,x) **Q** can be related to CONDITION(P, **Q**). The use of abstraction and application to represent the equivalence between question-answer pairs and declarative sentences has been independently proposed by several researchers (see [3]).

Apart from the technical benefit of being able to express information equivalence on RST structure precisely, abstraction also provides us with a generic tool for generating question-answer pairs from declarative sentences and larger units. The general formula for question formation over a subexpression E of P is: $P \longmapsto \lambda x.P' E$, where $P' = P[E := x]$. This allows us to generate various types of question-answer pairs via abstraction over different parts of the input, e.g.:

(A) Over the first argument of a relation: If it rains, the tiles get wet. $\mapsto$ Under what circumstances do the tiles get wet? If it rains.

(B) Over the second argument: If it rains, the tiles get wet. $\mapsto$ What if it rains? Then the tiles get wet.

(C) Over a relation (higher-order): John is at home because I saw his car outside. $\mapsto$ What is the relation between John being at home and his car being outside? The latter is evidence for the former.

(D) Over a subexpression of a simple proposition: John is at home. $\mapsto$ Where is John? At home.

Note that the mapping in (D) corresponds with that proposed in [12]. Our approach provides the formal underpinning for that work, and also presents a significant generalization of it, showing its relation to many other declarative to question-answer pair mappings.

So far, we have implemented mappings for some of the most common relations – CONDITIONAL, CONCESSION, ELABORATION, SEQUENCE, and DISJUNCTION – and we are continually adding mappings for new relations. It is straightforward to add mappings for additional discourse relations to T2D. We have developed a generic format for specifying such mappings. Our methodology for adding mappings and evaluating them on naturally occurring text is described in the next section.

ROBUSTNESS of the current version of T2D is limited by the performance of the underlying DAS parser. An evaluation of DAS's performance is described in section 3.4. DAS failed for 39% of the inputs that it was presented with. Failure took different forms: a) DAS crashed or produced no analysis, b) ill-formed input, as a result OCR errors,[3] led to an incorrect analysis by DAS, or c) the input was well-formed but DAS nevertheless produced an incorrect analysis. Currently, for the 39% of cases where DAS fails, our system produces no or an incorrect output. We are working on a number of strategies to address this problem: Firstly, we are exploring whether, when DAS crashes or produces no mapping, running it only on carefully selected subspans of the input might still yield useful results. Secondly, we intend to do some preprocessing of the input to check for OCR errors. Finally, for those cases where there was a well-formed input but an incorrect analysis, we are investigating post-processing on the DAS output to spot these (e.g., we observed that for the cases where DAS produces an incorrect analysis, the resulting tree often contains unnecessarilly many nestings).

The mapper, which is the main topic of this paper, is successful for almost all of the inputs (see section 3.4). Although we are deriving the mappings from a specific corpus, we anticipate that they are portable to other text genres, since they are defined in terms of domain-independent RST and syntactic constraints. There might, however, be problems with specific genres. For instance, narratives will typically be annotated mainly in term of TEMPORAL-AFTER relations, which makes for rather uninteresting dialogue.

VARIATION is addressed by allowing for multiple mappings for one and the same discourse relation. Currently, how to deal with CONTROL of variation is still an open issue. We are planning to investigate contextual factors that might determine the choice between different mappings.

3.2 Authoring of Mapping Rules

In this section we describe our methodology for authoring mapping rules by discussing a particular discourse relation, i.e., CONDITION. Evaluation is dealt with in Section 3.4. The development is empirically driven. We start out with a large collection of instances of the discourse relation in question. For this purpose, we use the PIL corpus,[4] a corpus consisting of 465 Patient Information Leaflets. We identified conditionals in the corpus by searching it with the regular

---

[3] The PIL corpus was created by scanning a collection of paper leaflets.

[4] Available at: http://mcs.open.ac.uk/nlg/old_projects/pills/corpus/

expression [I|i]f\b. This yielded a total of 4214 instances. We took a random sample of 100 sentences. Manual examination of the sample sentences led to their classification into two main categories: (1) nucleus of the conditional in (negative) imperative form, and (2) nucleus of the conditional in declarative form with modal auxiliary. For each case, we distilled separate mapping rules that are paraphrased below:

MAPPING RULES: **Condition with Imperative Nucleus**

> CONDITION(P,Q) & imperative(P) $\Longrightarrow$
> Layman: Under what circumstances should I P^*?
> Expert: If Q.

> CONDITION(P,Q) & neg-imperative(P) $\Longrightarrow$
> Layman: Under what circumstances should I not P^*?
> Expert: If Q.

where P^* is P[I:=you,you:=I,my:=your,your:=my,mine:=yours,yours:=mine]

MAPPING RULE: **Condition with Nucleus in Declarative Form with Modal Auxiliary**

> CONDITION(P,Q) & declarative-modal-aux(P) $\Longrightarrow$
> Layman: Under what circumstances $flip(P^*)$?
> Expert: If Q.

P^* is P[I:=you, you:=I, my:=your, your:=my, mine:=yours, yours:=mine], and $flip(X)$ is a function that performs the "interrogative flip" [19] inversing subject and auxiliary.

Here is an example for conditions where the nucleus is in (positive) imperative form. Given the input text 'If you experience any other unusual or unexpected symptoms consult your doctor or pharmacist', CONDITION(P,Q) is instantiated as CONDITION(*consult your doctor or pharmacist, you experience any other unusual or unexpected symptoms*). Syntactic analysis of the two clauses with the Machinese Syntax parser[5] tells us that P is in imperative form, i.e., P is the nucleus and Q is the satellite.

When the mapping rule provided above is applied, we obtain:

Layman: Under what circumstances should I consult my doctor or pharmacist?
Expert: If you experience any other unusual or unexpected symptoms.

Depending on the application, dialogue contributions are assigned to more specific role pairs of type Expert–Layman, such as Instructor–Student, Boss–Assistant, and so on.

---

[5] http://www.connexor.com/

An example of a condition with a declarative nucleus is 'It should not produce any undesirable effects if you (or somebody) accidentally swallows the cream'. This is represented as CONDITION(*it should not produce any undesirable effects, you (or somebody) accidentally swallows the cream*). The nucleus contains a modal auxiliary ("should").

After applying the interrogative flip, the resulting dialogue is:

Layman: Under what circumstances should it not produce any undesirable effects?

Expert: If you (or somebody) accidentally swallows the cream.

In order to introduce VARIATION into the dialogues, we also prepared alternate mappings. For example, for conditions we use the following additional mapping, which is independent of the form of the nucleus.

MAPPING RULE: **Alternate Mapping Rule for Conditional**

> CONDITION(P,Q) & nucleus(P) $\Longrightarrow$
> Layman: What if Q^*?
> Expert: Then P.

Here Q^* is Q[I:=you, you:=I, my:=your, your:=my, mine:=yours, yours:=mine]

When applied to 'It should not produce any undesirable effects if you (or somebody) accidentally swallows the cream', this mapping rule yields the following dialogue fragment:

Layman: What if I (or somebody) accidentally swallows the cream.

Expert: It should not produce any undesirable effects.

Note that this dialogue fragment appears to be more natural than the fragment produced by the other mapping (see above). One further strand of research we intend to pursue, is to develop a version of the system that creates and compares alternative mappings and selects the best one based on independent criteria (e.g., a measure of fluency).

3.3   Algorithm

The mapping algorithm performs prefix-parsing on the RST tree. The final dialogue is composed of sub-dialogues generated by recursively parsing the tree. The transitional words or expressions spoken by the Expert or the Layman are decided on the basis of the relation type of the current node. For instance, parsing an ELABORATION node will result in the concatenation of the dialog generated when parsing the left-hand child node, then the sentences 'Expert: Should I tell you more? – Layman: Yes, please.', followed by the Expert speaking the dialogue generated when parsing the right-hand child node. This algorithm, while simple, provides a good level of flexibility. It allows us to incrementally enrich the list of relation types for our system. Hence, we can evaluate the MAPPER on progressively richer samples every time a previous mappings have been validated.

3.4   Preliminary Evaluation

We conducted separate evaluations on both the DAS discourse parser and the MAPPER from the RST tree to DialogueNet. To evaluate DAS, we took a random sample of one hundred sentences from the PIL corpus. When compared to the analyses of a single human judge[6], DAS achieved correct discourse parse results for 61%. The failed parse outcomes for the remaining 39% can divided into four categories: (1) well-formed input, but incorrect analysis (40%), (2) ill-formed input (as a result of OCR errors; the corpus was created by scanning a large number of leaflets) and incorrect analysis (19%), (3) no mapping performed (19%), and (4) DAS crashes (22%).

In order to evaluate the MAPPER we took another random sample of one hundred condition sentences from the PIL corpus which was then manually annotated in terms of RST by one of the authors. The dialogue was correctly mapped, according to a single judge, in 92% of the cases. In the 8% of remaining cases, the generated dialog was incorrect for one of the following reasons: (1) the structure of the sentence was not correctly analyzed due to incorrect output from the Machinese Syntax parser (4%), or (2) the mapping rules were not precise enough (4%).

4   Walk-Through of Example

In this section, we describe the operation of T2D on a multi-sentence text by looking in detail at a specific input text and the DialogueNet and multi-modal dialogue that T2D can produce. We take three sentences from the PIL corpus that are also discussed in [14]: *(i) To take a tablet, you should first remove it from the foil and then swallow it with water. (ii) Your doctor will tell you the dosage. (iii) Follow his advice and do not change it.*

The text is input into our ANALYZER component as plain text, and processed by the DAS Discourse Analyzing System. DAS outputs an XML file consisting of tagging structures for RST relations, which encodes the RST tree corresponding to the input text. The Identification Module for nucleus/satellite determines the relative importance of two clauses between which a (mononuclear) rhetorical relationship holds, by syntactic analysis. For instance, if the relation is CONDITION, the nucleus is identified by the occurrence of a verb in imperative form or the presence of a modal auxiliary (see Section 3.2). The output of the ANALYZER can be visualized by an RST tree, as shown in Fig. 1. Sentence (i) and sentences (ii) and (iii) are connected by the multinuclear SEQUENCE relation, which is often used when no more specific relationship can be identified. The satellite of a MEANS relation specifies '[...] a method, mechanism, instrument, channel or conduit for accomplishing some goal.' [4, p. 62]. ELABORATION is a common way to modify the nucleus by providing additional information.

Next, the MAPPER Module is called to transform the RST tree into a DialogueNet structure. An example dialogue reads as follows:

---

[6] In this preliminary study, we used a single judge. We are planning further studies with two judges to assess interjudge agreement.

(1) Layman: How should I take the tablet?
(2) Expert: You should first remove it from the foil and then swallow it
             with water.
(3) Expert: Your doctor will tell you the dosage.
(4) Expert: Should I tell you more?
(5) Layman: Do I have to follow his advice?
(6) Expert: Yes.
(7) Expert: And do not change the dosage.

The nucleus of the MEANS relation sentence (i) is mapped to a question, dialogue contribution (1), explicating the intention of this relation. The answer, contribution (2), can be organized as a TEMPORAL-AFTER relation. However, (2) is not turned into a question–answer pair, since this relationship (similar to SEQUENCE) does not justify the formation of a question. This can be contrasted to the situation in sentence (iii). Here the nucleus of the ELABORATION relationship is turned into a question with an *induced* answer ("Yes"), followed by the satellite information, contribution (7). Note that anaphora resolution was applied in (7) for disambiguation. Besides induced answers, we also implement induced questions, such as dialogue contribution (4). Both types are intended to smooth the course of the dialogue. We are currently investigating a principled method to introduce them into the dialogue.

Finally, the purpose of the PRESENTER Module is to translate the DialogueNet structure into MPML3D [13], our Multimodal Presentation Markup Language for highly realistic 3D agents (see Fig. 2). The agents were created by a profes-

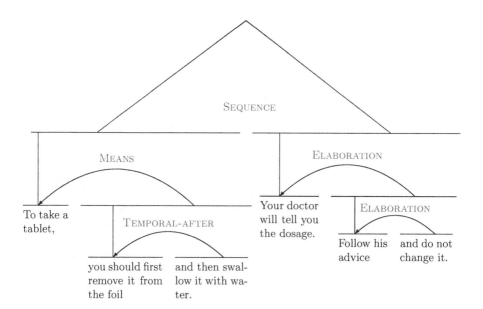

Fig. 1. RST tree of sample input sentences

Fig. 2. Multi-modal dialogue

sional Japanese character designer for "digital idols". They can perform around thirty gestures, express facial emotions, and speak with proper lip-synchronization. While MPML3D provides an easy-to-use, intuitive, and powerful scripting language for the definition of agent behavior, conversational gestures and gaze behavior have to be added manually. Since our T2D system is intended as a fully automated system, we are currently conducting extensive research in also automating this process.

5   Conclusion

We have developed a first working prototype of our Text2Dialogue system. In this paper, we presented both the theoretical grounding of the mapping that the system performs from Rhetorical Structure Theory structures to DialogueNet structures, and the system implementation. We introduced several requirements (ROBUSTNESS, EXTENSIBILITY, and VARIATION and CONTROL) and described how these are addressed. We also reported on the evaluation of the mapping rules that the system uses. In our future work, we aim to extend the system to mappings for further discourse relations, and to increase the naturalness of the dialogue by special devices, such as inserting induced questions. In this way, we want to advance the ease of generating high-quality multi-modal contents for non-professional and and expert digital content creators alike.

Acknowledgements. We would like to thank Huong Le Thanh for making the DAS system available to us, and Abdul Ahad and Christian Pietsch helping us with the installation of DAS. We would also like to acknowledge the helpful comments and suggestions of the three anonymous IVA07 reviewers.

References

1. André, E.: The generation of multimedia presentations. In: Dale, R., Moisl, H., Somers, H. (eds.) Handbook of Natural Language Processing, pp. 305–327. Marcel Dekker, Inc. (2000)
2. André, E., Rist, T., van Mulken, S., Klesen, M., Baldes, S.: The automated design of believable dialogue for animated presentation teams. In: Cassell, J., Sullivan, J., Prevost, S., Churchill, E. (eds.) Embodied Conversational Agents, pp. 220–255. The MIT Press, Cambridge (2000)
3. Bäuerle, R., Zimmermann, T.: Fragesätze. In: von Stechow, A., Wunderlich, D. (eds.) Semantics. An International Handbook of Contemporary Research, Mouton de Gruyter, Berlin/New York, pp. 333–348 (1991)
4. Carlson, L., Marcu, D.: Discourse tagging reference manual. Technical Report ISI-TR-545, ISI (September 2001)
5. Cox, R., McKendree, J., Tobin, R., Lee, J., Mayes, T.: Vicarious learning from dialogue and discourse: A controlled comparison. Instructional Science 27, 431–458 (1999)
6. Craig, S., Gholson, B., Ventura, M., Graesser, A.: Tutoring Research Group: Overhearing dialogues and monologues in virtual tutoring sessions: Effects on questioning and vicarious learning. International Journal of Artificial Intelligence in Education 11, 242–253 (2000)
7. Davis, R.: Writing for Dialogue Scripts. A & C Black Ltd, London (1998)
8. Hofstadter, D.: Gödel, Escher, Bach: an Eternal Golden Braid. Basic Books, USA (1979)
9. Le, H.T., Abeysinghe, G.: A study to improve the efficiency of a discourse parsing system. In: Gelbukh, A. (ed.) CICLing 2003. LNCS, vol. 2588, pp. 101–114. Springer, Heidelberg (2003)
10. Mann, W.C., Thompson, S.A.: Rethorical structure theory: Toward a functional theory of text organization. Text 8(3), 243–281 (1988)
11. Mitkov, R., Ha, L.A., Karamanis, N.: A computer-aided environment for generating multiple-choice test items. Natural Language Engineering: Special Issue on using NLP for Educational Applications 12(2), 177–194 (2006)
12. Nadamoto, A., Tanaka, K.: Complementing your TV-viewing by web content automatically-transformed into TV-program-type content. In: Proceedings 13th Annual ACM International Conference on Multimedia, pp. 41–50. ACM Press, New York (2005)
13. Nischt, M., Prendinger, H., André, E., Ishizuka, M.: MPML3D: a reactive framework for the Multimodal Presentation Markup Language. In: Gratch, J., Young, M., Aylett, R., Ballin, D., Olivier, P. (eds.) IVA 2006. LNCS (LNAI), vol. 4133, pp. 218–229. Springer, Heidelberg (2006)
14. Piwek, P., Power, R., Scott, D., van Deemter, K.: Generating multimedia presentations. From plain text to screenplay. In: Stock, O., Zancanaro, M. (eds.) Multimodal Intelligent Information Presentation, Text, Speech, and Language Technology, pp. 203–225. Springer, Heidelberg (2005)
15. Piwek, P., Power, R., Williams, S.: Generating scripts for personalized medical dialogues for patients. Technical Report 2006/06, Department of Computing, Faculty of Mathematics and Computing, The Open University, UK (2006)

16. Piwek, P., van Deemter, K.: Towards automated generation of scripted dialogue: some time-honoured strategies. In: Proceedings 6th Workshop on the Semantics and Pragmatics of Dialogue (EIDLOG-02), pp. 141–148 (2002)

17. Reitter, D.: Rhetorical theory in LaTeX with the rst package, `http://www.reitter-it-media.de/`

18. Sumi, K., Tanaka, K.: Transforming E-contents into a storybook world with animations and dialogues using semantic tags. In: Online Proceedings of WWW-05 Workshop on the Semantic Computing Initiative (SeC-05) (2005), `http://www.instsec.org/2005ws/`

19. Tenny, C.L., Speas, P.: The interaction of clausal syntax, discourse roles, and information structure in questions. In: ESSLLI 2004 Workshop on Syntax, Semantics and Pragmatics of Questions, Université Henri Poincaré, France (2004)

So Let's See: Taking and Keeping the Initiative in Collaborative Dialogues

Sabine Payr

Austrian Institute for Artificial Intelligence OFAI
sabine.payr@ofai.at

Abstract. In order to create and maintain social relationships with human users in mixed-initiative dialogues, IVAs have to give off coherent signals of claiming or relinquishing leadership in discourse. Quantitaive and qualitative analyses of human-human collaborative task-solving dialogues from the Ohio State University Quake Corpus reveal that discursive dominance is a shared achievement of speakers and given, taken or kept in a consensual way, up to the point where they incur "costs" in terms of efficiency in solving the task. Some verbal signals can be identified as relevant to this process.

1 Introduction

In the course of longer-term research work on emotions and social relationships in human-machine interaction, at a certain point my attention was drawn to the concept of mixed-initiative dialogue. The larger question then was whether mixed-initiative dialogue also characterizes a certain type of social relationship.

Mixed initiative has been in the focus of research on conversational interaction between users and intelligent virtual agents for some years now. It has been defined as "a flexible interaction strategy, where each agent can contribute to the task what it does best." (Allen 1999). This definition has to be kept in mind against more recent uses of the concept, where it is applied in a much broader sense to human-machine dialogues whether they deserve the name or not. Evidence for mixed initiative is gathered from human-human dialogues in experimental settings, e.g. (Fischer 2006, Byron 2005, Byron & Fosler-Lussier 2006, Ferguson et al. 1996, Chu-Carroll & Brown 2003) and tested in several human-machine environments (Brind^pke et al. 1995, Ferguson & Allen 1998). What is common to both types of experimental arrangements is the asymmetric setting of the dialogue. There is a pre-defined "leader" – either the human in the human-machine dialogues or one of the humans in human-human dialogues who typically sets out with more information and knowledge of the task to accomplish.

This asymmetric setting is criticized by Guinn (1999), as "the resulting conversation, then, might have very few changes in initiative." By contrast, Byron & Fosler-Lussier (2005) claim for the Quake Corpus that while the "partners have asymmetric knowledge of the goals ... both partners have equal capabilities within the task world to move about and manipulate the world. Therefore, the task initiative is equally shared between the partners." In section 2 of this paper, I present a comparative analysis of three of the Quake dialogues that puts both statements into

C. Pelachaud et al. (Eds.): IVA 2007, LNAI 4722, pp. 175–182, 2007.
© Springer-Verlag Berlin Heidelberg 2007

question. It also shows that initiative, as an analytic concept for dialogues, has to be distinguished from dominance, and that the characterization of dialogues as "mixed-initiative" does not predict the power relationships that exist or develop among participants.

Allen (1999) has set mixed initiative against "system control", exemplified by automated call centers that achieve not much more than form-filling dialogues (Fairclough 2001), to the dissatisfaction or even annoyance of numerous users. Nevertheless, IVAs or automated call systems have to take and keep the initiative sometimes. Users are familiar with passing over initiative to an agent, be it human or automated, and ready to be guided e.g. through procedures of ordering, information retrieval, tutoring, and the like. User dissatisfaction, then, need not be a consequence of system control, but rather of how initiative is taken and kept by the system. Section 3 gives examples, taken from the qualitative analysis of the data, of human dialogue partners' "techniques" to take and keep initiative.

2 Initiative and Dominance

The Quake Corpus
The OSU Quake 2004 Corpus (Byron & Fosler-Lussier 2006) contains English spontaneous task-oriented two-person situated dialogue. The corpus was collected using a first-person display of an interior space (rooms, corridors, stairs), created using a multi-player computer game engine called Quake II, in which the partners collaborate on a treasure hunt task. Pairs of students served as test persons and chose off-the-shelf avatars as their representations in the virtual world. Each one saw the virtual world on the screen from first person view. After an individual training session, one person was arbitrarily selected as the "leader" and given information about the tasks to fulfill collaboratively that the other person did not have.

The test persons communicated via headsets. Sound recordings were synchronized with video recordings resp. logfiles, and are available together with orthographic transcripts. The dialogues are between 220 and 580 turns long, and are here referred to as Quake 5 (the longest), 6 and 7.

The analysis presented here is qualitative in its outlook, even if a few phenomena are quantitatively compared among the dialogues. Qualitative analysis is the method of choice in a "specimen", not a "population" perspective on sampling: the reality to be studied is represented by the specimens. The specimens selected should be representative not of the whole "population" of data, but of the category. (tenHave 1999). The result then should be a description of a phenomenon in dialogue, not a theory, e.g. in the form of a rule which predicts its occurrence and form.

Comparing Dominance
Does the appointed leader indeed keep the initiative so that there are only few changes, as Guinn (1999) claims for this type of experiment, or is initiative equally distributed, as Byron & Fosler-Lussier (2006) suppose?

The first step was therefore to annotate the three dialogues manually for initiative. The distinction introduced by Chu-Carroll and Brown (2003) between dialogue and task initiative was not made for this study. For the present purpose, manual annotation seemed sufficient, because recognition of initiative per se was not the goal. Questions (if acknowledged and answered), suggestions (if acknowledged), commands and command-like structures, narratives of the speaker's own actions, and change of topic (e.g. through statements of new facts or perceptions) were considered as signs of initiative. Unsuccessful, i.e. non-acknowledged, attempts at initiative-taking were not counted. In this definition, initiative therefore assumes consent by speaker and hearer, even if it is for a very short span of dialogue, i.e. one question-answer sequence. A count of utterances shows a distribution that closely reflects the manually annotated initiative. In other words: who holds the initiative also has longer turns, which is only to be expected (Fig. 1).

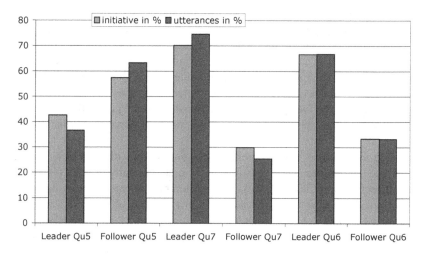

Fig. 1. Initiative turns and utterances in percent

In both Quake 6 and 7, the pre-defined leaders take the initiative for a longer period. The ratio is 2:1 in Quake 6, and 2,34:1 in Quake 7. But in Quake 5 the relationship is reversed. Here it is the follower who is more initiative, at a ratio of 1,34:1. The video and audio recordings show that in Quake 5, both players are similarly unfamiliar with this kind of game environment, so that dominance is not grounded on an expert-novice relationship.

It was also of interest to compare how often inititiative changes: the average length of a sequence in which one speaker remains initiative is 5,7 turns in Quake 5 vs. 7,2 in Quake 6 and 8,3 in Quake 7. The Quake 5 dialogue hence does not only stand out by the role reversal, the more equal distribution, but also by the more frequent changes of initiative. On this basis, it can be characterized as the most collaborative dialogue among the three, but it is still far from an equal distribution of initiative. It can however be said for all the dialogues that initiative changes frequently, so that the goal of achieving equal initiative can be said to have been partially achieved in this corpus.

The results show that it is not necessarily the appointed leader of the experiment who also leads the dialogue. In order to avoid confusions between the two kinds of leadership, I will call, in what follows, "dominant speaker" the speaker who leads in the conversation. "Dominance" here means a power relationship between participants but does not specify what kind of power is at work (cf. Payr 2006a). If, as we can assume in this case, the dialogue participants are in principle peers and there is no recognizable reason for a power disequilibrium, dominance is purely "discursive", i.e. situationally and personally established.

3 Friendly Takeover

The focus of the qualitative analysis was on the methods participants in a dialogue employ to gain and keep initiative, but also to signal and endorse acceptance of the other's initiative. In none of the dialogues under study the issue of dominance is addressed explicitly. There is no meta-discourse on who should lead or give instructions. This is, of course, most striking in the case of Quake 5, the dialogue with the reversal of dominance: although the appointed leader has key information about the task, she allows the follower to take over most of the initiative. But neither do the followers in the other two dialogues demand more initiative than what the leader grants.

Although the speakers are on familiar, informal terms with each other, they take care to frame instructions and suggestions to the other carefully in order to avoid face-threatening acts (Watts 2003). Proposals are preferably expressed as questions that are moreover not directed at the other speaker, but at both of them, using an inclusive "we". In Quake 6 and 7, expressions such as "we need to ..." and "we're supposed to ..." are mostly used by the leaders who are also dominant in these two dialogues. They thus refer to the experimental setting as an external, legitimizing force. In these cases, we can say that the leaders establish themselves as representatives of an institutional power to which both submit. This technique of appeal to authority is almost absent in Quake 5, where we have to assume that the speakers define their "subject positions" (Fairclough 2001) independently and consensually. As this is not done by negotiation, the question is if there are strategies that speakers use to signal dominance and consent.

"So ...": Taking the initiative
Speakers in the Quake Corpus dialogues use "so" frequently:

```
133-1: f: so we already did something
134-1: l: we didn't do anything
134-2: l: but it's there anyway
135-1: f: okay so
136-1: l: but we're also supposed to put one of the uh quake logos in this room
137-1: f: oh okay
137-2: f: so we have to find the quake logo
(Quake 5)
```

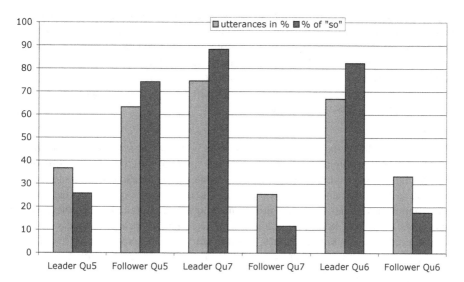

Fig. 2. Distribution of expressions with "so"

The distribution of occurrences (Fig. 2) shows that dominant speakers use it more often than their share of utterances lets expect. The function of "so", in general, is to sum up and to express continuity, and to frame the own turn as a consequence of what has been said before. The distribution leads us to assume that "so" here also serves as a signal for taking the initiative. This becomes apparent in turn 137 of the excerpt: after an unsuccessful attempt at re-assuming initiative in turn 135, the follower now endorses the information given by the leader in 136 and takes the initiative by transforming it into a plan.

"Let's see ...": keeping the initiative

Use of imperative forms is rare in the dialogues. A notable exception are those sequences where the (keyboard and mouse) commands for operating the simulation are at issue. No danger of face-threat seems to be involved where one speaker provides instructions of this kind on demand. Another exception are formulaic expressions such as "let's see", "hold on" or "wait":

> 11-4: f: so I just moved into a room that has a {sil}
> 11-5: f: hold on {sil}
> 11-6: f: let me see where I
> 11-7: f: I think I'm out on a balcony {sil}
> (Quake 5)

This sequence is broken by pauses during which the action goes on. The speaker does not see or do anything worth reporting, but keeps the turn and the dialogue initiative using these expressions.

Two kinds of repetition

One kind of repetition observed in the corpus has the character of an endorsement of the other's action, and to take the lead on from there. Functionally, it is a more explicit but similar form of the initiative-taking accomplished with "so". However, a repetition of a negative statement leaves the initiative to the other speaker. The differences in intonation of these two examples, and the negative form, make it clear to the hearer which is intended. There are not enough cases in this corpus to study this phenomenon more closely. Given that repeating user input is a frequently used technique in dialogue systems (e.g. Let's Go, DARPA Communicator), the effect of repetition however deserves more attention.

Acts of Naming

The virtual world of the experiment is new to both participants. They have to find means to communicate about and act in it, and to do so they use descriptions of the rooms, but also give them names. The borderline between descriptions and names is not easy to draw, because many of the names are descriptive (e.g. "the blue room"). Other namind strategies (e.g. "the dungeon room"), later uptake by the other speaker and use as a referring noun phrase allow us to say that the speakers actually orient to these expressions as a kind of names. Naming activities are most obvious in Quake 5, and again it is the dominant speaker who leads them: of the 12 naming acts, 8 are done by the dominant speaker.

The dominant speaker also suggests, at one point, to introduce a reference system for directions (east, west etc.). The suggestion is tentative, and quickly withdrawn when the other speaker hesitates. Names and orientations as ways of representing the world are not introduced lightly, because agreement of both speakers is needed to ensure further communication. If we consider naming acts as an exercise of representational power (Fairclough 2001), one-sided naming is also face-threatening, which can account for the care taken by the name-giver.

In most human-machine conversations to date humans have to guess at and adapt to the representations and capabilities programmed into the machine. The capability of negotiating representations of the world is still beyond most dialogue systems.

4 Discussion

The underlying assumption about mixed initiative is a relationship between the human and the machine where the machine should ideally take the role of an assistant who does not only give correct and helpful answers, but also takes initiative where this appears to be necessary and fruitful for the advancement of the task (Allen 1999). This definition implies that each agent continuously evaluates its own and the other's capacities and resources against an ideal of efficiency in task-solving. It presupposes that human-human collaborative dialogues come close to this ideal and lead to optimal solution of the task. Our analysis of just such dialogues has shown that they can fall considerably short of this ideal. Discursive dominance (Thornborrow 2002) also emerges in peer-to-peer informal dialogues and does not necessarily correspond to the intended and predicted leadership in communicative problem solving. The interesting finding, however, is that this can happen in a perfectly friendly, consensual way – without resistance or, in fact, any meta-discourse at all. Participants appear to orient towards their relationship as much as they orient towards task achievement (Payr 2006b).

Initiative is taken and given up constantly and smoothly. Most often, initiative is taken by introducing a new topic, which may be an observation, a suggestion or a report on actions undertaken. But there are also explicit signals with which the speakers take or keep the initiative, respectively give up or refuse it, of which the paper discusses a few specimens.

This exploration of discursive dominance is relevant for several areas of application of conversational IVAs, for example:

- "Service" applications, such as sales, booking or information applications: relationships between clients (users) and service persons (systems) appear paradoxical. On the one hand, service IVAs should display friendly submission, on the other hand, they are more efficient if they lead the dialogue which often amounts to form-filling. In this, they are no different from humans in a similar situation: both hold a certain power in the sense of valued resources. Human service providers and customers manage this tension and the related power shifts remarkably well and, in most cases, succeed in avoiding or mitigating the potentially face-threatening acts involved.
- Role-play applications, e.g. educational simulation games: IVAs have to take diverse roles and simulate different relationships with human players. Change and maintenance of such relationships may be the very point of such simulation games (see e.g. http://www.l2c.info/learning_to_collaborate/), and dialogues have to reflect these social states and processes in order to allow for a coherent game and learning experience.

Findings from human-human conversation cannot be simply transferred to human-computer interaction, for at least two reasons.

1. It has been argued that humans do not transfer their conversational behaviour mindlessly to the interaction with IVAs (cf. Fischer 2006a, b).
2. The rules that conversation analysis formulates as results are neither causal nor constraining. Rather, they are rules that people display an orientation to in their conversational behaviour (ten Have 1999, Eggins & Slade 1997).

Nevertheless, and keeping these caveats in mind, there are lessons to learn for the design of initiative-taking and -giving in conversational interaction with IVAs.

The broader research goal of which this study is only one small part is to relate verbal and non-verbal conversational behaviours to their socio-cultural meaning, and from there on to develop conversational artifacts that are able to assess, predict and handle their social relationship with the user. Power (or dominance, or control) is an ubiquitous factor in this relationship (the perfect peer-to-peer encounter is the exception, not the rule, and even there we rather find shifting patterns of situational dominance than plain equality), and the challenge to incorporate it grows as IVAs migrate to "serious" applications where users' identities and needs are at stake.

Acknowledgments

The Austrian Research Institute for Artificial Intelligence is supported by the Austrian Federal Ministry for Education, Science and Culture and by the Austrian Federal

Ministry for Transport, Innovation and Technology. This research is carried out within the project „Advanced Knowledge Technologies: Grounding, Fusion, Applications", sub-project 4, which is partially funded by the Austrian Society for the Advancement of Research (FFG) under contract no. 811593.

References

Allen, J.F.: Mixed-initiative interaction. In: IEEE Intelligent Systems, pp. 14–16 (1999)

Brindöpke, C., Häger, J., Johanntokrax, M., Phade, A., Schwalbe, M., Wrede, B.: Darf ich Dich Marvin nennen? Instruktionsdialoge in einem WoZ-Szenario. Szenario-Design und Auswertung. Bielefeld: Universität Bielefeld (1995)

Byron, D.K., Fosler-Lussier, E.: The OSU Quake 2004 corpus of two-party situated problem-solving dialogs. In: Proceedings of the 15th Language Resources and Evaluation Conference (LREC'06) (2006), available from http://www.cse.ohio-state.edu/ dbyron/pubs.html

Chu-Carroll, J., Brown, M.K.: Tracking Initiative in Collaborative Dialogue Interactions. In: Proceedings of the 35th Annual Meeting of the Association for Computational Linguistics (ACL/EACL-97), pp. 262–270 (1997)

Eggins, S., Slade, D.: Analysing Casual Conversation. Equinox, London (1997)

Fairclough, N.: Language and Power, 2nd edn. Longman, Harlow (2001)

Fischer, K.: The Role of Users Preconceptions in Talking to Computers and Robots. In: Fischer, K. (ed.) How People Talk to Computers, Robots, and Other Artificial Communication Partners, SFB/TR 8 Spatial Cognition. pp. 112–130 (2006b) (What Computer Talk Is and Isn't. AQ-Verlag, Saarbrücken, 2006a)

Ferguson, G., Allen, J.F.: TRIPS: An Integrated Intelligent Problem-Solving Assistant. In: Proc. AAAI-98, pp. 567–573. Madison, WI (1998)

Ferguson, G., Allen, J.F., Miller, B.: TRAINS-95: Towards a mixed-initiative planning assistant. In: Drabble, B. (ed.) Proc. 3rd Conference on Artificial Intelligence Planning Systems AIPS-96, Edinburgh, pp. 70–77 (1995)

Guinn, C.I.: Evaluating mixed-initiative dialog. IEEE Intelligent Systems, 21–23 (1999)

Payr, S.: Social Role Management in Human-Computer Interaction I. Vienna: Österreichisches Forschungsinstitut für Artificial Intelligence TR-2006-15. 2006b. Seriously Socially Situated Agents. In: Trappl, R.(ed.) Proceedings EMCSR 2006, OGKS Vienna (2006a)

ten Have, P.: Doing Conversation Analysis. Sage, London (1999)

Thornborrow, J.: Power Talk. Language and Interaction in Institutional Discourse. Longman, Harlow (2002)

Watts, R.J.: Politeness. Cambridge University Press, Cambridge (2003)

Health Document Explanation by Virtual Agents

Timothy W. Bickmore[1], Laura M. Pfeifer[1], and Michael K. Paasche-Orlow

[1] Northeastern University College of Computer and Information Science
360 Huntington Ave WVH202, Boston, MA 02115
(bickmore,laurap)@ccs.neu.edu
http://www.ccs.neu.edu/research/rag/
[2] Boston University School of Medicine
91 East Concord St, Suite 200, Boston, MA 02118
mpo@bu.edu

Abstract. We describe the design and evaluation of a virtual agent that explains health documents to patients. The prevalence and impact of low health literacy is presented as a motivation for such agents, given that face-to-face interaction with health providers is cited as one of the most effective means of communicating with these patients. We analyze the form and distribution of pointing gestures used by experts in explaining health documents, and use this data to develop a computational model of agent-based document explanation. This model is evaluated in a randomized controlled trial. Preliminary results indicate that patients with low health literacy are more satisfied with health document explanation by a virtual agent compared to a human.

Keywords: Virtual agent, relational agent, embodied conversational agent, health literacy, hand gesture.

1 Introduction

Many professionals provide their lay clients with documents that are, to varying degrees, incomprehensible. Whether due to technical jargon, obscure concepts, or poor writing on the part of the professional, or low literacy, cultural barriers, or cognitive impairment on the part of the client, documents often fail to serve their intended communicative function.

Perhaps nowhere is this problem more important and pervasive than in healthcare. The consequences of a patient failing to understand a prescription, hospital discharge instructions, or pre-surgery instructions can have serious, even fatal, consequences. The inappropriate complexity of documents has been discussed in the medical literature for over 50 years and in the past two decades this has been broadly recognized as a serious problem within the US medical community [5]. Indeed, a significant and growing body of research has emerged relating to the problem of "health literacy", which has brought attention to the ethical and health impact of overly complex documents in healthcare [30]. Virtual agents may provide a particularly effective solution for addressing this problem, by having the agents describe health documents to patients using exemplary techniques that an expert health provider might use, given that

C. Pelachaud et al. (Eds.): IVA 2007, LNAI 4722, pp. 183–196, 2007.

they had training in communicating with patients with low health literacy and had un-bounded time available.

In this paper we describe our initial efforts in building and evaluating a virtual agent designed to explain health documents to patients.

1.1 Health Literacy

Health literacy is the ability to perform the basic reading and numerical tasks re-quired to function in the health care environment, and it affects patients' ability to understand medication labels and instructions, hospital discharge instructions, instruc-tions for assistive devices and medical equipment, and health education material [1]. Patients with inadequate health literacy report lower health status [40], are less likely to use screening procedures, follow medical regimens, keep appointments, or seek help early in the course of a disease [39], have greater difficulties naming their medi-cations and describing their indications [4,41], more frequently hold health beliefs that interfere with adherence [18], have higher health-care costs [39], and have higher rates of hospitalization [4]. Fully 90 million American adults have limited literacy skills and limited literacy has been shown to be more prevalent among patients with chronic diseases, those who are older, minorities, and those who have lower levels of education [31]. Seminal reports about the problem of health literacy include a sharp critique of current norms for overly complex documents in health care such as in-formed consent [1,28].

1.2 Virtual Agents to Address Low Health Literacy

Evidence suggests that face-to-face encounters with a health provider—in conjunction with written instructions—remains one of the best methods for communicating health information to patients in general, but especially those with low literacy levels [11,23,25,33]. Face-to-face consultation is effective because it requires that the pro-vider focus on the most salient information to be conveyed [33] and that the informa-tion be delivered in a simple, conversational speaking style. Protocols for grounding in face-to-face conversation allow providers to dynamically assess a patient's level of understanding and repeat or elaborate information as necessary [10]. Face-to-face conversation also allows providers to make their communication more explicitly in-teractive by asking patients to do, write, say, or show something that demonstrates their understanding [14]. Finally, face-to-face interaction allows providers to use ver-bal and nonverbal behaviors, such as empathy [15] and immediacy [34], to elicit pa-tient trust, enabling better communication and satisfaction.

Of course, one problem with in-person encounters with health professionals is that all providers function in health care environments in which they can only spend a very limited amount of time with each patient [12]. Time pressures can result in pa-tients feeling too intimidated to ask questions, or to ask that information be repeated. Another problem is that of "fidelity": providers do not always perform in perfect ac-cordance with recommended guidelines, resulting in significant inter-provider and in-tra-provider variations in the delivery of health information.

Given the efficacy of face-to-face consultation, one technology that shows particu-lar promise for conveying health information to patients with low health literacy is the use of virtual agents that simulate face-to-face conversation with a provider. These systems can recognize and produce verbal and nonverbal conversational behaviors that signify understanding and mark significance, and can convey information in redundant channels of information (e.g., hand gestures, such as pointing, facial display of emotion, and eye gaze), to maximize message comprehension. They can use the verbal and nonverbal communicative behaviors used by providers to establish trust and rapport with their patients in order to increase satisfaction and adherence to treatment regimens [6]. They can adapt their messages to the particular needs of patients and to the immediate context of the conversation. Virtual agents can provide health information in a consistent manner and in a low-pressure environment in which patients are free to take as much time as they need to thoroughly understand it. This is particularly important as health providers frequently fail to illicit patients' questions, and patients with low literacy are even less likely than others to ask questions [19].

Virtual agents can also consistently evaluate patient comprehension of the material presented. Physicians infrequently evaluate patients' understanding, and when they do it is mostly simply to ask "do you understand?" without waiting for a reply [36].

2 Related Work

Virtual pedagogical agents and virtual agents that use deictic (pointing) hand gestures to refer to objects in their virtual or physical environment represent the two areas of previous research that are most relevant to our work. An agent that explains a document is essentially teaching the user about the topics covered in the document, and thus pedagogical strategies pioneered by other developers of virtual agents are of interest. The appropriate use of deictic gestures is particularly important for document explanation, since they are required to orient the user to the part of the document under discussion.

Virtual pedagogical agents include Autotutor [16], Steve [35], Cosmo [21], Persona [3], Sam [7] and others. Evaluations of these agents have largely shown mixed educational outcomes. For example, users rated the Persona agent as more entertaining and helpful than an equivalent interface without the agent [3]. However, there was no difference in actual performance (comprehension and recall of presented material) in interfaces with the agent vs. interfaces without it. On the other hand, researchers evaluating the Cosmo agent found that: 1) students who interacted with an educational software system with a pedagogical agent produced more correct solutions and rated their motivation to continue learning and interest in the material significantly higher, compared to the same system without the agent; 2) students who interacted with an agent that used speech output, rated the lessons more favorably and recalled more compared with students who interacted with an agent that used text output; and 3) students who interacted with an agent that used personalized dialogue recalled more than students who interacted with an agent that communicated using nonpersonalized monologues (as in video-based education) [24]. In another study, students using the AutoTutor pedagogical agent in addition to their normal coursework outperformed both a control group (no additional intervention), and a group directed to re-read relevant material from their textbooks [32].

Deictic gestures represent perhaps the most common type of hand gesture implemented in virtual agents. Early examples include the Persona agent, which could point to parts of images on web pages, and Jack, the virtual meteorologist, who could point at weather images that he stood in front of (in his virtual environment) while giving a weather report [29]. However, the interaction and gesture specifications in these early systems were mostly scripted. The BEAT system incorporated a simple rule that generated deictics whenever a new object in the agent's virtual world was referenced in speech and was "visible" to both the agent and user [9]. Perhaps the most sophisticated model of "deictic believability" was implemented for the Cosmo agent [22]. This system utilized a separate deictic planner that would determine the generation of deictics on the basis of speech act, gesture referent, speech referent, world model (including possible distractors) and discourse history. Virtual agents that can use alternative modalities have also used deictic gestures: MACK could highlight a paper map that was "shared" with a user by means of an overhead projector [8], and Steve accompanied users into a virtual reality world where he could point out virtual objects that the user needed to manipulate [35].

To our knowledge, with the exception of the maps used by MACK, no virtual agent has been designed to date for the task of explaining physical documents to users.

3 Health Document Explanation by Human Experts

In order to develop a virtual agent that can emulate expert document explanation behavior, we analyzed four example interactions in which experts were explaining health documents to others (Fig. 1). Two of these conversations involved a hospital discharge procedure, in which a nurse reviewed diagnoses, medications, follow-up appointments, and self-care procedures with a patient by explaining an "After Hospital Care Plan" (AHCP) document. The other two conversations involved a research assistant explaining a research informed consent (CONSENT) document. The CONSENT document was two pages long and consisted entirely of text, mostly in non-technical language, whereas the AHCP was eleven pages long and consisted of a mixture of text and images. While the AHCP was explicitly designed for patients with low health literacy, it is full of medical terminology (medication names, medical

Fig. 1. Explanation of AHCP (left) and CONSENT (right) by experts

condition names, etc.). We created a single standard instance of AHCP and CONSENT documents that were used in these studies and all subsequent evaluations. All four interactions were "mock" conversations in that the listener was another research assistant, but the four individuals doing the explaining were experts in their respective areas. In the two AHCP examples, the nurse and "patient" are seated next to each other at a table with the document on the table between them. In the CONSENT examples, the research assistant and "patient" are seated facing each other, and the research assistant holds the document up for the patient. All four interactions were videotaped for subsequent analysis.

The videos were transcribed and broken into utterances, following [27]. Speech acts were coded for each utterance using the DAMSL coding scheme [2]. Table 1 provides an overview of the four conversations.

Table 1. Conversations Analyzed

Conversation	Document	TRT	Utterances		
			Expert	**Patient**	**Total**
1	CONSENT	2:08	93	1	94
2	CONSENT	2:24	103	8	111
3	AHCP	6:46	282	32	314
4	AHCP	6:53	277	39	316

3.1 Analysis of Nonverbal Behavior During Human Document Explanation

Given the importance of face-to-face interaction in communicating with low literacy patients, we focused our initial analysis and modeling efforts on the nonverbal behavior of the expert in these conversations. Initial reviews of the videos indicated that one expert behavior was ubiquitous: deictic (pointing) gestures referencing the document. Thus, we further focused our initial analysis on the occasioning and form of these deictic gestures.

The start and end of each expert gesture was coded from the video, along with the form of gesture. The timing of gesture stroke relative to utterance was also coded as: before utterance, beginning of utterance (first three words), ending of utterance (last 3 words), middle of utterance, or continued from previous utterance (following [26]). We observed a wide range of deictic forms, but decided to initially collapse these into POINT (pointing and underlining) and REGION (whole hand) gestures.

Preliminary analyses indicated that a verbal reference to a new part of the document (relative to the one currently under discussion) seemed to be a good predictor for deictic gesture. Consequently, we also coded the part of the document under discussion by the expert. The documents were broken up into topic level by identifying pages, regions and items within each document. Each topic was represented by an ID number in the format "<page>.<section>.<item>", eg. "1.4.2". We also created a code to indicate the topic level being introduced (PAGE, SECTION, or ITEM), as well as a code that indicated relative navigation in the document (IN, OUT, FORWARD, etc.), both based on changes in the topic ID,

Chi-squared tests for independence indicated that speech act, topic level, and document navigation were all strongly associated with the occurrence and form of deictic gesture performed during a given utterance (NONE, POINT or REGION, $p<.001$). We then used a commercial decision tree modeling tool (DTREG.com) to evaluate models based on various combinations of these coded predictors. The lowest error rate found (15.5%) was for a model that considered all available information (speech act, topic level, etc.). However, the model based on topic level alone was only slightly worse (15.6% error rate), so we decided to base our initial computational model on topic level alone to simplify implementation.

3.2 Resulting Model of Deictic Gesture During Document Explanation

Our preliminary model generates a deictic gesture according to the model in Table 2.

Table 2. Document Deictic Generation Model

New Topic Level	Gesture		
	NONE	POINT	REGION
No Change	92.8%	4.4%	2.8%
PAGE	57.7%	3.8%	38.5%
SECTION	23.7%	36.8%	39.5%
ITEM	23.7%	21.1%	55.3%

We found that 83% of the time, deictic gesture stroke occurred at the beginning of an utterance. Thus, in our model, all document deictic gestures are generated with their stroke at the beginning of the related utterance.

4   A Computational Model of Document Explanation

An existing virtual agent framework designed for health counseling [6] was modified to provide explanation of health documents. The framework features a vector-graphics-based virtual agent whose nonverbal behavior is synchronized with a text-to-speech engine (Fig. 2). User contributions to the conversation are made via a touch screen selection from a multiple choice menu of utterance options, updated at each turn of the conversation.

Dialogues are scripted, using a custom hierarchical transition network-based scripting language based on Augmented Transition Networks (ATNs) [42]. ATNs are used both to model the hierarchical structure of dialogue [17] as well as to enable common sub-dialogues to be factored out and re-used. In addition to network branching operations, ATN actions can include saving values to a persistent database or retrieving and testing values from the database, in order to support the ability to remember and refer back to information from earlier turns and prior conversations. Agent utterances can be tailored at runtime through the inclusion of phrases derived from information in the database or other sources (template-based text generation).

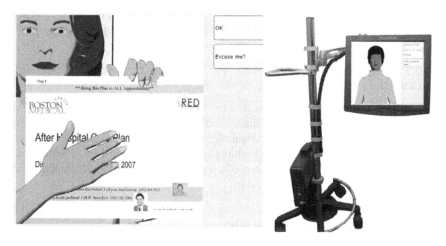

Fig. 2. Virtual Agent Interface   **Fig. 3.** Hospital Cart

The virtual agent has a range of nonverbal behaviors that it can use, including: hand gestures, body posture shifts, gazing at and away from the user, raising and lowering eyebrows, head nods, different facial expressions, and variable proximity (wide to close-up camera shots). Co-verbal behavior is determined for each utterance using the BEAT text-to-embodied-speech system [9], with several enhancements to support health dialogues. One such enhancement is that conversational frame [38] (task-oriented, social, empathetic, or encouraging) can be specified in the script and automatically translated into appropriate changes to facial expression, proximity, speech synthesizer intonation, and gesture frequency output by BEAT. While we are aware of some of the limitations of BEAT [20], we find that it is adequate for our purposes (e.g., we have yet to encounter a need for partially-overlapping temporal spans of verbal and nonverbal behavior).

The framework was extended for document explanation in several ways. Two new characters ("Elizabeth" and "Louise") were developed for this application that were more concordant with the hospital population we intend to deploy it in (middle aged, female, Caucasian and African American). A set of animation system commands was added to allow document pages to be displayed by the character (Fig. 1), with page changes automatically accompanied by a page-turning sound. A set of document deictic gestures was added so that the agent could be commanded to point anywhere in the document with either a pointing hand or an open hand. While the document is displayed, the agent can continue using its full range of head and facial behavior, with gaze-aways modified so that the agent looks at the document when not looking at the user (in our corpus, the expert gazed at the document 65% of the time and at the patient 30% of the time). However, hand gestures were limited to document deictics, and posture and proxemic shifts were disabled while the document is displayed.

In the first version of the system, we were primarily interested in the generation of document deictics given the verbal content of the document explanation script. In order to provide the information needed by BEAT for this, we introduced the use of an additional XML tag in every agent utterance that referenced the document. These tags specified the document location ID described in Section 3.1, and the X,Y coordinates (normalized to 100%, 100%) of the page corresponding to the location ID, for example:

```
<DOC PART="2.1.1" LOC="25,40"> It is for your blood
pressure. </DOC>
```

A BEAT behavior generator was created that tracked document context (current and previous document locations under discussion) and annotated the utterance parse tree with: page change specifications (whenever the document location ID indicated a change in page); document deictic gestures (per the rules described in Section 3.2); and additional gaze-aways (at the start of all utterances in which a document deictic gesture or page change is indicated).

5 Preliminary Evaluation Study

We conducted a pilot evaluation study to test the efficacy of our agent-based document explanation system, compared with a standard of care control (explanation by a human) and a non-intervention control (self study of the document in question). The study had a 3 (AGENT vs. HUMAN vs. SELF) x 2 (AHCP vs. CONSENT) between-subjects experimental design, in which each participant evaluated two different conditions in a single session, always AHCP followed by CONSENT, with the presentation of the other conditions randomized. This document ordering was intended to minimize carryover effects from the informed consent procedure for the pilot study itself to the CONSENT treatment of the study. To further minimize carryover, we used an informed consent document from an entirely different area of medical research (acquisition of blood samples for genetic banking). The study was approved by Northeastern University's IRB.

5.1 Apparatus

Two interaction scripts were created, one for the AHCP and one for CONSENT, based on the videotapes described in Section 3. In each script, users could simply advance linearly through the explanation (by selecting "OK"), ask for any utterance to be repeated ("Could you repeat that please?"), request major sections of the explanation to be repeated, or request that the entire explanation be repeated. Any number of repeats could be requested and, although the scripting language has the ability to encode rephrasings when an utterance is repeated, for the current study the agent would repeat the exact same utterance when a repeat was requested for any state in the script. The agent was deployed on a mobile cart with a touch screen attached via an articulated arm (Fig. 2), since this is the platform we will be using in the hospital for pre-discharge patient education (the articulated arm enables the screen to be positioned in front of a patient in a hospital bed). Study sessions were held in an observation room of our HCI laboratory, with the interactions videotaped using four closed-circuit video cameras.

5.2 Measures

In addition to basic demographics, we assessed health literacy using the REALM instrument, which categorizes individuals into 3rd grade and below, 4th-6th grade, 7th-8th grade, and high school [13]. We also created knowledge tests for each of the two documents, with the one for CONSENT based on the BICEP evaluation [37]. Note that these tests were always administered in an "open book" fashion with the participant able to refer to a paper copy of the document during the test. We augmented the BICEP with scale measures of likelihood to sign the consent document and perceived pressure to sign the consent document.

Evaluation questionnaires were also developed for the HUMAN and AGENT study conditions, assessing satisfaction with the instructor and with the overall instructional experience, desire to continue working with the instructor, trust in the instructor, and how knowledgeable the instructor was, all evaluated on 7-point scales.

5.3 Participants

Eighteen subjects participated in the study, were recruited via fliers posted around the Northeastern University campus, and were compensated for their time. Participants had to be 18 years of age or older and able to speak English. Participants were 74% male, aged 19-33. Two were categorized as 4th-6th grade, three as 7th-8th grade, and the rest as high school level, according to the REALM health literacy instrument.

5.4 Procedure

Participants arrived at the HCI laboratory, were consented, filled out the demographic questionnaire and then had the REALM health literacy evaluation administered.

Following this they were exposed to one of the three experimental conditions for the AHCP document. For the AGENT condition, they were given a brief training session on how to interact with the agent, the experimenter then gave the participant a paper copy of the document, left the room and closed the door. At the end of the interaction the virtual agent informed the participant that they could take as much time as they liked to review the document before signaling to the experimenter that they were ready to continue. For the HUMAN condition, a second research assistant in our lab explained the document to the study participant. This instructor did not have a health care background, but routinely administered informed consent for HCI studies and was allowed to watch the videotapes described in Section 3 to learn about the AHCP. The instructor was blind to the virtual agent interaction script content and evaluation instruments, and was simply asked to explain the document in question to the participant. For the CONTROL condition, the participant was simply handed the document and told to take as much time as they needed to read and understand it, and were then left alone in the observation room until they signaled they were ready to continue.

Following the first intervention, the research assistant verbally administered the AHCP knowledge test and instructor evaluations. The previous two steps were then repeated with the CONSENT document.

5.5 Results

We conducted full-factorial ANOVAs for all measures, with condition (AGENT, HUMAN, SELF), document (AHCP, CONSENT) and health literacy (four categories) as independent factors, and LSD post-hoc tests when applicable.

There was one main effect of document on test score (66.3 vs. 87.1, $F(1,18)=14.5, p<.001$) indicating that participants scored significantly higher on the AHCP test compared to the CONSENT test. There were no significant effects of condition or literacy on test score.

Instructor evaluations for the AGENT and HUMAN conditions indicated a number of significant effects. There was a significant interaction between condition, document and literacy on satisfaction with the overall experience ($F(1,14)=5.0$, $p<.05$) such that those in the highest literacy level were more satisfied with the agent compared to the human for CONSENT, but were more satisfied with the human for AHCP (Fig 4). However, lower literacy participants were more satisfied with the agent in all situations (5.14 for HUMAN vs. 6.33 for AGENT).

All participants rated the agent as more knowledgeable than the human for CONSENT, but the human more knowledgeable for AHCP (Fig 5, $F(1,140)=6.0$, $p<.05$).

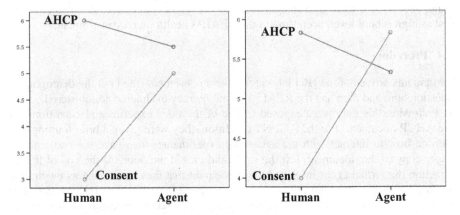

Fig. 4. Satisfaction with Overall Experience by Participants with High School Level Literacy   **Fig. 5.** Knowledge of Instructor Ratings by All Participants

There were also several main effects for literacy, with the lowest literacy participants scoring significantly lower on trust in the instructor (whether human or agent, $F(2,14)=4.4$, $p<.05$), how knowledgeable the instructor was ($F(2,14)=3.8$, $p<.05$), and desire to continue working with the instructor ($F(2,14)=4.2$, $p<.05$). For the CONSENT document, there were significant effects of health literacy on likelihood to sign ($F(2,12)=6.4$, $p<.05$) and perceived pressure to sign ($F(2,12)=132.0$, $p<.001$), such that those with lowest literacy were significantly less likely to sign and felt significantly more pressure to sign, compared to those with higher levels of literacy.

Six participants interacted with both the human and the agent in a single session, so we also compared ratings from these participants using a matched-pair analysis for increased power. These participants rated the agent significantly higher on satisfaction with the instructor (6.0 vs. 5.17, paired $t(5)=2.7$, $p<.05$) and satisfaction with the overall experience (6.17 vs. 5.0, paired $t(5)=2.9$, $p<.05$), compared to the human.

6 Conclusion

Although we did not see significant differences in test scores across intervention conditions, this was not too surprising given the relatively high literacy status of the participants and the fact that the tests were "open book". However, in a busy clinic, especially with low literacy patients, the agent may actually outperform a time constrained and impatient clinician. As some participants put it:

- "I'd rather have Elizabeth. I liked the interface. I liked the way the tone has been set to explain to people. It doesn't kind of exert too much pressure on the person who's listening, so I like that."
- "Elizabeth was cool, I would have taken that again. She was just so clear, she just went page by page so it wasn't missed. And then, I mean you can always just ask them [human] if you don't understand anyway, but it's different on a screen, I guess, because some people don't want to say that they don't understand. On a screen it's less embarrassing, no one's here so you can say 'Ok, let me hear that again.'"
- "Honestly I would have rather had Elizabeth explain them to me, just because of uh, maybe a situation with a conflict of interest, or maybe the distractions or something like that. Because everybody has distractions that keep us astray from the concept underlying the document."

While we did not see effects on test scores, we did see clear patterns emerge on satisfaction, with direct comparisons by participants who interacted with both the agent and human, as well as all evaluations by low literacy participants, indicating a preference for the agent.

The higher scores for the human describing the AHCP (satisfaction for high literacy participants and ratings of how knowledgeable the instructor was for all participants) may be due to the increased length and complexity of the AHCP and its much higher density of medical terms:

- Researcher: "Did you feel that Elizabeth did a better job explaining one of the documents to you versus another?" Participant: "Probably, yes, the second one. Well, maybe because it was easier to understand because it had less terminology."

One interpretation of these results is that the script for agent-based AHCP explanation was inadequate along one or more dimensions, and that only participants with high literacy were able to notice the deficiencies. A more likely explanation (referring to Figs. 4 and 5) is that participants did not like the human research assistant's explanation of the consent document.

In sum, we feel that the pilot study indicates that document explanation may be a very important application domain for virtual agents, and health document explanation to patients with low health literacy may be particularly significant.

Our future work is focused on extending the study with participants in the lowest literacy category. We also plan to revise the computational model using data from real provider-patient interactions (especially patients with low literacy), expand the repertoire and precision of the models of nonverbal behavior, and begin to investigate the automatic generation of explanation dialogue given a document as input. Finally, the preliminary results from this first study must be further validated through additional testing with a broader range of explanation scripts and a larger sample of human experts performing document explanation for comparison.

Acknowledgements. Thanks to Francisco Crespo and Thomas Brown for their assistance in conducting the evaluation study, and to our collaborators at Boston Medical Center—Dr. Brian Jack and Anna Johnson—for providing the example After Hospital Care Plan and videotaping the mock hospital discharge consultations. Jennifer Smith provided many helpful comments on the paper. This work was supported by a grant from the NIH National Heart Lung and Blood Institute.

References

1. Ad Hoc Committee on Health Literacy for the Council on Scientific Affairs, A.M.A.: Health literacy: report of the Council on Scientific Affairs. JAMA 281(6) 552–557 (1999)
2. Allen, J., Core, M.: Draft of DMSL: Dialogue Act Markup in Several Layers (1997)
3. Andre, E., Rist, T., Muller, J.: Integrating reactive and scripted behaviors in a life-like presentation agent. In: Proceedings of AGENTS'98, pp. 261–268 (1998)
4. Baker, D., Parker, R., Williams, M., Clark, S., Nurss, J.: The relationship of patient reading ability to self-reported health and use of services. Am. J. Public Health 87, 1027–1030 (1997)
5. Beecher, H.K.: Ethics and clinical research. N. Engl. J. Med. 274(24), 1354–1360 (1966)
6. Bickmore, T., Picard, R.: Establishing and Maintaining Long-Term Human-Computer Relationships. ACM Transactions on Computer Human Interaction 12(2), 293–327 (2005)
7. Cassell, J., Ananny, M., Basu, A., Bickmore, T., Chong, P., Mellis, D., Ryokai, K., Smith, J., Vilhjálmsson, H., Yan, H.: Shared Reality: Physical Collaboration with a Virtual Peer. In: Proceedings of CHI '00 (2000)
8. Cassell, J., Stocky, T., Bickmore, T., Gao, Y., Nakano, Y., Ryokai, K., Tversky, D., Vaucelle, C., Vilhjálmsson, H.: MACK: Media lab Autonomous Conversational Kiosk. Imagina '02 (2002)
9. Cassell, J., Vilhjálmsson, H., Bickmore, T.: BEAT: The Behavior Expression Animation Toolkit. In: SIGGRAPH '01, pp. 477–486 (2001)
10. Clark, H.H., Brennan, S.E.: Grounding in Communication. In: Resnick, L.B., Levine, J.M., Teasley, S.D. (eds.) Perspectives on Socially Shared Cognition, American Psychological Association, Washington, pp. 127–149 (1991)
11. Clinite, J., Kabat, H.: Improving patient compliance. J. Am. Pharm. Assoc. 16, 74–76 (1976)
12. Davidoff, F.: Time. Ann. Intern. Med. 127, 483–485 (1997)
13. Davis, T.C., Long, S.W., Jackson, R.H., Mayeaux, E.J., George, R.B., Murphy, P.W., Crouch, M.A.: Rapid estimate of adult literacy in medicine: a shortened screening instrument. Fam. Med. 25(6), 391–395 (1993)
14. Doak, C., Doak, L., Root, J.: Teaching patients with low literacy skills, 2nd edn., JB Lippincott, Philadelphia, PA (1996)

15. Frankel, R.: Emotion and the Physician-Patient Relationship. Motivation and Emotion 19(3), 163–173 (1995)
16. Graesser, A., al, e.: AutoTutor: A simulation of a human tutor. Cognitive Systems Research 1 (1999)
17. Grosz, B., Sidner, C.: Attention, Intentions, and the Structure of Discourse. Computational Linguistics 12(3), 175–204 (1986)
18. Kalichman, S., Ramachandran, B., Catz, S.: Adherence to a combination antiretroviral therapies in HIV patients of low health literacy. J. Gen. Intern. Med. 14, 267–273 (1999)
19. Katz, M.G., Jacobson, T.A., Veledar, E., Kripalani, S.: Patient Literacy and Question-asking Behavior During the Medical Encounter: A Mixed-methods Analysis. J. Gen. Intern. Med. (2007)
20. Kopp, S., Krenn, B., Marsella, S., Marshall, A.N., Pelachaud, C., Pirker, H., Thórisson, K., Vilhjálmsson, H.: Towards a Common Framework for Multimodal Generation: The Behavior Markup Language. In: Gratch, J., Young, M., Aylett, R., Ballin, D., Olivier, P. (eds.) IVA 2006. LNCS (LNAI), vol. 4133, Springer, Heidelberg (2006)
21. Lester, J., Towns, S., Callaway, C., Voerman, J., Fitzgerald, P.: Deictic and Emotive Communication in Animated Pedagogical Agents. In: Cassell, J. (ed.) Embodied Conversational Agents, MIT Press, Cambridge (2000)
22. Lester, J., Voerman, J., Towns, S., Callaway, C.: Deictic Believability: Coordinating Gesture, Locomotion, and Speech in Lifelike Pedagogical Agents. Applied Artificial Intelligence 13(4-5), 383–414 (1999)
23. Madden, E.: Evaluation of outpatient pharmacy patient counseling. J. Am. Pharm. Ass. 13, 437–443 (1973)
24. Moreno, R., Lester, J.C., Mayer, R.E.: Life-Like Pedagogical Agents in Constructivist Multimedia Environments: Cognitive Consequences of their Interaction. In: ED-MEDIA, pp. 741–746 (2000)
25. Morris, L., Halperin, J.: Effects of Written Drug Information on Patient Knowledge and Compliance: A Literature Review. Am. J. Public Health 69(1), 47–52 (1979)
26. Nakano, Y.I., Reinstein, G., Stocky, T., Cassell, J.: Towards a Model of Face-to-Face Grounding. In: Annual Meeting of the Association for Computational Linguistics (2003)
27. Nakatani, C., Traum, D.: Coding discourse structure in dialogue (version 1.0). University of Maryland (1999)
28. Nielsen-Bohlman, L., Panzer, A.M., Hamlin, B., Kindig, D.A.: Institute of Medicine. Health Literacy: A Prescription to End Confusion. In: Committee on Health Literacy, Board on Neuroscience and Behavioral Health, National Academies Press, Washington DC (2004)
29. Noma, T., Zhao, L., Badler, N.I.: Design of a virtual human presenter. Computer Graphics and Applications, IEEE 20(4), 79–85 (2000)
30. Paasche-Orlow, M., Greene, S.M., Wagner, E.H.: How health care systems can begin to address the challenge of limited literacy. J. Gen. Intern. Med. 21(8), 884–887 (2006)
31. Paasche-Orlow, M.K., Parker, R.M., Gazmararian, J.A., Nielsen-Bohlman, L.T., Rudd, R.R.: The prevalence of limited health literacy. J. Gen. Intern. Med. 20(2), 175–184 (2005)
32. Person, N.K., Graesser, A.C., Bautista, L., Mathews, E.C.: Evaluating Student Learning Gains in Two Versions of AutoTutor. In: Moore, J.D., Redfield, C.L., Johnson, W.L. (eds.) Artificial intelligence in education: AI-ED in the wired and wireless future, pp. 286–293. IOS Press, Amsterdam (2001)
33. Qualls, C., Harris, J., Rogers, W.: Cognitive-Linguistic Aging: Considerations for Home Health Care Environments. In: Rogers, W., Fisk, A. (eds.) Human Factors Interventions for the Health Care of Older Adults, pp. 47–67. Lawrence Erlbaum, Mahwah (2002)

196 T.W. Bickmore, L.M. Pfeifer, and M.K. Paasche-Orlow

34. Richmond, V., McCroskey, J.: Immediacy. In: Nonverbal Behavior in Interpersonal Relations, pp. 195–217. Allyn & Bacon, Boston (1995)
35. Rickel, J., Johnson, W.L.: Animated Agents for Procedural Traning in Virtual Reality: Perception, Cognition and Motor Control. Applied Artificial Intelligence (1998)
36. Schillinger, D., Piette, J., Grumbach, K., Wang, F., Wilson, C., Daher, C.: Closing the loop: physician communication with diabetic patients who have low health literacy. Arch.Intern.Med. 163(1), 83–90 (2003)
37. Sugarman, J., Lavori, P.W., Boeger, M., Cain, C., Edson, R., Morrison, V., Yeh, S.S.: Evaluating the quality of informed consent. Clinical Trials 2(1), 34 (2005)
38. Tannen, D.: Framing in Discourse. Oxford University Press, New York (1993)
39. Weiss, B.: Illiteracy among Medicaid recipients and its relation to health care costs. J. Health Care Poor Underserved 4(5), 99–111 (1994)
40. Weiss, B., Hart, G., McGee, D., D'Estelle, S.: Health status of illerate adults: relation between literacy and health status among persons with low literacy skills. J. Am. Board Fam. Parct. 5, 254–257 (1992)
41. Williams, M., Parker, R., Baker, D., Coates, W., Nurss, J.: The impact of inadequate functional health literacy on patients understanding of diagnosis, prescribed medications, and compliance. Acad. Emerg. Med. 2, 386 (1995)
42. Woods, W.A.: Transition Network Grammars for Natural Language Analysis. In: Grosz, B.J., Jones, K.S., Webber, B.L. (eds.) Readings in Natural Language Processing, pp. 71–88. Morgan Kaufmann Publishers, Los Alamitos (1986)

Virtual Patients for Clinical Therapist Skills Training

Patrick Kenny, Thomas D. Parsons, Jonathan Gratch,
Anton Leuski, and Albert A. Rizzo

Institute for Creative Technologies,
University of Southern California
13274 Fiji Way Marina Del Rey, CA 90292, USA
{kenny,parsons,gratch,leuski,rizzo}@ict.usc.edu

Abstract. Virtual humans offer an exciting and powerful potential for rich interactive experiences. Fully embodied virtual humans are growing in capability, ease, and utility. As a result, they present an opportunity for expanding research into burgeoning virtual patient medical applications. In this paper we consider the ways in which one may go about building and applying virtual human technology to the virtual patient domain. Specifically we aim to show that virtual human technology may be used to help develop the interviewing and diagnostics skills of developing clinicians. Herein we proffer a description of our iterative design process and preliminary results to show that virtual patients may be a useful adjunct to psychotherapy education.

Keywords: Virtual Humans, Virtual Patients, Psychopathology.

1 Introduction

Virtual human technology may provide mental health professionals with a powerful tool for assessment, intervention, and training. This technology offers exciting potential for rich interactive experiences. Current therapeutic training systems resort to using real people (hired actors or resident students) acting as simulated patients to portray patients with given medical problems. The problem could be physical or psychological. Whilst the use of technology to replace or augment simulated patients has not been widely applied or accepted, a search of the literature of interactive virtual characters reveals only a handful of studies. Part of the problem has been the difficulty of building complex interactive virtual characters that can act as simulated patients. An additional complication has been the technological issues involved in trying to get interactive virtual characters to act like real patients. On top of all this has been the expertise in designing effective training systems that can teach the relevant material. The work presented here is a preliminary attempt at what we believe to be a large application area. Herein we describe an initial endeavor to apply our virtual characters as virtual patients (VP).

We present an approach that allows novice mental health clinicians to conduct an interview with a virtual character that emulates an adolescent male with conduct disorder. The paper will also describe the theory and praxes involved in creating the character with psychological problems along with issues and lessons learned as to

C. Pelachaud et al. (Eds.): IVA 2007, LNAI 4722, pp. 197–210, 2007.

how it can be applied in training novice therapists to perform interviews and differential diagnosis. Aspects of preliminary subject testing of the system will be discussed along with a few example dialog sessions with the character. The final section will discuss proposals for future work and modifications to the current system to make the VP more engaging. Although we are in the early stages of developing this system, the initial outcome of the tests was favorable. The paper also illustrates how a variety of core research components developed at the University of Southern California facilitates the rapid development of mental health applications.

2 Related Work

Virtual humans are increasingly being recognized as useful tools for training, education, research, and entertainment. Work in virtual humans covers a broad array of tasks that require an integrated system for a fully embodied conversational character.

Fully embodied conversational characters have been around for since the early 90's [4]. There has been much work on full systems to be used for training [9,20,21], intelligent kiosks [16], and virtual receptionists [2]. We have had previous involvement with systems that use virtual reality for PTSD [22] and ADHD [18,23].

VPs are virtual interactive agents who are trained to simulate a patient's particular clinical presentation with a high degree of consistency and realism. VPs have commonly been used to teach bedside competencies in bioethical decision making, basic patient communication and history taking, and clinical decision making [6,10,17,26]. VPs can provide valid, reliable, and applicable representations of live patients [29]. For example, in an application from Lok's research group, instead of having novice medical students practice on professional patients, they constructed a virtual environment to represent an examination room where a VP could be interviewed verbally with speech recognition [1]. The goal in this application was to determine, via clinical interview, whether the VPs ailment was due to appendicitis. Results suggested that the virtual interaction was similar to the real interaction on content measures and participants gathered the same information from the virtual human and real patient.

Research into the use of VPs in psychotherapy training is very limited [8,11]. Beutler and Harwood [3] describe the development of a VR system for training in psychotherapy and summarize training-relevant research findings. We could not find reference to any other use of VPs in a psychotherapy course to date, despite online searches through MEDLINE, Ovid, and the psychotherapy literature. Designing VPs that have human-to-human interaction and communication skills would open up possibilities for clinical applications that address interviewing skills, diagnostic assessment and therapy training.

3 Virtual Patient Domain

We choose the medical field domain for this application, specifically cognitive behavior therapy (CBT). The mental health domain offers some interesting challenges to both the design of the characters and the design of the training system to enhance skills in interviewing, differential diagnosis, and therapeutic communication. The domain also offers a plethora of modeling issues including: verbal and non-verbal behavior, cognition, affect, rational and irrational behavior, personality, and psychopathology.

For our application we choose to model a character with the history and symptoms of conduct disorder (described below). We wanted to take on a problem that wasn't too hard to model and could be structured as an interview, where one could ask questions and get responses. We endeavored to constrain the domain so that the character would only discuss certain topics, which were decided upon a priori. To approach this problem we gathered data about patients with conduct disorder so that we could include their characteristics. We also spoke with experienced psychologists to develop a library of typical questions that a novice clinicians might ask a person with conduct disorder and the kinds of responses (verbal and nonverbal) persons with conduct disorder might give. Additionally, we needed something that was relevant to the types of training we would like to exemplify in the system, specifically clinical interviewing skills and diagnosis of a problem.

The data was gathered through role-playing exercises, subject testing, consulting manuals, and soliciting knowledge from subject matter experts. The methodology used was an iterative process of data collecting, testing, and refining. While the preliminary goal of the project was to use the VP to teach diagnostic skills training, the eventual goal is to have the VP be utilized in individual trainee interviews, small group and classroom settings.

3.1 Skills Training

Teaching interviewing skills with virtual humans and VPs is still a young discipline. The common practice is to use real humans (i.e simulated patients) to play the roles of the patients. A general complication involved in teaching general interviewing skills is that there are multiple therapeutic orientations and techniques to choose from and it is not well understood how to properly implement each of these with a VP. There are no standard methods and metrics to measure what works for the different types of interviews given to patients in the multitude of different mental health problems. To alleviate this problem we are concentrating on teaching skills required to diagnose a particular type of mental disorder called conduct disorder. Our goal is to obtain objective data from an initial intake interview. An intake interview is the first interview that a clinician conducts with a patient. The clinician may have some knowledge of why the patient is there (i.e. a referral question), but needs to ask the patient further questions to obtain a detailed history to narrow down the problem for differential diagnosis and treatment planning. The system is designed to allow novice clinicians to practice asking interview questions in an effort to create a positive therapeutic alliance with this very challenging VP.

3.2 Conduct Disorder

The project involved the construction of a natural language-capable VP named "Justin." The clinical attributes of Justin were developed to mimic a conduct disorder profile as found in the Diagnostic and Statistical Manual of Mental Disorders DSM-IV-TR [5]. Justin portrays a 16-year old male with a conduct disorder who is being forced to participate in therapy by his family. Justin has a history of a chronic pattern of antisocial behavior in which the basic rights of others and age-appropriate societal norms are violated. He has stolen, been truant, broken into someone's car, been cruel to animals, and initiated physical fights.

For conduct disorder the trainee's interview questions should be guided by eliciting information regarding the four general symptom categories prevalent in conduct disorder:

- Aggressive behavior – e.g. fighting, bullying, being cruel to others or animals
- Destructive behavior – e.g. arson, vandalism
- Deceitful behavior – e.g. repeated lying, shoplifting, breaking into homes or cars
- Violation of rules – e.g. running away, engaging in non appropriate behavior for age

The VP system is designed to provide answers to questions that target each of these categories and will respond to a variety of questions pertinent to these areas. More detail of how this is accomplished is seen in the architecture section. Some responses by the VP may be on target, off target, involve "brush away" responses, and in some cases, they may be irrelevant replies. For example if the trainee asks: "How are things going at home" or "Are you having any problems at home" or "How are things going?", the system will respond with "My parents think I messed up." Further questions will lead to finding out that the patient has been running away. This will lead to marking one of the above categories true for the diagnosis in the trainees' interview. In order for the trainee to pass, it will require responses in all of the categories. One important distinction between this VP system and a general question response text or speech based system is the ability to use multimodal presentation in the interaction with the patient. The character will respond with gestures along with speech. The dialog of the embodied character is synchronized with non-verbal behavior when the patient answers questions. For example a brush off response would trigger an arm to swing out as to push the issue aside. Being able to develop more multimodal behavior for each of the categories is anticipated to make this a powerful asset over just a text interface. The total set of questions, responses, behavior patterns and interview interactions are extracted from role-playing exercises, initial subject testing, interviews with doctors and common sense. In total the question set consists of over 100 questions and 70 responses. The current set of gestures consists of over 20 distinct gestures in a sitting pose and 30 standing gestures in 4 poses; hands at sided, crossed arms and right and/or left hand on hip.

4 Virtual Patient Architecture

The VP system is based on our existing virtual human architecture [9,27]. The general architecture supports a wide range of virtual humans from simple question/answering to more complex ones that contain cognitive and emotional models with goal oriented behavior. The architecture is a modular distributed system with many components that communicate by message passing. Because the architecture is modular it is easy to add, replace or combine components as needed. For example in the larger virtual human architecture the natural language section is divided into three components: a part to understand the language, a part to manage the dialog and a part to generate the output text. This is all combined into one component for the VP system.

Interaction with the system works as follows and can be seen in Figure 1. A user talks into a microphone which records the audio signal that is sent to a speech recognition engine. The speech engine converts that into text. The text is then sent to a statistical response selection module. The module picks an appropriate verbal response based on the input text question. The response is then sent to a non-verbal behavior generator that selects animations to play for the text, based on a set of rules. The output is then sent to a procedural animation system along with a pre-recorded or a generated voice file. The animation system plays and synchronizes the gestures, speech and lip syncing for the final output to the screen. The user then listens to the response and asks more questions to the character.

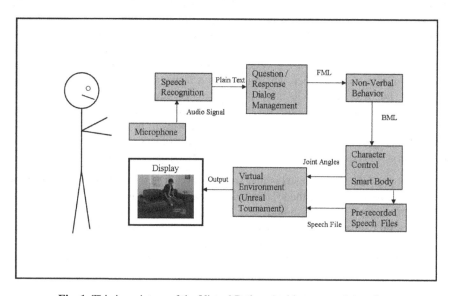

Fig. 1. This is a picture of the Virtual Patient Architecture and data flow

4.1 Human Speech Input

A human user talks to the system using a head-mounted close-capture USB microphone. The user's speech is converted into text by an automatic speech recognition system. We used the SONIC speech recognition engine from the University of Colorado, Boulder. [19]. We customized the engine's acoustic and language models for the domain on interest [25]. In general a language model is tuned to the domain word lexicon. We collect user's voice data during each session, it allows us to go over the data to collect words not recognized to enhance the lexicon and also to get error rates to compare the input speech with the processed output speech. The speech recognition engine processes the audio data and produces the text of the user's utterance. It then packages the text into a message and sends it to the response selection module.

4.2 Response Selection

The response selection module receives a text message from the speech recognition module, analyzes the text, and selects the most appropriate response. The virtual human system has a number of pre-defined response lines and given a user's utterance, the response selection module has to choose a single answer among them. This response selection process is based on a statistical text classification approach developed at the Natural Language group at ICT [14]. The approach requires a domain designer to provide some sample questions for each system response. When a new question comes from the speech recognition module, the system uses the mapping between the answers and sample questions as a "dictionary" to "translate" the question into a representation of a "perfect" answer. It then compares that representation to all known text answers and selects the best match. This approach was developed for the SGT Blackwell virtual human project [15] and has been shown to outperform traditional state-of-the-art text classification techniques.

To facilitate rapid development and deployment of virtual human agents with similar capabilities the Natural Language group created NPCEditor, a user friendly software package for editing the system answers, adding sample questions, training and running the text classifier. There is no limit to the number of answers or sample questions, but it is advised to have at least two or three sample questions for each answer. The system allows for several answer categories. Sometimes the system combines the text from answers of different categories to produce the final response. The only category required is on-topic responses, the others are optional, but make the system more interactive and realistic. The category types are as follows:

- On-topic – These are answers that are relevant to the domain of the conversation. These are the answers the system has to produce when asked a relevant question. Each on-topic answer should have a few sample questions and single sample question can be linked to several answers. The text classifier generally returns a ranked list of answers and the system makes the final selection based on the rank of the answer and whether the answer has been used recently. That way if the user repeats his questions, he may get a different response from the system.
- Off-topic – These are answers for questions that do not have domain-relevant answers. They can be direct, e.g., "I do not know the answer", or evasive, e.g., "I will not tell you" or "Better ask somebody else". When the system cannot find a good on-topic answer for a question, it selects one of the off-topic lines. More details on off-topic answer classification can be found elsewhere [24].
- Repeat –If the classifier selects an answer tagged with this category, the system does not return that answer but replays the most recent response. Sample questions may include lines like "What was that?" or "Can you say that again?" Normally, there is at most one answer of this category in the domain answer set.
- Alternative – If the classifier selects an answer tagged with this category, the system attempts to find an alternative answer to the most recent question. It takes the ranked list of answers for the last question and selects the next available answer. Sample questions may include lines like "Do you have anything to add?" Normally, there is at most one answer tagged with this category in the answer set.

- Pre-repeat – Sometimes the system has to repeat an answer. For example, it happens when a user repeats a question and there is only one good response available. The system returns the same answer again but indicates that it is repeating itself by playing a pre-repeat-tagged line before the answer, e.g., "I told you already." There is no need to assign sample questions to these answer lines.
- Delayed – These are the lines from the system that prompt the user to ask about a domain related thing, e.g., "Why don't you ask me about…" Such a response is triggered if the user asks too many off-topic questions. The system would return an off-topic answer followed by a delayed-tagged answer. That way the system attempts to bring the conversation back into the known domain. This category has no sample questions assigned.

Once the output response is selected, it is packaged up into a FML (Functional Markup Language) message structure. FML allows the addition of elements such as affect, emphasis, turn management, or coping strategies. For the VP, the response selection module does not add any additional information besides the text.

4.3 Behavior Generation

The FML message is sent to the non-verbal behavior (NVB) generator which applies a set of rules to select gestures, postures and gazes for the virtual character. Since the VP in this application was sitting down, the animations mainly consisted of arm movements, wave offs and head shakes or nods. The VP character does not do any posture shifts or go into standing posture, although in the next version more gestures and postures will be added. Once the NVB selects the appropriate behavior for the input text, it then packages this up into a Behavioral Markup Language (BML) [12] structure and sends it to a procedural animation system. For more detail on how the NVB works, see the paper on this at last years IVA06 [13].

4.4 Character Control and Output

This last part of the process is the execution and display of the characters multimodal behavior. This is accomplished with a procedural animation system called Smartbody [28]. Smartbody takes as input the BML message that contains the set of behaviors that need to be executed for the head, facial expressions, gaze, body movements, arm gestures, speech and lip syncing and synchronizes all of this together. These behaviors need to be in sync with the output speech to look realistic. Smartbody is capable of using generated or pre-recorded speech. The VP used pre-recorded speech.

Smartbody is hooked up to a visualization engine, in this case the Unreal Tournament game engine for the graphics output. Smartbody controls the character in the game engine and also specifies which sound to play for the characters speech output. Smartbody is also capable of having controllers that perform specific actions based on rules or timing information, such as head nods. The controllers are seamlessly blended in with the input animations specified in the BML. The VP does not make extensive use of controllers, however, future work is to design controllers for certain behavior patterns such as gaze aversion or ticks the character might have. A motex, which is a looping animation file, can be played for the character to give is a bit of sway, or in the VP case, finger tapping.

Fig. 2. Virtual Patient "Justin" in the clinician's office

4.5 Artwork

The artwork plays a crucial role in defining the characters behavior, attitude and condition. People are able to make a judgment about someone within the first few seconds. The project involved the development of a VP named "Justin", see Figure 2. We wanted a sixteen year old boy that has some kind of mental problem, but we wanted to keep the character design general so that the artwork would not be tied to a specific medical condition, for example giving him a broken arm. For the boy we wanted a typical teenager with a T-shirt, blue jeans and baseball hat. One must be careful with the design of the character as everything can lead to questions by the users. For example the character has a rip in the pants. This was seen, but not realized until one of the subject testers asked the patient where he got the rip in the pants. Since this was not anticipated, there were no appropriate responses except a brush-off.

The project also involved the development of a clinical virtual environment in which the trainees learn interviewing techniques. The environment was modeled after a typical clinician's office and was meant to represent a place that would make the patient feel at home.

5 Evaluation and Discussions

The purpose of the evaluation was two fold: 1) General assessment of the system's capacity for interactive response to questions posed to the VP; and 2) Specific application of the system's performance when interacting with a novice clinician as he or she conducted an intake interview and relevant psychiatric history of the VP. The sample of participants included six persons from the University of Southern

California's Keck School of Medicine. Two staff members associated with the project administered the evaluations. Initial inclusion criteria for these evaluations required that participants have previous clinical therapy skills. The desired level of clinical competence, however, was not readily available. As a result, our sample size was limited to an N of 3.

The method of evaluation was conducted in three phases: 1) Pre-Questionnaire Phase: an initial pre-questionnaire assessed the participant's skill level for spoken dialog systems and clinical skill set relevant to differential diagnosis of adolescent behavior problems; 2) Interview Phase: a 30 minute interactive interview with the VP (i.e. Justin); and 3) Post-Questionnaire Phase: following the interview a post-questionnaire assessed the participant's knowledge of the VPs condition, the interaction with the VP and the system in general. The post-questionnaire had questions ranked on a 7 point Likert scale with some area for comments. In total there were 35 questions that made up the pre and post forms. The initial results presented here will be used to adjust the system for a more formal evaluation.

5.1 Assessment of the System

Assessment of the system was completed by 1) experimenter observation of the participants as they communicated with the VP in addition; 2) the questionnaires. In order that the system be adequately evaluated, we determined a number of areas that needed to be addressed.

- The behavior of the VP should match the behavior one would expect from a patient in such a condition. Specific behaviors included: verbalization, gesture, posture, and appearance.
- Adequacy of the communicative discourse between the VP and the participants.
- Proficiency (e.g. clarity, pace, utility) of VPs discourse with the participant.
- Quality of the speech recognition of utterances spoken.

The results from the survey suggest that the system performed well and participants reported that the system simulated the real-life experience (i.e. ranked 5 or 6). The verbal and non-verbal behavior also ranked high (i.e. between 5 and 7).

Some participants found aspects of the experience "frustrating", mainly because they were not able to receive anticipated responses and the system's tendency to repeat some responses too many times. This was due to the speech recognition's inability to evaluate some of the stimulus words. Further, there were too many "brush off" responses and questions asked that were outside the dialog set previously constructed. The VP seems to be slightly more resistant than anticipated. As a result, it was difficult for participants to get the VP to elaborate on matters that were initially presented. This occurred, for example, when a participant attempted to acquire more detailed information related to the VPs peer-relations, drug use, and familial relations. The level of depth in a topic area limited the VPs response set to only a cursory level and as a result, further details were not forthcoming. When the participants tried to ask questions about the familial relations from a different vantage point the same responses or "brush off" responses were chosen. Whilst this is desirable in that it pushes the participant to apply multiple interviewing tactics, the system may also seem rigid and unresponsive if there is not enough feedback from the VP, This could be alleviated if an observer or instructor was watching the trainee and provided necessary feedback in those instances in which the system cannot.

There is a concern that participants ascribe characteristics to the VP which in fact are not present. For example, although the VP responded "Yes" to a question about whether the VP hurt animals, in actuality the system did not recognize the input speech. This can lead to confusion later on if the character then responds differently. In fact one of the most substantial lessons learned was the amount of conversation state that needed to be tracked for the topics and questions asked by the participant so that the VP's responses would be consistent throughout the session.

5.2 History Taking and Interviewing Assessment

If the system was to be used in helping to train clinicians then we would want to know if the subjects could identify a behavior problem in the VP. Specifically, we would want to assess the clinician's ability to differentially diagnose the VPs conduct disorder. We asked several questions about what condition the participants thought the VP had, what led to this conclusion, how early they diagnosed the condition, and if the condition was believable to them.   Additionally we had them select from conduct disorder categories, what they gathered from interaction with the character, and what problems they thought the VP had. These were multiple choice questions where participants could choose from home, school, parents, friends or life in general. Most participants selected school, parents, and life in general. Although there were responses in all categories, the ones the participants selected were the ones with the most responses. The participants tended to focus more on a single area, rather than asking questions that would allow them to have a broad understanding of the VPs psychiatric history. This may reflect the fact that these were novice clinicians, easily swayed by a desire for a quick diagnosis instead of a full clinical picture for differential diagnosis. The data from the initial intake interview suggests that overall the participants were able to establish that the VP was resistant, had problems with his family, school and life, but could only attribute this to a behavior problem and not conduct disorder. The participants did not ask appropriate questions, which would have elicited information regarding the four general symptom categories prevalent in conduct disorder. As a result, they were unable to prompt the system to offer the correct responses. Again, this reflects the novice level of these clinicians and the need for a qualified supervisor to help direct their development.   A more experienced clinician would know the importance of seeking a full clinical picture so that she may then explore in more depth the referral issues.

5.3 Results and Lessons Learned

Based on the subject testing the question and response set needs to be expanded to include more detail about the conditions in each of the conduct disorder categories, and have the system offer up more information that would lead them to asking more questions about topics that are covered in the domain.

People unfamiliar with speech systems tend to have run-on or multi-subject sentences, i.e. ask many questions in one speech utterance. The current system does not deal with this well and usually ends up with a brush off or incorrect response choice. This can frustrate the user as they expect the system to be able to do more then it can. This can lead to negative training, or it could also be seen as good training to get the user to think about the questions they are asking. There are some proper ways to conduct an interview as described in [7], but everyone has their own questioning style they are comfortable with and the system would need to be able to handle each type. The subjects enjoyed the experience, thought it could be useful tool, and it gave them freedom to think and explore the problem space.

One question that should be discussed is; Can you participate in a clinical interview without discourse memory, or the ability for the patient to remember more then the last one or two questions. One of the complaints that we saw in subject using these kinds of question response systems are the number of repeat responses. Having a way to track the discourse would ultimately benefit the usability, however it would make authoring the dialog more complex as this would increase the questions and response lines required. It is unclear how much discourse memory is needed in this application and future studies are required for that.

6 Conclusion

This study was our initial prototype of building an interactive VP that was capable of discourse with novice clinicians so that they may establish the VPs clinical history and differential diagnosis. We described the domain, the architecture, the subject testing and evaluation conducted. The plan is to take the results and lessons learned from the evaluation and apply those to a more formal study. For the current study, we acknowledge that this may have some bearing on the overall interpretation of results. Furthermore, these findings are based on a fairly small sample size. As a necessary next step, the reliability and validity of the test needs to be established using a larger sample of participants. This will ensure that the current findings are not an anomaly due to sample size.

This is an initially prototype system that we are currently using as an assessment tools to make a differential diagnosis of a virtual patient. In order to build a system like this to be effective for general clinical interviewing a minimal set of requirements should be considered. It's hard to state all that is needed without more subject testing and evaluations. But these requirements should address the technology, the learning objectives and the virtual patients. The technology needs to support face to face interaction, ideally using speech recognition. The system needs to respond in a natural amount of time for the character, response times that are too slow distract from the process. The system needs to allow the characters to respond and express themselves with verbal and non-verbal behavior. Understanding the learning objectives and how best to enable that in the system is valuable, however it can be quite a complex and difficult process. The technology needs to support those objectives. The characters need to be believable and responsive for the type of mental disorder they posses and designing the surface level verbal and nonverbal behavior is still an area of research.

Are embodied characters better then just speech or text interfaces? We believe that having the ability for a character to show verbal and non-verbal behavior is a powerful mechanism. Clinicians rely on certain nonverbal cues to understand the behavior of the patients and to make a diagnosis. Increasing the believability of these characters will draw the clinician into a closer engagement then just analyzing text.

Future work with the system should include: 1) addition of a camera for more user input into the system. This would enable the character to see the users' movement, e.g. if they are gazing at them. The more interaction the better; 2) addition of more personality to the character; this would allow training with different types of characters, for example an aggressive vs. a passive one. The kinds of questions the user asks may change based on some personality characteristics. The personality would be reflected in the verbal and non-verbal behavior; 3) maintain more conversation and discourse memory about what is being discussed in the interview to reduce brush off or incorrect responses; 4) addition of intonation, prosody, and affect to the speech output (e.g given that persons with Conduct Disorder are prone to anger, it may be appropriate to have him shout his responses when the same question is asked several times); 5) addition of tools to build characters that have several different behavior problems, the dialog they would use and the non-verbal behavior they would manifest; 6) Compare an interview of a real clinician and a real patient to a VP and see how the questions asked to the real patient respond when asked to the VP.

For interview training a series of small vignettes that guide one particular interviewing technique such as reflective listening and following would be useful. Additional enhancements to the system would include the building of an agent that tracks the dialog, affective behaviors, and other state information of interviewers. Such enhancements would also augment the VPs behaviors based on the system's capacity for representing various psychological problems.

Characters should be built that don't fit neatly into one specific category, as no one ever does. They should have the core criteria of a normal person but can deviate from that norm into one of the mental disorder categories. Ascribing this kind of verbal and non-verbal behavior to a fully embodied multimodal character will ultimately increase the believability, interactivity and effectiveness of the system. In most therapy session talking to the patient is the cure, a clinician that tries to understand the problem and offer up a solution will lead to a clinician that can enhance their skill set.

Acknowledgments. This work was sponsored by the U.S. Army Research, Development, and Engineering Command (RDECOM), and the content does not necessarily reflect the position or the policy of the Government, and no official endorsement should be inferred. We wish to thank Keck School of Medicine at USC and Cheryl StGeorge for helping with the test subjects.

References

1. Andrew, R., Johnsen, K., Dickerson, R., Lok, B., Cohen, M., Stevens, A., Bernard, T., Oxendine, C., Wagner, P., Lind, S.: Comparing Interpersonal Interactions with a Virtual Human to those with a Real Human. IEEE Transactions on Visualization and Computer Graphics (2006)
2. Babu, S., Schmugge, S., Barnes, T., Hodges, L.: What Would You Like to Talk About? An Evaluation of Social Conversations with a Virtual Receptionist. In: Gratch, J., Young, M., Aylett, R., Ballin, D., Olivier, P. (eds.) IVA 2006. LNCS (LNAI), vol. 4133, pp. 169–180. Springer, Heidelberg (2006)

3. Beutler, L.E., Harwood, T.M.: Virtual reality in psychotherapy training. Journal of Clinical Psychology 60, 317–330 (2004)
4. Cassell, J., Bickmore, T., Billinghurst, M., Campbell, L., Chang, K., Vilhjálmsson, H., Yan, H.: An Architecture for Embodied Conversational Characters. In: Proceedings of the First Workshop on Embodied Conversational Characters, Tahoe City, California, October 12-15 (1998)
5. Diagnostic and Statistical Manual of Mental Disorders DSM-IV-TR 4th Ed, (Text Revision), American, Psychiatric Association (1994)
6. Dickerson, R., Johnsen, K., Raij, A., Lok, B., Hernandez, J., Stevens, A.: Evaluating a script-based approach for simulating patient-doctor interaction. In: Proceedings of the International Conference of Human-Computer Interface Advances for Modeling and Simulation (2005)
7. Evans, D., Hern, M., Uhlemann, M., Lvey, A.: Essential Interviewing: A Programmed Approach to Effective Communication, 3rd edn. Brooks/Cole Publishing Company (1989)
8. Frank, G., Guinn, C., Hubal, R., Pope, P., Stanford, M., Lamm-Weisel, D.: JUSTTALK: An application of responsive virtual human technology. In: Proceedings of the Interservice/Industry Training, Simulation and Education Conference, USA (2002)
9. Gratch, J., Rickel, J., André, E., Badler, N., Cassell, J., Petajan, E.: Creating Interactive Virtual Humans: Some Assembly Required. IEEE Intelligent Systems (July/August 2002)
10. Johnsen, K., Dickerson, R., Raij, A., Harrison, C., Lok, B., Stevens, A., et al.: Evolving an immersive medical communication skills trainer. Presence: Teleoperators and Virtual Environments 15(1), 33–46 (2006)
11. Kiss, B., Szijarto, G., Benedek, B., Simon, L., Csukly, G., Takacs, B.: CyberTherapy: Applications of virtual reality and digital humans in clinical psychology. In: 2nd International Conference on Computer Animation Geometric Modeling, Hungary (2003)
12. Kopp, S., Krenn, B., Marsella, S., Marshall, A., Pelachaud, C., Pirker, H., Thorisson, K., Vilhjalmsson, H.: Towards a Common Framework for Multimodal Generation: The Behavior Markup Language. In: Gratch, J., Young, M., Aylett, R., Ballin, D., Olivier, P. (eds.) IVA 2006. LNCS (LNAI), vol. 4133, Springer, Heidelberg (2006)
13. Lee, J., Marsella, S.: Nonverbal Behavior Generator for Embodied Conversational Agents. In: 6th International Conference on Intelligent Virtual Agents, Marina del Rey, CA (2006)
14. Leuski, A., Patel, R., Traum, D., Kennedy, B.: Building effective question answering characters. In: Proceedings of the 7th SIGdial Workshop on Discourse and Dialogue, Sydney, Australia (2006)
15. Leuski, A., Pair, J., Traum, D., McNerney, P.J., Georgiou, P., Patel, R.: How to talk to a hologram. In: Edmonds, E., Riecken, D., Paris, C.L., Sidner, C.L. (eds.) Proceedings of the 11th international conference on Intelligent user interfaces(IUI'06), Sydney, Australia, pp. 360–362. ACM Press, New York (2006)
16. McCauley, L., D'Mello, S.: MIKI: A Speech Enabled Intelligent Kiosk. In: Gratch, J., Young, M., Aylett, R., Ballin, D., Olivier, P. (eds.) IVA 2006. LNCS (LNAI), vol. 4133, pp. 132–144. Springer, Heidelberg (2006)
17. McGee, J.B., Neill, J., Goldman, L., Casey, E.: Using multimedia virtual patients to enhance the clinical curriculum for medical students. Medinfo 9(2), 732–735 (1998)
18. Parsons, T.D., Bowerly, T., Buckwalter, J.G., Rizzo, A.A.: A controlled clinical comparison of attention performance in children with ADHD in a virtual reality classroom compared to standard neuropsychological methods. Child Neuropsychology (2007)
19. Pellom, B.: Sonic: The University of Colorado continuous speech recognizer. Technical Report TR-CSLR-2001-01, University of Colorado, Boulder, CO (2001)

20. Prendinger, H., Ishizuka, M.: Life-Like Characters - Tools, Affective Functions, and Applications. Springer, Heidelberg (2004)
21. Rickel, J., Gratch, J., Hill, R., Marsella, S., Swartout, W.: Steve Goes to Bosnia: Towards a New Generation of Virtual Humans for Interactive Experiences. In: AAAI Spring Symposium on Artificial Intelligence and Interactive Entertainment, Stanford University, CA (2001)
22. Rizzo, A.A., Pair, J., Graap, K., Treskunov, A., Parsons, T.D.: User-Centered Design Driven Development of a VR Therapy Application for Iraq War Combat-Related Post Traumatic Stress Disorder. In: Proceedings of the 2006 International Conference on Disability, Virtual Reality and Associated Technology, pp. 113–122 (2006)
23. Rizzo, A., Bowerly, T., Buckwalter, J., Klimchuk, D., Mitura, R., Parsons, T.D.: A Virtual Reality Scenario for All Seasons: The Virtual Classroom. CNS Spectrums 11(1) (2006)
24. Patel, R., Leuski, A., Traum, D.: Dealing with out of domain questions in virtual characters. In: Gratch, J., Young, M., Aylett, R., Ballin, D., Olivier, P. (eds.) IVA 2006. LNCS (LNAI), vol. 4133, Springer, Heidelberg (2006)
25. Sethy, A., Georgiou, P., Narayanan, S.: Building topic specific language models from webdata using competitive models. In: Proceedings of EUROSPEECH, Lisbon, Portugal (2005)
26. Stevens, A., Hernandex, J., Johnsen, K., et al.: The use of virtual patients to teach medical students communication skills. The Association for Surgical Education Annual Meeting, April 7-10, New York, NY (2005)
27. Swartout, W., Gratch, J., Hill, R., Hovy, E., Marsella, S., Rickel, J., Traum, D.: Toward Virtual Humans. AI Magazine 27(1) (2006)
28. Thiebaux, M., Marshall, A., Marsella, S., Fast, E., Hill, A., Kallmann, M., Kenny, P., Lee, J.: SmartBody: Behavior Realization for Embodied Conversational Agents. In: IVA07 (2007)
29. Triola, M., Feldman, H., Kalet, A.L., Zabar, S., Kachur, E.K., Gillespie, C., et al.: A randomized trial of teaching clinical skills using virtual and live standardized patients. Journal of General Internal Medicine 21(5), 424–429 (2006)

Integrating a Virtual Agent into the Real World: The Virtual Anatomy Assistant Ritchie

Volker Wiendl, Klaus Dorfmüller-Ulhaas, Nicolas Schulz, and Elisabeth André

University of Augsburg, Lab for Multimedia Concepts and their Applications,
Eichleitnerstr. 30, 86159 Augsburg, Germany

Abstract. Augmented realities, which are partially real and partially virtual, open up new ways for humans to interact with Embodied Conversational Agents (ECAs) since they allow users to meet ECAs in the physical space. Nevertheless, attempts to integrate ECAs as digital overlays in a physical space have been rare. Obvious reasons are the high demands such an integration puts to the animation of ECAs as virtual augmentations of the physical space, their capabilities to perceive not only the virtual, but also the physical world as well as reactive behavior control. In this paper, we describe our technical contributions towards solving these challenges. To illustrate our ideas, we present the virtual anatomy assistant Ritchie that monitors the user's actions in a physical space and dynamically responds to them.

1 Introduction

Augmented realities [1], which are partially real and partially virtual, offer great promise to educational software because they help users to perform real-world tasks in space and may provide useful additional information by enhancing the users' natural surroundings with digital overlays. They allow users to interact with physical and virtual 3D objects in a physical environment and may contribute to a better understanding of spatial concepts than a pure virtual space by conveying spatial cues in a direct manner, see also [2].

Embodied conversational agents (ECAs) bear great potential for educational software because of their motivating and engaging effect, see for example [3]. They may positively influence the learners' interaction experience by rendering presentations more lifelike and appealing and helping learners to reduce fear of failure. Most ECAs developed so far reside on the learner's desktop, have been integrated into web applications or co-habit a 3D virtual environment with learners. Hardly any attempt has been made to integrate them in the learner's real environment.

In this paper, we report on first efforts to combine the benefits of ECAs and augmented realities by employing the metaphor of a digital mirror. The user's physical environment is projected on a screen, and the video image of the real scene is augmented by virtual objects. In addition, a virtual character is rendered into the video image. The character responds to the user's actions in the real world, e.g., by providing instructions or commenting on the user's performance.

C. Pelachaud et al. (Eds.): IVA 2007, LNAI 4722, pp. 211–224, 2007.
© Springer-Verlag Berlin Heidelberg 2007

The smooth integration of virtual agents into the user's physical environment raises particular challenges to audio-visual rendering, the acquisition and analysis of context data as well as reactive behavior planning. In particular, the following requirements have to be met:

- **Seamless Integration of the Physical and the Real World**
  In order not to destroy the illusion of co-existing virtual and real worlds, we have to make sure that digital overlays are correctly rendered into the video image of the real scene. This includes the accurate handling of occlusions between digital and real objects as well as the generation of realistic shadows for digital objects falling onto real objects and vice versa. In addition, updates of the virtual world have to be performed in real-time in the case of changes in the physical world that affect the virtual world.
- **Context Sensors for the Real and the Digital World**
  Characters that inhabit Augmented Realities need to be aware of the physical as well as the digital context. As a consequence, specific support for the handling of context data is required to fuse the results from the synthetic and real vision processes. Context data may refer to user actions, but also to environmental factors, such as temperature or luminosity.
- **Context-Sensitive Behavior Control**
  The agent needs to be able to dynamically adapt its behavior to changing circumstances with and without explicit user interaction. In order to ensure that the agent spontaneously reacts to external events, it should be possible to interrupt actions, such as animations of the agent, in a natural manner and to provide smooth transitions to follow-up actions.

In the next section, we first provide an overview on existing work aiming at integrating virtual characters in the user's physical environment. We then describe the setup of the Virtual Anatomy Assistant Ritchie which teaches anatomy of the human body using a real skeleton. In the subsequent three sections, we detail our technical contributions to meet the challenges identified above. We first focus on the registration problem between the virtual and real world as well as graphical issues that have to be handled in order to smoothly embed ECAs in augmented reality scenarios. After that, we describe the employed context sensors, the ACOSAS Core Engine handling context data for dynamic behavior behavior control as well as the ACOSAS Player that implements the connection to the graphical rendering and text-to-speech synthesis. Finally, we report on the results of a user study conducted at CeBIT 2007, the world's largest computer fair.

2   Related Work

Various attempts have been made to integrate virtual characters into the user's physical world - either by projecting virtual displays on real objects or vice versa by integrating video images of real objects into a virtual scene.

Cassell and colleagues [4] present a system which allows children to play with natural figurines inhabiting a physical castle in collaboration with a virtual character. The character is projected on the screen and a digital image of physical castle on the screen provides the user with the impression that the castle continues into the screen. The authors make use of RFID technology in order track which figurines in the castle the child moves.

Kruppa and colleagues [5] developed a character that is capable of freely moving along the walls of a real room by making use of a steerable projector mounted at the ceiling of the room and a spatial audio system. The character is aware of the user's position and orientation in the room and thus may provide situated advice, but unlike Ritchie it is not able to track the user's pointing gestures in space. Furthermore, the application does not make use of any additional digital overlays apart from the character.

Barakonyi and Schmalstieg [6] present an Augmented Reality framework that integrates work on autonomous agents with work on ubiquitous computing. The framework supports the creation of a large variety of agent-based applications, such as mobile agents embodied by virtual and physical objects as well as agents that are able to migrate from one Augmented Reality application to another. Unlike Ritchie, their agents do, however, not integrate sophisticated conversational skills that include dynamically generated gestures, mimics and speech.

In our earlier work, we made use of a video see-through Head-Mounted Display (HMD) to combine video recordings from the real scene with digital overlays including the virtual character Ritchie [7]. In this Augmented Reality application, Ritchie jointly explores with the user a table-top application that combines virtual buildings of the city center of Augsburg with a real city map being laid out on a real table. The benefit of the approach followed in this paper in comparison to our earlier work lies in the fact that the user may move freely around without having to wear obtrusive equipment or being wired. Furthermore, several users may participate in the installation at the same time taking on the role of an observer or actor.

Most similar to the work described in this paper are applications with agents making use of the mirror paradigm. A very early example is the ALIVE system [8] that incorporates body gestures influencing the behavior of a virtual dog called Silas. In contrast to our setup, virtual objects appear only in front of the video image since occlusion problems between real and virtual objects are not handled. In our application setup, we integrate a real skeleton that gives tactile feedback while the user is positioning virtual organs. Herewith, virtual objects are occluded by the real skeleton and virtual organs cast shadows on real objects in order to enhance a mixed reality impression. A more recent application example that is based on the mirror paradigm includes the Invisible Person [9] which is only visible in the mirror, but not in the real world. In one application, the Invisible Person is acting as a game partner in the TicTacToe game where both the user as well as the Invisible Person may select pads of a game board by moving to a certain position and conducting specific postures. Neither Silas nor the Invisible Person make use of speech and communicative gestures to interact with the human user, however. Cavazza and colleagues [10] employed the mirror paradigm for digital story telling to enable users to participate in a story both as an actor and a spectator. In their application, a video image of the user is integrated in a virtual world while in our case a virtual character is integrated as a digital overlay in the real world. The application by Cavazza and colleagues therefore rather falls in the area of augmented virtuality as opposed to ours which is an augmented reality application. In addition, our approach allows not only for the interaction with digital, but also for the interaction with physical objects.

3   The Virtual Anatomy Assistant

As an example of an educational virtual agent application, we have designed and implemented Ritchie, a Virtual Anatomy Assistant, that helps the user to locate organs of the human body. As shown in Fig. 1 the user stands in front of a backprojection screen where a real-time camera image of the user's physical environment is shown. The attendance of a user is detected by a recognition sensor built on top of the whole installation. Next to the user is a real skeleton. The user's task is to attach virtual organs rendered into the video image to the real skeleton using a tangible pointing device. In Fig. 2 one can see the typical interaction procedure. The user first selects one of the organs from a menu and then moves it to the skeleton position where he or she wishes to place it. In addition, users may explore the virtual organs as part of their physical environment. For example, by rotating the pointing device, they may look at the organs from different sides. The position and rotation of the pointing device is tracked by an optical tracking system called IRTraX and offered by inoptech[1]. It also tracks the position of the skeleton to enable the system to update the transformations of the organs already being placed.

To avoid a possible dominance of the virtual character we have rendered Ritchie smaller than the user on a real socket next to the skeleton. Additionally, the socket helps to avoid occlusion problems between the user and the character.

Fig. 1. The setup of the Virtual Anatomy Assistant application

---

[1] http://www.inoptech.com

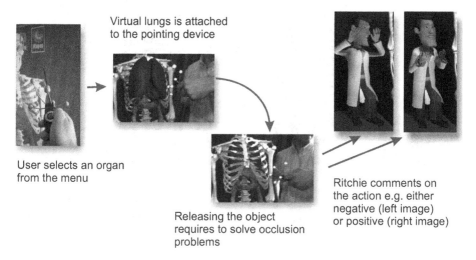

Virtual lungs is attached
to the pointing device

User selects an organ
from the menu

Releasing the object
requires to solve occlusion
problems

Ritchie comments on
the action e.g. either
negative (left image)
or positive (right image)

Fig. 2. A typical interaction between user, skeleton, and the virtual character Ritchie

4   Seamless Integration of Physical and Real Worlds

Augmented Reality should appear to the user as if the virtual and real objects coexisted in the same space. In order to achieve this, a basic process called registration is needed that requires the use of tracking systems. The process of registration is divided into two subtasks. First, a calibration step is needed to estimate static offset and tracking parameters. Calibration can be done offline. Second, the manipulation of objects and typically the user's viewing position have to be tracked in real-time. In the proposed digital mirror setup, the latter is unimportant due to the fact that the user views the real scene from the position of the video camera capturing the real world.

Our digital mirror setup uses an infrared-based stereoscopic tracking system to track the skeleton and a pointing device similar to a mouse with six degrees of freedom. Unfortunately, tracking coordinates are calculated in the coordinates of the stereoscopic tracking system, typically. However, to coincide the virtual objects manipulated by the pointing device with the video image of the projection screen, we need to know the spatial transformation between the video camera and the stereoscopic tracking system. We solved this problem as follows:

1. Calibrate the video camera with the GMLCamera calibration tool.[2]
2. Integrate a system (such as ARToolkitPlus [11]) that recognizes an artificial marker and estimates its pose from the perspective of the video camera.
3. External camera calibration of the stereoscopic tracking system that estimates the relative transformation parameters between infrared cameras.

---

[2] http://research.graphicon.ru/calibration/gml-c++-camera-calibration-toolbox.html

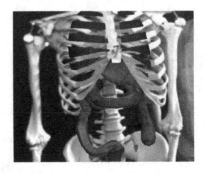

Fig. 3. The integration of virtual shadows on real objects improves the impression of a seamless integration

Fig. 4. For a realistic impression of augmented reality virtual objects have to be occluded by real ones

4. Mount an artificial marker perpendicular to the calibration angle of the stereoscopic tracking system [12] such that the relative offset between the two coordinate systems can be easily measured using a ruler.
5. Move this calibration rig into the interaction volume and ensure that there is no line-of sight problem. Then, store pose parameters of the marker and calibration angle. Finally, calculate the world transformation parameters that represent the transformation between objects in the video camera space and the coordinate system of the calibration angle.

As a result of this offline calibration, objects tracked by the infrared-based tracking system are given in the world coordinate system and can be precisely projected onto the video image by using the inverse world transformation matrix.

Apart from rendering the virtual objects and the video image, the graphical renderer has to account for techniques to convey the illusion of an augmented reality. The video image of the real environment is rendered as a full screen background image using a virtual camera model incorporating the parameters of the physical video camera, e.g. focal length, and the principal point. As a consequence, virtual objects are registered properly, however, they appear always in front of the real objects resulting in the shortcoming that the viewer does not have the impression of the virtual objects being integrated into the scene. To overcome this problem and reduce the gap between the real and virtual world, we rely on a technique which is also known under the term "black object rendering". To this end, we create three dimensional models of some real objects (e.g. the skeleton) that are visible in the video image. The virtual copies are placed in the scene in a way that their screen projection exactly overlaps with the corresponding real objects in the video image. The models are just rendered to the depth buffer and not the color buffer so that they get their color from the video texture but occlude the other virtual objects which are intersecting them. Collisions between the character and the user have been avoided by placing the character on a socket (see Section 3).

To further improve the illusion of a consistent scene, we have the virtual objects cast shadows on the real world objects. To this end, we do not draw the video texture as a simple background full screen quad, but project the video image onto the occlusion objects, modulating the video texture with the shadow intensity of the occlusion models. The resulting shadows give important clues regarding the distance between the virtual objects and the real objects and result in the impression of a better integration.

5 Context Sensors

Situated agents need to take the user's physical context into account. Recent projects equip animated agents with a set of sensors to detect and track people in front of the screen. Examples include kiosk agents, such Mack [13] or Max [14]. For the anatomy assistant, we have included four different sensors that are connected through the Virtual Reality Peripheral Network (VRPN)[3] library:

1. Mouse Sensor: handles button clicks of the pointing device
2. Keyboard Sensor: for administrative purposes
3. Person Detection: indicates the attendance of a user
4. 3D Optical Tracking System: measures the 6DOF of a pointing device and the skeleton.

While the keyboard sensor is only used for administrative purposes (e.g. to reset the application), the person detection and the pointing device has direct influence on the character's behavior. The person attendance detection is realized by a camera that is mounted above the skeleton and was already used in the COHIBIT system described in [15]. If it indicates the presence of a user, it forwards the changed state to ACOSAS that triggers a transition from the "Start Idle Phase" to the "Visitor Arrived" state (see Section 6).

The context data of the tracking system and the mouse button sensor is primarily used for selecting and placing a virtual organ, but secondarily a change of an organ's state also has an influence on the character's comments. The fusion of the real context data with the virtual state of the world is being done by our ACOSAS system (see Section 6).

6 Context-Sensitive Behavior Control

In order to enable a human author to easily specify context-sensitive stories with ECAs, we designed and implemented the ACOSAS (**A CO**ntext **S**ensing **A**uthoring **S**ystem) framework. Similar to the approach presented by Gebhard and colleagues [16], ACOSAS models the flow of a reactive story by means of cascaded finite state machines. However, unlike their system, ACOSAS [17] provides specific support for the integration of context data. The fact that ACOSAS is able to access context information from the user's physical environment and to fuse real with virtual context makes it in particular suitable for the realization of the Virtual Anatomy Assistant.

---

[3] http://www.cs.unc.edu/Research/vrpn/index.html

6.1   The ACOSAS Core Engine and the ACOSAS Player

For improved reusability we have split ACOSAS in a core module handling the
story and context sensors, and a player application for the connection to the
different output modules, such as rendering and text-to-speech. Figure 5 shows
the interaction between the ACOSAS Core Engine, the context sensors as well
as the ACOSAS player.

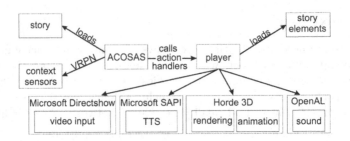

Fig. 5. Module Layout of the ACOSAS Core Engine and the ACOSAS Player: The
different output modules are linked by the player application. The ACOSAS Core
Engine can control their functionalities by calling registered action handlers.

As input, the ACOSAS Core Engine expects a story file. The header of this
file contains links to context sensors as well as a world description file containing
the story elements loaded by the player. The body of the story file essentially
consists of a specification of the finite state machine representing the story.

The connection between the ACOSAS Core Engine and the ACOSAS Player
is established via so-called action handlers that are triggered by the ACOSAS
Core Engine during the traversal of the finite state machine. The ACOSAS Player
loads story elements, such as the character, the organs and specific sounds, and
provides action handlers to manipulate these elements. The main consideration
behind the introduction of action handlers was to abstract from the technical
details of the underlying output modules.

6.2   Modeling the Story with ACOSAS

The nodes of the finite state machines correspond to scenes while the edges
represent transitions between scenes. Figure 6 shows the story nodes created
for the Virtual Anatomy Assistant. There are two major story states. The first
one is "Start Idle Phase" which refers to a situation when no user is present.
In this state, the story loops through different sub nodes in which the character monologizes or performs specific animations to attract visitors. The second
one is "Visitor Arrived" which refers to a situation when a user approaches the
booth. To ensure that Ritchie is permanently alive, we also included a "Game
Idle Phase" in which Ritchie encourages the user to start or continue with the
placement task. The utterances used are chosen by a script that takes into account the state of the interaction device. While the user is placing an organ the

character would not disturb him or her. The states "User placed organ" and "All organs placed" specify Ritchie's behaviors when commenting on the user's actual performance. By using these fixed states with variable scripted actions we achieve great flexibility. Even if the user responds in an unexpected manner, for example, by starting a conversation with people closeby, the character would not get lost since it always remains in valid predefined states. According to the state machine created for the Virtual Anatomy Assistant, it would then try to get the user's attention back. For the Virtual Anatomy Assistant, the user's perceivable actions are restricted to approaching and leaving the installation and the placement of objects. It is important to note, however, that the ACOSAS system enables us to model character responses to arbitrary user actions including not only vision-based, but also audio-based context sensors. For the european project CALLAS[4], for example, we have developed an emotion recognition sensor based on acoustic features.

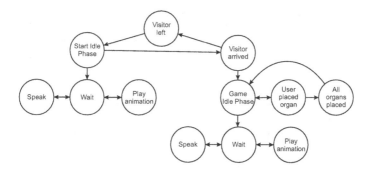

Fig. 6. The Virtual Anatomy Assistant as realized within ACOSAS. In each node various actions for controlling Ritchie are triggered. Some of them have random parameters to offer a greater variety in the character's behavior.

A transition between story nodes is taken if all corresponding conditions are satisfied and all blocking actions (see below) have been finished. Conditions may refer to parameters that are received via context sensors. For example, the transition between the "Start Idle Phase" and the "Visitor arrived" state depends on data received by the person detector. Other possible sources for the parameter values are LUA scripts or just hard-coded constant values. We opted for the choice of LUA [18] as a scripting language since it is employed by a number of commercial games (such as World of Warcraft), it's very fast and also easy to use. Another advantage is the fact that values or actions provided by LUA functions can be changed on the fly without restarting the application.

For each story node, we may specify actions that will be triggered if the corresponding node is entered, left or interrupted. In the latter case, there are actions that were activated when entering the node, but not yet finished when

---

[4] http://www.callas-newmedia.eu/

leaving it. In the Virtual Anatomy Assistant, such a situation may occur when Ritchie is waiting for visitors. If the person attendance detector signals that a user has arrived, the current animation of the character has to be interrupted and the "Visitor arrived" node is entered. To interrupt a story node, we may, for example, specify an action that ends the character's current animation by fading the animation to a neutral state. Next to the predefined actions implemented in the player, the designer can also create more complex ones by using the scripting language that can access various LUA binding functions (e.g. accessing context values) provided by the ACOSAS core module and the player.

6.3   Behavior Output

As mentioned in Section 6.1 the ACOSAS Player has to implement the handlers for actions triggered by the ACOSAS Core Engine and the connection to the output libraries, such as graphics, sound and text-to-speech.

For the graphical duties, we are using the Horde3D rendering engine[5] developed at our lab. Among other things it supports morph targets that can be easily used for the synchronisation of synthesized speech based on a text-to-speech library, such as the Microsoft Speech API, and the virtual agent's lip movements.

A morph target defines the final positions of some vertices. Beginning from a base pose, the vertex positions are linearly interpolated. By setting the interpolation factors it is possible to control the strength of a facial expression and to mix several targets. Our implementation uses a morph target system to fade between the previous and current viseme of the text to be spoken.

Another challenge is the animation of the character's body. Our objective was to create convincing movements of the character and smooth transitions between separate animation clips. The movements of the character were realized using a skeletal animation system. The animations were created with a 3D modeling package and applied directly to the model.

To enable smooth transitions from one animation to another, we make use of a technique called animation blending. With our system, it is possible to put several animation clips on discrete channels. A weight for each channel determines how much the associated animation contributes to the final result relative to the other channels. To perform a transition between two channels, we do blending by fading one channel towards zero and the other towards one.

Another important requirement is the possibility to play several animations at the same time. This is called animation mixing. In our case, we have a rather long subtle idle animation where Ritchie performs slight movements of his head, blinks with its eyes and breathes. This animation is played by using an endless action and has to be combined with some randomized and casual gestures. To achieve this effect, we use additive animations. We calculate the difference in translation and rotation of the gesture animation relative to the character's standard pose. This difference is added to the base animation which is in our case the idle clip.

---

[5] http://www.nextgen-engine.net/

Therewith we have a simple way to combine arbitrary independent gestures with very satisfying visual quality and a minimum amount of effort.

7 Evaluation

The Virtual Anatomy Assistant was evaluated at CeBIT 2007, the world's largest annual trade show for information and telecommunication technology.

7.1 Method

Over a period of 8 days, hundreds of people interacted with the Virtual Anatomy Assistant out of which 71 (56 male and 15 female) participated in the evaluation and filled in the questionnaire. All subjects were native speakers of German. 19 participants were under 18 years old, 52 over 18 years old.

All participants were given an individual introduction to the system. In particular, they were shown how to select menu options using the pointing device and how to place organs in the skeleton. After that, they had the chance to try out the system themselves. On average, the experiment took about 10 minutes per participant. After the experiment, each participant filled in an anonymous post-questionnaire.

The post-questionnaire used 14 attitude statements with a 5-ary rating scale (disagree, somewhat disagree, neutral, somewhat agree, agree) to evaluate how the participants perceived the interaction with the system (9 questions) and the behavior of the agent (5 questions).

7.2 Results for the Interface

To show that the mean value of a rating was significantly above or below the neutral value of 3, we applied t-tests for one sample. Overall, the interface was perceived as positive. The participants thought it was illustrative to place organs in the real skeleton with a mean value of 4.48 ($t(70)=13.723$, $p<0.001$), they found it not too difficult to concentrate both on the real skeleton and the presentation on the screen with a mean value of 2.61 ($t(70)=-2.293$, $p<0.03$), and they did not find the interface confusing with a mean value of 1.92 ($t(70)=-8.469$, $p<0.001$). The participants found it easy to select menu options with a mean value of 3.92 ($t(70)=7.633$, $p<0.001$). They found it less easy (mean 3.32) to place the organs at the wanted position ($t(70)=2.529$, $p<0.02$).

We did not find any empirical evidence that the females experienced the interaction with the system differently than the males. We noticed, however, that different age groups (i.e. participants under 18 years old and participants over 18 years old) responded differently to the mirror metaphor. In particular, we compared the responses of participants under 18 years old with those of participants over 18 years old. The average age of the first age group was 13.63. The youngest participant in this group was 10 and the oldest 17. For the second age group, we did not record the exact age because we assumed that people were reluctant to give that information.

Table 1. Mean Ratings for Age-Specific Perception of the Interface

Mean Scores	Children	Adults
Interface was illustrative	4.84	4.35
Reminded me of a mirror	3.95	2.87
Found it helpful to see myself on the screen	3.79	2.65
Overlooked that I was visible on the screen	1.74	2.73

Applying a two-tailed t-test to the two age groups showed that there were significant differences between the two age groups for 4 out of 9 statements. Overall, the younger age group developed a better understanding of the mirror metaphor and gave it a more positive rating (see Table 1). In particular, the younger participants found it more illustrative to place organs in the real skeleton ($t(69)=2.086$, $p<0.05$) than the older participants, they felt rather reminded of a mirror ($t(69)=2.929$, $p<0.006$) than the older participants, they found it more helpful to see themselves on the screen ($t(69)=3.227$, $p<0.003$) than the older participants , and they were less likely to overlook that they were visible on the screen than the older participants ($t(69)=-2.391$, $p<0.03$).

7.3   Results for the Character

Overall, the results of the experiment indicate that the participants perceived the character as intended. It was rated above mean in regard to its entertaining value with a mean value of 3.92 ($t(70) = 6.284$, $p<0.001$). Furthermore, the participants had the impression that the character was aware of them with a mean value of 4.23 ($t(70) = 10.936$, $p<0.001$). Even though the character was permanently talking, it was not regarded as distracting with a mean value of 1.83 ($t(70) = -10.141$, $p<0.001$). Nevertheless, the participants did not consider Ritchie as superiorly helpful. As a reason, we indicate that the character commented on the actions by the participants, but it did not provide any hints regarding where to place the objects. Its main purpose was to encourage the participants to start with their task and to entertain them by witty comments. We also thought Ritchie's special kind of humor would make the participants feel less embarrassed about making mistakes. However, this could not be confirmed by our experiments.

Interestingly, we did not find any significant gender or age differences regarding the perception of the character. The results regarding gender are in line with the results obtained by Kipp and colleagues [15] for the Autostadt scenario. For adults, we observed, however, a medium correlation between the participants' ratings of the task and their ratings of the character which could not be attested for the younger age group. The easiest the placement task was for the adults, the more they appreciated Ritchie's entertaining value (Pearson Product-Moment Correlation: $r=0.501$; $p<0.001$). Obviously, the adults had more sense for Ritchie's humor when figuring out less difficulties with the task. For young people under 18, there was no significant correlation between the two variables.

We ascribe this effect to the heterogeneous composition of this age group. Especially, younger children might have problems with Ritchie's sarcastic nature which probably had a stronger influence on their ratings than the difficulty of task.

8 Conclusion

In this paper, we reported on our efforts to integrate an embodied conversational agent into the user's real world. The technological contributions of this paper include (1) the combination of sophisticated tracking systems with state-of-the art rendering techniques to achieve a seamless integration of the physical and the real world and (2) a module for context-aware behavior control that enables spontaneous character responses to a user's actions in the physical world which may even include interruptions of a character's ongoing actions. To illustrate our ideas, we presented the Virtual Anatomy Assistant Ritchie which is based on these technologies. An evaluation of Ritchie confirmed that it contributed to a positive perception of the interaction experience by its entertaining value without being distracting. The participants had the impression that the character was aware of their presence and noticed what they were doing. Furthermore, the users found it illustrative to place virtual objects in a real skeleton.

Future work will concentrate on the conduction of a controlled experiment in order to shed light on the benefits of augmented realities for spatial learning tasks. Furthermore, we will equip the virtual character with a component for spatial reasoning so that it will be able to provide hints to the users regarding the placement of objects.

Acknowledgments. This work was partly funded by the European Commission, project IST-2005-2.5.7 Callas.

References

1. Azuma, R.T.: A survey of augmented reality. Presence: Teleoperators and Virtual Environments 6, 355–385 (1997)
2. Shelton, B.E., Hedley, N.R.: Exploring a cognitive basis for learning spatial relationships with augmented reality. Technology, Instruction, Cognition and Learning 1, 323–357, 154 (2002)
3. van Mulken, S., André, E., Müller, J.: The persona effect: How substantial is it? In: Proceedings of the Thirteenth Conference of the British Computer Society Human Computer Interaction Specialist Group - People and Computers XIII, Sheffield, pp. 53–66 (1998)
4. Cassell, J., Ananny, M., Basu, A., Bickmore, T., Chong, P., Mellis, D., Ryokai, K., Smith, J., Vilhjálmsson, H., Yan, H.: Shared reality: physical collaboration with a virtual peer. In: CHI '00 extended abstracts on Human factors in computing systems, pp. 259–260. ACM Press, New York, USA (2000)
5. Kruppa, M., Spassova, M., Schmitz, M.: The virtual room inhabitant - intuitive interaction with intelligent environments. In: Zhang, S., Jarvis, R. (eds.) AI 2005. LNCS (LNAI), vol. 3809, Springer, Heidelberg (2005)

6. Barakonyi, I., Schmalstieg, D.: Ubiquitous animated agents for augmented reality. In: Proceedings of IEEE and ACM International Symposium on Mixed and Augmented Reality (ISMAR'06), IEEE Computer Society Press, Los Alamitos (2006)
7. Dorfmüller-Ulhaas, K., André, E.: The synthetic character ritchie: First steps towards a virtual companion for mixed reality. In: Proceedings of IEEE International Symposium on Mixed and Augmented Reality (ISMAR'05), IEEE Computer Society Press, Los Alamitos (2005)
8. Maes, P., Darrell, T., Blumberg, B., Pentland, A.: The alive system: full-body interaction with autonomous agents. Computer Animation, 11 (1995)
9. Psik, T., Matković, K., Sainitzer, R., Petta, P., Szalavari, Z.: The invisible person: advanced interaction using an embedded interface. In: EGVE '03: Proceedings of the workshop on Virtual environments 2003, pp. 29–37. ACM Press, New York, USA (2003)
10. Cavazza, M., Charles, F., Mead, S.J., Martin, O., Marichal, X., Nandi, A.: Multimodal acting in mixed reality interactive storytelling. IEEE-Multimedia 11, 30–39 (2004)
11. Wagner, D., Schmalstieg, D.: ARToolKitPlus for pose tracking on mobile devices. In: Proceedings of 12th Computer Vision Winter Workshop (CVWW'07) (2007)
12. Dorfmüller-Ulhaas, K.: Optical Tracking - From User Motion To 3D Interaction. PhD thesis, Institut 186 für Computergraphik und Algorithmen, Vienna (2002)
13. Nakano, Y.I., Reinstein, G., Stocky, T., Cassell, J.: Towards a model of face-to-face grounding. In: Dignum, F.P.M. (ed.) ACL 2003. LNCS (LNAI), vol. 2922, pp. 553–561. Springer, Heidelberg (2004)
14. Kopp, S., Jung, B., Leßmann, N., Wachsmuth, I.: Max - a multimodal assistant in virtual reality construction. Künstliche Intelligenz 17, 11–17 (2003)
15. Kipp, M., Kipp, K.H., Ndiaye, A., Gebhard, P.: Evaluating the tangible interface and virtual characters in the interactive cohibit exhibit. In: Gratch, J., Young, M., Aylett, R., Ballin, D., Olivier, P. (eds.) IVA 2006. LNCS (LNAI), vol. 4133, pp. 434–444. Springer, Heidelberg (2006)
16. Gebhard, P., Kipp, M., Klesen, M., Rist, T.: Authoring scenes for adaptive, interactive performances. In: AAMAS '03: Proceedings of the second international joint conference on Autonomous agents and multiagent systems, pp. 725–732. ACM Press, New York, USA (2003)
17. Erdmann, D., Dorfmüller-Ulhaas, K., André, E.: Integrating VR-authoring and context sensing: Towards the creation of context-aware stories. In: Göbel, S., Malkewitz, R., Iurgel, I. (eds.) TIDSE 2006. LNCS, vol. 4326, pp. 151–162. Springer, Heidelberg (2006)
18. Ierusalimschy, R., de Figueiredo, L.H., Filho, W.C.: LUA — an extensible extension language. Software Practice and Experience 26, 635–652 (1996)

Proactive Authoring for Interactive Drama: An Author's Assistant

Mei Si, Stacy C. Marsella, and David V. Pynadath

Information Sciences Institute
University of Southern California
Marina del Rey, CA 90292
meisi@isi.edu, marsella@isi.edu, pynadath@isi.edu

Abstract. Interactive drama allows people to participate actively in a dynamically unfolding story, by playing a character or by exerting directorial control. One of the central challenges faced in the design of interactive dramas is how to ensure that the author's goals for the user's narrative experience are achieved in the face of the user's actions in the story. This challenge is especially significant when a variety of users are expected. To address this challenge, we present an extension to Thespian, an authoring and simulating framework for interactive dramas. Each virtual character is controlled by a decision-theoretic goal driven agent. In our previous work on Thespian, we provided a semi-automated authoring approach that allows authors to configure virtual characters' goals through specifying story paths. In this work, we extend Thespian into a more proactive authoring framework to further reduce authoring effort. The approach works by simulating potential users' behaviors, generating corresponding story paths, filtering the generated paths to identify those that seem problematic and prompting the author to verify virtual characters' behaviors in them. The author can correct virtual characters' behaviors by modifying story paths. As new story paths are designed by the author, the system incrementally adjusts virtual characters' configurations to reflect the author's design ideas. Overall, this enables interactive testing and refinement of an interactive drama. The details of this approach will be presented in this paper, followed by preliminary results of applying it in authoring an interactive drama.

1 Introduction

Interactive drama allows people to participate actively in a dynamically unfolding story, by playing a character or by exerting directorial control. Because of its potential for providing interesting stories as well as allowing user interaction, it has been proposed for a wide range of training applications (e.g. [1,2,3,4,5]) as well as entertainment applications (e.g. [6,7,8,9,10,11]). A variety of approaches have been taken to build interactive dramas. These approaches can be roughly divided into two categories, character-centric and narrative-centric designs (when speaking from the agent's perspective, they are also referred as using autonomy and story-based agents for interactive dramas [12]). In character-centric

C. Pelachaud et al. (Eds.): IVA 2007, LNAI 4722, pp. 225–237, 2007.
© Springer-Verlag Berlin Heidelberg 2007

approaches, e.g. FearNot! [2], MRE [4], SASO [13], and Thespian [14,3], the emphasis is on building plausible characters. The narrative ideally emerges from the characters' behaviors. Narrative-centric designs on the other hand focus more on the narrative structure of the overall story instead of the design of individual characters. Systems deploying this type of approach include Façade [15], Mimesis [16] and IDA [8]. These systems employ some representations of narrative structure that are used to control how the story unfolds.

One of the central challenges faced in the design of interactive dramas is how to reduce authoring effort resulting from the merge of narrative and interaction. This challenge is especially significant when a variety of users are expected. Different users may interact with the system in very different ways. To ensure that the desired (pedagogical and/or dramatic) effect will be experienced, or the experience is appropriately tailored for different types of users, the system needs to be repeatedly tested with different user behaviors. In most of the existing systems, this step is performed by hand. However, a thorough examination by hand is extremely time consuming and impossible in many cases. Consider a short scene consisting of 5 rounds of interaction between a user and virtual characters, if at each step the user has 10 reasonable moves, there are 10^5 possible user action sequences or paths through the story!

To address this problem, the work discussed here presents a proactive, automated approach to assist the author in evaluating and incrementally refining the performance of an interactive drama system. The key to our approach is modeling types of users in order to limit the number of story paths the author must evaluate.

The approach we take is based on extending Thespian [14,3], a multi-agent system for authoring and simulating interactive dramas. The user is modeled as a decision-theoretic goal-driven agent. This allows the authoring procedure to restrict the generation of users' behaviors to ones that are *well-motivated* in the sense that they have consistent motivations throughout the story. The selective generation based on this well-motivated criterion can greatly reduce the number of possible user action sequences because it spares the author from testing the system with user behaviors that are unlikely to happen. In addition, because it is often the case that most of the generated paths are consistent with the author's expectations and therefore do not need special attention, the authoring procedure can filter story paths using either default or author defined criteria that characterize types of stories worthy of inspection. Due to the selective generation combined with the post-generation filtering, the system can proactively prompt the author to pay attention to only a small set of paths that are most likely to be problematic. The author's changes to these paths can then be passed back to Thespian to incrementally refine the story's design.

The rest of this paper is structured as follows. Section 2 gives an overview of Thespian's proactive authoring procedure. Section 3 introduces the example domain. Section 4 and 5 describe the current architecture of the Thespian system and its extension to proactive authoring. Section 6 provides a detailed example of applying the proactive authoring procedure. Finally, in section 7 the results are discussed and followed by proposed future work.

2   Overview

The approach we take to proactive authoring is based on extending Thespian's original authoring process. The new approach exploits two aspects of Thespian's design. First, each story character in Thespian is modeled as a decision-theoretic, goal-driven agent, with the character's personality/motivations encoded as goal preferences. Characters' behaviors in the story, their policies of actions, are automatically generated based on these goal preferences. Second, Thespian has a fitting algorithm that allows a character's goal preferences to be derived automatically from example story paths (in effect, sequences of character actions). Thus, an author can provide Thespian with example story paths and then Thespian can fit the behavior of the characters to perform according to those paths.

Figure 1 shows the overall structure of Thespian's new proactive authoring procedure. As in previous work on Thespian, the author provides story paths to the fitting procedure in order to fit the virtual characters. The system then systematically simulate potential users' behaviors interacting with the virtual characters. To reduce the number of paths generated, the simulation is restricted to consider only potential users whose behavior is well-motivated (See Section 5.2 for a discussion on how we use fitting to operationalize "well-motivated"). Next, the authoring procedure filters the story paths generated by this simulation in order to select those that are most likely to be problematic. The resulting paths are passed to the author. The author's feedback can then be passed back to Thespian's fitting procedure, in the form of modified story paths, to further refine the design of the story's characters. This overall process can proceed iteratively to design the interactive story.

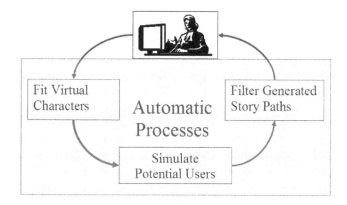

Fig. 1. Thespian's Proactive Authoring Procedure

3   Example Domain

The example domain of this work is a Grimms' fairy tale, "Little Red Riding Hood". The story contains four main characters, Little Red Riding Hood, Granny, the hunter and the wolf. The story starts as Little Red Riding Hood (Red) and the wolf meet each other on the outskirt of a wood while Red is on her way to Granny's house. The wolf has a mind to eat Red, but it dare not because there are some wood-cutters close by. At this point, they can either have a conversation or choose to walk away. The wolf will have a chance to eat Red at other locations where nobody is close by. Moreover, if the wolf heard about Granny from Red, it can even go eat her. Meanwhile, the hunter is searching the woods for the wolf to kill it. Once the wolf is killed, people who got eaten by it can escape. In our modeling of the story, the numbers of possible actions per move for Red, Granny, the hunter and the wolf are 14, 2, 4, and 10 respectively. The role of Red is assumed to be taken by the user. The user can interact with virtual characters through a text based interface.

4   Thespian's Current Architecture

Thespian is a multi-agent system for authoring and controlling virtual characters in an interactive drama. It is built upon PsychSim [17], a multi-agent system for social simulation based on Partially Observable Markov Decision Problems (POMDPs) [18].

4.1   Thespian Agent

Thespian's basic architecture uses POMDP based agents to control each character, with the character's personality and motivations encoded as agent goals. Each Thespian agent consists of five components, its state, action dynamics, goals, policies, and beliefs about self and others.

An agent's state is defined by a set of state features, such as its location and degree of hunger. The values of these state features change as events (actions of characters) happen in the story. The agent's action dynamics define how its state is affected by actions. An agent's goals are expressed as a reward function over the various state features the agent seeks to maximize or minimize. We model a character's personality profile as its various goals and their relative importance (weight). For example, the wolf character can have goals of satisfying its hunger (increasing the value of its state feature "full") and keeping itself alive, with the latter goal having higher importance. Thespian agents have a "Theory of Mind" that allows them to form mental models about other agents, including the user. An agent's belief (subjective view) of the world includes its belief about the state, action dynamics, goals and policies of itself and other agents and *their* subjective views of the world, a form of recursive agent modeling [19]. Policies tell the agent what to do given its current state. Currently, all agents use a bounded lookahead policy. Following this policy, when an agent selects its next action it projects limited steps into the future to evaluate the effect of each option. The agent considers not just the immediate effect of an action, but also the expected responses of other characters and, in turn, the effects of those responses, and its reaction to those responses and so on. The agent evaluates the overall effect with respect to its goals and then chooses the action that has the highest expected value.

4.2   Fitting Procedure and Authoring

Thespian's fitting procedure enables an author to define characters' roles in a story by creating alternative desired paths (sequences of characters' actions) of the story. The fitting procedure [20,14] can tune agents' goal weights so that they will re-create the paths if the user behaves following the paths. When the user deviates from the paths, the virtual characters will respond using the same motivations fitted from the story paths.

Algorithm 1. FIT-SEQUENCE(S_0, $char\_name$, seq, $fixedgoals$)

1: S_0 : initial state set by author at initialization
2: $char\_name$: character whose role is to be fitted
3: seq : time sequence of $action$ - preferred path
4: $fixedgoals$: goals whose weights should not be changed in this process
5: $C \leftarrow [\ ]$: constraint on goal weights
6: $S \leftarrow S_0$
7: **for** each action A in seq **do**
8:    **if** $A.actor == char\_name$ **then**
9:       # adding constraints
10:      **for** each action a in $char\_name$.**getOptions**() **do**
11:         $new\_C \leftarrow$ **Reward**$(A,S) \geq$ **Reward**(a,S)
12:         C.**Append**(new_C)
13:    # update state
14:    $S \leftarrow S \times$ **Dynamics**(A)
15: **Return AdjustGoalWeights**$(char\_name, C, fixedgoals)$
16:
17: **Dynamics**(action) as defined in PsychSim
18: **Reward**(action,state) calculated similar to PsychSim, with modifications to take turn-taking into account
19: **AdjustGoalWeights**$(char\_name, constraints, fixedgoals)$ returns if the characters' goal weights, except the weights of the $fixedgoals$, can be adjusted so that all the $constraints$ are satisfied

---

In fitting, Thespian proceeds iteratively for each story path, fitting the goals of one agent at a time and holding all other agents' goals as fixed. Specifically, for each story path and each character, Algorithm 1 is invoked to fit that character so that it performs its actions in the story path. The algorithm proceeds down the sequence of actions in the story path (Step 7). If the current action is performed by the agent that is currently being fitted (Step 8), the fitting process simulates the agent's lookahead process, and automatically calculates constraints on goal weights to ensure the desired action receives highest utility among all candidate actions (Step 11). By the end, the constraints resulting from fitting each path can be merged into one common constraint set. By default, in fitting, the weights of all of the agent's goals can be adjusted. The author can also specify a set of goals whose weights should not be adjusted, e.g. characters should always have a high goal weight on keeping themselves alive. Typically, there are multiple candidate goal weight values that are consistent with the story paths defined by the author. Any of these solutions guarantees that the characters will follow the preferred paths of the story. Thespian will pick the goal weights as close to the original ones as possible. When fitting results in no candidate goal weight values, it is not possible for the characters to be motivated to behave following all the story paths and the author has to exclude some of the paths.

5   Proactive Authoring Procedure

In this section, we will present our new proactive authoring procedure which can help the author to examine the interactive drama system's performance when facing a variety of users. This procedure can systematically simulate potential users' behaviors, filter correspondingly generated story paths, and proactively prompt authors to verify virtual characters' behaviors in paths that are most likely to be problematic. Furthermore, the author can specify the granularity of the exploration to control the number of story paths that will be simulated as well as criteria that determine which paths the system identifies for the author to inspect. In particular, the author can specify the achievement (or lack of achievement) of plot points as filtering criteria, where plot points can be defined in terms of events in the story, and characters' (including the user's) beliefs or their actual states in the story. Thus, the author can easily tell if the desired user experience is achieved with the current configuration of virtual characters. If it is not, the author can correct virtual characters' behaviors by specifying new story paths to be fitted.

5.1   Model Potential Users

Thespian models the user as a decision-theoretic goal-driven agent similar to other characters in the story. The users' different interaction styles are reflected by their different preferences over the set of goals they have and their different beliefs about other characters.

Similar to how other characters are designed, the user agent's initial values of state features, action dynamics and beliefs are based on the story being modeled. Most of this information is either common-sense knowledge, e.g. social norms, or conveyed to the user before the interaction through a back story, e.g. action dynamics, beliefs about self and other characters. Therefore, this part of the model is fixed for simulating all types of users unless the author purposely leaves some information uncertain to the user, e.g. tells the user that there is 50% of the chance that the wolf is a good character and will not eat anybody.

Table 1. An Example of User's Possible Goals

Category	Example Goals
Character (Role) Goals	keep self alive
	give cake to Granny
Social Norm Goals[1]	complete adjacency pair
	keep appropriate conversational flow
	be succinct
Personal Goals	like to explore the environment
	like to converse

Though we can usually assume the user has the goals of the character which he/she takes the role of, the user's goals are seldom limited to the role. People may have various personal goals, and habits to behave in certain ways, which can be cast as goals in Thespian. Currently we consider users' additional goals from two possible sources. Firstly, as a member of a society, people's behavior usually follows social norms. In Thespian, we cast these norm-following behaviors of a character as goals to maximize relevant state features that keep track of how consistent the norms and behaviors are. Secondly, people may have various personal goals during the interaction. Curiosity is a basic human need and a common goal in virtual environments; often a user wants to explore the environment more and converse more with the virtual characters. Table 1 lists some of the possible user goals we model in the "Little Red Riding Hood" story. In this example, the role of Red is assumed to be taken by the user.

5.2   Simulate Interactions with Potential Users

This section presents Thespian's automated approaches for simulating interactions with potential users. The basic approach can exclusively generate all story paths that can be encountered by a well-motivated user, a user who has consistent motivations through out the interaction. A special case of applying this approach is to simulate "protypical" users who have fixed sets of goals as their prototypes. The prototypes are either designed by the author or are derived by discretizing the user's possible goal space. The basic approach assumes that the user only has one possible mental model of other characters. This can be extended to simulate users having alternative mental models.[1]

Generate Story Paths for Well-Motivated Users. Algorithm 2 shows the pseudo code of this process. This process moves in a stepwise fashion. First, we find all actions of the user that are well-motivated at the current state (well-motivated actions are determined by invoking the fitting procedure as described in section 4.2), then for each of these actions other characters' responses are

---

[1] Note that only a subset of the goals in Thespian's model of social normative behaviors apply to this domain. For detailed description of this model, see [21].

Algorithm 2. Generate-All-Paths(S_0, *user*, *fixedgoals*, *maxstep*, *existPath*)

1: S_0 : initial state set by author at initialization
2: *user* : the name of the user character
3: *fixedgoals* : goals whose weights should not be changed in this process
4: *maxstep* : maximum number of actions the user performs
5: *existPath* : path that has already happened
6: **for** each action a in *user*.**getOptions**() **do**
7:     *pathnew* ← *existPath*.**append**(a)
8:     *res* ← **Fit-Sequence**(S_0,*user*,*pathnew*,*fixedgoals*)
9:     # if this is a possible path
10:    **if** *res* == 1 **then**
11:        # simulate other characters' responses to the user's action
12:        **while** *user* does not have the next turn **do**
13:            *other_character's_action* ← **getResponse**()
14:            *pathnew* ← *pathnew*.**append**(*other_character's_action*)
15:        *maxstep_new* ← *maxstep* - 1
16:        **if** *maxstep_new* > 0 **then**
17:            **Generate-All-Paths**(S_0,*user*,*fixedgoals*,*maxstep_new*,*pathnew*)
18:        **else**
19:            # this is a path we want
20:            **Output-to-File**(*pathnew*)

---

simulated. When it is the user's turn to act again, the same process will be repeated until the length of story paths specified by the author is reached.

This process is implemented as a recursive function. When the function is called to generate story paths starting from the very beginning of the story, *existPath* is empty. If the author wants to simulate possible story paths starting from the middle of the story, *existPath* should contain all the actions that have already happened by that point.

Note that unlike the fitting procedure in the authoring process, in which actions with equal utility as others are regarded as not motivated enough, the fitting procedure in this function will treat the actions as well-motivated. The reason for this difference is that here we want to simulate all actions the user can possibly perform instead of ensuring certain actions will be picked by an agent. In fact, the author can make this simulation process more tolerant to inaccurate user modeling by passing an epsilon value to the fitting procedure to relax the **AdjustGoalWeights** function (see Algorithm 1 for definition). This way, actions will be treated as well-motivated even though their utilities are slightly lower than the maximum utility the agent might achieve via some other action(s).

Generate Story Paths for Protypical Users. It is often sufficient and interesting to test a system's behaviors with protypical users. The prototypes can be designed by the author. Alternatively, Thespian models protypical users by systematically varying the user agent's preference over its goals. The granularity preference set by the author will define the fineness of the discretization. For each set of the user's goal weights, the **Generate-All-Paths** procedure will be called to generate all story paths that can be encountered by users with these goal weights. While calling this process, the *fixedgoals* parameter needs to be set to all of the agent's goals. This way the **AdjustGoalWeights** function will only perform a test on whether the action is motivated by the agent's current goal weights, and will not try to adjust the agent's goal weights.

Generate Story Paths for Users with Alternative Mental Models. To simulate potential users with different goals and different mental models about other characters, the author needs to supply users' alternative mental models in terms of beliefs about other characters' goals and initial states. The author can either design the alternative mental models by hand or derive them using automated means (see [22] for a possible approach). Thespian will then set the user agent's belief according to each of the models (as shown in [22], the number of distinct models in a story environment is limited), and call the **Generate-All-Paths** procedure to generate all story paths that can be encountered by users with that mental model. Finally, story paths generated by simulating users with different mental models will be merged.

5.3   Filter Generated Story Paths

The number of story paths resulting from simulating well-motivated users may still approach a large number. In addition, it is often the case that most of the generated paths are consistent with the author's expectations and therefore do not need special attention. So Thespian has a special mechanism for selecting story paths to present to the author.

Thespian can use both its default heuristics and author specified criteria for filtering story paths. Currently, Thespian provides two default heuristics. The first one picks story paths in which the virtual characters repeat the same behaviors more than a certain percentage, e.g. 75% of the time. The second heuristic selects story paths in which the virtual characters repeat the same behavior continuously more than a certain number of times, e.g. 3 times. These two heuristics are designed based on the observation that it is usually not a good interactive experience if the virtual characters always respond to the user with the same actions. Both heuristics are configurable by the author. The author can specify the names of the characters to be watched for (by default all the virtual characters' behaviors will be included in the analysis), the thresholds for reporting, e.g. instead of 75% the threshold can be lowered to 60% for the first heuristics, and the actions to be watched for, e.g. paths will be selected only if the wolf repeats "do nothing" all the time. In addition to the default heuristics, the author can specify the achievement (or lack of achievement) of plot points as additional filtering criteria. Plot points can be defined in terms of events in the story, e.g. pulling out story paths in which the wolf eats Granny and is not killed by the end, and characters' (including the user's) beliefs or their actual states in the story, e.g. pulling out story paths in which Red believes she has a close social distance with the wolf by the end. The paths selected by different criteria often overlap with each other. As the last step, the filtering procedure will merge paths selected by all the criteria and present the distinct paths to the author.

To complete the authoring process, the author needs to review the paths being selected, and make modifications to them (correct virtual characters' behaviors) if the paths are different from his/her expectations. For example, in one of the paths generated in the examples given in Section 6, the hunter arrives at the place where Red and the wolf are. The hunter would have killed the wolf, but Red keeps on talking to him. While the hunter is entrapped in the conversation with Red, the wolf runs away. The author may want to design a new story path that forces the hunter to kill the wolf instead of talking to Red in that situation. Next, the newly corrected story paths together with the originally designed story paths are passed to the **Fit-Sequence** function to reconfigure the virtual characters. When necessary, additionally rounds of evaluation (by simulating potential user's behaviors) and reconfiguration of the virtual characters can be iteratively performed.

6   Example Authoring Process

This section provides an example of using the proactive authoring approach to facilitate the design of an interactive drama, the story of Red Riding Hood.

Step 1: Tune characters' goals to story paths specified by the author. The following story path is passed to the **Fit-Sequence** function. Sentences in parentheses describe the status of the story that can not be seen easily from the characters' actions.

Red greets the wolf. − > the wolf greets back. − > Red tells the wolf that she is on her way to visit Granny. − > the wolf says bye to Red. − > Red says bye to the wolf. − > Both Red and the wolf walk away. − > (Red and the wolf meet outside of Granny's house) the wolf eats Granny. − > (the hunter arrives) the hunter kills the wolf. − > Granny escapes from the wolf.

Step 2: Simulate potential users' behaviors. To demonstrate simulating users with alternative mental models of other characters, we assume the users are informed that in this story the wolf might be a good character and will never eat people. These users might have this mental model or the default mental model of the wolf being evil. Thespian generated story paths that can be encountered by users with 5 rounds of interaction. In addition, Thespian simulated protypical users' behaviors. Due to space limitation, only the results of simulating the following two prototypes are listed in Table 3: the user has a dominant goal of giving the cake to Granny and the user has a dominant goal of NOT giving the cake to Granny (This is the case that the user does not adapt the character's goals). When simulating each of these prototypes, the user agent's other goal weights are set to the results of fitting to the story path described above.

Step 3: Filter the generated story paths and present to the author. When filtering the paths to present to the author, the wolf is selected as the only character to be examined because in this story both the hunter and Granny are expected to have repeated actions, e.g. the hunter moves around searching for the wolf all the time. In addition to the default filtering heuristics, we define the achievement of the following plot point as a filtering criterion: the wolf eats Granny and is not killed by the end. The summaries of results are given in Table 2 and Table 3. Note, because the user is playing Red, the total number of paths in the story is 14^5!

Table 2. Results of simulating users with alternative mental models

Mental model	Well-motivated paths	Selected by heuristics	Selected by plot point
the wolf is good	2456	181	72
the wolf is evil	1837	95	56

Table 3. Results of simulating protypical users

Mental model	Want Granny to have cake	Well-motivated paths	Selected by heuristics	Selected by plot point
the wolf is good	Yes	1688	98	68
the wolf is good	Opposite	2318	175	72
the wolf is evil	Yes	1513	86	56
the wolf is evil	Opposite	1729	92	56

7   Discussion and Future Work

Though we have not formally evaluated this proactive authoring procedure, the numbers reported in Section 6 are very informative. In this domain, simulating a 5-round interaction with a well-motivated user results in thousands of possible story paths. Though these numbers are already dramatically smaller than the total number of paths (14^5), it is still impossible for a human author to exam each of these paths. Fortunately, the filtering process further cuts the numbers of paths that need to be reviewed into about 1/10 of all the paths that have been generated, and allows the author to specify his/her own filtering criteria using plot points. The numbers being reported here are story dependent and filtering criteria dependent. Nevertheless we feel this proactive authoring procedure is potentially a very helpful tool for evaluating and refining the design of an interactive drama. It enables automatic testing of the performance of the interactive drama, and the author only needs to pay attention to a limited set of story paths that are likely to be problematic. It is also worth mentioning that by extensively testing the virtual characters' behaviors, the modeling deficits in the virtual characters are also more easily revealed.

On the other hand, this authoring procedure is still at its early stage. We currently foresee three parts in future work. Firstly, we plan to build richer syntax which allows the author to specify more complex filtering criteria, e.g. a partial order of events is violated. Secondly, we seek to find more efficient automatic and domain independent algorithms for identifying potentially problematic story paths and assigning priorities to paths that need to be reviewed. These algorithms can help authors who are not familiar with a domain to start authoring. Finally, the current fitting procedure in Thespian can only fit characters' motivations to sequences of actions. As plot points can be specified in terms of not only actions (events), but also characters' beliefs, and actual states, we plan to extend the fitting procedure to enable automated character configuration using this information.

8   Conclusion

In this paper, we made our initial movement towards building a proactive authoring procedure within the Thespian framework. The proactive authoring procedure presented in this paper can automatically generate story paths that can be encountered by a well-motivated user, who may have alternative mental models about other characters. The authoring procedure can also simulate protypical users' behaviors. Further, the story paths generated by simulating potential users are filtered before being presented to the author, so that the author only needs to pay attention to paths identified as problematic. Two default, but configurable filtering heuristics are provided by Thespian. In addition, the author can specify the achievement (or lack of achievement) of plot points as filtering criteria. Finally, the author's feedback will be used to fine tune the virtual characters. This approach can reduce authoring effort resulting from open-ended user interaction. Especially, it can help the author design interactive dramas for a wide range of users for either ensuring the same desired effect will be experienced in all types of users, or tailoring the experience for different types of users.

Acknowledgments

We thank our colleagues, especially John Gratch, Mark Riedl, Bill Swartout for their support and thoughtful discussions.

References

1. Marsella, S.C., Johnson, W.L., Labore, C.: Interactive pedagogical drama for health interventions. In: AIED (2003)
2. Paiva, A., Dias, J., Sobral, D., Aylett, R., Sobreperez, P., Woods, S., Zoll, C.: Caring for agents and agents that care: Building empathic relations with synthetic agents. In: Kudenko, D., Kazakov, D., Alonso, E. (eds.) Adaptive Agents and Multi-Agent Systems II. LNCS (LNAI), vol. 3394, pp. 194–201. Springer, Heidelberg (2005)
3. Si, M., Marsella, S.C., Pynadath, D.V.: Thespian: An architecture for interactive pedagogical drama. In: AIED (2005)
4. Swartout, W., Hill, R., Gratch, J., Johnson, W., Kyriakakis, C., LaBore, C., Lindheim, R., Marsella, S.C., Miraglia, D., Moore, B., Morie, J., Rickel, J., Thiúbaux, M., Tuch, L., Whitney, R., Douglas, J.: Toward the holodeck: Integrating graphics, sound, character and story. In: Agents, pp. 409–416 (2001)

5. Riedl, M.O., Andrew, S.: Believable agents and intelligent scenario direction for social and cultural leadership training. In: the 15th Conference on Behavior Representation in Modeling and Simulation, Baltimore, Maryland (2006)
6. Riedl, M.O., Saretto, C.J., Young, R.M.: Managing interaction between users and agents in a multi-agent storytelling environment. In: AAMAS, pp. 741–748 (2003)
7. Cavazza, M., Charles, F., Mead, S.J.: Agents interaction in virtual storytelling. In: Proceedings of the International WorkShop on Intelligent Virtual Agents, pp. 156–170 (2001)
8. Magerko, B.: Story representation and interactive drama. In: Artificial Intelligence and Interactive Digital Entertainment (AIIDE), Marina del Rey, CA (June 2005)
9. Louchart, S., Aylett, R.: The emergent narrative theoretical investigation. In: the 2004 Conference on Narrative and Interactive Learning Environments (2004)
10. Szilas, N.: IDtension: a narrative engine for interactive drama. In: 1st International Conference on Technologies for Interactive Digital Storytelling and Entertainment, Darmstadt Germany (2003)
11. Braun, N.: Storytelling in collaborative augmented reality environments. In: Proceedings of the 11th International Conference in Central Europe on Computer Graphics, Visualization and Computer Vision (2003)
12. Mateas, M., Stern, A.: Towards integrating plot and character for interactive drama. In: Working notes of the Social Intelligent Agents: The Human in the Loop Symposium. AAAI Fall Symposium Series (2000)
13. Traum, D.R., Swartout, W., Marsella, S.C., Gratch, J.: Fight, flight, or negotiate: Believable strategies for conversing under crisis. In: Panayiotopoulos, T., Gratch, J., Aylett, R., Ballin, D., Olivier, P., Rist, T. (eds.) IVA 2005. LNCS (LNAI), vol. 3661, Springer, Heidelberg (2005)
14. Si, M., Marsella, S.C., Pynadath, D.V.: Thespian: Using multi-agent fitting to craft interactive drama. In: AAMAS, pp. 21–28 (2005)
15. Mateas, M., Stern, A.: Integrating plot, character and natural language processing in the interactive drama Façade. In: the International Conference on Technologies for Interactive Digital Storytelling and Entertainment (2003)
16. Young, R.M., Riedl, M.O., Branly, M., Jhala, A.H., Martin, R.J., Saretto, C.J.: An architecture for integrating plan-based behavior generation with interactive game environments. Journal of Game Development (2004)
17. Marsella, S.C., Pynadath, D.V., Read, S.J.: PsychSim: Agent-based modeling of social interactions and influence. In: Proceedings of the International Conference on Cognitive Modeling, pp. 243–248 (2004)
18. Smallwood, R.D., Sondik, E.J.: The optimal control of partially observable Markov processes over a finite horizon. Operations Research 21, 1071–1088 (1973)
19. Gmytrasiewicz, P., Durfee, E.: A rigorous, operational formalization of recursive modeling. In: ICMAS, pp. 125–132 (1995)
20. Pynadath, D.V., Marsella, S.C.: Fitting and compilation of multiagent models through piecewise linear functions. In: Kudenko, D., Kazakov, D., Alonso, E. (eds.) Adaptive Agents and Multi-Agent Systems II. LNCS (LNAI), vol. 3394, pp. 1197–1204. Springer, Heidelberg (2005)
21. Si, M., Marsella, S.C., Pynadath, D.V.: Thespian: Modeling socially normative behavior in a decision-theoretic framework. In: Gratch, J., Young, M., Aylett, R., Ballin, D., Olivier, P. (eds.) IVA 2006. LNCS (LNAI), vol. 4133, Springer, Heidelberg (2006)
22. Pynadath, D.V., Marsella, S.C.: Minimal mental models. In: AAAI (2007)

The Effects of an Embodied Conversational Agent´s Nonverbal Behavior on User´s Evaluation and Behavioral Mimicry

Nicole C. Krämer[1], Nina Simons[2], and Stefan Kopp[3]

[1] University Duisburg-Essen, Forsthausweg 2, 47057 Duisburg, Germany
[2] University of Cologne, Herbert-Lewin-Str. 2, 50931 Köln, Germany
[3] University Bielefeld, PO box 100131, 33501 Bielefeld, Germany
`nicole.kraemer@uni-due.de, skopp@techfak.uni-bielefeld.de,`
`nina.simons@web.de`

Abstract. Against the background that recent studies on embodied conversational agents demonstrate the importance of their behavior, an experimental study is presented that assessed the effects of different nonverbal behaviors of an embodied conversational agent on the users´ experiences and evaluations as well as on their behavior. 50 participants conducted a conversation with different versions of the virtual agent Max, whose nonverbal communication was manipulated with regard to eyebrow movements and self-touching gestures. In a 2x2 between subjects design each behavior was varied in two levels: occurrence of the behavior compared to the absence of the behavior. Results show that self-touching gestures compared to no self-touching gestures have positive effects on the experiences and evaluations of the user, whereas eyebrow raising evoked less positive experiences and evaluations in contrast to no eyebrow raising. The nonverbal behavior of the participants was not affected by the agent's nonverbal behavior.

Keywords: Evaluation, nonverbal behavior, mimicry, social effects of ECAs.

1 Introduction

When evaluating embodied conversational agents, it has not only been shown that they usually are accepted and efficient but that the perceptions and effects are dependent on the agent´s appearance, abilities and behaviours. Recent studies especially show that the agent's behavior is indeed a crucial variable influencing an agent's effects on the user [1, 2, 3, 4], and that especially subtle nonverbal behaviors are pervasive [5]. Yet, systematic studies that investigate the particular effects of an agent´s specific nonverbal behavior are still scarce, especially for subtle behavioral cues [for an exception see 6]. Likewise, only few studies combine the usual self-report data on subjective evaluation with measurements of the behavior of the user, e.g., to identify social effects [7].

Against this background, the study reported here focuses on the effects of two kinds of subtle nonverbal behaviors of the agent on the human user's evaluation, feelings, and behaviors during the interaction. The nonverbal behaviors studied are

C. Pelachaud et al. (Eds.): IVA 2007, LNAI 4722, pp. 238–251, 2007.
© Springer-Verlag Berlin Heidelberg 2007

eyebrow raising and adaptors, i.e. self-touching gestures like scratching. In addition to the users´ subjective experiences, it is assessed whether users tend to pick up any of those behaviors of the agent, i.e., whether one can find effects of behavioral mimicry in human-agent interactions. The study was carried out with the conversational agent Max [8], as it has been permanently applied since January 2004 as an information kiosk agent in a public computer museum (the Heinz-Nixdorf-MuseumsForum in Paderborn, Germany). Partly, the study was conducted at the museum site, with visitors to the museum as participants, and partly with university students who met the agent in the laboratory of the Artificial Intelligence Group of the University of Bielefeld (Germany).

1.1 Effects of Nonverbal Behavior

Nonverbal behavior of humans (e.g., facial expressions, gaze, gestures, postures, and head and body movements) has a strong impact on the process and the results of our communicative efforts and plays a vital role in person perception processes. Summarizing findings from different studies Burgoon [9] suggests that overall approximately 60-65% of social meaning is derived from nonverbal behaviors.

It has also been demonstrated and acknowledged that the nonverbal behavior of an embodied agent has sustainable effects [3]. With regard to specific behaviors, several studies demonstrated the importance of the agents´ gaze behavior. Rickenberg and Reeves [3] empirically showed that participants experienced more anxiety and performed worse when the interface agent appeared to observe the user. Heylen, van Es, Nijholt, and van Dijk [10] proved that human-like gaze behavior of a cartoon-like talking face is evaluated more positively with regard to usability, satisfaction, involvement and naturalness than when displaying a small amount of gaze movements or random movements. But also the amount of gaze has been demonstrated to play a crucial role: Bailenson, Beall, Loomis, Blascovich, and Turk [11, 12] show in their "non-zero sum gaze" application with avatars that people react more positive when they experience to be gazed at 100% of time: Not only did people look at the avatar more often [12] but female participants were persuaded to a greater amount by a text that was read by the avatar. Finally, it has been shown that gaze behavior and eyebrow movements, especially in combination, are perceived as indicators of extraversion of the virtual character [13, 14].

Concerning bodily movements, it could be documented that agents exerting several language supporting gestures (deictic, iconic, metaphoric and beat) are evaluated as more useful, more friendly and more natural (although the amount of gestures was seen as overdoing) than agents only displaying pointing gestures [15]. However, a word of caution is in order since gesture was confounded with presentation as 2D or 3D agent in this study. Buisine, Abrilian, and Martin [16] reported that male participants rated redundant speech and gesture (relevant information was given in both modalities) more positive than complementary speech and gesture (information was given either in speech or in gesture). Cassell and Thórisson [17] showed that process-oriented nonverbal behavior such as turn taking and beat gestures leads to smoother language interactions and better ratings of the agent's usefulness and speech comprehension capabilities, compared to solely presenting emotional feedback (showing confusion or smiling). However, it was shown that already subtle behavioral aspects are influential, e.g., an increased head movement activity [5].

1.2 Social Effects of Agents and Mimicry

Early evaluation studies with conventional computers characterized by human-like attributes [18] as well as with embodied conversational agents [19] showed that machines and agents are readily perceived as social entities: already minimal cues and conditions in terms of similarity with humans lead users to show behavior that would be expected in human-human interaction. Person perception was shown to be like that of real humans [20], cooperation and trust is fostered [19, 21], tasks are facilitated or inhibited by "social" presence of a virtual agent [3], and socially desirable behavior is triggered [19, 22]. Likewise, Blascovich et al. [23] and Bailenson et al. [1] demonstrated that interactions with artificial humans in virtual environments follow the rules of spatial use in human-human interaction: People approach a virtual non-human-figure closer than a human-like virtual person, especially if this virtual person showed realistic behavior such as eye gaze. With regard to users' communicative behavior, it has been demonstrated that the presence of an agent triggers behavior known from human-human-dialogue: users are inclined to interact more in natural language (instead of e.g. a remote control) [7, 22] and moreover employ polite behaviors such as small-talk and etiquettes [7, 8].

One aspect of human communication that has not yet been examined systematically with regard to the social effects of virtual agents is interpersonal coordination as it appears in interactional synchrony and mimicry. This behaviour can broadly be defined as "mimicry is having one individual is doing what another individual does" [24, p. 11]. Recently, the automaticity of these phenomena has been stressed [25]: It is seen as unaware, efficient, uncontrollable (i.e. cannot be stopped) and unintentional.

Interactional synchrony and mimicry are often assumed to be connected to rapport or positive evaluations of the interaction partner. Although many findings support this notion [26, 27, 28, 29] this has not been proven consistently and the direction of causality is not assured. But what kind of behavior is being mimicked? In an experimental study, Chartrand and Bargh [30] demonstrated that rubbing one's face or shaking one's foot is mimicked). Also, congruent arm, body and leg postures have been demonstrated to be adopted [31, 32]. Although fewer studies have dealt with facial mimicry, the mimicry of smiling, tongue protruding, mouth opening and yawning was demonstrated [see 33, for a summary]. Furthermore, there is anecdotal evidence that eye brow movements are mimicked [34].

It is an open question if mimicry effects also arise when humans interact with virtual embodied agents. However, mimicry has also been shown to occur when another person is presented via media [35, 36, 37]. With regard to interactive agents, however, mostly anecdotal evidence has been reported suggesting that the behavior of an agent or robot gets mimicked [38, 39]. Thórisson [39], for example, observed that "in general, participants tended to mimic the agents' behaviors: If the agent was rigid, they tended to stand still; if the agent was more animated, they tended to be animated" (p. 175). In the opposite direction mimicry by agents was shown to affect humans: When the head movements of human participants were mimicked by the virtual interaction partner, the latter was not only more influential and persuasive but was also rated more favourably [40]. Also, a virtual rapport agent engaging in mimicry of the user was shown to increase speaker fluency and engagement [29].

Against this background, the study presented here aims to contribute to a better understanding of both, effects of nonverbal behavior and social effects. Eyebrow raising [14, 34] and self-touching gestures (so-called adaptors) are chosen as behavioral cues on the part of the agent. Our research questions are: (1) What are the effects of an agent´s eyebrow movements and adaptors on the experiences and evaluations of the user? and (2) Is one of the behaviors or are both mimicked when they are presented?

2 Method

The embodied conversational agent: Max. Within this study, the participants were confronted with the embodied conversational agent Max (see figure 1). This virtual agent developed by the Artificial Intelligence Group of the University of Bielefeld (Germany) has a humanoid appearance as well as verbal and nonverbal dialog skills [8]. Max is displayed in human-like size on a screen and his synthetic voice is presented via loud speakers. In contrast to previous applications, in which users had to use a keyboard to communicate with Max, participants in this study could address Max in spoken language via microphone. Since speech technology is so far not able to reliably recognize spoken language input in noisy environments, a so-called "Wizard of Oz" scenario [41, 42] was used. The human Wizard acted as "speech recognizer" in that he entered by keyboard what the participants said and thus made the participant's natural language utterances accessible for Max. Nevertheless, the Wizard had no influence on the verbal and nonverbal reactions of Max, which were autonomously generated by the system. A disadvantage of this procedure was, however, a considerable time delay of Max's reactions to subject's utterances. In order to avoid confusion or turn-taking problems, a red point was shown on the screen, right to Max's head, to indicate that the system is processing the statement and that a reaction is prepared.

Independent variables: Variations of Max´s nonverbal behavior. Since both facial expression and gesture are of interest with regard to mimicry, a facial as well as a gestural behavior aspect of Max were varied to test the research questions of this study: self-touching gestures and eyebrow raising. The nonverbal behaviors were selected according to previous experimental findings from interpersonal communication [14, 24, 30]. With respect to self-touching gestures, four different gestures were implemented within this study (see figure 1). Following Chartrand and Bargh [30] and van Baaren [24] the first self-touching gesture was a scratching at the left cheek. Additionally, a scratching below the neck (in the area of the décolleté), a scratching at the left side of the upper body and a scratching in the right half of the belly were employed. The occurrence of all four gestures (self touching) was compared with the absence of all four gestures (no self touching). When presenting self-touching gestures, Max showed the self-touching behavior on average every 23 seconds, each time randomly selecting one gesture out of the four possibilities. The eyebrow raising was also varied in two levels: eyebrow raising or no eyebrow raising. The eyebrow raising was presented depending on the prosody of simultaneous speech, such that Max raised his eyebrows with a probability of 50% on every accentuation peak in his speech. The frequency of all further nonverbal behaviors of Max (emblematic, metaphoric, iconic and deictic gestures, emotional facial expressions, head and eye movements) did not differ between conditions.

Fig. 1. Max´s different self touching gestures

Overall, a two-factorial experimental design with four different conditions resulted, and a between subjects design was chosen.

Dependent variables: Evaluation of Max. With respect to the evaluation of the agent a questionnaire was used to assess the feelings of the participants during the interaction, the person perception of Max and the general evaluation. The questionnaire was designed based on existing questionnaires which were developed and repeatedly employed in other studies [5, 43]. By means of a 20-item questionnaire the feelings of the participants during the interaction were determined (e.g., "attentive", "amused", "cheerful", "relaxed" and "lethargic"). The questions on general evaluation, for example, included to what extent the participants enjoyed the communication with Max, to what extent they could control the conversation, or whether they could imagine to complete tasks with Max or other virtual characters, such as programming a video recorder. For both evaluation aspects participants had to state their level of agreement by means of five-point Likert-scales, with the extremes "strongly disagree" and "strongly agree". The person perception of Max was measured with the help of a 34-item semantic differential (seven point bipolar rating scales, whose extremes are designated by two opposite adjectives, based on [5]). It was assessed, for example, whether Max was perceived rather as "warmhearted" or "cold", "self-confident" or "shy", "competent" or "incompetent", "wooden" or "animated", "believable" or "unbelievable".

Dependent variables: Nonverbal behavior of the participant. In order to determine whether the participants imitated Max's behavior during the interaction, the interactions were recorded on video with the consent of the participants. To assess how frequently every participant raised his/her eyebrows and how often he/she touched him/herself, the video recordings were analyzed by counting the eyebrow raisings and self-touching gestures of each participant. Both, self-touching gestures in the face and self-touching gestures on the neck and upper body were rated as self-touching gestures. Likewise, not only identical behavior between Max and the participants, but all self-touching gestures on the upper body and in the face were assessed. Furthermore, it was not required that the matching behavior took place at the same time. Instead of this, in accordance with Chartrand and Bargh [30] and van Baaren [24], merely the frequency of the same or similar behavior during the interaction was observed. In order to ascertain comparability between subjects, frequencies were related to individual interaction duration.

Procedure. Participants were requested to engage in a 10-minute small talk with Max and to additionally play the "animal game" with him. For the game the participants had to choose an animal which Max attempted to guess by asking questions that must be answered with "yes" or "no". In order not to direct the attention of the participants to Max's nonverbal behavior, the participants were informed that the goal of the study was to test whether Max is suited for certain applications in its current form. After the interactions, which lasted between 8 and 14 minutes (mean value = 10.71 minutes, standard deviation = 1.24 minutes) participants were handed the questionnaire on experiences and evaluations. After filling out the questionnaire, the participants were fully debriefed (with regard to the actual goals of the study) and asked for consent to analyze their data.

Participants. 50 persons aged from 15 to 72 years volunteered to participate in the study (age mean value = 27.73 years; standard deviation = 11.53 years). The sample consisted of 28 female and 22 male persons. As mentioned above, the data were partly collected in a public computer museum (10 participants) and partly at a laboratory (40 participants). To avoid any confounding of the data the participants from the different locations were distributed uniformly over the different conditions.

3 Results

3.1 Evaluation of Max

The consideration of the mean values of the four experimental conditions for the items showed that the participants experienced and evaluated the interaction with Max positively by reporting positive feelings during the interaction, perceived Max positively in reference to the majority of items, as well as rated the interaction with Max positively. However, results also showed consistently that Max was judged as rather wooden, stiff, artificial, incompetent and feeble, but also as rather dominant (see mean values in tables 1 and 2).

However, comparisons of the mean values of the experimental conditions showed several differences. Before the mean value comparisons were calculated by means of the general linear model, a factor analysis (main component analysis with varimax rotation) was first calculated for each of the three evaluation aspects. Nevertheless, all significant results with regard to both, factors and items, are depicted in the following.

For the items concerning the feelings of the participants during the interaction, the factor analysis yielded four factors which together clarify 59.83% of the total variance. The factors were labeled according to their positive item loadings with the concepts "interest/amusement", "strain", "attention" and "negative feelings".

The factor analysis for the person perception of Max determined six factors explaining 58.74% of variance. The factors were designated with the terms "social-communicative competence", "activity", "naturalness", "sympathy", "strain" and "reservation". Due to the fact that items are bipolar and negative poles in most cases were associated with higher values, all factors had to be named contrary to their positive item loadings.

With regard to the general evaluation the factor analysis identified two factors explaining for 61.38% of variance. The factors were termed "acceptance" and "control".

Effects of the self touching gestures. With regard to the feelings of the participants during the interaction, there were no significant main effects of the independent variable "self-touching gestures", neither for the items nor for the factors. However, for the item "nervous", a tendency on the 10% level of significance was discernible: subjects exposed to Max's self-touching gestures tended to be more nervous than subjects in the experimental conditions without self-touching gestures (see table 1).

With respect to the influence of the self-touching gestures on the person perception of Max, several significant main effects could be identified (see table 1): With regard to the item level Max was perceived as more aggressive, but also as more warmhearted, more agile and more committed when presenting self-touching gestures than when he showed no self-touching gestures. Concerning the extracted factors, Max was evaluated as more natural when he touched himself with several gestures than when this behavior was not presented. Furthermore, several tendencies could be observed on the 10% level of significance: When Max's nonverbal behavior included self-touching gestures the participants tended to rate him as inspiring more confidence and being more animated as well as more strained on the factor level, than when this behavior was not shown. There were no significant effects of the self-touching gestures with regard to the general evaluation.

Effects of eye-brow raising. For the feelings of the participants during the interaction significant differences could be determined when comparing the levels of the independent variable "eyebrow raising" (see table 2): if Max raised his eyebrows during the interaction, the participants felt more nervous and more diverted, but also more tired than participants who were not exposed to eyebrow raising. In reference to the extracted factors a corresponding significant difference was shown: participants exposed to Max raising his eyebrows reported more negative feelings than subjects not exposed to this behavior. Moreover, participants tended to be more irritated when Max raised his eyebrows than when not presenting this behavior. The latter difference was however only significant on the 10% level.

With reference to the person perception of Max, several significant main effects were visible with regard to the independent variable "eyebrow raising" (see table 2): if Max raised his eyebrows during the interaction, he was perceived as colder, stiffer, stiller, more powerless and more serious. In addition, a significant main effect for the factor "naturalness" could be determined: subjects in the experimental conditions without eyebrow raising evaluated Max as more natural than participants exposed to his eyebrow raising. Concerning the item "inspiring confidence-disquieting" likewise a difference between the behavior variations was noticeable, which however was only significant to the 10% level: when raising his eyebrows, Max was evaluated as less "inspiring confidence" than when there was no eyebrow raising.

Table 1. Main effects of the independent variable self-touching gestures

Item/factor	Mean values		Standard deviations		Analysis of variance				η^2
	S_1	S_2	S_1	S_2	F-ratio	df within	df between	p-value	
Feelings of the participants during the interaction									
Nervous	2.59	1.93	1.37	1.09	3.813	1	46	.057	.077
Person perception of Max									
wooden-animated	3.62	2.86	1.75	1.38	3.316	1	45	.075	.069
warmhearted-cold	2.95	4.21	1.43	1.26	10.900	1	45	.002	.195
inspiring confidence-disquieting	2.86	3.39	1.25	0.99	2.871	1	46	.097	.059
agile-stiff	3.77	4.82	1.80	1.54	5.195	1	46	.027	.101
aggressive-peaceful	5.36	6.25	1.50	0.97	6.566	1	46	.014	.125
committed-not involved	2.68	3.25	0.89	1.04	4.392	1	46	.042	.087
Factor: naturalness	-0.436	0.342	1.057	0.818	9.535	1	46	.003	.172
Factor: strain	-0.307	0.241	0.941	0.995	3.771	1	46	.058	.076

S_1: self-touching gestures: yes; S_2: self-touching gestures: no

Interactions between self touching gestures and eye-brow raising. With regard to the users´ feelings during the conversation a significant interaction for the item "indifferent" could be determined (see table 3): the participants felt more indifferent when Max showed one of the two varied nonverbal behaviors, than when Max presented both or none of the two behavior patterns. Furthermore, a tendency for the item "bored" was discernible, which showed the same evaluation pattern (see table 3).

Two significant interactions were visible with reference to the interaction between the independent variables "self-touching gestures" and "eyebrow raising" (see table 3): it was shown that Max was perceived as more attentive if he presented both or neither of the two behavior patterns than if he showed one of the two behavior patterns. The second significant interaction resulted for the factor "social-communicative competence": here the picture emerged that the social-communicative competence was regarded as higher if Max showed both or neither of the two behavior patterns than when he showed one behavior pattern. Especially when both behavior patterns were presented the social-communicative competence was evaluated higher.

Beside these significant interactions, further interactions appeared which were significant on the 10% level (see table 3): a tendency for the item "aggressive-peaceful" emerged: this interaction was a semi-disordinal or hybrid interaction. The mean values show that when Max presented self-touching gestures, he was evaluated as more aggressive on both levels of the independent variable "eyebrow raising" than when he did not touch himself. Still, when Max did present self-touching gestures he was perceived as more aggressive without eyebrow raising than when he did raise his

Table 2. Main effects of the independent variable eyebrow raising

Item/factor	Mean values		Standard deviations		Analysis of variance				η^2
	S_1	S_2	S_1	S_2	F-ratio	df within	df between	p-value	
Feelings of the participants during the interaction									
Irritated	1.92	1.46	1.19	0.66	3.020	1	45	.089	.063
Tired	2.04	1.28	1.14	0.54	9.157	1	46	.004	.166
Nervous	2.56	1.88	1.42	0.97	4.196	1	46	.046	.084
Diverted	2.24	1.60	1.13	0.87	5.305	1	46	.026	.103
Factor: negative feelings	0.291	-0.291	1.107	0.800	4.158	1	46	.047	.083
Person perception of Max									
warmhearted-cold	4.08	3.28	1.44	1.40	4.351	1	45	.043	.088
inspiring confidence-disquieting	3.44	2.88	1.00	1.20	3.309	1	46	.075	.067
agile-stiff	4.84	3.88	1.57	1.76	4.572	1	46	.038	.090
vigorous-powerless	4.40	3.60	1.41	1.19	4.558	1	46	.038	.090
lively-still	4.12	3.28	1.48	1.10	4.383	1	46	.042	.087
serious-cheerful	3.32	4.24	1.57	1.23	5.640	1	46	.022	.109
Factor: naturalness	0.285	-0.285	0.923	1.010	5.908	1	46	.019	.114

S_1: eyebrow raising: yes; S_2: eyebrow raising: no

eyebrows, while participants not exposed to self-touching gestures judged Max as more aggressive if he raised his eyebrows. For the item "wooden-animated", however, a disordinal interaction was visible: if Max showed both or neither of the two behavior patterns participants tended to perceive him as more "wooden" according to the mean values than when he presented one of the two behavior patterns.

With reference to the items for the general evaluation, a significant interaction could be determined for the item "it was interesting to communicate with Max" (see table 3). The mean values showed that the participants evaluated the communication with Max as more interesting if either both or neither of the two behavior patterns were presented, while they regarded him as less interesting if only one behavior was presented. Moreover, the same evaluation pattern emerged when considering the interaction for the factor "acceptance". This interaction missed the 5% but not the 10% level of significance (see table 3).

3.2 Nonverbal Behavior of the Participants

With regard to the nonverbal behavior of the participants, the frequencies of the coded behaviors per minute between the levels of the independent variables were compared

Table 3. Interactions between the independent variables

Item/Factor	Mean values				Standard deviations				Analysis of variance				H^2
	S_1	S_2	S_3	S_4	S_1	S_2	S_3	S_4	F-ratio	df_1	df_2	p	
Feelings of the participants during the interaction													
Bored	2.36	2.79	2.55	1.93	1.43	1.12	0.93	0.73	2.91	1	46	.095	.059
Indifferent	1.36	1.93	2.09	1.29	0.51	0.92	1.30	0.47	8.00	1	46	.007	.148
Person perception of Max													
wooden-animated	3.00	3.07	4.30	2.64	1.79	1.49	1.49	1.28	3.94	1	45	.053	.081
aggressive-peaceful	5.64	5.93	5.09	6.57	1.50	1.00	1.51	0.85	2.95	1	46	.093	.060
attentive-diverted	2.18	2.79	3.18	1.64	0.75	1.31	1.33	0.50	13.3	1	46	.001	.225
Factor: social-communicative competence	-.060	.214	.507	-.565	.664	1.10	1.24	.634	6.26	1	46	.016	.120
General evaluation													
It was interesting to communicate.	4.27	3.43	3.36	4.00	1.10	1.34	1.12	1.04	4.99	1	46	.030	.098
Factor: acceptance	0.39	-.271	-.204	0.12	1.11	1.01	1.12	0.73	3.04	1	46	.087	.062

S_1: eyebrow raising: yes - self-touching gestures: yes; S_2: eyebrow raising: yes - self-touching gestures: no;
S_3: eyebrow raising: no - self-touching gestures: yes; S_4: eyebrow raising: no - self-touching gestures: no
df_1: within; df_2: between

by means of the general linear model. The consideration of the mean values of all four experimental conditions led to the result that the frequency of the self-touching gestures on the part of the participant was small. Significant main effects of the self-touching gestures or the eyebrow raising on the nonverbal behavior of the participant were not visible. Thus, mimicry was not observable.

4   Discussion

The goal of the present study was to broaden the findings on the effects of virtual agents´ nonverbal behavior since these have repeatedly been demonstrated to affect the users´ experiences and evaluations. Eyebrow raising and self-touching behavior were selected as independent variables since previous studies from interpersonal as well as agent-human interaction already demonstrated their potential to affect both the evaluations and the behavior (e.g., with regard to the mimicry of the behavior) of the participants.

Main effects of self-touching gestures consistently demonstrated that the presence of this behavior indeed affects the evaluation of the agent: He was rated as more natural, more warmhearted, more agile and more committed when presenting self-touching gestures than when he showed no self-touching gestures. Nevertheless, there also seems to be a downside of frequent self-touching. The agent is additionally evaluated as more strained and aggressive. Further studies should vary the frequency of the behavior on different levels in order to ascertain whether a linear relation can be determined. If this is the case, there might be an optimal frequency that potentially leads to positive effects but not (yet) to negative outcomes. The positive effects in general also suggest that behaviors do not have to be directly functional in terms of process-oriented gestural behaviors [17, 39] but that also in terms of dialogue functions seemingly "useless" behaviors might contribute to a positive evaluation [44]. The feelings of participants during the interaction, however, have barely been affected by the agent´s self-touching behavior.

With regard to eyebrow movements both, feelings during interaction and evaluation were consistently affected by the subtle cue. Surprisingly, the number of significant differences and corresponding effect sizes are not smaller than with regard to the effects of self-touching – although eyebrow movements can be classified as more subtle behaviors. Nevertheless, results are different from those obtained for self-touching: Here, the presence of the behavior does not lead to increased liking but to more negative evaluations and more negative feelings during the interaction. This is also inconsistent with the results of Krahmer et al. [14] who obtained positive effects of eyebrow raising. The conflicting results might be due to the usage of completely different agents or due to the specific form of the behavior (frequency, intensity). In both cases, the implication for further research is that nonverbal behavior and its effects are complex. Results suggest that the attributes of nonverbal behavior in human-human-communication, that is, their subtlety, the importance of the quality of movements, and their context dependency [5, 45] can also be found with regard to the behavior of agents. Also, results on the interaction of self-touching and eye-movement behaviors suggest that the agent is rated most positive when he either displays none of the behaviors or both. This, again, indicates that the effect of specific cues might be dependent on the presence or absence of others. This complexity with regard to effects will certainly render future research more difficult since contexts and specific quality of movements and cues will have to be taken into account. On the other hand, research that rigorously considers and systematically varies these aspects might also contribute to basic research on nonverbal communication [20].

With regard to mimicry participants did not imitate any of the varied behaviors. This might indicate that social effects of embodied agents have been overestimated and that the effects found so far are merely "as though" reactions (as posited by Kiesler & Sproull [46]) instead of caused by automatic application of social rules [47]. Since the lack of mimicry reactions might, however, simply be due to the fact that the specific agent did not sufficiently evoke social effects, further studies should continue to address this question. Specifically, the short time-delay during the agent´s turn-taking might have resulted in the fact that participants did not really feel "in conversation". Additional studies will have to overcome this handicap and also vary task and situation.

In sum, the results can be seen as promising in the sense that they show that further research is worthwhile and important. By analyzing an embodied agent´s nonverbal behavior not only applied findings (e.g., with regard to the optimal frequency of self-touching gestures) but also results important for basic research on nonverbal behavior (e.g., tackling the question whether there is linear relation between self-touching and rating as aggressive or natural) might be gained.

References

1. Bailenson, J.N., Blascovich, J., Beall, A.C., Loomis, J.M.: Interpersonal distance in immersive virtual environments. Personality and Social Psychology Bulletin 29, 1–15 (2003)
2. Cowell, A.J., Stanney, K.M.: Embodiment and interaction guidelines for designing credible, trustworthy embodied conversational agents. In: Rist, T., Aylett, R., Ballin, D., Rickel, J. (eds.) IVA 2003. LNCS (LNAI), vol. 2792, pp. 301–309. Springer, Heidelberg (2003)
3. Rickenberg, R., Reeves, B.: The effects of animated characters on anxiety, task performance, and evaluations of user interfaces. In: Letters of CHI 2000, pp. 49–56 (2000)
4. Slater, M., Steed, A.: Meeting People Virtually: Experiments in Shared Virtual Environments. In: Schroeder, R. (ed.) The Social Life of Avatars: Presence and Interaction in Shared Virtual Environments, pp. 145–171. Springer, Heidelberg (2002)
5. Krämer, N.C.: Bewegende Bewegung. Sozio-emotionale Wirkungen nonverbalen Verhaltens und deren experimentelle Untersuchung mittels Computeranimation. Pabst, Lengerich (2001)
6. Kaiser, S., Wehrle, T.: Animating and analyzing facial expressions in human-computer interactions: An appraisal based approach. Paper presented at the ISRE General Meeting, July 2005, Bari (2005)
7. Krämer, N.C.: Social communicative effects of a virtual program guide. In: Panayiotopoulos, T., et al. (eds.) Intelligent Virtual Agents 2005, pp. 442–453. Springer, Hamburg (2005)
8. Kopp, S., Gesellensetter, L., Krämer, N.C., Wachsmuth, I.: A conversational agent as museum guide - design and evaluation of a real-world application. In: Panayiotopoulos, T., Gratch, J., Aylett, R., Ballin, D., Olivier, P., Rist, T. (eds.) IVA 2005. LNCS (LNAI), vol. 3661, pp. 329–343. Springer, Heidelberg (2005)
9. Burgoon, J.K.: Nonverbal signals. In: Knapp, M.L., Miller, G.R. (eds.) Handbook of interpersonal communication, 2nd edn., pp. 229–285. Sage, Thousand Oaks (1994)
10. Heylen, D., van Es, I., Nijholt, A., Dijk, B.: Experimenting with the gaze of a conversational agent. In: van Kuppevelt, J., Dybkjaer, L., Bernsen, N. (eds.) Proceedings of the International CLASS Workshop on Natural, Intelligent and Effective Interaction with Multimodal Dialogue Systems, Kluwer Academic, New York (2002)
11. Bailenson, J.N., Beall, A.C., Loomis, J., Blascovich, J., Turk, M.: Transformed Social Interaction: Decoupling Representation from Behavior and Form in Collaborative Virtual Environments. PRESENCE: Teleoperators and Virtual Environments 13, 428–441 (2002)
12. Beall, A.C., Bailenson, J.N., Loomis, J., Blascovich, J., Rex, C.: Non-Zero-Sum Mutual Gaze in Collaborative Virtual Environments. In: Proceedings of HCI International, Crete (2003)
13. Fukayama, A., Hagita, N., Mukawa, N., Ohno, T., Sawaki, M.: Messages embedded in gaze of interface agents: impression management with agents gaze. In: Proceedings of the SIGCHI conference on Human factors in computing systems: Changing our world, changing ourselves, pp. 41–48 (2002)
14. Krahmer, E., van Buuren, S., Ruttkay, Z., Wesselink, W.: Audio-visual Personality Cues for Embodied Agents: An experimental evaluation. In: Proceedings of the AAMAS03 Workshop on Embodied Conversational Characters as Individuals, Melbourne, Australia (July 15, 2003)

15. McBreen, H., Jack, M.: Empirical evaluation of animated agents in a multi-modal e-retail application. In: Proceedings of the AAAI Fall Symposium on socially intelligent agents (2000)
16. Buisine, S., Abrilian, S., Martin, J.-C.: Evaluation of multimodal behaviour of agents. Cooperation between speech and gestures in ECAs. In: Ruttkay, Z., Pelachaud, C. (eds.) From Brows to trust. Evaluating Embodied Conversational Agents, Kluwer, New York (2004)
17. Cassell, J., Thorisson, K.R.: The Power of a Nod and a Glance: Envelope vs. Emotional Feedback in Animated Conversational Agents. Applied Artificial Intelligence 13, 519–538 (1999)
18. Reeves, B., Nass, C.I.: The media equation: How people treat computers, television, and new media like real people and places. Cambridge University Press, New York (1996)
19. Sproull, L., Subramani, M., Kiesler, S., Walker, J.H., Waters, K.: When the interface is a face. Human Computer Interaction 11, 97–124 (1996)
20. Bente, G., Krämer, N.C., Petersen, A., de Ruiter, J.P.: Computer Animated Movement and Person Perception. Methodological Advances in Nonverbal Behavior Research. Journal of Nonverbal Behavior 25, 151–166 (2001)
21. Parise, S., Kiesler, S., Sproull, L., Waters, K.: Cooperating with life-like interface agents. Computers in Human Behavior 15, 123–142 (1999)
22. Krämer, N.C., Bente, G., Piesk, J.: The ghost in the machine. The influence of Embodied Conversational Agents on user expectations and user behaviour in a TV/VCR application. In: Bieber, G., Kirste, T. (eds.). IMC Workshop 2003, Assistance, Mobility, Applications, Rostock, pp. 121–128 (2003)
23. Blascovich, J., Loomis, J., Beall, A.C., Swinth, K.R., Hoyt, C.L., Bailenson, J.N.: Immersive virtual environment technology as a methodological tool for social psychology. Psychological Inquiry 13, 103–124 (2002)
24. Van Baaren, R.B.: Mimicry: a social perspective (10.02.2006) (2003), Available: http://webdoc.ubn.kun.nl/mono/b/baaren_r_van/mimi.pdf
25. Lakin, J.L., Jefferis, V.E., Cheng, C.M., Chartrand, T.L.: The chameleon effect as social glue: Evidence for the evolutionary significance of nonconscious mimicry. Journal of nonverbal behavior 27, 145–162 (2003)
26. Bernieri, F.J., Rosenthal, R.: Interpersonal coordination: Behavioral matching and interactional synchrony. In: Feldman, R.S., Rimé, B. (eds.) Fundamentals of nonverbal behavior, pp. 401–432. Cambridge University Press, Cambridge (1991)
27. LaFrance, M.: Posture mirroring and rapport. In: Davis, J. (ed.) Interaction rhythms: Periodicity in communicative behaviour, pp. 279–298. Human Sciences Press, New York (1992)
28. Van Baaren, R.B., Holland, R.W., Kawakami, K., van Knippenberg, A.: Mimicry and pro-social behavior. Psychological Science 15, 71–74 (2004)
29. Gratch, J., Okhmatovskaia, A., Lamothe, F., Marsella, S., Morales, M., van der Werf, R., Morency, L.P.: Virtual Rapport. In: Gratch, J., Young, M., Aylett, R., Ballin, D., Olivier, P. (eds.) IVA 2006. LNCS (LNAI), vol. 4133, Springer, Heidelberg (2006)
30. Chartrand, T.L., Bargh, J.A.: The chameleon effect: The perception-behavior link and social interaction. Journal of Personality and Social Psychology 76, 893–910 (1999)
31. LaFrance, M.: Postural mirroring and intergroup relations. Personality and Social Psychology Bulletin 11, 207–217 (1985)
32. LaFrance, M., Ickes, W.: Posture mirroring and interactional involvement: Sex and sex typing effects. Journal of Nonverbal Behavior 5, 139–154 (1981)

33. Chartrand, T.L., Maddux, W.W., Lakin, J.L.: Beyond the perception-behavior link: The ubiquitous utility and motivational moderators of nonconscious mimicry. In: Hassin, R.R., Uleman, J.S., Bargh, J.A. (eds.) The new unconscious, pp. 334–361. Oxford University Press, Oxford (2005)
34. Goodwin, C.: Conversational Organization: Interaction between hearers and speakers. Academic Press, New York (1991)
35. Bavelas, J.B., Black, A., Lemery, C.R., Mullett, J.: I show how you feel: Motor mimikry as a communicative act. Journal of Personality and Social Psychology 50, 322–329 (1986)
36. Hsee, C.K., Hatfield, E., Carlson, J.G., Chemtob, C.: The effect of power on susceptibility to emotional contagion. Cognition and emotion 4, 327–340 (1990)
37. Neumann, R., Strack, F.: Mood contagion: The automatic transfer of mood between persons. Journal of Personality and Social Psychology 79, 211–223 (2000)
38. Cañamero, L.: Playing the emotion game with Feelix: What can a LEGO robot tell us about emotion? In: Dautenhahn, K., Bond, A., Canamero, L., Edmonds, B. (eds.) Socially intelligent agents: Creating relationships with computers and robots, pp. 69–76. Kluwer, Norwell (2002)
39. Thórisson, K.R.: Communicative humanoids. A computational model of psychosocial dialogue skills. PHD-Thesis. MIT, Cambridge (1996)
40. Bailenson, J.N., Yee, N.: Digital chameleons. Automatic assimilation of nonverbal gestures in immersive virtual environments. Psychological Science 16, 814–819 (2005)
41. Dahlbäck, N., Jönsson, A., Ahrenberg, L.: Wizard of Oz studies – why and how. In: Proceedings of the ACM International Workshop on Intelligent User Interfaces, ACM Press, New York (05.07.2006) (1993), available: http://citeseer.ist.psu.edu/45570.html
42. Oviatt, S.L., Adams, B.: Designing and evaluating conversational interfaces with animated characters. In: Cassell, J., Sullivan, J., Prevost, S., Churchill, E. (eds.) Embodied conversational agents, pp. 319–345. MIT Press, Cambridge (2000)
43. Rüggenberg, S.: Virtueller Helfer sucht Nutzer. Die Bedeutung der Technikexpertise der Benutzer für die Akzeptanz von anthropomorphen Schnittstellen. Unveröffentlichte Diplomarbeit, Universität zu Köln (2002)
44. Bickmore, T., Cassell, J.: Social Dialogue with Embodied Conversational Agents. In: van Kuppevelt, J., Dybkjaer, L., Bernsen, N. (eds.) Natural, Intelligent and Effective Interaction with Multimodal Dialogue Systems, Kluwer Academic, New York (3.9.2006) (2004), available: http://www.soc.northwestern.edu/justine/jc_papers.htm
45. Burgoon, J.K., Buller, D.B., Woodall, W.G.: Nonverbal communication: The unspoken dialogue. Harper & Row, New York (1989)
46. Kiesler, S., Sproull, L.: Social Human-Computer Interaction. In: Friedman, B. (ed.) Human Values And The Design of Computer Technology, pp. 191–199. Cambridge University Press, Cambridge (1997)
47. Nass, C., Moon, Y.: Machines and mindlessness: Social responses to computers. Journal of Social Issues 56, 81–103 (2000)

Spatial Social Behavior in Second Life

Doron Friedman[1,2], Anthony Steed[1], and Mel Slater[1,3]

[1] University College London
{d.friedman,a.steed,m.slater}@cs.ucl.ac.uk
[2] The Interdisciplinary Center, Herzliya, Israel
[3] ICREA-Universitat Politecnica de Catalunya, Spain

Abstract. We have developed software bots that inhabit the popular online social environment SecondLife (SL). Our bots can wander around, collect data, engage in simple interactions, and carry out simple automated experiments. In this paper we use our bots to study spatial social behavior. We found an indication that SL users display distinct spatial behavior when interacting with other users. In addition, in an automated experiment carried out by our bot, we found that users, when their avatars were approached by our bot, tended to respond by moving their avatar, further indicating the significance of proxemics in SL.

1 Introduction

Social virtual environments, as envisioned in cyberpunk literature [12,4], are now becoming widely popular. At the time of writing these lines the SecondLife (SL) web site brags there are approximately 5.9 million registered users and 25,000 online visitors[1]. SL is not the first such online 3D persistent community, and it is by no means flawless; we are definitely going to see SL and rival products change and evolve significantly. However, SL's increasing popularity have already made it an interesting target of research in its own right; it is an interesting opportunity to study the behavioral patterns of people in such virtual universes.

In highly immersive virtual-reality (VR) environments we have evidence that participants have a strong sense of presence; at least some of them for some of the time. We follow Sanchez-Vives and Slater's operative definition of presence [17] in that we expect people to behave in the same way in the virtual environment as they would in an equivalent real-world situation. Note that presence is, thus, very different from engagement. There is no question whether SL is engaging, our question is: do people have a sense of presence in SL? do they behave as if they were in a real world, and to what extent?

One of the main features distinguishing SL from online chat environments is that is it is supposed to induce a sense of being in a three-dimensional space. Therefore, we set out to study the spatial behavior of SL users, and specifically, their social spatial behavior.

Since SL is a commercial product, we do not have access to statistical data, and it is unlikely that such data would be made public by Linden Labs (the

---

[1] http://www.secondlife.com

C. Pelachaud et al. (Eds.): IVA 2007, LNAI 4722, pp. 252–263, 2007.

company behind SL). Thus, we have developed automated software bots that are able to wander around SL and systematically collect data. In addition, we have built these bots to have some social capabilities of their own; this allows them not only to observe and collect data, but also to participate in social interactions, thus essentially carrying out social experiments within SL.

2 Background

The study of the social significance of space, and in particular the distance between people as they interact, was initiated by Hall [5,6], who termed it proxemics. Hayduk [7] provides a more recent survey.

Video games have been recognized in the past as a potential for artificial intelligence research (for example, see [10] and [9]). As Loomis et al. [11] note, collaborative virtual environments (CVEs) are also a useful tool for research in psychology.

CVEs provide each user with an avatar that embodies them in the virtual world. This avatar serves several purposes: it should be distinctive to convey identity, at least over a short period of time, it indicates the user's chosen position, and possibly their attention and some indication of their emotional state, through verbal or non-verbal communication (NVC) [2].

However, almost exclusively in these environments, the user must "act" at least some of these: they must chose their appearance, position their own avatar and indicate their emotional state. Depending on the system, some of this may be automatic or semi-automatic. In an immersive system, or other tracked system, some NVC may occur automatically, because some of the participant's limbs are tracked. In a desktop system, attention and position are conveyed semi-automatically because the nature of the interface means that the user must normally get their view close to an object to interact with it. Some CVEs support 1st-person views, but most support 3rd-person views, or 3rd-person is the most prevalent view if there is an option. In fact, some CVEs have very rigid constraints between the 3D view and the avatar position. SL is slightly looser in this respect, in that the user can rotate and zoom the camera around their avatar's location.

The avatar thus "grounds" the user in the environment. A CVE system may enable communication between users if their avatars are nearby, though this is typically determined only by proximity, not by facing direction. Despite this, experience with early CVEs found that users would naturally form social groups and face users they were communicating with [3]. Even experienced CVE users, who know that avatar proximity is neither necessary nor sufficient to enable communication, adopt socially-aware spatial behaviors: these behaviors help manage what could otherwise be quite confusing situations with many people attempting to interact at once [13]. Several studies of immersive systems have found evidence that users treat social space very naturally, attending to the gaze of others and watching body language [8].

Recently, Yee, Bailenson and colleagues have studied social space within SL. In [18] they uncover patterns of social space use that would be expected, such as gender differences, and eye-gaze avoidance for situations where the interpersonal difference is only 2-4m.

The previously discussed studies were all conducted with avatars of users. Bailenson et al. [1] studied approach of an immersed user to both agent avatar and user avatars. They found that users would keep distance, but that knowledge that the avatar was a user avatar would deter personal space invasions. Vinayagamoorthy et al. [15] studied the situation of a user of an immersive system approaching agent avatars, which were programmed to represent different emotional states. The agent avatars would respond when the user approached, and the user would subsequently adopt a socially-acceptable position. Comments from interviews, indicated that some users felt they should respect the social conventions, even though they knew the avatars were autonomous [16].

3   The SL Bots

SL is intended to be built first and foremost by its users, and it thus provides facilities for content creation. Programming is achieved with the Linden Scripting Language (LSL), which provides a wide range of capabilities; at this time LSL includes 330 built-in functions, including: vehicles, collision detection, physics simulations, communication among users, inventory management, playing audio and video files, and more. However, LSL was clearly not designed to construct bots; scripts are only attached to objects, not to the user's avatar directly. We have come around this limitation by attaching a ring to our avatar. The ring object can then run a script, and the script can then be used to move the avatar and animate it, so that it appears walking while moving, as well as performing other tasks required by our bot.

Our bot has a basic capability for wandering around and finding locations or objects of interest. The implementation is as follows: the bot selects a random direction and starts walking in that direction, until it either reaches an obstacle (such as a wall) or the target. If it reaches an obstacle it selects another random direction and keeps moving in the new direction. While this approach is simple and not necessarily efficient, it has proved successful in practice, and even allowed our bot to occasionally wander in and out of closed buildings, passing through doors. Typically, as in the study described here, the bot is instructed to locate other avatars. When it detects one or more avatars it stops and carries out its social task, until it is terminated, or until it find itself alone again.

The bot has simple interaction capabilities: when it encounters other avatars it greets them using their name. The bot can also play a large range of approximately 50 pre-recorded animations. However, we have found out that such animations do not play an important role in SL. While users are able to allow their avatar to play pre-recorded animations, this is not similar to real-life NVC. For example, users very rarely use these animations, and when they do, these are typically high-level animations, such as dancing. In the real world, NVC is a continuous process, which plays an important part in communication, and is mostly unconscious.

Our bot has capabilities for data collection: it can be instructed to collect information about the objects and avatars it encounters on the way, log this information, and send it to us. Currently it uses email to send us the information, but SL allows other forms of communication with external software, such as HTTP or XML-RPC[2].

4   Experiment 1: Proxemity in Dyadic Interactions

SL adopts the approach, typical of non-immersive VEs, of conversational characters [14]: the avatars display autonomous NVC, with a possibility for the users to override their avatars' gestures and postures. In SL, users very rarely use this possibility. Such autonomous NVC may or may not contribute to the sense of presence of SL users, but it clearly does not allow us to study the level of presence based on the users' behavior. Thus, instead of NVC, we study a subset of NVC, namely proxemics.

Most proxemics research is focused on dyadic interactions (interaction between two people). Hall [6] distinguished among several distance categories, measured as circles around a person:

1. intimate space: for touching — up to 1.5 feet.
2. personal space: for interaction among friends — 1.5-4 feet.
3. social space: interactions among acquaintances — 4-12 feet.
4. public space: for public speaking — over 12 feet.

If indeed users copy this social behavior into SL, we expect to see similar distances among interacting avatars. SL avatars are, by default, of the same height as average adults (measured, of course, in virtual units). While users can create very small or very large avatars, it is rare to see such cases[3]. Thus, we expect the virtual distance in SL to match the corresponding real distance in a social real-world interaction, with real units replaced by virtual units. Generally, SL does not allow touching (with the exception of unique devices for "adult" interaction, which were not studied here). We thus do not expect to see avatars within intimate space.

4.1   Method

We have sent our bot on a mission to collect spatial data in SL, from 20 different locations, selected arbitrarily. It is not possible to follow Yee et al. [18], who sampled all SL regions, because: i) SL is growing fast, and ii) some areas in SL

---

[2] http://rpgstats.com/wiki/index.php?title=XMLRPC

[3] The same goes for non-human avatars; while it is common to see humanoid avatars with fancy or unique clothing, it is quite rare to encounter non-humanoid avatars (such as animals).

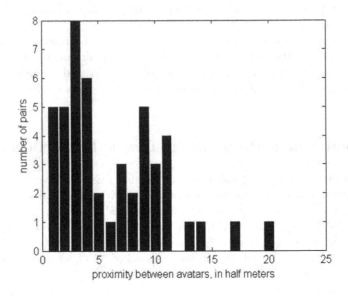

Fig. 1. The distribution of the number of pairs of interacting avatars by distance, in half meter units

block our script from running. We are still looking for a method to ensure that our sample of SL is balanced. Similar to Yee et al. [18], we have excluded from the study specific regions such as dance clubs, sex clubs, or other locations that may pose special constraints on spatial behavior.

From this data, we first isolated cases of dyadic interactions. Two avatars are considered interacting if they were in the same area for over one minute and if they were facing each other. By facing each other, we mean that their orientation was no more than 90 degrees away from the line connecting their positions.

Note that, unlike Yee et al. [18], we only look at couples of avatars that are alone (i.e., all other avatars are over 10 meters away), and not couples that may be a part of a group; our assumption is that dyadic interaction and group interaction should first be studied separately. We take the distance when our bot first spots the avatars in range, otherwise our bot might affect the interaction, and it would no longer constitute a dyadic interaction.

Also, unlike Yee et al. [18], we do not rely on the chat texts to judge whether the avatars are talking, because users could be communicating via a private instant-messaging channel, hidden from our bot.

4.2   Results

Our bot ran a few days and nights and collected 205 samples of pairs of avatars. Based on the criteria mentioned above we consider 49 of these couples to be interacting. An analysis of the distances reveals an interesting pattern (Figure 1):

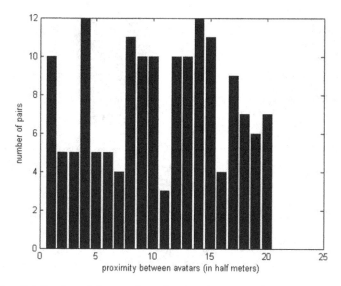

Fig. 2. The distribution of the number of pairs of avatars who are not interacting with each other, by distance, in half meter units

the distance between two avatars seems to have two distinct peaks: one around 1-1.5 meters and the other around 4.5 meters. Figure 3 shows a couple of avatars in these two distances. As a comparison, if we look at the distances of the 156 pairs of avatars assumed not to be interacting, the distances seem to be uniformly distributed (see Figure 2).

The precise interpretation of these results is not clear. Possibly, avatars first communicate when they are close enough to draw attention to each other (around 4-5 meters in SL), and if they feel close they move to a more personal distance (1-1.5 meters in SL). In any case, the important result is that the proximity among interacting avatars does not seem arbitrary. The null hypothesis that the samples are taken from a Gamma distribution is not rejected (Chi-squared = 36.9 on 48 degrees of freedom). In order to evaluate the fit we treat the distance (y) as the response variable with a Gamma distribution in a generalized linear model (GLIM), and then fit a constant as the independent variable. In such a case, if the fit was not good the deviance (which is the chi-squared value) would be high (at least 2 * the degrees of freedom); in this case the fit is good. This fit suggests that the distances are drawn from a random population with mean 2.85 and standard deviation 2.2 (although manual inspection suggests it may be a mix of two Gamma distributions). This implies that the distances follow the pattern of distribution of points randomly in space according to a Poisson process, i.e., there is some regularity in the spatial social behavior of avatars in SL, not unlike what we would expect in a real life social setting, such as a cocktail party.

We have tested whether there is a difference in proxemity related to (virtual) gender; Yee et al. [18] found such differences among male-male, female-female,

(a)

(b)

Fig. 3. (a) Screenshots of two avatars interacting: (a) social distance — approximately 5 meters, and (b) personal space — approximately 1 meter

and mixed dyads. As SL does not provide the gender of an avatar (neither virtual nor real), this information was not available to our bot. We deduced the gender of 44 out of the 49 pairs based on the avatar's first name[4]; in our case there

---

[4] In the future we recommend recording the display on the screen, for such post-hoc analysis.

was no significant effect of gender on distance. As Yee et al. [18] mention, the evidence for such a gender effect in real life is mixed.

5   Spatial Response: An Automated Experiment

In real life, when two people are engaged in conversation, they typically respond to each other's "body language". One of the common effects is posture shift; when one person changes posture, the other would typically respond by changing their posture as well. If both are in rapport they would often mimic each other's posture, but even if not there would almost always be a posture shift within a few seconds.

As mentioned earlier, posture is meaningless in SL, and we cannot test whether there is a posture-shift effect. Instead, our hypothesis is that if our bot would move towards the user it is interacting with, then the other user would also move in response. We do not predict what type of movement will take place; we merely predict there will be a movement response.

5.1   Method

In order to test this hypothesis we used our bot to carry out an automated experiment. We have programmed it to look for spatially isolated avatars and approach them. Based on the previous section, our instructions to our bot were as follows: stand 4 meters and face the other avatar. Then greet them (e.g., say "hello *name*, how are things?"), wait 2 seconds, and move towards them to a personal distance, of 1.2 meters. During the 10 seconds following this approach the bot observes whether the other avatar moves, and sends us the results.

It is possible, of course, to carry out such experiments with an experimenter controlling the avatar. One advantage of an automated experiment is accuracy and less experimental noise. Another advantage is that the researcher can spend time on the beach while the bot performs the experiment... It is still recommended to watch the screen (or record it and watch afterwards). For example, in one case our bot approached an avatar that was sitting inside a vehicle; naturally there was no spatial reaction from that avatar.

First, in order to establish a baseline, We have analyzed the data obtained from 49 interacting pairs of avatars (in Section 4) to find out how often avatars change position during interaction. We found out that the rate of movement is very slow, and many couples did not move at all. On average, we have observed 65 position changes in 172 minutes of interaction logged, or an average of one motion every 2 minutes and 39 seconds.

Next, we sent our bot to carry out the experiment, in 10 different locations selected arbitrarily. Our bot approached 28 avatars, and sampled for avatar motion in the 10 seconds after approaching them.

5.2   Results

The results indicated that 12 out of the 28 opponent avatars moved within the 10 seconds duration following the approach. On the one hand, this is not a very reliable response; it means that only 42% of the users responded as we expected them to[5]. On the other hand, this is significantly more than position shifts in typical SL interactions: based on the baseline, we could expect 1 or 2 motions (280 seconds divided by $159 = 1.76$) overall; we found the response to be 6 times larger than the baseline, so we regard this as an indication that many of the users did respond to our bot's approach.

As a side note, our bot recorded the contents of the chat channel after greeting the avatars, and sent us the data. 20 out of the 28 users responded to our bot's greetings ("Hello *name*, how are you doing?"). These were always short casual responses, mostly "hi", or slightly more sophisticated response such as "hmm... doing what?". We could see this as an indication that the majority of people respond to the verbal (chat) channel, more so than to the non-verbal, spatial channel.

6   Discussion and Future Work

We have described how our SL bots can systematically collect data from SL, and even carry out automated experiments. Ideally, we would like our SL bots to be able to socialize successfully in SL. Currently they are able to approach single avatars and, with a high rate of success, illicit some response (either verbal or position change). Such studies are, in general, useful for designing avatars and autonomous virtual agents with intelligent spatial behavior.

We have used scripting language (LSL) for our study, and it provided for most of our needs. The SL client have been recently released as open source, and there is an intention on behalf of Linden Labs to release the server source code as well. Note that this would allow more flexibility in implementing the agents, but would not address our main needs. First, we would still not have access to statistics available on Linden servers (with its very large number of users). Second, it is not clear if the information we need is explicitly available in the SL system. For example, we would like to know what avatars look like (e.g., are they male, female, or non-human). Using the client source one can extract scene information, including both the 3D model or the 2D rendered view. However, we would still require significant (virtual) machine vision effort to be able to determine what the avatar looks like, e.g., whether the avatar is attractive or not.

Furthermore, if we want our bots to be able to engage in more meaningful interactions, we hit the natural-language dialogue barrier. This is notoriously difficult, but we suggest SL may be an interesting domain for studying natural-language interaction. Unlike online chat environment, the conversation is often situated; for example, a user may tell another user: "do you see that green sign above our heads? click it to participate in the lottery." To further study non-verbal mediated communication we need to stay in the realm of

---

[5] We did not find equivalent numeric data regarding the frequency of posture shifts in real life, but we assume the response is close to a 100%.

highly-immersive VR settings, including at least some information on postures and gestures, extracted from trackers.

Bots collecting information, and even carrying out experiments, raise methodological issues. For example, we need to find ways to ensure that we are sampling SL properly. We need to find ways to know who are the users behind the avatars we are interacting with: are they currently socializing, or are they working? in the future we might need to make sure they are not bots themselves...

Such research may also raise ethical, and even legal considerations. Carrying experiments with human subjects generally requires following ethical guidelines and experiments require formal approval from an official committee. For example, informed consent is always required from a subject before participating in an experiment. As long as the study is purely observational there is no problem. In our case the manipulation of the subjects (in Section 5) is clearly insignificant. If there were direct information being asked about the subjects, then it may be necessary to get institutional ethics approval, and also to make it clear to the subjects that this is a study, and they have the right to refuse, as in any real-life experiment. There is still a a difference from real-life experiments, since everyone is anonymous. However, some people put enormous resources into maintaining online personas, and would rightly object to using that persona's name in records. Another concern will need to be addressed if the bots would be able to carry out more meaningful social interactions, since this would involve deception. In some virtual environments users are happy to accommodate bots in the condition that they declare themselves to be bots.

We have found some evidence of spatial social behavior in SL. Although these are early results, we see that: i) users tend to keep their avatars in non-arbitrary proximity from the other avatars they are interacting with, and ii) almost half of the users responded in to an approach by our bot into their personal space by changing their position.

We agree with Yee et al. [18] that even in such a non-immersive experience as SL (small avatars observed on a computer screen, controlled by mouse and keyboard), users assign some social significance to the spatial context of their avatars. However, we do not agree with their conclusion that spatial social behavior in SL is identical to real-world behavior. Rather, we suspect that such virtual proxemics is a result of a transformation of real life proxemics. For example, while psychological literature bounds interaction distance by 12 feet, or 3.66 meters [6,7], we found a significant number of avatars intracting with distances of up to 5 (virtual meters); such differences would not be surprising, since SL lacks the richness of the NVC channel, and relies of text chat rather than speech. Also, these differences could be due to a small field of view in SL, as compared with real life.

As another example, SL avatars rarely move while interacting, while we expect people in real life to change positions much more frequently within an interaction. These pieces of evidence testify to the possibility that SL users do not have a high sense of presence.

Nevertheless, we still see it important to study social behavior in non-immersive environments such as SL. People are now spending a lot of time in such environments (not only in SL but more so in multi-user video games), and we suggest there is both theoretical and practical reasons for comparing people's behavior in such environments with their behavior in real life, and also with their behavior in highly-immersive VR. Practically, such research will inform us how to construct improved interfaces, which preserve more of the social nuances of real-life interactions. Theoretically, such research may provide us with new insights about the human brain and psychology, from the way they adapt to new types of experiences.

Acknowledgements

This work has been supported by the European Union FET project PRESENCCIA, IST-2006-27731.

References

1. Bailenson, J.N., Blascovich, J., Beall, A.C., Loomis, J.M.: Interpersonal distance in immersive virtual environments. Personality and Social Psychology Bulletin 29, 1–15 (2003)
2. Benford, S., Bowers, J., Fahlen, L.E., Greenhalgh, C., Snowdon, D.: User embodiment in collaborative virtual environments. In: Proc. of CHI'95, pp. 242–249 (1995)
3. Bowers, J., Pycock, J., O'Brian, J.: Talk and embodiment in collaborative virtual environments. In: Proc. of CHI'96, pp. 58–65 (1996)
4. Gibson, W.: Neuromancer. Voyager (1984)
5. Hall, E.T.: The Silent Language. Doubleday, New York (1959)
6. Hall, E.T.: The Hidden Dimension. Doubleday, New York (1966)
7. Hayduk, L.: Personal space: Where we now stand. Psychological Bulletin 94, 293–335 (1983)
8. Heldal, I., Schroeder, R., Steed, A., Axelsson, A.S., Spante, M., Widestrom, J.J.: Immersiveness and symmetry in copresent scenarios. In: IEEE Virtual Reality 2005, pp. 171–178 (2005)
9. Kaminka, G.A., Veloso, M.M., Schaffer, S., Sollitto, C., Adobbati, R., Marshall, A.N., Scholer, A., Tejada, S.: Gamebots: A flexible test bed for multiagent team research. Commun. ACM 45(1), 43–45 (2002)
10. Laird, J.E.: Research in human-level AI using computer games. Commun. ACM 45(1), 32–35 (2002)
11. Loomis, J.M., Blascovich, J.J., Beall, A.C.: Immersive virtual environments as a basic research tool in psychology. Behavior Research Methods, Instruments, and Computers 31(4), 557–564 (1999)
12. Stephenson, N.: Snowcrash. ROC Publishing (1991)
13. Tromp, J.G., Steed, A., Wilson, J.R.: Systematic usability evaluation and design issues for collaborative virtual environments. Presence: Teleoper. Virtual Environ. 12(3), 241–267 (2003)
14. Vilhjlmsson, H.H., Cassell, J.: Bodychat: Autonomous communicative behaviors in avatars. In: Int'l Conf. Autonomous Agents, Minneapolis, Minnesota, pp. 269–276 (1998)

15. Vinayagamoorthy, V., Brogni, A., Steed, A., Slater, M.: The role of posture in the communication of affect in immersive virtual environments. In: The 2nd ACM SIGGRAPH International Conference on Virtual Reality Continuum and Its Applications (2006)
16. Vinayagamoorthy, V., Steed, A., Slater, M.: The impact of a character posture model on the communication of affect in an immersive virtual environment (submitted 2006)
17. Sanchez Vives, M.V., Slater, M.: From presence to consciousness through virtual reality. Nature Reviews Neuroscience 6(4), 332–339 (2005)
18. Yee, N., Bailenson, J.N., Urbanek, M., Chang, F., Merget, D.: The unbearable likeness of being digital; the persistence of nonverbal social norms in online virtual environments. Cyberpsychology and Behavior 10, 115–121 (2007)

Generating Embodied Descriptions Tailored to User Preferences

Mary Ellen Foster

Informatik VI: Echtzeitsysteme und Robotik
Fakultät für Informatik, Technische Universität München
Boltzmannstraße 3, 85748 Garching bei München, Germany
foster@in.tum.de

Abstract. We describe two user studies designed to measure the impact of using the characteristic displays of a speaker expressing different user-preference evaluations to select the head and eye behaviour of an animated talking head. In the first study, human judges were reliably able to identify positive and negative evaluations based only on the motions of the talking head. In the second study, subjects generally preferred positive displays to accompany positive sentences and negative displays to accompany negative ones, and showed a particular dislike for negative facial displays accompanying positive sentences.

1 Introduction

The facial displays and body language that accompany embodied speech can have a significant effect on all aspects of how the content is perceived. A number of recent studies have demonstrated that the non-verbal behaviour of an embodied agent can affect users' perceptions and reactions at a number of levels, ranging from prosodic stress to affective content. For example, Swerts and Krahmer [1] have demonstrated in a series of studies that nodding and raising the eyebrows on prosodically stressed syllables can enhance users' ability to perceive stress in speech. Rehm and André [2] found that users judged an embodied agent that used deceptive facial displays to be less trustworthy and less certain about what it was saying than an agent that did not use such displays. Marsi and van Rooden [3] implemented selected facial displays of certainty and uncertainty on a talking head in the context of a multimodal question-answering system. In an experiment, users generally rated the videos intended to show certainty as being more certain than those intended to show uncertainty, even when the spoken content was identical.

The above studies all measured how facial displays can add dimensions of meaning that are not present in the speech signal. A related experimental strategy is to generate combinations of speech and body language where the message expressed on the two channels is either consistent or inconsistent. Such studies can be used to measure the relative impact of the two communication channels. For example, in some experiments, Swerts and Krahmer [1] showed judges stimuli with visual stress on one syllable and spoken stress on another and asked them

C. Pelachaud et al. (Eds.): IVA 2007, LNAI 4722, pp. 264–271, 2007.
© Springer-Verlag Berlin Heidelberg 2007

to select the stressed syllable; they found that the visual channel has greater impact for this task. Studies of this type can also compare users' reactions to stimuli with consistent or inconsistent cues, by measuring such factors as task performance or subjective preferences. A study of this latter type is that of Berry et al. [4], who compared several versions of an embodied agent in the context of a recall task and found that subjects performed best when the affective content was consistent between the language and the facial displays.

In this paper, we examine the impact of using corpus-derived rules to select the non-verbal behaviour of a talking head in a multimodal dialogue system. We first recorded and annotated the head and eye movements of a speaker reading a number of sentences in the domain of the target dialogue system. We then implemented a simple rule-based method to select displays for the embodied agent based on this corpus data and performed two studies to test the effectiveness of the rules, using both of the experimental strategies mentioned above. In the first study (Section 3), subjects were asked to identify the intended evaluation based only on the facial displays and were generally able to do so. In the second study (Section 4), users were asked to give subjective preferences between consistent and inconsistent combinations of speech and facial displays, and tended to prefer the consistent combinations.

2   A Corpus of Conversational Facial Displays

The COMIC multimodal dialogue system[1] adds an embodied dialogue interface to a CAD-like application used in sales situations to help clients redesign their bathrooms. When COMIC generates a description of a tile design, it uses information from a model of user preferences to help make choices at all levels.

(a) Positive   (b) Negative

Fig. 1. Characteristic facial displays from the corpus

To help select appropriate facial displays for the COMIC talking head to use when presenting the descriptions, we recorded the face of a speaker reading approximately 450 sentences generated by the system and annotated his facial displays; details of the recording and annotation process are given in [5]. The single biggest influence on the speaker's facial displays was the user-preference

---

[1] http://www.hcrc.ed.ac.uk/comic/

evaluation—that is, whether the user was expected to like or dislike the object being described. When he described a feature with a positive evaluation, he was more likely to turn to the right and to raise his eyebrows (Fig. 1(a)); on the other hand, on a feature with a negative evaluation, he was more likely to lean to the left, lower his eyebrows, and narrow his eyes (Fig. 1(b)).

3   Experiment 1: Recognisability

To test the recognisability of the facial displays of the recorded speaker, we performed a user study designed to measure whether subjects were able to identify the evaluation expressed in a sentence based only on the accompanying facial displays, where the displays were selected using a simple rule based on the findings from the corpus.

3.1   Subjects

This experiment was run over the web; subjects were recruited through the Language Experiments Portal,[2] a website dedicated to online psycholinguistic experiments. There were a total of 26 subjects: 14 females and 12 males. 20 of the subjects were between 20 and 29 years old, 4 were over 30, and 2 were under 20. 11 described themselves as expert computer users, 14 as intermediate users, and one as a beginner. 11 were native speakers of English, while the others had a range of other native languages.

3.2   Methodology

Each subject was shown 16 videos in which a talking head described a tile design. There were four different types of videos: with no facial displays, using only nodding, and using the positive and negative displays from the corpus. After viewing each video, the subject was asked to indicate whether they thought the speaker believed that the user liked or disliked the design being described; they could also choose *don't know* if they were unable to determine the intended evaluation. All subjects saw videos for the same 16 sentences, in an individually randomly-chosen order. The schedule types were randomly allocated to the videos so that each subject saw four schedules of each type.

3.3   Materials

To create the materials for this study, we used the COMIC text planner to generate 16 neutral sentences. For each sentence, we then created a set of facial-display schedules, using a simple rule that added a display to every mention of a tile-design feature (style, colour, decoration, and manufacturer). There were four schedule types: one using the characteristic positive displays from the corpus (Fig. 1(a)), one using the negative displays (Fig. 1(b)), one using only nodding, and one that did not assign any motions at all. The following are the facial-display schedules created for one of the sentences in this study, where $tn=r$

---

[2] http://www.language-experiments.org/

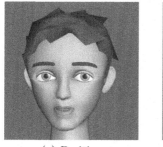

(a) Positive   (b) Negative

Fig. 2. Synthesised version of characteristic facial displays

indicates a right turn, $ln=l$ a left lean, $bw=u$ and d upward and downward brow motions, $nd=d$ a downward nod, and sq narrowing the eyes:

	This	*design*	*features*	*orange*		*in*	*the*	*colour scheme.*
Positive				tn=r, bw=u				
Negative				ln=l, bw=d, sq				
Nodding				nd=d				
Nothing								

We then created a video for each generated schedule using the RUTH talking head [6] and the Festival speech synthesiser [7]. The start and end of each display were coordinated with the relevant words: for example, in the above sentence, all displays would start and finish at the same time as the word *orange*. Fig. 2 shows how the facial displays from Fig. 1 were reproduced on the RUTH head.

3.4   Results

The overall results of this study are presented in Fig. 3. The x axis in this graph shows the actual facial displays that were used; for each display type, the bars indicate the number of times that the subjects believed that the speaker was being positive or negative, or whether they could not tell, respectively. For example, the videos with negative facial displays were identified as positive on 28 trials and as negative on 69 trials, while on the remaining 7 trials the judges were unable to make a decision.

We can assess the significance of these results using a binomial test, which provides an exact measure of the statistical significance of deviations from a theoretically expected classification into several categories (in this case, three). The results of this test indicate that subjects were successful at identifying both the positive and negative facial displays (66% and 63%, respectively; both $p < 0.0001$), and also tended to identify the schedules with nodding as positive (64%, also $p < 0.0001$). There was a weaker but significant tendency to identify the schedules with only lip-synchronisation as negative (45%, $p < 0.05$). The difference between the response patterns for the different video types is statistically significant: $\chi^2 = 87.4$, $df = 6$, $p < 0.0001$.

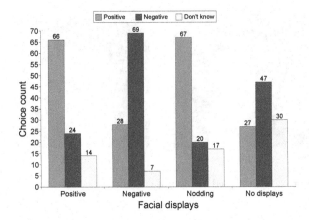

Fig. 3. Response counts for the recognition study

3.5   Discussion

The results of this experiment indicate the subjects were able to identify the intended evaluation when the talking head used the characteristic positive and negative displays of the corpus speaker. The tendency of subjects to identify a sentence with only a nod as positive could be due to several factors. First, while nodding is common across the entire corpus, particularly on words with predicted pitch accents, its frequency is relatively higher in positive contexts. The subjects could have been interpreting the nodding as a positive signal even though it was not intended as such. Another possibility is that the default interpretation of descriptions in COMIC—which operates in a sales domain—is that a design being described is assumed to be something that the user will like unless it is explicitly marked otherwise.

4   Experiment 2: Consistency

In this second experiment, we tested whether subjects' ability observed in the preceding study to identify the polarity of facial displays translates into any preferences regarding the consistency between the evaluation expressed on the verbal and non-verbal channels.

4.1   Subjects

Like the previous study, this one was also run over the web, again using the Language Experiments Portal to recruit subjects. In this case, there were 18 subjects: 8 females and 10 males. 14 of the subjects were between 20 and 29 years old, 3 were over 30, and one was under 20. 11 described themselves as expert computer users, 5 as intermediate users, and 2 as beginners. 8 of the subjects were native English speakers.

4.2 Methodology

Each subject was shown 12 pairs of videos. Both videos in a pair had identical speech content, but the face-display schedules differed: each trial included two of the three possible types of facial displays (positive, negative, or nodding only). For each trial, the subject was asked to indicate which video they preferred; subjects were encouraged to go with their first instincts and were not otherwise instructed on the selection criteria. All subjects saw videos of the same 12 sentences, in an individually-chosen random order. Six of the sentences suggested a positive evaluation, while the other six indicated a negative evaluation. The trials were balanced so that a subject made each pairwise comparison between schedules twice per sentence type (positive or negative), once in each order, while the allocation of comparisons to items was made randomly for each subject.

4.3 Materials

To create the materials for this experiment, we used the COMIC text planner to generate a further 12 sentences, again based on neutral user preferences. We then created a positive version of six of the sentences and a negative version of the other six by prepending either *You will like this* or *You will not like this*. For each sentence, we then used the rule-based method described in Section 3.3 to create three face-display schedules (positive, negative, and nodding); we also added a nod on the initial *this* in all cases. We then created videos of each version of each sentence, using the RUTH head and the Festival synthesiser as in the previous experiment. The following are the three schedules generated for one of the positive sentences in this study:

	You	*will*	*like*	*this:*	*it*	*is*	*classic.*
Positive				nd=d			tn=r, bw=u
Negative				nd=d			ln=l, bw=d, sq
Neutral				nd=d			nd=d

4.4 Results

The results of this study are shown in Fig. 4. On each graph, the bars on the left indicate the choices made in a positive context, while the right-hand bars show the choices made in a negative context. For example, when comparing positive facial displays against negative displays (Fig. 4(a)), subjects preferred the positive displays in a positive context 31 out of 36 times, while in a negative context they preferred the negative displays 20 times out of 36. There is a clear pattern: in a negative context, subjects generally preferred the less positive facial displays (negative over positive; negative over nodding; nodding over positive), while in a positive context these preferences were all reversed. The only preferences that were individually significant on a binomial test were those for positive displays over each of the others in a positive context (both $p < 0.05$). Using a χ^2 test, the preference between schedules using positive and negative displays (Fig. 4(a)) was

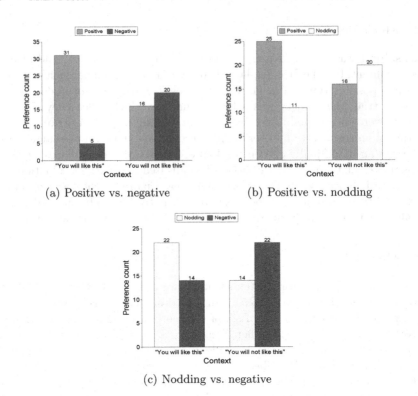

(a) Positive vs. negative

(b) Positive vs. nodding

(c) Nodding vs. negative

Fig. 4. Choice counts for the consistency study

found to be significantly different in the two contexts ($\chi^2 = 12.0$, $p < 0.001$); for the positive-nodding choice (Fig. 4(b)), the context had a marginally significant impact ($\chi^2 = 3.63$, $p \approx 0.06$); while for the nodding-negative choice (Fig. 4(c)), the effect was further from being significant ($\chi^2 = 2.72$, $p \approx 0.1$).

4.5   Discussion

The subjects showed a marginally significant difference between their responses to the videos with positive displays and those with nodding; the difference for the neutral vs. negative choice showed a similar trend but was not statistically significant. This suggests that, although videos with nodding may appear to be positive when presented in isolation, when they are contrasted with displays that are explicitly positive, the difference becomes apparent. As well, there appears to be a general preference across all of the trials for the positive facial displays: the strongest preferences are those for the positive displays over the others, while adding a negative context only reduces the preference to just under 50%.

5   Conclusion

The speaker recorded for our corpus showed characteristically different facial displays in positive and negative contexts. To test whether these displays are recognisable, we performed two user studies using talking-head videos generated using a simple corpus-derived rule. In the first experiment, subjects were reliably able to identify positive and negative evaluations based on the facial displays; they identified displays with only nodding (a common display in all contexts) as positive, and also had a weaker tendency to identify videos with no motion as negative. In the second study, subjects generally preferred consistent combinations of spoken and visual content.

The results of these studies extend findings from other studies of the influence of non-verbal behaviour on the interpretation of embodied speech (e.g., [1,2,3,4]) to show that varying the body language based on the user-model evaluation has a similar effect. They also confirm that the most marked behaviours of the speaker recorded for the corpus—namely, the facial displays he used in positive and negative contexts—are identifiable to human judges, and that people also prefer embodied descriptions where the facial displays are consistent with the polarity expressed in the speech. Knowing that the displays in the corpus are identifiable when resynthesised on the talking head indicates that this corpus is suitable for use in tasks such as the data-driven generation of non-verbal behaviour, which was the main motivation for creating the corpus.

References

1. Swerts, M., Krahmer, E.: On the perception of audiovisual cues to prominence (In press)
2. Rehm, M., André, E.: Catch me if you can – exploring lying agents in social settings. In: Proc. AAMAS '05 (2005)
3. Marsi, E., van Rooden, F.: Expressing uncertainty with a talking head. In: Proc. MOG 2007 (2007)
4. Berry, D.C., Butler, L., de Rosis, F., Laaksolathi, J., Pelachaud, C., Steedman, M.: Final evaluation report. Deliverable 4.6, MagiCster project (2004)
5. Foster, M.E.: Associating facial displays with syntactic constituents for generation. In: Proc. ACL 2007 Linguistic Annotation Workshop (2007)
6. DeCarlo, D., Stone, M., Revilla, C., Venditti, J.: Specifying and animating facial signals for discourse in embodied conversational agents. Computer Animation and Virtual Worlds 15(1), 27–38 (2004)
7. Clark, R.A.J., Richmond, K., King, S.: Festival 2 – build your own general purpose unit selection speech synthesiser. In: Proc. ISCA Speech Synthesis Workshop (2004)

Scrutinizing Natural Scenes: Controlling the Gaze of an Embodied Conversational Agent

Antoine Picot, Gérard Bailly*, Frédéric Elisei, and Stephan Raidt

GIPSA-Lab, Dept. of Speech & Cognition, UMR 5216 CNRS/INPG/UJF/Stendhal
46 av. Félix Viallet, 38031 Grenoble, France
gerard.bailly@icp.inpg.fr

Abstract. We present here a system for controlling the eye gaze of a virtual embodied conversational agent able to perceive the physical environment in which it interacts. This system is inspired by known components of human visual attention system and reproduces its limitations in terms of visual acuity, sensitivity to movement, limitations of short-memory and object pursuit. The aim of this coupling between animation and visual scene analysis is to provide sense of presence and mutual attention to human interlocutors. After a brief introduction to this research project and a focused state of the art, we detail the components of our system and confront simulation results to eye gaze data collected from viewers observing the same natural scenes.

Keywords: Embodied conversational agents, face-to-face interaction, eye gaze, talking face, visual scene analysis.

1 Introduction

We produce around 250.000 saccades per day. The eyes of the authors of this paper cover approximately 7m per second when screening computer screens. Multiple factors influence the intensive activity of our gaze control system: perceptive salience of various elements of our field of view (color, shape, motion, etc), their pertinence according to the purpose of the current scan (searching for a particular object or face, decoding the intentions of a human agent, etc) or the *a priori* knowledge we have on each element of the multimodal scene (familiarity, expectations, etc). The main objective of this work is to determine automatically the successive centers of interest that will likely attract the attention and the gaze of our Embodied Conversational Agent (ECA) observing a dynamic natural scene. We particularly propose a gaze control system that identifies and tracks regions of interest, weights their salience and pertinence regarding to the cognitive task, handles a stack of attention and couples visual analysis with an effective gaze control.

Such a strong coupling between a detailed multimodal scene analysis and motor control is necessary for developing ECA sensitive to changes of their real or virtual environment. The environment includes of course the interlocutors: the objective of this grounding of cognitive states and actions is to give to human partners tangible signs of presence and awareness. These cues have an important impact on information processing during interaction in terms of comprehension, belief and cognitive load.

---

* Corresponding author.

C. Pelachaud et al. (Eds.): IVA 2007, LNAI 4722, pp. 272–282, 2007.

After a brief state of the art where we will detail two major contributions that have inspired this work, we will describe our own proposal and illustrate its properties with concrete examples. This technical presentation is followed by a comparative evaluation with eye-tracking data collected on human subjects.

2   State of the Art

In order to plan their displacements, mobile robots have multiple sensors to build and analyze representations of their surrounding environment. Designing human-aware planning strategies is now a very challenging issue [1]. Most of anthropoid robots or companion robots are sophisticated scene analysis systems (mostly using vision) to analyze human behavior, identify their activities and plan adequate motor responses. Social robots developed at MIT [6] control sensory-motor loops where mutual attention is essential for acquiring and maintaining a common representation space. Maintaining eye contact as well as moving the head and eyes to signal interest or desire to take or leave turn are essential cues for signaling that the loop is effective. Robots developed at Waseda University exhibit such multimodal attention: Robita for example is able to follow a multi-speaker conversation, signal with head and gaze movements that it effectively tracks turns and is thus in a position to take part in the conversation [18]. It is also able to understand and generate multimodal deictic gestures.

Fig. 1. The Rackham robot interacting with a child (© LAAS Toulouse)

Most virtual conversational agents have often poor or none information on the actual environment where the interaction takes place. In absence of a grounded perception, their control model of gaze is often based on statistical regularities such as probability density functions of blinking frequency, amplitudes of ocular saccades or durations of eye fixations. Lee et al. [16] have thus proposed a statistical control model that takes into account the current cognitive activity of the talking agent (notably listening vs. speaking). If the generated saccades are preferred to a fixed or random gaze, the model should benefit from a finer description of the cognitive activities [see 4 and Raidt et al., this volume] as well as an effective coupling with a scene analysis. Proposals made by Courty [10] for virtual scenes or by Gu and Badler [12] for static natural scenes do not address exactly the problem of scrutinizing dynamic natural scenes.

The robot Rackham, developed by LAAS in Toulouse, combines advantages of sense of presence obtained by the performative actions of its body and the communicative actions of our virtual talking face displayed on a screen embedded in the robot (see Fig. 1.). A first coupling of the multimodal scene analysis performed by Rackham with the gaze controller of the talking face has been performed and evaluated [9].

The objective of the present work is to endow this coupling with a more sophisticated gaze controller, capable of reproducing essential characteristics of human visual attention (this paper) and face-to-face interaction (Raidt et al., this volume).

2.1 Behavioral Data

The process by which our eyes explore our field of vision consists in a series of saccades and fixations. A fixation here includes an optional smooth pursuit occurring when fixating a moving region of interest. Saccades are rapid movements of the eyes (approx. 25-40ms, 200°/s) that bring the region of interest (ROI) in the central receptive field of the retina (fovea) for further high resolution spectral analysis. Saccades are thus followed by a first fixation (approx. 300ms) followed by corrective fixations [or refixations as amplified by 27 in reading] or a smooth pursuit in case of a slowly moving object of interest. These two main components of gaze trajectory correspond coarsely to two complementary cortical pathways: a dorsal-temporal "where" pathway responsible for localizing multisensorial events in the scene – often termed as the fly detector - and a ventral-parietal "what" pathway responsible for object identification [19]. Jeannerod [14] prefers a more specific differentiation between a pragmatic (perception for action) vs. a semantic (perception for comprehension) analysis of the scene.

Scrutinizing a scene (still image or video) does not only consist in producing saccades towards the most salient object to the next: cognitive demands have a strong impact on the gaze trajectory and object selection [28]. Vatikiotis-Bateson et al. [26] have also shown that eye movements during audiovisual speech perception are also influenced both by the comprehension task and environmental listening conditions (signal-to-noise ratio). Attention mechanisms have also a strong impact on scene analysis [see 24 for impressive experiments on inattention blindness].

2.2 Computational Models of Visual Attention and Scene Analysis

Several computational models of visual attention and scene analysis have been proposed to mimic behavioral data. Numerous models for computing salience maps for still images and videos have been proposed to analyze, encode or summarize visual scenes. We pre-sent briefly two models that have attracted our attention because they both have exogen-ous and endogenous pathways while offering very complementary approaches (cf. Fig. 2.).

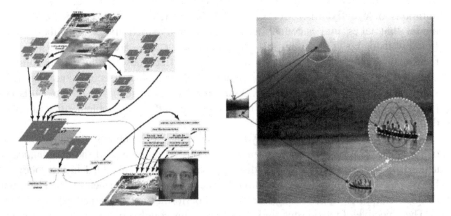

Fig. 2. Models for observing natural scenes. Left: eye saccades of the ECA developed by Itty et al. [13] are sequenced by points of interest computed from a video input. Right: Sun [25] uses a multi-scale segmentation to scrutinize an image by successive zoom-ins and -outs.

Itti et al. [13] propose a neurobiological model of visual attention for the control of the movement of the head and eyes of a video-realistic avatar. This model has three main components: (a) a map that associates a degree of intrinsic salience to each pixel of an image by combining several elementary salience maps (movement, orientation, intensity, and color) computed at different scales (using a pyramidal decomposition of the image); (b) a pertinence map that weights this previous map according to the cognitive demand [for an updated proposal, see 20] and (c) an attention map that takes in charge the sequencing of interest points computation by inhibiting zones of interest already scanned (often called inhibition of return mechanism or IOR).

The model of visual attention proposed by Sun [25] is based on a prior hierarchical segmentation of the scene into objects. Elementary processing units are not pixels but segments. The model also performs a syntactic scene analysis organizing segments by salience (from the most salient segment at the largest scale to the smallest) and embedding (from the object to its constituents). Sun also introduces a temporary IOR that restores attention when the appearance of a given segment changes.

3   Our Model of Visual Attention

Similarly to Itti et al., the front-end of our model (see Fig. 3.) is a saliency map without prior segmentation. A segmented object is however attached to the most salient interest point in the image by thresholding locally the map. Descriptors of the texture of the segment (notably in contrast with the surrounding region using linear discriminant analysis) are stored in a stack of attention. They are used to track the segment when in motion and also detect segment changes for temporary IOR.

Visual attention is implemented as a stack of attention that temporarily memorizes the position and textural characteristics of segments previously scanned. The stack can function as a FIFO (First-In First-Out) or a LIFO (Last-In First-Out). The most frequent usage is FIFO: it implements a temporary IOR. Each time a new ROI is detected, it is analyzed by the visual system (gaze is directed to it and a minimum fixation interval is planned for object recognition) and pushed on the stack. When the stack is full, the oldest ROI is popped off the stack and discarded. For determining the next most salient object in the scene, we subtract the saliency of all stored items in the stack from the saliency map. A stored item can thus only be scrutinized again if it has been popped off the stack by new incoming items or if its salience (thus its position or appearance) has changed.

The analysis of the current ROI can however be interrupted in order to process an exogenous stimulus that is particularly salient. In this case the stack functions as a LIFO: the current ROI is pushed on the stack and popped from the stack once the exogenous stimulus has been processed [11].

Our implementation of temporary IOR consists in reactivating a ROI that has changed compared to its stored characteristics or that gains back focus after its removal of the stack due to its limited storage capabilities (the stack has only 4 slots, i.e. possibility of maintaining attention to only 4 ROIs). We also added a smooth pursuit mechanism based on a ROI tracker using Kalman filtering. A module for recognizing and scrutinizing specific objects has also been added to enhance attention towards ROI with high potential interest such as faces.

Note finally that this system includes an effective coupling between saccade generation and visual analysis: a retinal filtering centered on the current position of the fovea cone is applied to the image before computing the saliency map that is thus sensitive to the eye movements. This differs from Itti et al. [13] implementation where the center of the retinal filter is always placed at the center of the screen. We do not assume that the camera is monitored by the eye gaze controller as it is usually the case for anthropoid robots [5].

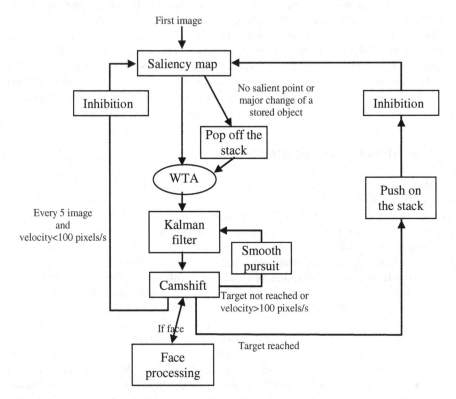

Fig. 3. Synopsis of the proposed system of visual attention. The saliency map is computed using the same scheme as Itti et al. [13] except the fact that the retinal filter is centered on the current point of gaze interest.

3.1 Saliency Map

The saliency map combines the responses of two image processing modules: (a) a "where" module combines orientation (0° and 90°) and movement maps computed at different scales on the raw image and combined by a simple addition; (b) a "what" module combines color and intensity maps computed after the retinal filter. This filter convolves the raw image with a Gaussian filter centered on the current convergence of the eye gaze. The resulting image is blurred according to the distance of the pixel to the center of the field of view. The final saliency map is obtained by summing these two maps normalized by their respective variance (obtained experimentally using a 10mn video). The pixel that is the next target of visual attention is the pixel with maximum salience (Winner Take All or WTA).

3.2 Attention Stack

Contrary to Itti et al. where the interest region is first removed of the attention map and returns slowly to attention using a relaxation process, we adopt an attention stack where the position and characteristics of the current ROI is temporally stored. This scheme is very alike the STM (short-term memory) system proposed by Peters & O'Sullivan [22] except that not all salient objects are stored in the stack and that their locations are effectively stored. The attention drop is just obtained by subtracting the memorized salience of the ROI to the global saliency map. It will thus inhibit the relevant ROI even if its salience is high or will reactivate it if its characteristics changes. The stack has only 4 elements and functions normally as a FIFO: storing a new ROI pops the oldest stored ROI off the stack. An element is thus popped off the stack either if it is too old or because its characteristics has changed (an object passing in the foreground may for example hide the object in the background stored in the ROI or lightening conditions of the ROI may change and enlighten the object for bringing renewed attention to this area). The stack may also function as a LIFO, when the fixation of the current ROI (average 160ms) is interrupted by the coming out of a very salient object in the scene: the current ROI is pushed on the stack, the new ROI is then processed immediately and eventually pursued, and then the memorized ROI is popped off the stack for finishing the WHAT processing.

3.3 Smooth Pursuit

In the Itti et al. and Sun's proposals, the only module that underlies a possible smooth pursuit is the movement map: the most salient pixel or ROI is expected to coincide with the object in motion. But this is rarely the case, especially when several objects are moving in the scene: this could result in alternating between several points of attention. We have thus added a special module dedicated to smooth pursuit – based

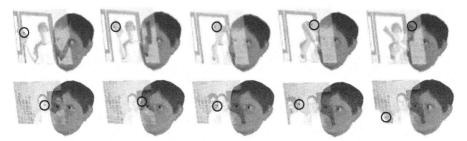

Fig. 4. Our ECA scrutinizing natural scenes. For sake of presentation, the image currently processed is incrusted in a semi-transparent screen placed in front of the ECA. A black circle materializes the current interest point determined by our model of visual attention. The results are given for a few key images of two videos. Top: the subject waves a book in front of the ECA and the smooth pursuit module takes in charge the gaze controller. Bottom: another subject passes in the back of the interlocutor and triggers a saccade to pursue this new and important object of interest.

on a Kalman filter – that updates the characteristics of the current ROI. The pursuit stops when the estimated speed of the object reaches a minimum threshold. In this mode, the gaze is anchored to the object trajectory and the pursuit has priority over salience computation: the saliency map is only renewed every 5 images in order to be able to process very salient exogenous stimuli (see previous section).

Note also that the control module of the eyes direction uses the estimated speed of the object to anticipate the next position of the object.

3.4 Specific Objects: Face Detection

Human vision system is face-aware: the neural activity in a specific zone of the temporal lobe significantly increases when we observe faces (even truncated) *vs.* images without faces or with destructured faces [21]. Such hardwired detectors enable us to focus rapidly on objects of the scene that are semantically very important. The saliency map receives thus a third input: a face detector [we used the built-in OpenCV detector based on 17]. Eyes and mouth detectors are also used [15] to verify the hypothesis and trigger a face-aware gazing of the main elements of the face [26, see also Raidt et al., this volume].

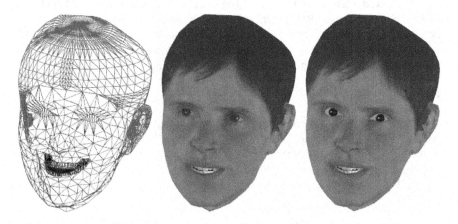

Fig. 5. Our virtual talking face is driven by 12 facial degrees-of-freedom [2]. The eyes and eyelids movements are controlled by 5 degrees-of-freedom that capture the correlations between gaze and eyelids deformations [3].

3.5 Results and Evaluation

We present here results obtained on two live videos. The model of visual attention has been coupled with a model of control of the eye gaze of an ECA [3, 7] (see also Fig. 5) that takes care of binocular coordination, saccade generation and micro-saccades during fixations. The trajectories generated by this coupled control (see Fig. 4) have been compared with eye tracking data collected on 5 viewers. Subjects were instructed to view the same videos for further description of each scene to the experimenter. Fig. 4 shows the superposition of the screen coordinates of computed and captured centers of attention.

In Scene 1, one subject first waves a blue book in front of him with his right arm, then a red book with his left arm and then the two books with both arms. This first scene aims at validating our system handling smooth pursuit and the attention stack (since we can only gaze at one object at one time!). Fig. 4 illustrates the results when the subject moves the two books at the same time: the gaze follows the blue book while the red book is ignored and will never be stored in the stack. This inattentional blindness [24] is also present in the occulometric data. The major differences between computed and observed gaze (see Fig. 6) is due to reaction time (our system detects changes more rapidly than human observers) and pursuit of movements (our system pursue the arm gesture although the carried object is outside of the field of view whereas the human viewers exploit causal links between these two movements and switch rapidly back to the subject's face).

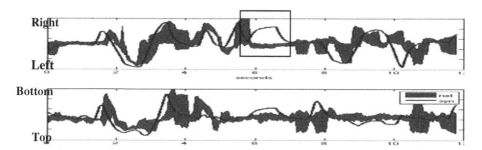

Fig. 6. Comparing the displacement of the gaze focus (top: horizontal; bottom: vertical) predicted by our system with oculometric data (displayed as gauges with means and standard deviations) for scene 1. The major discrepancies are underlined. At t=6s, our system follows the arm movement while viewers go back to the face of the subject (see text for explanation).

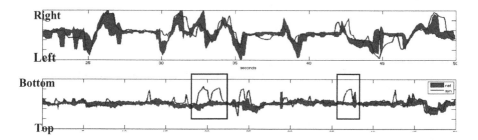

Fig. 7. Same as Fig. 6. but for scene 2. The gaze is often attracted by T-shirts (lower coordinates than faces, see text for explanation).

In Scene 2, one subject in the foreground faces the camera while several other subjects walk in the background, stop behind his shoulders and look at the camera. This scene aims at validating our face detector and the stack in LIFO mode (the examination of the face of the main subject is often interrupted by the other subjects passing through). Fig. 4 illustrates the push and pop of the main ROI of the scene to treat an interruption.

The major differences between computed and observed gaze (see Fig. 7) concern the ordinates: the saliency map is too sensitive to saturated colors of the T-shirts that override the salience provided by the face detector.

3.6 Performances

This algorithm has been implemented in C language under Linux Red Hat 9. It uses the OpenCV 0.9.9 Intel library. The tests have been run using a 2002 Pentium 4 desktop at 3.2 GHz. We are close to real time: the processing rate is close to 0.08s per image i.e. 12 images per second.

4 Conclusions and Perspectives

We described here a system for scrutinizing natural scenes and its coupling with a controller of the gaze of an ECA. Original components for this model of visual attention have been proposed and implemented: a stack of attention, an integrated face detector and a module for smooth pursuit. This system has been confronted to natural scenes and its prediction has been compared with oculometric data. This confrontation has shown the efficiency of the system in predicting a large part of the observed human behavior. It has also shown limitations and tracks for improvement, notably the importance of top-down processes, cognitive processes and *a priori* knowledge. Mirroring the attention stack and the saliency map, we are planning to add an intention stack [8] and a pertinence map [20] so that the ECA can concentrate its attention to the objects and events directly concerned with its cognitive tasks. Both will determine what to do with salient objects: task-dependent irrelevant ROI should be discarded from the saliency map with a different mechanism than the stack of attention. The pertinence map provides an efficient way to smooth out unimportant ROIs.

A long-term memory component [22] should be also added to feed the intention stack with desired characteristics of the search (location, aspect, etc) for matching objects. The face detector is part of this component: faces and facial expressions are in fact expected to bring more information and comprehension of the scene than other salient ROIs. We have already considered its coupling with a model of mutual attention developed for face-to-face conversation (see Raidt et al., this volume).

Our objective is to develop a real-time implementation of such a sophisticated model of visual attention to quantify its impact on live situated face-to-face interactions where ECA and subjects are involved in collaborative tasks. We have already shown that a pertinent control of multimodal deictic gestures of an ECA has a strong influence on reaction time [23] and plan to use a similar evaluation paradigm for assessing mutual attention.

Acknowledgements. This work has been financed by the project « scrutation de scènes multimodales » supported by ELESA, the project « Deixis Multimodale » supported by GIS PEGASUS, and the project « Présence » of the cluster ISLE supported by Rhones-Alpes. A first implementation of the model proposed by Itti et al. has been done by Romain Rossi.

References

1. Alami, R., Clodic, A., Montreuil, V., Sisbot, E.A., Chatila, R.: Toward human-aware robot task planning. In: AAAI Spring Symposium. To boldly go where no human-robot team has gone before (2006)
2. Bailly, G., Elisei, F., Badin, P., Savariaux, C.: Degrees of freedom of facial movements in face-to-face conversational speech. In: International Workshop on Multimodal Corpora, Genoa - Italy (2006)
3. Bailly, G., Elisei, F., Raidt, S., Casari, A., Picot, A.: Embodied conversational agents: computing and rendering realistic gaze patterns. In: Pacific Rim Conference on Multimedia Processing, Hangzhou (2006)
4. Bilvi, M., Pelachaud, C.: Communicative and statistical eye gaze predictions. In: International conference on Autonomous Agents and Multi-Agent Systems (AAMAS), Melbourne, Australia (2003)
5. Breazeal, C.: Designing Sociable Robots. MIT Press, Cambridge (2002)
6. Brooks, R.A., Breazeal, C., Marjanovic, M., Scassellati, B., Williamson, M.: The Cog Project: Building a Humanoid Robot. In: Nehaniv, C.L. (ed.) Computation for Metaphors, Analogy, and Agents. LNCS (LNAI), vol. 1562, pp. 52–87. Springer, Heidelberg (1999)
7. Casari, A., Elisei, F., Bailly, G., Raidt, S.: Contrôle du regard et des mouvements des paupières d'une tête parlante virtuelle. in Workshop sur les Agents Conversationnels Animés, Toulouse - France (2006)
8. Chopra-Khullar, S., Badler, N.I.: Where to look? Automating attending behaviors of virtual human characters. In: Annual Conference on Autonomous Agents, New York (1999)
9. Clodic, A., Fleury, S., Alami, R., Chatila, R., Bailly, G., Brèthes, L., Cottret, M., Danès, P., Dollat, X., Elisei, F., Ferrané, I., Herrb, M.: Rackham: an interactive robot-guide. In: IEEE International Workshop on Robots and Human Interactive Communications, Hatfield, UK (2006)
10. Courty, N.: Animation référencée vision : de la tâche au comportement, in IRISA. 2002, INSA: Rennes. p. 198 (2002)
11. Godijn, R., Theeuwes, J.: The relationship between exogenous and endogenous saccades and attention. In: Hyönä, J., Radach, R., Deubel, H. (eds.) The mind's eye: cognitive and applied aspects of eye movement research, pp. 3–26. North-Holland, Amsterdam (2003)
12. Gu, E., Badler, N.I.: Visual attention and eye gaze during multipartite conversations with distractions. In: IVA 2006, pp. 193–204 (2006)
13. Itti, L., Dhavale, N., Pighin, F.: Realistic avatar eye and head animation using a neurobiological model of visual attention. In: SPIE 48th Annual International Symposium on Optical Science and Technology, San Diego, CA (2003)
14. Jeannerod, M.: The cognitive neuroscience of action, p. 236. Blackwell, Oxford, UK (1997)
15. Jiang, X., Binkert, M., Achermann, B., Bunke, H.: Detection of glasses in facial images. In: Jiang, X. (ed.) Asian Conference on Computer Vision, Hong Kong - China (1998)
16. Lee, S.P., Badler, J.B., Badler, N.: Eyes alive. ACM Transaction on Graphics 21(3), 637–644 (2002)
17. Lienhart, R., Maydt, J.: An extended set of haar-like features for rapid object detection. In: IEEE International Conference on Image Processing, Rochester - NY, IEEE Computer Society Press, Los Alamitos (2002)
18. Matsusaka, Y., Tojo, T., Kobayashi, T.: Conversation robot participating in group conversation. IEICE Transaction of Information and System E86-D(1), 26–36 (2003)

19. Mishkin, M., Ungerleider, L.G., Macko, K.A.: Object vision and spatial vision: two cortical pathways. Trends in Neuroscience 6, 414–417 (1983)
20. Navalpakkam, V., Itti, L.: Modeling the influence of task on attention. Vision Research 45(2), 205–231 (2005)
21. Perrett, D., Rolls, E., Caan, W.: Visual neurones responsive to faces in the monkey temporal cortex. Exp Brain Research 47, 329–342 (1982)
22. Peters, C., O'Sullivan, C.: Bottom-up visual attention for virtual human animation. In: Computer Animation and Social Agents, Rutgers University, New York (2003)
23. Raidt, S., Bailly, G., Elisei, F.: Does a virtual talking face generate proper multimodal cues to draw user's attention towards interest points? In: Raidt, S. (ed.) Language Ressources and Evaluation Conference (LREC), Genova, Italy (2006)
24. Simons, D.J., Chabris, C.F.: Gorillas in our midst: sustained inattentional blindness for dynamic events. Perception 28(9), 1059–1074 (1999)
25. Sun, Y.: Hierarchical object-based visual attention for machine vision, in Institute of Perception, Action and Behaviour. School of Informatics. University of Edinburgh, Edinburgh, p. 169 (2003)
26. Vatikiotis-Bateson, E., Eigsti, I.-M., Yano, S., Munhall, K.G.: Eye movement of perceivers during audiovisual speech perception. Perception & Psychophysics 60, 926–940 (1998)
27. Vergilino-Perez, D., Collins, T., Dore-Mazars, K.: Decision and metrics of refixations in reading isolated words. Vision research 44(17), 2009–2017 (2004)
28. Yarbus, A.L.: Eye movements during perception of complex objects. In: Riggs, L.A. (ed.) Eye Movements and Vision, pp. 171–196. Plenum Press, New York (1967)

Attentive Presentation Agents

Tobias Eichner[1,2], Helmut Prendinger[1], Elisabeth André[2],
and Mitsuru Ishizuka[3]

[1] National Institute of Informatics
2-1-2 Hitotsubashi, Chiyoda-ku,Tokyo 101-8430, Japan
helmut@nii.ac.jp
[2] Institute of Computer Science, University of Augsburg
Eichleitnerstr.30, D-86135Augsburg, Germany
tobias.eichner@gmail.com, andre@informatik.uni-augsburg.de
[3] Graduate School of Information Science and Technology, University of Tokyo
7-3-1 Hongo, Bunkyo-ku, Tokyo 113-8656, Japan
ishizuka@i.u-tokyo.ac.jp

Abstract. The paper describes an infotainment application where life-like characters present two MP3 players in a virtual showroom. The key feature of the system is that the presenter agents analyze the user's gaze-behavior in real-time and may thus adapt the presentation flow accordingly. In particular, a user's (non-)interest in interface objects and also preference in decision situations is estimated automatically by just using eye gaze as input modality. A formal study was conducted that compared two versions of the application. Results indicate that attentive presentation agents support successful grounding of deictic agent gestures and natural gaze behavior.

1   Introduction

Advances in multi-modal user interfaces allows us to develop exciting new applications. Keyboard and mouse are no longer the sole input devices for interacting with computers. More subtle and natural ways of interaction can be supported and hence enrich the experience of the user interacting with an application.

In our work we propose a so-called infotainment (information and entertainment) application in which two life-like characters present two MP3 players of a fictitious company as co-presenters. The key feature of the system is that the agents are 'aware' of the user seated in front of the screen, which is achieved by the use of a video-based eye tracker. The system analyzes the gaze behavior of users in real-time and is capable of adapting the presentation flow according to the user's interest or non-interest. The system aims to imitate human presenters who typically receive (visual) feedback from their audience. If, e.g., a museum guide notices that people are distracted or interested in an object different from the one currently presented, the human guide can either try to regain the attention or shift the focus of the presentation to the other object.

This paper is structured as follows. Section 2 discusses related work. Section 3 sketches the MPML3D and Java Real-Time Component. Section 4 describes

C. Pelachaud et al. (Eds.): IVA 2007, LNAI 4722, pp. 283–295, 2007.

our methods to recognize (visual) interest and preference. Section 5 provides details about the application scenario, available agent responses, and our notion of 'grounding'. In Section 6 we put forth hypotheses about attentive presentation agents. Section 7 describes our empirical study using two versions of the application. The results are presented in Section 8. Section 9 concludes the paper.

2   Related Work

One of the early uses of human gaze in human–computer interaction was as a pointing device [8]. Similar to positioning a mouse pointer on an interface object in order to activate it, a user might trigger an action in the interface by simply looking at the object. Rather than using gaze for controlling or manipulating interface objects, Attentive User Interfaces (AUIs) [21] and "visual attentive interfaces" [16], by contrast, are geared toward recognizing the user's intention from natural gaze behavior. For instance, the InVision system described in [16] processes a user's gaze directed at an interface depicting a kitchen environment, and infers whether the user is hungry or intending to rearrange the kitchen items, and so on, from the gaze path.

The "gaze-responsive self-disclosing display" [19] is one of the first systems which analyzes the user's gaze behavior in real-time and responds to it in an appropriate way. The application shows a small 3D planet, where a 2D virtual agent tells something about the items one can see on the planet. When the user looks on some specific object, e.g. a staircase, the virtual narrator will talk about the staircase. If the user's gaze switches between two staircases, the agent will talk about staircases as a group. Additionally, the current object of interest is zoomed-in. The FRED system [20] makes use of 3D animated facial agents and combines them with a conversational gaze model in a multi-agent setting. The agents have the capability to notice if the user (or another agent) is looking at them. Together with the speech data they can determine if they have to listen to someone else or if they can talk. The focus of that work is the regulation of conversional flow in a multi-agent environment, whereas we focus on detecting interest and attentiveness in a virtual presentation.

Another application using an virtual agent is the MACK system described in [10]. The authors uses a head tracker to determine a user's gaze in a direction-giving task. The animated agent explains directions on a map and monitors the user's head. In that application, lack of negative feedback indicates successful grounding. If grounding fails, the agent will perform a repair action to help the user. The difference of our work to the MACK system is that we do not assume verbal input to drive the presentation of the agent. Furthermore, we analyze and interpret eye movements rather than head movements.

3   MPML3D and Java Real-Time Component

Our application is based on (1) the MPML3D framework for animating the agents and defining the content of the presentation, (2) a Java Real Time

Component for receiving and analyzing the eye data in real-time, and (3) the eye-tracking system. (1) and (2) will be introduced in this section, and (3) in Sect. 7.

3.1 MPML3D Framework

When setting up a virtual presentation, the focus of the author should be on creating content and not on technical issues. The Multimodal Presentation Markup Language for 3D agents (MPML3D) provides a easy-to-use XML scripting language to define both the content of the presentation as well as the animations of the agents [7,11]. The main concept of MPML3D are *actions*: every (speech) utterance of an agent, every gesture and mimic expression, etc. is defined as an action. Actions can be performed sequentially or in parallel. Hence it is possible that an agent performs, e.g. a deictic gesture during an utterance. Actions can be broken down into sub-actions, which allows synchronization word by word.

An important feature of actions is that they can be interrupted by other actions anytime and thus react to certain events triggered by user input instantly. An interruption can be induced by the concept called *perceptions*: unlike actions, they run in the background and wait for an event to occur. Perceptions can be defined for arbitrary objects. So it is possible that the agents perceive themselves or, e.g., which screen object the user is attending to. Perceptions can be seen as a core feature of MPML3D by which agents sense their virtual environment and the real world (using sensors).

The main difference between MPML3D and other character markup languages, such as the Affective Presentation Markup Language (APML) [2] is that MPML3D focusses on the control and interaction between two (or more) agents rather than a single agent.

3.2 Java Real Time Component

The second basic component of our application is the Java Real-Time Component (JRTC). An eye tracker provides huge amounts of data during tracking, amongst others gaze coordinates, pupil size, eye closure, direction vector of the head, etc. In order to access all these data in an easy and convenient way, we have developed the JRTC component. It provides a form of API, making it simple to integrate the data of the eye tracker into any application. At the moment, JRTC supports the Seeing Machines eye tracker [15] and a device for bio-signal processing. JRTC not only receives data from devices, but also performs computations on the data. It can deliver both raw data and classification results or smoothed data. To be even more flexible and powerful, a Bayesian Net can be included with the Netica library [12]. In our application, we only made use of the gaze coordinates. All the computations (introduced in the next section) were also integrated in the JRTC.

4   Gaze-Based Recognition of Interest and Preference

A basic functionality of our presentation system is to recognize the visual inter-est of the user, i.e. which interface object the user pays attention to. Another, independent capability of the system is to determine the preferred visual object among two by only analyzing the gaze behavior. Both were introduced in [6].

In our system, *visual interest* was determined by a slightly simplified ver-sion of the algorithm introduced in [14], where two interest metrics have been introduced: The *Interest Score* (IScore) metric indicates the 'arousal' of a vi-sual stimuli, i.e. the probability that the user is interested in that visual object. When the IScore value passes a certain threshold, the object becomes 'active'. The *Focus of Interest Score* (FIScore) calculates the amount of interest in an active object over time. If the FIScore for an active object falls below a certain threshold, it becomes deactivated (the user lost interest in that object).

The main component to calculate the IScore metric is $p = \frac{T_{ISon}}{T_{IS}}$, where T_{ISon} is the accumulated time on a visual object within a sliding time window of the size T_{IS} (set to 1000 ms). To allow for other factors influencing the calculation of interest, [14] suggest the following, extended equation: $p_{is} = p(1+\alpha(1-p))$. Here, α represents a set of parameters increasing the accuracy of interest estimation. Our simplified version has two out of the four parameters defined in [14]:

$$\alpha = c_0 \frac{c_f \alpha_f + c_s \alpha_s}{c_f + c_s}$$

α_f represents the frequency of entering and leaving an object with the gaze. The more often the user's gaze switches to an object, the higher is the chance of excitation. It is calculated with the formula $\alpha_f = \frac{N_{sw}}{N_f}$, where N_{sw} denotes the number of times eye gaze enters and leaves the object and N_f denotes the maximum possible N_{sw} in the preset time window. α_s is calculated as $\alpha_s = \frac{S_b - S}{S}$, where S_b denotes the average size of all defined interest objects and S the size of the currently calculated object. It is assumed that larger visual objects have a higher chance to be hit by chance than smaller objects because of noise in the eye data. The factor compensates for this issue.

FIScore calculates the continued interest of the user in the active object over time. Like in IScore, the basic component is the gaze intensity on the active object. Additional, gaze intensity on other interest objects is considered. The sliding time window is twice as big as for IScore computation (2000 ms).

To estimate *(visual) preference*, we exploited the so-called "gaze cascade" effect in two-alternative forced choice (2AFC) situations. This effect was discov-ered in a study where users had to choose the more attractive face from two faces [17]. It could be demonstrated that there was a distinct gaze bias towards the chosen stimulus in the last one and a half seconds before the decision was made. The decision formation process was completed within six to seven seconds. Based on these results, the AutoSelect was developed for real-time estimation of preference [1]. Thus gaze points are calculated in a time window of 1500 ms length. If 90% (or more) of all gaze points within this time window are on one visual object, the system chooses that object. AutoSelect was tested in a study where users had to select their preferred necktie from two presented neckties by gaze. The system achieved an accuracy of 72%.

5 Gaze-Based Presentation

Our application consists of a virtual sales scenario where two MP3 players are presented by a team of a female and a male agent, which was first described in [13]. The models of our agents were designed by a professional Japanese artist. They can perform several gestures like greeting, counting with fingers, deictic and beat gestures, and facial expressions (happy, sad, surprised). Speech output is generated using Loquendo Text-to-Speech [9], and lips are adequately animated.

The course of the presentation can be summarized as follows: Yuuki, the female agent, starts the presentation by introducing the (fictitious) company and her colleague Ken (the male agent). After that, Ken promotes the first MP3 player, the MP3PodAdvance, by providing a description of its features, which includes an example of navigating the menu of the player to select a particular song. After Yuuki presents the other MP3 player, the EasyMP3Pod, both agents argue over the benefits and drawbacks of each player. During that discussion they realize that the device presented by the other character would fulfill their particular needs better than what they have presented themselves. Hence, the agents address the user directly, and ask him or her to choose one of the two MP3 players. Finally, the two agents say good bye and the presentation ends.

5.1 Reacting to the User's Interest State

The key feature of the application is that the user experiences that the virtual agents are aware of him or her and react to interest and non-interest. The user should not have the impression of watching a static presentation. To achieve this goal, we defined gaze-sensitive areas on the screen, so-called "interest objects". In these areas, the user's gaze is analyzed regarding (non-interest in the presentation. The defined objects are (from the left to the right): (i) SideAds, a total of four slides that advertise the MP3 players and are exchanged every five seconds; (ii) male agent ("Ken"); (iii) 3D model of MP3PodAdvance; (iv) virtual slide; (v) 3D model of EasyMP3Pod; (vi) female agent ("Yuuki"); (vii) the view out of the window. Their bounding rectangles can be seen in Fig. 1.

For the following four screen objects, agent reactions are defined when the user shows interest in them.

SideAds: Motivated by the experimental design (described in Sect. 7), the changing side ads should distract the user. If the user looks at the ads for the second time, the currently not speaking agent will interrupt the presentation asserting that the user is distracted. Afterwards, the side ads are turned off.

Ken and Yuuki: Both agents know when the user is looking at them. There will be an interruption if the user is looking at the non-speaking agent. E.g., Ken

Fig. 1. Bounding areas of interest objects. (The displayed computer screen area is clipped for convenience and does not show the view the user has).

will state "Is there something wrong with my necktie? I think you are looking at me, even if Yuuki is explaining something."

View: If the user shows interest in the view out of the window over Tokyo, the agents will interrupt the presentation, the camera of the 3D scene will focus the skyline and Yuuki will talk about some landmarks. This is the only exception where the camera focuses an interest object.

Off-screen: As a sign of general non-interest can be seen when the user takes the gaze off the screen area. In that case, the agents wonder what they can to to regain the user's attention. After a short chat they continue the presentation.

Notice that these interruptions can occur anytime during the presentation depending on the user's gaze behavior, i.e. they are context-independent. In the following, we will describe context-dependent interruptions.

5.2   Responding to Failed Grounding

An important indicator of a user's attentiveness is successful grounding. In human face-to-face communication, grounding relates to the process of ensuring that what has been said is understood by the conversational partners, i.e., there is "common ground" [4,3]. During the presentation, the agents repeatedly perform referential gestures to link their spoken content to a visual stimulus. Our system checks grounding in these situations as follows:

– If the grounding situation lasts for less than 2000 ms, it is treated as a *short grounding situation*. In this case, the user is supposed to look at the grounding object (the referred visual stimuli) during the utterance or within one second after the utterance or gesture terminated for at least 150 ms. This situation typically occurs when the agents perform deictic gestures or explain a changing region on the virtual slides.

– In *long grounding situations* (longer than two seconds), the user is supposed to look at the grounding object for 45% of the time of the duration of the utterance. This situation occurs when an agent explains facts on the (virtual) slides with no changing content.

In our application, the two agents, the two virtual models of the MP3 players and the slides are possible grounding objects. If the system classifies a grounding situation as failed, the agents will react on this. In total, 15 grounding situations are defined, whereby the slides are defined as grounding object in nine cases, the two player models in two cases each, and Ken and Yuuki in one case each.

Here are some examples of available reactions:

Yuuki's self-introduction: At the beginning of the presentation, Yuuki introduces herself. The user is assumed to look at her during this time. If not, Ken will interrupt and ask the user to look at Yuuki.

Ken's introduction: When Yuuki introduces Ken, the user's gaze should transit from Yuuki to Ken during the deictic gesture. Otherwise, Ken will wave his hand and 'help' the user to find him on the screen.

Slides: The majority of grounding situations is related to the slides. Here the agent explains the slide content, often accompanied by a deictic gesture. If the user does not attend to the slide, an agent will ask the user for more attention.

MP3 players: When the agents refer to the players by using a deictic gesture, the user's focus should turn to the model. The agents monitor whether the user attends to the player and react, if he or she is not looking there.

5.3 Preference Estimation

At the end of the presentation, the agents ask the user to choose the preferred player. For that purpose, images of both players are shown on the slide and the agents perform deictic gestures towards them (see Fig. 2). A pre-study showed that the gaze cascade phenomenon will occur naturally in this situation: Users will alternately look left and right on the slide and exhibit a bias for one player. The gaze-sensitive bounding boxes include both the images on the slide and the two models of the player in

Fig. 2. Bounding areas for selecting the preferred MP3 player

case that users consider the virtual models in the decision making process. At the end of the automatic decision time of the system (7.5 seconds), the user is asked to declare the decision by a key press on a keyboard. This allows us to compare the decision calculated by our system with the user's decision. Finally, the agent with the preferred player expresses happiness about its successful promotion.

6   Theory

The general hypothesis of our research on attentive presentation agents is that they can provide a more natural interaction experience such that the user will experience the presentation agents as more mindful and exhibit a more natural gaze behavior towards the presentation. We suggest the following hypotheses:

Grounding Hypothesis: Grounding is more successful with attentive agents.

Mindfulness Hypothesis: It is speculated that users experience the interaction with attentive agents as similar to human face-to-face communication and more engaging, inducing a sense of involvement and co-presence with the presentation agents. Our operationalization of 'mindfulness' is based on the concepts of "face-to-face"(communication), "involvement", "co-presence", and "partner evaluation" proposed in [5], and "engagement" as described in [18].

Gaze Cascade Hypothesis: Based on our previous finding [1], we predict that the gaze cascade effect generalizes to the virtual product presentation scenario.

7   Method

Experimental Design. The experiment had a between-subjects design. Two versions were implemented.

- *Interactive (I) version*: The system analyzes the user gaze and the agents react accordingly. Agent interruptions cannot be foreseen in this version.
- *Pseudo-interactive (PI) version*: The agents interrupt the presentation at seven pre-defined points, independent of user gaze. Since agents *do* react, even in a seemingly random way, this version is called "pseudo-interactive".

Note that all interruptions that could occur in the interactive version, actually do occur in the pseudo-interactive version. This allows us to compare the two versions, because there are no reactions which can only occur in one version.

Subjects. Thirty-five subjects, all students, researchers, or staff from NII, participated in the study. Their age ranged from 19 to 41 yrs (average 27.5 yrs). They received 1,000 Yen for participation. There were technical difficulties with ten subjects due to lacking experience of the experimenter with the eye tracking setup. Four subjects could not be calibrated because of reflections of contact lenses or glasses. All of those subjects were excluded from the study beforehand. The remaining twenty-one subjects (twelve female, nine male) were randomly assigned to the interactive and pseudo-interactive versions.

Apparatus. The presentation was shown on an IBM 20.1 inch screen with a resolution of 1600 × 1200 pixels and ran on a Dell workstation with dual-core

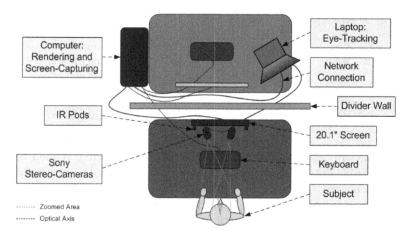

Fig. 3. Experimental system setup

processor. The eye-tracking software faceLAB from Seeing Machines [15] ran on a separate laptop which was connected to the workstation via network. Sony stereo cameras of the faceLAB eye tracker and loudspeakers were positioned below the screen. The user was seated in front of the screen (80 cm distance). Two infrared pods were attached at the upper part of the display for illuminating the eyes. The system has a sampling rate of 60 Hz. In real-time modus of faceLAB, data processing has a delay of 30 ms. Each presentation was captured as a video file. The schematic setup can be seen in Fig. 3.

Procedure. Subjects entered the experiment room individually and received a written instruction about the procedure. The instruction given to the subjects was to watch the presentation as they would watch a presentation given by human presenters. At that time, the experimenter was available for queries. Subsequently, each subject was calibrated for eye tracking. The subject was asked to assume a comfortable sitting position, and the experimenter started the calibration process by first determining reference points for head tracking, and then for eye (and pupil) tracking. Calibration is a step-by-step process following the menu-based instructions of the faceLAB software. The experimenter receives feedback on the accuracy of the calibration process, and may repeat some step, if necessary. Calibration of a subject took five minutes on average.

Then the subjects were shown the presentation, which lasted for about seven to eight minutes. During that time, only the experimenter and an assistant were present in the room and silence was kept. After the presentation finished, subjects were asked to fill out a questionnaire with nineteen questions that addressed their impression of the presentation.

8 Results

We start with some general results. The mean length of the presentation in the interactive version was 423.68 sec, and 477.13 sec in the pseudo-interactive

Table 1. Results of grounding success rate by version and category of grounding object

Grounding Category	I Version	PI Version
Yuuki	85.7%	100.0%
Ken	14.3%	50.0%
Slides	92.0%	76.0%
MP3 Players	53.5%	4.0%

version. One subject was removed from the pseudo-interactive version because of partly missing data. The interactive version was significantly shorter than the pseudo-interactive version $(t(18) = 2.33; p < 0.02)$. These values confirm our prediction as interruptions in the interactive version were gaze-dependent. It is also reflected in the standard deviation (SD) of 70.1 seconds for the length of the interactive version. The interactive version had 5.7 interruptions per subject (vs. 7 in the pseudo-interactive version). It is worth mentioning that 31.6% of the interruptions were triggered by a failed grounding with respect to one of the virtual MP3 players. The 3D models might have been too small or the deictic gestures to them were not sufficiently precise. Another explanation might be their simplicity as graphical objects and short visual encoding time.

To test the *Grounding Hypothesis*, we counted successful grounding situations in both versions. In the interactive version, fifteen grounding situations were defined that may lead to an agent reaction in case of negative evidence (failed grounding). The same grounding situations are also present in the pseudo-interactive version (although agents will not react to failed grounding unless by coincidence). Overall, grounding was successful in 77% of the cases in the interactive version, and in 56.67% in the pseudo-interactive version. The detailed grounding success for defined grounding objects (summarized in Table 1) shows that success is depending on the grounding object. In the interactive version, the agents were able to lead the user's attention to the slides and also to the MP3 players. We do not have an explanation for the low success rate for groundings on Ken, but the comparatively high success rate in the pseudo-interactive version is delusive: shortly after Ken's introduction by Yuuki, Ken alerts the user to look at him. An explanation for the lower success rate of Yuuki can be that in the interactive version the presentation was startet by the user's gaze on the slides and not like in the pseudo-interactive version by keystroke of the experimenter. Hence, some users were maybe looking a little bit clueless at the beginning of the presentation where the grounding situation occured.

In order to test the *Mindfulness Hypothesis*, we relied on questionnaires as a standard evaluation method. A seven point Likert scale was used, ranging from "−3" (strongly disagree) to "3" (strongly agree), with "0" as the neutral attitude. Fifteen questions in the dimensions face-to-face, involvement, co-prescence and agent evaluation have been borrowed from [5], the engagement dimension was derived from the description in [18]. Interestingly, the only significant results relate to questions that address the salient feature of each version in a quite direct way. Subjects in the interactive version felt that the agents were aware of them to a significantly higher extent ($t(19) = 2.48; p < 0.05$), and in the pseudo-interactive version, they thought that the agents react to them in a strange way ($t(19) = -1.78; p < 0.05$). (All t-tests are one-tailed.) Moreover, we can interpret the result to the question "I had the impression that the agents cared about my interest." as a tendency that subjects consider their interest being taken into account better in the interactive than in the pseudo-interactive version ($t(19) = 1.38; p = 0.09$).

Finally, we turn to the results for the *Gaze Cascade Hypothesis*. In eight cases (out of twenty-one), the system could not make a decision within the 7.5 seconds for automatic preference estimation. These subjects might have needed more time to select their preferred MP3 player. For the remaining 13 decision situations, the system achieved an accuracy of 76.9%. Table 2 shows the results split up for the interactive and pseudo-interactive version. It is noticeable that the result in the pseudo-interactive version is much better. We can only speculate about the reason. Subjects in the interactive version might have noticed that the agents react to their gaze behavior and have a certain "anticipation". Consequently, subjects might have felt restricted and uncertain in how they 'should' look. By contrast, subjects in the pseudo-interactive version experienced ill-timed agent reactions and therefore might have felt less guided.

Table 2. Results of automatic preference estimation. ("n/a" means "not applicable")

System Decision	I Version	PI Version
correct	30.0%	63.6%
wrong	20.0%	27.3%
n/a	50.0%	9.1%

9 Conclusion

We described an agent-based presentation system that relies on eye gaze (1) to adapt the presentation to the user's interest, and (2) to react if the user is inattentive. For this purpose, we implemented appropriate agent feedback to guide the user or to ask him or her for more attentiveness. Gaze was also used to assess preference among two presented visual stimuli. Visual interest was estimated using a previously developed algorithm [14]. Preference estimation was based on our previously developed algorithm for analyzing the case cascade effect in real-time [1]. Furthermore, the system implemented an algorithm for testing successful grounding related to interface objects. This is achieved by the agents' deictic gestures, verbal comments, or a combination of both.

Our interface using attentive presentation agents is intended to provide a personalized experience. Users should have the feeling that their interest (or lack of interest) matters to the agents. User statements like "In the beginning I was bored. And then suddenly Yuuki waved her hand and asked for more attention." or "She [Yuuki] was yelling at me!" provide informal evidence that this aim was achieved. We conducted an empirical study where two versions of the system were compared: an interactive version analyzing the user's gaze behavior in real-time with appropriate agent reactions to interest/disinterest, and a pseudo-interactive version based on randomly assigned interruptions. It could be shown that in the interactive version, grounding was more successful, and that users in this version felt that the agents were aware of them. An open issue is to find an optimal level of agent attentiveness. The poor results regarding the gaze cascade effect indicate that gaze-based agents may carry a certain risk of 'overdoing' attentiveness. We will address this issue in our future research.

Our work has demonstrated the power of using eye gaze as input. The next step is to complement gaze with an additional modality, e.g. to recover from situations where the system could not classify the user's (non-)interest correctly. Another interesting issue might be to adopt the visual attention methods developed for our infotainment application to other scenarios like virtual worlds or interactive games.

Acknowledgments

The first author was supported by an Int'l Internship Grant from NII under a Memorandum of Understanding with the Faculty of Applied Informatics at the Univ. of Augsburg. The research was supported by the Research Grant (FY1999–FY2003) for the Future Program of the Japan Society for the Promotion of Science (JSPS), by a JSPS Encouragement of Young Scientists Grant (FY2005–FY2007), and an NII Joint Research Grant with the Univ. of Tokyo (FY2006).

References

1. Bee, N., Prendinger, H., Nakasone, A., André, E., Ishizuka, M.: AutoSelect: What You Want Is What You Get. Real-time processing of visual attention and affect. In: André, E., Dybkjær, L., Minker, W., Neumann, H., Weber, M. (eds.) PIT 2006. LNCS (LNAI), vol. 4021, pp. 40–52. Springer, Heidelberg (2006)
2. Carolis, B.D., Pelauchaud, C., Poggi, I., Steedman, M.: APML: Mark-up language for communicative character expressions. In: Prendinger, H., Ishizuka, M. (eds.) Life-like Characters. Tools, Affective Functions and Applications, Cognitive Technologies, pp. 65–85. Springer, Heidelberg (2004)
3. Clark, H.H.: Using Language. Cambridge University Press, Cambridge (1996)
4. Clark, H.H., Brennan, S.E.: Grounding in communication. In: Resnick, L.B., Levine, J.M., Teasley, S.D. (eds.) Perspectives on Socially Shared Cognition, pp. 127–149. APA Books, Washington (1991)
5. Garau, M., Slater, M., Bee, S., Sasse, M.A.: The impact of eye gaze on communication using humanoid avatars. In: Proceedings SIGCHI Conference on Human Factors in Computing Systems (CHI-01), pp. 309–316. ACM Press, New York (2001)
6. Hoekstra, A., Prendinger, H., Bee, N., Heylen, D., Ishizuka, M.: Highly realistic 3d presentation agents with visual attention capability. In: Proceedings 7th International Symposium on Smart Graphics (SG-07). LNCS, vol. 4569, pp. 73–84. Springer, Heidelberg (2007)

7. Ishizuka, M., Prendinger, H.: Describing and generating multimodal contents featuring affective lifelike agents with MPML. New Generation Computing 24, 97–128 (2006)
8. Jacob, R.J.K.: The use of eye movements in human-computer interaction techniques: What You Look At is What You Get. ACM Transactions on Information Systems 9(3), 152–169 (1991)
9. Loquendo Vocal Technology and Services, URL (2006), http://www.loquendo.com
10. Nakano, Y.I., Reinstein, G., Stocky, T., Cassell, J.: Towards a model of face-to-face grounding. In: Proceedings of Association for Computational Linguistics (ACL-03), pp. 553–561 (2003)
11. Nischt, M., Prendinger, H., André, E., Ishizuka, M.: MPML3D: a reactive framework for the Multimodal Presentation Markup Language. In: Gratch, J., Young, M., Aylett, R., Ballin, D., Olivier, P. (eds.) IVA 2006. LNCS (LNAI), vol. 4133, pp. 218–229. Springer, Heidelberg (2006)
12. Norsys Software Corp. Netica, URL (2003), http://www.norsys.com
13. Prendinger, H., Eichner, T., André, E., Ishizuka, M.: Gaze-based infotainment agents. In: Proceedings ACM SIGCHI International Conference on Advances in Computer Entertainment Technology (ACE-07), pp. 87–90. ACM Press, New York (2007)
14. Qvarfordt, P., Zhai, S.: Conversing with the user based on eye-gaze patterns. In: Proceedings of the SIGCHI Conference on Human Factors in Computing Systems (CHI-05), pp. 221–230. ACM Press, New York (2005)
15. Seeing Machines. Seeing Machines, URL (2005), http://www.seeingmachines.com/
16. Selker, T.: Visual attentive interfaces. BT Technology Journal 22(4), 146–150 (2004)
17. Shimojo, S., Simion, C., Shimojo, E., Scheier, C.: Gaze bias both reflects and influences preference. Nature Neuroscience 6(12), 1317–1322 (2003)
18. Sidner, C.L., Kidd, C.D., Lee, C., Lesh, N.: Where to look: A study in human-robot engagement. In: International Conference on Intelligent User Interfaces, pp. 78–84. ACM Press, New York (2004)
19. Starker, I., Bolt, R.A.: A gaze-responsive self-disclosing display. In: Proceedings CHI-90, pp. 3–9. ACM Press, New York (1990)
20. Vertegaal, R., Slagter, R., van der Veer, G., Nijholt, A.: Eye gaze patterns in conversations: There is more to conversational agents than meets the eyes. In: Proceedings of CHI-01, pp. 301–308. ACM Press, New York (2001)
21. Zhai, S.: What's in the eyes for attentive input. Communications of the ACM 46(3), 34–39 (2003)

The Rickel Gaze Model: A Window on the Mind of a Virtual Human

Jina Lee[1], Stacy Marsella[1], David Traum[2], Jonathan Gratch[2], and Brent Lance[1]

[1] Information Sciences Institute, University of Southern California, USA
{jinal,marsella,brent}@isi.edu
[2] Institute for Creative Technologies, University of Southern California, USA
{traum,gratch}@ict.usc.edu

Abstract. Gaze plays a large number of cognitive, communicative and affective roles in face-to-face human interaction. To build a believable virtual human, it is imperative to construct a gaze model that generates realistic gaze behaviors. However, it is not enough to merely imitate a person's eye movements. The gaze behaviors should reflect the internal states of the virtual human and users should be able to derive them by observing the behaviors. In this paper, we present a gaze model driven by the cognitive operations; the model processes the virtual human's reasoning, dialog management, and goals to generate behaviors that reflect the agent's inner thoughts. It has been implemented in our virtual human system and operates in real-time. The gaze model introduced in this paper was originally designed and developed by Jeff Rickel but has since been extended by the authors.

1 Introduction

Research on gaze has shown that it plays a large number of cognitive, communicative and affective roles in face-to-face human interaction [1] [2] [3]. Gaze is of course central to attentional mechanisms, helping to provide information to and regulate cognitive processes accordingly, but also can be an intentional or unintentional signal to others about these processes. It similarly informs, reflects and conveys underlying emotional processes and attitudes. And as a powerful nonverbal signal, it plays a critical role in regulating dialog and social processes in general. Given its myriad roles, it is not surprising that gaze has been called the window on the soul of a human.

We envision a similar role for gaze in virtual humans, as a window on the "mind" of a virtual human. The gaze model introduced in this paper was originally designed and developed by Jeff Rickel. It has evolved through the work of the authors but clearly within the structure developed by Rickel. The model is driven by a virtual human architecture [4] [5] that interleaves behaviors related to planning and execution of tasks and attention capture. Task-related behaviors (e.g., checking the status of a goal or monitoring for an expected effect or action) trigger a corresponding gaze shift, as does attention capture (e.g., hearing a new sound in the environment). Gaze during social interactions is driven by the dialogue state and the state of the virtual human's own processing, including gaze at an interlocutor who is speaking, gaze aversion during utterance planning (to claim or hold the turn), gaze at an addressee when speaking, and gaze when expecting someone to speak.

C. Pelachaud et al. (Eds.): IVA 2007, LNAI 4722, pp. 296–303, 2007.
© Springer-Verlag Berlin Heidelberg 2007

The tight integration of gaze behaviors to our underlying cognitive model ensures that the outward attention of the virtual humans is synchronized with their inner thoughts. Thus the gaze behavior reveals virtual human processes as opposed to human cognitive processes and may differ in timing from average human gaze behavior. Nevertheless, those differences in gaze, if properly realized, should ideally help a human adjust or entrain. This is in contrast to approaches that focus more on mimicking the physical properties of human gaze [6] [7] [8]. When our virtual human takes longer to understand speech, the gaze reflects that. Ideally, the virtual human is perceived as slower in that regard than a native (human) speaker and the human user will ideally adjust.

A key aspect of our approach is that it is part of a virtual human with highly-detailed models of socio-cognitive processes. This in turn supports myriad connections between those processes and gaze, allowing the gaze to play a large number of cognitive, communicative and affective roles, as it does in people. This essentially makes gaze a sparse resource and raises the question of how to regulate or prioritize those connections so that contentions for the virtual human's gaze are resolved.

In this paper, we describe our approach for a gaze model for virtual humans. The gaze behavior generated by our model is realized through the SASO research prototype (Stabilization and Support Operations) [9], which grew out of the Mission Rehearsal Environment [10], to teach leadership and negotiation skills under high stress situations. In this system, the trainees interact and negotiate with a life-size virtual human that resides in a virtual environment.

The next section summarizes the different functions of gaze and various gaze models implemented in other virtual human systems. Section three provides the details of our gaze model and its implementation. We end by discussing issues in our model and future directions, including extensions to the model and experiments we are preparing to conduct.

2   Related Work

There has been extensive psychological study of the functions of gaze behaviors. Argyle and Cook [11] provides an overview of the various movements and functions of gaze. The following summarizes a few of those functions.

Gaze is used to exchange social signals. Even when two people are not interacting, if one is being looked at by another, he/she expects something to happen or an interaction to start [11, p.85]. A request for attention may also be signaled through gaze. After making mutual gaze, one may shift gaze to a third object and return to mutual gaze to draw the other person's attention to the third object silently.

Argyle and Cook also identified a number of important functions and patterns of gaze during conversation [11, p.114-124]. Conversational gaze serves to send social signals, open a channel to receive visual non-verbal messages, and control the synchronization of speech. Gaze aversion occurs at the beginning of utterances, while speaking, when asked a question, and during hesitant pieces of speech. In general, gaze aversion can serve to avoid overload of information and external distraction. Gaze is also used to regulate turn-taking between the speaker and the addressee. As a speaker ends his utterance, he makes a prolonged eye gaze at the listener, at which point the listener makes a gaze aversion and starts speaking.

There have been many implementations of gaze behaviors in virtual agents. One of the first of these was Animated Conversation [12], which implemented a real-time interaction between two virtual agents. The gaze model was based on conversational behaviors such as turn taking. Many gaze implementations in virtual humans are similarly based on communicative signals, such as REA, the Real Estate Agent [13]. Pelachaud et al. [8] use Bayesian belief nets to determine when to gaze in conversation, based on frequency data collected from human interaction. Our approach models both conversational gaze and environmental interaction with an emphasis on revealing the cognitive state of the virtual human.

3 The Gaze Model

The approach to modeling gaze in the Rickel model assumes that gaze is closely tied to the agent's cognitive operations that are at any time vying for processing time. These operations may include perceptions of events, the update of beliefs, understanding speech, planning, and taking actions in the world, of which the selected operation serves to determine both the type of gaze as well as its physical manner.

In this section, we begin with describing the various types of gazes in the model. Then we describe the different cognitive operations and how they determine gaze. Finally, we provide an example to demonstrate the generation of gaze behaviors.

3.1 Different Types of Gaze and Their Properties

Our gaze model produces a wide range of gaze behaviors. Different gazes specified through a set of properties that describe the type, style, speed, as well as the agent's rationale behind the gaze behaviors. Figure 1 summarizes the various gaze properties that can be specified.

- **Gaze-type:** A symbol describing the type of gaze at the target. It can be one of avert, cursory, look, focus, or weak-focus. Focus requires having the body oriented towards the target and may cause stepping whereas weak-focus avoids stepping towards the target.
- **Target:** The name of an object that the agent is gazing at or shifting gaze to, or averting in the case of gaze aversion.
- **Priority:** A symbol describing the priority of the cognitive operation that triggered this gaze command.
- **Speed:** The desired speed of the gaze shift. It can be one of slower, slow, normal, fast, or default.
- **Track:** If the gaze type is glance, look, or focus, this slot specifies whether the object should be continuously tracked, or looked at once but not tracked. If the gaze type is avert, this slot holds a symbol that describes the type of aversion (offset from eyes, down, sideways-down, up, sideways-up).
- **Reason:** A token that represents the rationale behind why we are doing the gaze. This specifies the cognitive operations or the sub-phases of the operations associated with gaze.

Fig. 1. Properties of Gaze Commands

Gaze-type, target, and track define the physical properties of gaze. In addition, reasons specify the underlying rationale for the gaze. Examples of reason are *planning_speech_hold_turn*, *speaking*, *monitor_expected_action*, etc. In the original implementation, reason did not play a functional role; the manner of the gaze was specified in the gaze properties as noted. In a more recent work, we have begun to pass the "reason" for the gaze to the animation system that realizes the body. This provides the animation system with more information to specialize the manner. However, the basic idea behind the implementations remains. The model of gaze should have a large space of gaze types with varying physical manner. With such a model, the inner intricacies of the agent's reasoning can be revealed by different gaze manners.

3.2 Cognitive Operations Associated with Gaze Commands

In our model, we assume that a set of cognitive operations in turn produce a variety of gaze behaviors. Gaze requests are associated with and are made by these operations. For instance, there are different gaze behaviors for the sub-phases of outputting speech depending on whether the agent is about to speak, intends to hold turn, etc. Table 1 provides a partial overview of the mapping between cognitive operations and their impact on gaze. Some processes are not listed for space reasons. In particular, appraisals and coping operations also impact gaze (e.g., there are 13 different types of coping strategies, such as shifting responsibility to other person or resigning from achieving the goal, with various manners of gaze associated).

The cognitive operations can be largely grouped into categories that are based on their functions. There are operations to manage the conversation such as *planning speech*, *listen to speaker*, and *interpret speaker's utterance*. These operations describe the different phases of conversational interaction and may show a pattern of sequence. For example, the agent may listen to someone, interpret the speech, plan and execute speech, and then wait for grounding. There are also cognitive operations that are tied to updating of the agent's beliefs, desires, and intentions, as well as operations associated with perceptual processes such as monitoring for events and attending to sound in the environment.

An important point to note about this model is that there is a large set of distinct cognitive operations. The role of the gaze model is to reflect and convey what cognitive operations the agent is engaged in. Therefore, the properties of the gazes will differ according to the current cognitive operation.

Gaze behaviors in category 3 reflect the gathering of visual information about the world. These include both top-down processes such as monitoring objects/events for changes as well as bottom-up processes such as orienting towards the source of sound [15].

In addition to gaze behaviors associated with different cognitive operations, there is a priority scheme among them to allow one operation to interrupt another. For instance, the agent might be delivering an utterance when there is an explosion. The agent then needs to choose whether to respond to the unexpected event or continue with the current operation. The priorities among operations will resolve the contention and the model will generate gaze behaviors associated with the selected operation.

Table 1. Association between cognitive operations and gaze behaviors

CATEGORY 1: CONVERSATION REGULATION

Cognitive Operation	Behavior	Quality	Reference
Planning speech	Gaze aversion	Slower, offset from eyes	[2]
Start an utterance	Look at hearer	Focus, track	[2]
During speech	Look at hearer	Slow, focus, track	[11, p.99]
Utterance is a rejection or counter-proposal	Gaze aversion (Avoid threat)	Slow, Sideways-down	[11, p.92-99]
Utterance is reluctant acceptance	Gaze aversion	Slow, Sideways-down	[2]
Utterance is about past event	Gaze aversion	Slow, Sideways-up	[2]
Done speaking	Look at hearer	Slow	[2]
Hold turn	Gaze aversion	Slow, offset from eyes	[2]
Listen to speaker	Look at speaker	Weak-focus, track	[11, p.101]
Interpret speaker's utterance	Look at speaker	Weak-focus, track	[11, p.121]
Expect speech from the other	Look at speaker	Weak-focus, track	[11, p.121]
Wait for grounding (acknowledgement or repair)	Look at other	Weak-focus, track	[2]

CATEGORY 2: UPDATE INTERAL COGNITIVE STATE

Cognitive Operation	Behavior	Quality	Reference
Update desire, relevance, intention while planning	Gaze aversion (Cognitive load)	Slower, offset from eyes	[14]
Update belief while planning	Look at object (Gather info.)	Look, track	[1]

CATEGORY 3: MONITOR FOR EVENTS / GOAL STATUS

Cognitive Operation	Behavior	Quality	Reference
Check status of precondition object when planning is blocked	Look at object (Gather info.)	Look, track	[15]
Monitor surroundings for unexpected changes	Look at object (Gather info.)	Look, track	[15]
Monitor for expected changes in the environment or actions by others	Look at other (Gather info.)	Look, track	[15]
Attend to a loud or unusual sound	Look at object (Gather info.)	Slow, look, track	[15]

3.3 Example

Let us go through an example from SASO to demonstrate how gaze behaviors are generated. In this scenario, a human user plays the role of a captain whose mission is to move a local clinic to a safer location. To complete the mission, she needs to negotiate with the doctor and the mayor of the city. Note that this is a multi-party setting and the gaze model is able to produce gaze shifts among different participants.

The following contains the transcript of user and virtual humans along with the cognitive operations that drive the gaze behaviors of each agent. Figure 2 shows the screenshots of the behaviors (the doctor is the left character with crossed arms and the mayor is the right character).

(1) CAPTAIN: **Hello, I am captain Kirk.**
     DOCTOR: *[planning-speech-look-at-hearer: Look at hearer (captain)]*
(2) DOCTOR: **Hello, captain.**
     DOCTOR: *[expect-speech: Look at the speaker (captain)]*
        ...
(11) MAYOR: **(to captain) We have many things to attend to.**
     DOCTOR: *[listen-to-speaker: Look at speaker (mayor)]*
(12) CAPTAIN: **It is imperative that we move the clinic out of this area.**
        ...
(18) DOCTOR: (to elder) **This conflict is madness. It is killing people.**
     DOCTOR: *[monitor-expected-action: Look at agent (captain)]*
(19) CAPTAIN: **Doctor would you be willing to move the clinic downtown? We can give you supplies.**
        ...

(a) Line 2: Doctor and the mayor are looking at the captain

(b) Line 11 Doctor looks at the mayor while mayor is speaking to the captain

Fig. 2. Gaze behaviors from SASO

4 Conclusion

In this paper, we have described the Rickel gaze model for embodied conversational agents. The basic vision behind the model is that gaze should reflect the inner state of the agent's cognitive processing. The model achieves this by having a large set of distinct gaze behaviors whose physical characteristics reflect or serve cognitive operations. The model has successfully been implemented within our virtual human system and drives the agent to change its gaze as both the situation and its own internal cognitive processing evolve. For example, it exchanges grounding with other agents, monitors for expected events, or attends to unusual sounds.

There are a range of possible improvements we envision for the model. As the model was originally developed, gaze manner was specified within the model and that provided parameters to a procedural animation of gaze. We are currently testing an approach that passes the *reason* parameter to the styles that generates nonverbal behaviors [16] [17] so that the animation system is not tied to specific parameterization but can explore more expressive variations that may also be tied to other aspects of the body's state as well as the capabilities of the animation system.

Cultural and individual variation is another aspect we hope to model. The amount of mutual gaze, duration, and target of gaze are influenced by individual's personality or cultural background. For example, prolonged gaze during face-to-face interaction could be considered as showing interest in one culture while in another, it could be interpreted as being hostile. Rich case-by-case studies highlighting the cultural variation will be required to model the differences.

To evaluate the model, we also plan to conduct a number of experiments with human users. We are particularly interested in the user's responses to the behaviors and what they infer from the behaviors. We are also interested to find out how effective the gaze behaviors are in improving the quality of interaction between virtual humans and human users.

Acknowledgements. This work was sponsored by the U.S. Army Research, Development, and Engineering Command (RDECOM), and the content does not necessarily reflect the position or the policy of the Government, and no official endorsement should be inferred.

References

1. Argyle, M., Ingham, R., Mccallin, M.: The different functions of gaze. Semiotica, 19–32 (1973)
2. Kendon, A.: Some functions of gaze direction in social interaction. Acta Psychologica 26, 22–63 (1967)
3. Abele, A.: Functions of gaze in social interaction: Communication and monitoring. Journal of Nonverbal Behavior 10, 83–101 (1986)
4. Rickel, J., Johnson, L.L.: Animated agents for procedural training in virtual reality: Perception, cognition, and motor control. Applied Artificial Intelligence 13, 343–382 (1999)
5. Marsella, S., Gratch, J., Rickel, J.: Expressive Behaviors for Virtual Worlds. In: Prendinger, H., Ishizuka, M. (eds.) Life-Like Characters Tools, Affective Functions, and Applications, Springer, Heidelberg (2003)
6. Peters, C., Pelachaud, C., Bevacqua, E., Mancini, M., Poggi, I.: A model of attention and interest using gaze behavior. In: Panayiotopoulos, T., Gratch, J., Aylett, R., Ballin, D., Olivier, P., Rist, T. (eds.) IVA 2005. LNCS (LNAI), vol. 3661, pp. 229–240. Springer, Heidelberg (2005)

7. Fukayama, A., Ohno, T., Mukawa, N., Sawaki, M., Hagita, N.: Messages embedded in gaze of interface agents: Impression management with agent's gaze. In: Proc. of SIGCHI conf. on Human factors in computing systems, pp. 41–48. ACM Press, New York (2002)

8. Pelachaud, C., Bilvi, M.: Modelling gaze behavior for conversational agents. In: Rist, T., Aylett, R., Ballin, D., Rickel, J. (eds.) IVA 2003. LNCS (LNAI), vol. 2792, pp. 93–100. Springer, Heidelberg (2003)

9. Traum, D., Swartout, W., Marsella, S., Gratch, J.: Fight, Flight, or Negotiate: Believable Strategies for Conversing under Crisis. In: Panayiotopoulos, T., Gratch, J., Aylett, R., Ballin, D., Olivier, P., Rist, T. (eds.) IVA 2005. LNCS (LNAI), vol. 3661, Springer, Heidelberg (2005)

10. Swartout, W., Gratch, J., Hill, R.W., Hovy, E., Marsella, S., Rickel, J., Traum, D.: Toward virtual humans. AI Magazine 27, 96–108 (2006)

11. Argyle, M., Cook, M.: Gaze and Mutual Gaze. Cambridge University Press, Cambridge (1976)

12. Cassell, J., Pelachaud, C., Badler, N., Steedman, M., Achorn, B., Becket, T., Douville, B., Prevost, S., Stone, M.: Animated conversation: rule-based generation of facial expression, gesture & spoken intonation for multiple conversational agents. Computer Graphics 28, 413–420 (1994)

13. Bickmore, T., Cassell, J.: Social Dialogue with Embodied Conversational Agents. In: Bernsen, N. (ed.) Natural, Intelligent and Effective Interaction with Multimodal Dialogue Systems, pp. 23–54. Kluwer Academic Publishers, Dordrecht (2004)

14. Doherty-Sneddon, G., Phelps, F.G.: Gaze Aversion: A Response to Cognitive or Social Difficulty? Memory & Cognition 33, 727–733 (2005)

15. Chopra-Kullar, S., Badler, N.: Where To Look? Automating Attending Behaviors of Virtual Human Charactors. In: Proc. of 3rd Annual Conf. on Autonomous Agents, pp. 9–23 (1999)

16. Kallmann, M., Marsella, S.: Hierarchical Motion Controllers for Real-Time Autonomous Virtual Humans. In: Panayiotopoulos, T., Gratch, J., Aylett, R., Ballin, D., Olivier, P., Rist, T. (eds.) IVA 2005. LNCS (LNAI), vol. 3661, Springer, Heidelberg (2005)

17. Lee, J., Marsella, S.: Nonverbal Behavior Generator for Embodied Conversational Agents. In: Gratch, J., Young, M., Aylett, R., Ballin, D., Olivier, P. (eds.) IVA 2006. LNCS (LNAI), vol. 4133, Springer, Heidelberg (2006)

Embodied Creative Agents:
A Preliminary Social-Cognitive Framework

Stéphanie Buisine[1,*], Améziane Aoussat[1], and Jean-Claude Martin[2]

[1] ENSAM-LCPI, 151 bd de l'Hôpital, 75013 Paris, France
stephanie.buisine@paris.ensam.fr
[2] LIMSI-CNRS, BP 133, 91403 Orsay Cedex, France

Abstract. The goal of this paper is to open discussion about industrial creativity as a potential application field for Embodied Conversational Agents. We introduce the domain of creativity and especially focus on a collective creativity tool, the brainstorming: we present the related research in Psychology which has identified several key cognitive and social mechanisms that influence brainstorming process and outcome. However, some dimensions remain unexplored, such as the influence of the partners' personality or the facilitator's personality on idea generation. We propose to explore these issues, among others, using Embodied Conversational Agents. The idea seems original given that Embodied Agents were never included into brainstorming computer tools. We draw some hypotheses and a research program, and conclude on the potential benefits for the knowledge on creativity process on the one hand, and for the field of Embodied Conversational Agents on the other hand.

Keywords: Embodied Conversational Agents, Creativity, Brainstorming, Facilitator, Expressivity, Personality.

1   Introduction

This paper presents a potential application field for Embodied Conversational Agents (ECAs) which has not been explored yet, namely the field of industrial creativity and computer-supported brainstorming. The paper is structured as follows: in section 2 we define the field of industrial creativity, and expose the brainstorming process and state of the art. In section 3 we show that ECAs were never included in the existing creativity-supporting tools although they would raise interesting research questions. We elaborate on several examples of hypotheses and present the related research program. We expose the expected benefits of such a research program for both fields of industrial creativity and ECA design, before concluding on our general iterative approach between a social-cognitive framework of creativity and experimental investigations.

---

* Corresponding author.

C. Pelachaud et al. (Eds.): IVA 2007, LNAI 4722, pp. 304–316, 2007.
© Springer-Verlag Berlin Heidelberg 2007

2 Industrial Creativity

2.1 Scope Definition

Creativity is a high-level cognitive process which has given rise to researches in various fields such as Psychology [14, 63], Engineering [6, 33, 50, 68] or Human-Computer Interaction [12, 24, 61, 62]. Creativity applies to artistic work (e.g. fine arts, literature, architecture, music), educative domain (e.g. early-learning and playing activities), scientific skills (e.g. problem resolution, discoveries, epistemological breakthroughs), and industrial applications (e.g. creation of product functions, stylistic design of artifacts).

In this paper we consider creativity in industrial applications, for example when some people design products that contribute to changing our everyday habits with new technologies or innovative functions (e.g. global positioning systems in cars to find one's way, or in mobile phones to be easily located, portable players radically changing our relations to our multimedia contents, etc.). Understanding and supporting this kind of creativity is not only an interesting research challenge: industrial innovation being one of the few ways for western countries to remain competitive, the product life cycle is getting shorter and shorter and new products have to be constantly developed and timely placed to market.

2.2 Brainstorming

Group Creativity. To improve creativity, a wide-spread practice in companies is the group brainstorming. Although creativity fundamentally remains an individual capacity, many collective creativity phenomena were demonstrated. For example, cognitive stimulation (i.e. the exposition to others' ideas) proved to enhance idea generation in individuals [21, 22, 45]. Moreover, social comparison (i.e. the possibility to compare one's own performance to the others') was shown to be motivating for brainstorming participants and to improve idea generation [2, 32, 38, 43, 53]. Therefore creativity appears worth implementing in groups, for example in the form of a brainstorming. This is especially true for industrial creativity which can benefit from multiple, or even multidisciplinary viewpoints [8].

The Brainstorming Method. Although brainstorming is sometimes practiced wildly, some methodological toolkits [33, 50, 68] have been formalized to structure the reflection and manage groups' dynamics. For example, the preparation (e.g. decomposing the problem, formulating the questions to address) is fundamental to the quality of outcome from the session. Besides, for efficient idea generation and a smooth running of the group, Osborn [50] recommends stating and displaying the following rules during the whole course of the session: *Criticism is ruled out; Free-wheeling is welcomed; Quantity is wanted; Combination and improvement are sought.* These rules need to be formalized and periodically reminded to the brainstorming participants because such attitudes are not spontaneous, and the use of Osborn's rules actually proved to enhance brainstorming productivity [52, 54, 65, 71]. The brainstorming is also more efficient when leaded by a "facilitator", i.e. someone who does not participate in the idea generation but manages speech turns, encourages the participants individually and collectively, ensures that the focus on the problem and the brainstorming rules are kept observed [36, 49, 50, 51, 54]. Today, being a facilitator can be a full-time occupation since many consulting services specialized in creative problem solving were set up to assist companies in their conducting of creativity sessions.

Electronic Brainstorming. A major shortcoming of classical brainstorming sessions as previously defined is the absolute necessity of managing speech turns: each participant has to wait for her/his turn to give an idea and can give only one idea within a turn. However, it was demonstrated that ideas do not come one by one but rather by "trains of thought" (i.e. by automatic and rapid accumulations of semantically related ideas [46]). Verbal brainstorming therefore interferes with idea generation process in several ways: due to the coordination needs and time constraints, the participants have to rehearse some of their ideas, which stops further idea generation and prevents them from listening to the ideas of others, or they select the ideas they will give to the group (which implies a self-censorship that should normally be ruled out). These phenomena occurring during verbal brainstorming are referred to as "production blocking" [19, 43, 46].

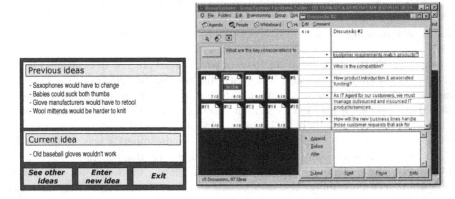

Fig. 1. Examples of collective electronic brainstorming systems: On the left panel, a research tool adapted from Gallupe et al. [27], here used in the Thumbs Problem (a classical problem in brainstorming research about the practical benefits or difficulties that would arise if everyone had an extra thumb on each hand). On the right panel, the commercial software GroupSystems I (www.groupsupport.com).

To counteract production blocking while keeping the advantages of group brainstorming (e.g. the positive effects of cognitive stimulation and social comparison), electronic brainstorming procedures were created. They consist in making the participants simultaneously generate ideas on individual computers networked together and located in the same room [17]. The ideas typed in by the participants are displayed on a large-screen in the front of the room, as well as on each workstation (Fig. 1). The role of the facilitator is the same as in traditional brainstorming except that s/he does not have to manage speech turns. In the field of

Computer-Supported Cooperative Work (CSCW), electronic brainstorming tools fall into the category of group decision systems and electronic meeting rooms [23]. They are rather simple systems relative to other co-located or distant groupware, and the context of creativity does not suppose any special needs.

Electronic brainstorming were shown to actually improve idea production in comparison to control brainstorming sessions [16, 27, 28, 34, 42, 58, 66], and this benefit increases with group size [17, 18].

Personality Issues in Brainstorming. Beside modeling general brainstorming mechanisms applying to all groups whatever their composition, many researchers examined the influence of participants' personality on idea generation and creativity [5, 7, 11, 25, 26, 31, 56]. The close analysis of these results is beyond the scope of the present paper but we may mention for example that the following personality traits were shown to influence creativity: psychoticism, social anxiety, openness, impulsivity, individualism, extroversion, etc.

The previous studies all concerned participants' personality. Likewise, we may wonder whether facilitator's personality would also influence idea production from the brainstorming participants. However, to our knowledge, this issue has never been investigated. Although the usefulness of facilitators was confirmed [36, 49, 51, 54], their behavior and recommended personality was always kept constant. A good facilitator is expected to always stay neutral, to express professionalism and self-confidence, to be dynamic and demonstrate great communication and listening skills, to be friendly and show a sense of humor [20, 70]. What if the facilitator was more emotionally involved in her/his relation to the group? What if s/he showed extreme sympathy or, conversely, disagreeableness? The question is not straightforward since participant's creativity is likely to be triggered off by both positive feelings (through e.g. social facilitation or the experience of positive affects [10]) and negative feelings (because it is fundamentally an adaptive capacity for solving problems in contexts of fear, discomfort, aggression, competition, etc. [50]).

3 How Can Embodied Agents Help?

The possibility to employ Embodied Conversational Agents (ECAs) in electronic brainstorming interfaces is never evoked in the previous state of the art. Yet, some of those systems originally designed to be used in a co-located setup have evolved to applications for distant asynchronous brainstorming through the Internet [17, 43]. But the interface of these systems was never embodied.

The same observation applies more generally in the broad field of computer-supported creativity. Corporate needs for creativity gave rise to a market for computational tools of creativity and a lot of research prototypes and commercial software have been developed[1]. According to Shneiderman [61], the existing computer solutions can be categorized into three approaches: inspirational tools (e.g. favoring visualization, free association, or sources of inspiration), structural tools (e.g. databases, simulations, methodical techniques of reasoning), and situational tools (e.g.

---

[1] Examples of commercial software include Goldfire Innovator (www.invention-machine.com), ThoughtOffice (www.ideacenter.com), MindManager (www.mindjet.com).

based on the social context, enabling peer-consultation, or dissemination). Lubart [39] adopted a classification grounded on the role played by the computer in the creative process: systems assisting the user in the management of creative projects (computer as nanny), those supporting communication and collaboration within a team (computer as pen-pal), systems implementing creativity enhancement techniques (computer as coach) and those contributing to the idea production (computer as colleague). But these roles were never personified and such a possibility is never mentioned is the literature related to creativity-assisting tools.

Likewise in the field of ECAs, industrial creativity was never studied as a potential application framework. ECAs are used in contexts of games, education, personal assistance, commercial websites, etc. The domain closest to creativity may be the use of ECAs as partners of storytelling for children [13, 59].

3.1 Hypotheses

The idea to integrate ECAs into creativity-supporting tools, and especially into brainstorming tools, seems relevant for several reasons we develop in the following paragraphs.

Personification. Personifying the interface can be interesting in itself, as it was shown with pedagogical agents whose presence can be sufficient to improve subjective experience and also sometimes performance [3, 44, 67]. Therefore it could be interesting to investigate whether this kind of effect would also arise for a creativity application in which either the brainstorming participants or the facilitator are represented by ECAs.

Dialog. The domain of ECAs is still considered as lacking believability because current technologies of artificial intelligence do not meet users' requirements in terms of dialog. But in the field of creativity, especially if the ECA represents a partner in the brainstorming, such a weakness can become a strength [39]. Indeed the contribution of ECAs would not rely on exact reasoning but could be related to suggesting new ways for idea searching, to diverging by associative thinking, using e.g. databases and semantic networks. In such a context, a weird idea association made by an ECA could be useful and efficient; in fact, an artificial diverging agent was previously implemented in a brainstorming system [47], but this agent was not personified. Therefore we assume that the effect of interface personification could be tested without being biased by ECA's poor reasoning capacities.

This argument applies for a partner ECA but not for a facilitator ECA, who would have to understand all the interaction and react adequately and timely. In this case the solution could be to include an ECA and a model of nonverbal behavior into the system and control the verbal behavior by a wizard-of-oz setup.

Expressivity, Personality, Role-Playing. A major research interest in ECA community concerns agents' capacity to mimic human affective behaviors [4, 9, 15, 40] and personality expression (with e.g. the adaptation of FFM and OCC personality models [1]). ECA personalities can be used to control the expression of emotion (intensity or modalities), to represent the importance of goals, or to modify the probability of occurrence of certain behaviors [69]. The interrelations between emotions, mood and personality are especially focused on [57, 64]: for example some models of personality featuring several interdependent layers with different timescales were proposed [29, 37]. The final goal of such research is to endow virtual characters with individual personalities [41, 60]: how different characters cope differently with emotions, which weights they use for evaluating events, etc. Gesture style dictionaries [48] and character profiles [30] were also studied.

Some of these expressive agents were included into teams of ECAs in which each one has his role (see Rist et al. [55] for a review): for example, the eShowroom generates commercials by using several presentation agents with different roles, different attitudes towards the product, different personality traits, etc. Pedagogical applications were also designed with teams of ECAs [35] representing different instructional roles such as the expert, the tutor, the mentor, the motivator, the learning companion (or peer tutee), the helper, the competitor, the troublemaker, etc. Sometimes human users can join the team as in multi-party gatherings and conversations in virtual space: for example the Magic Monitor [55] is a multi-user conferencing system in which ECAs represent the conversation partners, be they humans or virtual conversational agents, and the system includes a virtual facilitator agent who provides meta-information about the conversation. Some recent online games[2] are also built on a similar architecture: the players choose their character, collaborate together with other players and with virtual agents towards the achievement of a common goal.

In the context of creativity sessions, there are only two roles (potentially associated with multiple personality dimensions): the partner and the facilitator. A few studies examined the influence of group members' personality on the creativity of their partners, showing e.g. that the presence of social anxious people in a group made their partners spontaneously lower their performance [11]. However, personality research has been concerned mainly with the relation between individuals' personality and their own creativity, and the influence of the facilitator's personality was never tested.

The use of ECAs for representing brainstorming partners or facilitator could enable us to further study the effects of social and affective interactions in a brainstorming task. In comparison to protocols involving acting experimenters, ECAs would have the advantage of being more easily controllable and of displaying repeatable behaviors. They could thus constitute a new experimental tool for exploring creativity processes.

3.2 Research Program

Evaluating creativity. In the following research program we intend to collect creativity metrics that are classically used in the literature [45], such as: the quantity of ideas generated (which is correlated to the quality of the production [52]), the width of production (i.e. the number of semantic categories represented), the depth of production (i.e. the number of semantically-related ideas), the semantic distance (i.e. originality) between the ideas and the initial problem. These metrics are generally submitted to inter-judge agreement procedures.

---

[2] See e.g. Guild Wars, www.guildwars.com

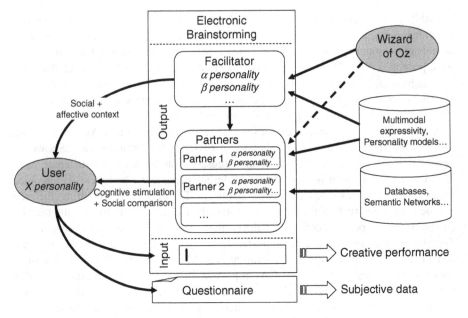

Fig. 2. General architecture of the experimental setups

Personification. The first step could be to introduce existing ECA models into a simple electronic brainstorming system. The goal would be to merely implement the personification hypothesis with ECAs' personality set to neutral (cf. Fig. 2 with expressivity and personality models deactivated). To justify the presence of ECAs and facilitate experimental control, we may test only distant electronic brainstorming situations: indeed, such a procedure would enable us for example to simulate the behavior of all group members and test only one user at a time (instead of groups of users).

By combining different features of our system we could create the following range of experimental conditions:

- Collective distant electronic brainstorming (with no personification),
- Collective distant electronic brainstorming with an ECA facilitator,
- Collective distant electronic brainstorming with ECA partners and facilitators (the test user would first have to choose an avatar),
- Individual electronic brainstorming (cf. Fig. 2 with partners removed) with a non-personified facilitator,
- Individual electronic brainstorming with an ECA facilitator.

These experimental conditions would enable us to evaluate the effects of personifying the facilitator both on individual and collective creativity, and the effects of personifying the partners on collective creativity. The effects of personification should also be evaluated on users' subjective impressions. Furthermore, the collection of gender and personality data from the test users could enable us to identify potential relations between individuals' personality and their reactions (both on performance and subjective dimensions) to the presence of ECAs.

Personality. The following step would consist in manipulating the social and affective environment of electronic brainstorming by giving ECAs a strong personality. The most influencing character in the brainstorming might be the facilitator: therefore we assume that the effects of personality would be more clear-cut when implemented in ECA facilitators (in comparison to ECA partners). That is why we chose to especially emphasize this hypothesis in the present section.

To help us model the expression of personalities in the facilitator's role, we should first conduct a few pilot tests with human brainstorming participants and human facilitators acting within different communication styles, personalities, emotions, etc. Those (costly) pilot studies are not expected to produce significant experimental results because they may not be repeated a sufficient number of times. Their aim would rather be to feed a computational model of multimodal expressive behavior for ECAs.

With a trained model (eventually validated with replay procedures [9]) the large-scale experiments could be conducted by creating the following conditions (see Fig. 2):

- Collective distant electronic brainstorming with an ECA facilitator, α personality,
- Collective distant electronic brainstorming with an ECA facilitator, β personality,
- Individual electronic brainstorming (cf. Fig. 2 with partners removed) with an ECA facilitator, α personality,
- Individual electronic brainstorming with an ECA facilitator, β personality.

It should be noticed that several control conditions would be provided by the first research step (collective and individual conditions with no personification and with a neutral ECA facilitator).

For the moment the α and β (and so on...) personality traits have not been determined because this requires a closer literature analysis. However, we intend to test at least a positive (i.e. socially desirable) personality trait and a negative one. We wish to examine their effects on both the idea generation performance and the subjective experience of users. Finally, theses data would be crossed with user's gender and personality in order to investigate interaction effects between user's and facilitator's individual characteristics.

Extension to Other Kinds of Creativity. An example of medium- to long-term perspective to such a research could be to extend the experimental focus to other kinds of creativity, for example educational creativity (early-learning activities) dedicated to children, in individual or in collective modes. According to the results obtained in the previous research steps, some of the experiments could be replicated in order to test the generalization of the effects to other populations and other kinds of creativity. For example we could imagine that the cognitive and social mechanisms of creativity and their relation to the affective context could be different between children and adults.

4   Expected Outcomes

We think that the exploratory developments envisioned in this paper could have significant contributions to both the fields of creativity research and ECA design.

4.1 Contribution to Creativity Research

The potential benefits to the study of creativity process can be formulated as follows:

- Further modeling of cognitive, affective and social mechanisms of creativity: especially, the results about the influence of the affective context on creativity could help us understand the nature of creativity (an archaic capacity related to a feeling of danger or a modern evolution related to social comfort).
- Comparison between individual and collective creativity processes: are those the same and only mechanism? Does the environment of a group change the individual's reaction and adaptation?
- Comparison between children's and adults' creativity processes: to obtain reliable data on this topic we will have to ensure that the tasks (related to industrial and educative creativity) will remain fairly comparable. The creative educative task for children will have to be designed as an adaptation of the task submitted to adult users.
- Perspectives for new creativity-supporting tools: if the results appear to be easily transferable to a commercial development (e.g. a positive effect of personification, or of simple expressivity parameters), we could imagine to promote the design of more efficient tools to improve creativity, and indirectly industrial innovation.

4.2 Contribution to ECA Research

Finally, the research directions presented in this paper could be beneficial to the ECA community by the following aspects:

- Providing a context for modeling the behavioral expression of affects, of personality traits and social interactions from the way human facilitators behave.
- Comparison of the way users perceive a human / an ECA: do they reliably decode and interpret multimodal behaviors and personality?
- Providing improvement directions for the design of ECAs (based on the previous observations).
- Exploration of a new application field, and potentially identification of new usefulness elements.

5   Conclusion

Inspired by Kim and Baylor's approach with pedagogical agents [35], our goal in this paper was to introduce a preliminary social-cognitive framework to serve as a theoretical basis for and a guide to the optimal design of Embodied Creative Agents. In this respect, creative agents could be developed both as cognitive tools and as social tools for supporting creative processes: creative agents as cognitive tools could be equipped with databases and semantic networks for associative thinking and take turns when the user does not generate ideas. Besides, creative agents as social tools would be present on the screen, exhibit their own performance (ECA partners), express their personality and react to the user's behavior (ECA facilitator) in order to provide a social context for the creative practice.

The first set of agents that would be designed to afford these social-cognitive dimensions could then enable us to conduct a series of experimental studies that would in turn expand the social-cognitive framework: research on creative processes will be expected to progress through such a spiral iterative approach.

References

1. André, E., Klesen, M., Gebhard, P., Allen, S., Rist, T.: Integrating models of personality and emotions into lifelike characters. In: Workshop on Affect in Interactions Towards a new Generation of Interfaces, pp. 136–149 (1999)
2. Bartis, S., Szymanski, K., Harkins, S.G.: Evaluation and performance: A two-edged knife. Personality and Social Psychology Bulletin 14, 242–251 (1988)
3. Beun, R.J., de Vos, E., Witteman, C.: Embodied conversational agents: Effects on memory performance and anthropomorphisation. In: Rist, T., Aylett, R., Ballin, D., Rickel, J. (eds.) IVA'2003 International Conference on Intelligent Virtual Agents. LNCS, vol. 2792, pp. 315–319. Springer, Heidelberg (2003)
4. Bevacqua, E., Pelachaud, C.: Expressive audio-visual speech. Journal of Visualization and Computer Animation 15, 297–304 (2004)
5. Bolin, A.U., Neuman, G.A.: Personality, process, and performance in interactive brainstorming groups. Journal of Business and Psychology 20(4), 565–585 (2006)
6. Bonnardel, N.: Créativité et conception: Approches cognitives et ergonomiques. Solal Editions, Marseille (2006)
7. Bouchard, T.J.: Personality, problem-solving procedure, and performance in small groups. Journal of Applied Psychology Monograph 53(1), 1–29 (1969)
8. Brown, V.R., Paulus, P.B.: Making group brainstorming more effective: Recommendations from an associative memory perspective. Current Directions in Psychological Science 11(6), 208–212 (2002)
9. Buisine, S., Abrilian, S., Niewiadomski, R., Martin, J.C., Devillers, L., Pelachaud, C.: Perception of blended emotions: From video corpus to expressive agent. In: Gratch, J., Young, M., Aylett, R., Ballin, D., Olivier, P. (eds.) IVA 2006. LNCS, vol. 4133, pp. 93–106. Springer, Heidelberg (2006)
10. Burleson, W.: Developing creativity, motivation, and self-actualization with learning systems. International Journal of Human-Computer Studies 63, 436–451 (2005)
11. Camacho, L.M., Paulus, P.B.: The role of social anxiousness in group brainstorming. Journal of Personality and Social Psychology 68(6), 1071–1080 (1995)
12. Candy, L., Hori, K.: The digital muse: HCI in support of creativity. Interactions 10, 44–54 (2003)
13. Cooper, B., Brna, P.: Fostering cartoon-style creativity with sensitive agent support in tomorrow's classroom. Educational Technology & Society, vol. 4 (2001)
14. Csikszentmihalyi, M.: Creativity: Flow and the psychology of discovery and invention. Harper Perennial, New York (1996)
15. De Rosis, F., Pelachaud, C., Poggi, I., Carofiglio, V., De Carolis, B.: From Greta's mind to her face: Modelling the dynamics of affective states in a conversational embodied agent. International Journal of Human-Computer Studies 59, 81–118 (2003)
16. Dennis, A.R., Valacich, J.S.: Computer brainstorms: More heads are better than one. Journal of Applied Psychology 78(4), 531–537 (1993)
17. Dennis, A.R., Williams, M.L.: Electronic brainstorming: Theory, research and future directions. Kelley School of Business, Technical Reports TR116-1 (2002)

18. DeRosa, D.M., Smith, C.L., Hantula, D.A.: The medium matters: Mining the long-promised merit of group interaction in creative idea generation tasks in a meta-analysis of the electronic group brainstorming literature. Computers in Human Behavior 23, 1549–1581 (2007)
19. Diehl, M., Stroebe, W.: Productivity loss in brainstorming groups: Toward the solution of a riddle. Journal of Personality and Social Psychology 53(3), 497–509 (1987)
20. Ditkoff, M.: The ten personas of a brainstorm facilitator (2004), http://www.innovationtools. com
21. Dugosh, K.L., Paulus, P.B.: Cognitive and social comparison processes in brainstorming. Journal of Experimental Social Psychology 41, 313–320 (2005)
22. Dugosh, K.L., Paulus, P.B., Roland, E.J., Yang, H.C.: Cognitive stimulation in brainstorming. Journal of Personality and Social Psychology 79(5), 722–735 (2000)
23. Ellis, C.A., Gibs, S.J., Rein, G.L.: Groupware: Some issues and experiences. Communications of the ACM 34, 38–58 (1991)
24. Farooq, U.: Eureka! Past, present, and future of creativity research in HCI. ACM Crossroads 12, 6–11 (2005)
25. Feist, G.J.: A meta-analysis of personality in scientific and artistic creativity. Personality and Social Psychology Review 2(4), 290–309 (1998)
26. Furnham, A., Yazdanpanahi, T.: Personality differences and group versus individual brainstorming. Personality and Individual Differences 19(1), 73–80 (1995)
27. Gallupe, R.B., Bastianutti, L.M., Cooper, W.H.: Unblocking brainstorms. Journal of Applied Psychology 76(1), 137–142 (1991)
28. Gallupe, R.B., Cooper, W.H., Grisé, M.L., Bastianutti, L.M.: Blocking electronic brainstorms. Journal of Applied Psychology 79(1), 77–86 (1994)
29. Gebhard, P.: ALMA - A Layered Model of Affect. In: AAMAS'05 International Conference on Autonomous Agents and Multiagent Systems, pp. 29–36 (2005)
30. Gillies, M., Ballin, D.: A model of interpersonal attitude and posture generation. In: Rist, T., Aylett, R., Ballin, D., Rickel, J. (eds.) IVA 2003. LNCS (LNAI), vol. 2792, Springer, Heidelberg (2003)
31. Goncalo, J.A., Staw, B.M.: Individualism-collectivism and group creativity. Organizational Behavior and Human Decision Processes 100, 96–109 (2006)
32. Harkins, S.G., Jackson, J.M.: The role of evaluation in eliminating social loafing. Personality and Social Psychology Bulletin 11(4), 457–465 (1985)
33. Isaksen, S.G., Dorval, K.B., Treffinger, D.J.: Creative approaches to problem solving: A framework for change. Kendall Hunt (2000)
34. Kerr, D.S., Murthy, U.S.: Divergent and convergent idea generation in teams: A comparison of computer-mediated and face-to-face communication. Group Decision and Negotiation 13, 381–399 (2004)
35. Kim, Y., Baylor, A.L.: A social-cognitive framework for pedagogical agents as learning companions. Educational Technology Research & Development 54, 569–590 (2006)
36. Kramer, T.J., Fleming, G.P., Mannis, S.M.: Improving face-to-face brainstorming through modeling and facilitation. Small Group Research 32, 533–557 (2001)
37. Kshirsagar, S.: A multilayer personality model. SMARTGRAPH '02 International symposium on Smart Graphics, pp. 107–115. ACM Press, New York, USA (2002)
38. Leggett Dugosh, K., Paulus, P.B.: Cognitive and social comparison processes in brainstorming. Journal of Experimental Social Psychology 41, 313–320 (2005)
39. Lubart, T.: How can computers be partners in the creative process. International Journal of Human-Computer Studies 63, 365–369 (2005)

40. Martin, J.C., Niewiadomski, R., Devillers, L., Buisine, S., Pelachaud, C.: Multimodal complex emotions: Gesture expressivity and blended facial expressions. International Journal of Humanoid Robotics 3, 269–292 (2006)

41. Maya, V., Lamolle, M., Pelachaud, C.: Influences on embodied conversational agent's expressivity: Towards an individualization of the ECAs. In: AISB'04 (2004)

42. McLaughlin Hymes, C., Olson, G.M.: Unblocking brainstorming through the use of a simple group editor, pp. 99–106. ACM Press, New York, USA (1992)

43. Michinov, N., Primois, C.: Improving productivity and creativity in online groups through social comparison process: New evidence for asynchronous electronic brainstorming. Computers in Human Behavior 21, 11–28 (2005)

44. Moreno, R., Mayer, R.E., Spires, H., Lester, J.: The case for social agency in computer-based teaching: Do students learn more deeply when they interact with animated pedagogical agents? Cognition and Instruction 19, 177–213 (2001)

45. Nijstad, B.A., Stroebe, W., Lodewijkx, H.F.M.: Cognitive stimulation and interference in groups: Exposure effects in an idea generation task. Journal of Experimental Social Psychology 38, 535–544 (2002)

46. Nijstad, B.A., Stroebe, W., Lodewijkx, H.F.M.: Production blocking and idea generation: Does blocking interfere with cognitive processes? Journal of Experimental Social Psychology, 39, 531–548 (2003)

47. Nishimoto, K., Sumi, Y., Mase, K.: Toward an outsider agent for supporting a brainstorming session - An information retrieval method from a different viewpoint. Knowledge-Based Systems 9, 377–384 (1996)

48. Noot, H., Ruttkay, Z.: Gesture in style. In: Camurri, A., Volpe, G. (eds.) GW 2003. LNCS (LNAI), vol. 2915, p. 324. Springer, Heidelberg (2004)

49. Offner, A.K., Kramer, T.J., Winter, J.P.: The effects of facilitation, recording, and pauses on group brainstorming. Small Group Research 27, 283–298 (1996)

50. Osborn, A.F.: Applied Imagination. Principles and procedures of creative problem-solving. Charles Scribner's Sons (1953)

51. Oxley, N.L., Dzindolet, M.T., Paulus, P.B.: The effects of facilitators on the performance of brainstorming groups. Journal of Social Behavior and Personality 11(4), 633–646 (1996)

52. Parnes, S.J., Meadow, A.: Effects of "brainstorming" instructions on creative problem solving by trained and untrained subjects. Journal of Educational Psychology 80(4), 171–176 (1959)

53. Paulus, P.B., Dzindolet, M.T.: Social influence processes in group brainstorming. Journal of Personality and Social Psychology 64(4), 575–586 (1993)

54. Paulus, P.B., Nakui, T., Putman, V.L., Brown, V.R.: Effects of task instructions and brief breaks on brainstorming. Group Dynamics: Theory, Research, and Practice 10(3), 206–219 (2006)

55. Rist, T., André, E., Baldes, S., Gebhard, P., Klesen, M., Kipp, M., Rist, P., Schmitt, M.: A review of the development of embodied presentation agents and their application fields. In: Prendinger, H., Ishizuka, M. (eds.) Life-Like Characters: Tools, Affective Functions, and Applications, pp. 377–404. Springer, Heidelberg (2003)

56. Rothenberg, A.: Creativity: Complex and healthy. Psychological Inquiry 4(3), 217–221 (1993)

57. Rousseau, D., Hayes-Roth, B.: A social-psychological model for synthetic actors. International Conference on Autonomous Agents, pp. 165–172. ACM Press, New York, USA (1998)

58. Roy, M.C., Gauvin, S., Limayem, M.: Electronic group brainstorming: The role of feedback on productivity. Small Group Research 27, 215–247 (1996)
59. Ryokai, K., Vaucelle, C., Cassell, J.: Virtual peers as partners in storytelling and literacy learning. Journal of Computer Assisted Learning 19, 195–208 (2003)
60. Sandercock, J., Padgham, L., Zambetta, F.: Creating adaptive and individual personalities in many characters without hand-crafting behaviors. In: Gratch, J., Young, M., Aylett, R., Ballin, D., Olivier, P. (eds.) IVA 2006. LNCS (LNAI), vol. 4133, pp. 357–368. Springer, Heidelberg (2006)
61. Shneiderman, B.: Creating creativity: User interfaces for supporting innovation. ACM Transactions On Computer-Human Interaction (TOCHI) 7, 114–138 (2000)
62. Shneiderman, B., Fischer, G., Czerwinski, M., Resnick, M., Myers, B.: Creativity support tools: Report from a U.S. National Science Foundation sponsored workshop. International Journal of Human-Computer Interaction 20, 61–77 (2006)
63. Sternberg, R.J.: Handbook of Creativity. Cambridge University Press, Cambridge (1998)
64. Trappl, R., Petta, P.: Creating personalities for synthetic actors. Towards autonomous personality agents. Springer, New York (1997)
65. Turner, W.M., Rains, J.D.: Differential effects of "brainstorming" instructions upon high and low creative subjects. Psychological Reports 17, 753–754 (1965)
66. Valacich, J.S., Dennis, A.R., Connolly, T.: Idea generation in computer-based groups: A new ending to an old story. Organizational Behavior and Human Decision Processes 57, 448–467 (1994)
67. Van Mulken, S., André, E., Müller, J.: The persona effect: How substantial is it? In: HCI'98 International Conference on Human-Computer Interaction, pp. 53–66. Springer, Heidelberg (1998)
68. VanGundy, A.B.: 101 activities for teaching creativity and problem solving. John Wiley & Sons, Inc, Chichester (2005)
69. Vinayagamoorthy, V., Gillies, M., Steed, A., Tanguy, E., Pan, X., Loscos, C., Slater, M.: Building expression into virtual characters. In: Eurographics Conference, State of the Art Reports (2006)
70. Wallgren, M.K.: Reported practices of creative problem solving facilitators. Journal of Creative Behavior 32, 135–148 (1998)
71. Weisskopf-Joelson, E., Eliseo, T.S.: An experimental study of the effectiveness of brainstorming. Journal of Applied Psychology 45(1), 45–49 (1961)

Feel the Difference: A Guide with Attitude!

Mei Yii Lim and Ruth Aylett

School of Mathematical and Computer Sciences,
Heriot Watt University,
Edinburgh, EH14 4AS, Scotland
{myl,ruth}@macs.hw.ac.uk

Abstract. This paper describes a mobile context-aware 'intelligent affective guide with attitude' that guides visitors touring an outdoor attraction. Its behaviour is regulated by a biologically inspired architecture of emotion, allowing it to adapt to the user's needs and feelings. In addition to giving an illusion of life, the guide emulates a real guide's behaviour by presenting stories based on the user's interests, its own interests, its belief and its current memory activation. A brief description of the system focusing on the core element - the guide's emotional architecture - is given followed by findings from an evaluation with real users.

1 Introduction

In interaction with current virtual guides, users tend to lose interest rapidly due to lack of 'life' and unmet expectations of the character's intelligence. This problem must be solved in order to prolong interaction between the guide and user and make it more engaging and natural, thus increasing appreciation of heritage sites. Picard [1] argues that "a machine, even limited to text communication, will be a more effective communicator if given the ability to perceive and express emotions". They will have to have emotion-like mechanisms working in concert with their rule-based systems to be truly effective. Dautenhahn [2] added that the better computational agents meet our human cognitive and social needs, the more familiar and natural they are and the more effectively they can be used as tools. Hence, intelligence and emotions work in parallel to create an effective computer system.

2 The Affective Guide

The Affective Guide is an attempt to create a guide with personality and beliefs, to provide a more natural and engaging interaction during a tour visit, advancing the development of existing context-aware tourist guidance systems (eg. [3, 4, 5], etc.). It addresses the frustration that usually occurs in the interaction with an emotionless computerised system that does not react intelligently to a user's feelings. The Affective Guide is implemented on a PDA integrated with

C. Pelachaud et al. (Eds.): IVA 2007, LNAI 4722, pp. 317–330, 2007.

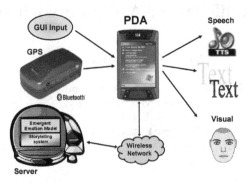

Fig. 1. The System Architecture

Loquendo embedded text-to-speech system[1]. The user's position is determined by a Global Positioning System while the user's orientation is calculated based on previous and current location information. An ice-breaking session prior to a tour extracts information about the user's name and interests. This information is used to choose attractions that match the user's interests and plan the shortest route to them. The guide navigates the user to the chosen locations via directional instructions as well as via an animated directional arrow. Upon arrival, it notifies the user and starts the storytelling process. The system links electronic data to actual physical locations so that stories are related to what can be immediately seen. A server performs the processing and holds the guide's memories, both long-term and current memories and sends the results of processing to the PDA on demand through wireless communication as shown in Figure 1. The user provides input through the graphical user interface and the system outputs are in the form of speech, text and an animated talking head.

2.1   The Emergent Emotion Model

The core element of this research is the emotional architecture of the guide which is biologically inspired, based on the 'PSI' model [6] where the interest lies in modelling the conditions for the emergence of emotions. The emotions of the Affective Guide are not explicitly defined but emerge from modulation of information processing such as perception, intention selection, planning and memory access. The emerging emotions avoid rigidness in behaviour, provide more colour to the resulting emotions and produce a natural agent that adapts to the interaction enviroment flexibly. By adapting its behaviour, the guide's emotional responses mirror those of biological systems, consistent with what a human might expect, hence should seem plausible to a human.

This model bridges the gap between models that focus solely on physiological-level of emotions (eg. [7, 8, 9]) and those that concentrate on higher-appraisal level (eg. [10, 11]). Blumberg's [9] model is interesting but it was developed

[1] http://www.loquendo.com/en/technology/tts_embedded.htm

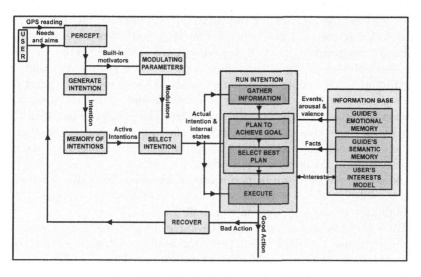

Fig. 2. The Emergent Emotion Model

with only animals in mind. The level to which it is implemented is too low for the Affective Guide which requires planning and storytelling capabilities. It concentrates on geometry manipulation for behaviour expressions, not on creating internal emotional states. The Hap architecture in the Oz project [12] used the OCC model [10] and focused on building unique believable characters, as an artistic abstraction of reality, not biologically plausible behaviour. On the other hand, we argue for successful linking between the lower-physiological and higher-cognitive systems to create a guide that possesses variable emotions, acts appropriately and effectively and appears an interesting and distinctive individual.

Figure 2 illustrates the emotion model of the Affective Guide. The guide has two built-in motivators to maintain, *competence* and *certainty*. The *level of competence* refers to the guide's ability to cope with the user's differing perspective about an issue whereas the *level of certainty* is the degree of predictability of the user interests. The user's confirmation or not of the guide's prediction about their interest, contributes to its *level of certainty* while the degree to which the user agrees with its argument, contributes to its *level of competence*. These built-in motivator values will affect the modulator values, such as *arousal level, resolution level* and *selection threshold*. *Arousal level* is the guide's readiness to act while *resolution level* determines the carefulness of the guide's behaviour. The *selection threshold* on the other hand, is the limit competing motives have to cross in order to become active. *Arousal level* is inversely related to *resolution level* while directly proportional to *selection threshold*. The interaction between the built-in motivators and the modulators produces wide variation of emotions and behaviours in the guide, expressed through a 2D animated talking head.

The guide continuously reads user inputs (feedback on the degree of interest in the story and degree of agreement to the guide's argument), together with system feedback (success or failure) and the GPS information. The user gives feedback through two trackbars (one for the degree of interest and the other for the degree of agreement) that allow rating from 1 to 10. The rating of 1 means not interested in the story or total disagreement to the guide's argument, while the rating of 10 represents high interest in the story or total agreement to the guide's argument. Then, it generates an intention and stores it in a memory of intentions together with the built-in motivators. More than one intention can be active at the same time and depending on the importance of the need and its *selection threshold* value, one of the active intentions is selected for execution. The execution of an intention will produce a success or failure feedback into the system and recovery will be performed as necessary. Basically, the guide has three possible intentions - update its beliefs about the user's interests; adjust the story presentation; or perform storytelling.

In order to execute an intention, the guide decides whether to explore for more information, to design a plan using the available information or to run an existing plan, depending on which intention is selected and its emotional state. A standard prompt is generated when there is no story to tell or the story for the current location has finished at which point the guide informs the user of the unavailability of any story. Planning is performed for storytelling and the extensiveness of planning depends on the guide's *resolution level*. In the case of updating its beliefs or story adjustment, the guide will explore the database for information so that appropriate changes to its beliefs and story topic may take place. By doing this, it adapts its behaviour according to its internal states and the environmental circumstances.

For example, if the guide's prediction about the user's interests is correct (high certainty) and the user perspective is consistent with that of the guide (high competence), the guide may experience low to medium *arousal level* and *selection threshold* with a medium *resolution level*. In this case, the guide can master the situation. The guide will perform planning and provide an elaborated story on the current subject. When the *resolution level* is high enough, it will also include its own viewpoints in the narration. On the other hand, if the guide's prediction about the user's interests is wrong (low certainty) and the user's perspective is in conflict with the guide's viewpoint (low competence), the *arousal level* of the guide will be very high. It is reasonable to react quickly. In this situation, the guide tends to give a brief story without details.

2.2   Storytelling System

Results from our survey of human tour guides show that factors like role, interest, experience, the guides beliefs, the guides personality, type of tour and visitor group all affect the information presentation. Most guides tend to incorporate beliefs and past experiences whether his/her own or that of others while narrating a story since a life story is always more interesting than just bare facts. Hence, personality plays an important role in a tour guide. Furthermore, one of the most striking features of historical investigations is the coexistence of multiple interpretations of the same event, depending on the storyteller's perspective [13]. In accordance with these findings, the presentation of information from different perspectives by different guides is emphasized. Contrasting views and a distinct personality are achieved in the Affective Guide through emotional memories, a manifestation of the guide's past experiences.

The guide's long-term memory is made up of declarative memories, both semantic and emotional. Semantic memory contains facts, including location-related information and the user's profile. Emotional memory contains events that have emotional impact on the guide and holds the guide's beliefs. The emotional memory is tagged with 'arousal' and 'valence' [14] tags analogous to the *Emotional Tagging* concept [15], which recorded the guide's emotional states for an event. When interacting with the user, the guide reconstructs its own past, at the same time presenting facts about the site of attraction. The recollective experience of the guide is related to the evocation of previously experienced emotions through the activation of emotion tags. Hence, it re-experiences the emotions when a particular event happened, though there might be a slight variation due to the user's input.

This research moves away from the concept of a guide that recites facts about places or events towards a guide that utilises improvisational story-telling techniques [16]. The storytelling process, presented in Figure 3 starts upon arrival at a particular site of interest or upon user activation. At every step, the Affective Guide decides what to tell dynamically. The guide takes the user's responses plus its own beliefs, interests and its current memory activation into consideration for story narration. It selects a memory spot based on these factors, that will lead to further extension of facts as well as emotional memory elements depending on its current *resolution level*. The retrieval of memory pieces continues until the combined memory pieces is large enough to generate a story. All these extension processes are performed by Jess[2]. For more information on the Affective Guide, please refer to [17].

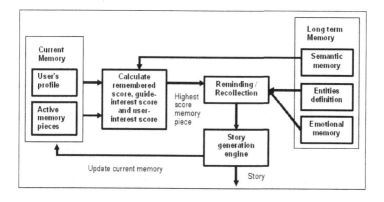

Fig. 3. The Storytelling Process

---

[2] http://herzberg.ca.sandia.gov/jess/

2.3 Prototype System

A prototype version of the Affective Guide has been developed. The 'Los Alamos' site of the Manhattan Project[3] was chosen as the narrative domain, where the buildings are mapped onto Heriot-Watt Edinburgh campus buildings. The Manhattan Project was chosen because it contained many characters with different personalities and ideologies that can be used as Affective Guides. All stories are related to the 'Making of the atomic bomb'.

2.4 Example Stories

Some examples of the stories generated by the non-emotional guide and the emotional guide with different *resolution level* are provided below:

Presentation by a non-emotional guide or an emotional guide's with low *resolution level*:
The Japanese bombing targets were chosen to be places the bombing would most adversely affect the will of the Japanese people to continue the war and military in nature. The targets were places that had not been previously damaged by air raids to enable accurate assessment of the effects of the bomb.

Presentation by an emotional guide's with medium *resolution level*:
The Japanese bombing targets were chosen to be places the bombing would most adversely affect the will of the Japanese people to continue the war and military in nature. It seemed brutal to be talking about burning homes. But we were engaged in a life and death struggle for national survival, and we were therefore justified in taking any action that will save the lives of American soldiers and sailors. We must strike hard with everything we have at the spot where it will do the most damage to the enemy. The targets were places that had not been previously damaged by air raids to enable accurate assessment of the effects of the bomb.

Presentation by an emotional guide's with high *resolution level*:
The Japanese bombing targets were chosen to be places the bombing would most adversely affect the will of the Japanese people to continue the war and military in nature. It seemed brutal to be talking about burning homes. But we were engaged in a life and death struggle for national survival, and we were therefore justified in taking any action that will save the lives of American soldiers and sailors. We must strike hard with everything we have at the spot where it will do the most damage to the enemy. The targets were places that had not been previously damaged by air raids to enable accurate assessment of the effects of the bomb. The scientists became extremely active trying to stop the military use of the bomb over a city, urging a harmless demonstration instead. My own position was that

---

[3] http://www.lanl.gov/

the atom bomb is no worse than the fire raids which our B 29s were doing daily in Japan and anything to end the war quickly was the thing to do.

3   Evaluating the Affective Guide

The main aim of the evaluation is to measure the effect of the inclusion of emotions and attitudes on users' tour experiences. Three versions of the Affective Guide were tested - emotional, non-emotional and random emotions. The emotional version consists of a guide that expresses emotions through facial animation and reflects its attitude by including its perspective and experiences in the narration. The guide's perspective is retrieved from its emotional memory which lead to re-experience of emotions as discussed in Section 2.2. This information are related to the selected facts and can be about the guide itself or others.

Mulken *et al.* [18] found that the mere presence of an interface character makes interaction more entertaining and improves the interaction experience. In order to prevent a biasing representation effect, a guide agent also presents in the non-emotional version. The non-emotional guide has a neutral emotional state, achieved by fixing the values of the modulating parameters. Its processing and internal state are not affected by the user feedback and it does not present any perspective related stories. Additionally, in order to verify that it is not the facial expressions of the guide alone that causes the guide to be perceived as more interesting, a variation of the non-emotional version is included where the guide generates random facial expressions, but presents no perspective information. Hence, the three versions for the guide are:

- Guide A: The guide shows emotions and attitude
- Guide B: The guide shows neither emotions nor attitude (the control group)
- Guide C: The guide shows emotions but no attitude (the placebo group)

Furthermore, we would like to determine if the emotional guide is better able to foster learning in the user. Are the users more motivated to learn about the subject when the presentation is make by the emotional guide? Does the emotional guide embody a higher level of intelligence that prolongs the participant's attention? Does the inclusion of perspective and life experience make the stories more interesting? The goal is to verify if the emotional guide is able to create a greater long term memory effect in the user compared to the non-emotional guide.

In the experiments, the participants were asked to interact with the Affective Guide. Prior to the tour, the participants were required to answer some general questions about their previous experiences with mobile technologies and guided tours as well as their interest in the topic of presentation. The participants were not told the purpose of the experiments, hence, they could not predict and would not be affected by any prior assumptions about the guide's behaviour. The participants were provided with instructions for use as well as background information about the Manhattan Project and were told that they would be tested on their knowledge about the Los Alamos site after the tour. The guide takes each participant around Heriot-Watt University campus which is the pretended Los Alamos site. The participants can choose one of the three areas - 'Science', 'Military' or 'Social' as their interest for the guide's narration. To prevent distraction, the participant is allowed to carry the PDA and laptop and go on the tour on their own. The participants were requested to listen to at least three stories at each location. During the tour, the participants have to rate the degree of interest of the stories as well as how much they agreed with the guide's argument after each storytelling cycle. This step was performed by all participants, including those interacting with the non-emotional and random emotions guide. For these two groups, the participants' input does not affect the processing of the guide in any way, but acts as a control that gives the participants an impression that the guide is reacting to their feedback. Upon completion of the tour, each participant was asked to answer two sets of questionaires.

3.1 Questionaires

In the experiments, the independent variable (IV) is the Affective Guide's emotions and attitude (absence or presence). We defined as the dependent variables (DVs), the guide's storytelling performance, the guide's facial expressiveness, the guide's character and the participants' tour experience. The DVs are measured using 7-point, Likert scale using Questionaire A. Rating of 1 indicates the worst or a negative answer while 7 indicates the best or a positive answer. Five questions assessed the guide's storytelling performance (Q1: intelligence, Q2: believability, Q3: emotional content, Q4: interest relation, Q5: stories adjustment), five questions assessed the guide's facial expressiveness (Q6: intelligence, Q7: believability, Q8: naturalness, Q9: emotional reaction, Q10: appropriateness), two questions assessed the guide's character (Q11: personality, Q12: resemblance to real guide) and four questions assessed the participant's experience (Q13: interestingness, Q14: meaningfulness, Q15: engagement, Q16: overall experience).

Questionaire B was generated after the tour to test the recall level. It contains multiple choices questions based on what the participants have listened to during the tour. Subjects could take as long as necessary to complete the test. Each correct answer for the multiple choices questions is awarded one point. Participants were also asked to indicate whether they found the information overloading, so as to avoid that subjects' answers on the retention questionaire being confounded by lack of interest and information overload.

3.2 Results

A total of 30 participants took part in the experiment, 10 participants for each guide. A one-way Multivariate Analyses of Variance (MANOVA) was performed to examine the effect of the different guides on linear combination of the DVs altogether. ANOVAs with Bonferroni adjustment (overall $\alpha < 0.05$) were employed for follow-up analyses on those dependent variables that showed significance in the omnibus F-test. The Bonferroni tests are reported by giving the mean differences in the dependent variables between any two groups with A, B and C representing the observed means for Guide A, Guide B and Guide C respectively.

The MANOVA was significant with Wilks' lambda=0.011, F=3.463, P=0.005. and partial η^2=0.895. The overall F-test indicated significant difference in intelligence of storytelling (F(2, 27)=4.192, P<0.05), believability of storytelling (F(2, 27)=3.498, P<0.05), stories adjustment (F(2, 27)=4.314, P<0.025), naturalness of facial expressions (F(2, 27)=4.776, P<0.025), emotional rating of facial expressions (F(2, 27)=8.830, P<0.025) and overall tour experience (F(2, 27)=4.500, P<0.025). Differences in interestingness of stories (F(2, 27)=3.054, P=0.064) missed the statistical significance at α=0.05. Figure 4 compares the participants' rating for Guide A, B and C. The mean (standard deviation) for the DVs are shown in Table 1.

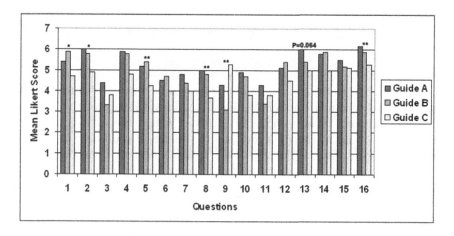

Fig. 4. Significant differences between Guide A, B and C (* P<0.05, ** P<0.025)

Table 1. Mean and standard deviation for significant DVs

DV	Guide A (n=10)	Guide B (n=10)	Guide C (n=10)
Q1:intelligence	5.40 (.699)	5.90 (.876)	4.70 (1.160)
Q2:believability	6.00 (.667)	5.80 (.632)	4.90 (1.449)
Q5:stories adjustment	5.20 (1.135)	5.40 (.843)	4.25 (.791)
Q8:naturalness	5.00 (1.054)	4.80 (.919)	3.70 (1.059)
Q9:emotional reaction	4.30 (1.160)	3.10 (1.101)	5.30 (1.252)
Q13:interestingness	6.00 (.816)	5.40 (.699)	5.00 (1.155)
Q16:overall experience	6.20 (.632)	5.90 (.568)	5.30 (.823)

In the Bonferroni test, Guide A is perceived as more emotional than Guide B (A-B=1.20, P=0.090), but missed statistical significance. No other significant effect was detected for Guide A and Guide B. For comparison between

Guide A and Guide C, participants observed Guide A's facial expressions to be more natural than Guide C's (A-C=1.30, P<0.025). Participants found Guide A's discourse more believable (A-C=1.10, P=0.059) and the stories better adjusted than Guide C's (A-C=0.95, P=0.094). Stories presented by Guide A were also found to be more interesting than those presented by Guide C (A-C=1.00, P=0.062). Although these tests missed statistical significance, overall, participants who interact with Guide A had a significantly better experience than those who interacted with Guide C (A-C=0.90, P<0.025). Comparing Guide B and Guide C, the participants found Guide B's discourse more intelligent (B-C=1.20, P<0.025) and its capability in adjusting the story is significantly better than Guide C's (B-C=1.15, P<0.05). In terms of facial expressions, Guide B is more natural (B-C=1.10, P=0.066) than Guide C whereas Guide C is significantly more emotional than Guide B (C-B=2.20, P<0.025). Guide B and Guide C do not differ in terms of participant's experience. As for the recall test, no significant difference is observed. The average mark for Guide A is 54.46, Guide B is 50.49 and Guide C is 51.89.

3.3   Discussion

The results show that in terms of facial expressions (Q9), a random emotions guide is perceived as the most emotional, followed by a guide with normal emotions and lastly the non-emotional guide. The average rating for the emotional guide is slightly more than 4 on the Likert scale, which reflects that the guide is expressing emotions at the right level, not too much or too little. The random emotions guide's rating on the other hand is above neutral, more than 5, while the non-emotional guide's rating falls below neutral, slightly above 3.

The facial expressions in the random emotions guide can change quite drastically, hence is the most emotional. This might explain why the comparison between the emotional guide and the guide with random emotions showed that the emotional guide is perceived as more natural (Q8) than the random emotions guide. The participants who interacted with the random emotions guide questioned the believability of the stories (Q2) it presented according to their feedback. They believed the emotional guide's discourse more than the random emotions guide. This could be due to the fact that the inclusion of attitude in the guide causes its stories to be more realistic and absorbing. Furthermore, the emotional guide was given a higher rating on its ability in adjusting the stories (Q5) based on their interests.

Comparing the non-emotional guide and the random emotions guide, the participants rated the non-emotional guide's facial expressions as more natural (Q8) than those of the random emotions guide. They also perceived the non-emotional guide discourse to be more intelligent (Q1) than that of the random emotions guide. Since most of the participants in these two groups selected 'Science' and 'Military' rather than 'Social' as their interest, this might explain why they perceived the non-emotional guide as more natural and intelligent than the random emotions guide as scientists and military personnel are usually quite serious. As for the participants perceptions on the guide's ability to adjust stories (Q5) in these two groups, it could be solely an influence of the questionaire. The participants might not have any clue whether the guide is adjusting the stories or not but because they were being asked to rate how well the guide is adjusting the stories based on their feedback, they interpret that the guide must have done so.

Degree of emotional content in the stories (Q3) recorded no significant difference. This may be due to the fact that the topic is a serious one, though from the graph in Figure 4 we can see that the stories presented by the emotional guide were given a higher emotional rating. Besides, changes in voice tone are important for emotional detection, and the text-to-speech system used lacks this. Next, the participants found the stories highly related to their chosen interest (Q4) resulting in no significant difference between the groups. This could be due to the fact that all the spots of attraction were chosen based on the participants selected interest during the start of the tour, leading to a high relation between stories and interests.

The result showing insignificant differences for the intelligence of the guide's appearance (Q6), may be a judgment based on first impressions rather than interaction behaviour. Furthermore, in this experiment, facial expression changes are the same for all guides except in the intensity of changes, leading to equivalent degrees of believability (Q7) and appropriateness (Q10) for the guide's facial expressions. The personality (Q11) comparison between the guides did not differ significantly but observing Figure 4 again, the emotional guide's participants expressed higher confidence in identifying the guide's personality. The inclusion of attitude may have made the guide character's more distinctive. The emotional guide is described as interesting, helpful, funny, friendly, hardworking, opinionated towards others, enthusiastic, happy, accurate, patriotic, loyal, sociable, outspoken, confident, cautious, reactive, patient, open-minded, straighforward and frank. In contrast, the non-emotional guide is described as calm, intelligent, informative, serious, friendly, confident, trustworthy, giving, sad and knowledgeable. Participants described the random emotions guide as sad, unenthusiastic, proud, susceptible, expressive, bitter, sad, angry, unbiased, flat, observant, intelligent, sharp, shrewd and not friendly.

Overall, no significant difference was detected for the guide's degree of resemblance to the real guide (Q12). One reason that the reported differences between guides did not achieve significance may have been due to the granularity of the rating scale employed in the experiment. Each guide is rated as highly analogous to its real counterpart with an average rating of about 5. Using a 7 point Likert scale meant that there was proportionally little room to express any further improvements. The participants judged the guide's attributes for resemblance based on the guide's knowledge about the subject, information presentation and the navigation instructions. Notwithstanding, participants who interacted with the emotional guide commented on the guide's emotional responses and ability to present stories and anecdotal information rather than just facts as analogous to the real guide.

In terms of tour experience, the test showed significant differences for interestingness of stories (Q13) and tour experience (Q16). The participants who interacted with the emotional guide found the stories more interesting and had a better overall tour experience than those who interacted with the random emotions guide. From the figure, it can also be observed that the emotional guide has a higher rating for Q13, Q15 and Q16, followed by the non-emotional guide and finally the random emotions guide. Those who interacted with the emotional guide liked the sense of having a companion capable of tailoring stories to their interests. Regarding the lack of significance in meaningfulness of tour (Q14), most participants reported an overload of information because they lost track of the guide's discourse easily. Most of them had problems keeping up with the guide's discourse due to the less-than-natural and high speed voice generated by the text-to-speech system.

As for the recall test, no significant difference is observed. Problems with guide's speaking speed, which could not be successfully slowed, and with the lack of expressiveness in its voice, would be the most obvious cause. Many of the participants too were non-native English speakers which complicated their comprehension of information further. Evaluation was carried out in November-December and the Scottish cold winter is another factor which reduced the participants' concentration level as many of them pointed out. The availability of multiple choices may have also allowed the participants to guess the answer when they were unsure. Additionally, the number of questions that each participants had to answer varied depending on the number of stories they listened to. Thus performance may also vary with participants answering fewer questions scoring better than those with more questions.

4   Conclusion and Future Work

This paper provides evidence that an affective guide with personality can improve tour experience. It proves that it is not the addition of facial expression alone that makes an interaction more interesting, but the intelligence and attitude of the guide. Although the differences between the emotional and non-emotional guide are not significant enough, the graphs reflect a better rating for the emotional guide in terms of participants' experiences. The participants may simply not notice an improved performance in the emotional guide to a significant enough degree due to the short interaction time. As in human social interaction, it takes time to know an individual personally.

In this study the effects have been represented in a limited fashion due to the number of participants tested. Furthermore, the between-subjects design and the adjustment of alpha level in the post-hoc test make it relatively difficult to get significant differences, but there is no obviously preferable alternative. It is very possible that other effects could be found if subjects are asked to interact with the agent for a longer time. In order to improve the reliability of the test, a larger group of subject is required and the technical problems with the current technologies have to be solved. It would be desirable to replace the text-to-speech system with one that can generate a more natural and emotional voice with a slower speed.

Acknowledgements

Work supported by the European Union's Sixth Framework Programme, in the IST (Information Society Technologies) Thematic Priotity IST-2002-2.3.1.6 Multimodal Interfaces, HUMAINE (Human-Machine Interaction Network on Emotion) [19] (Contract no. 507422). The authors are solely responsible for the content of this publication. It does not represent the opinion of the European Community and the European Community is not responsible for any use that might be made of data appearing therein.

References

[1] Picard, R.W.: Affective Computing. MIT Press, Cambridge (1997)
[2] Dautenhahn, K.: The art of designing socially intelligent agents – science, fiction and the human in the loop (1998)
[3] Abowd, G.D., Atkeson, C.G., Hong, H., Long, S., Kooper, R., Pinkerton, M.: Cyberguide: A mobile context-aware tour guide. Wireless Networks 3(5), 421–433 (1997)
[4] Sumi, Y., Etani, T., Fels, S., Simone, N., Kobayashi, K., Mase, K.: C-map: Building a context-aware mobile assistant for exhibition tours. The First Kyoto Meeting on Social Interaction and Communityware (1998)
[5] O'Grady, M.J., O'Rafferty, R.P., O'Hare, G.M.P.: A tourist-centric mechanism for interacting with the environment. In: Proceedings of the First International Workshop on Managing Interactions in Smart Environments, Dublin, Ireland, December, 1999, pp. 56–67. Springer, Heidelberg (1999)
[6] Dörner, D.: The mathematics of emotions. In: Frank Detje, D.D., Schaub, H., eds.: Proceedings of the Fifth International Conference on Cognitive Modeling, Bamberg, Germany, 75–79 (2003)
[7] Canamero, D.: A hormonal model of emotions for behavior control. In: VUB AI-Lab Memo 97-06, Vrije, Universiteit Brussel, Belgium (1997)
[8] Velásquez, J.: A computational framework for emotion-based control. In: Proceeding of the Grounding Emotions in Adaptive Systems Workshop, SAB '98, Zurich, Switzerland (1998)
[9] Blumberg, B.: Old Tricks, New Dogs: Ethology and Interactive Creatures. PhD thesis, Massachusetts Institute of Technology, MIT, Cambridge, MA (1996)
[10] Ortony, A., Clore, G., Collins, A.: The cognitive structure of emotions. Cambridge University Press, Cambridge, UK (1988)
[11] Scherer, K.R.: Appraisal considered as a process of multilevel sequential checking. In: Scherer, K.R., Schorr, A., Johnstone, T. (eds.) Appraisal Processes in Emotion: Theory, Methods, Research, pp. 92–120. Oxford University Press, New York (2001)
[12] Bates, J.: The nature of characters in interactive worlds and the oz project (1992)
[13] Tozzi, V.: Past reality and multiple interpretations in historical investigation. Stud Social Political Thought 2 (2000)
[14] Kensinger, E.A., Corkin, S.: Two routes to emotional memory: Distinct neural processes for valence and arousal. PNAS 101(9), 3310–3315 (2004)
[15] Richter-Levin, G., Akirav, I.: Emotional tagging of memory formation - in the search for neural mechanisms. Brain Research Reviews 43, 247–256 (2003)

[16] Ibanez, J.: An Intelligent Guide for Virtual Environments with Fuzzy Queries and Flexible Management of Stories. PhD thesis, Departamento de Ingenieria de la Informacion y las Communicaciones, Universidad de Murcia, Murcia, Spain (2004)

[17] Lim, M.Y., Aylett, R.: Intelligent mobile tour guide. In: Symposium on Narrative AI and Intelligent Serious Games for Education, AISB'07, Newcastle, UK (2007)

[18] van Mulken, S., André, E., Muller, J.: The persona effect: How substantial is it (1998)

[19] Humaine: Human-machine interaction network on emotion (2004), http://emotion-research.net

It's All in the Anticipation

Carlos Martinho[1] and Ana Paiva[2]

[1] Instituto Superior Técnico, Taguspark Campus,
Av. Prof. Cavaco Silva, 2744-016, Porto Salvo, Portugal
carlos.martinho@tagus.ist.utl.pt
[2] INESC-ID, Rua Alves Redol 9,
Apartado 13069, 1000-029 Lisboa, Portugal
ana.paiva@inesc-id.pt

Abstract. Since the beginnings of character animation, *anticipation* has been an effective part of the repertoire of tricks used to create believable animated characters. However, anticipation has had but a secondary role in the creation of synthetic virtual life forms. In this paper, we describe how a simple anticipatory mechanism that generates an affective signal resulting from the mismatch between sensed and predicted values — the *emotivector* — can help in the creation of consistent believable behaviour for intelligent virtual characters.

Keywords: Believable Synthetic Characters, Anticipation, Emotion.

1 Introduction

Artificial intelligence (AI) researchers have long sought to create characters that appear to have a life of their own. In their quest to create the *illusion of life*, a term coined by the prominent animators from Disney Studios [17], AI researchers opened the door for traditional character animator techniques to become part of the synthetic character inheritance. One of the first concept to be transferred from traditional character animation to AI was the idea of a *believable* character, a character that "provides the illusion of life and thus permits the audience's suspension of disbelief" [1]. In the late 1920's, Disney studios developed a set of practices that became the fundamental principles of traditional animation to achieve believability [17]. This reference is relevant for AI researchers interested in building believable behaviour, as it promotes the mind of the character as the driving force of the action, and stresses the importance of the character's personality in the creation of such behaviour.

The pioneering work by Bates' group on the role of emotions in believable agents brought two important concepts from Disney guidelines to the field of synthetic characters: *emotion* and *exaggeration*. Bates [1] argued that the clear expression of emotions was a central requirement for believable characters. This findings have been confirmed by subsequent work [2] and, as a result, most synthetic characters have an underlying affective model [14]. Exaggeration appears as a means to convey more effectively a certain emotion that otherwise could go unnoticed and break the suspension of disbelief.

C. Pelachaud et al. (Eds.): IVA 2007, LNAI 4722, pp. 331–338, 2007.

This paper describes the current results of our research that is inspired in another important principle from Disney studio guidelines: *anticipation* [7]. Following the idea that the "mind is the driving force for the action", we have explored the relation between anticipation and emotion, and designed a simple anticipatory affective mechanism [10], that we call *emotivector*, inspired in the psychology of emotion and attention that automatically generates affective states and attention grabbing potential from sensor signals. The emotivector is a fusion of ideas from the fields of affective computing [14] and anticipatory computing [16], using the concept of surprise (inherent to anticipatory systems) implemented as an automatic reaction to a mismatch between expectation and perception [8], that has proven effective in creating simple believable characters.

The paper is organized as follows. Section 2 describes the emotivector in some detail, explaining how anticipation is used to automatically generate affective states and the models from the psychology of attention and emotion supporting our approach. Section 3 describes a synthetic character built with emotivectors, the interactive experimental scenario used to validate our approach, and the results of the experiment. Finally, section 4 draws some conclusions.

2   Emotivector

The emotivector is a simple anticipatory affective mechanism coupled with a sensor[1] that: (1) monitors the values of the sensor[2] and predicts its next state; (2) determines the affective state that arises from the mismatch between the prediction and the sensed input value and; (3) sends this information along with the sensor value. When a value from the sensor reaches the processing module of the agent, the tag provides a recommendation such as 'this signal value is much worse than we expected: you should look at it carefully', or 'nothing new here: it is slightly becoming brighter, as expected'. The agent can then take these recommendations into account for its further processing. Each step is described in more detail in the next subsections.

2.1   Predicting the Next Sensor Value

The computation of the emotivector relies on its capacity to predict the next sensor value. Each time a new signal reaches the sensor, its value is fed to the emotivector. Based on the history of values, the emotivector computes the sensor next expected value. Our predictor implements an hybrid algorithm based on the Kalman filter [6] and the general recirculation algorithm [5], whose learning rate was altered to be mediated by the current affective state (i.e. experiences associated with intense affective states will have a greater influence on the prediction). This algorithm provided us with a simple and efficient generic predictor which does not require any initial fine-tuning to work. More details on the implementation of the prediction algorithm can be found in [11].

---

[1] We assume that the synthetic character is developed as a software agent.

[2] For the sake of simplicity, all the sensors discussed in this paper are unidimensional and their values varies within the interval $[0, 1]$.

2.2 Interpreting the Mismatch: Salience

When a new value reaches the emotivector, it is confronted with its previously computed expected value. The emotivector then estimates the signal a-priori *salience* by computing two components inspired by Posner's two-system model of attention [15]: the exogenous component and the endogenous component. The *exogenous* component is inspired in bottom-up, automatic reflex control of attention, and emphasizes unexpected values of a signal: the greater the difference between the expected value and the input value, the greater the exogenous salience. The *endogenous* component is inspired in top-down, voluntary control of attention, and emphasizes the closeness of a signal value to any actively searched values. In other words, if we are looking for something, similar things will likely attract our attention: the closer the value of the signal gets to a searched value, the greater the endogenous component will be. The interaction of both components define the attention grabbing potential of the signal, by adding or subtracting a component from the other [13].

2.3 Interpreting the Mismatch: Sensations

The existence of a desired value for a sensor allows the emotivector to associate a certain 'quality' to the signal in the form of a basic affective state that we refer to as a *sensation* [4]. To generate such a sensation, we use a model inspired in early behavioural theories of emotions. Our sensations are defined across two dimensions, as in [18]: valence and change. The model works as follows. The emotivector anticipates a reward (if the prediction is closer to the desired value than the current value) or a punishment (in the opposite situation). When the 'real' reward or punishment reaches the emotivector, it is confronted with the reward or punishment expectation. As a result, and following an approach inspired in the behavioural synthesis of Hammond [3], one of the four following basic sensations is triggered[3]: S+ or positive increase, if reward is stronger than expected; $+ or positive reduction, if reward is weaker than expected; S- or negative increase, if punishment is stronger than expected, and; $- or negative reduction, if punishment is weaker than expected.

2.4 Selecting the Relevant Signals

When all signals from the sensors finally reach the processing module of the agent, each one with a tag from the associated emotivector, how does the agent select which are relevant? To answer this question, we added *error prediction* to the emotivector. We added a second (identical) predictor to the emotivector which receives the error prediction each time a new value enters the emotivector and is compared with the expected value. Based on the history of error predictions, and using the same algorithm as the first predictor, this second predictor

---

[3] We use Millenson's notation to define our sensations. If we would use a name to designate a certain affective state, we would be implying a certain intensity. Symbols have a desired neutral quality to them.

estimates the next prediction error. When the 'real' prediction error is greater than the estimated prediction error, the emotivector marks the signal as *relevant*.

2.5 Uncertainty

Error prediction provides an error margin for the estimation of the next sensor value. Each time the first predictor estimates the next value of the sensor, the second predictor estimates how thrustworthy this prediction is, by estimating the prediction error. As such, the emotivector is able to model, in a certain sense, the *uncertainty* associated with the prediction.

The introduction of uncertainty allowed us to extend our four-sensation model to a nine-sensation model. In the four-sensation model, when the emotivector is expecting a reward (i.e. is expecting the value of the signal to move closer to a desired value), the outcome can only be two-fold: the reward can be better (a S+ sensation) or worse (a $+ sensation) than expected. With the uncertainty associated with a prediction, the outcome can now be three-fold: 'significantly better than expected', 'significantly worse than expected' or 'better, as expected'. This approach allowed us to more than double the sensations automatically generated by the emotivector. Figure 1 represents the nine-sensation model.

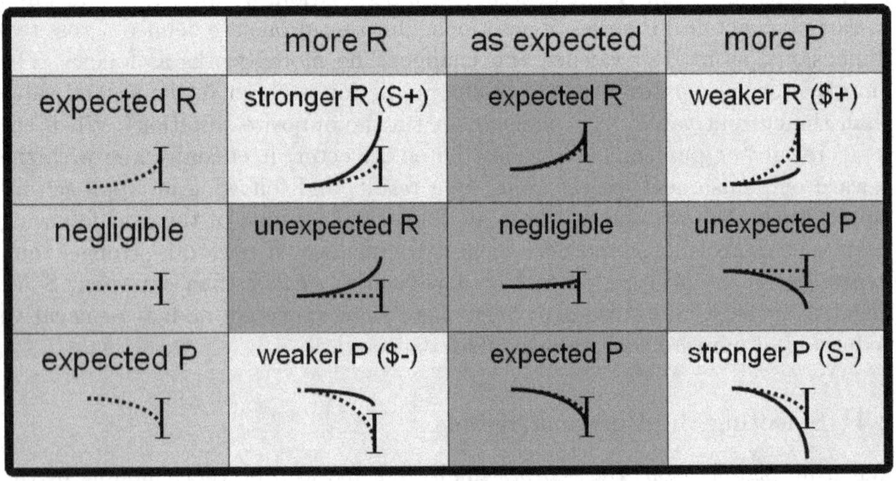

	more R	as expected	more P
expected R	stronger R (S+)	expected R	weaker R ($+)
negligible	unexpected R	negligible	unexpected P
expected P	weaker P ($-)	expected P	stronger P (S-)

Fig. 1. Nine-sensation model: In the figure, R stands for reward and P for punishment. The first line shows possible outcomes when the emotivector is expecting reward: 'significantly better than expected', 'better, as expected', and 'significantly worse than expected'. The use of uncertainty allowed five new sensations (represented by darker cells) to be introduced. From top to bottom, and left to right, they are: 'reward is as good as expected', 'unexpected reward', 'no significant reward nor punishment, as expected', 'unexpected punishment', and 'punishment is as bad as expected'.

3   Aini

Aini is a synthetic flower living in a stretch of shallow water, a synthetic character created to evaluate the adequacy of the emotivector mechanism in the creation of believable behaviour. Aini is a situated, embodied virtual agent which dynamics are controlled by a physics engine. A detailed description of the implementation of Aini's virtual body can be found in [12].

To test our model, we designed an interactive task: a word puzzle game in which Aini helps the user to uncover a four-letter word by reacting consistently to the user's actions in the virtual environment. To complete the word, the user has to place a set of letter cubes onto wooden platforms representing the word letters and their relative position in the word. To allow for a more immersive interaction and account for situatedness and embodiement, the simulation is fully three-dimensional and physics controlled. Figure 2 shows Aini in her virtual environment. For a fully detailed description of the experimental settings and the challenges involved in such a game, please refer to [9].

Fig. 2. Aini and the Word Puzzle Game. The three last letters of the word ('I', 'L' and 'A') are uncovered (they are read from Aini's perspective). Aini is currently expressing an 'unexpected reward' sensation towards the last introduced letter ('L'). The user had been playing around with the cubes for so much time (instead of performing the task) that Aini was not expecting any progress to happen so soon.

3.1   Emotivectors in Action

For this experiment, a grid of 25 emotivectors was used to build Aini's synthetic vision system. Each emotivector was associated with a sensor measuring the distance to the nearest object in a predefined direction within Aini's field of view, linearly normalized to the interval $[0, 1]$. By using emotivectors in such a way, we verified that this approach automatically implemented behaviours such as 'casually look around' and 'quickly look at something new' [10]. Additionally, another emotivector was associated with task progress[4] and generated the task related sensations, each one mapped onto particular animation parameters. An interesting fact is that, for the user, these sensations seemed to account for the history of the interaction. This is best understood through an example.

Consider the case of a user trying to uncover the word 'ZEAL'. Aini starts in a neutral state. The user starts playing around in the environment rather than concentrating on the task. Because no change occurs in the task progress, Aini's prediction accuracy increases (i.e. the predicted error margin decreases), representing the fact that Aini expects (with a high certainty) the task progress to remain unchanged. When the user finally places her first letter ('L') in the wrong place, Aini expresses an 'unexpected punishment' sensation, as the sensed punishment falls outside of the predicted error margin. Aini stops moving and lowers its 'head'. Aini now expects more 'punishment' to come although she is very uncertain about it (Aini just failed to predict the value, as such the uncertainty associated with the prediction increased). Influenced by Aini's negative expression, the user removes the letter 'L' from the word. As the task progress increases by a significant amount, Aini expresses a 'weaker punishment' sensation: it rises its 'head' and waves encouragingly. It is important to note that *if* the user decides to place the letter 'L' again in the same (wrong) placeholder, Aini will react differently from the first time, as the emotivector state has changed in the meantime: the sensor history has changed, as well as the prediction for the next value and its associated error margin. The user now places the 'L' letter cube in the correct position. As there is still a great uncertainty associated with the emotivector prediction, an 'expected reward' sensation is triggered and Aini expresses her confidence regarding the user progress in the task. Afterward, the user places the 'A' letter in the right position. As the margin of error for prediction has now dimished, the value entering the emotivector is outside the error prediction margin, and a 'stronger reward' sensation is triggered, making Aini express total bewilderment to the user.

This simple example shows how rich an interaction can become by simply mapping the emotivector basic sensations onto a set of affective expressions. The history of the interaction and the timing of the different actions will make the emotivector trigger different basic sensations in response to a same user action.

---

[4] The progress of the task is measured on an unidimensional scale from '0' ('none of the letters belong to the word') to '1' ('all the letters are in the correct position') using an approach inspired in the game 'mastermind' (M. Meirovitz, 1971). The initial value is '0.5' ('no letters on the wooden platforms').

3.2   Results

The subjective nature of believability makes its experimental assessment a non-trivial task. Believability is usually a measure of the subject satisfaction regarding the interaction with a synthetic character and is generally evaluated through questionnaires. To help evaluating believability, we additionally designed the experiment in such a way that for the user to finish the task, the behaviour of the synthetic character had to be emotionally consistent (i.e. how the synthetic character express 'its' affective state should be consistent with the user actions) and demonstrate intentionality (i.e. how the character express 'its' affective state has to be consistent with 'its' perceived intentions).

We asked the users to perform four word puzzles with four synthetic characters sharing a same graphical appearance but behaving differently. Two were control characters (with idle and random behaviour) and two others were comparatively evaluated: the emotivector approach and an approach used by the current generation of computer games, that can be resumed as "attend to the closest/last event in the environment and react adequately to it" [9]. A total of 280 word puzzles were played by more than 60 male and female subjects from 5 to 79 years old, belonging to different groups according to their computer skills. The results confirmed the adequacy of the emotivector approach: no subject was able to finish the game with the two control characters (which suggests that it is impossible to finish the game without the help of the synthetic character) and; while all subjects succeeded at the task with the emotivector-based synthetic character, only 20.6% finished the task using the game-based approach.

This experiment revealed three interesting results. First, that emotivector based synthetic vision provides with a natural form of interaction (e.g. by waving an object to draw the character's attention to it). Second, that even a single emotivector (in this case, the emotivector connected to the task progress) can create rich and non-repetitive behaviour that seems to account for the history of past interactions in a meaningful manner. Third, that the emotivector based behaviour may, in certain situations, outperform significantly the approach used in the current generation of computer games. A detailed description of the results can be found in [9].

4   Conclusion

Successful animation as gauged by an audience does not necessarily require completely realistically animated characters, but it does always require characters with a consistent personality. In this paper, we have described the emotivector, an anticipatory mechanism that automatically generates an affective signal resulting from the mismatch between sensed and predicted values. We explained how the emotivector was used to build a synthetic character and presented the experiment putting the concept to the test. The obtained results suggest that the emotivector can be a useful tool for the creation of consistent and non-repetitive behaviour and the creation of believable characters.

Acknowledgments

This work is supported by EU project MindRACES: from reactive to anticipatory cognitive embodied systems (IST-511931).

References

1. Bates, J.: The Role of Emotions in Believable Agents. CMU-CS-94-136 School of Computer Science. Carnegie Mellon University, Pittsburgh, PA 15213 (1994)
2. Elliott, C., Rickel, J., Lester, J.: Lifelike Pedagogical Agents and Affective Computing: An Exploratory Synthesis. In: Veloso, M.M., Wooldridge, M.J. (eds.) Artificial Intelligence Today. LNCS (LNAI), vol. 1600, pp. 195–212. Springer, Heidelberg (1999)
3. Hammond, L.: Conditioned emotional state. In: Physiological Correlates of Emotion, Academic Press, London (1970)
4. Harlow, H., Stagner, R.: Theory of emotions. Psychological Reviews (1933)
5. Hinton, G., McClelland, J.: Learning representations by recirculation. In: Anderson, D. (ed.) Neural Information Processing Systems. American Institute of Physics (1988)
6. Kalman, R.: A new approach to linear filtering and prediction problems. Transactions of the ASME Journal of Basic Engineering 82(D), 3545 (1960)
7. Lasseter, J.: Principles of Traditional Animation Applied to 3D Computer Animation. Computer Graphics 21(4), 35–44 (1987)
8. Lorini, E., Castelfranchi, C.: The cognitive structure of Surprise: looking for basic principles. To appear in Topoi: An International Review of Philosophy, vol. 26(1) (2007)
9. Martinho, C.: Anticipatory Believability. Instituto Superior Técnico. PhD Thesis draft (2005)
10. Martinho, C., Micelli, M., Dias, J., Paiva, A., Castelfranchi, C.: Anticipation and emotion. MindRACES Technical Report (2005)
11. Martinho, C., Paiva, A.: Using Anticipation to Create Believable Behaviour. In: Proceedings of the 21st National Conference on Artificial Intelligence and the 18th Innovative Applications of Artificial Intelligence Conference, AAAI Press, Stanford, California, USA (2006)
12. Martinho, C., Paiva, A.: Aini: Achieving Believability Through Anticipation. In: Proceedings of Nineteenth Conference on Computer Animation and Social Agents (2006)
13. Muller, H., Rabbit, P.: Reflexive orienting of visual attention: time course of activation and resistance to interruption. Journal of Experimental Psychology: Human Perception and Performance 15 (1989)
14. Picard, R.: Affective Computing. MIT Press, Cambridge (1997)
15. Posner, M.: Orienting of attention. Quaterly Journal of Experimental Psychology 32 (1980)
16. Rosen, R.: Anticipatory Systems. Pergamon Press, Oxford (1985)
17. Thomas, F., Johnston, O.: Disney Animation: The Illusion of Life. Abbeville Press, New York (1981)
18. Young, P.: Motivation and Emotion. Wiley, Chichester (1961)

Incorporating Emotion Regulation into Virtual Stories

Tibor Bosse, Matthijs Pontier, Ghazanfar F. Siddiqui, and Jan Treur

Vrije Universiteit Amsterdam, Department of Artificial Intelligence,
De Boelelaan 1081a, 1081 HV Amsterdam, The Netherlands
{tbosse,mpontier,ghazanfa,treur}@few.vu.nl
http://www.few.vu.nl/~{tbosse,mpontier,ghazanfa,treur}

Abstract. This paper presents an approach to incorporate emotion regulation as addressed within psychology literature into virtual characters. To this end, first Gross' informal theory of emotion regulation has been formalised using a dynamical system style modelling approach. Next, a virtual environment has been created, involving a number of virtual agents, which have been equipped with the formalised model for emotion regulation. This environment has been used to successfully generate a number of emergent virtual stories, in which characters regulate their emotions by applying regulation strategies such as situation selection and attentional deployment. The behaviours shown in the stories were found consistent with descriptions of human regulation processes.

1 Introduction

In recent years, there has been an increasing interest in the area of *virtual storytelling*, addressing the development of computer systems that generate fictive stories in which the characters show realistic behaviour. In order to develop virtual stories, a large variety of approaches have been proposed, e.g., [4], [5], [13]. A trend that can be observed in many of these approaches is the movement from stories with a fixed, pre-scripted storyline towards *emergent narrative*, i.e., stories in which only a number of characters and their personalities are fixed, rather than the precise script of the story [1]. In the latter type of storytelling, ideally, all the designer (or writer) has to do is to determine which (types of) characters will occur in the play (although usually it is still needed to roughly prescribe the course of events). Hence, advantages of emergent narrative are the reduced amount of work that has to be spent by the writer, and the non-deterministic and unpredictable behaviour of the story.

In parallel with the shift from fixed storylines to emergent narrative, there has been a development in the nature of the involved characters as well. Recently, the characters (or agents) that are present in virtual stories are transforming more and more from shallow avatars to complex personalities with human-like properties such as emotions and theories of mind, e.g., [15]. To accomplish this, researchers have started to incorporate cognitive models within virtual characters, e.g., [10], [12]. Despite these first promising attempts, there is still a wide area to explore when it comes to enhancing virtual agents with cognitive capabilities.

In line with the development described above, this paper explores the possibilities to equip the characters involved in virtual stories with the capability of *emotion*

C. Pelachaud et al. (Eds.): IVA 2007, LNAI 4722, pp. 339–347, 2007.

regulation. Informally, emotion regulation can be described as the process humans undertake to increase, maintain or decrease their emotional response, see e.g., [7], [8], [11], [14]. The idea is that, by offering virtual agents the capacity to actively regulate their emotions, they will be able to select those kinds of behaviours that they feel most comfortable with. As a result, such agents will 1) behave more realistically and 2) have more freedom in the choice of their actions, which enhances the emergent narrative effect. This approach is similar to the approach taken in [9], which aims at incorporating coping behaviour into virtual humans.

In order to build emotion regulation into virtual stories, in this paper the informal model by Gross [7] as found in psychology literature was taken as a basis. This model describes a number of strategies humans use to adapt their emotion response levels, varying from situation selection to cognitive change and response modulation. Next, this model has been formalised using a dynamical system style modelling approach (see also [3] for some initial steps). In addition, a virtual environment has been created, incorporating a number of virtual agents, and these agents have been equipped with the formalised model for emotion regulation. To test the behaviour of the model, a series of simulation experiments has been performed using the LEADSTO simulation language [2]. The model has been connected to the Vizard Virtual Reality Toolkit [16], to visualise the resulting stories in a graphical environment.

2   Emotion Regulation in the Virtual Agent Context

Gross [8] describes a process model of emotion regulation using the following definition: 'Emotion regulation includes all of the conscious and nonconscious strategies we use to increase, maintain, or decrease one or more components of an emotional response'. In his model, Gross distinguishes four different types of emotion regulation strategies, which can be applied at different points in the process of emotion generation. First of all, when applying *situation selection*, a person chooses to be in a situation that matches the emotional response level the person wants to have for a certain emotion. For example, you can stay home instead of going to a party, because you are in conflict with someone who is going to that party. Second, when applying *situation modification*, a person modifies an existing situation so as to obtain a different level of emotion. For instance, when watching an irritating television program, you zap to another channel. Third, *attentional deployment* refers to shifting your attention to a certain aspect. For example, you close your eyes when watching an exciting penalty shoot-out. Finally, *cognitive change* refers to selecting a cognitive meaning to an event. For example, when a person loses a tennis match and blames the weather circumstances, instead of his own capacities.

To incorporate these strategies into virtual characters, a modelling approach was used that is based on the LEADSTO simulation environment [2] and the Vizard Virtual Reality Toolkit [16]. Due to space limitations, the technical details of LEADSTO and Vizard are not shown here. However, they can be found in Appendix A in [17]. Below, in Section 2.1, at a language-independent level a global overview is given of the model, of which an initial version can be found in [3]. Next, in Section 2.2, for each of the regulation strategies it is shown how it is used in the virtual agents playing as characters in virtual stories. The complete formal specification of the model (in LEADSTO notation) is shown in Appendix B in [17].

2.1 Global Overview

In order to incorporate emotion regulation strategies into virtual agents, a virtual environment is created that is populated by a number of agents. Each agent is equipped with a mechanism to regulate its emotions, which is based on the model as described informally by Gross [7]. To create a formal model, for any given type of emotion a number of variables have been introduced. For convenience, the model concentrates on one specific type of emotion. In principle, this can (at least) be any emotion that is considered to be a basic human emotion, e.g., sadness, happiness, or anger [6]. In order to describe the regulation of such an emotion, the model takes into account the four strategies discussed by Gross are used (i.e., *situation selection, situation modification, attentional deployment*, and *cognitive change*). Based on the four strategies mentioned, in the formalisation four corresponding *elements* (denoted by k) are introduced, for the objects that are affected by the particular strategies: *situation, sub-situation, aspect*, and *meaning*.

The model assumes that each agent aims at an optimal level of emotion. The regulation process in the virtual agents starts by comparing the actual *emotion response level* ERL to the emotion response level ERL_norm aimed at. The difference between the two is the basis for adjustment of the choices made for each of the elements k; based on these adjusted choices, each element k will provide an adjusted *emotional value* EV_k.

To obtain a quantitative model, the emotion response level and the emotional values for the different elements for a given type of emotion are represented by real numbers in the interval [0, 2] (where 0 is the lowest possible ERL (e.g., extreme sadness), and 2 the highest (e.g., extreme happiness)). In the model, the level of emotion to aim at (the ERL norm), is also expressed in a real number in the domain [0, 2]. Based on these concepts, the ERL is recalculated each step by the following difference equation formula:

$$new\_ERL = (1-\beta) * \Sigma_k (w_k * EV_k) + \beta * ERL$$

In this formula, new_ERL is the new emotion response level, and ERL is the old emotion response level. The persistency factor β is the proportion of the old emotion response level that is taken into account to determine the new emotion response level. Initial tests have indicated that values for β around 0.9 deliver realistic results. The new contribution to the emotion response level is calculated by the weighted sum of the emotional values: $\Sigma_k w_k * EV_k$. By normalisation, the sum of all the weights w_k is taken to be 1. The following section describes how the different strategies influence the values of EV_k.

2.2 Emotion Regulation Strategies

Situation selection: which agent to meet. Every step, each agent chooses to be alone, or to contact another agent, by comparing the EVs it attaches to being alone and to being with other agents. The agent will always choose the option with the EV that is closest to its optimal ERL. When two agents contact each other, they decide to meet. When the agents are meeting, their EV for situation is set to the EV they attach to the other agent. When an agent chooses to be alone, its EV for situation is set to its EV for being alone.

Situation modification: what to talk about. When two agents are in a meeting, they will talk about a certain conversation subject. To decide which of the agents will start talking, each agent has a personal *dominance factor*. The agent with the highest dominance factor will choose the first conversation subject. Each step after this, the agent who has not chosen the current conversation subject will choose the next conversation subject. When an agent gets to choose which conversation subject to talk about, it will compare the EVs it attaches to each conversation subject, and select the one that is closest to its optimal ERL. The EV for subsituation is set to the EV the agents attach to the conversation subject they are currently talking about. When an agent is not in a meeting, its EV for subsituation will be set to the neutral value of 1, since the agent is not in a subsituation. When an agent A talks to another agent B about a certain conversation subject CS, this will affect the way agent B thinks about agent A. Agent B's EV for agent A will change using the following formula:

$$\text{new\_EV}_{\text{agent\_A}} = \beta_{\text{friendship}} * \text{EV}_{\text{agent\_A}} + (1-\beta_{\text{friendship}}) * \text{EV}_{\text{CS}}$$

In this formula, new_EV$_{\text{agent\_A}}$ is the new EV agent B will attach to agent A and EV$_{\text{agent\_A}}$ is the old EV agent B attached to agent A. The persistency factor $\beta_{\text{friendship}}$ is the proportion of the old EV that is taken into account to determine the new EV. Here, values for $\beta_{\text{friendship}}$ bigger than 0.9 (where $\beta_{\text{friendship}}$ will get bigger when an agent knows another agent for a longer time) deliver realistic results. The new contribution to the ERL is determined by EV$_{\text{CS}}$: the EV agent B attaches to the conversation subject agent A is talking about. So how much an agent likes another agent, depends on how much an agent likes the conversation subjects another agent talks about.

The extent to which an agent likes to talk about a certain conversation subject can be changed by external events. For example, an agent will start to like a sports team more when this team wins a match. To accomplish this, the following formulas are used:

$$\text{new\_EV}_{\text{CSn}} = \text{EV}_{\text{CSn}} + \Delta\text{EV}_{\text{CSn}}$$

When a positive event occurs: $\Delta\text{EV}_{\text{CSn}} = \eta * \text{EV}_{\text{CSn}} * (d_{\text{max}} - \text{EV}_{\text{CSn}})$

When a negative event occurs: $\Delta\text{EV}_{\text{CSn}} = -\eta * \text{EV}_{\text{CSn}} * (d_{\text{max}} - \text{EV}_{\text{CSn}})$

In these formulas, new_EV$_{\text{CSn}}$ is the new EV the agent attaches to the conversation subject, and EV$_{\text{CSn}}$ is the old EV the agent attached to the conversation subject. Here η is a variable that determines the speed of adjusting EVs to conversation subjects. A lower η will result in slower adjustment. Here, an η of 0.02 delivers realistic results. The part EV$_{\text{CSn}} * (d_{\text{max}} - \text{EV}_{\text{CSn}})$ prevents EV$_{\text{CSn}}$ from under- or overadjustment.

Attentional deployment: on which aspect to focus. When an agent is in a conversation, it can choose to pay attention to, or to distract its attention from the conversation. Every step, the agent chooses the option with the EV closest to its optimal ERL. The EVs the agent attaches to paying attention or distracting its attention, depend on the conversation subject the agent is currently talking about, according to the following formulas:

$$\text{new\_EV}_{\text{pay\_attention}} = \beta_{\text{asp}} * \text{EV}_{\text{pay\_attention}} + (1-\beta_{\text{asp}}) * \text{EV}_{\text{CS}}$$
$$\text{new\_EV}_{\text{distract}} = \beta_{\text{asp}} * \text{EV}_{\text{distract}} + (1-\beta_{\text{asp}}) * (-\text{EV}_{\text{CS}} + d_{\text{max}})$$

In these formulas, new_EV$_{\text{pay\_attention}}$ and new_EV$_{\text{distract}}$ are the new EVs for pay_attention and distract, and EV$_{\text{pay\_attention}}$ and EV$_{\text{distract}}$ are the old EVs for pay_attention and distract. The persistency factor β_{asp} is the proportion of the old EV that is taken into account to determine the new EV. The new contribution to the EV for pay_attention is determined by EV_{CS}, the EV the agent attaches to the conversation subject it is talking about. The new contribution to the EV for distract is calculated by ($-EV_{CS} + d_{max}$). This will reach a high value when the agent attaches a low EV to the conversation subject, and a low value when the agent attaches a high value to the conversation subject. So when the agent likes the conversation subject, it will be more likely to pay attention to the conversation. The agent chooses to distract from, or pay attention to the conversation, by comparing the two EVs for paying attention and distracting, and picking the option with the EV closest to its optimal ERL.

Cognitive change: which meaning to attach. Every step, agents can choose to apply self-talk. An agent can use self-talk to relativise its current state of mind, or on the other hand, to attach more meaning to its current state. Every step, an agent chooses to relativise, attach a stronger meaning, or to apply no self-talk, by picking the option with the EV closest to the optimal ERL of the agent. The EV for not applying self-talk always has the neutral value of 1. The EVs for relativising and attaching more meaning depend on the ERL of the agent, and are updated every step according to the following formula's:

$$new\_EV_{relativise} = d_{max} - ERL$$
$$new\_EV_{attach\_more\_meaning} = ERL + (ERL-1) * (1 - abs(1-ERL))$$

When an agent has a high ERL, the EV for relativising will be low, and when an agent has a high ERL, the EV for relativising will be high. So relativising always influences the ERL of the agent to reach a more neutral value.

When the ERL of the agent has the neutral value of 1, (ERL-1) will be 0, and the EV for attaching more meaning will be 1. When the ERL of the agent is smaller than 1, then ERL-1 will have a negative value, and the EV for attaching more meaning will have a value that is smaller than the current ERL. When the ERL of the agent is bigger than 1, then ERL-1 will be bigger than 1, and the EV for attaching more meaning will have a value that is bigger than the current ERL. So attaching more meaning always influences the ERL of the agent to a more extreme value than the current one. Multiplying by (1 – abs(1-ERL)) prevents the EV from reaching values that are out of the domain.

3 Simulation Experiments

Several experiments have been done to test the simulation model's ability to generate interesting scenarios. To obtain movies in Vizard, events in the LEADSTO simulations were translated to visualisations in Vizard. The exact mapping that was used for this translation is shown in Appendix C in [17]. For example, the fact that an agent is happy is visualised by a certain type of smile, and the fact that an agent distracts from a conversation is visualised by this agent moving its head away from its conversation partner.

In all of the simulations, three agents are involved, which will be called Barry, Gary, and Harry. The particular emotion these agents will try to regulate during the scenario's is their amount of happiness. To enable this, the particular topics they are allowed to talk about are football (in particular, the Dutch football teams Ajax and Feyenoord) and hockey. The parameter settings of all agents used in three specific experiments are shown in Appendix D in [17].

Due to space limitations, only one of the simulation experiments is discussed in this paper. The results of the LEADSTO simulation of this experiment can be seen in

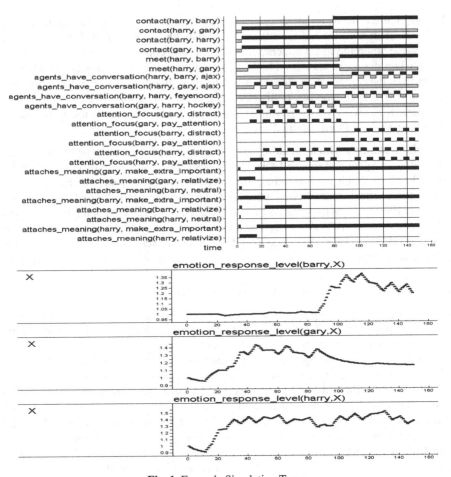

Fig. 1. Example Simulation Trace

Figure 1. Here, time is on the horizontal axis, whereas different events are displayed on the vertical axis. A dark box on top of a line indicates that an event is true at that time point; a light box below a line indicates than an event if false. A detailed description of what happens in this scenario is provided in Appendix E in [17].

As mentioned earlier, using a specific conversion program that has been implemented, LEADSTO simulations were translated into movies in Vizard. A screenshot of an example Vizard movie (which corresponds to the scenario shown in Figure 1) is shown in Figure 2. This figure shows a situation in which (on the foreground) two agents are having a conversation. The left agent is talking about hockey, but the right agent tries to distract from the conversation by moving its head away from the conversation. The cognitive meaning that each agent attaches to its current thoughts is displayed (in red) above the heads of the agents. Meanwhile, in the background a third agent is standing alone. The full Vizard movie of this scenario (as well as the movies that correspond to the two other experiments described in Appendix D) can be found on [17].

Fig. 2. Screenshot of an example scenario in Vizard

The resulting movies provide a first indication that the emotion regulation strategies as described by [7] have been implemented successfully within the virtual agents used as characters. To be specific, the agents are able to perform *situation selection* by selecting different conversation partners, and withdrawing from conversations if desired. Moreover, they can perform *situation modification* by changing conversation topics, they can perform *attentional deployment* by changing the amount of attention they pay to a conversation, and they can perform *cognitive change* by changing the cognitive meaning they assign to their thoughts (e.g., by stating to themselves that something is not very important). These behaviours were found consistent with predicted behaviours for situations as described by Gross [7], [8] (which are based on empirical evidence).

4 Discussion

Within the domain of virtual storytelling, the idea of *emergent narrative* has become more and more popular [1]. Moreover, there is a growing trend to incorporate cognitive models within the characters involved in virtual stories (e.g., [10], [12]). As a next step in that direction, the current paper aims at building emotion regulation as known from psychology literature into virtual characters. To this end, the informal model by Gross [7] was taken as a basis, and has been formalised using a dynamical system style modelling approach (see also [3] for some initial steps). A virtual environment has been created, which includes a number of virtual agents that have been equipped with the formalised model for emotion regulation. To test the behaviour of the model in a prototyping phase, a series of simulation experiments has been performed using the LEADSTO simulation language [2]; in the Vizard Virtual Reality Toolkit [16], such simulations have been visualised in a graphical environment. The resulting movies provide a first indication that the emotion regulation strategies as described by [7] have been implemented successfully within the virtual characters. The simulation results have been compared with the behaviours for different situations as described by Gross [7], [8], and found consistent. Validation involving comparison with detailed empirical data is left for future work.

Concerning related work, an approach in the literature that has similarities to the current approach is [9]. In that paper, a computational model is introduced that can simulate several strategies about how humans cope with emotions, such as 'positive reinterpretation' and 'denial'. Their approach makes use of plan-based causal representations, augmented with decision-theoretic planning techniques, whereas our approach uses dynamical systems representations. Other differences are that they propose a "content model", in which appraisal and regulation operate on rich representations of the emotion-evoking situation, and that their work has been evaluated against clinical data.

Virtual stories involving characters with elaborated cognitive or psychological capabilities can be used for a number of purposes. On the one hand, they may be used for entertainment (e.g., for creating computer games with more complex, unpredictable and more human-like characters). On the other hand, they may be used for educational purposes (e.g., to create a virtual training environment for psychotherapists, which enables them to practice anger management sessions with virtual clients). Further research will investigate whether the model is suitable for such purposes. As soon as these types of challenges will be tackled, also a more precise evaluation will be performed of how humans perceive the current characters (e.g. in terms of believability).

References

1. Aylett, R.: Narrative in Virtual Environments: Towards Emergent Narrative. In: Working notes of the Narrative Intelligence Symposium, AAAI Spring Symposium Series, AAAI Press, Menlo Park, California (1999)
2. Bosse, T., Jonker, C.M., van der Meij, L., Treur, J.: A Language and Environment for Analysis of Dynamics by SimulaTiOn. International Journal of AI Tools. To appear (2007)
3. Bosse, T., Pontier, M., Treur, J.: A Dynamical System Modelling Approach to Gross' Model of Emotion Regulation. In: Proceedings of the 8th International Conference on Cognitive Modeling, ICCM'07, Taylor and Francis (to appear 2007)
4. Cavazza, M., Charles, F., Mead, S.: Interacting with virtual characters in interactive story-telling. In: Alonso, E., Kudenko, D., Kazakov, D. (eds.) Adaptive Agents and Multi-Agent Systems. LNCS (LNAI), vol. 2636, pp. 318–325. Springer, Heidelberg (2003)
5. Dautenhahn, K.: Story-Telling in Virtual Environments. In: Proceedings of the ECAI'98 Workshop on Intelligent Virtual Environments, Brighton, UK. (1998)
6. Ekman, P., Friesen, W.V., Ellsworth, P.: Emotion in the human face: guidelines for research and integration of Findings. New York: Pergamon (1972)
7. Gross, J.J.: The Emerging Field of Emotion Regulation: An Integrative Review. Review of General Psychology 2(3), 271–299 (1998)
8. Gross, J.J.: Emotion Regulation in Adulthood: Timing is Everything. Current directions in psychological science 10(6), 214–219 (2001)
9. Marsella, S., Gratch, J.: Modeling coping behavior in virtual humans: Don't worry, be happy. In: Proceedings of Second International Joint Conference on Autonomous Agents and Multiagent Systems, AAMAS'03, pp. 313–320. ACM Press, New York (2003)
10. Marsella, S.C., Johnson, W.L., LaBore, C.: Interactive Pedagogical Drama. In: Proceedings of the 4th International Conf. on Autonomous Agents, pp. 301–308. ACM Press, New York (2000)

11. Ochsner, K.N., Gross, J.J.: The cognitive control of emotion. Trends in Cognitive Sciences 9, 242–249 (2005)
12. Paiva, A., Machado, I., Prada, R.: Heroes, villains, magicians. In: Proceedings of the Conference on Intelligent User Interfaces, IUI'01, pp. 129–136 (2001)
13. Theune, M., Faas, S., Heylen, D., Nijholt, A.: The Virtual Storyteller: Story Creation by Intelligent Agents. In: Proceedings of Technologies for Interactive Digital Storytelling and Entertainment, pp. 204–215 (2003)
14. Thompson, R.A.: Emotion regulation: A theme in search of definition. In: Fox, N.A. (ed.) The development of emotion regulation: Biological and behavioral aspects. Monographs of the Society for Research in Child Development, vol. 59, pp. 25–52 (1994)
15. Van Vugt, H.C., Hoorn, J.F., Konijn, E.A., De Bie Dimitriadou, A.: Affective affordances: Improving interface character engagement through interaction. International Journal of Human-Computer Studies 64(9), 874–888 (2006)
16. Worldviz. Vizard Virtual Reality Toolkit. University of California. URL: http://www.worldviz.com/vizard.htm
17. http://www.cs.vu.nl/ tbosse/virtualstories

Endowing Emotional Agents with Coping Strategies: From Emotions to Emotional Behaviour

Carole Adam and Dominique Longin

Université Paul Sabatier, IRIT,
118 route de Narbonne, F-31062 Toulouse Cedex 9
{adam,longin}@irit.fr

Keywords: Emotions, coping strategies, "intelligent" agent models, BDI logics.

Introduction. Emotion takes an increasingly important place in the design of intelligent virtual agents. Designers of emotional agents build on theories from cognitive psychology, that describe the cognitive functioning of emotions with two indivisible processes [1,2]: the *appraisal* process triggers emotions, in particular intense negative emotions to point out threatening stimuli, and the *coping* process modifies the behaviour to manage these stimuli. Nevertheless, among the existing emotional agents, a lot express emotions triggered by an appraisal process [3] but few have a coping process allowing their emotions to impact their behaviour [4,5,6]. In previous work [7] we provided a formalization of Ortony *et al.*'s appraisal process [8] in a BDI logic, *viz.* a logic of mental attitudes. The next step is to formalize the coping process in the same framework. Our aim here is to provide the theoretical basis of an agent architecture rather than an implementation. We only give here an overview of our framework (*cf.* [9,10] for more details).

Applications for virtual agents endowed with coping strategies. A model of coping offers interesting application prospects. First, it could make embodied conversational agents once more realistic and believable by allowing them to expose coping behaviours that are considered irrational by standard models of dialogue. Second, an agent who knows some coping strategies could help the user to cope with his own emotions, either during his interaction with the system (intelligent interfaces, pedagogical agents) or during his everyday life (design of Ambient Intelligence Systems [11]). Third, the use of context-dependent coping strategies could increase the believability and unpredictability of human-like characters for virtual worlds or video games, and thus improve the user's immersion and pleasure in the virtual world.

Existing work. Meyer [4] describes the triggering of emotions following [12] and represents their influence on behaviour through unconscious action tendencies (in the sense of [13], for example anger induces aggression), that differ from the conscious coping efforts that we want to formalize here. Gratch and Marsella [5] implement some coping strategies from the COPE model [14] in the EMA agent. This agent's behaviour is very believable, but its mental state is represented by a complex structure inspired from planning, while we propose to use BDI logics, a more generic formalism. Elliott's Affective Reasoner [6] computes the agent's emotions according to the OCC typology [8] and matches them with an action from a database mixing coping strategies with other types of reactions. This is a functional agent architecture, but what we want to provide here is a generic formal model that could be a basis for such implementations.

C. Pelachaud et al. (Eds.): IVA 2007, LNAI 4722, pp. 348–349, 2007.

Psychological basis. We refer to Lazarus and Folkman's definition of coping [2] as "constantly changing cognitive and behavioral efforts to manage specific external and/ or internal demands that are appraised as taxing or exceeding the resources of the person". We then build on the COPE model [14], a set of fifteen *coping* strategies, *viz.* particular kinds of reaction against a negative emotion (for example denying the reality of a situation that makes us sad, or planning actions against a situation that makes us angry).

Our formalism. We consider coping strategies as actions, and express their conditions and effects in terms of the agent's mental attitudes. We then propose a process leading the agent to the choice and application of a particular strategy in a given situation, depending on his personality. Our logic allows us to prove some indirect effects of the use of coping strategies on the agent's subsequent behaviour. We illustrate the functioning of our framework on an example from a virtual world for the training of firemen.

Conclusion. For now, our BDI framework does not manage the intensity of emotions; as a consequence we assume that the execution of a coping strategy simply makes the emotion disappear, instead of making its intensity decrease. But we believe that BDI logics also offer interesting properties: first they have a great explanatory power of the agent's behaviour and allow to reason about it; second they are one of the most widely used tools for describing agents architectures [15].

References

1. Lazarus, R.S.: Emotion and Adaptation. Oxford University Press, Oxford (1991)
2. Lazarus, R.S., Folkman, S.: Stress, Appraisal, and Coping. Springer, Heidelberg (1984)
3. Pelachaud, C., Carofiglio, V., Carolis, B.D., Rosis, F.D., Poggi, I.: Embodied contextual agent in information delivering application. In: Adaptive Agents and Multi-Agent Systems, ACM, New York (2003)
4. Meyer, J.J.C.: Reasoning about emotional agents. Int. Journal of Intell. Systems 21(6) (2006)
5. Gratch, J., Marsella, S.: A domain independent framework for modeling emotion. Journal of Cognitive Systems Research 5(4), 269–306 (2004)
6. Elliott, C.: The Affective Reasoner: A process model of emotions in a multi-agent system. PhD thesis, Northwestern University, Illinois (1992)
7. Adam, C., Gaudou, B., Herzig, A., Longin, D.: OCC's emotions: a formalization in a BDI logic. In: Euzenat, J., Domingue, J. (eds.) AIMSA 2006. LNCS (LNAI), vol. 4183, pp. 24–32. Springer, Heidelberg (2006)
8. Ortony, A., Clore, G., Collins, A.: The cognitive structure of emotions. Cambridge (1988)
9. Adam, C., Longin, D.: Endowing emotional agents with coping strategies: from emotions to emotional behaviour. Research report IRIT/RR–, -15–FR, IRIT, UPS, Toulouse (June 2007) (2007), available at ftp://ftp.irit.fr/IRIT/LILAC/iva-coping.pdf
10. Adam, C.: The emotions: from psychological theories to logical formalization and implementation in a BDI agent. Phd thesis, INP Toulouse, France (July 2007), available at ftp://ftp.irit.fr/IRIT/LILAC/2007_Adam_Phd_Thesis.pdf
11. Adam, C., Gaudou, B., Herzig, A., Longin, D.: A logical framework for an emotionally aware intelligent environment. ECAI workshop on Artif. Intell. Techniques for Ambient Intelligence (2006), ftp://ftp.irit.fr/IRIT/LILAC/Adam_aitami2006.pdf
12. Oatley, K., Jenkins, J.M.: Understanding emotions. Blackwell publishing, Oxford (1996)
13. Frijda, N.: The emotions. Cambridge University Press, Cambridge (1986)
14. Carver, C.S., Scheier, M.F., Weintraub, J.K.: Assessing coping strategies: a theoretically based approach. Journal of Personality Psychology 56(2), 267–283 (1989)
15. Wooldridge, M.: Reasoning about rational agents. MIT Press, Cambridge (2000)

From IVAs to Comics
Generating Comic Strips from Emergent Stories with Autonomous Characters

Tiago Alves[1], Ana Simões[1], Marco Vala[1], Ana Paiva[1],
Adrian McMichael[2], and Ruth Aylett[2]

[1] IST - Technical University of Lisbon, Avenida Professor Cavaco Silva, Tagus Park
2780-990 Porto Salvo, Portugal
[2] MACS, Heriot-Watt University, Riccarton, Edinburgh EH10 4ET
{tiago.alves,ana.simoes}@tagus.ist.utl.pt,
{marco.vala,ana.paiva}@inesc-id.pt, awm1@hw.ac.uk,
ruth@macs.hw.ac.uk

Abstract. Emergent narrative systems create stories which are always different from each other. Creating summaries of these stories is a challenge especially if we want to capture the richness of the characters. Our goal is to automatically generate summaries from emergent narrative using comics as the visual medium for the summary. We identify the most important situations in the story log looking at the emotional state of the characters, transform the resulting summary into a comics description and create the comic. We believe that a good summarization of a story that maintains the emotions of the characters together with an expressive visual representation is essential for the user to remember the story.

Keywords: Emergent narrative, story summarization, comics description language, comics generation.

1 The Comics Generation System

The comics generation system aims at generating summaries of emergent narrative using comics. As a case study we used FearNot! [1].

FearNot! allows children to explore what happens in bullying situations using a friendly environment. It uses emergent narrative and a cast of autonomous characters to create improvised bullying situations which are unscripted by nature. FearNot! generates complete logs for each episode.

In order to create a visual summary of an episode of FearNot! we need to summarize the main events (as in [3]), describe these events using a comics description language (similar to [2]) and then generate the comic strips (as in [4]).

Our comics generation system is divided into four main components. The first component is the log summarizer in which the log produced by FearNot! is analysed and the most important events are extracted. The summarization consists in analysing the emotional state of the characters. Strong emotions will lead to important actions.

C. Pelachaud et al. (Eds.): IVA 2007, LNAI 4722, pp. 350–351, 2007.

Additionally, the actions that led to these strong emotions are also considered important.

The second component creates descriptions of those important actions using our Comic Strip Description Language (CSDL). The CSDL is an XML-based markup language that semantically describes a story like a comic strip.

The next component analyses and transforms the comic strip descriptions into comics. It is coupled with the last component: the library. The library stores all the resources needed to generate the comic which include backgrounds, characters and items.

Fig. 1. An example of the results that can be expected from our system

2 Future Work

The comics generation system is a work in progress but preliminary results are encouraging. We believe that a good summarization of log files together with an expressive comics representation can help readers to better visualize and understand the important events in a story. The next steps are the completion of the system prototype and then doing a pilot evaluation with the children that have already had contact with FearNot!.

References

1. Aylett, R., Louchart, S., Dias, J., Paiva, A., Vala, M., Woods, S., Hall, L.: Unscripted Narrative for Affectively Driven Characters. In IEEE Computer Graphics and Applications 26(3), 42–52 (2006)
2. Comic Book Markup Language (CBML) (in, 2007-03-30) (2007), http://www.cbml.org
3. Friedman, D., Feldman, Y., Shamir, A., Dagan, Z.: Automated Creation of Movie Summaries in Interactive Virtual Environments. In: Proceedings of IEEE Virtual Reality, pp. 191–199. IEEE Computer Society Press, Los Alamitos (2004)
4. Kurlander, D., Skelly, T., Salesin, D.: Comic Chat. In: Proceedings of the 23rd Annual Conference on Computer Graphics and interactive Techniques SIGGRAPH '96, pp. 225–236. ACM Press, New York (1996)

Emotional Agents with Team Roles to Support Human Group Training

Raúl A. Aguilar[1], Angélica de Antonio[2], and Ricardo Imbert[2]

[1] Universidad Autónoma de Yucatán, Mathematics School
Periférico Norte Tablaje 13615, A.P. 172, Cordemex, C.P. 97110, Mérida, México
avera@uady.mx
[2] Universidad Politécnica de Madrid, Computer Science School
Campus Montegancedo, 28660, Boadilla del Monte, Madrid, Spain
{rimbert,angelica}@fi.upm.es

Abstract. In the teamwork research area there is an increasing interest about the principles behind team effectiveness and effective team training; for Intelligent Virtual Agents (IVAs) Team Training is an excellent application area; nevertheless, the few reported works about IVAs in team training, illustrate both the use for the individualized teaching (Pedagogical Agents) of procedural tasks and the substitution of missing team members (Teammate Agents) to promote the practice of team tasks in relation to functional roles (Taskwork) [1].

Our interest on Intelligent Virtual Environments for Training (IVETs) has led us to propose a Team Training Strategy (TTS) whose purpose is to promote social skills as well as knowledge and skills related to tasks of socio technical nature. The alternatives that we are evaluated to improve the performance of human groups and to promote effective teams deal with: the use of scaffolding as the best tutoring approach, the promotion of social skills before technical skills, and especially, the selection of the best nonfunctional roles (team roles) balance according to the task.

In addition, our aim is to incorporate into an IVA called Pancho (Pedagogical AgeNt to support Colaborative Human grOups) the particular behaviors of Team Roles defined by Belbin [2]; Pancho, with a selected team role —according to a team model— will join the human group with the intention of improving the performance of the team (Teamwork) and providing scaffolding to the trainees (Taskwork). The Belbin's categorization is the earliest and still the most popular. He states that the team role can be defined as a tendency to behave, contribute and interrelate with each others at work in a certain distinctive ways; he also states that in teamwork, a good mix of team roles in the group is necessary for groups to use their technical skills optimally. The team roles defined by Belbin have very particular behaviors; we have selected a generic cognitive architecture for agents with emotionally influenced behaviors —called COGNITIVA— to realize those roles [3]. The constructs provided by this architecture (Personal traits, Concerns, Moods, Attitudes and Physical states) are being properly instantiated to generate the desired behaviors.

C. Pelachaud et al. (Eds.): IVA 2007, LNAI 4722, pp. 352–353, 2007.
© Springer-Verlag Berlin Heidelberg 2007

References

1. Rickel, J., Johnson, L.: Extending Virtual Humans to Support Team Training in Virtual Reality. In: Lajkemeyer, G., Nebel, B. (eds.) Exploring Artificial Intelligence in the new Millenium, ch. 7 (2002)
2. Belbin, M.: Management Teams. John Wiley & Sons, New York (1981)
3. Imbert, R., de Antonio, A.: When emotion does not mean loss of control. In: Panayiotopoulos, T., et al. (eds.) IVA 2005 LNCS (LNAI), vol. 3661, pp. 152–165 (2005)

Context Awareness in Mobile Relational Agents

Timothy W. Bickmore, Daniel Mauer, and Thomas Brown

Northeastern University College of Computer and Information Science
360 Huntington Ave WVH202, Boston, MA 02115
{bickmore,daniel}@ccs.neu.edu, brown.tho@neu.edu
http://www.ccs.neu.edu/research/rag/

1 Introduction

The development of virtual agents designed to draw users into personal and professional relationships with them represents a growing area of research [1]. Mobility and
context awareness represent important directions of research for these relational
agents, since they offer unique affordances for relationship development. A mo-
bile/wearable agent has the potential to be with a user for a significant period of time,
and frequency of contact alone has been shown to be associated with increased solidarity between people. The ability to sense some aspects of the user's environment
(context awareness) may also provide mobile agents with unique relational affordances. Automatically recognizing and commenting on situations in the user's life can
amplify many relational perceptions, including familiarity, common ground, solidarity
and intimacy. In addition, an agent's ability to proactively interrupt and help a user in
a situation that is automatically sensed by the agent may lead to increased perceptions
of trust and caring by the user.

2 Experimental Platform

We have developed a general purpose relational agent interface for use on handheld computers such as PDAs (Fig. 1).
The animated agent appears in a fixed
close-up shot, and is capable of a range
of nonverbal conversational behavior, including: facial displays of emotion; head
nods; eye gaze movement; eyebrow
raises; posture shifts and visemes. These
behaviors are synchronized in real time
with agent output utterances, which are
displayed in a text balloon rather than using speech, for privacy reasons. User inputs are constrained to multiple choice
selections at the bottom of the display.
    Interaction dialogues are scripted in an
XML-based hierarchical state-transition

Fig. 1. Mobile Virtual Agent Interface

C. Pelachaud et al. (Eds.): IVA 2007, LNAI 4722, pp. 354–355, 2007.

network, which allows for the rapid development and modification of system behavior. Scripts consist primarily of agent utterances, the allowed user responses to each agent utterance, and instructions for state transitions based on these responses and other system events (timers, sensor input, etc.). Scripts are authored using a visual design tool, and are then processed using the BEAT text-to-embodied-speech engine [2], which automatically adds specifications for agent nonverbal behavior. In addition, visemes are generated using an extension of the *freeTTS* text-to-speech engine.

Interruption behavior can be very flexibly defined using a variety of wait states and state transitions conditioned on events. During specified wait states, the PDA's display shuts off, and the interface remains dormant until some condition is met, while sensor inputs and other background processes remain active. Example wake up conditions include specific times of day, changes in user behavior as measured by sensor input, or hardware key presses by the user.

The initial application domain for the handheld agent is exercise promotion using an integrated 2D accelerometer enabling the agent to tell whether a user is currently walking at a moderate intensity or not (based on a speed calibrated for each user).

3 Pilot Study on Awareness and Social Bonding

In order to explore the relational efficacy of context awareness, we conducted a small study to compare a mobile context aware agent with an otherwise identical agent without sensing ability. Both agents attempted to motivate users to walk more, but in one condition (AWARE) the agent could sense whether the user was walking at moderate intensity or not and automatically provided feedback to the user whenever they finished a walk, while in the other condition (NON-AWARE) the user had to explicitly tell the agent when they were starting and ending a walk. The study was a counter-balanced within-subjects design experiment in which each treatment lasted four days. Eight males, aged 19-23, participated in the study.

Results indicated that context awareness led to greater user-agent bonding ($F(1,4,)=8.6$, $p<.05$), but less walking (minutes of moderate intensity walking, $F(1,4)=74.3$, $p<.001$) in study participants. This difference in walking behavior may have been due to perceptions of low reliability in the sensing mechanism, or to the psychological effect of making a commitment to the NON-AWARE agent when walk starts were declared. Ongoing work will address these issues in future versions.

Acknowledgements. This work was supported by NIH National Library of Medicine grant R21LM008553.

References

1. Bickmore, T., Picard, R.: Establishing and Maintaining Long-Term Human-Computer Relationships. ACM Transactions on Computer Human Interaction 12(2), 293–327 (2005)
2. Cassell, J., Vilhjálmsson, H., Bickmore, T.: BEAT: The Behavior Expression Animation Toolkit. In: SIGGRAPH '01, pp. 477–486 (2001)

Implicit Training of Virtual Agents

Anton Bogdanovych[1], Marc Esteva[2], Simeon Simoff[1], and Carles Sierra[2]

[1] Faculty of Information Technology,
University of Technology Sydney 2007 NSW, Australia
{anton,simeon}@it.uts.edu.au
[2] Artificial Intelligence Research Institute (IIIA-CSIC)
Campus UAB, Barcelona, Catalonia, Spain
{esteva,sierra}@iiia.csic.es

Abstract. This paper provides a brief overview of an implicit training method used for teaching autonomous agents to represent humans in 3D Virtual Worlds without any explicit training efforts being required.

1   Introduction

Many scholars, whose work is focused on intelligent virtual agents face the problem of making them believable. The believability has a lot of different characteristics, e.g. personality, social role awareness etc [1]. In our work, instead of trying to discover and implement different characteristics of believability, we use imitation learning [2]. The main hypothesis behind it can be best summarized by the cliche "to know a man is to walk a mile in his shoes" [2]. To increase the believability of agents we suggest that they constantly observe the behavior of humans and learn to imitate it. Efficient imitation can be achieved when a human is fully immersed into an environment based on the 3D Electronic Institutions technology [3]. This technology utilizes 3D Virtual Worlds, used for the visualization purposes, together with Electronic Institutions that help to establish the rules of the interactions among participants. Such approach valuably facilitates the training of autonomous agents. 3D representation of the environment provides as much possibilities to observe the behavior of the humans as the real world does. It assumes similar embodiment for all participants, including humans and autonomous agents who imitate the humans, so every action that a human performs can be easily observed and then reproduced by an autonomous agent, without a need to overcome the embodiment dissimilarities. Moreover, the use of Electronic Institutions provides context and background knowledge for learning, helping to explain the tactical behavior and goals of the humans.

2   Implicit Training

An important feature of 3D Electronic Institutions is that every human participant is always supplied with a corresponding software agent that communicates the desires of the human to the institutional infrastructure. While a human drives an avatar and acts in the Virtual World, the agent observes those actions and learns how to make the decisions on human's behalf. 3D Electronic Institutions

C. Pelachaud et al. (Eds.): IVA 2007, LNAI 4722, pp. 356–357, 2007.
© Springer-Verlag Berlin Heidelberg 2007

separate the actions that happen in the Virtual World into two different kinds: normative level actions (operations that require institutional validation) and visual level level actions (no validation required). An example of a normative level action is opening a door to enter a secure auction. An example of a visual level action can be a gesture or any other kind of avatar movement.

Based on these actions, the learning-related information for each of the agents is stored in a separate learning graph. The nodes of this graph correspond to normative level actions. Each node is associated with two variables: the action name together with parameters and the probability ($P(Node)$) of this action to be executed. The arcs connecting the nodes are associated with prerecorded sequences of visual level actions ($s_1, \ldots, s_n$) and the attribute vectors that influenced them ($a_1, \ldots, a_n$). Each pair $\langle a_n, s_n \rangle$ is stored in a hashtable, where a_i is the key of the table and s_i is the value. Each a_i consists of the list of parameters: $a_i = \langle p_1, \ldots p_k \rangle$. We assume that the behaviour of the principle is only influenced by what is currently visible through the field of view of the avatar and limit the visible items to the objects located in the environments and other avatars. So, the parameters that can be used for learning are recorded in the following form: $p_i = \langle V_o, V_{av} \rangle$. Here V_o is the list of visible objects; V_{av} is the list of visible avatars. Each time an institutional message is executed, the autonomous agent records the parameters it is currently able to observe, creates a new visual level sequence and every 50 Ms adds a new visual level message into it. The recording is stopped once a new institutional message is executed.

The nodes of the learning graph are seen as internal states of the agent, the arcs determine the mechanism of switching from one state to another and the probability $P(Node)$ determines how likely it is for the agent to change its current state to the state determined by the next node. Once the agent reaches a state $S(Node_i)$ it checks all the other nodes connected to the $Node_i$, selects the node ($Node_k$) with the highest probability and changes its current state to $S(Node_k)$ by executing the best matching sequence of the visual level actions recorded on the arc that connects $Node_i$ and $Node_k$. The best matched sequence is selected through the employment of a classifier, which compares the currently observed parameters to the parameters associated to the recorded sequences.

3 Conclusion

We presented the implicit training method and described an approach to implement it using a learning graph. Future work includes further development of this concept and its evaluation.

References

1. Magnenat-Thalmann, N., Kim, H., Egges, A., Garchery, S.: Believability and interaction in virtual worlds. In: MMM, pp. 2–9 (2005)
2. Breazeal, C.: Imitation as social exchange between humans and robots. In: AISB Symposium on Imitation in Animals and Artifacts, pp. 96–104 (1999)
3. Bogdanovych, A., Berger, H., Simoff, S., Sierra, C.: E-Commerce Environments as 3D Electronic Institutions. In: Proc. of IADIS e-Commerce 2004, Portugal (2004)

Human Actors and Virtual Agents Playing Together to Transform Stage Direction Practices

Alain Bonardi[1] and Christine Zeppenfeld[2]

[1] Ircam, 1, place Igor-Stravinsky, 75004 Paris, France
[2] Stage director, 21 Cité Leclaire, 75020 Paris, France
alain.bonardi@ircam.fr, christinezeppenfeld@wanadoo.fr

Abstract. In this article, we show how approaches based on interactive data-mining may inspire new conceptions of theatre staging. They may be applied thanks to virtual agent systems interacting with comedians. We then give an example of such a theatre production, *La Traversée de la nuit*.

Keywords: Multimedia theatre, new practices of staging, intelligent virtual agents, ontologies, interactive data-mining.

1 Interactive Data-Mining *Versus* Dramaturgical Ontologies

In this article, we are wondering about new practices of theatre combining intelligent virtual agents and human actors. Contrary to traditional approaches of theater based on dramaturgical ontologies of characters (defined as types) or situations (defined as paradigms), we have explored new ways considering interactive data-mining as the basis of staging.

2 The Inter-media Play *La Traversée de la nuit*

Our research is based on an example of staging from a non-dramatic text, *La traversée de la nuit*, by Geneviève de Gaulle-Anthonioz [3], telling her imprisonnment in the bunker of the Ravensbrück camp at the end of the World War II. The stage direction is based on an autarkic human to machine system [1]: an actress tells the whole text. A danser performs a certain number of gestures inspired by Nô theatre; there is a multimedia computer, as an artificial actor. The computer projects images onto a very large screen at the back of the stage (the actress and the dancer can see part of it at any time), provoking the reaction of the comedians who may adapt their play. To complete the loop, the computer grasps the emotional states of the actress's voice.

The technical implementation of the human-machine system is based on a neural network to analyse the actress's voice as an input and a multi-agent system to generate projected images as an output. The neural network was trained in supervised mode during several months. The actress would impose herself a list of twenty emotional states and read the whole text using one of them. The input voice is computed one sentence after another, giving a twelve-component vector.

C. Pelachaud et al. (Eds.): IVA 2007, LNAI 4722, pp. 358–359, 2007.
© Springer-Verlag Berlin Heidelberg 2007

The multi-agent system [1] enables the realtime generation of images projected on a screen at the back of the stage. The one hundred autonomous agents may be compared to dynamic "billstickers" that would generate images (each of them carries a small part of image, still or animated collected from image banks). Each agent has a small psychological model of sensitivity, that reacts to the emotional states provided by the neural network according to the text sequences. The result is a "mood" that conditions the agent. The agents cooperate towards one goal by optimizing an utility function computed from the appearance qualities of the images generated (evaluated by as specific agent, the observer agent). Agents may move, twist, enlarge, reduce, make more or less transparent their own small images.

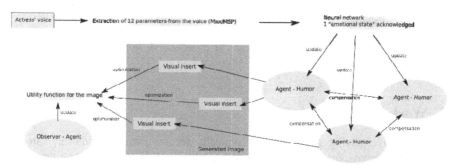

Fig. 1. Overall organization of the computerized processes in *La Traversée de la nuit*

3   Conclusion

We have shown how the approaches based on interactive data mining may inspire new modalities of stage direction associating actors and computers. The purpose of the multiagent system we have described is to provoke the action and participation of the performers on stage, to enrich the common field of digital and performance arts.

References

1. Becker Villamil, M., Raupp Musse, S., de Oliveira, L.P.L.: A Model for Generating and Animating Groups of Virtual Agents. In: Rist, T., Aylett, R., Ballin, D., Rickel, J. (eds.) IVA 2003. LNCS (LNAI), vol. 2792, pp. 15–17. Springer, Heidelberg (2003)
2. Bonardi, A., Rousseaux, F.: New Approaches of Theatre and Opera Directly Inspired by Interactive Data-Mining. In: the proceedings of the International Conference Sound & Music Computing (SMC'04), Paris, pp. 1–4. October 20-22 (2004)
3. de Gaulle, G.: La Traversée de la nuit, Éditions du Seuil (1998)
4. Pelachaud, C., Poggi, I.: Multimodal Embodied Agents. The Knowledge Engineering review 17(2), 181–196 (2002)

Towards Characters with a Full Episodic Memory

Cyril Brom[1], Klára Pešková[2], and Jiří Lukavský[3]

[1,2] Charles University, Faculty of Mathematics and Physics, Prague, Czech Republic
[3] Institute of Psychology, Academy of Sciences, Prague, Czech Republic
brom@ksvi.mff.cuni.cz

Abstract. A typical present-day virtual actor is able to store episodes in an *ad hoc* manner, which does not allow for reconstructing the actor's personal stories. We have prototyped a virtual RPG actor with a *full* episodic memory, which allows for this reconstruction. The paper overviews the work done and sketches the work in progress.

1 Work Detailed

Computer role-playing games (RPGs) typically feature virtual worlds large in size, lifetime and behavioural possibilities. These worlds, both in off-line and on-line RPGs, are usually inhabited by thousands of virtual actors ("non-player characters", NPCs).

An innate challenge of these games is to provide a player with a believable story. Though there is likely more narration in RPGs then in any other kind of commercial games, storytelling in RPGs is still far from novels or films. The generating of story in RPGs is a multi-dimensional problem. One facet of this problem is unfolding the story and keeping it consistent when a player speaks with NPCs, i.e. letting the actors tell believable stories about themselves.

To be able to answer questions like "What were you doing the last week? And please, focus on the most important things." according to their personal histories, and not using a text written in advance by a designer, the NPCs must be simulated (at least to some extent) even if no player is around and they must be equipped with a *full episodic memory* and a *linguistic module* transferring the outcome of the memory to syntactically correct sentences. By "full" we mean a generic memory that stores more or less everything happening around the actor tagged with the actor's own relevance estimation, as opposed to an *ad hoc episodic memory* storing only the events specified in a hardwired fashion inside the actor's script or reactive plan (this kind of episodic memory is almost always present in current intelligent actors).

As the first step towards such actors, we have prototyped a shaman NPC with this kind of episodic memory as a part of our on-going work on a large educational storytelling game [1]. For experimental purposes, the actor inhabits a simplified grid world that contains about 50 objects of 18 different classes, and carries out 14 different tasks. These tasks are relatively complex (e.g. herborising, extinguishing a fire) with a hierarchical nature, and they typically include manipulation with several objects. They are represented by AND-OR trees.

Because of innate characteristics of RPGs (large worlds, many actors), our main priorities were the memory consumption and the fast storage and retrieval times.

C. Pelachaud et al. (Eds.): IVA 2007, LNAI 4722, pp. 360–361, 2007.

We have settled several requirements on the episodic memory, which are based on the current psychological view about this kind of memory. The proposed characteristics of the system are stemming from these requirements:

1. short and long-term episodic memory distinction,
2. storage of both the objects the actor encountered and tasks he/she performed, including time information,
3. storage only of the objects that passed an "attentional filter"
4. simplified forgetting,
5. an ability to answer the following questions: "where is something?", "when did the actor see the thing x?", "what did the actor do from t_1 to t_2?", "why did you do the action a?"; mostly in constant or linear time.

Several issues remain as work in progress, most notably:

1. determining emotional relevance of episodes and implementation of forgetting based on this relevance,
2. determining trustfulness (or reliability) of memory records in dynamic worlds,
3. storing episodes about other actors.

Several tests have been carried out with the prototyped actor, focusing both on the actors' efficiency (in terms of time spent in searching for objects), and size of its memory (in terms of memory records). We have tested the shaman in a 5 day scenario, and in worlds with different dynamics (measured as a fraction of objects that changed during a day). The tests revealed two main findings. First, the memory consumption is acceptable, but deeper forgetting may be needed particularly in scenarios lasting for a longer period. Second, the efficiency of the actor is better than the efficiency of an actor without memory, but only in worlds with relatively low dynamic. This is caused mostly by the insufficient reliability assessment of the records in the present model.

An example of the answer to question: "What did you do between t_1 and t_2?" in the current implementation is: *"I was doing SearchRandom for smokeability because of Smoke. I was doing go from room 1 to room 2 because of SearchRandom. I was doing look in environment because of SearchRandom. I was doing go from room 2 to room 5 because of SearchRandom. I was doing pick up Calumet1 because of Smoke. I was doing Smoke."*

The work is fully detailed in [2]. The progress made with the issue (2), i.e. with determining trustfulness of records in the memory, is described in [3].

Acknowledgment. This research was partially supported by the Program "Information Society" under project 1ET100300517, and **GA UK 351/2006/ A-INF/MFF**.

References

1. Brom, C., Abonyi, A.: Petri-Nets for Game Plot. In: Proceedings of AISB Artificial Intelligence and Simulation Behaviour Convention, Bristol, vol. 3, pp. 6–13 (2006)
2. Brom, C., Pešková, K., Lukavský, J.: What does your actor remember? Towards Characters with a Full Episodic Memory. Technical Report No. 2007/4 of the Dept. of Software and Computer Science Education. Charles University, Prague (2007)
3. Brom, C., Pešková, K., Lukavský, J.: Where did I put my glasses? Determining trustfulness of records in episodic memory by means of an associative network. In: Brom, C., Pešková, K., Lukavský, J. (eds.) Proceedings of European Conference on Artificial Life 2007. LNCS, vol. 4648, pp. 243–252. Springer, Berlin (2007)

Towards Fast Prototyping of IVAs Behavior: Pogamut 2

Ondřej Burkert, Rudolf Kadlec, Jakub Gemrot, Michal Bída, Jan Havlíček,
Martin Dörfler, and Cyril Brom

Charles University in Prague, Faculty of Mathematics and Physics
Dept. of Software and Computer Science Education, Prague, Czech Republic
ondra@atrey.karlin.mff.cuni.cz, brom@ksvi.mff.cuni.cz
http://artemis.ms.mff.cuni.cz

Abstract. We present the platform for IVAs development in the human like environment of the first-person shooter game Unreal Tournament 2004. This environment is extendible and supported by vast community of users. Based on our previous experience the problem of fast verification of models of artificial intelligence or IVAs is in implementation issues. The developer spends most of his time solving technical environment dependent issues and malfunctions, which drives him away from his goals. Therefore our modular platform provides a tool, which helps solving those problems and the developer can spend saved time by solving another AI based issues and model verification. The platform is aimed for research and educational purposes.

1 Introduction

The development of a complex behavior of an *intelligent virtual agent* (IVA) acting in a human-like 3D world is in general very hard. IVA is an embodied agent, which is graphically represented by an avatar in the environment. There are a lot of aspects to the IVA aside from the behaviors like skeletal animations, face expressions, etc. but our platform is focused only on prototyping of the IVA's behavior.

Nowadays, there are a lot of applications featuring IVAs including serious games [1], therapeutic tools [2], etc. There are some tools both commercial [3] and freeware [4, 5] that can be used for creation of IVA's behavior. Commercial tools are expensive and lack connection to 3D world while freeware tools lack IDE.

There is no such a platform that would combine mature and extensible virtual world and IDE for developing IVAs. In this paper, we present the toolkit Pogamut 2 that aims at filling this gap.

2 Pogamut 2

Pogamut 2 integrates five main modules: (1) Unreal Tournament 2004 (UT04), (2) Gamebots2004 (GB04), (3) Parser, (4) Agent library, (5) IDE.

Unreal Tournament 2004 is a commercial game, which is used as a virtual world. Main feature is extensibility and environmental editor that comes out of the box.

C. Pelachaud et al. (Eds.): IVA 2007, LNAI 4722, pp. 362–363, 2007.

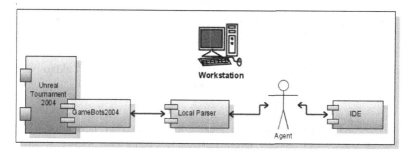

Fig. 1. Platform architecture overview

The *Gamebots 2004* is a built-in server in the UT04, which export information from UT04 for the *Agent*. We have extended the old version of GameBots [5] and added new functionalities containing exporting navigation points, ray tracing, etc.

The *Parser* translates text messages of the GB04 to Java objects.

The *Agent library* is a package of Java classes. It provides (a) a memory storing variety of sensory information, (b) functional primitives for the control of IVA's body, (c) an inventory to manage items the agent picks up, (d) methods for movement around the map that are solving navigation issues, including A*.

The *IDE* is made as a plug-in for NetBeans^{TM} development environment. It provides help in important stages of work – development, debugging and experimenting. It contains: (a) scripting of agent's behavior (Java, Python) (b) tools for debugging – an inspector of internal agent variables, a viewer of agent's memory, viewers for logs, etc., (c) supports experiments with declarative rules [6].

The Pogamut 2 beta version is available at our webpage [7].

Acknowledgements

This work is supported by grant GA UK 1053/2007/A-INF/MFF and partially supported by grants GA UK 351/2006/A-INF/MFF and "Information Society" 1ET100300517.

References

1. Tactical Iraqi [25. 6. 2007], http://www.tacticallanguage.com
2. Hodges, L.F., Anderson, P., Burdea, G.C., Hoffman, H.G., Rothbaum, B.O.: Treating Psychological and Physical Disorders with VR. IEEE Computer Graphics and Applications, 25–33 (2001)
3. X-Altment GmbH: X-Altment [25. 6. 2007], http://www.x-aitment.net
4. [25. 6. 2007], http://fear.sourceforge.net
5. [25. 6.2007], http://www.planetunreal.com/gamebots
6. [25. 6. 2007], http://labs.jboss.com/jbossrules
7. [25. 6. 2007], http://artemis.ms.mff.cuni.cz/pogamut

Towards a Multicultural ECA Tour Guide System

Aleksandra Cerekovic[1], Hung-Hsuan Huang[2], Igor S. Pandzic[1], Yukiko Nakano[3],
and Toyoaki Nishida[2]

[1] Faculty of Electrical Engineering and Computing, Zagreb, Croatia
[2] Graduate School Informatics, Kyoto University, Japan
[3] Department of Computer, Information and Communication Sciences, Tokyo
University of Agriculture & Technology, Japan
{aleksandra.cerekovic,igor.pandzic}@fer.hr,
{huang,nishida}@ii.ist.i.kyoto-u.ac.jp,
nakano@cc.tuat.ac.jp

In this article we present an ongoing project in our research group, an ECA based multicultural tour guide system. Tour guide ECA agent provides information about the city of Dubrovnik and dynamically changes its behaviors among Japanese, Croatian and general western cultures speaking in English.

The tour guide system architecture is being carried out by a generic ECA framework (GECA framework) we introduced in our prior work [1]. Based on the low-level OpenAIR's XML routing protocol [2], GECA framework provides a seamless integration of various components; the consistency of communication channels, timing synchronization of all components, and handling streaming data from sensors in a real-time. Most importantly, system architecture has a possibility for extension with another cultural domain.

Fig. 1. Configuration of the tour guide system

Combination of devices depicted in figure 1. collects verbal and non-verbal input from the human user. Speech recognition component recognizes specific keywords in the natural speech language (Japanese, English, Croatian) and motion sensor devices detect non-verbal behaviors which are not culture dependent (nodding, shaking, head orientation, pointing or five fingers straight). Since no general purpose speech recognizer/ synthesizer for Croatian exists, to recognize Croatian keywords we are using an English speech recognition component adopted with grammar rules for Croatian.

In the deliberate phase of the system, we introduce GECA Scenario Markup Language (GSML) script based on AIML [3]. GSML script defines an interactive scenario between the human user and ECA agent; a states of a

C. Pelachaud et al. (Eds.): IVA 2007, LNAI 4722, pp. 364–365, 2007.

conversation and transition between the states. Script unifies input pattern matching cases for the each of 3 modes.

In the system output, in English and Japanese mode ECA's speech is generated by TTS engine. For Croatian we use pre-recorded audio files of a real human voice and lip-sync animations generated by Lip Sync system we had on out disposal [4]. ECA's speech is accompanied with cultural dependent non-verbal behaviors. In Japanese mode gestures are supported by the CAST engine [5] and look more natural. CAST generates type and timing information of spontaneous gestures from Japanese text string by using a statistical model built from analyzing human presentation video. To generate ECA's non-verbal expressions, we provide animation database with set of various non-verbal behaviors; culture dependent and non dependent animations that each developer has on his disposal when extending the system. This is practical issue because some gestures are widely used in many cultures (i.e. nodding to say that something is prohibited). Within the database we had implemented our findings on behaviors of actual Japanese and European tour guides we observed at sightseeing spots. This presents only beginning of the research on the cross-culture issue in the ECA-human interaction domain. We have started CUBE-G project [6] with the University of Augsburg to explore the cross-culture issues in depth.

GECA framework enables simple modification of an existing version of the system. In order to expand the system with another cultural domain, developer should integrate speech recognition/synthesizer engine by using one of GECA libraries we provide, and extend GSML script with specific patterns and corresponding cases for that culture. In the system output, he could also use animations from the animation database. If no recognition/synthesizer for preferred language exists, we propose solutions we used in Croatian version of the system.

Regarding the future work, besides mentioned CUBE-G project, we are concerned on detection of culture dependent non-verbal behaviors in the system input. GSML syntax is being improved to cover more complex situations in ECA-human conversations and we also intend to extend animation database with more expressions.

References

[1] Huang, H., Masuda, T., Cerekovic, A., Tarasenko, K., Pandzic, I., Nakano, Y., Nishida, T.: Toward a Universal Platform for Integrating Embodied Conversational Agent Components. In: Gabrys, B., Howlett, R.J., Jain, L.C. (eds.) KES 2006. LNCS (LNAI), vol. 4252, pp. 220–226. Springer, Heidelberg (2006)

[2] OpenAIR protocol, http://www.mindmakers.org/openair/airPage.jsp

[3] AIML (Artificial Intelligence Markup Language), http://www.alicebot.org/

[4] Zoric, G., Pandzic, I.S.: A Real-time Language Independent Lip Synchronization Method Using a Genetic Algorithm. In: The Proceedings of ICME 2005 (6-8 July, 2005)

[5] Nakano, Y., Okamoto, M., Kawahara, D., Li, Q., Nishida, T.: Converting Text into Agent Animations: Assigning Gestures to Text. The Human Language Technology Conference (HLT-NAACL04) (2004)

[6] Culture-adaptive Behavior Generation for interactions with embodied conversational agents (CUBE-G), http://mm-werkstatt.informatik.uni-augsburg.de/projects/cube-g/

Towards the Specification of an ECA with Variants of Gestures

Nicolas Ech Chafai[1,2], Catherine Pelachaud[1], and Danielle Pelé[2]

[1] University of Paris 8
[2] France Télécom R&D

1 Context of the Study

The animation of an ECA, for most of animation systems, implies that its behaviour is encoded in a representation language, giving a form for each modality of a behavior. Interested in gestures, several representation languages exist already that that usually give a physical description of the necessary information for the production and reproduction of gestures, and for its synchronization with the other modalities. In our work, we aim at enriching the SAIBA description of gestures with semantic considerations, enabling an ECA to use a gesture for a wide range of applications.

2 Relevant Semantic Dimensions of Gestures

To determine which are the semantic information we need to encode in a gesture description, we have studied some families of gestures from a taxonomy specified by Calbris (1983). For the moment we have chosen to concentrate on few families of gestures, namely the ones expressing temporal meaning or temporal relations, and gestures expressing a negation for their large range of variants. For instance, if an ECA wants to deny something, it expresses a negation, and has various ways to express it. It may shake the raised hand, or the head, or just the forefinger. It may do it with one or both hands, positioning the hand at the level of the shoulder or of its chest, etc. Thus, in a particular family, we might distinguish two types of information: the dimensions of gestures that are consistent in each variant of gesture, called CD for Consistent Dimensions; the dimensions of gestures that suggest nuances in the semantic value of the global meaning, called VD for Variant Dimensions.

	Consistent dimensions
Negation	*The vertical axis of the hand position* (the hand is raised)
	Palm direction (toward the interlocutor)
	The finger direction (up)
Temporal meaning	*Hand movement* (linear along an axis)
	Relative palm direction (toward the starting position of the movement)
	Variant dimensions
Negation	*Laterality* (with one or both hands to give emphasis)
	The frontal axis of the hand position
	The vertical axis of the hand position
	The hand configuration (extended forefinger, or open hand)

C. Pelachaud et al. (Eds.): IVA 2007, LNAI 4722, pp. 366–367, 2007.

Temporal	*The frontal axis of the movement* (personal timeline)
meaning	*The vertical axis of the movement* (personal progress)
	The horizontal axis of the movement (absolute timeline)
	Hand configuration (flat hand, or extended finger)
	The action of the wrist (to specify sections in a timeline)

The choice of which variant to produce may depend on high level information such as: the personality of the ECA, the social relation that it shares with its interactants (another ECA, or the user), or even it may depend on user's conditions of viewing (*e.g.* its point of view), etc.

3 A Representation of Gestures Based on the Notion of Families of Gestures

The online version of the volume will be available in LNCS Online. Members of institutes subscribing to the Lecture Notes in Computer Science series have access to all t The ECA systems usually propose to have, on the one hand, the definition of a given gesture (stored in a repository) and to have, on the other hand, the rendering of this gesture. If we want to have the rendering of another gesture, we have to define a new complete gesture. For gestures with a slight difference, or with specific nuances, we may want to define one complete gesture, and then to define or render the others from this one. That is, we may want to integrate the notion of family presented in section 3. We have proposed a representation based on the notions of CD and VD that is fairly simple but that allows us to easily define gesture variants of a gesture, and then to allow an ECA to render variants of gestures based on higher level information as stated previously (social relations, personality of the ECA, etc.). In the near future, we aim at enlarging the scope of this study by taking into account more gestures and gesture families to precise the CD and VD elements, and then to implement the representation of gestures in an ECA in order to allow this ECA to render variants of gestures.

Acknowledgments. This research is partially supported by the FP6 Network of Excellence HUMAINE (IST-2002-2.3.1.6). We would also like to thank G. Calbris for bringing us her expertise on the domain, and for her relevant insight and advises.

References

1. Calbris, G.: Contribution à une analyse sémiologique de la mimique faciale et gestuelle française dans ses rapports avec la communication verbale. PhD thesis, vol. II (1983)
2. Kopp, S., Krenn, B., Marsella, S., Marshall, A., Pelachaud, C., Pirker, H., Thórisson, K., Vilhjalmsson, H.: Towards a Common Framework for Multimodal Generation: The Behavior Markup Language. In: Gratch, J., Young, M., Aylett, R., Ballin, D., Olivier, P. (eds.) IVA 2006. LNCS (LNAI), vol. 4133, Springer, Heidelberg (2006)

AI-RPG Toolkit: Towards A Deep Model
Implementation for Improvisational Virtual Drama

Chung-Cheng Chiu[1], Edward Chao-Chun Kao[2],
Paul Hsueh-Min Chang[1], and Von-Wun Soo[1,2,3]

AI laboratory in
[1] Department of Computer Science
[2] Institute of Information System and Applications
National Tsing Hua University
[3] Department of Computer Engineering and Information Science,
National University of Kaohsiung
{redjava,edkao,pchang,soo}@cs.nthu.edu.tw

The form of improvisational drama allows participants to have their own choices to influence the ongoing story, and each play results in a different ending. However, authoring such story contents requires ad hoc scripting, and static story structures lose ingenuity once users hacked through them. Our purpose is to develop a toolkit for: (1) fast authoring the story content, and (2) allow it for repeated plays yet retaining fresh interactive experience. While most similar applications have explicit, sophisticated story structures to ensure the number of possible interactions and endings in specific situations, we argue that characters should have enough background knowledge to make any improvisational choices. The more knowledge they have, the more sophisticated course of actions they may express. As a result, we take a deep-model approach to implement virtual agents, allowing them to deliberate and act with established knowledge in unexpected situations.

Our methodology integrates the standardized web ontology language (OWL) from W3C into the game engine. OWL is utilized to define relations of concepts in descriptions of environments, e.g. the functionalities of objects, and personal traits in virtual dramas, e.g. motivation rules which map beliefs to desires in BDI agent structure. In a fashion of three-layered architecture which divides the system into agents, settings, and actual data, the character agents may infer their course of actions according to their strategies, sustained by settings defined in OWL to conceptualize the actual data. Defining background settings and possible storylines in OWL has many advantages, as OWL has many predefined classes of relations to build a well-structured knowledge base, and is portable to any other characters as long as they support this standard. As a result, the development of agent architecture and storylines can be separated as the situation when using scripts, but the knowledge created in OWL can be easily ported to any other applications effortlessly. The reuse of knowledge enables fast authoring of the story contents, and the accumulating background knowledge behind scenarios potentially allows characters to perform different behaviors. As this toolkit is still in an early stage of development, and knowledge base is far from exhaustive, it is sufficient for virtual agents to start an improvisational drama defined in OWL.

Acknowledgments. This research is supported by National Science Council of ROC under grant number NSC 93-2213-E-007-061.

Attention Based, Naive Strategies, for Guiding Intelligent Virtual Agents

Damien Clauzel[1], Claudia Roda[1], Laurent Ach[2], and Benoît Morel[2]

[1] American University of Paris, Paris, France
{dClauzel,cRoda}@AUP.fr
[2] La Cantoche, Paris, France
{lAch,bMorel}@Cantoche.fr

1 General Aspect

The AtGentive project[1,2] focuses on the support of attention in learning environments. To achieve this objective the system analyses the learners' computer activities and physical states and, on the basis of this analysis, it generates interventions. Such interventions either supply learners with information useful to support their current attentional focus, or are aimed at attracting the user's attention to new foci.

The AtGentive system communicates with the user using a wide range of modalities including an IVA controlled by an external Reasoning Module (the system's component generating the interventions). The IVA's behaviour is guided by parametrized scripts. The scripts' parameters (mood, strength) are computed by the Reasoning Module based on models of the users and of the tasks they are performing.

2 The Reasoning Module

The Reasoning Module is in charge of processing the data sent by the application and other external components in order to produce interventions aimed at supporting users' attentional processes. These interventions are used for providing suggestion to the application and triggering the IVA (see figure 1).

Several studies have demonstrated that human's feelings towards virtual agent's interventions play an important role on whether the help and suggestions will actually be taken in consideration by the user. Supplying useful information is a necessary but not sufficient condition for a successful interaction. A study conducted on the intervention types generated by the AtGentive system suggests that, in order to establish productive interactions, the IVA should be likeable and offer advice that is timely and believable[3].

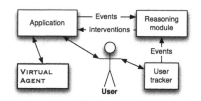

Fig. 1. General communication between the components

C. Pelachaud et al. (Eds.): IVA 2007, LNAI 4722, pp. 369–370, 2007.

AtGentive systems select the time of the intervention depending on the desired impact on the user's current attentional state[4]. Several strategies can be used to setup the strength and mood of IVA's interventions (empathy, positive reinforcement...) based on the learning method employed in the application. The AtGentive system chooses the mode of intervention depending on the user activity and the information that needs to be communicated.

3   The IVA

The purpose of the IVA Module is to receive and process requests for IVA interventions according to a previously defined general intervention model and to adapt these interventions to different environments and graphical contexts. This module is integrated in the application in a way that clearly separates the content of IVA's generic interventions from application processes, and also separates the necessary references to graphical user interface from the generic intervention data.

Two components constitute the AtGentive Embodied Agent Module: the script generator which produces a page describing an Embodied Agent intervention, and the script player which is responsible for playing the script in the browser.

An intervention of the embodied agent is described by an XML script (or template script). It is composed of speech, animations, expressions and other actions. Any action in the script may be assigned a name (as an XML attribute) so that it can be changed from a context script (another XML file). Context scripts control the selection of actions in template scripts, according to parameters mood (of the virtual character) and strength (of the intervention).

References

1. Roda, C., Nabeth, T.: The atgentive project: Attentive agents for collaborative learners. In: Nejdl, W., Tochtermann, K. (eds.) EC-TEL 2006. LNCS, vol. 4227, Springer, Heidelberg (2006)
2. The AtGentive Consortium: The AtGentive project. Partially sponsored by the European Community under the FP6 framework project IST-4-027529-STP (2005-2007) http://www.AtGentive.com
3. Rudman, P., Zajicek, M.: Autonomous agent as helper - helpful or annoying? In: IAT 2006 - IEEE/WIC/ACM International Conference on Intelligent Agent Technology, Honk Kong (2006)
4. Bailey, B., Konstan, J.: On the need for attention aware systems: Measuring the effects of interruption on task - performance, error rate, and affective state. In: Computers in Human Behavior, pp. 685–708 (2006)

Behavioural Reactive Agents for Video Game Opponents with Personalities

Carlos Delgado-Mata[1,2,3] and Jesús Ibáñez-Martínez[4]

[1] Nibbo Studios, Michoacán 200-B, CP 20270, Aguascalientes,México
[2] Universidad Panamericana, Campus Bonaterra, Aguascalientes, CP 20290, México
[3] Heriot Watt University, Riccarton Campus, Edinburgh, EH14 4AS, UK
[4] Department of Technology, University Pompeu Fabra, Barcelona, Spain

Abstract. Nowadays, the video gaming experience is shifting from merely realistic to believable. The behaviour of the computer driven player and non-playing characters is often poor when compared to their visual appearance. In this sense, there has been a recent interest in improving the video gaming experience with novel Artificial Intelligence (AI) techniques. This paper presents a robotics inspired behavioural AI to simulate characters' personalities in a commercial video game.

1 AI to Produce Personality Traits

The model described here is applied to control the user's opponent in the video-game Überpong, which is somehow an evolution of the classic Pong. Überpong provides different characters with distinctive personality profiles. The aim of the game is to score more points than the opponent. The game is played via a paddle composed of a spring and two small spheres. The paddle spring is affected by spring physics, and thus, the ball can be affected in several ways. One is by tightening and loosening the tension of the spring as the ball collides with it. Another is by moving the paddle direction as the ball collides with paddle, and thus, change the direction of the ball by applying an effect. The computer driven player uses different strategies to affect the ball's acceleration and direction, depending on their personality trait. The players are also provided with special items (power ups) that can be used to affect the properties of the ball, one's own paddle, and the opponent's paddle. It is important for the computer driven player to use effective and compelling strategies to attack, defend, apply effects to the ball and also use items according to its personality profile. The AI is defined using four kind of parameters which are described next.

How the opponent approaches the ball's destination. There are three methods used. The first is simply to follow the ball. The second one is an erratic version of the first one, and the third one is a predictive algorithm that computes where the ball is estimated to arrive when it crosses the plane described by the x position of the AI driven player. In all the cases, there is a simple vision system to restrict vision between a near and a far plane. Parameters were also added to simulate decay in the quality of perception close to the far plane.

C. Pelachaud et al. (Eds.): IVA 2007, LNAI 4722, pp. 371–372, 2007.

First Set of Parameters to define Personality. These parameters define the personality traits aggressive, sad and fearful. The opponent with an aggressive personality trait tries to accelerate the ball by loosening the paddle before the ball approaches and then it tightens the paddle as the ball is colliding with the paddle's spring. The fearful opponent tries to de-accelerate the ball by tightening the paddle before the ball approaches and then loosening the paddle as the ball collides, and the sad player just plays a safe game and keeps the paddle stretched all the time.

Second Set of Parameters to define Personality. These parameters define the personality traits audacious and cautious. The opponent with an audacious personality trait applies ball effects (and therefore changes the flow of the expected answer), whilst the AI driven player with a cautious personality trait does not.

Third Set of Parameters to define Personality. These parameters define the personality traits impulsive, predictable and analytic. The opponent with an impulsive personality trait uses the power-up as they receive it (a knee jerk reaction), the opponent with a predictable personality trait will wait x seconds to apply the power up. The opponent with an analytic personality trait 'analyses' the moment to cause the most damage to the opponent.

2   Conclusion

The video game Überpong was developed by Nibbo Studios (figure 1 shows a screenshot). This game has won several awards; one is the first place for a video game company of the 2006 video game development competition organised by the Mexican chapter of the International Game Developers Association, the Electronic Gamming Show, and the Economy Secretary. It has also been praised by two Independent Game Festival judges.

Fig. 1. Opponent (on the right) is preparing its move

Acknowledgements

The authors would like to thank the developers and artists involved in Überpong. Special thanks to Oscar Miguel Guillén Hernandez (Creative Lead) and Pier Paolo Guillén Hernandez (Programming Lead).

Adapting Hierarchical Social Organisation by Introducing Fear into an Agent Architecture

Pablo Lucas dos Anjos, Ruth Aylett, and Alison Cawsey

Heriot-Watt University, Edinburgh, EH14 4AS,
School of Mathematical and Computer Sciences
{anjos,ruth,alison}@macs.hw.ac.uk

Abstract. This paper considers possible affective roles in an agent-based social simulation, and in particular the effect of adding a simple model of fear into a replication of an agent-based social simulation.

Keywords: Agent architecture, emergence, organisation, and action-selection.

Agent models have been used for studying social interaction, both in human and in primate societies [1, 2, 5]. It has been shown how individual aggressive behaviours can contribute to the formation of groups and social rank adaptation in primate societies [3, 4]. In this paper we present a study investigating the effect of adding fear-based reaction to a replication of the Dominance World (DomWorld) model [3] since research has not yet explored this type of affect using a computational model.

DomWorld [3, 4] and its precursor framework MIRROR [5, 6] are the most analysed agent simulations of rank-based social organisation using aggressive interactions in social primate behaviour. DomWorld focuses on homogeneous agents that execute differentiated male and female pre-fixed behavioural rules in a grid. These include a one-unit forward move, direction rotations and interactions with other entities occupying adjacent cells. The rank dynamics is dependent on the agent settings, as they influence the intensity and frequency of dominance interactions. Each agent initially checks if its personal space of 2 cells was invaded, and may execute grouping or dominance related behaviours that adjust the social hierarchy. The model was extended for the current study by: (a) increasing the maximum executable agents to 40, and (b) introducing the concept of reactive fear as a local interference to female behaviour during the attractive period to male agents.

Ten runs of the extended model containing 160 epochs of 200 simulation cycles were executed for six different configurations. The results showed that when female fear is activated (+F) in cases of both high (>AGG) and low aggressive configurations, the numbers of interactions are significantly lower than without fear (-F). While total male interactions and aggressions are high throughout the simulations with enabled attraction (+ATT), simulating agents without fear (-F) increase their chance of interacting as no female will attempt to avoid males approaching their nearby personal space of 2 units. When fear is introduced in a highly aggressive configuration with attraction (>AGG, +ATT, +F), female agents perform much more dominance interactions than in simulations with high aggression and attraction but without fear (>AGG, +ATT, -F). Conversely, the total number of non-aggressive interactions tends to decrease under the same conditions of >AGG, +ATT, +F.

C. Pelachaud et al. (Eds.): IVA 2007, LNAI 4722, pp. 373–374, 2007.
© Springer-Verlag Berlin Heidelberg 2007

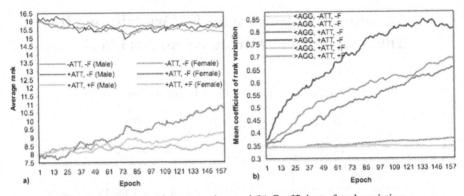

Fig. 1. (a) Ranks in high aggression, and (b) Coefficient of rank variation

Figure 1 (a) shows how male and female average ranks evolve over the simulated epochs in different configurations of high aggression; while (b) indicates their average variation. Higher values represent a steeper social hierarchy. Occasionally some females have higher ranks than males. However, the non-dashed lines in (a) shows the supremacy of male ranks. Female ranks tend to improve most when the simulation is configured with attraction and without fear (+ATT, -F), but (b) shows the coefficient practically stable in these conditions. When fear is introduced in highly aggressive configurations with attraction (b) >AGG, +ATT, +F, females tend to have better ranks than without attraction or fear. The coefficient is smaller than >AGG, +ATT, -F, and somewhat higher than in simulations configured as >AGG, -ATT, -F. This revised model occasionally favours the ability of some agents to achieve –or maintain– higher ranks. This was better observed in female ranks, as in configurations of enabled attraction, together with fear and intense aggression, males engage in more aggressive interactions among themselves but conflicts between genders are less frequent than without fear. When fear is introduced, the difference between ranks can decrease simply by interfering in the pattern of aggressive interactions. This is an example of how reactive behavioural rules and differences in internal state can play an important role on action-selection and the primate-like social organisation of artificial agents.

References

1. Dunbar, R.I.M.: Modeling Primate Behavioural Ecology. International Journal of Primatology 24(4) (2002)
2. Huffman, M.A.: Acquisition of innovative cultural behaviours in nonhuman primates: a case study of stone handling, a socially transmitted behaviour in Japanese macaques. In: Cecilia, M.H., Bennett, G., Galef, J. A. (eds.) Social Learning in Animals, pp. 267–289 (1996)
3. Hemelrijk, C.K.: Understanding Social Behaviour with the Help of Complexity Science (Invited Article). Ethology 108(8), 655–671 (2002)
4. te Boekhorst, I.J.A., Hogeweg, P.: Self-structuring in artificial CHIMPs offers new hypotheses for male grouping in chimpanzees. Behaviour 130, 229–252 (1994)
5. Flack, J.C., de Waal, F.B.M.: Dominance style, social power, and conflict management in macaque societies: A conceptual framework. In: Thierry, B., Singh, M., Kaumanns, W. (eds.) Macaque Societies: A Model for the Study of Social Organization, pp. 157–181. Cambridge University Press, England (2004)

Roles of a Talking Head in a Cooperative Human-Robot Dialogue System*

Mary Ellen Foster

Informatik VI: Echtzeitsysteme und Robotik
Fakultät für Informatik, Technische Universität München
Boltzmannstraße 3, 85748 Garching bei München, Germany
foster@in.tum.de

The JAST human-robot dialogue system [1] is designed as a platform to integrate empirical findings on cognition and cooperative dialogue with research on autonomous robots by supporting multimodal human-robot collaboration on a construction task. The robot consists of a pair of mechanical arms with grippers, mounted in a position to resemble human arms, and a Philips iCat animatronic talking head [2]. The user and the robot work together to assemble construction toys on a common work area, coordinating their actions through speech, gestures, and facial displays. Fig. 1 shows the set-up of the robot.

The talking head has three distinct functions in the JAST system. It moves its lips to accompany the synthesised speech; it produces a range of facial expressions; and it modifes its gaze direction to look at the user or at specific locations on the table. Lip-synchronisation is straightforward to implement in the iCat software and plays a clear role in adding to the naturalness of the output. However, the other two functions of the animated head require more sophisticated implementations and have a more complex effect on the system output.

The facial expressions of the talking head may accompany specific parts of the speech—for example, the head might raise its eyebrows to emphasise a particular word or phrase in the output, or look pleased while thanking the user for helping with a task. Other displays may be produced independent of speech to provide non-verbal feedback or back-channeling, such as displaying a "thinking" expression while processing the user input, nodding to indicate agreement, or looking confused to indicate that there are problems with the speech-recognition system. Producing appropriate facial expressions requires a mechanism for choosing the correct commands and coordinating them with the output on other channels and with the user's behaviours.

The gaze direction of the talking head can be controlled to look at objects on the table when it manipulates or refers to them, and to look at the user's face when it addresses them directly. As well, gaze direction can be used as a form of fast, imprecise pointing, as the head is able to change position much more quickly than the robot arms. To include all of these behaviours in the system, the output planner must have access to the location of the user and of all objects in the world; it must also select appropriate gaze changes to include in the output

---

* This research was supported by the EU project JAST (FP6-003747-IP).

C. Pelachaud et al. (Eds.): IVA 2007, LNAI 4722, pp. 375–376, 2007.

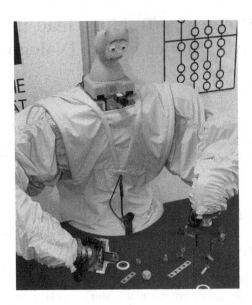

Fig. 1. Set-up of the robot in the JAST dialogue system

and, as for facial expressions, must coordinate the selected behaviours with the output on other channels and with the user's behaviours.

A number of studies have demonstrated that the expressiveness of an embodied agent—physical or virtual—has a significant effect on the experience of users of interactive systems. For example, a version of the Mel robot agent that used a full range of expressive and gaze behaviours increased user engagement the system [3]; the expressive facial displays of the animated virtual agent in the COMIC dialogue system mitigated the slowness of the system [5]; while the Leonardo robot [4] actually communicates entirely through body language and gestures. We expect the facial displays and gaze feedback of the embodied head in the JAST human-robot system to have a similarly positive effect on users' interactions with the system.

References

1. Foster, M.E., By, T., Rickert, M., Knoll, A.: Human-robot dialogue for joint construction tasks. In: Proceedings, 8th International Conference on Multimodal Interfaces (ICMI '06), pp. 68–71 (2006)
2. van Breemen, A.J.N.: iCat: Experimenting with animabotics. In: Proceedings, AISB 2005 Creative Robotics Symposium (2005)
3. Sidner, C.L., Lee, C., Kidd, C.D., Lesh, N., Rich, C.: Explorations in engagement for humans and robots. Artificial Intelligence 166(1-2), 140–164 (2005)
4. Breazeal, C., Brooks, A., Gray, J., Homan, G., Kidd, C., Lee, H., Lieberman, J., Lockerd, A., Chilongo, D.: Tutelage and collaboration for humanoid robots. International Journal of Humanoid Robotics 1(2), 315–348 (2004)
5. White, M., Foster, M.E., Oberlander, J., Brown, A.: Using facial feedback to enhance turn-taking in a multimodal dialogue system. In: Proceedings, HCI International 2005. (2005)

Modeling Imitational Behavior Via Social Comparison Theory
(Extended Abstract)

Natalie Fridman and Gal A. Kaminka

The MAVERICK Group
Computer Science Department
Bar Ilan University, Israel
fridman@cs'.biu.ac.il, galk@cs.biu.ac.il

Abstract. Modeling crowd behaviors is an important challenge for intelligent virtual agents. We propose a general cognitive model of simulating crowd behaviors, based on Festinger's Social Comparison Theory (SCT), a prominent social psychology theory. We present the use of the SCT model (using the Soar cognitive architecture) in the generation of imitational behavior in loosely-coupled groups and show that SCT generates behavior more in-tune with human crowd behavior.

1 Introduction

Existing computer science models of crowd behavior often focus only on a specific phenomenon (e.g., flocking, pedestrian movement), and thus must be switched depending on the goals of the simulation. We propose a novel model of crowd behavior, based on Social Comparison Theory (SCT) [1], a popular social psychology theory. The key idea in this theory is that humans, lacking objective means to evaluate their state, compare themselves to others that are similar.

Elsewhere [2], we described the SCT algorithm and showed that SCT covers a variety of pedestrian movement phenomena. In this short abstract we describe the implementation of SCT model in Soar cognitive architecture. We evaluate the use of SCT in the generation of imitational behavior and show that SCT generates behavior more in-tune with human crowd behavior.

2 SCT Implementation in Soar

We implemented SCT in the Soar [4]. Soar was connected to the GameBots virtual environment [3]. SCT was implemented as a secondary parallel thread within Soar. Whereas normally, operators are proposed (and selected) by Soar based on their suitability for a current goal (e.g., through means-end analysis), in our agent operators were also proposed based on their suitability for SCT. The SCT thread proposed operators by following the algorithm described in [2], though in a way that is adopted for Soar's decision cycle: At every cycle, for each observed agent and for each difference with the agent, the SCT process would propose an operator that would minimize the difference. Then, a set of preference rules is triggered that ranks the proposals based on the SCT algorithm. At the end, only one SCT operator is supported.

C. Pelachaud et al. (Eds.): IVA 2007, LNAI 4722, pp. 377–378, 2007.

3   Evaluation of Imitational Behavior

We conducted experiments to evaluate whether SCT can account for imitational behavior in groups. We rely on experiments with human subjects, which judged the human crowd behavior and the resulting SCT behavior in comparison to completely individual behavior (i.e., arbitrary decisions by each agent, independently of its peers), and to completely synchronized behavior (i.e.,all agents act in complete unison).

The first hypothesis underlying the experiments was that groups controlled by SCT would generate behavior that would be ranked somewhere in-between the individual and perfect-coordination models. Another hypothesis is that human crowd behavior would also be ranked somewhere in-between the individual and perfect-coordinated behaviors.

To examine the first hypothesis, we created three screen-capture movies of 11 Soar agents in action. In all, the agents were fixed to their initial locations, and the only actions available to them were to do nothing, or turn at some angle. In all screen-capture movies there is one blue agent that stands in a front and turn up to 90° left or right. All others are red agents that act according to one of the models. We asked 12 subjects to fill a questionnaire after each movie, based on what they saw. The questions examined different aspects of the coordination of the agents, using an ordinal scale of 1–6, with 1 being a low result (associated with more individual behavior), and 6 being a high result (associated with perfect unison).

To examine the second hypothesis, we used a TV news clip, which showed a group of people standing and waiting for some event to occur; the only action they performed was to occasionally turn. 12 new subjects were asked to fill the same questionnaire after seeing *only the news clip*.

In general, the responses to the questions placed the SCT model and the human crowd in between the individual and unison models. Across all questions, the responses for the SCT model were found to be significantly different from the results of the individual-choice and unison models. The human crowd results appears to be significantly different from the individual model in all questions, however, it is significantly different from the unison model in the coordination and non-random questions but not in the relationship question.

References

1. Festinger, L.: A theory of social comparison processes. Human Relations, 117–140 (1954)
2. Fridman, N., Kaminka, G.A.: Towards a cognitive model of crowd behavior based on social comparison theory. AAAI, Stanford, California, USA (2007)
3. Kaminka, G.A., Veloso, M.M., Schaffer, S., Sollitto, C., Adobbati, R., Marshall, A.N., Scholer, A., Tejada, S.: GameBots: A flexible test bed for multiagent team research. Communications of the ACM 45(1), 43–45 (2002)
4. Newell, A.: Unified Theories of Cognition. Harvard University Press, Cambridge, Massachusetts (1990)

Social Animation in Complex Environments*

Francisco Grimaldo, Miguel Lozano, and Fernando Barber

Computer Science Department, University of Valencia,
Dr. Moliner 50, (Burjassot) Valencia, Spain
{francisco.grimaldo,miguel.lozano,fernando.barber}@uv.es

This work presents a market-based social model to produce good quality behavioral animations for groups of intelligent virtual agents. The social model coordinates the activities of groups of virtual characters and also includes social actions in the agent decision-making. We follow the Multi-Agent Resource Allocation approach presented in [2], where agents express their preferences using utility functions. The dynamics of social interactions is inspired by the theory of Piaget [3] over which we have implemented reciprocal task exchanges.

The social model proposed allows any agent to auction tasks in order to reallocate them so that the global social welfare can be increased. Tasks are exchanged between agents using a first-price sealed-bid (FPSB) auction model where the agents express their preferences using performance and social utility functions. The performance utility function $U_{perf}^i(\langle i \leftarrow t \rangle)$ of a bidder agent i reflects the efficiency achieved when the task t is allocated to the agent i ($\langle i \leftarrow t \rangle$). There can be many reasons for an agent to be more efficient: it may perform the task faster than others because of his know-how or it may be using a resource that allows several tasks to be performed simultaneously – e.g. a coffee machine in a virtual bar can be used by a waiter to make more than one coffee at the same time. Furthermore, we introduce two additional social utilities to represent the social interest in exchanging a task. We define the following social utility functions:

- Internal social utility ($U_{int}^i(\langle i \leftarrow t, j \leftarrow t_{next} \rangle)$): is the utility that a bidder agent i assigns to a situation where i commits to do the auctioned task t so that the auctioneer agent j can execute his next task t_{next}.
- External social utility ($U_{ext}^i(\langle j \leftarrow t \rangle)$): is the utility that a bidder agent i assigns to a situation where the auctioneer agent j executes the auctioned task t while i continues with his current action.

Therefore, the winner determination problem has two possible candidates coming from performance (see equation 1) and sociability (see equation 2). The social winner is determined looking at the maximum social utility received to pass the task to a bidder ($U_{int}^*(t)$) and the maximum social utility given by all bidders to the situation where the task is not exchanged but performed by the auctioneer j ($U_{ext}^*(t)$). To balance task exchange, social utilities are weighted

---

* Supported by the Spanish MEC under grants TIN2006-15516-C04-04 and Consolider Ingenio 2010 CSD2006-00046.

C. Pelachaud et al. (Eds.): IVA 2007, LNAI 4722, pp. 379–380, 2007.

with a reciprocity matrix (see equations 3 and 4). We define the reciprocity factor w_{ij} for two agents i and j, as the ratio between the number of favors – i.e.tasks – that j has made to i (see equation 5).

$$winner_{perf}(t) = \left\{ k \epsilon Agents | U^i_{perf}(t) = \max_{i \epsilon Agents} \{U^i_{perf}(\langle i \leftarrow t \rangle)\} \right. \tag{1}$$

$$winner_{soc}(t) = \begin{cases} j & U^*_{ext}(t) >= U^*_{int}(t) \\ i & U^*_{ext}(t) < U^*_{int}(t) \wedge U^i_{int}(t) = U^*_{int}(t) \end{cases} \tag{2}$$

$$U^*_{int}(t) = \max_{i \epsilon Agents} \{U^i_{int}(\langle i \leftarrow t, j \leftarrow t_{next} \rangle) * w_{ji}\} \tag{3}$$

$$U^*_{ext}(t) = \max_{i \epsilon Agents} \{U^i_{ext}(\langle j \leftarrow t \rangle) * w_{ij}\} \tag{4}$$

$$w_{ij} = Favours_{ji}/Favours_{ij} \tag{5}$$

Agents choose between performance and sociability in accordance with their *Sociability* factor, which is the probability to select the social winner instead of the performance winner. *Sociability* can be adjusted in the range [0,1] to model intermediate behaviors between efficiency and total reciprocity. This can provide great flexibility when animating characters, since *Sociability* can be dynamically changed thus producing different behaviors depending on the world state.

The social model has been tested successfully in dynamic environments using a multi-agent simulation framework [1] that allows the definition of social BDI agents. The snapshots shown in figure 1 correspond to the simulation of a virtual bar, where groups of waiters and customers can interact and finally display complex social behaviors such as negotiation among waiters to gain access to a resource, assumption of external actions/favors, or animation of simple chats.

Fig. 1. Animating interaction situations

References

1. Bordini, R.H., da Rocha, A.C., Hübner, J.F., Moreira, A.F., Okuyama, F.Y., Vieira, R.: MAS-SOC: a Social Simulation Platform Based on Agent-Oriented Programming. Journal of Artificial Societies and Social Simulation 8 (2005)
2. Hogg, L.M., Jennings, N.: Socially intelligent reasoning for autonomous agents. IEEE Transactions on System Man and Cybernetics 31(5) (2001)
3. Piaget, J.: Sociological studies. Routledge, London (1995)

A Script Driven Multimodal Embodied Conversational Agent Based on a Generic Framework

Hung-Hsuan Huang[1], Aleksandra Cerekovic[2], Igor S. Pandzic[2], Yukiko Nakano[3], and Toyoaki Nishida[1]

[1] Graduate School of Informatics, Kyoto University, Japan
[2] Faculty of Electrical Engineering and Computing, University of Zagreb, Croatia
[3] Department of Computer, Information and Communication Sciences,
Tokyo University of Agriculture & Technology, Japan
{huang,nishida}@ii.ist.i.kyoto-u.ac.jp,
{aleksandra.cerekovic,igor.pandzic}@fer.hr, nakano@cc.tuat.ac.jp

Embodied Conversational Agents (ECAs) are life-like CG characters that interact with human users in face-to-face conversations. To achieve natural conversations, they need to understand the inputs from human users, deliberate the responding behaviors and realize those behaviors in multiple modalities. They are sophisticated, require numbers of building assemblies and are thus difficult for individual research groups to develop. To facilitate result sharing and rapid prototyping of ECA researches, a Generic ECA Framework that is meant to integrate ECA assemblies seamlessly is being developed by our group. This framework is composed of a low-level communication platform (GECA Platform), a set of communication API libraries (GECA Plugs) and a high-level protocol (GECA Protocol, GECAP).

GECA Platform is an architecture based on blackboard model and XML message exchanging by subscribe-publish mechanism. There is a server that provides common services include naming service, message subscription and message forwarding managements. For the benefits of the support of two-way communication and explicit temporal model that is essential in real-time applications, a light weight protocol, OpenAIR [1] is adopted as the low-level routing protocol for the communication among the components running on the platform, GECA server and blackboard managers.

GECA Plug libraries absorb the differences caused by operation systems and programming languages to facilitate the development of the wrappers for plugging software tools into the platform. They are basically the AIR Plugs in OpenAIR context coupled with additional GECA original routines.

GECAP is a specification of core message types and XML message format exchanged among the components upon the GECA platform. Its syntax is not fixed and can be freely extended depends on the applications. Because the main interests on human-agent interactions, we currently treat the deliberate process as a black box and focus on multimodal inputs and outputs of ECA systems. In GECAP, there are three categories of messages in input phase, output phase and the ones for system uses.

The components generating input phase messages acquire sensing data of human users' behaviors and interpret them in multiple channels of modalities such as natural language speech, pointing gesture, nodding and gazing. In addition to interpreted

C. Pelachaud et al. (Eds.): IVA 2007, LNAI 4722, pp. 381–382, 2007.

sensor data, temporal information and alternative hypothesizes of the interpretation results are transferred. The only actuator of software based ECAs is the character animation player. Components send output phase messages to drive the virtual character in the player to speak and perform non-verbal animations as well as typical controls over the virtual environment such as changing the scenes where the character is in. Verbal utterance is the master channel and non-verbal behaviors that are configurable in run-time are synchronized with it. Several system message types such as the ones for component status querying are also defined.

GECA Scenario Markup Language (GSML) describing human-agent interactions and its executing component are developed to supple GECAP. It is inspired from AIML's [2] pattern-template pair that describes human-agent interactions. In addition to that, it also describes conversation states, matches multimodal patterns of user's input and triggers multimodal templates of agent's behaviors. A simplified fusion method which partially solves the ambiguities of multimodal inputs is possible with the information sent in GECAP input phase messages.

The development of the first GECA server prototype as well as C#, C++ and Java versions of GECA Plug have been completed. We have also implemented several example ECA systems for different applications, by introducing components such as Japanese spontaneous gesture generator [3], head tracker [4], hand shape recognizer, head nodding recognizer, GSML executor, speech recognizer and an animator implemented with visage|SDK [5]. The example systems include an application for experiencing cross-culture gesture differences with one avatar of the user and multiple computer controlled agents, a multimodal Dubrovnik City tour guide agent developed in the eNTERFACE'06 workshop [6], and a quiz kiosk for food science knowledge is used in the National Food Research Institute of Japan open lab events.

The goal of this project is to make the framework publicly available as a handy ECA toolkit which includes a reference agent and can be extended to more complex agent easily by it users.

References

1. OpenAIR 1.0, http://www.mindmakers.org/openair/airPage.jsp
2. Artificial Intelligence Markup Language (AIML), http://www.alicebot.org/
3. Nakano, Y., Okamoto, M., Kawahara, D., Li, Q., Nishida, T.: Converting Text into Agent Animations: Assigning Gestures to Text. In: Proceedings of The Human Language Technology Conference (2004)
4. Oka, K., Sato, Y.: Real-time modeling of a face deformation for 3D head pose estimation. In: Proc. IEEE International Workshop on Analysis and Modeling of Faces and Gestures (AMFG2005), IEEE Computer Society Press, Los Alamitos (2005)
5. visage|SDK, visage technologies, http://www.visagetechnologies.com/index.html
6. Huang, H., Cerekovic, A., Tarasenko, K., Levacic, V., Zoric, G., Treumuth, M., Pandzic, I.S., Nakano, Y., Nishida, T.: An Agent Based Multicultural User Interface in a Customer Service Application. In: the Proceedings of the eNTERFACE'06 workshop on multimodal interfaces (2006)

A Quiz Game Console Based on a Generic Embodied Conversational Agent Framework

Hung-Hsuan Huang[1], Taku Inoue[1], Aleksandra Cerekovic[2], Igor S. Pandzic[2], Yukiko Nakano[3], and Toyoaki Nishida[1]

[1] Graduate School of Informatics, Kyoto University, Japan
[2] Faculty of Electrical Engineering and Computing, University of Zagreb, Croatia
[3] Department of Computer, Information and Communication Sciences,
Tokyo University of Agriculture & Technology, Japan
{huang,inoue,nishida}@ii.ist.i.kyoto-u.ac.jp,
{aleksandra.cerekovic,igor.pandzic}@fer.hr, nakano@cc.tuat.ac.jp

This article describes an attempt to build a quiz game kiosk for show-room use based on the Generic Embodied Conversational Agent (GECA) Framework [1] that provides a general purpose architecture for connecting modularized ECA functional components for multimodal human-agent interactions.

GECA Framework is composed of three parts: GECA Platform provides common services and the facilities for low-level communication among components via XML message exchanging on shared blackboards, GECA Plugs are communication and utility APIs that absorb the differences caused by operating systems and programming languages to facilitate the development of component wrappers, GECA Protocol (GECAP) is an extensible specification of core message types and XML message format exchanged among the components. To simplify the problem, available agent-human interactions are described in a script language, GSML (GECA Scenario Markup Language) that is inspired from AIML [2]. So far, a mediating server and a set of standard GECA components include Japanese spontaneous gesture generator [3], head tracker, hand shape recognizer, head nodding recognizer, GSML executor, speech recognizer and an animator [4] have been developed.

On the other hand, the quiz game kiosk project is initiated to fulfill the demands of our client, the National Food Research Institute (NFRI) of Japan. They hold several open lab events every year and concern how to attract more visitors and how to improve the efficiency in knowledge conveyance of their research results and general educational materials to public audiences. What we conducted is to build a game console with an ECA issuing quizzes based on the following hypothesizes: comparing to static exhibits, an exhibition which the visitors can participate in should be more attractive, an embodied character who issues quizzes and explains the correct answers should make the contents more understandable and earn the visitors' concentration.

The resulted prototype is built by combining standard GECA components, GSML executor, animator and the GECA server with two additional components, a touch panel component and an emotion component. Touch panel was chosen here as the user interface because the nature of public exhibition is not appropriate to use complex sensors. To enhance the life-likeliness of the agent, the emotion component is introduced to control the agent's facial expression and the background music. It

C. Pelachaud et al. (Eds.): IVA 2007, LNAI 4722, pp. 383–384, 2007.

Fig. 1. The configuration of the NFRI quiz agent and actual circumstance of the open lab event

is basically an implementation of the PAD space model proposed in Becker et al. [5]. The quiz agent gets positive stimulation on emotion and mood axes when the visitor tries to answer the quiz, gets even higher values if the answer is correct and perceives negative stimulation when the answer is wrong. The value on boredom axis grows when there is no input from the visitor while time goes by. The emotion component continuously changes its internal state to drive the agent to shows 8 facial expressions and play 14 background melodies depending on the current state like angry, bored, concentrated, friendly, etc.

This quiz kiosk (see Fig. 1) was shown in a one-day public open lab event of NFRI on April 20th, 2007 and was the first real-life use of GECA agents. Typical visitors were the people who study or live in the neighborhood. Each game session contains 10 quizzes relating to general knowledge about food science. The quizzes are selected randomly from a total number of 43. In the six-hour event time, there were totally 307 visitors in small groups played the kiosk and initiated 87 game sessions. Almost during the whole day, there were dozens of visitors waiting for playing the game, therefore we considered that the basic idea was very successful in attracting the visitors. Besides, from questionnaire investigation, most of the visitors reported that they enjoyed the game and felt that the knowledge explained by the agent is trustable. Overall, because the success obtained in this event, the constant setup of this kiosk in the showroom of NFRI is scheduled from October 2007.

References

1. Huang, H., Cerekovic, A., Pandzic, I., Nakano, Y., Nishida, T.: A Script Driven Multimodal Embodied Conversational Agent Based on a Generic Framework. In: IVA 2007. LNCS, vol. 4722, pp. 381–382. Springer, Heidelberg (2007)
2. Artificial Intelligence Markup Language (AIML), http://www.alicebot.org/
3. Nakano, Y., Okamoto, M., Kawahara, D., Li, Q., Nishida, T.: Converting Text into Agent Animations: Assigning Gestures to Text. In: Proceedings of The Human Language Technology Conference (2004)
4. visage|SDK, visage technologies, http://www.visagetechnologies.com/index.html
5. Becker, C., Kopp, S., Wachsmuth, I.: Simulating the emotion dynamics of a multimodal conversational agent. In: Proceedings on Tutorial and Research Workshop on Affective Dialogue Systems (ADS-04), pp. 154–165 (2004)

AVSML: An XML-Based Markup Language for Web Information Integration in 3D Virtual Space

Yasuhiko Kitamura[1], Yatsuho Shibata[2], Keisuke Tokuda[2], Kazuki Kobayashi[2], and Noriko Nagata[1]

[1] School of Science and Technology, Kwansei Gakuin University
[2] Graduate School of Science and Technology, Kwansei Gakuin University
2-1 Gakuen, Sanda, Hyogo 669-1337, Japan
{ykitamura,scbc1030,tokuda,kby,nagata}@ksc.kwansei.ac.jp

3D virtual space can visually represent the spatial structure to users and it has been applied to many fields such as city planning, navigation, education, entertainment and so on. In the 3D virtual space, an agent can navigate a user in an interactive manner [5]. Various platforms to build a 3D virtual space and languages to control the agents have been proposed [1,2,3,4]. For example, VKSC (Virtual Kobe Sanda Campus) is a 3D virtual space of Kobe Sanda Campus, Kwansei Gakuin University [1]. In VKSC, an agent called Suzie guides a user in the campus upon his/her request.

3D virtual space gets more reality by integrating the real-world information such as the time, weather and the corresponding information of objects in it. Various sensor data can be used to represent the real-world information, but the Web information also can be used though it may be indirect and incomplete real-world information. If the virtual space is tightly connected to the corresponding Web information, it gets more reality [1]. Web information suppliers can inform the latest information to the users through the 3D virtual space and the users experience it in the virtual space.

How to integrate a 3D virtual space and the corresponding Web information is an interesting research issue. It is not good to hard-code the integration process but the process should be open in order that anybody can be involved in the integration. We are developing an XML-based markup language called AVSML (Agent and Virtual Space Markup Language) to integrate Web information that is distributed in a number of Web sites in a 3D virtual space. When a 3D virtual space is tightly connected to the Web information, it changes depending on the update. This means that an agent that inhabits in the space should be adaptive to the change. We are developing a guide agent that autonomously adapts to changes of the 3D virtual space.

We assume that 3D virtual space is composed of objects and agents. Objects are passive entities like buildings, gates and the background. Agents are active entities that can move in the virtual space and interact with the user through chatting. In our work, the Web information related to the objects in the virtual space is integrated as shown in Fig. 1. Some Web information can be visually represented in the virtual space. For example, a gate of building in the virtual space can be open or closed according to the Web information about the building and the background changes depending on the weather information from the Web. The other information may not be represented visually, but it can be presented by an agent. For example, an agent can explain that the School of Science and Technology is located in the building.

C. Pelachaud et al. (Eds.): IVA 2007, LNAI 4722, pp. 385–386, 2007.

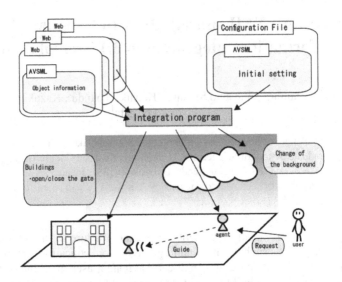

Fig. 1. Integrating Web information in 3D virtual space

As shown in Fig. 1, the integration program collects the related Web and reflects it in the 3D virtual space. If a user gives a request to an agent, the agent guides him/her in the virtual space.

To integrate the Web information in a virtual space, we need a language to describe that. It is not good to hard-code the process by using a programming language such as Java, because it is not easy to maintain the relation between the virtual space and the Web information. We are so developing an XML-based markup language called AVSML. XML is easy to be understood by human and easy to be attached to Web pages. Agents move around in the 3D virtual space and guide a user. If the virtual space changes according to the Web information, the agents need to adapt to the change. We can describe agent behavior as rules in AVSML to cope with this problem. For example, if a gate is closed on the way to a destination, the agent can choose an alternative route that is written in rules.

References

1. Kitamura, Y., et al.: Toward Web Information Integration on 3D Virtual Space. In: Kishino, F., Kitamura, Y., Kato, H., Nagata, N. (eds.) ICEC 2005. LNCS, vol. 3711, pp. 445–455. Springer, Heidelberg (2005)
2. Nischt, M., et al.: MPML3D: A Reactive Framework for the Multimodal Presentation Markup Language. In: Gratch, J., Young, M., Aylett, R., Ballin, D., Olivier, P. (eds.) IVA 2006. LNCS (LNAI), vol. 4133, pp. 218–229. Springer, Heidelberg (2006)
3. T.Ishida, Q.: Description Language for Interactive Agents. IEEE Computer 35(11), 42–47 (2002)
4. Ishida, T.: Digital City Kyoto: Social Information Infrastructure for Everyday Life. CACM 45(7), 76–81 (2002)
5. Prendinger, H., Ishizuka, M. (eds.): Life-Like Characters: Tools, Affective Functions, and Applications. Springer, Heidelberg (2004)

Simulation Environment for Anticipatory Behaving Agents from the Artificial Life Domain

Karel Kohout and Pavel Nahodil

Department of Cybernetics, Czech Technical University in Prague,
Karlovo náměstí 13, 121 35 Prague, Czech Republic
{kohoutk,nahodil}@fel.cvut.cz

Abstract. Our research is focused on simulation of agents - animates. The architecture of these agents is mainly inspired by nature therefore they are sometimes called artificial creatures. The main contribution of this paper is the description of designed simulation environment architecture for the Artificial Life (ALife) domain. It was named the World of Artificial Life (WAL). Our platform incorporates results of research in domain of hybrid agent architectures.

Keywords: Anticipation, ALife, Hybrid Architecture, Behavior, Animate, Artificial creatures.

1 Introduction - State of the Art

The field of ALife simulators is very diverse. Most of freely available simulators are concerned with only one phenomenon of ALife i.e. cellular automaton, boids or bimorph simulators. There are only few general simulators such as StarLogo [2], Swarm [4] or Cormas [5]. These simulators still did not suit our requirements. There is a successor of StarLogo called StarLogoTNG [3]. Preview version has been released in April 2007. Our need for robust simulation environment emerged three years ago and first implementation of WAL appeared in 2004 hence StarLogo TNG was not considered.

2 Designed Architecture

We divided the work in two parts. WAL Abstract Architecture (WALA^2) was separated from its implementation (WAL) for even more robustness and modularity (this was inspired by FIPA Abstract Architecture). WALA^2 provides implementation free description of the simulation environment and its interfaces with the program surroundings (modules). The implementation of this architecture is described in detail in [1]. The simulator consists of engine (data representation), layers, agents and interface to modules (visualization, analysis, parameterization). The core is the engine (platform). It controls run of the simulation on a program level (synchronization, data structure maintenance). There are two components of the environment layers and agents. In one simulation step engine asks all layers to

C. Pelachaud et al. (Eds.): IVA 2007, LNAI 4722, pp. 387–388, 2007.

evaluate actions of all agents and perform environmental changes as an effect of these actions if there are any. The distribution of action evaluation to layers means distribution of simulation control so that each layer can run in different computation thread. Layers define the virtual world and its "physical" laws. The layer is a logically separable part of the environment which combined with other layers defines the virtual environment as whole. According to the executed actions of the agents the layer will modify its own values and will provide a new sensory data. There were two types of layers point (past states not considered) and gradient (past states considered). Under "agent" we understand any object in simulation either virtually alive (creature) or virtually non-living (trees, food, water, etc...). The agent consists of two parts the body and the mind. The mind of an agent communicates with the body through data from sensors and action of effectors, communication between body and mind is done via message sending. Even agents own state has to be observed by sensors. This covers also the state of agent's sensors and effectors (some of them can be damaged or partially malfunctioning). With our simplified sensors we avoid recognition problem, which is every living creature performing. Also effectors execute the effect of the selected action directly (for example motion is done by moving to the desired position). Agent mind and control are not part of the environment. For visualization external visualization module (3D) or internal (2D, default) can be used.

3 Results and Conclusion

In this paper, we have introduced the simulation environment architecture. It was used by several agent architectures designed in various programming languages (C, Java, Matlab). With respect to the abstract architecture they were capable of running in WAL environment. In the near future we want to extend this architecture to fully distributed. Our goal now it to program WAL server application capable of running agents implemented on client side or hosted on the server itself. This way we want to compare our results in the field of agent design with other researchers.

Acknowledgment. This research has been supported by the Ministry of Education, Youth and Sports of the Czech Republic as a part of the specific research at the CTU in Prague.

References

[1] Kohout, K.: The Simulation of Animates Behavior and its Visualization. Diploma Thesis at the CTU, FEE, Dept. of Cybernetics, supervised by Nahodil, P., Prague (2004)

[2] StarLogo on the Web [online]. Last Rev: (March 2007), http://education.mit.edu/starlogo/

[3] StarLogo, TNG,: [online]. Last Rev. (March 2007), http://education.mit.edu/starlogo-tng/

[4] The Swarm Development Group [online]. Last Rev. (June 2007), http://wiki.swarm.org

[5] Natural Resources and Multi-Agent Simulations [online]. Last Rev. (November 2006),http://cormas.cirad.fr/indexeng.htm

Towards an Architecture for Aligned Speech and Gesture Production

Stefan Kopp and Kirsten Bergmann

Artificial Intelligence Group, University of Bielefeld,
P.O. Box 100131, 33501 Bielefeld, Germany
{skopp,kbergman}@techfak.uni-bielefeld.de

The automatic production of speech and gesture is one of the most challenging issues in building embodied conversational agents, due to the intricacy of how the two modalities seem to "align" with each other. Based on experiences from computational approaches and inspired by current theoretical modeling attempts, we propose an architecture to simulate how on-the-spot speech and gesture production might run and bring about more natural multimodal behavior.

Many empirical findings indicate that the interplay between speech and gesture in forming multimodal utterances is complex and highly influenced by contextual aspects like the given communicative intention, the information state, or verbalizability constraints (cf. [1]). From the models that Psycholinguistics offers in order to explain these data, the model proposed by Kita & Özyürek [2] currently seems to be most adequate. This model is characterized by a close interaction between processes that form and balance linguistic and gesture meaning. In contrast, computational models usually employ, inadequately, predefined lexicons of coarse-grained language and gesture templates. To overcome this shortcoming recent systems break down the production process in an unidirectional, three-staged architecture inherited from natural language generation (content planning, microplanning, surface realization).

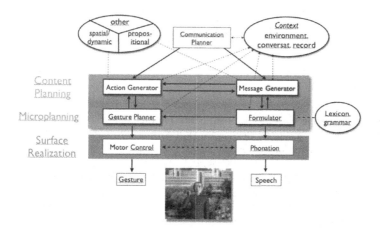

Fig. 1. The architecture for the production of aligned speech and gesture

C. Pelachaud et al. (Eds.): IVA 2007, LNAI 4722, pp. 389–390, 2007.

The architecture we propose for aligned speech and gesture production (see Figure 1) allows for a decisive interplay between both modality strands. Further, the stages of content planning and microplanning are connected bidirectionally and are simultaneously engaged in the iterative process of working towards a multimodal utterance. At first, an underlying communicative intention is generated by the *Communication Planner* and forwarded to both an *Action Generator* and a *Message Generator*. The former selects a visuo-spatial representation of the referent and a "gesture practice". This is due to the fact that the same referent may be depicted, e.g., by contouring its shape (practice shaping) or by a static configuration standing for the object itself (modelling). Characteristic features of the refernt are now filtered and used to attune the chosen gesture practice. The Message Generator selects propositional knowledge from the underlying knowledge base. Both generators interface with each other and reconcile their respective content representations. The resulting distribution of meaning depends on the modality-specific capacity for representing certain types of information (visuo-spatial vs. propositional), as well as the communicative goals at hand or the dialog context.

The *Formulator* receives the propositions generated by the Message Generator and carries out sentence planning. This processing can impact the distribution of meaning, since the Formulator reports back to the Message Generator on whether a message is verbalizable and to which degree. Similarly, the *Gesture Planner* receives the imagistic representation from the Action Generator and reports back on what semantic structures can be expressed within a gesture. The four modules interact until an adequate multimodal encoding of the intended message is achieved (trying to encode as much semantic features as possible–starting with the most important, focused ones–as fast as possible). Temporal coordination of coexpressive verbal and gesture elements is achieved via a direct link between Formulator and Gesture Generator. *Motor Control* and *Phonation* are concerned with the realization of synthetic speech and hand/arm animation and are realized by our existing virtual human Max [3]. Informed by an empirical study on spontaneous speech and gesture in direction-giving, ongoing work is addressing the four core parts and their workings in this architectural framework.

Acknowledgements. This research is partially supported by the Deutsche Forschungsgemeinschaft (DFG) in the Collaborative Research Center 673 "Alignment in Communication".

References

1. Bergmann, K., Kopp, S.: Verbal or Visual: How Information is Distributed across Speech and Gesture in Spatial Dialog. In: Schlangen, D., Fernandez, R. (eds.) Proceedings of the 10th Workshop on the Semantics and Pragmatics of Dialogue, pp. 90–97 (2006)
2. Kita, S., Özyürek, A.: What Does Cross-Linguistic Variation in Semantic Coordination of Speech and Gesture Reveal? Evidence for an Interface Representation of Spatial Thinking and Speaking. Journal of Memory and Language 48, 16–32 (2003)
3. Kopp, S., Wachsmuth, I.: Synthesizing Multimodal Utterances for Conversational Agents. Computer Animation and Virtual Worlds 15(1), 39–52 (2004)

Avatar Puppetry Using Real-Time Audio and Video Analysis

Sylvain Le Gallou[1,2], Gaspard Breton[1], Renaud Séguier[2],
and Christophe Garcia[1]

[1] France Telecom, TECH/IRIS Team,
rue du Clos Courtel, Cesson-Sévigné, France
`firstname.lastname@orange-ftgroup.com`
[2] Supélec/IETR, SCEE Team, avenue de la Boulaie,
Cesson-Sévigné, France
`firstname.lastname@supelec.fr`

Abstract. We present a system which consists of a lifelike agent animated in real-time using video and audio analysis from the user. This kind of system could be used for Instant Messaging where an avatar controlled like a puppet is displayed instead of the webcam flow. The overall system is made of video analysis based on Active Appearance Models and audio analysis based on Hidden Markov Model. The parameters from these two modules are sent to a control system driving the animation engine. The video analysis extracts the head orientation and the audio analysis provides the phonetic string used to move the lips.

1 System Overview

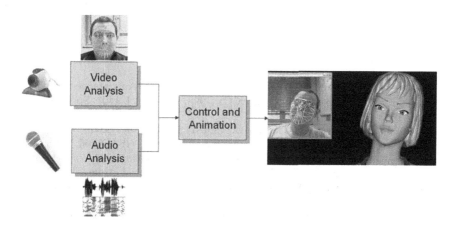

Fig. 1. Overview of the pupettry system

C. Pelachaud et al. (Eds.): IVA 2007, LNAI 4722, pp. 391–392, 2007.

2   Video Analysis

In order to do video analysis of faces, we carried out a face alignment based on the Active Appearance Model (AAM) method [1]. AAM is a deformable model method which allows shape and texture to be jointly synthesized by statistical shape and texture models. The creation of the statistical shape and texture model is performed by learning from a database of different examples of faces. In order to be able to compute the orientation of the head, the model has learned from a database containing various faces with different expressions and orientations. We also implemented a preprocessing step in order to improve the robustness of the AAM illumination variations. Indeed we carried out the adaptive histogram equalization as a preprocessing on images before the AAM method like [2]. This method provides a good video flow analysis of faces without limitations in background and illuminations.

3   Audio Analysis

The audio analysis is performed using a common HMM model learned from several speakers in a noisy environment. The system is multi-speaker and works for both genders. The phonetic segmentation is performed in real time on 64ms buffers allowing a really short delay.

4   Control and Animation

The animation is performed using the FaceEngine 3D animation system [3] which works in real-time. The head movements are computed using a behavior engine [4] taking into account biological constraints such as the vestibulo-ocular reflex and the head inertia. Lips movements are performed using a co-articulation algorithm [5] blending the visemes corresponding to the phonetic string returned by the audio analysis.

References

1. Cootes, T.F., Edwards, G.J., Taylor, C.J.: Active Appearance Models. In: Burkhardt, H., Neumann, B. (eds.) ECCV 1998. LNCS, vol. 1407, Springer, Heidelberg (1998)
2. Le Gallou, S., Breton, G., Garcia, C., Sguier, R.: Distance Maps: a robust illumination preprocessing for active appearance models. VISAPP'06, International Conference on Computer Vision Theory and Applications (2006)
3. Breton, G., Bouville, C., Pel, D.: FaceEngine: A 3D Facial Animation Engine for Real Time Applications. Web3D Symposium, Paderborn. Germany (2000)
4. Breton, G., Pel, D., Garcia, C.: Modeling gaze behavior for a 3D ECA in a dialogue situation. In: Proceedings of the 11th international conference on intelligent user interfaces, Sydney, Australia (2006)
5. Cohen, M.M., Massaro, D.W.: Modeling Coarticulation in Synthetic Visual Speech. Models and Techniques in Computer Animation. Springer, Heidelberg (1993)

Double Appraisal for Synthetic Characters

Sandy Louchart[1], Ruth Aylett[1], and Joao Dias[2]

[1] MACS, Heriot-Watt University, Riccarton, Edinburgh. EH14 4AS, UK
{Sandy,Ruth}@macs.hw.ac.uk
[2] INESC-ID and IST, Rua Prof. Cavaco Silva, Porto Salvo, Portugal
joao.assis@tagus.ist.utl.pt

Abstract. The paper describes a double appraisal-based emotion system for synthetic characters. This approach gives intelligent agents the ability to make decisions with respect to the emotional states of others, thus implementing aspects of the theory of mind concept and laying the basis for cognitive empathy.

Keywords: Double-appraisal, Emotions, Synthetic Characters.

This paper describes the implementation of an emotion-based system for synthetic characters to support their use in interactive storytelling as synthetic actors. This work relates to the Emergent Narrative (EN) concept [1, 2] in which the role played by a synthetic character is quite different from that in more traditional plot-based structures given that narrative is generated on the fly by their interactions. The internal structure of characters must therefore include complex autonomous action-selection mechanisms.

This work exploits the hypothesis that the emotional impact of an action stands as a surrogate for its dramatic value and allows the characters to conjointly assume in a distributive manner the dramatic weight of an unfolding story without relying on a pre-determined plot structure. A novel agent action-selection mechanism featuring a double appraisal cycle, as opposed to the single appraisal system of many other appraisal-based agent architectures was implemented within the FAtiMA [3] agent architecture which includes the OCC [4] cognitive appraisal taxonomy.

Cognitive appraisal theory asserts that humans evaluate events, objects and other people in relation to their own goals, and that affective states result from this process depending on whether, for example, an event supports or undermines their goals. FAtiMA [3] implements cognitive appraisal with associated coping mechanisms both for reactive and planned actions

1 Double Appraisal [DA]

[DA] features an action-selection mechanism in which the agent makes decisions based firstly on the emotion associated with its goals, and then secondly also on the emotional impact the action would have if directed at itself. This action selection mechanism adds another invocation of the appraisal process and re-appraises potential actions according to the agent's own set of emotional reactions. The agent uses its

C. Pelachaud et al. (Eds.): IVA 2007, LNAI 4722, pp. 393–394, 2007.

own set of values to assess how an action is perceived by others to make a choice between competing potential actions. Thus the decision is made as if the action was directed towards the agent itself. In order not to affect the *actual* emotional state of the agent, this re-appraisal cycle is executed in parallel to the "appraisal-coping" cycle and takes place within a second instance of the agent's mind that is not connected with the agent's running emotional state.

2 Double Appraisal with Modelling [DAM]

[DAM] adds another dimension to the re-appraisal approach by actually conducting the re-appraisal with respect to a representation of the emotional reaction sets of all the agents present in a scenario. It aims to select the action that would have the highest overall emotional impact on any character present within the scenario. It considers the impact of actions on each character and picks the one that scores the highest value for some character in the scene.

3 Conclusion

The work reported here was carried out as a first step in implementing a novel story management approach that draws on interactive practices rather than non-interactive theoretical approaches. The "Double-Appraisal" (DA/DAM) approach is an affectively driven action-selection mechanism that exploits the close relationship between emotions and drama in order to generate dramatically interesting events. It links cognitive appraisal modelling to specific narrative functions and drama (i.e. dramatic action-selection mechanism) and specifically integrates bottom-up emergent structures within a character-based narrative framework. It extends characters from the simple playing of their dramatic role into actors that evaluate the dramatic impact of what they do.

Acknowledgement. This work was partially supported by European Community (EC) and is currently funded by the eCIRCUS project IST-4-027656-STP. The authors are solely responsible for the content of this publication. It does not represent the opinion of the EC: the EC is not responsible for any use that might be made of data appearing therein.

References

1. Aylett, R., Dias, J., Paiva, A.: An affectively driven planner for synthetic characters.ICAPS 2006. AAAI Press, Stanford, California, USA (2006)
2. Aylett, R., Louchart, S.: Towards a narrative theory of VR. Special issue on storytelling. Virtual Reality. Journal 7, 2–9 (2003)
3. Dias, J., Paiva, A.: Feeling and Reasoning: a Computational Model. In: Bento, C., Cardoso, A., Dias, G. (eds.) EPIA 2005. LNCS (LNAI), vol. 3808, pp. 127–140. Springer, Heidelberg (2005)
4. Ortony, A., Clore, G., Collins, A.: The cognitive structure of emotions. Cambridge University Press, Cambridge (1988)

An Expressive Avatar for Instant Messaging Endowed with Emotional Intelligence

Alena Neviarouskaya[1], Helmut Prendinger[2], and Mitsuru Ishizuka[1]

[1] University of Tokyo, Department of Information and Communication Engineering, Japan
lena@mi.ci.i.u-tokyo.ac.jp, ishizuka@i.u-tokyo.ac.jp
[2] National Institute of Informatics, Japan
helmut@nii.ac.jp

Abstract. In this paper, we propose to endow a graphical representation of a user in Instant Messaging – an avatar – with the ability to recognize and to express emotions and to play social nonverbal behaviour, on the basis of textual affect sensing and interpretation of communicative functions conveyed by online conversations. The developed Affect Analysis Model integrated with Instant Messaging (IM) media supports the recognition of affect from text to ensure avatar animation in an appropriate and expressive manner.

Keywords: Affect sensing from text, affective user interface, animations, avatar.

Recently, a wide variety of approaches to visualizing the affective content of documents can be observed. The underlying idea is to associate each emotion with a particular pattern of expressive reaction. It has been demonstrated that affect can be represented by means of color [3], expressive text [2,5], static or animated emoticons, cartoon-like characters or human-like avatars, and images of human faces.

In our research, a 2D avatar was designed to automatically represent a user's affect and social nonverbal behaviour in an Instant Messaging (IM) system. Animations of avatar expressive patterns are driven by the output of the developed Affect Analysis Model [4], which is capable of recognizing and interpreting the conveyed emotions and communicative behaviour from not only correctly written text, but also informal messages written in abbreviated or expressive manner. The proposed rule-based approach to affect sensing from text at a sentence-level is described in [4]. For affect categorization, we use the subset of emotional states defined by Izard [1]: 'anger', 'disgust', 'fear', 'guilt', 'interest', 'joy', 'sadness', 'shame', and 'surprise'. As to communicative functions, 'greeting', 'thanks', 'posing a question', 'congratulation', and 'farewell' form the basis for communicative behaviour identification.

After the dominant emotion of the sentence is determined (according to the highest intensity in the resulting emotion vector) and communicative functions are detected, the relevant parameters are sent to the animation engine, which decides the sequence of animations and their duration depending on sentence length, intensity of dominant emotion, personality type of a user, and 'overall mood' of a conversation.

Emotional states of avatar were designed conformably to the relevant expressive means. For example, 'fear' is characterized by: widely open eyes; raised eyebrows;

C. Pelachaud et al. (Eds.): IVA 2007, LNAI 4722, pp. 395–396, 2007.

open mouth with crooked lips; trembling chin; hands in front of the body quasi pushing the source of fear away. In our work, we consider one personality trait, extraversion, to differentiate ways and strength of avatar expressiveness. In order to enable the avatar to display emotions of different intensity degrees, animations were created according to low, middle, and high level of emotion intensity.

As examples, facial expressions of 'joy', 'anger' and 'fear' of the female avatar designed by us are shown in Fig. 1.

Fig. 1. Examples of emotions displayed by female avatar

The richness of the information cues is a salient aspect of effective interpersonal communication. This holds true also within the virtual environment context. Based on their automatic identification from text, our avatar can act out the five communicative functions listed above. They can be displayed in sequence with emotional animations. However, the communicative function 'posing a question' is an exceptional case. Each of the five communicative functions has an associated specific lexicon and nonverbal behaviour. For example, relevant lexicon and expressive means for 'congratulation' are, respectively: 1) "congratulation", "praiseworthy", gj [good job], llta [lots, lots of thunderous applause], d=(^o^)=b [thumbs up] etc.; 2) admiring gaze, smile, clap of the hands. The animations of our avatar also include idle movements so as to provide a sense of liveliness: eye blinks; changing of gaze direction to avoid "dull stare"; yawning; playing with fingers; smoothing hair; folding arms, etc.

In our work, we strive to provide vivid and expressive visual signals to enhance socially oriented online communication media through the visualization of affective states and nonverbal behaviour of an avatar on the basis of textual affect sensing.

References

1. Izard, C.E.: Human Emotions. Plenum Press, New York, NY (1977)
2. Kalra, A., Karahalios, K.: TextTone: Expressing Emotion Through Text. In: Costabile, M.F., Paternó, F. (eds.) INTERACT 2005. LNCS, vol. 3585, pp. 966–969. Springer, Heidelberg (2005)
3. Liu, H., Selker, T., Lieberman, H.: Visualizing the Affective Structure of a Text Document. In: Proceedings of the Conference on Human Factors in Computing Systems, CHI'03, pp. 740–741 (2003)
4. Neviarouskaya, A., Prendinger, H., Ishizuka, M.: Textual Affect Sensing for Sociable and Expressive Online Communication. In: Paiva, A., Prada, R., Picard, R.W. (eds.) ACII 2007. LNCS, vol. 4738, pp. 218–229. Springer, Heidelberg (2007)
5. Strapparava, C., Valitutti, A., Stock, O.: Dances with Words. In: Proceedings of the International Joint Conference on Artificial Intelligence, India, pp. 1719–1724 (2007)

ALICIA
An Architecture for Intelligent Affective Agents

Marco Paleari[1], Brian Duffy[2], and Benoit Huet[1]

[1] Eurecom Institute, B.P. 194,
F-06294 Sophia Antipolis Cedex, France
{paleari,huet}@eurecom.fr
[2] The SmartLab, University of East London
London, UK
brd@media.mit.edu

Abstract. One of the most important social ability for effective social interaction with people is the capacity to understand, feel and ultimately express emotions. In this paper we present an architecture, based on the BDI paradigm, employing a three layered approach and coupling an emotion engine which simulates the generation of affective states based on Scherer's component process theory and influences decision making.

1 ALICIA's General Architecture

ALICIA's architecture (Fig. 1) is based on the well known BDI (Belief, Desire and Intention) paradigm. The work is also inspired by the classically rational element in the SOAR architecture [1]. Knowledge of the environment is modeled through Dynamic Belief Networks (DBN), emotions are described through Scherer's component process theory of emotions [2].

The architecture is based on a three layer model (i.e. *reactive*, *schematic* and *conceptual* layers) of agent cognition [2,3]. A fourth layer is added, the physical, which is tailored to the platform on which ALICIA is implemented.

The autonomous agents developed using this architecture are able to appraise emotions as reactions to events and objects in the surrounding and to react through physically triggered fast reactions, schema and planned decisions. The choice of the best future action is influenced by the most relevant emotions felt (emotion mixture approach) as well as by the agent preferences and personality.

Some characteristics of the databases containing beliefs, desires, and intentions facilitate this process of emotional influence. For example the fact of splitting the desires' DB in two parts (desires and aversions) makes it very simple to simulate influences of mood on decision making and affective state's appraisal by pruning the number of desires and aversions which are considered.

This process also works thanks to the fact that desires, as beliefs, intentions, possible behaviors, actions, and plans are sorted so that the more emotionally relevant ones are found first. This approach, thanks also to somatic markers [4], allows for fast decision making, by pruning non emotionally-relevant decision branches, which follows in some way agent's preferences.

C. Pelachaud et al. (Eds.): IVA 2007, LNAI 4722, pp. 397–398, 2007.

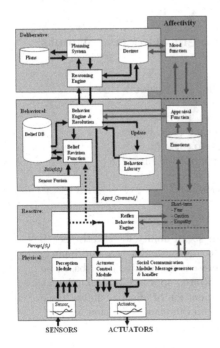

Fig. 1. ALICIA's architecture

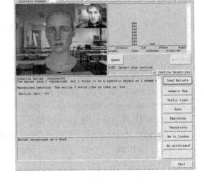

Fig. 2. Demo Interface

We have tested the architecture by deploying a software agent (Fig. 2) and simulating inputs describing different, more or less emotionally relevant, situations to test the different level of the architecture. In all these preliminarily proposed scenarios the agent behaved as expected.

The results of these preliminary experiments have shown the importance of adopting an integrative approach when dealing with different sensor modalities. We are therefore currently evolving the architecture by implementing a multimodal sensor fusion system [5].

References

1. Lehman, J.F., Laird, J., Rosenbloom, P.: A gentle introduction to soar: An architecture for human cognition. 2006 Update (2006)
2. Scherer, K.R.: Appraisal Considered as a Process of Multilevel Sequential Checking. In: Appraisal processes in emotion: Theory, methods, research, pp. 92–120. Oxford University Press, New York, US (2001)
3. Leventhal, H., Scherer, K.R.: The relationship of emotion to cognition: A functional approach to a semantic controversy. Cognition and Emotion 1, 3–28 (1987)
4. Damasio, A.R.: Descartes Error: Emotion, Reason, and the Human Brain. Avon books, NY (1994)
5. Paleari, M., Lisetti, C.L.: Toward multimodal fusion of affective cues. In: HCM 2006 First International Workshop in Human Centered Multimedia at ACM Multimedia 2006, S.Barbara, California (2006)

Towards a Unified Model of Social and Environment-Directed Agent Gaze Behaviour

Christopher Peters

IUT de Montreuil
Université de Paris 8
c.peters@iut-univ.paris8.fr

Abstract. When considering the gaze behaviours of embodied agents, and necessarily the underlying processes of visual attention that help to guide them, most work to date has been focused either on models aimed at controlling gaze in social situations, for example when one or more ECA's and humans are interacting, or for controlling gaze directed at the environment in a more general sense, typically for helping AVA's accomplish tasks such as navigation. We are designing a model of visual attention that attempts to amalgamate these concepts into a unified design in order to produce intelligent virtual agents that can behave in a social manner with social stimuli while also being attentive to events when mobile in the more general environment.

1 Purpose

The modelling of visual attention is an important element in simulating human interaction behaviours. While work involving autonomous virtual agents, or AVA's, and virtual humans has produced models capable of dealing in a general manner with the virtual environment [1], [3], [5], these models alone are not sufficient for modelling social situations. They do not detect or treat social stimuli in a special manner and do not incorporate top-down rules for mediating visual attention during social interaction. On the other hand, work involving ECA's (see for example [2], [6]) often considers as relevant only those social entities involved in conversation (and in some cases, a subset of objects related to the conversation also). As would be expected, these gaze models produce good results for face-to-face social scenarios, but do not extend to handle broader dynamic environments in which the agents are mobile. In such environments, elements from both of these domains are desirable for creating more capable intelligent virtual agents: this is the focus of our modelling efforts.

2 Model

We are creating a unified model of visual attention that can account for social stimuli as a special category when calculating the influence of general environmental stimuli on gaze. The model is 'unified' in the sense that all processing, social or otherwise, is conducted in a single framework using the same generic processing pipelines and representations (see for example [4] for the case of memory). Our model is designed so

C. Pelachaud et al. (Eds.): IVA 2007, LNAI 4722, pp. 399–400, 2007.
© Springer-Verlag Berlin Heidelberg 2007

that the agent can be active in two modes relating to the context: general and conversational. The mode of the agent is related to its perception of its level of engagement with others, inferred through their gaze behaviours based on perceptual theory of mind. When an agent deems itself to be engaged with another, it enters conversational mode, whereby top-down rules bias attention so that gaze follows patterns similar to conventional face-to-face systems. For example, the agent behaves so as to gaze at the other, or gaze upwards to signal thinking, as dictated by social rules embodied in a dialogue file. An important note is that bottom-up attention remains active during this process in order permit interruption from events in the environment.

3   Prototype Scenario

A prototype scenario for testing purposes involves two agents positioned within a virtual environment, allocated roles of speaker and listener. The listener runs the model of visual attention with which it can become distracted by other events happening in its field-of-view. The speaker infers the interest of the listener from its gaze behaviour as the dialogue progresses. If it detects a lack of interest, it may adapt the dialogue in a simple manner, for example by saying 'Are you paying attention to me?' or by following the gaze of the listener.

Acknowledgements

Thanks to Catherine Pelachaud for her guidance in this work, which is being funded by the Network of Excellence HUMAINE, IST-2002-2.3.1.6 and the Integrated Project CALLAS, IST-2005-2.5.7.

References

1. Chopra, S., Badler, N.: Where to look? automating attending behaviors of virtual human characters. Autonomous Agents and Multi-Agent Systems 4(1/2), 9–23 (2001)
2. Poggi, I., Pelachaud, C., de Rosis, F., Carofiglio, V., De Carolis, B.: Multimodal Intelligent Information Presentation. In: Stock, O., Zancarano, M. (eds.) chapter GRETA. A Believable Embodied Conversational Agent, Kluwer Academic Publishers, Dordrecht (2005)
3. Kim, Y., Hill Jr, R.W., Traum, D.R.: A computational model of dynamic perceptual attention for virtual humans. In: 14th Conference on Behavior Representation in Modeling and Simulation (BRIMS) (2005)
4. Peters, C.: Designing synthetic memory systems for supporting autonomous embodied agent behaviour. In: Proceedings of the 15th International Symposium on Robot and Human Interactive Communication (RO-MAN), pp. 14–19 (2005)
5. Peters, C., O' Sullivan, C.: Bottom-up visual attention for virtual human animation. In: Proceedings of Computer Animation for Social Agents (CASA) 2003 (2003)
6. Rehm, M., Andre, E., Wissner, M.: Gamble v2.0 - social interactions with multiple users. In: Proc. of the Int. Conf. on Autonomous Agents and Multiagent Systems (AAMAS) (2005)

Automatic Generation of Expressive Gaze in Virtual Animated Characters: From Artists Craft to a Behavioral Animation Model

Rossana B. Queiroz[1], Leandro M. Barros[1], and Soraia R. Musse[2]

[1] Universidade do Vale do Rio dos Sinos (UNISINOS)
São Leopoldo, RS, Brazil
fellowsheep@gmail.com, leandromb@unisinos.br
[2] Pontifícia Universidade Católica do Rio Grande do Sul (PUCRS)
Porto Alegre, RS, Brazil
soraia.musse@pucrs.br

Abstract. We present a model for automatic generation of expressive gaze in virtual agents. Our main focus is the eye behavior associated to expressiveness. Our approach is to collect data from animated Computer Graphics films, and codify such observations into an animation framework. The main contribution is the modeling aspects of an animation system, calibrated with empirical observations in order to generate realistic eyes motion. Results show that this approach generates convincing animations that improve the empathy of virtual agents.

1 Introduction

This work investigates eye behavior patterns and their relation with some affective states. Our model is mainly based on the hypothesis that Computer Graphics (CG) films can provide us a good parametrization of eyes motion in function of character emotion. This could be also observed in real life, however, we believe that CG films are more useful in the sense that they use the same language we are dealing with. We follow a methodology inspired by Lance et al. [1]. However, our intention, for now, is not to generate accurate eye movements by precise eye measurements, but to identify the observed behaviors and codify them into a computational system, in order to improve character's empathy.

2 From Artists' Craft to Behavioral Model

We build our model based mainly on three ideas: *i)* the statistical model of Lee [2], for realist saccade generation; *ii)* the idea of gaze *lexicon* from Poggi et al. work [3], for mapping of signals and meanings of agent's internal state; and *iii)* the idea of extracting gaze data from CG films, from Lance's work.

The overall architecture consists in five modules: *i)* *Gaze Storyboard*: is the input of our system, a script file with one or more gaze actions; *ii)* *Behavioral*

C. Pelachaud et al. (Eds.): IVA 2007, LNAI 4722, pp. 401–402, 2007.
© Springer-Verlag Berlin Heidelberg 2007

Database is the collection of agent's internal states parameters. According to the Gaze Storyboard actions, this module provides animation parameters for emotion expressions; *iii) Expressive Gaze Generator* is the module that interprets Gaze Storyboard files, loads script files required from Behavioral Database and generates FAP (MPEG-4 Facial Animation Parameters) files according to Behavioral Database files or just-eye behavior specification. This module communicates with Default Model module to generate saccade parameters; *iv) Default Model:* it is our implementation of Lee's statistical model and some other auxiliary methods that generate isolated parameters when behavior requires alterations in magnitude, direction or inter-saccadic interval; and *v) Facial Animation Module* is our visualization platform, that follows MPEG-4 Facial Animation standard.

From film observations, we propose four eye behaviors: *i) Concentration*: gaze shifts are smaller and less frequent. Internal affective states that requires a fixed gaze can be described with this behavior, such as angry, liking and surprise or simply to denote attention (mutual gaze); *ii) Discomfort*: gaze shifts are more frequent with great (glances, escapes) or small magnitudes (out of control sensation). Internal affective states which requires a loss of control sensation or confused/hidden feelings such as commotion, annoyance, nervousness, gratitude and fear should be described with this behavior; *iii) Distress*: gaze direction tends to down. Internal affective states such as sadness and shame should be described with this behavior; *iv) Irony*: gaze direction tends to up. Internal states such as impatience and reproach should be described with this behavior.

We also created a language for description of facial parameters we called Gaze Description Language (GDL). We can use the implemented behaviors without facial expression (directly on Storyboard file) or in specific expression GDL files.

3   Experimental Results and Final Remarks

We presented a model for automatic generation of expressive gaze in virtual agents, whose main focus is the eye behavior associated to expressiveness. Our system is implemented and functional. Experimental videos are available on the web (http://www.fellowsheep.wait4.org/2007-1/IVA2007-Results). Preliminary results showed that our model allows automatic gaze generation associated with facial expressions through different eye behaviors. As future work, we intend to evaluate our animations qualitatively, in order to know the users' view point and improve the robustness of our system.

References

1. Lance, B., Stacy, M., Koizumi, D.: Towards expressive gaze manner in embodied virtual agents. In: AAMAS Workshop on Empathic Agents (2004)
2. Lee, S.P., Badler, J.B., Badler, N.I.: Eyes alive. In: SIGGRAPH '02: Proceedings of the 29th annual conference on Computer graphics and interactive techniques, pp. 637–644. ACM Press, New York (2002)
3. Poggi, I., Pelachaud, C., de Rosis, F.: Eye communication in a conversational 3D synthetic agent. AI Communications 13(3), 169–182 (2000)

Analyzing Gaze During Face-to-Face Interaction

Stephan Raidt, Gérard Bailly, and Frédéric Elisei

Dept. of Speech & Cognition, GIPSA-Lab, Grenoble Universities, France
{Stephan.Raidt,Gerard.Bailly,Frederic.Elisei}@gipsa-lab.inpg.fr

Abstract. We present here the analysis of multimodal data gathered during realistic face-to-face interaction of a target speaker with a number of interlocutors. Videos and gaze have been monitored with an experimental setup using coupled cameras and screens with integrated eye trackers. With the aim to understand the functions of gaze in social interaction and to develop a coherent gaze control model for our talking heads we investigate the influence of cognitive state and social role on the observed gaze behavior.

Keywords: Face-to-face interaction, talking head, gaze control model.

Gaze is an essential component of face-to-face interaction. When interacting with a human interlocutor, the gaze patterns of an Embodied Conversational Agent (ECA) carry important cues not only for signaling the ECA's own communicative intentions but also its awareness of the environment as well as of the cognitive and emotional state of its interlocutors. The aim of our research is to understand the functions of gaze in social interaction and to develop a coherent gaze control model for our talking heads taking into account the results of detailed multimodal scene analysis.

Bilvi and Pelachaud [1] propose a gaze model for dyadic conversations. Textual input to the system augmented with tags indicating communicative functions drives a statistical model to generate eye movements alternating between direct and averted gaze. Lee et al. [4] propose also a similar statistical model based on analysis of video recordings of monologues uttered by one subject. Both models take into account the cognitive activity of the ECA (e.g. speaking vs. listening, etc) but do not integrate any detailed scene analysis: they do not determine exactly where their target speakers are looking. Itti et al. [3] developed a gaze control model coupled with a visual attention system that detects salient and pertinent points of interest in a natural scene and triggers exogenous saccades. There is however no detection nor separate treatment of faces in this system.

We developed an experimental platform where two subjects can interact via a crossed camera–screen setup, with the aim to give interlocutors the impression to be facing each other across a table. Video and audio signals as well as gaze directions are recorded during the interaction for later analysis. The experiment involves dyadic interactions between a female reference subject (for whom we build a virtual speaking clone) and several naïve subjects with same social status and sex. The interaction consists in a sentence-repeating game. One partner utters semantically unpredictable sentences that the other is asked to repeat. Roles are further exchanged. With this rather restricted scenario we try to capture the main elements of face-to-face

C. Pelachaud et al. (Eds.): IVA 2007, LNAI 4722, pp. 403–404, 2007.

interaction and to enhance the gaze cues of mutual attention. It also imposes a clear chaining of cognitive states (reading, speaking, listening, waiting, thinking...) and simplifies complex negotiation of turn taking and state dependent gaze analysis. According to our knowledge this is the first experimental setup that monitors both subjects during such a mediated face-to-face interaction.

Based on the audiovisual and gaze data saccades and fixations of each speaker with reference to the respective position of the face of their interlocutor are automatically computed. Analysis of these data clearly confirms the triangular pattern of fixations scanning the eyes and the mouth previously obtained by Vatikiotis-Bateson, Eigsti et al. [5] for perception of prerecorded audiovisual speech. The fixations

Left: Experimental setting. Right: distributions of fixations towards our reference speaker.

towards four regions of interest (left and right eyes, mouth, and face) have been further distinguished and impact of role and cognitive state of each interlocutor are examined. We show that both factors have a significant impact on distributions of gaze fixations and blinking rate of our reference subject. We show for example that speakers never fixate the mouth of their interlocutors when speaking and that blink rate is accelerated when 'speaking', whereas 'reading' and 'listening' slow it down and often inhibit blinks.

Following general results obtained by Gullberg and Holmqvist [2] we also show that pre-recorded stimuli produce significantly different gaze behavior of the interlocutors compared to live interaction.

Based on the measured data we built a first gaze control model for our talking head by training a Hidden Markov Model. Given a succession of cognitive states with associated durations it computes parameters describing the fixations of the ECA towards the various regions on the face of its interlocutor. An initial state in each HMM has been added to cope with the particular distribution of the first fixation. The observation probabilities determine the duration of the fixation emitted by the HMM at each transition. They are computed from fixations gathered from the interactions. Fixations to the mouth are for instance longer than fixations to the eyes.

References

[1] Bilvi, M., Pelachaud, C.: Communicative and statistical eye gaze predictions. In: International conference on Autonomous Agents and Multi-Agent Systems (AAMAS), Melbourne, Australia (2003)

[2] Gullberg, M., Holmqvist, K.: Visual attention towards gestures in face-to-face interaction vs on screen. In: International Gesture Workshop, London, UK (2001)

[3] Itti, L., Dhavale, N., Pighin, F.: Realistic avatar eye and head animation using a neurobiological model of visual attention. In: SPIE 48th Annual International Symposium on Optical Science and Technology, San Diego, CA (2003)

[4] Lee, S.P., Badler, J.B., Badler, N.: Eyes alive. ACM Transaction on Graphics 21(3), 637–644 (2002)

[5] Vatikiotis-Bateson, E., et al.: Eye movement of perceivers during audiovisual speech perception. Perception & Psychophysics 60, 926–940 (1998)

Affect and Metaphor in an ICA: Further Developments

C.J. Smith, T.H. Rumbell, J.A. Barnden, M.G. Lee, S.R. Glasbey,
and A.M. Wallington

School of Computer Science, University of Birmingham, Birmingham, B152TT, UK
A.M.Wallington@cs.bham.ac.uk

Abstract. We describe a computational treatment of certain sorts of affect-conveying metaphorical utterances. This is part of an affect detection system used by intelligent conversational agents (ICAs) operating in an edrama system.

1 Introduction

At IVA06, we described a system [1] for text-based, on-line, improvisational, role-playing (*eDrama*). We discussed an ICA, as a minor character in the drama, that made largely content-free, but affectively sensitive, responses, named EMMA (EMotion, Metaphor and Affect). Affect includes emotions/moods e.g. embarrassment, hostility and evaluations of goodness, importance, etc. Analysing metaphor for affect was not fully investigated or implemented but we can now report the implementation of some types of metaphor analysis and an important, related, architectural change to EMMA.

2 A Blackboard Architecture and Metaphor Processing

The different textual conveyors of affect used by EMMA interact. Now metaphor, and its extreme context-sensitivity, is being implemented as a major source of affect, the potential for interaction has greatly increased. We now use a blackboard architecture, with hypotheses arising from a process going onto a central blackboard where they can cooperate and compete flexibly with hypotheses posted by other processes.

Many have noted that metaphor and affect interact, e.g. 'he hungered for her', 'you slimy X' (see [1]; [2]), but metaphor seems to have been ignored by ICA research. Indeed, there are few computational treatments of it at all. We describe the processing here, of two important types of metaphorical phenomena found in edrama transcripts.

1) Casting someone as either: a special type of human without claiming literal truth (e.g. 'you baby,' 'you freak'); or a monster, mythical or supernatural creature, etc. (e.g 'Lisa is an angel'); or an animal. Note, the latter often conveys affect -negative or positive- but interestingly the young form ('piglet', 'pup' etc.) may be affectionate, even when the adult form is negative. EMMA deals with cases with a conventional metaphorical sense but also with those without one, for one might still determine a particular affective connotation from, e.g. the young form, or size. The latter because:

2) The metaphorical use of size adjectives. 'A little X' often conveys affective qualities of X such as unimportance and contemptibility, but may convey affection,

C. Pelachaud et al. (Eds.): IVA 2007, LNAI 4722, pp. 405–406, 2007.

even if the X is usually negative as in 'little devils' for children. 'Big X' can convey the importance of X ('big event') or intensity of X-ness ('big bully'). See [3].

Our approach splits processing into two: (A) recognition of potential metaphors and (B) analysis of recognised elements to determine affect. The basis for (A) is a list of phrases and syntactic structures, observed in edrama scripts and elsewhere, which often include metaphors or have metaphors as collocates. We currently focus on three syntactic structures, 'X is/are a Y', 'You Y' and 'like [a] Y' and on the lexical strings, 'a bit of a', 'such a' and 'look[s] like'. These structures/phrases are found by parsing the actors' utterances for Grammatical Relations (GR) using the RASP parser [4].

Once the (X and) Y nouns have been recognised, WordNet is used to analyse them, checking for example whether Y is a kind of animal. In simple cases (e.g. with 'cow') Y has an alternative sense (or synset) as an 'unpleasant person'. However, 'person' senses are not always found, in which case Y is still marked as a metaphor but the affect labelled 'positive or negative'. Further processing may determine which. We illustrate here the process with the example 'You piglet'. Others to be discussed include: *You cow*; *Lisa is an angel*; *You little rat*; *You little piggy*; *You're a lamb*.

1. The metaphor detector recognises the GRs of the 'You Y' signal (i.e. |ncmod| |you_ppy| |piglet_nn1|) and puts the noun 'piglet' on the blackboard.
2. The metaphor analyser reads 'piglet' from the blackboard and detects that it is a hyponym of 'animal' i.e., it is a 'kind of' animal.
3. 'Piglet' is not encoded with a specific metaphorical meaning (i.e. it is not also a hyponym of 'person'). So the analyser retrieves the gloss from WordNet.
4. It finds 'young' in the gloss and retrieves all of the words that follow it. In this example the gloss is 'a young pig' so 'pig' is the only following word.
5. The analysis process is repeated for each of the words captured from the gloss and the metaphor labelled with the appropriate polarity.
6. This example would result in the metaphor being labelled as an animal metaphor which is negative but affectionate with the affection label having a higher numerical confidence weighting than the negative label.

Future analyses involve checking and comparing the hypernym trees of both X and Y.

Acknowledgments

Supported by EPSRC grant EP/C538943/1 and ESRC grant RES-328-25-0009.

References

1. Zhang, L., Barnden, J.A., Hendley, R.J., Wallington, A.M.: Exploitation in Affect Detection in Improvisational E-Drama. In: Gratch, J., Young, M., Aylett, R., Ballin, D., Olivier, P. (eds.) IVA 2006. LNCS (LNAI), vol. 4133, pp. 68–79. Springer, Heidelberg (2006)
2. Kövecses, Z.: Metaphor and Emotion: Language, Culture and Body in Human Feeling. Cambridge University Press, Cambridge (2000)
3. Sharoff, S.: How to Handle Lexical Semantics in SFL: A Corpus Study of Purposes for Using Size Adjectives. System & Corpus: Exploring Connections. Equinox, London (2006)
4. Briscoe, E., Carroll, J., Watson, R.: The Second Release of the RASP System. In: Proceedings of the COLING/ACL 2006 Interactive Presentation Sessions, Sydney (2006)

A Case-Based Approach to Intelligent Virtual Agent's Interaction Experience Representation

Haris Supic

Faculty of Electrical Engineering, University of Sarajevo,
Zmaja od Bosne bb, 71000 Sarajevo, Bosnia and Herzegovina
haris.supic@etf.unsa.ba

Abstract. In this paper we describe a case-based representation of intelligent virtual agent's interaction experience. This allows us to develop an approach to creation of IVAs by using case-based reasoning. We called this agent CBRIVA. We can define a CBRIVA as an entity that selects the next step based on previous interaction experience. A CBRIVA's interaction experience is represented in the form of the three types of cases: *plan, contextual, and action cases.*

Keywords: Case-based reasoning, interaction experience, simulated vision.

1 Introduction

Case-based reasoning (CBR) is a type of reasoning based on the reused past experiences called cases [1]. In general, a case consists of a *problem*, its *solution,* and *an outcome.* The basic idea of CBR is that the solution of successful cases should be reused as a basis for future similar problems. In this paper we present a case-based approach to creation of IVAs that we called CBRIVA. A CBRIVA's interaction experience is represented in the form of cases.

2 Case-Based Representation of the IVA's Interaction Experience

The CBRIVA and environment interact at each of a sequence of interaction loops. We first introduce the basic terms: *steps, intentions,* and *behavior routines.*

Steps. A step is any action selected and/or taken by the CBRIVA. According to the interaction model, there are three types of steps as follows: a) the act of shifting the attention is called *the focus of attention;* b) the act of changing the state of the CBRIVA is called an *action step*, and c) the act of asking for help or defining the new mission is called *a step for user intervention* [2].

Intentions. In our model, there are two types of intentions: *plan intentions* and *contextual intentions.* Plan intentions are planned in advance at the beginning of the current mission due to the fact that the environment contains certain static structures that do not change over time. This is an opposite of the contextual intentions. A

C. Pelachaud et al. (Eds.): IVA 2007, LNAI 4722, pp. 407–408, 2007.

contextual intention represents a CBRIVA's desire that is the most appropriate for the given contextual conditions.

Behavior Routines. A CBRIVA does not use case-based reasoning throughout each interaction loop. Instead, throughout certain interaction loops, a CBRIVA routinely selects steps based on behavior routines that are generated by case-based reasoning throughout certain previous interaction loop. Behavior routines are defined as n-tuples $b=(b_1, b_2, ...b_i, ...b_n)$, $1 \leq i \leq n$, where elements b_i are intentions or action steps depending of the type of the behavior routine. The three types of behavior routines are possible: *plan, contextual,* and *action behavior routine.*

Plan, Contextual, and Action Cases. Cases include observations of the world as well as behavior routines that represent the solution component of cases. In our representation scheme, cases are classified as *plan* and *situation cases.* Furthermore, situation cases are classified as *contextual* and *action cases.* Plan cases are used to support reasoning processes at planning abstraction level. As a result of reasoning processes at plan level a CBRIVA selects an appropriate plan behavior routine. On the other side, situation cases are used to support reasoning processes at contextual and action abstraction levels. As a result of reasoning processes at contextual and action levels, a CBRIVA selects appropriate contextual and action behavior routines.

In order to qualitatively evaluate the described case-based approach to IVA's interaction experience representation, we have developed an approximate model for a simulated vision that can provide an appropriate means for a CBRIVA to reason based on what it perceives. Simulated visual perception involves determining which object surfaces in the environment are currently visible to a CBRIVA. We adopt an approach to the simulated vision similar to the one described in [3].

3 Conclusions and Future Work

In this paper we have presented an approach to intelligent virtual agent's interaction experience representation by using three types of cases: *plan, contextual,* and *action cases.* Each type of cases represents an interaction experience at different abstraction levels. The next step in this line of research should concentrate on developing an appropriate indexing scheme for efficient case retrieval.

References

1. Aamodt, A., Plaza, E.: Case-Based Reasoning: Foundational Issues, Methodological Variations and System Approaches. AICOM 7(1), 39–59 (1994)
2. Supic, H., Ribaric, S.: Autonomous Creation of New Situation Cases in Structured Continuous Domains. In: Munoz-Avila, H., Ricci, F. (eds.) ICCBR 2005. LNCS (LNAI), vol. 3620, pp. 537–551. Springer, Heidelberg (2005)
3. Terzopoulos, D., Rabie, T.: Animat vision: Active vision in artificial animals. In: Proc. Fifth Int. Conf. on Computer Vision, pp. 801–808. Cambridge, MA (1995)

Modeling Spatiotemporal Uncertainty in Dynamic Virtual Environments

S. Vosinakis[1], G. Anastassakis[2], and T. Panayiotopoulos[2]

[1] University of the Aegean, Department of Product and Systems Design Engineering
Hermoupolis, Syros, Greece
spyrosv@syros.aegean.gr
[2] University of Piraeus, Department of Informatics
Piraeus, Greece
{ganast,themisp}@unipi.gr

Current virtual agent [1] control architectures involve representations of the environment that must be adequate for effective deliberative behaviour rather than simple encoding of the environment's state. Hence, they must take into account the element of uncertainty that is inherent to perceptual processes, in the form of predicting the future state of perceivable parts of the environment or the current state of non-perceivable parts. A number of approaches have been proposed to deal with uncertainty. A large proportion introducing uncertainty as a means towards increased perceptual believability [2]. A different group attempts to deal with inherent uncertainty in a variety of ways [3,4]. Although substantial benefits are gained in both cases, prediction over time is rarely addressed, while potential knowledge on targets' intentions remains largely unexploited.

In this paper we propose a model of spatiotemporal uncertainty as an enhancement to current virtual agent control architectures. Our model is based on a fuzzy set representation and has been designed to participate in a generic VA control architecture focusing on the real-time nature of the target domain. Based on a distilment of the great variety of VA architectures available today, the architecture contains, among other components, Sensors that are the VA's means to perceive the virtual environment. These provide environment knowledge to a Control component which, in co-operation with a Knowledge Base, generates autonomous behaviours executed consequently by Effectors.

A question arises as to where within such a VA architecture the mechanisms to handle spatiotemporal uncertainty should fit. Sensors seem to be a suitable choice, for a number of reasons. Firstly, predicted knowledge is seamlessly and transparently available to other components just as solid, explicitly-sensed knowledge is. Secondly, a real-world metaphor is introduced, that clarifies and de-centralizes design. Humans, for instance, do not exercise conscious thinking to predict the trajectory of a ball thrown to them or the course of a moving car. Technical benefits are gained, too.

The proposed model uses three dimensional fuzzy sets to represent the uncertainty about the motion of animated entities in the environment. This representation is constructed based on the agent's perceptual information and on its beliefs about the other entities' intentions. The basic element of the proposed representation is the

C. Pelachaud et al. (Eds.): IVA 2007, LNAI 4722, pp. 409–410, 2007.

Fuzzy Position, which stands for the position of an entity in the environment. It is a 3D Fuzzy Set which represents the plausibility of an entity e to be positioned in (x, y) at time t. The membership function $\mu_{P_e}(x, y, t) \rightarrow [0,1]$ takes into consideration the agent's knowledge of the geometry of all static entities observed, its beliefs about the motion abilities of the entity e and its estimation about the possible intention(s) -if any- of e.

Concerning the motion abilities of an entity, the proposed model requires from the agent to know its maximum velocity v_{max}, its maximum acceleration a_{max} and its maximum angular velocity ω_{max}. These values could be a priori knowledge of the agent or they could be learned from observation. Also, based on its high-level knowledge and reasoning, the agent might have an estimation of the intentions of the observed entity. There might be places or elements it might want to approach or avoid, e.g. in a game environment a player might approach a gun and avoid an enemy. We call these positions *attractors* and *distractors* respectively and they could be static or animated. Each entity can have an arbitrary number of attractors and distractors associated to it.

The Fuzzy Position of an entity can be used to estimate its location at time t, given that the uncertainty increases as the interval $(t - t_0)$ increases, t_0 being the time of the last sensed position. Furthermore, the time at which an entity is expected to reach a certain position or area can be estimated. These estimations can take place using a defuzzification method, such as centroid or average of maxima. This analysis can lead to higher level knowledge, such as possible future positions of entities or actual positions of non visible entities. Even more important is the fact that the agent can extract knowledge about locations where an entity can certainly not be after time t, provided that the motion abilities of that entity are known. This is especially useful if fuzzy spatial knowledge is to be used by a planner as part of a behavior-generation procedure, for action precondition evaluation, etc.

The authors have set up an experimental evaluation in order to assess the efficiency of the proposed representation to predict future positions of animated entities in non-deterministic environments. A 3D space representing a virtual museum has been constructed and a number of 20 participants have been asked to move freely around and observe the contents. The evaluation results indicate that the estimations of future locations of animated entities can be precise enough, given that an agent's beliefs about possible attractors and distractors and about motion capabilities of the entities are correct.

References

[1] Aylett, R., Luck, M.: Applying artificial intelligence to virtual reality: Intelligent virtual environments. Applied Artificial Intelligence 14(1), 3–32 (2000)

[2] Kim, Y., Hill, R.W., Traum, D.R.: A Computational Model of Dynamic Perceptual Attention for Virtual Humans. In: Proc. 14th Conference on Behavior Representation in Modeling and Simulation (2005)

[3] Hill, R., Kim, Y., Gratch, J.: Anticipating Where to Look: Predicting the Movements of Mobile Agents in Complex Terrain. In: Proc. 1st International Joint Conference on Autonomous Agents and Multi-Agent Systems (2002)

[4] Conde, T., Thalmann, D.: An Integrated Perception for Autonomous Virtual Agents: Active and Predictive Perception. Computer Animation and Virtual Worlds 17, 457–468 (2006)

Avatars Contributions to Commercial Applications with Living Actor™ Technology

Laurent Ach and Benoît Morel

Cantoche. 68 rue d'Hauteville 75010 Paris, France
{lach,bmorel,info}@cantoche.com

Abstract. The technology and commercial experience of Cantoche put a new light on applications using avatars.

Keywords: avatar applications, intelligent behaviors, video streaming, real time, customer feedback.

1 Context

While nonverbal cues would be communicated directly by a video, the 3-D animated avatars let people extend their self expression with a personalized "alter ego" that can be used in innovative services over Internet and phone. Avatars allow people to be represented by an image that masks or emphasizes their actual character, behavior and even gender.

They already are used as interactive assistants or brand ambassadors for explaining, presenting, guiding or getting attention and also as an "alter-ego" for everyone to express emotions and feeling.

Avatars that behave in a credible manner as pseudo-realistic or fictitious characters, in all these different scenarios, need some sort of intelligence. Living Actor™ technology developed by Cantoche is based on the notion of actor considered as a semi-autonomous agent capable of being controlled through high-level instructions. Living Actor™ is a software suite that provides users and companies with sophisticated full body avatars that are easy-to-use.

2 Technology

Living Actor™ behaviors are determined by scripting commands and adapt to features detected in dialog text or voice. But having automatic or high-level behaviors does not mean all avatars should behave the same. They have different personalities that filter through their animations and facial expressions and they interpret all actions in their manner. To be credible, virtual characters should also show smooth animations while reacting in real-time to input events. When they speak, their movements must be consistent with their voice. The poor animations often seen when avatars speak is an important factor of non-acceptance. Living Actor™ combines automatic and high-level commands with a high quality of animations.

C. Pelachaud et al. (Eds.): IVA 2007, LNAI 4722, pp. 411–412, 2007.

Creating virtual characters that are well accepted by the users also involves some artistic skill and scenarist work. The virtual character production line and the real-time animation software must be capable of including all these elements. Building the useful software components and writing avatar intervention scripts requires a lot of practice with commercial and academic users. Applications using avatars range from the creation of static video content to real-time sound-synchronized visualization, through interactive virtual character embedded in web or intranet sites.

The most advanced application built on top of Living Actor™ technology is SpeechToVisio. It combines several important features: use of avatars from a production line that respects the different skilled involved in the creation process, intelligent behaviors based on voice analysis, real-time video streaming. It is used to replace the real image of a user by the image of his avatar. This is done in real time with all computations on server side. SpeechToVisio takes as input an audio stream and creates an audio-video output stream with an animated avatar. Avatar animations are selected according to the following principals: some features are extracted from the audio signal along dimensions of interest, like the sound volume, the pace of the speech, and others. These features are compared with the characteristics associated with the virtual character's animation data and the best behaviors are selected in real time, using artificial intelligence techniques.

3   Benefits

We distinguish two main markets, companies' and consumers' markets and analyze the benefits using avatar:

Companies' benefits: Avatars are an image for a company brand or serve as a point of contact for its project, as well as be a personal representation for communication with PCs, TV, or cellular phones. Benefits of avatars are myriad. Avatars work 24 hours a day, provide a consistent brand and approach across all customers, and receive contacts across interactive voice response (IVR), VoIP, text chat, IM, SMS and MMS. Avatar embodies the voice and message of the company.

Consumer's applications: Driven by the young generation and primed by virtual communities, people can create new forms of virtual communications using avatars especially on mobile phone in videotones, video calls, messaging, etc. Avatars are a new fun manner for people to create their own content and to express themselves. Avatars are a means for more effective communication.

The CereVoice Characterful Speech Synthesiser SDK

Matthew P. Aylett and Christopher J. Pidcock

Cereproc Ltd, Edinburgh, UK
matthewa@cereproc.com
http://www.cereproc.com

Abstract. CereProc®Ltd. have recently released a beta version of a commercial unit selection synthesiser featuring XML control of speech style. The system is freely available for academic use and allows fine control of the rendered speech as well as full timings to interface with avatars and other animation.

1 Introduction

CereVoice®is a unit selection speech synthesis software development kit (SDK) produced by CereProc Ltd., a company founded in late 2005 with a focus on creating characterful synthesis and massively increasing the efficiency of unit selection voice creation. The system is designed with an open architecture, has a footprint of approximately 70Mb (below 16Mb if flash is used to store the voice database), for a 16Khz voice and runs at approximately 10 channels realtime. The system is a diphone based unit selection system with pre-pruning and a Viterbi search for selecting candidates from the database. (see [?]).

Current systems are acceptable for reading neutral material such as bank balances but sound unacceptable if you use them to read longer texts or more personal information. We believe this is caused by current approaches to voice building. Most state-of-the-art synthesisers use unit selection to synthesise speech. This approach is based on recording a large database of speech and concatenating small sections of speech together to create new utterances.

The process for recording the database is time consuming (20-30 hours of studio time) and resource intensive. Thus, for commercial systems, a strong focus is made on creating neutral multiple-use voices. In addition, in order to improve concatenation there is an emphasis on reducing the variance of the speech within the database leading, for example, to requesting the source speaker to alter their natural speaking style to make it unnaturally neutral.

This results in voices which are completely inappropriate for expressive characters.

This leads to a vicious circle: commercial synthesis companies don't produce expressive voices so commercial customers can't develop systems using expressive voices. In turn, this forms the perception that there is no market for expressive voices and thus commercial synthesis companies don't create them.

C. Pelachaud et al. (Eds.): IVA 2007, LNAI 4722, pp. 413–414, 2007.

2   Expressive Synthesis: Breaking the Deadlock

Four key elements are required for breaking the vicious circle of dull speech synthesis:

1. Voice building must be made more efficient.
   If it becomes possible to build a voice with 10 hours or 6 hours of studio time the incentive for building more voices and making them more expressive is greater. In addition it becomes possible to record a wider variety of speech styles while maintaining a sufficient commercial standard.
2. Control of speech style
   In order to make use of the variation recorded in the voice, it needs to be categorised, or automatically coded, when the voice is built, and the system needs to be able to select material based on this categorisation during synthesis.
3. Semi-automatic synthesis
   Although we don't yet understand how to completely control expressive voices we can use a limited amount of manual intervention to create expressive and characterful cues and prompts. Inserting automatic synthesis between these stock phrases is a pragmatic way of generating expressive dynamic synthesis.
4. Development of applications which require characterful synthesis
   In order to move the technology forwards we need pressure from innovative application developers who can see and harness the enormous potential of characterful synthesis.

CereProc has addressed the first issue by developing a completely automatic voice generation and capture system. This has made the general voice building process more efficient. For example a George Bush voice was successfully developed completely automatically from web based material.

In addition CereProc reduces the amount of material required for sound coverage using a process we term 'voice bulking' where unusual diphones (the basic unit used in the synthesis) can be synthetically generated offline. This allows more material to be recorded for prosodic and speech style coverage.

The ability to select and mimic speech styles is accomplished with the use of a rich XML control language. Finally, by making the system freely available to the academic community as well as allowing innovative commercial enterprises to take part in an extensive beta test program, CereProc hopes that application developers will make use of this functionality and in turn drive the technology forward.

Reference

1. Aylett, M.P., Pidcock, C.J.: The cerevoice characterful speech synthesiser sdk. In: AISB, pp. 174–178 (2007)

Virtuoz Interactive Agents

Aurélie Cousseau

Virtuoz
acousseau@virtuoz.com
http://www.virtuoz.com

1 The Business of Virtuoz

Virtuoz is a software company that develops and sells an interactive agent technology capable of efficiently collaborating with clients' customer service departments in order to provide its users with an innovative, immediate, assistance service based on artificial intelligence.

Virtuoz designed its interactive agents as real interfaces between man and machine capable of conversing with internet users and ceding to a human operator when necessary. In cases of a constantly-growing mass of available information on sites, these intelligent avatars play the role of a human-like assistant that replies to questions 24/7 in a personalized and cordial manner.

2 Virtuoz Technology

The technology developed by Virtuoz is founded on a combination of a lexical and semantics analysis and a syntax analysis which is based on "unification grammar" making it possible to decipher the meaning of the phrase.

The agent will formulate the best response by using the semantic representation of the phrase and combining it with information about context, business environment, and its conversational strategy.

Once a response is formulated, a message is sent to the avatar informing it that it can post the correct response (or say it in the case of speech synthesis), play the animated sequence, and prompt the customer to navigate the site. It can also be proactive and lead the conversation. When a new situation arises in conversation regarding the creation of the response, the automatic, guided learning tutorial increases the agent's domain of knowledge.

3 Performance

The reasoning and comprehension capabilities of the agents allow them to carry out complex conversations. This is how Virtuoz agents are capable of fulfilling all of its clients' various missions - from acquisition(Coca Cola or Crédit Cetelem agents. . .), to client relationship development (like Téa's on Discountéo).

The utilisation of agents allows companies to handle a large part of their incoming messages automatically and immediately. Thanks to these virtual agents,

C. Pelachaud et al. (Eds.): IVA 2007, LNAI 4722, pp. 415–416, 2007.

the call center can dedicate itself to high value-added tasks and traffic peaks are incurred without harming the image or customer service quality of the company because there is no added congestion to other communication channels.

On sites that face strong flows of communication such as Nine AOL Assistance, the agent, Chloé in this case, holds about 150 000 conversations per month. Regardless of whether one addresses it in technical terms or in modern language, it will interpret its interlocutors' questions and supply them with an instantly customised response. Véronique Biguet, Manager of Selfcare and Online Support at Neuf-Cegetel, believes the agent proved itself, "Chloé reached the goals we set for her by responding to 75 % of the questions she was asked." It's a very efficient tool that proved its usefulness in the very first month after its launch."

4   Utilisation of Corpus

The agents' activities make it possible for VirtuOz to compile a large corpus that is put to use in different ways.

The agents' conversations are exploited by companies through the use of a help tool. This help tool offers Dialog Mining opportunities by permitting access to information through data searches and knowledge extractions. At Neuf-AOL Assistance, the agent is used as a warning indicator capable of signalling, in actual time, the occurrence of technical problems and solving them as quickly as possible.

Due to actual-time reporting, emphasis can also be placed on the expectations of the non-satisfied customers. Analysis of saved conversations (anonymous) on Voyages-sncf.com allowed the website team to discover the large incurrence of questions about travelling with pets. Thus, marketing and sales teams compiled information regarding animal travel and made it readily available to its clients.

A corpus such as this allows VirtuOz to make its agents and technology evolve by running test on its own large information database. On the other hand, one part of the research at VirtuOz is dedicated to developing the human aspect of its agents by giving the agents a personality, a sense of humor, or even a resistance to flirtatious comments.

5   How are VirtuOz Agents Perceived?

All the work that has been put into personifying VirtuOz agents gives the internet sites a humanized aspect. "Léa is considered to be part of the team because she is capable of dealing with the most current questions and redirecting the concerns," remarks Julien Nicolas, Manager of Agency Operations at Voyages-sncf.com. From an outsider's point of view, he adds, "we are often asked if a human is actually typing the responses." Thus, more than 2 or 3 people say "hello," "thank you," or "goodbye" to VirtuOz agents proving that they are perceived as real assistants and not just machines or mere search agents.

Finger Tracking for Virtual Agents

Gerrit Hillebrand and Konrad Zuerl

Advanced Realtime Tracking GmbH Weilheim, Germany

Abstract. Tracking is an essential tool for virtual agents. It provides
(a) the pose of the interacting person for a correct 3d view of the virtual
agent, (b) Motion Capture data of real persons that can be transferred to
an avatar to obtain realistic movements or for interacting, (c) details of
such movements like hands and fingers. This can be used for interactions
like gesture recognition, too. With the example of tracking hands and
fingers, the related problems and solutions are discussed: wireless active
markers, addressing for identification, marker positions at finger tips,
finger calibration etc.

1 Introduction

This article is meant to accompany a technical demonstration of an optical tracking system from Advanced Realtime Tracking GmbH at IVA 2007. It describes
some general aspects of optical tracking systems and their influences on the
application of finger tracking.

Although the idea of determining the hands pose dates from 1983 by AT&T
Bell Labs, the principal implemetation is still based on a glove like input device
with several bending sensors. The main problem of this type of gloves is the
error propagation in the kinematic chain from the wrist to the fingertip.

In our setup we only measure the position of the fingertips and the pose of
the back hand. Further information such as bending and spreading angles of
the fingers is calculated by an inverse kinematic hand model. This approach
improves the accuracy for the fingertips. It also allows the device to be built
without a closed glove and thus improving hygienic aspects.

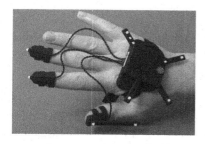 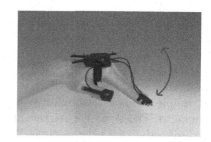

Fig. 1. Fingertracking device   **Fig. 2.** Movement for calibration process

C. Pelachaud et al. (Eds.): IVA 2007, LNAI 4722, pp. 417–419, 2007.

2   Fingertracking

We examined the flexibility of the human hand and and found out that, without external forces applied to the finger, there is a relation between the bending angles of the outermost and middle finger joint. This relation is independent from the pose of the fingers base joint. This reduction of the finger from four degree of freedom (2dof base joint, 1dof middle joint, 1dof outermost joint) to three dof allows us to calculate the fingers pose from a single 3dof information of the tip position. There is an unavoidable offset between fingertip and marker since we cannot place a marker directly inside the fingertip to measure it. Placing the marker on the top of the finger is best for AR because the tip is free to perform actions on real objects. However this marker position comes along with an ambiguous calculation of the fingers bending (fig.3). We propose a position directly on the length axis of the outermost phalanx as a compromise.

Due to a different type of base joint the thumb has a higher flexibility compared to the other fingers. The saddle joint allows the thumb to be rotated and reach an opponent position to the fingers. To correctly measure its pose we added a second marker for it (fig.1).

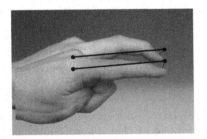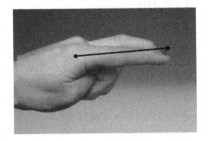

Fig. 3. Ambiguity at top marker position

3   Marker

Speaking of optical tracking systems in general, any object except cameras that is added to the environment in order to enable or to ease tracking is called a marker. Those markers are typically designed to be easily recognizable by cameras and image processing software.

In our terminology a marker provides 3d information. A rigid arrangement of at least four markers is called a target and also provides orientation information (6dof).

For our infrared tracking system we can distinguish two types of markers. The most simple one is a retroreflective sphere to be used with flash lights built in the cameras. Those passive markers are cheap and do not need any power supply or sychronization with the cameras. The second type are light emitting markers. In our case they consist of an IR LED and a diffusor to improve the angular visibility. These active markers need at least power supply.

Principally there is one problem for any type of marker. If the images of two markers in the camera get very close they cannot be separated by image processing any more. Both markers will be lost for that frame. This merging marker problem becomes crucial for the markers at the fingertips because they get very close especially at gripping gestures.

By synchronizing active markers with the cameras of the tracking system we achieve two important improvements. First synchronized active markers are much more energy efficient and secondly there is the possibility to switch off markers for certain frames. This sequential addressing of single fingermarkers not only avoids merging markers, but also makes the assignment of a marker to the appropriate finger well defined. For instance this enables an easy detection of crossed fingers.

To allow wireless synchronization the device contains an IR receiver and a micro controller. It automatically adjusts to the systems framerate and counts autonomously the frames whenever the IR synchronazation fails. Currently we can use up to four hands in one tracking system which can be scaled up to 16 cameras. The hand pose can be tracked at a framerate of 60Hz whereas the framerate of the relative finger poses is divided by the number of tracked fingers.

4   Calibration

To correctly calculate the finger angles from the position of the fingertip it is crucial to determine the length of each finger and the position of the base joint. We also experienced that every user mounts the 6dof hand target in a slightly different way. The exact transformation from the target to a defined hand coordinate system must also be calculated within the calibration process (fig.2).

5   Summary

The inverse kinematic fingertracking focusses on accurate measurement of the fingertips. With this device we open the hand interaction for applications where not only a rough shape or defined gestures are needed but also exact positions. Primarily theses are augmented reality applications where a precise conformance between reality and virtual augmentation is required.

Originally designed for interaction tasks in 3d space such as gripping or pointing, the first version was restricted to three fingers. To also fulfill the requests of gesture recognition and avatar animation we enhanced the fingertracking device and developed a complete five finger version.

Techniques of Dialogue Simulation

Fred Roberts and Björn Gülsdorff

Artificial Solutions, Altonaer Poststraße 13b,
22767 Hamburg, Germany
{fred.roberts,bjoern.guelsdorff}@artificial-solutions.com

Abstract. We claim that it is more effective to simulate intelligence than it is to recreate it. To this end several of the classic social psychological theories suggest strategies to transform the dialogue into an encounter with a consistent and cohesive personality. The secret is to use the mind-set of the user to the advantage of the conversation, and to provoke the user into showing typical behavior. This is presented in an online system: Elbot.com.

Keywords: Dialogue simulation, social psychology, interactive customer assistants, Artificial Solutions, Elbot.

1 Intelligence in Interactive Assistants (IA)

IAs are commercial dialogue systems with a well-defined area of expertise. They are designed to recognize classes of inputs in all their synonymous variations and associate them with a desired response in respect to context information. These responses are written to conform to a meaning, and not a particular literal formulation. The rules for input classification originate from a core knowledge base and are fully customizable. This gives the IA designer complete control over the IA's character and range of expression. Providing information in the area of expertise is a must. Dealing with open range inputs is an entirely different task. Our IA Elbot is devoted to this.

Elbot is a sarcastic, award-winning robot trying to comprehend the human way of life. Systems like Elbot require the development of various new techniques. Several social psychological theories have helped us enhance the conversational experience by presenting a character with consistent attitude, thereby creating the illusion of an intelligent personality. Elbot also demonstrates the main virtues of our IAs: be prepared for typical inputs and induce users to behave in a predictable manner.

2 Schemata and Social Comparison

Using schemata the IA can establish personality: First, in social perceptions we tend to imagine non-existent details according to stereotypical expectations. Secondly, people react to inconsistencies in schemata. For IAs this means: with a consistent sketch of personality details users perceive a complete and cohesive personality while well-chosen inconsistencies draw them into predictable patterns of reaction.

In the theory of social comparison we constantly compare ourselves with others to test our affinity and to see where we stand in the norm. So users will often confront

C. Pelachaud et al. (Eds.): IVA 2007, LNAI 4722, pp. 420–421, 2007.

the IA with questions about its likes, dislikes, and opinions. To write a response for everything would require an infinite amount of time. Our IA technology enables us to recognize complete classes of expressions and synonyms. Each class is associated with a series of text phrases to initiate a short dialogue. Presenting an attitude (or personality) and at the same time pleasing the user with responsiveness creates a strong illusion of intelligence. For example, this response would be given for synonyms of drinkable liquids: <u>User</u>: Do you like water? <u>Elbot</u>: I'm afraid drinkable liquids might be dangerous for robots. What is your opinion on this?

3 Reactance and Provocation

A well known social psychological principle is reactance: people will often do the opposite of what they are told to do. Our IAs model reactance for certain user inputs. Elbot's refusal to do something the user wants brings about typical responses. On the other hand, we provoke users with suggestive questions or present topics of interest to draw them into goal-driven dialogues. Altogether this brings users to react predictably while at the same time retaining their illusion that their reactions are unique and original.

4 Conclusion

It is more important to know your user and have something to say than to have an answer to everything. We invite you to visit Elbot at elbot.com.

5 About Artificial Solutions

Artificial Solutions develops interactive customer assistants to answer natural language inquiries via web, e-mail, voice and mobile applications. As of June 2007, more than 200 IAs have been launched in more than 20 languages for a wide range of industries around the globe.

Author Index

Lecture Notes in Artificial Intelligence (LNAI)